Cieza de León, Pedro de
The Incas.

DATE DUE

MAR 24 '77			
NOV 23 77			
FEB 8 '79			
JUN 6 79			
APR 29 '81			
May 20			
June 10			
JUN 17 '83			
MAR 3 '82			
MAY 11 '88			

THE CIVILIZATION OF THE AMERICAN INDIAN SERIES

(Complete list on pages 395-99)

THE INCAS

of Pedro de Cieza de León

THE
INCAS

of Pedro de Cieza de León

Translated by Harriet de Onis

Edited, with an Introduction, by

Victor Wolfgang von Hagen

NORMAN : UNIVERSITY OF OKLAHOMA PRESS

Some of the other books by Victor W. von Hagen

EXPLORATION:

Off With Their Heads (New York, 1937)
Ecuador the Unknown (New York, 1938)
Jungle in the Clouds (New York, 1940)
Ecuador and the Galápagos Islands (Norman, 1949)
Highway of the Sun (New York, 1955)

BIOGRAPHY:

South America Called Them (New York, 1945)
*Maya Explorer: John Lloyd Stephens and the Lost Cities
of Central America and Yucatán* (Norman, 1947)
Frederick Catherwood, Architect (New York, 1950)
The Four Seasons of Manuela (New York, 1952)

ARCHAEOLOGY AND ETHNOLOGY:

The Tsátchela Indians of Western Ecuador (New York, 1939)
The Jicaque (Torrupan) Indians of Honduras (New York, 1943)
The Aztec and Maya Papermakers (New York, 1943)
Realm of the Incas (New York, 1957)
The Aztec: Man and Tribe (New York, 1958)
(Editor) *Incidents of Travel in Yucatan*, by John L. Stephens
(Norman, 1959)
The World of the Maya (New York, 1960)
The Ancient Sun Kingdoms of the Americas (New York, 1960)

Library of Congress Catalog Card Number: 59–7955

Copyright 1959 by the University of Oklahoma Press,
Publishing Division of the University.
Manufactured in the U.S.A.
First edition, June, 1959.
Second printing, June, 1960.
Third printing, March, 1969.

For more than four hundred years Cieza—Pedro de Cieza de León, to give his full and sonorous name—has conducted his readers over the Royal Road of the Incas.

This seventeen-year-long journey gave countless generations the story of a people out of the reaches of time dwelling in the mountain fastness of the Andes and living a strange way of life which Cieza detailed in custom and history, describing their strange folkways and their destruction, which he chronicles even as they were being decimated and destroyed.

This chronicle, which had been often republished throughout the sixteenth century, is not alone one of the most widely printed books on Peru's conquest; it also—in this all scholars agree—possesses the greatest objectivity of any history ever written about the Incas.

I myself followed, four hundred years later, this Pedro de Cieza de León over the same Royal Road of the Incas, that road which he so wonderfully described, in a search for the remains of this well-famed highway and the stone-built cities that lay near to it. Thus I can attest to his accuracy and precise reporting. Moreover, I think I know Pedro de Cieza, for I carried his books for many years over thousands of miles of the land which he traversed, and now those self-same books lie before me, soiled, dog-eared, and worn from use; Cieza has always been my enchiridion in these travels.

Cieza, in constant use in one way or another in my researches, has been a continual reminder that in some later day an effort had to be made so that Pedro de Cieza de León might be available to all of those who, although moved by the here and now, were also interested in the loom of the past. Cieza's Inca chronicles were no longer available in English; they have never been translated into French or German, and those Spanish editions that *are* now available suffer from execrable scholarship. After numerous editions in Italian and in Spanish (albeit issued from Flanders), Cieza was cast into English in 1709 by one John Stevens and titled *The Seventeen Years Travels of Peter de Cieza*. The alembic, however, was poor; the chapters are castrated and whole portions telescoped together in the most arbitrary fashion. Moreover, the editor ignored the authentic illustrations that appeared in the original Cieza and made his own in high-blown sententious fantasy; the edition's only merit is that it was the first in English of the "Prince of Chroniclers."

In 1864, Sir Clements Markham, urged to do so by Prescott, translated Cieza anew, published the whole of the two chronicles; whole, that is, if one excepts deletions of entire sections which he found "unfit for translation," and furthermore, written in a style that is often broken and limping in its threadbare prose. Yet this is not to denigrate Markham's pioneer work; it is only to stress that with the passage of a century that has so enriched our understanding of the Inca realm, I felt the need for an edition of Pedro de Cieza de León, a work which could avail itself, by explanatory notes, of all that is now known. Moreover, each generation should reinterpret for itself the classics of other years, as George Santayana had it: "Foreign classics have to be re-translated and re-interpreted for each generation, to render their old naturalness in a new way and keep their perennial humanity living and capable of assimilation. It is this continual digestion of the substance supplied by the past that alone renders the insights of the past still potent in the present and the future."

And so to render the old naturalness of Cieza in a new way, Harriet de Onis, one of the finest scholar translators of our time, undertook to give Cieza that which he had not enjoyed in his four centuries of life—a faithful rendering in English in a prose so unaffectedly simple that at times it rises to epic grandeur; at the same time, a rendering that includes all that Pedro de Cieza saw fit to write and the Holy Office sanctioned—without deletion and excised chapters "unfit for translation."

In this edition the two *Crónicas,* the first and the second, which appeared three hundred years apart, have been arranged as one great work. The realities of the moment—i.e., the excessive cost of publication, the desire to escape repetition, and the need to bring Pedro de Cieza's observations on the Incas into one available volume—has brought about the plan to interjoin both; now the two *Crónicas* can be read as one.

That *Crónica* published in Cieza's lifetime (1553) and the second discovered and published in 1880, I found could be synchronized as one because the first is, in the main, geographical: a description of the verdant valleys, of titanic desolation of Andes and desert, and of people and places; the second is concerned with the institutions of the Inca realm, with emphasis on the varied aspects of this strange and haunting story of a people who, without writing or the wheel, conquered space and time. The first portion of the *Prima Crónica,* ix that is, Chapters I–XXXV, is about the land that is now Colombia, and as this was not within the Inca empire, it has not been included in the present volume, being reserved for later publication.

Thus this edition has been arranged as one great work, interlaced and combined so that it reads as one; nothing save repetition has been deleted. However, so that the reader remains aware of precisely which of the *Crónicas* form the subject of each chapter, two series of numerations are used. In this manner, following Cieza ("I always honor the hands of my reader"), I have brought him together with himself after four hundred years of excision.

Who was Pedro de Cieza de León?

The mystery of Pedro de Cieza de León, the man, pressed itself upon us as the pages of his Chronicles of Peru were translated and edited. Certainly such painstaking literary labor as we were giving Cieza should not appear without inexhaustible search to pierce the mystery of his identity. Anonymity when he lived was the rule in that robust century; unless a man were well born and had official scribes to embellish his deeds, little attention was paid to him, and few were bold enough to speak of themselves. Still, Pedro de Cieza was sufficiently uncommon. He was, he said, "chronicler of the Indies"; moreover, he stated, and time has proved, that he did write eight histories—which cover the entire epoch of Peru from discovery to conquest, from civil wars to the coming of the viceroys. So buried somewhere, I was certain, must be the details of Cieza's existence, for a man cannot have walked for seventeen years throughout so chronicled a time as the conquest of Peru without leaving impress.

First the *Archivos Nacionales del Perú* in Lima yielded up Pedro de Cieza's marriage contract (dated a few months before he left Peru), and thereon was his signature, bold and flowing, with an enveloping rubric; this showed him to have been very much alive. Then the research pointed toward the famous *Archivos de Protocolos Notariales de Sevilla,* a depository for an unfathomed number of documents that relate to the Americas. There, following the first positive evidence, we were led to Cieza's personal documents, and I held at long last the extraordinary document which was his "Last Will and Testament." But at that very moment I was made aware of the fact that a young Peruvian scholar, Señor Miguel Marticorena, had been working in the same archives and had found numerous other documents of Pedro de Cieza; moreover, he was in the very act of preparing them for publication.

Man inevitably desires priority. It is a fundamental human instinct since life ever reaches out for newness: to do a new thing or even to be a new thing is very human. Scholars had sought for many centuries to know something of this Pedro de Cieza de León and when they could not find the documents, they invented the facts; all biographical details about Cieza that have been published are contrived. Prescott, for all his thoroughness, never penetrated the mystery; the late Philip Ainsworth Means, one of our finest archaeological historians, could not offer a single new fact. The most indefatigable Spanish scholars, who knew their way through the mould and confusion that are the Spanish Archives, never located the Cieza documents. So here we were, Señor Marticorena and I, colliding at the hour of truth. Yet it delights me to record, in this decade of private and public perversity, that we did not try to outrun each other to the printer; instead we emulated Mr. Wallace and Mr. Darwin.[1] Señor Marticorena gallantly turned over to me such as I did not have of the fascinating documents of Cieza, those which had eluded all before him, and I aided him to finish his work and, as well, delayed this book so that he would have, as he should have, the undenied priority of first publishing the Cieza documents.[2]

Pedro de Cieza de León lives again because of many helpful hands.

[1] While Charles Darwin was working on his first evolutionary essay in 1858, he received in the mail an article, "On the Tendency of Varieties to Depart Indefinitely from the Original Type," by Alfred R. Wallace, with the pleading request that if Darwin found it new, would he suggest where it might be published? Wallace, whose name is connected with Pacific exploration, had hit upon the "missing factor" of the origin of species independent of Darwin. After days of torturing doubts, Darwin presented both his own and Wallace's historical papers to be read at a meeting in Kew Gardens. On that evening of July 1, 1859, the theory of evolution by natural selection was publicly announced.

[2] Miguel Marticorena Estrada, "Cieza de León en Sevilla y su Muerte en 1554," Documentos, *Anuario de Estudios Americanos,* Vol. XII, (Seville, 1955), 615–74.

I wish to record my gratitude for the aid of Mr. John Davis Lodge, U. S. Ambassador to Spain, who helped me in finding someone who knew his way about the labyrinth of papers which form the Archives in Spain—which reminds one that Prescott in 1838 wrote to the then United States Minister to Spain, Arthur Middleton, in a similar vein: "I now begin to think seriously of the Conquest of Mexico and Peru," and he asked for the same aid as that which I begged for, over one hundred years later. Mr. Frederick Cromwell of Casa Americana, Seville, helped to seek out Dr. Enrique Dorta and others, who led me to Señor Miguel Marticorena, for whose aid in all this I remain most grateful, especially for his trust in allowing me the Cieza documents long before he himself published them.

xi

I must thank Harriet de Onis, not alone for her superb translation, for our exchange of letters helped me form an idea of the man; and, too, Mr. Savoie Lottinville, the editor-publisher of the University of Oklahoma Press, who believed when I first doubted that the two Chronicles could be edited into one.

The Henry E. Huntington Library of San Marino, California microfilmed for me and allowed me the use of the entire 3,000 documents that form the Pizarro–La Gasca collection—the self-same papers which Pedro de Cieza de León examined in 1550 whilst in Peru ("and I remember they were so numerous that three secretaries did not finish reading them in four days"). As they have always in the past when I worked on other books in progress, Mr. Shultz and Miss Haydeé Noya of that library were of invaluable assistance, as was Mr. Robert Hill, Keeper of Manuscripts at the New York Public Library, who aided me to copy some of their rareties to be used here.

And finally to my daughter Bettina, who allowed herself to be born on time so as not to throw off the publishing schedule, and to my secretary Mrs. Gladys Bryson, who has doggedly gone over Cieza manuscripts so often, typing, retyping, correcting, and translating, that she could now be enshrined as his amanuensis—to all those gracious hands who helped me to flesh the bare bones of Pedro de Cieza de León, to breathe into them and give them life—my deepest gratitude.

"Silvania"   *Victor Wolfgang von Hagen*
La Molina, Lima, Peru

Part I

Contents

Part II

Contents

Contents

Part III

THE INCAS

LIST OF MAPS

—I—

EVER SINCE he was rediscovered by William H. Prescott in the nineteenth century while he carried on research for his *History of the Conquest of Peru,* Pedro de Cieza de León has been widely esteemed. But it was not until his lost histories were found, gathering dry rot and dust in the Escorial, and were published and his *Crónicas* reissued after a lapse of three hundred years, that he came into his own and emerged as the "Prince of Chroniclers."

William Prescott, since he was half-blind and forced to read with trained ogre-eye, had developed that superior "feel" of materials which seems to come as an acquired characteristic of the benighted; with this quality and the touch of experience gained from going through veritable mountains of Spanish manuscripts which his amanuensis had copied for him in Madrid, he was able to give the first critical evaluation of Cieza: ". . . an author of particular note . . . the conception of his histories . . . was, of itself, indicative of great comprehensiveness of mind in its author. . . . The literary execution of the work, moreover, is highly respectable . . . even rich and picturesque."

All, or almost all, scholars who have followed Prescott now consider the pioneer work of Pedro de Cieza de León "as the cornerstone when writing of Inca achievements." His observations and descriptions of nature and peoples, rare in any man, were extraordinary, for he was a man of war and paralleled (so thought R. B. Cunninghame Graham) only by Bernal Díaz del Castillo, the companion of Cortés in the conquest of Mexico. Díaz, who was blunt, honest, and forceful, vowed that he "would describe [the conquest of Mexico] quite simply, as a first witness, without twisting events one way or another." Cieza, who came as a boy to the Americas, began his journal at twenty, because "there came over me a great desire to relate the admirable things that have existed, and much of what I have written I have seen with my own eyes."

How did Pedro de Cieza produce, not one, but eight books of living history, writing history even as it was being made? How was it that coming to the New World as a boy of thirteen and being matured on death and rapine, he found the time to write, or, a greater paradox, how did he acquire the knowledge to write—and, moreover, to write so well? While other boys of this age had leisure to acquire learning, his was gained in battles, going with his captains "who were lancing and disemboweling Indians." Moreover, and again, who was Pedro de Cieza de Leon? No one, not even his contemporaries, who freely plagiarized from him, seems to have known; that is, they knew no more about him than those crumbs of autobiography that he had left at the table. Cieza was never mentioned in a contemporary document, even though he spent seventeen years in the Indies. His name never appears in letters or reports, and although he avers that he was appointed *"Cronista de las Indias"* in 1548 by Pedro de la Gasca—the King's famous gray eminence—and was given letters by him to all officials throughout Peru with orders to aid him in searching out the history of events, past and present, no such documents have been found, and this despite the fact that the papers of La Gasca[1] have been minutely examined, and yet——And yet Pedro de Cieza de León had connections so powerful that he obtained immediate audience with Philip II, king-prince of Spain, on his return to the Peninsula, in order to bring him his first *Crónica*. Some had opined that "Pedro de Cieza" was in reality two people: one the soldier who traveled and took down the raw material, the other a learned writer who fashioned it into literature. This is here disproven; warrior and writer were one.

Whether he was anonymous or not did not prevent Cieza's contemporaries from dipping into his manuscripts and appropriating such portions as were needed for their own publications. Those of

xxvi

[1] The three thousand or more pages of manuscript which compose the Pizarro–La Gasca manuscript collection in the Huntington Library formed part of the personal archives of Pedro de la Gasca and, as well, the sequestered papers of Gonzalo Pizarro. These documents, full of detail and anecdote, provide a picture of the final war in which Pedro de Cieza de León took part. This collection lay first in the library at Madrid, from which they were borrowed by the well-known scholar, Marcos Jiménez de la Espada. Found after his death in 1898 by his heirs, the documents eventually came into the hands of Maggs Bros. in London, who issued a catalog and then sold them as a complete collection to the Henry E. Huntington Library, San Marino, California. See "From Panama to Peru: the Conquest of Peru by the Pizarros, the Rebellion and the Pacification by La Gasca. An epitome of the original signed documents" (London, Maggs Bros., 1925); and "The Pizarro–La Gasca MSS Collection in the Huntington Library," by Clarence H. Haring, *Huntington Library Quarterly*, Vol. XVIII, No. 4 (August, 1955).

his manuscripts which remained unpublished were often plagiarized in their entirety down until the eighteenth century. This was a form of literary trespass which the learned Master Jacobus Thomasius of St. Nicolaus College at Leipzig (who wrote the celebrated *De Plagio Litterario* in 1684) would scarcely have deemed proper. Yet, despite the plagiarisms, Cieza remained unknown. The biographer historian Nicolás Antonio, who wrote of the "worthies" of Seville in 1788,[2] was then not even certain of his place of birth: *"Petrus de León, patria, an dumtaxat domicilio incolutave Hispaniensis"*—meaning that he did not know (even his name was wrongly written) whether Cieza was born in Seville or was a citizen by adoption. Thus, as was to be expected, his dates of entreé and egress from life are wrong.

xxvii

Those archaeological historians who work on South American cultures lean heavily on Cieza because almost all we know about the prehistoric tribes of Colombia in the Sinú, in the Cauca and beyond, come from him; all that exists on the coastal tribes of Ecuador was set down by him. He was the first to make a methodical study of the Inca realm and to distinguish between the tribes within it, pointing out distinct forms of customs, manners, and dress. He was the first to describe the ruins of Tiahuanacu, outlining them as they are in fact, the work of another people, long anterior to the Incas, and he discerned that the ruins of Huari near Ayacucho were not Inca, but bore resemblance to those of Tiahuanacu; the quipu, that ingenious Andean mnemonic device, was first explained by him.

In Colombia he wrote for the first time, of the actions and reactions of curare, that poison which curdled the blood of its victims; we owe the first description of the potato to him: "... earth nuts ... of good flavor, very acceptable to the Indians and a dainty dish even for Spaniards." Also he detailed the vicuña (which he did not like his fellow-soldiers to call "sheep") and the llama. He wrote of the coca leaf masticated by the Indians since time immemorial, of Inca roads and their tambo stations on the way, and of the whole system of *chasqui* couriers which he studied and which has been quoted by almost everyone who wrote after him. Not alone is Cieza our best authority, noting each

2 Which illustrates Francis Bacon's ironic observation that "the stream of life lets every solid substance sink and carries down with it only the froth and the foam," for when another writer compiled *Hijos de Sevilla, illustres en Santidad, Letras, Armas, Artes o Dignidad* (Seville, 1791), the author, one Fernando Díaz de Valderrama, showed that, like Nicolás Antonio, he knew nothing of Pedro de Cieza de León.

THE INCAS

thing down meticulously without conscious bias and threading his way through the morass of the unknown, but he was one of the earliest writers; only a few first notices were printed before him.[3]

Finally, it must be stressed here that Cieza was not mere amanuensis, one of those who with blackened scrivener's fingers wrote loose volumes full of contumely; Cieza was a historian and geographer

[3] The importance and primacy of Pedro de Cieza's history can only be correctly understood if all of the published material on Peru is put in chronological order:

1528: Le Relación Sáamano-Xérex. The first authentic notice of Peru, without date or province, addressed to *"Vuestra Alteza"* (Your Highness) and signed by Juan de Sáamano. Written in 1527 by one of the men sent to succor Pizarro on the Isle of Gallo, it exists as manuscript (No. CXX) in the State—formerly Imperial—Library in Vienna.

1533 (November 23): *The Report of Hernando Pizarro* to the Royal Audience of Santo Domingo on the capture of Atahualpa and the Inca empire. The report was published by Gonzalo Fernández Oviedo y Valdéz, the resident historiographer of the Indies. It is available to English readers in *Reports of the Discovery of Peru* (London, Hakluyt Society, 1852).

1534 (April): [Anonymous] *La Conquista del Perú . .. cima ventura del Emperador y por la prudencia y esfuerzo del muy magnífico y valeroso caballero Capitán Francisco Pizarro . . . y de su hermano Hernando Pizarro y de sus animosos capitanes—y fieles y esforzados compañeros que con él se hallaron.* Printed in Seville, 1534. The first detailed report on the conquest of Peru, of such rarity that there are only two surviving copies of the original edition, and the New York Public Library copy can be classified as a manuscript. It bears on its title page Atahualpa, carried on a litter, being offered a Bible by Padre Vicente de Valverde. There is much dispute over the authorship; the most probable suggestion is that offered by Raúl Porras, the Peruvian scholar, that it was the work of Cristóbal de Mena, one of the most literate members of the expedition. See Alexander Pogo, "The Anonymous *La Conquista del Perú,*" *Proceedings* of the American Academy of Arts and Sciences, Vol. LXIV, No. 8 (July, 1930); Joseph Sinclair, *Le Conquista del Perú, a facsimile copy* (New York, 1929); Raúl Porras, *Las Relaciones Primitivas de la Conquista del Perú Paris,* (1937).

1534 (July): Francisco de Xérez, *Verdadera Relación de la Conquista del Perú . . .,* part title of the famous report by Francisco Pizarro's secretaries (which included that of Miguel de Estete), issued in July, 1534, by the same printer who issued the anonymous report, Bartolomé Pérez. There were many versions of this book in Italian, Dutch, German, and Flemish. In France it appeared in Lyons under the title (1534) *Nouvelles Certaines des Isles du Perou.*

1552: Francisco López de Gómara, *Hispanic Victrix: Primera y Segunda Parte de la Historia General de las Indias.* Published in Medina del Campo in 1553 (the same year as Pedro de Cieza's book was published in Seville). Gómara was Cortes' chaplain and was given all the details for his book by the conquistador of Mexico. The style of the work is good, it has the merit of elegant brevity, and it is clear and concise, but Gómara never was in the New World. Part of the book concerns Peru; and the author was taken to task for errors by Cieza in the second (Antwerp) edition of his *Chronicle,* which makes it certain that Cieza himself revised his own book. Gómara's book because of its literary merit, was republished several times in his lifetime. Another edition appeared in Zaragoza (1554–55) which contains thirty-two large wood engravings —the earliest series of woodcuts illustrating American history with the exception of those of Pedro de Cieza de León. There were many translations; it appeared in London in 1578 as *The Pleasant Historie of the Conquest of the West India, now called new Spayne, Atchieved by the worthy Prince Hernando Cortez.*

setting down, in a grand concept, the whole history of two separate races of men and chronicling the while the rise and fall of the Inca empire. He was to the New World what Herodotus had been to his. Cieza might well have written the same words of that Greek geographer: "I hope to do two things: to preserve the memory of the past by putting on record the astonishing achievements of our own men and of the Asiatic peoples, and second: and more particularly, to show how the two races came into conflict."[4]

Cieza wrote simply, but he also wrote well, with an apt turn of phrase performing, as the Spaniard said, *"Con el alma en la pluma"* —with his soul in his pen.

—2—

Pedro de Cieza de León was born at the Villa of Llerena, Spain, in 1520. We know little more than that, except that his father, who bore the name of Lope de León, was a small shopkeeper and, like his mother, born Leonor de Cazalla, a native of Llerena.[5]

The Villa of Llerena (it was not a city until the seventeenth century) was at the time of Cieza's birth on an important axis of commerce, being on the main highway to Portugal, only a few miles from the frontier city of Badajoz. Llerena lay at the outer edge of Extremadura province, that harsh land known for the naked misery of its soil and its surfeit of poverty, that province which gave the New World many of its conquerors, such as the Pizarros and the Belalcázars —hard-bitten peasants delighted to go abroad for succor from this bald and eroded land.

Llerena was not too distant from the great Roman silver road, the Via Argenta, which connected Seville, running through Mérida, to Salamanca. Llerena was first a Roman village, *Dagina Turulorum,* and then in the tenth century it was occupied by the Saracens. It changed back and forth in the tides of battle until it was finally taken by the Spanish Knights of Santiago in 1241. Although the Spanish victors laid about in earnest and Alfonso XI thought Llerena sufficiently Hispaniolized to hold his parliament there in 1340, still a

---

4 These are the opening lines of *The Histories,* by Herodotus, as translated by Aubrey de Selincourt (London, 1954).

5 The documentation of Cieza de León's last years in Seville is given by Señor Miguel Marticorena in his "Cieza de León en Sevilla y su Muerte."

large percentage of Arab population remained; there were also large community cells of Sephardic Jews. Llerena remained in fact so Arab that when a new church was erected in the fifteenth-century plateresque style, the tower was decorated with a strong Arab flavor; the interior was unmistakably Mudejar.

xxx

All this is important in Cieza's heritage.

The Inquisition had a tribunal at Llerena and lists of the condemned are still extant. It exhibits how deep lay the suspicions of nonconformity, for Llerena was a focal point of heterodoxy. The Spaniard posited that the Jews aided the Arabs in their invasion of Spain and in the holding down of the Christians, so there was a concentrated effort to induce those of alien corn to become Christians. The Jewish converts were henceforth known as *conversos*. Ferdinand and Isabella, in the first part of their reign over a united Spain, were surrounded by *conversos,* who held high office in finance, diplomacy, the army, the church, and even in the royal household.[6] The plaint and wail of the triumphant Spaniard was that assimilation did not always follow conversion, enlivening their arguments for indiscriminate expulsion by quoting from the Talmud: ". . . drops of oil in water—no matter how well we wash the jar, it will forever remain oily." Such arguments eventually prevailed, and the Jews were expelled from Spain in January, 1492.

Pedro de Cieza de León, *converso* or not, read Erasmus and was this event and was brought up in a region well peopled with such *conversos*. The Inquisition, boring ceaselessly into their daily lives, used all the subtle tricks of dialectic to pry out what they then characterized as "false Christians," and so, throughout Pedro de Cieza's histories one will find an excessive appeal to God and the mysteries of the Church ("Satan . . . for Cieza," says Prescott, "had a full measure of ancient credulity"), so that this canting rubbish stands in glaring contrast to his precise observation on primitive peoples. Some have averred that this excessive appeal to God and Church was used to cover up the fact that he himself was a *converso*—and thus suspect.

[6] "In many districts the Jews acted as auxiliaries to the invaders. The captured towns were entrusted to Jewish garrisons with a stiffening of Mussulmans, to hold down the Christians" (Louis Bertrand and Sir Charles Petrie, *The History of Spain*). In the chapter entitled "Jews, Christians, and Conversos" (in his *Christopher Columbus*), Salvador de Madariaga summarizes the whole complicated social history of the origin of the Spanish-Jewish pogroms and dispersions.

This, however, is unproved; Pedro de Cieza's vision of God was of his time and well within the orbit of the Spanish microcosm. Men, moreover, are rare who are free from the foibles of their time. Cieza accepted the idea of God as furnished him by the Roman Catholic faith; he referred all to God, leaving the term in its infinite vagueness, and relying for the rest on theology, which, as we know, treats the unknowable with minutest accuracy.[7]

xxxi

While it is true that the Inquisitorial lists record some "Cazallas" under suspicion of being *conversos,* they were not of the same province nor of the same family, for the "Cazallas" on Cieza's maternal side had been minor merchants, public notaries; many were connected with the Church. Still, the Cazallas of Llerena were not conformists; they were in fact Catholic deviationists with Protestant leanings, marked as *alumbrados* and *Erasmistas;* Cieza's family was of this sect. This will explain Pedro de Cieza's comity and simplicity and his gift of sympathy for the natives, whom he regarded as human beings and whose culture he described in humane terms.

Pedro de Cieza de León, *converso* or not, read Erasmus and was a humanist.[8]

How did Cieza find the time—seeing that he left for the New World "at so tender an age that I hardly rounded out thirteen years" —to acquire an education? And wherefrom this display of learning he exhibits in his books? That he had books with him must be taken for granted and that he found time to read "in the many histories that I have seen" must be accepted. He obviously did not attend a university, for he often deprecates his "small learning"; he freely confesses that his attempt to write histories was a "temerity on the part of one of so few letters." Still his youth must have been fostered in learning, and like many others of his time he attained intellectual strength very early and his keen understanding came well clad to ripen in the sun of the busy human world. One must not be dubious of this; Hernán Cortés was considered for his time and the circum-

7 ". . . always bear in mind that a sound intelligence rejects everything that is contrary to reason except in matters of faith, where it is necessary to believe blindly," says l'abbé Jerome Coignard in Anatole France's *La Rôtisserie de la Reine Pédauque.*

8 Desiderius Erasmus (b. 1469), Dutch humanist ordained as a Catholic priest; studied and taught in Paris. He wrote many satirical and critical works combining wide erudition with malicious humor. A humanist, often critical of clerical abuse and lay ignorance, he still remained a believing Roman Catholic. His influence was vast and was the origin of heterodoxy in Spain which was condemned by the Church.

stances of his employment—i.e., a conquistador—a man of learning, for he had attended the University of Salamanca at the age of fourteen. Even then it was for only a matter of months, "where in the short lapse of time he read grammar ... perhaps law ... then leaving his studies soon returned home." Yet Cortés' "Five Letters" to his king, written while making the conquest of Mexico, are ingenious pieces in their precise grasp of people and geography. Besides, many of those who participated in the American conquest could read and write. They were not all knuckleheads, like Francisco Pizarro, who after sixty years of life could only make the rubric beside his signature.

Cieza's education, wherever he had it and whatever it was, certainly was not scanty for that period. He was familiar with Herodotus and Cicero and he read Erasmus; he tosses about the names of Alexander, Hector, Titus Livy, Valerius, and even those of a certain obscurity such as Diodorus Siculus, not as a parade of names but in direct relation to the point he is making. His family doubtlessly had some connections, and whether he had schooling in Seville, Mérida, or elsewhere, it seems to have been adequate; besides, the mere attending of a university would not in itself have made him a good observer or, even more, a good writer, for "what nature does not give," so runs the Spanish proverb, "Salamanca lends not."

Seville, since the beginning of the discovery of the New World, had been its center; the ships going out and returning made for the riverport of Sanlúcar de Barrameda (which fronted the Atlantic beyond the Strait and the Pillars of Hercules), entered the river, and were borne up by tide and tow less than fifty miles inland to Seville. In Seville was the *Casa de Contratación,*[9] a sort of Colonial Office Board of Trade contrivance where almost all business with the New World was conducted; here, too, one obtained permission to travel abroad.

---

[9] The *Casa de Contratación,* explains Salvador de Madariaga (*The Rise of the Spanish American Empire* [London 1947], 60–61), had been founded on January 20, 1503. Through conquest and discovery it grew apace throughout the sixteenth century until there was an Admiralty Board of Trade for Indian Affairs formed as a sort of tribunal.

It was composed of a president, with accountants, clerks, lawyer magistrates, even jailers; there was a chief pilot, who explained claims of conquistadores, made grants to those who sought new lands, trained pilots, studied and published maps, and recast and designed and manufactured ship's instruments. Although subordinated to the Council of the Indies, it had control of all who ventured abroad.

Seville reflected in the sumptuousness of its buildings its position as the entrepôt of the Americas; its cathedral was embellished by gifts from those *tercios* who, having won fame and renown in the "newfounde worlde," sought regal entry into the next by handsome donations to the church. The university, the houses of the factors who engaged in commerce, the presence of agents of the banking houses of the Welsers and the Fuggers, whose destinies were tied to the rise and fall of the Spanish Hapsburgs—all in their way gave Seville its glittering place in the sun.

Over the ancient Roman roads still in use, Pedro de Cieza must have made his way often enough to Seville and beyond, traveling with his father, a merchant of Llerena. Those years would have been the only years granted him to travel, for when describing Inca stonework, he wrote: *"In all Spain* I have not seen anything that could be compared with the masonry of these walls"; and again when speaking of the Inca roads, "The roads were more crowded than the Roman road between Seville and Trian, and I could not say more." This suggests that he made his way about very early in life.

On January 9, 1534, the galleon *Santa María del Campo* wharfed in Seville, the self-same treasure ship which brought the ransom gold of the Inca Atahualpa; it carried aboard millions of pesos of gold and silver bullion. Along with it, to explain the whole extraordinary business of Inca conquest, was Hernando Pizarro, the literate member of the Pizarro clan. Those in Seville who meddled in American affairs knew that Francisco Pizarro had discovered in 1527 the ramparts of the "kingdom of gold" and that he had made his way back to Spain in the summer of 1528 bearing with him llamas, some Quechua-speaking Indians taken from Tumpiz or Tumbes, and enough gold and silver to give his astonishing tale of the "first contact" with that Inca realm a metallic reality. On July 26, 1529, Queen Juana the Mad had signed the famous *Capitulación* which opened up the conquest of Peru and defined the powers and privileges of Pizarro.[10] That is all that Seville had of Pizarro after he departed from Spain that same

[10] Juana the Mad, the addle-brained mother of Charles V, signed the famous *Capitulación* with Francisco Pizarro for the conquest of Peru on July 26, 1529. In this he was given rights of discovery in Peru, title and rank of governor and captain-general, permission to erect fortresses, to assign commanderies (encomiendas) of Indians under the limitations of the law, and to exercise all the authority incident to a viceroy. His annual salary was to be 725,000 *maravedís,* or $725.

year until now, and here was the *Santa María del Campo,* loaded with golden spoils, the like of which Spain had never seen.

Among those who witnessed the arrival of this golden ship and watched with wondering eyes as its bullion was being removed to the countinghouses of the King, was young Pedro de Cieza: "I remember the rich pieces of gold that I saw in Seville, brought from Cajamarca, where the treasure that Atahualpa promised the Spaniards was collected." His imagination naturally was fired by the glitter of the gold and the swaggering, commanding presence of Hernando Pizarro, who only a few years before had been no more than a human cipher in the harsh lands of Extremadura. Now he was dressed in velvets with glittering ear-ornaments and with small Negro pages to do his bidding. Like his contemporary, who was in Peru during Cieza's time (and one who also wrote a *History of the New World*), he could have explained his actions thus: "When I was a youth, being like many others anxious to see the world and hearing of those countries recently found . . . I determined to go there."[11]

Not alone the mere sight of this treasure stirred his imagination; there were exciting things to read, for within four months of the arrival of the *Santa María del Campo,* the press of Bartolomé Pérez in Seville had printed *La Conquista del Peru.* It was the first report (by a soldier who did not name himself) of the capture, ransom, and death of the Lord-Inca, Atahualpa.

The printer-publisher, hurried as he was to satisfy the public demand for information, delayed it long enough to include on its title page a crude, yet effective illustration of the whole memorable scene —Atahualpa being borne on his litter, Vicente de Valverde handing him a Bible (the throwing down of which was the signal for his capture), and the armed Pizarros standing by attired in slashed velvet. These booklets, read by countless people, passed from hand to hand

---

[11] Girolamo Benzoni, born in Milan in 1519, traveled widely in the Americas between 1542 and 1556. He was involved in the same civil wars as Pedro de Cieza; yet his grasp of what he saw was slight, his information superficial, and the Italianate orthography of names of the land as well as all names of persons borders on the ludicrous. Still the book had an immense vogue throughout Europe, largely because of the illustrations of Theodore de Bry. A Flemish engraver, goldsmith by profession, De Bry fled the lowlands during the infamous Council of Blood (1570) and settled at Frankfurt, where he illustrated and issued a large folio volume of Belzoni (the first illustrated book on the conquest of Peru), as well as early books on Florida and Virginia. Here he began in 1590 his *Grands et Petits Voyages.* (See *The New World,* edited by Stefan Lorant [New York, 1946].)

until, worn and torn from use, all disappeared except one unique copy. As Europe clamored for news of this fabulous discovery of the "kingdom of gold" and the news was printed throughout Europe, in France the pamphlet appeared under the naïve title of *Nouvelles Certaines des Isles du Perou.*

In March, 1535, Pedro de Cieza petitioned, with the aid of his father **XXXV** and his uncle, Alonso de Cazalla, a well-known public notary in Seville, for permission to sail for the New World, as right of passage was vigorously controlled. If further proof be needed that his family was not *conversa* and not on the wanted list of the Inquisition, it is found in the fact that his petition was quickly granted. In the books of the *Asientos de Pasajeros,* under date of April 2, 1535, there appears this entry: "Pedro de León, son of Lope de León and of Leonor de Cazalla, citizens of Llerena, sailed with Juan del Junco to Cartagena in the vessel of Cifuentes; Rodrigo Pérez and Luis de Llerena swore that he is not of the forbidden ones."[12]

On that date or close to it, the ship of "Cifuentes" sailed down the Guadalquivir River from Seville; passing the river seaport of San-lúcar de Barrameda, it made the first swells of the Atlantic, carrying the boy "who scarcely rounded thirteen years"—the future *Cronista de las Indias*—out into the Ocean-Sea toward South America.

—3—

In the same year, after a passage of thirty-five days, during which time the galleon of "Cifuentes" touched at the Azores,[13] and a month later at the Antilles, Pedro de Cieza arrived at Cartagena.

An immense natural harbor and soon destined to be the entrepôt of the Americas, which would make it for centuries the focal point of foreign envy, Cartagena had only recently been founded by Captain Pedro de Heredia. An ambitious, active, energetic man, not held back by any scruples, Heredia had already laid out the city with a church and storage houses, and by the time of the arrival of the gal-

[12] *Archivo General de Indias,* Seville. *Contratación,* leg. 5.536, Book 3, Passenger List. Folio 168, April 2, 1535. Also see Cristóbal Bermúdez Plata *Catálogo de Pasajeros a Indias,* Vol. II (1535–38), No. 434 (Seville, 1942).

[13] The Azores were called *Terceras.* This explains an obscure passage in Pedro de Cieza's last will and testament where he says "Yten mando que se paguen a Diego Mexia yerno del jurado Venegas tres escudos que me presto en la tercera viniendo de Indias." Doubtlessly what was meant here (since Cieza only made one voyage) was that the money was lent to him at the Islas Terceras (Azores).

leon of "Cifuentes," it even had a landing pier. As for Heredia, he
was in the interior up the river Sinú (which debouched into the Carib-
bean not too far from Cartagena), where he busied himself "disemboweling Indians with great satisfaction."

Pedro de Cieza certainly was not given much time to acclimatize
himself to his surroundings. Within days of his arrival he was sent
along with a force to aid Pedro de Heredia with his "disemboweling,"
for Cieza records being "in that Cenú . . . where I was in the year
1535." There he saw his first gold —some of those wonderful imagi-
native castings which we know, since many somehow escaped the
Spanish crucibles. "I saw great and rich quantities removed . . . in
the burial places of Cenú from out of these tumuli." On the *llanos*
of the river Sinú—first called the Finzenú—lay fertile plains spotted
with large burial mounds. In these the dead were found surrounded
by golden images which rank among the finest in the Americas. The
discovery of these whetted the appetites of the conquistadors, and
from out of that golden hoard came the ironical couplet of how

> *It was an ill day for Peru*
> *When they found the river Sinú.*

This because Francisco Pizarro, then in that year of 1535 conqueror
of the Incas and founder of Lima, first acquired his spurs of conquest
when in the self-same Sinú in 1509, very early in the game, following
the famous Captain Ojeda into this land.

After the Sinú, Pedro de Cieza was sent along with an army of exploration—and conquest—to settle the large inland Urute (Urabá)
Gulf, into which flowed the waters of the river Atrato.

The Spaniards still searched for the "strait" which Columbus had
vainly sought, a natural canal that would lead to the Pacific. Apparently the Spanish crown dangled great rewards in front of their eyes
so they would expend all their energies trying to find a passage to
the Southern Seas and thus Pedro de Cieza trekked in search of it,
along with his Captain Alonso de Cáceres; he said of him: ". . . a
valorous man . . . of this I am a good witness, for in the discovery
of the Urute, I served under his banner."

Cieza nowhere mentions what he did in his first years. He was
certainly not a soldier; he must have been hired by some officer as a

page, or an arms-bearer, lacing his captain into his armor, keeping the weapons in repair, feeding the horses; or when on the rivers, paddling or poling; or when walking across the wide bare *llanos,* bearing his captain's necessities. For many of the captains who came to Colombia were fresh from the Italian wars and with the proceeds of the booty at the sack of Rome, and they had outfitted themselves in shining armor, embroidered doublets, and Perpignan hats, and arrived with a company of lackeys and pages and ofttimes scribes, so that their anticipated deeds might find a ready chronicler. As soon as they collided with the reality of the land, all this panoply was discarded. No one any longer wore full armor, or if he did in this ovenhot land, he found himself more or less like Don Quixote: *"molido i quebrantado"*—broken as if he had passed through a mill. Gone, too, were the illusions of sudden wealth. It was a frightful way to earn passage through life; still it was done and inspired by the Spanish sense of *missión* which made them endure horrible years. Cieza was one of them.

"I found myself in the village of San Sebastián de Buena Vista [now Urabá] in the year 1536." And he wrote with understandable pride, "We were the first Spaniards to travel this route to the Southern [i.e., Pacific] Sea." It was here that the youthful Pedro began to take mental notes on his first contacts with the Indians, those who lived in the Choco and on the Atrato River. They "lived in small villages, in houses like long sheds, sleeping in hammocks. . . . they are clean in their eating . . . the lords are obeyed and feared . . . and their women are the prettiest and most lovable of any that I have seen in the Indies."

After fruitless hammering at the green wall of vegetation in an attempt to locate a pass to the Pacific and wasting men and supplies, the expedition "to find a natural canal" came to an end. In the summer of 1537, Pedro de Cieza transferred—apparently with his captain, he does not say—to the army of Master Juan de Vadillo, he who promised to take them up to Antioquía, high and deep into the interior, where, rumor had it, a great chieftain called Nutibara surrounded himself with golden luxury.

Cieza began to fall under the spell of this country as they began to pole up the *"río verde* which lies forty-eight leagues from Antioquía."* They did not know where they were going. They had no maps. Their guides were naturally inconstant. They were always hungry. Trees, some with roots awash from the black earth, others bound together by lianas as thick as cordage, hung over the river. Still more, the heartwood eaten away by termites, stood bald and sere, like signposts on the roads of time. Along the banks the foliage was tenanted by iguanas "which look like the lizards of Spain except that they are larger and fiercer." There were enormous water snakes, "one of which I set down as true even though I did not see it—that one twenty feet long which Pedro Jimón ran through with a lance . . . which in its belly they found a young deer whole as it had been swallowed. . . . the Spaniards were so hungry they ate the fawn and even part of the snake." On the *llanos* there were snakes "which when they crawl make a noise that sounds like a rattle; if these bite a man, he dies," along with peccaries, jaguars, and tapirs. The trees were livened by colonies of red howling monkeys, parrots, macaws, and a bell-bird whose one-note song is as pure and golden as a clapped bell. And there was the annoying persistence of insects: "Great spiders . . . and ants, like the one which bit one Noguerol . . . the pain was so great that he became unconscious. . . . and worms, thick hairy worms . . . I shall never forget . . . for once while on guard by a river in the mountains of Abibe . . . one of these worms bit me on the neck and I spent the worst night in my whole life."

The crisp air was vibrant with the music of cicadas when their company quit the river, took to the *llanos,* and made their way overland toward the Cauca River, which would lead them to Antioquía. They did not know it then, but they were following the trail that led to El Dorado following the path of salt (for salt was so scarce a commodity it was used as currency), the small ceramic salt-filled dishes which were coming down as trade from the interior. The captured Indian traders told them that "where the salt comes, comes the gold"—but this riddle making no sense, they turned from that path and kept to the one that would bring them up the Cauca to that plateau ruled by the chief Nutibara.

The Indians were already giving trouble. The war horses emerged from the melee with enough arrows stuck in them to give them the look of hedgehogs. Cieza, now a full-fledged soldier of seventeen, being without armor, made a breastplate of articulated leather out of the tough hide of the tapir as a defense against poison arrows, for they had come in contact with Indians using curare, "A plant so evil," wrote Cieza, describing it for the first time, "that whenever it hits and draws blood, surely one dies, even though the wound be no more than a pinprick." Against Indians, poison darts, ambush, and hunger, the Spaniards had the horse, powder, crossbow, and petard. It was courage of an extraordinary sort, and no matter what the motives, whether the thirst for gold or the thirst for God, one can never cavil at their courage and their persistence. What remains amazing is that Cieza, even in such moments, was taking down notes of what he saw and heard: "Everywhere I turned aside to see what I could of the regions in order to learn and set down what they contained." Instead of killing time, he made time: *hacer tiempo,* as the Spaniards have it: "Often when the other soldiers were resting, I wearied myself writing. But neither this nor the difficulties of land, mountains, and rivers . . . intolerable hunger and trials ever stood in my way of two callings, that of writing and following my standard and my captain without abate." At first he said that he was moved to put down what was occurring for the reason that "time destroys the memory of events in such sort that soon there is no knowledge of what has passed." Whatever it was that gave him this impulse, we remain in eternal debt, for after all these four hundred years Cieza is still the best historical source on the Indians of the Cauca River and beyond; customs, description, dress, manners, people, animals, industry, were carefully observed. We can only be grateful that he "turned aside."

Even as Cieza occupied himself with conquest and note-taking, the small army of Captain Vadillo in 1539 was making its way up the Cauca valley. The first Spaniards to do so, they were made aware that matters in Peru had taken a dismal turn. Although the information they had was years old, they heard of the escape of the Inca, the siege of Cuzco by great armies of Indians, and that an appeal had been sent out by the Marquis Pizarro to all the Spaniards throughout the Americas to hurry down to Peru to aid in breaking the siege. The next news was that it had been broken. Then no sooner was that siege ended than the Inca fled with his army and retired to an unassailable part of the mountain at Vilcabamba. After this, a civil war, long in the making, had broken out between Pizarro and his partner, Diego de Almagro, resulting in the death of the latter at Las Salinas—and an open conflict between the two contending parties who were quar-

reling over the carcass of the Inca empire was in full progress. Even
if any of the Spaniards in the Cauca valley, though perspiring and
broken in their armor after climbing over savage and unknown
mountains, thought of going on to that golden empire of dubious
future, the means of movement toward Peru did not exist.

xl

By the year 1541, Cieza had rounded out twenty-one years of age.
He had taken part in the founding and settling of Antioquía and
was already setting off with his new captain, Jorge Robledo, to conquer and settle other cities farther up the Cauca valley.

Robledo was a *hidalgo* (i.e., a *hijo de algo,* a son of somebody).
Because of his birth and breeding, he appealed more to Cieza than
did all his other commanders, and he remembered his qualities even
after a long passage of time. Robledo's treatment of the Quimbayas
lacked the ferocity of the earlier conquests, and his men reaped gold
breastplates and goblets from the best goldsmiths in America. It was
a generous country, with game, fruits, a benign climate, and an altitude not much over three thousand feet; the Indians were well built,
"the men proper and tall—the women very loving."

Still the founding of cities and conquest of others' lands could
only be accomplished by blood and iron; the Indians who opposed
were so terrorized that when the Spaniards came into the valley of
Aburra, "the natives took such a horror of us that they and their
women hanged themselves from the trees by their hair or belts."

In the spring of 1541 the upper valley having been, if not fully
dominated, at least terrorized, and the lands of the defeated divided
among the deserving, the Spaniards returned to Cartago, which had
been previously settled. This they decided to put in a state of defense
while breaking in the natives to the yoke of peace. Jorge Robledo,
content that this was being done, turned his back on his conquests
and made his way with sundry members of a small force back to the
coast, there to take ship to Spain to attempt to have confirmed all
that he had conquered. Cieza and the rest (many names which turn
up again and again in the history of Peru) settled down in this
Cartago for six years; it was at this time, in the autumn of 1541, that
be began his history.

What made him set it down? Cieza himself gives answer: "for
traveling hither and yon and as I saw the strange and wonderful
things that exist in this New World . . . there came upon me a great

desire to write certain of them, those which I had seen with my own eyes and also what I heard from highly trustworthy persons . . . so . . . taking heart, with mounting confidence, I determined to devote a part of my life to writing history, being moved to do so by the following reasons: First, because I had taken notice that wherever I went, nobody concerned himself with writing aught of what was happening, and time destroys the memory of things; and second, because considering that we and the Indians all have the same origin . . . it was right that the world should know how so great a multitude of these Indians were brought into the sanctity of the Church." Such a history would have been difficult enough to write in a scholar's sanctuary. Then, under the circumstances, it was a small miracle. A few Spaniards with tenuous communications sat in their stockades ready to move out to repel attack from whatever quarter. The Quimbayas, "indomitable people . . . hard to subdue," were only one of the number of distinct tribes in the Cauca valley. They were in contest with the Spaniards as well as with each other. As the climate was mild, the Indians went about naked: "Neither men nor women wear anything but small aprons to cover their privities." Their large houses, of studs and fascine work thatched with grass, were communal, and fighting towers rose above the stockaded villages, "on top of which hung the heads of their enemies . . . a fearsome sight to behold."

For long it was war without quarter; any Spaniard who had the misfortune to fall alive to the enemy was, according to Cieza's observations, destined for the cooking pot. "These Indians are so given to eating of human flesh that they are known to seize women on the point of giving birth . . . and swiftly slit their belly with their knives . . . and extract the child . . . which they roast and eat. And again: "Once the Spaniards found a big cooking pot full of boiled meat. They were so hungry that their one thought was of eating. . . . when all had eaten their fill, one of the Spaniards fished out of the pot a hand with fingers on it." Prisoners, whether they were Spaniards or Indians, were never killed but placed "in a pen like a cage . . . and well fed, and once they were fattened, they brought them out . . . killed them with great cruelty, and ate them." Even then, Cieza's humanism must have impressed them, for they gave him money to invest; and on his death bed he remembered it: "I was entrusted with and am obliged to repay three hundred ducats that certain Indians whom I know gave me to invest which I did not, and because they are dead and in no wise can I make restitution to them."

He did not try to justify these conquests with any ape-faced devising or hypocrisy; for ironically, he speaks about their being "brought to justice [i.e., captured and subdued], though there was little need of killing, for it was only for the sake of getting this accursed gold from them." This fierce drama was unmatched by anything the soldiers had seen, many of them veterans of the Italian wars. To farm outside of the stockades, the Spaniards had to rely upon subdued Indians or Negro slaves (of which there seem to have been quite a few), and these they had under constant guard. Such an existence made cruelty as natural as breathing. What other relaxation was there but wenching with the Indian girls? Now and then (for Cieza, too) in this terrible life, there was a parenthesis for love. "As my Captain knew," wrote Cieza, "that I was curious to know the secrets of the Indians, he gave me Catalina [this being the name he gave a comely Indian] . . . that I might learn more easily." And when not women, it was carousal on liquor made from fermented corn mash, "a wine they made of corn which is so strong that too much of it leaves one senseless." In this sort of life Pedro de Cieza wrote, composing on top of a drumhead which served as a table and with a condor's quill for a pen. Yet he remained the careful, dispassionate observer. And even when his very existence was challenged anew each day, "my body spent through those long journeys and protracted vigils . . . climbing great and rugged mountains, so lofty that their summits were lost in the clouds and the accompanying scud . . . I was so done in that it was very difficult for me to reach the top and on turning to gaze down, it seemed that the ravines reached down into the bowels of hell."

Despite the fact that he took part in these actions, he covered finally more than three thousand miles, "seeing these things with my own eyes." He described what he saw with scientific exactitude, and he was doing what he vowed he would do at the beginning: "The things that I deal with in this history I have observed with great care and diligence." All this was started before Cieza had reached his majority.

Observation combined with precise description is a rare talent in any man. In Pedro de Cieza's case it is even more extraordinary since he was then very young, with little formal schooling and reared in

a theater of war. The only such person with whom he is comparable
is that wonderful Bernal Díaz del Castillo, a conquistador and com-
panion-in-arms of Hernán Cortes in the conquest of México. Still the
comparison is not apt; Bernal Díaz wrote as an octogenarian and
looking backward ("I am now an old man eighty and four years of
age and I have lost my sight and hearing and as luck would have it
I have gained nothing of value") and had the aid of a number of
published histories to jog his memory and give him an ordered sequence of events. Cieza began at twenty, while actually participating
in battle, and he had nothing on which to lean except the turn of
daily events; he wrote in a vacuum.

xliii

The scarcity of paper and ink only added to the problem. One
piece of paper cost then as much as a horse would fifty years later: "A
sheet of paper," Cieza complains, "cost me thirty pesos in Cali."[14]
Since the eight histories of Pedro de Cieza approximated eight thousand sheets of foolscap, one can from this form an idea of the immense
financial investment there was in paper alone. Cieza bought paper
when he should have used his money to buy a horse; when he should
have carried gold in his saddlebags, he was carrying books.

As the manuscript history began to pile up, during the years 1541-
47, Pedro de Cieza faced the problem of the transport of this burgeoning manuscript. He was still a foot soldier, he had to be alert
for attack on the march, he could not burden himself with too much,
and so the fear of the loss of his manuscripts was always before
him; he seemed somehow to have lost nothing despite the long
marches and the battles, except in the melee at Xaquixahuana, where
he lost some valuable papers and notebooks, "which I regretted very
much." The care and the solicitude for his papers is something like
that of William Dampier, pirate and navigator, whose career, too,
was hardly conducive to sustained literary effort. Still he composed
his *Discourses on Winds,* observations on the movements of air cur-

---

[14] Costs in the first years of the conquest were fantastic; there is no precise equivalent in purchasing power for Spanish pesos, ducats, *maravedís* (one cent), and other
forms of money. "A sow," said Cieza, "brought 1,600 pesos in Colombia" (one could
have purchased ten horses for that sum twenty-five years later); "common table knives
sold at 15 pesos each. . . . I heard that Captain Miguel Muñoz . . . bought a cobbler's
awl for 30 pesos, and I myself paid 8 gold pesos for a pair of sandals . . . soldiers bought
piglets for 100 pesos before they were born." (*Chronica del Perú* [Anvers, 1554], 53.)

rents, which for safety's sake he kept "in a large Joint of Bamboo . . . stop't at both ends with wax."[15]

The autumn of 1546 put an end to Pedro de Cieza's hegira in Colombia. His Captain Jorge Robledo ("so much liked for his goodness to us, that we looked upon him as a father") returned from Spain with the title of marshal and married to the well-born Doña María de Carvajal. He arrived in the company of Díaz de Armendáriz who came from Spain to enforce the "New Laws."[16] Conceived as a humanist measure to aid the Indians, as often happens to the best intentions, it caused instead war and completed the ruin of the Inca empire. In the Americas, where geographical lines were fluid, the territorial grants of various conquistadors frequently overlapped, and Jorge Robledo thought that he need only flourish a royal writ and bring Sebastián de Belalcázar, the conqueror of the realm of Quito, to submission; so with no more ado he entered into the disputed land about Popayán. On a dark night on October 4, 1546, Belalcázar surprised Jorge Robledo at Lomo de Pozo, summarily judged him, and summarily beheaded him, knowing full well that the Indians would subject his corpse to ritual cannibalism. Cieza was not there at the moment of attack, but his companions-in-arms were, and so "to prevent the body of Robledo and the others from being taken to the town of Arma and eaten by the Indians . . . [they] burned the house over their bodies." That was the bitter end for Cieza. "When I had notice of this . . . I abandoned my *repartimiento* of Indians, my hacienda at Arma, and left my mines to the wild Indians of Quimbaya."[17]

[15] William Dampier (d. 1715), buccaneer and navigator bent on piracy, sailed the Main, made his way around Cape Horn, and was marooned in the Nicobar Islands in the Pacific. His book, *A New Voyage Round the World,* which included "Discourses on the Winds" (1699), is a superb treatise which showed his skill as a hydrographer.

[16] The "New Laws" signed by Charles V, actually entitled *Leyes y Ordenanzas nuevamente hechas por S. M. para la gobernación de las Indias,* were principally passed to "conserve the Indians." The Indians were declared free and vassals of the crown; colonists could no longer have grants or encomiendas—that is, "commanderies of Indians" working under slave conditions. All religious orders and royal officials must give up such as they held at once and never again possess them. Others who had them, i.e., the conquistadors, could retain theirs, but these rights were not hereditary. Compulsory service by Indians was prohibited; they could be neither overworked nor overtaxed. (See Haring, *The Spanish Empire in America.*)

[17] "When the *repartimiento* was made . . . Arma was given to me in encomienda . . . I being a conquistador of these parts" (*War of Chupas,* 20). Arma, which lay twenty-three leagues from Cartago and twelve from Acerma (in the Cauca valley),

Popayán lies at the headwaters of the Cauca River, "neither high nor low, neither excessively cold nor hot"; it was destined to produce more poets, patricians, and prelates than any other place in all Colombia. In the autumn of 1546, Popayán was something else; it was filled with knights armed with pike and arquebus, a gathering of the very high and the very low, to hear the King's pleasure. They were commanded, said the royal decree, to place themselves under the orders of the officers loyal to the crown and proceed to Peru, there to put down the rebellion raised by Gonzalo Pizarro.

xlv

Why Cieza joined the group under Belalcázar so soon after he had murdered his captain is not explained. Perhaps he had no choice. However, this Belalcázar was a famed captain. Of equivocal antecedents (it is said of him that more than three-quarters of his life was a question mark), yet he was an efficient, predatory sort of man, one who took no more notice of the thousands of armed Indians than he would a handful of flies. He came early to Panama and was called out of retirement in Nicaragua at the beginning of the conquest of Peru; he was not at Cajamarca when the Inca was seized nor at the rape of Cuzco in 1534, but he made up for lost time after that pursuing the remaining Incaic hosts, which he defeated near snow-topped Chimborazo. He then moved north and founded Quito. Later, in pursuit of the myth of El Dorado, he was one of the "three" who made junction deep in Chibcha blood in the heartlands of Colombia. Balacázar was, as has been said, stronger than Quizquiz, the Inca chieftain he defeated; he was stronger than the wild tribes who blocked his way in Colombia; he was stronger than the mountains and the jungles, even more than disease and hunger. In a sense he had even conquered time.

"was one league from the big river that is the Cauca and was first situated on a slope leading down to the river and covered with big palm groves. The lands," Cieza wrote, "are fertile . . . a field of corn yields a hundred bushels or more and they plant it twice a year. . . . there are large deposits of [placer] gold in the big river. . . . with time this will become one of the richest lands of the Indies. The *repartimiento* of Indians in payment of my services was granted to me within the confines of this town. I wish that I could write more at length about this, for there is a good reason for it, but the nature of the reasons forbid it, most of all because of my comrades, we discoverers and conquerors who set out from Cartagena, are without Indians [i.e., income from their produce]; those who have them came by them for money or because they followed the fortune of those in power, which is no small wrong." (*Primera Crónica*, Harriet de Onis translation.)

What finally defeated him was a woman.[18]

It is with this Sebastián de Belalcázar and attached now as horseman that our chronicler, young Pedro de Cieza de León, rode into the furthermost northern corner of the kingdom of Peru.

The time was April 18, 1547.

—4—

Pedro de Cieza de León entered the Inca realm at Pasto. He went across the Angasmayo River, which was, as he knew, "the farthest point north reached by the Lord-Inca Huayna Capac," and then over the bridge of Rumichaca: "There is a bridge [Rumichaca] over this river which is natural, but seems man-made." Crossing the "bridge of stone," he set foot for the first time in the traditional boundaries of Peru.

They were now on full war footing. Gonzalo Pizarro, master of Peru, knew of their arrival and, as well, of the arrival of his nemesis, Pedro de la Gasca. A spy had reported that "Belalcázar had gone [to Quito] with four hundred men." Although Pedro de Cieza, who ought to have known, said, "Not quite two hundred of us Spaniards set out from the territory of Popayán with Belalcázar to support the cause of His Majesty against the tyrants."

By this time Pedro de Cieza knew all that had transpired in Peru. After involved verbal disputes and minor skirmishes, all of Peru was enmeshed in a civil war after the conquest. Diego de Almagro and Francisco Pizarro had quarreled over the division of the Inca spoils; there followed the battle of Salinas at the salt leaches outside of Cuzco, and Almagro was defeated—as is wonderfully recounted by Pedro de Cieza—"on the Saturday of St. Lazarus, 1538," and later beheaded. In the months that followed, Gonzalo Pizarro went off to find the "land of cinnamon" beyond Quito, and in that epic his second in command sailed down and discovered the Amazon River. In the meanwhile, Francisco Pizarro was assassinated at Lima in June, 1541, by the followers of Almagro's son. They then became masters of Peru.

---

[18] The man that Belalcázar "executed" was married to Maria Carvajal de Robledo. Delicately nurtured, she was implacable and pursued the old warrior relentlessly, and in 1550 summoned him to trial. He was being sent to Spain under bond when he sickened and died in Cartagena in 1551, deserted, broken, and seventy-five years of age. "A friend," said a chronicler, bought four yards of muslin and paid a nameless woman a peso and two *reales* to make a shroud."

Gonzalo Pizarro emerged from the jungles of the Amazon to find everything that he knew changed. The crown, anxious to settle these disputes, had sent Vaca de Castro, and he found the Pizarro camp fully willing to side with the King. Almagro the Younger, seeing nothing to be gained by acquiescence, moved into formal battle at Chupas, close to the newly founded city of Ayacucho. This battle marked the emergence of Francisco Carvajal, that septuagenarian and *pícaro* of high degree (a *pícaro* was one who saw the seamy side of life and remembered it with pleasure); he lent the only note of humor to the grim task of slaughter.

Almagro was defeated at Chupas on September 16, 1542, his army decimated, and he, as was the usual course, was beheaded. Then, no sooner had this phase ended than the "New Laws" were read to those conquistadors who had survived. There had been a rumor in the colonies of the preparation of these decrees, for after many years of propaganda Las Casas, Bishop of Chiapas, to secure the Indians' survival and to ease their lot, had finally seen these humane laws made into royal decrees. What now emerged were "laws and ordinances newly made for His Majesty for the better governing of the Indies" —which in effect spelled out the doom of those conquistadors who had gained the land by conquest and partitioned it among themselves. The conquistadors were violently aroused. Vaca de Castro was fortunate to have escaped with his life after that, and the next to arrive, a knight of Ávila named Blasco Núñez Vela, appointed as the first viceroy to Peru, had to bear the brunt. He was approached by sober-minded citizens and asked to consider some alleviation of the "New Laws." He replied frigidly, "I have come not to tamper with the laws nor to discuss their merits, but to execute them." Upon this, everyone flocked to the banner of Gonzalo Pizarro, and the Viceroy, instead of executing the laws, was himself executed by them; he was defeated in January, 1546, on the plains of Añaquito, near Quito, and stabbed to death on the field. Gonzalo Pizarro was now undisputed master of Peru.

Pedro de la Gasca, given title as president of the Royal Council in a royal decree dated February 16, 1546, was sent to deal with the rebellion in Peru. La Gasca was to play a significant part in this history, and he was also to loom very importantly in the life of Pedro de Cieza. He was no soldier. He had studied law and theology at Salamanca and had long been a member of the Council of the Spanish Inquisition. Frail, long in years, confessedly ignorant of military affairs and without knowledge about Peru, La Gasca offset these handicaps with a subtle intellect and executive ability. More, he was well endowed— and was impervious to bribery. His authority was plenary; he had a quire of Royal Decrees to be filled out according to his discretion.

xlviii

In a military pincers movement against the widely spread forces of Gonzalo Pizarro, the cavalry under Belalcázar, of which Cieza was one, moved down the backbone of the Andes following the Royal Road of the Incas. Another larger army under La Gasca's command landed on the coast at Tumbes. Pedro de Cieza, with ample time to "turn aside," as he did in Colombia, continued to make inquiry about all that concerned the Inca empire as they moved down through the famous cities from Quito southward—Pasto, Quito, Llactacunga, down the avenue of volcanoes and over the high *páramos* of the Andes into the valleys that lead to Tomebamba.

This Tomebamba (Cuenca now stands where it once was) had been one of the favorite lodging places of the last great Inca, Huayna Capac, "among one of the finest and richest in all Peru, and the buildings the largest and best." Atahualpa, his son by a woman of Quito, is said to have been born there.

Since the object was to defeat Gonzalo Pizarro quickly, before he knew what forces were being deployed against him, Belalcázar did not follow the royal mountain road of the Incas; instead, he took a lateral road which, turning beyond Tomebamba, led to the coast. This we know. For Pedro de Cieza states that "there was no direct route from Tomebamba to the [Peruvian coast] except by the way of San Miguel de Piura" [which was the first Spanish settlement in Peru.]

So into the coastal ramparts of the quondam empire of the Incas rode the "attachment of Quito, walking their horses at a Castilian pace." Although some of the names of the famous horses of the conquest were preserved,[19] Cieza, since he was an objective historian, failed to leave us the name of his own. Yet, like the rest, he mounted *á la gineta,* in a high Moorish saddle with mameluke bit, a single

[19] And these have been lovingly recalled by R. B. Cunninghame Graham (who himself rode Pampa, his "Black Argentine . . . for twenty years without a fall"). (See *The Horses of the Conquest* [Norman, 1949].)

rein, hand held high, and short Moorish stirrups. All rode in this fashion; the "Inca" Garcilaso de la Vega—who cribbed much from Cieza's histories—averred that "my country was won *á la gineta* [*mi tierra se ganó á la gineta*]."

The Quito contingent arrived at Tumbes some time in August, 1547, the captains having been summoned there to conference by the arrival of Pedro de la Gasca. It was agreed that they would advance in four columns toward their next gathering place at Jauja, seven hundred miles southward, once a large garrison city of the Incas and for a short period, in 1535, the first Spanish capital of Peru. Jauja, located in the cordilleras, more or less in the geographical center of Peru, was a hub of connections and served by three distinct Inca highways. The reasons for this cautious approach of four columns was so that the spies of Gonzalo Pizarro would not know where to place the main body of strength to oppose their passage through the Andes, and, if ambushed in the narrow defiles of the cordilleras, the whole army would not be overwhelmed. Such were La Gasca's tactics, as he explained later to his King-Emperor:[20] "One of the columns . . . troops under command of Juan de Saavedra . . . and those from Quito" were to go along the royal Inca road in the Andes. Cieza, however, did not go with "those from Quito"; instead, he went along the coast either with the main body of troops under La Gasca (who left Tumbes on the sixth of September) or immediately thereafter, for he writes, "I passed through the valley of Pacasmayo in the month of September, 1548,[21] to join the other soldiers who had come down from the government of Popayán."

Cieza's first view of the coast and the Inca domains was unhurried, since the army, encumbered by its supplies, moved at a pace which allowed Cieza, as he had often done in Colombia, to "turn aside." He had time to view the "great coastal highway, although in many places the road is now ruined and destroyed"; he was able to spend some

---

[20] La Gasca gave a forty-page summary to the King of his trip down from Panama and arrival at Tumbes (dated August 11, 1547) and a listing of the gathering of his forces throughout the northern kingdom (p. 421, La Gasca Papers); and later, after La Gasca had ascended the cordilleras, he wrote his "Most Illustrious Sir" (dated Jauja, December 27, 1547) to explain the tactics which he intended and did use in order to bring his troops in four columns safely to the valley of Jauja. (See p. 447, a summary of letters in *Pizarro–La Gasca Papers*, Maggs Bros. [London, 1925].)

[21] Pedro de Cieza is mistaken in his dates. As the battle of Xaquixahuana occurred on April 5, 1548, the correct date must be September, 1547.

days about the valleys that had formed the pre-Inca empire of Chimor and its capital, Chan-Chan, and to make inquiries into the customs of people of the coastal *yungas*. That which he did "not fully apprehend" was elaborated for him later by the friar Domingo de Santo Tomás, who was long resident in Peru. Cieza observed the strange weather phenomena on the coast, put down a description of coastal plants, the manner of native irrigation, and named all of the important oases along the desert road. Cieza "turned aside" to climb up into and describe the great Chimú fortress of Paramonga, whose bulk still stands, but without the "rooms and dwellings with walls painted with many wild animals and birds."

Pedro de Cieza went through the Lima valley about the beginning of December, 1547, coming to the sacred temple of Pachacamac: "There was none to compare with this . . . which is built upon a man-made hill of adobes . . . and on its summit the temple," and then went on to its valley, now called Lurin; thence he mounted and took the direct road—the wonderfully built main lateral road that connected this part of the coast direct with Jauja. This stone road beginning in the desert about Pachacamac is built into the side of the rock wall which borders the river canyon; the road rises in its relatively short 175 miles to a height of 16,000 feet when it crosses the *puna* and the desolation of Pariacaca. Pedro de Cieza leaves no doubt that he traveled this route: "Those who read this book and who have been in Peru will remember the road which goes from Lima [i.e., Pachacamac] to Jauja by the rugged mountains of Huarochirí and the snowy heights of Pariacaca . . . will understand . . . more than I write." Cieza followed this narrow and yet wonderfully engineered road—extensive sections of which still exist—gained the first and largest way-station in the Andes, to sleep "at the dwellings at Huarochirí, the halfway mark of the journey." Then he crossed the Pariacaca, a snow-bound and desolate land—doubtlessly experiencing *soroche,* the altitude sickness that assailed José de Acosta when he went over the same route[22]—he then mounted the Inca step-road which brought

---

[22] "There is in Peru," wrote José de Acosta, who traveled that way in 1570, "a high mountain which they call *Pariacaca* . . . when I came to mount the degrees, as they called them, which is the top of the mountaine, I was suddenly seized with so mortall and strange a pang . . . I was surprised with such pangs of straining and casting, as I thought to cast up my heart too, for having cast up meate, fleugme, and choller both yellow and greene, in the end I cast up blood. . . . it is the passage of this Pariacaca

him up and then down into the intermontane valley. There he crossed the suspension bridge which spanned the Mantaro River (its ramparts are still extant) and entered ancient Jauja, where La Gasca had some of his forces already assembled. He recorded the arrival of Captain Palomino over this route; mayhap Cieza was one of those "hundred men."

La Gasca, certainly aware that "Gonzalo Pizarro was at Cuzco making preparations for war," put the king's forces, which amounted to one thousand mounted and foot, in order and began the southward movement of his army. On the thirteenth of January, 1548, they reached Huamanga (now Ayacucho); a day later the army passed the plains of Chupas which had been the site of an earlier battle between the Spaniards—and which history Pedro de Cieza would tell—then, following the well-kept Inca road, they moved into the large ceremonial center of Vilcas-huamán; a wonderfully constructed stone city of which Cieza alone thought to give a good description. The army then descended a particularly precipitous Inca road and in the arid cacti-filled valley of the Vilcas, now the Pampas, River, Pedro de Cieza crossed the first of the gigantic Inca suspension bridges: "The bridge [of Vilcas]...is made of twisted fibers...so strong that horses can gallop over them as though they were crossing the bridge of Alcántara at Córdoba, in Spain."

At Andahuaylas they made rendezvous. They were now close on to Cuzco, and La Gasca awaited the arrival of further reinforcements; he records that "On the second of February, Belalcázar arrived at Andahuaylas with twenty horsemen, his presence giving great pleasure to the whole camp as he is held in much esteem."

The final battle for Peru began with La Gasca's attempt to take and hold the various suspension bridges which spanned the Apurímac River; these were the key to the taking of Cuzco. As was expected, the enemy had destroyed the four suspension bridges that crossed the Apurímac. The canyon was too sheer and the river too deep to allow either fording or sending over the equipment by raft, so they began to "collect the materials for bridges over the Apurímac." This meant no less than having hordes of Indians plait immense rope cables capable of sustaining a suspension bridge two hundred feet long.

that dothe have this propertie." (*The Naturall and Morall Historie of the East and West Indies,* 146.)

These immensely heavy and unwieldy cables were transported bodily by the Indians to the high banks of the Apurímac. The man who played a conspicuous part in this project was one Pedro Alonso Carrasco, an old conquistador. A friendship sprang up between Pedro de Cieza and this Carrasco during this operation on the banks of the Apurímac, and his name often appears as an informant in Cieza's history; "Peralonso Carrasco . . . one of the old conquistadors, told me . . . ."

lii

On the fifth of April the cables of a bridge, after various vicissitudes, were put up at Cotabamba near a bend in the Apurímac, and good tactics allowed La Gasca's troops to hold the other side while the bridge was finally put in order.

On the ninth of April, 1548, the opposing troops began to take position on the plains of Xaquixahuana, that field which had seen so many decisive battles in the past. La Gasca had arrayed in battle his "300 pikemen and 400 arquebusiers," and in the rear—presumably with Pedro de Cieza among them—220 cavalry." Soldiers firing four mortars from a hilltop which overlooked the massed enemy, rolled the cannon balls among the troops of Gonzalo Pizarro, and this was enough to bring them to that moment of truth. First singly, then in groups of two and three and then in a mass, the troops began to desert. When La Gasca's arquebusiers opened fire on those of the enemy with minds unmade to fight or flee, it precipitated a wholesale flight to the standard of the King. There, to one side, watching his army melt away—and laughing at the contretemps that would bring him to the headsman's axe—was Francisco de Carvajal. Very much alive at eighty-four years of age, he who had fought through Pavia, the sack of Rome, and the civil wars of Peru, festooning the unfruited trees with the bodies of men who had the ill luck to run counter to his wishes. Carvajal sat still on his horse "Boscanillo" (who like his rider was past his prime), and above the din of battle, all could hear him jest at his losses, singing an old nursery rhyme,

O mother, my hairs
One by one they fly away in the air
O, poor mother,
My hairs!

Then he belatedly took off, but his horse floundered in the marshes of Anta, and he was set upon and captured, well illustrating the Spanish proverb, *"Una cosa piensa el bayo y otra el que lo ensilla."* Fully knowing his end, he laughingly prepared for it.

When the last shot had been fired, Pedro de Cieza changed figuratively his soldier's attire for the cloak of the historian and "sharpened his quill."

liii

Unfortunately, in the melee Cieza lost some of his notebooks and papers, "which [he] regretted very much." Perhaps it was the loss of part of his manuscript which led to his recognition by Pedro de la Gasca, for certainly it was unusual enough that a common soldier was writing a history of Peru.[23] Even more unusual was the fact that he should carry the whole of the bulky manuscript into battle. More than likely he was brought to La Gasca's attention by one of his secretaries, for it so happened that of his four scriveners, one, Pedro López de Cazalla, was from Llerena; he was, as his name suggests,

[23] It is strange that Pedro de Cieza did not know, or if he knew, never mentioned, that three others were taking down notes that would eventuate into books on Peru. "I had taken notice," he wrote, "that wherever I went nobody concerned himself with writing aught of what was happening." Yet Girolamo Benzoni, an Italian from Milan, was then writing down his notes, which became a book (see footnote 11 above). He was there during the civil wars, in fact at the time of Cieza, quitting Lima on May 8, 1550, because "President de la Gasca had ordered all foreigners to quit the country." Another, Agustín de Zárate, long a member of the Royal Council of Castile, had arrived in Peru in 1544 to make an accounting of acts and accounts of the officers of the crown. He collected notes and material, particularly from Rodrigo Lozano of Trujillo and from many others, but his life being threatened, he left Lima in June, 1545. He composed his book in Spain; he is never mentioned by Pedro de Cieza. The third, and it is really inexplicable that he should not have been known and mentioned by Pedro de Cieza) was the Mexican-born Pedro Gutiérrez de Santa Clara. Born of a conquistador of Mexico and an Aztec woman, he came to Peru during the civil wars (1544–48) to serve under Captain Pablo de Meneses. He remained in Peru for at least four years (1544–48) during which time he took elaborate note on the occurrences of the civil wars. Almost all of the *dramatis personae* mentioned by Pedro de Cieza are here also, and someone must have informed Cieza that another was going over the same ground as himself, since he wrote some of his history in Cuzco after 1547. This immense manuscript, called by Pedro Gutiérrez "Quincenarios," remained in manuscript until published in 1904 under the title of *Historia de las Guerras Civiles del Peru* (5 vols., edited by Manuel Serrano y Sáenz). It deals almost exclusively with those wars, but the author does mention in passing the curious statues in Tiahuanacu (Book III, Chapter IX), the great abandoned ruined city of Huánuco (Book II, Chapter LXI), the burial *Chullpas* about Lake Titicaca, the feather-weaving, made from marine birds, "given me by a Curaca friend of mine that was the great Lord of the town of Chincha," and other details which are sandwiched between the heavier layers of military action. Like Cieza, he is never mentioned in any contemporary letter or report, and, as Cieza is to him, so is he to Cieza; they were unknown to each other, yet both were writing of the events transpiring before their eyes.

related to Cieza's mother. Whether it was this way or that, the matter is of no moment; La Gasca read that which Cieza had written. He had a patron.

Pedro de Cieza returned to Lima soon after the dismembering of the body of Francisco de Carvajal and the beheading of Gonzalo Pizarro. Presumably he journeyed in the official party to Lima, where La Gasca reported to the King that they were received on September 17, 1548 "with much joy and fun and dancing."

During the month of October, La Gasca was occupied with affairs of government and in giving rewards to the deserving and a variety of punishments to those who had the misfortune to lose. Cieza was appointed *Cronista de Indias;* although this document has not come to light, Cieza says he was in possession of such an appointment along with letters addressed to the authorities of Peru. This title did appear on his only published *Crónica* (1553), yet in his own hand he wrote *"primer Cronista de las Indias"* under his name in the history entitled the *War of Quito.*

He was allowed access to all the captured correspondence of Gonzalo Pizarro, much of which now forms the Pizarro–La Gasca manuscript collection in the Huntington Library, for he remembered that "I, being in [Lima] . . . saw the letters of Gonzalo Pizarro. . . . I remember that there were so many that three secretaries, continually reading to President La Gasca, did not finish for four days." He wearied himself copying down all he needed, confessing in the *War of Chupas* that "my mind is so confused in trying to comprehend . . . the affairs which we yet have to deal with, and my body so weary through the long journeys and protracted vigils I have passed through." Which arm-weariness, however, did not prevent him, after he had copied down all that pertained to his history, from returning to the cordilleras.

In the early months of 1549, now officially *"Cronista de Indias,"* Pedro de Cieza again took the Huarochirí road to the cordillera, to continue his search into history. "I was on my way . . . in the year 1549 to visit the provinces . . . carrying letters from President La Gasca to all the officials asking them to assist me in learning and finding out the most important things of these provinces."

Beyond Cuzco he continued along the Inca highway, pausing here and there to observe people or ruins, such as Piquillacta, "a large city

. . . bound by a great wall along the top of which . . . ran an aqueduct of water . . . there among the quarries of Rumi-colca . . . from which the Incas mined the stones they used in their buildings, which is a thing to see"; as always he put down his observations and, as well, information he gleaned from good informants, for "I have brought and compiled this history of what I saw and experienced . . . from reliable information I received from persons whose word could be relied upon." So he went on—southward to Ayaviri. It was near here that the Royal Road of the Incas bifurcated on both sides of Lake Titicaca. He rode about the Altiplano of the Colla, that vast area of Aymara-speaking peoples, the most populous in Peru, that lay in and about the basin of Lake Titicaca. He sought out the *chullpas*—houses of the dead—the large, beautifully made stone towers in which the demanding dead were placed with the food and things of their lives, including living women to accompany them. Cieza recalled that "while in the village of Nicasio [close to Titicaca] when we were on our way to Charcas, one Diego de Uceda . . . and I saw some women [immolated] as I have described." Cieza noted down all the things of their husbandry; he gave the first description of coca, the leaf that yielded the cocaine alkaloid, and its effect on the Indian as a person and on the fortunes of Spain, once it was openly allowed, after the conquest, for general addiction. "This coca was so valuable in Peru in the years 1548, 1549, and 1551 that there was never in the whole world a plant . . . so highly valued. There are those in Spain who became rich from this coca."

Titicaca, that immense body of water lying at 12,500 feet, had its first description from Cieza. He circled its end, made his trek away from the main Inca route to visit Tiahuanacu. In an analysis the structure of this pre-Inca ceremonial center was amazingly gauged by him: "I would say that I consider this the oldest antiquity in all Peru." As always, his own observation was enlarged by talking to others. At Tiahuanacu there was Juan Vargas. At Lake Titicaca he had details from Captain Juan Ladrillero. Although these and other of his informants seldom appear in most histories, they were, as evidenced in the seldom-used "Regulations for Tambos,"[24] Span-

---

[24] The *Ordenanzas de Tambos*, which may be translated as the "Ordering of Regulations of the Halting Stations [tambos]." Giving the distance from one to the other, the modes of conveyance by Indian carriers, and the obligation of the respective Spanish

iards long in the land, "old conquistadors," and Cieza knew by now how to separate those whose tales were seasoned with old saws, which is the wisdom of the unlettered, from those "whose word I could rely upon."

Cieza's southern journey ended in La Plata, now called Sucre. The Incas had called it Chuquisaca. There in 1545 a Spaniard, Villaroel by name, found, with an Indian named Gualpa, the fabulously rich silver mountain of Potosí; it became La Plata. Cieza made a sketch of the silver mountain of Potosí—the first illustration of it ever to appear—and gathered generously of the knowledge of what had transpired in the past from General Pedro de Hinojosa. He had been in Peru since 1545 and was then one of the richest men, having estates, said Cieza, "which yielded an annual income of a hundred thousand *castellanos.*" The famous conquistador, Captain Pedro Anzures, sometimes written "Peranzúrez," respected, liked, and very liberal, says Cieza of him, gave fully of his sagas, for he had been in all the important engagements and among the first to plunge into the eastern Amazon jungles on one of the great epics of exploration. Pedro de Cieza moved no farther; already his notes, his burgeoning manuscripts could take in no additional territory, and he readily admitted that "the affairs of Chile are so important and [they] would call for special attention."

Cieza had covered an immense swath of land. No one before him, in the double capacity of soldier and chronicler, had personally seen so much; no one since him—even with the advantages of time and space—ever repeated it. Cieza seemed fully aware of it: "What I have done is to set down what I have seen from Urabá in Colombia to Potosí [which is in Bolivia] . . . a distance . . . which I estimate at a good 1,200 leagues.[25]

---

overlords, it "was a report and regulation of the road and the tambos of the royal Inca road" ordered by the Spanish interim governor, Cristóbal Vaca de Castro, and completed in Cuzco on May 31, 1543. In this seldom-used document is the name of each conquistador who held the encomienda of each tambo along the route. Many of the informants of Pedro de Cieza, whose stations were too low to be mentioned in the histories, are found in this document, proving that they were the "old conquistadors" upon whom Cieza relied for his information. (See *Revista Histórica,* Vol. III, No. 4 (Lima, 1909), 427–92.)

[25] A Spanish league was two and one-half to three miles; it was measured by the pace of a horse or the distance a horse could walk in an hour. Cieza's 1,200 leagues would be around three thousand miles, which is about correct.

Cieza was the first human geographer of this land, a delineator of regions and climates, a naturalist examining species of animals and plants, an ethnographer looking into race and tribes, clothes, customs, industries, and forms of native governments and religious beliefs. Cieza was at pains to give a word picture of the physiognomy of the land, the sky, and the magnitude of this new world; the frigid desolation of the highlands—the *páramos, punas,* and *xallcas* and the persistent effect of geography on peoples, so as to acquaint his fellow men in Spain with the actions of their sons in an unknown land. He wrote not alone of the Incas, giving fulsome details of their lives; he wrote even more of the civil wars that plagued the land, when the contending conquistadors fell upon each other. He set down the deeds of knights as if he were writing a new *Iliad*—mourning for the unnecessary death of so many brave men: "I should have wished not to relate the cruelties of my countrymen. . . . I would rather escape from a narration of battles and leave them unwritten, [but] people must know about such great evils . . . that may occur in civil wars . . . and the brutal deaths inflicted by both sides." Very boldly he moralized on the origin of such wars, words which would pass his censors in Lima, yet would by their very sharp-edged truth become one of the factors which left his histories unpublished for centuries: "I will further say that one of the causes that have given rise to troubles and dissensions . . . in the Indies, has been the promotion by His Majesty and the high council of the Indies of illiterate men to govern, many without tact or prestige."

At the same time Cieza set down (they would have been lost otherwise) the histories of the great explorations of these self-same *tercios,* by whose personal audacity the world's landscape had been extended to infinity, "for who else would recount the unheard-of trials which such a small number of Spaniards underwent in so vast an area. Who else would have set down the amazing episodes that have taken place in the wars and discovery of 1,600 leagues of territory and the hunger, thirst, deaths, and fatigue."

Cieza had a superb grasp of this material, and he put it down in robust sixteenth-century style, with an economy of phrase and pattern. His deprecating remarks that it seemed "a temerity on the part of a man of so few letters to attempt what others more learned have not undertaken" is a mere *coup de maître,* for his description of people and events are deft and highly visual. For example, hear what he says in passing, of Diego Centeno: "He was a native of Ciudad Rodrigo. He was a gentleman, not very tall. He had a fair skin, pleasant countenance, with a red beard. Of noble condition, he was not very liberal as regards his own estate, but expended that of the King with largesse." It is the same Centeno who tried to protect Francisco de Carvajal from being set upon after his capture and which colloquy Cieza preserved:

"To whom," said Carvajal, in mock heroics, "am I indebted for this protection?"

"Do you not know me?" answered Centeno. "You have pursued me all these years, 3,000 leagues through the Andes."

"I crave your pardon," retorted Carvajal, giving knee. "It is so long since I have seen anything but your fleeing ass that I had fully forgotten your face."

The style is simple and bald and yet it has pungency. Perhaps it is the turn of a phrase that makes it seem more simple than it really was, or the feature of sixteenth-century style was to underwrite great events so that the event itself would not be lost in a display of verbiage.

Although Cieza de León took part in the destruction of the natives, he had no heart for it. He knew that the storms of cruelty the Spaniards used against the Indians were in large part due to their terror, cut off as they were from history and custom and surrounded by unfabled creatures in an unknown continent. Cieza, however, kept his purity of heart; his sympathy for the Indians expressed in humane terms are sentiments with which his contemporary, Erasmus, could have found no fault. ". . .those ill-treated unhappy natives . . . the captains of Pizarro were so remiss that they never thought of checking or lifting a hand to prevent the evils. . . . the consequence is that the country from Lima south to Nazca lost the greater part of its inhabitants." A conquistador himself, Cieza did not hypocritically bewail the use of Indians "when it is done with moderation; I would not condemn the employment of Indian carriers . . . but if a man had need of one pig, he killed twenty; if four Indians were wanted, he took a dozen . . . and there were many Spaniards who made the poor Indians carry their whores in hammocks borne on their shoulders. Were one ordered to enumerate the great evils, injuries, robberies, oppression, and ill treatment inflicted on the natives during these

operations . . . there would be no end of it . . . for they thought no
more of killing Indians than if they were useless beasts. . . . when I
came from Cartagena, I saw a Portuguese named Roque Martín,
who had the quarters of Indians hanging on a porch to feed his dogs
with, as if they were wild beasts. . . . Friar Bartolomé de las Casas,
afterwards Bishop of Chiapas, arrived in Spain . . . and asserted that
the Spaniards were treating natives in the manner so mentioned . . .
and His Majesty ordered the assembly of grandees and prelates . . .
to determine what should be provided for the good government . . .
of the Indies . . . and their deliberations resulted in the 'New Laws.' "
Yet Cieza balanced the picture: "I do not claim that these evil deeds
against the Indians were committed by all the Spaniards, for I know
and saw many instances of good treatment the Indians received at
the hands of kindly, God-fearing men. . . . Alonso de Alvarado was
a good administrator and ordered that the Indians should not be overworked and should be well treated. In this he truly showed himself
to be a father to the Indians . . . he even flogged two Spaniards for
robbing natives of their provisions. Robert B. Cunninghame Graham,
a nineteenth-century Cieza in his own right, observed that "among
Spaniards there were many honorable exceptions to the rule, a thing
often forgotten by the English historians [Graham was a Scot], willing to spread the idea of the black legend in order to justify piracy."

One will find it difficult in that century, or any that followed, to find
quite another such as Pedro de Cieza. Exact, charitable, and precise,
he put down only what he himself observed, and he kept record of
those, Indians or Spaniards, who gave him what he did not see with
his own eyes. He judged sanely of literary glory, lacking that valuable
illusion that sustained other great historians, that his remained the
ultimate truth. "If anyone can do this more accurately and in greater
detail, the road lies open to him." Literary glory comes only to those
who importune it, and Cieza was modest to a fault. Still, one knows
from him what he himself experienced and what he had from others.
He never fails to distinguish the various sources of his information,
for he said, "I always honor the hands of my readers." One walks
secure in the path of history with such a one.

Cieza's humanism, as a reading of his testament will reveal, re-
rained consistent to the end. A Catholic albeit a deviationist, he
knew, after a lyrical passage on the good governing of the Incas,

how to balance it, as equipoise, with some arrant nonsense about the will of God, so as to lull the censors into passing on his histories without excision. Like Rabelais, who died the same year as Cieza, he kept his opinions up to the burning point.

lx   At the end of 1549 or the beginning of 1550, Pedro de Cieza, "to insure greater accuracy," went again to Cuzco at the time when the Captain Juan de Saavedra was *corregidor*. This old partisan of Almagro, living next to the House of the Nazarenas, held high office in Cuzco, for this Saavedra always had the luck to change sides at the right moment; his life exhibited that while honor and profit cannot always be carried in one bag, it seemed that they sometimes could go together at least a portion of the way. Saavedra, who had taken part in most of the intrigues and battles of the civil wars, was to give Pedro de Cieza many important personal details for his histories.

Cuzco was much altered in appearance from what it was when first seen by the "three" who were sent in 1533 by Francisco Pizarro to hurry up the flow of gold to ransom the Lord-Inca Atahualpa.[26] The siege of Cuzco, which was begun in February, 1536, by an immense army led by Manco Inca II, had rained fire and destruction on it, materially altering original buildings. Many had been pulled down in that battle, and the Spanish occupancy of fifteen years naturally had brought about considerable change in Inca town planning. Most of the sacred Inca buildings that had withstood the siege had been partitioned by the conquistadors and new walls set up within them, disturbing the general architectural harmony of Incaic Cuzco. Still, only fifteen years having passed since the conquest, Cuzco preserved a generous echo of its past, enough at least for Pedro de Cieza, when he trod its narrow streets, to make out the Inca walls of precisely cut stone and to discern what it had been. The evidences of the 1548 battle were still about; gory quarters of the massive body of

[26] The "three" were Pedro Moguer, Francisco de Zárate, and Martín Bueno, sent, says the chronicler, "by Pizarro to fetch the gold . . . and to see the city of Cuzco." These three Christians were ordered to "get a sight of the city of Cuzco and to bring a report of all they saw." Thus these were the only Europeans ever to see Cuzco as it was before the change set in with the later arrival of the conquistadors. Hernando de Soto, who later achieved fame and glory as the discoverer of Florida and the Mississippi River, was then sent along with Pedro de Barco (one of those whom Carvajal hanged as fruit on the leafless trees), but none of them left any record of what they saw at Cuzco.

Francisco de Carvajal still hung at the four entrances to Cuzco, where they had been placed after he had been beheaded, drawn, and quartered. And close upon the main square the head of Juan de Acosta still dangled in its iron cage, giving out the odors of the King's justice.

Many old conquistadors were then living in Cuzco, having made for themselves large and seignorial doorways—an important element for a man climbing out of obscurity. Diego Maldonado, surnamed "the rich," had his home in what had been the palace of Topa Inca, directly across from the building that would emerge as the Cathedral of Cuzco. Juan de Betanzos, a galician and an old conquistador, the same who had married Pizarro's mistress—a sister of Atahualpa—had his house facing the square of Cusi-pata. He was then composing his book on the history of the Incas;[27] and within a crossbow-shot from him was the house of Pedro López de Cazalla, scrivener to the King and a kinsman of Pedro de Cieza. Cieza's other friends were there, those whom he had met in battle or travels, such as Juan de Pancorvo; he lived in an Inca palace along the canalized river Huatanay that cut through the heart of Cuzco. Tomás Vásquez, one of his dependable informants on things Inca, lived in Cusi-pata, as did Peralonso Carrasco, the same who had organized the bridging of the Apurímac in the battle of 1548. At the time that Pedro de Cieza was investigating the history of the Incas, putting down the notes which would become his immortal *Crónicas,* young Garcilaso de la Vega, then eleven years old, was walking about the streets of Cuzco, when not studying latin in the School of Nobles under Pedro Cuellar. And there, too (almost as large as his famous father), was Pedro de Candia the Younger, with the same name and same build as that Greek who, accoutred in a full suit of armor, walked ashore at Tumbes in 1527.

lxi

[27] It is strange that Cieza did not use Juan de Betanzos as one of his informants, since he had been in Peru as early as 1531, had been settled in Cuzco since 1540, and had married an Inca palla (baptized Doña Angélica), who was the sister of Atahualpa. Through her he acquired much information on the Incas. His contact with the Incas was the reason he was selected to try to worm the Lord-Inca Xairi Tupac Yupanqui out of his neo-Inca state in Vilcabamba. In 1551 he wrote, at the request of the first Viceroy, *Suma y naración de los yngas quelos yndios llamaron Capac cuna que fueron señores enla ciudad del/ cuzco y detodo loaella subieto que fueron mill leguas detierra/ losquales heran desdelrrio de maulle que esdelante de chile/ hasta deaquellaparte dela ciudad delquito* . . . ("Sum and narration of the Incas whom the indians called Capac cuna, that were masters in the city of Cuzco and of all to it subjected, which were one thousand leagues of land, from the river Maule which faces Chile up to that part of the city of Quito"). Like most such it was not published at the time; it was printed in 1880.

There were enough old conquistadors there to give loose tongue about the past; the problem was to select.

Cieza, when setting out to "inform himself from persons of complete credibility," did it methodically. To compile a history of the Andean people, he examined many of the Inca nobles then living in Cuzco. A captain of the late Inca Huayna Capac, named Pisca, gave Cieza the precise details of the siege of Cuzco in 1536, for that Indian had been with Manco Inca II throughout the war. Information of a different sort he had from a well-born Indian who had been intimate with Manco Inca II and was then a servant of Cieza's old friend Juan Ortiz de Zárate, who lived in La Plata, for, as he said, "I have always given great attention to painstaking accuracy in my history . . . I took trouble to obtain accurate information about events concerning the Indians." Of Manco Inca II, the young Inca who had raised a revolt against the Spaniards in 1536 and almost caused their downfall, he gathered additional information from a priest, Ortun Sánchez. Sánchez, who had had a part in the business, told him how Manco escaped to set up a neo-Inca state in the inaccessible parts of the mountains of Vilcabamba. Further, "the *Orejones* of Cuzco supplied me with information." In particular he searched out Cayu Tupac Yupanqui, one of the few surviving descendants of Huayna Capac, "to give me an account of the Incas that I relate."

His admiration for Inca polity expanded with the growth of his manuscript histories: "Few nations had a better government . . . one of the things most to be envied . . . is how well they knew how to conquer such vast lands . . . and bring them to the flourishing state in which the Spaniards found them. . . . I recall hearing my fellow-Spaniards say, when we were in some indomitable region outside of their kingdoms, 'Take my word for it, had the Incas been here, it would have been a different story.' . . . in many respects they were far ahead of us."

He recorded the manner in which they made their conquests ("they entered many lands without war") and the manner in which they collected tribute tax once the conquest was complete. The Lord-Inca gathered together the chieftains . . . addressed them with affectionate words . . . and they accepted the tribute tax . . . moderate and unvexing. . . . in some regions this was more than that now paid to the Spaniards, yet the system the Incas employed was so good that

lxii

the people did not feel it . . . but with the disorder and the greed of the Spaniards, the number of people has fallen off to such a degree that most of them have disappeared, and they will be wiped out completely as a result of the covetousness and greed of most or all of us here."

In this manner he went on, questioning, investigating, obtaining from Spaniard and Indian alike information which he balanced, after long years in the Indies, on the scales of his experience.

In the month of July, 1550, Cieza was in Lima. There, by the terms of his appointment, he had to turn over the whole of his manuscript to be read by the authorities. The president of the King's Council, Pedro de la Gasca, having put down the rebellion and reordered the kingdom, setting up again the flow of gold and silver to his King's coffers, then arranged for his successor[28] and sailed from Lima in the beginning of 1550. He left in his stead a council of three, to act as rulers of Peru until the coming of the Viceroy. Two of these were directed—one gathers from La Gasca's instructions—to read carefully what Pedro de Cieza had written to make certain that nothing entered his history that was unfavorable to either the King or La Gasca. Cieza says as much: "Most of what I have written was seen by Dr. Bravo de Saravia and the Lic. Hernando de Santillán, judges of the Royal Audience of the City of Kings [Lima]."[29]

[28] In a letter sent to Charles V by La Gasca, dated at Tumbes, August 11, 1547, La Gasca recommended Antonio de Mendoza, the viceroy of New Spain (Mexico) as a suitable candidate for viceroy of Peru. This admirable administrator, who had served in Mexico since 1550, reluctantly accepted the post because of his advanced age and failing health. A semi-invalid, Mendoza left Mexico City employing the Mexico-Veracruz road, then he was poled up by water to the Coatzacoalcos River, carried across the isthmus of Tehuantepec to Cortes' port of Huatulco, where he embarked in 1551 on the *San Andrés*. The voyage and Peru were too much for him; he died in Lima in July, 1552.

[29] These three, Bravo de Saravia, Santillán, and the Archbishop Loayza served as interim rulers of Peru from the departure of La Gasca until the arrival of Viceroy Toledo. Melchor Bravo de Saravia was one of the judges who came from Spain in the train of La Gasca. He was later president of the Audiencia of Chile. Hernando de Santillán, who also came from Spain to assist La Gasca, was a *licenciado*, i.e., an attorney and a judge. A man of mordant wit and "an incorrigible player of chess," Santillán was also a man of sharp intelligence. He was sent to Quito by Philip II to open an *audiencia* in 1564, but in time he fell into disgrace, returned to Spain, and whilst waiting for the wheels of justice to revolve, wrote a *Relación* on Peru. This is interesting since it was this same Santillán who read all of what Pedro de Cieza had written and knew, when he was in Spain, where most of the unpublished material lay, and had access to it. One need scarcely add that the manuscript went unprinted for three hundred years; it appeared as a *"Relación,"* edited by Marcos Jiménez de la Espada, in *Tres Relaciones Antiguas Peruanas* (Madrid, 1879).

How much these worthy gentlemen read of the eight thousand or more folio manuscript pages of Cieza's histories, including the irrevocably lost "Book of Foundations,"[30] we do not know. As Cieza turned the manuscript over to them, he remembered those who had warned that "a great reward cannot be obtained without great labor" and that Solomon had warned about riches and watchfulness and much working of the spirit, "for," he said finally, as he let the manuscript out of his hands for the first time in ten years, "in putting my hand to write a work so difficult as this upon which I am now engaged . . . I in no way could avoid passing long night vigils."

lxiv

Then he turned to his own personal affairs, preparing to return home, after an absence of seventeen years—and to arrange his marriage.

That marriage, which was to be Cieza's greatest joy and greatest sorrow, began with the signing of a marriage contract in Lima on August 19, 1550. A merchant, Pedro López (not to be confused with the other of the same name who was the secretary to La Gasca), representing his sister, agreed in this document that Pedro de Cieza would marry Isabel López on his return to Seville. That the name of the daughter in no wise conformed to either the name of her father or mother is one of the curiosities of Spain; even some notable names of history, the "Inca" Garcilaso de la Vega for one, took the name of a noted ancestor, leaving behind his very own (which, incidentally, was Gómez Suárez de Figueroa). The fact remains that Isabel was the daughter of Juan de Llerena, presumably from Cieza's own village but then a very-well-set-up merchant in Seville, with connections in the Americas; his son in fact was then in Peru, and Cieza, when he left, gave a power of attorney to "Juan de Llerena, citizen of Saña." Had Cieza wooed this Isabel López by letter, had it been an outgrowth of an epistolary romance, or did her brother, then in the Indies on business, think Pedro de Cieza a worthwhile catch? There must have been something about the historian of the Incas that caught the eye of the man of Seville, for he, in his sister's family's name, agreed

---

[30] What was the "Book of Foundations"? Presumably it had much to do with the date and founding of all the Spanish settlements in America. "The town of Plata was then founded and settled. In my *Book of Foundations* I have written what was needed concerning it." (*War of Salinas*, 245.); and again, "There are many things to tell of this province which I have written in my *Book of Foundations*, where the reader will have seen them." (*War of Chupas*, 30.) Cieza does not mention the book in his last will and testament. We know no more.

to turn over on the marriage as dowry the sum of four thousand golden crowns (quite a princely sum, for Gonzalo Pizarro tried to bribe La Gasca with only twenty thousand pesos, which was considerably less). "I grant and recognize by this letter that I undertake that as soon as thyself, the said Pedro de Cieza, should arrive at the aforesaid city of Seville, thou wilt wait on the aforesaid my father and the aforesaid Isabel López, my sister, so that thou mayest marry the aforesaid Isabel López my sister, and thou wilt receive besides herself, when thou dost so, as marriage dowry, four thousand crowns in the ordinary currency circulating in the aforesaid city of Seville."

Later, on the eleventh of September, he arranged that three acquaintances, "citizens of Llerena in the Kingdom of Spain," who presumably were sailing before himself, "especially and for me and in my name, representing my own person, may effect and do so effect a certain marriage with *Isabel López,* legitimate daughter of *Juan de Llerena,* citizen of Seville, and Maria Abreo, his wife, in accordance and in the tenor of a deed of contract signed between myself and *Pedro López.*[31]

Putting together other business affairs after this, Pedro de Cieza readied himself to return. He retrieved his manuscript history and put down the last words, "Concluded in Lima, City of Kings, in the Kingdom of Peru, on the eighteenth of September, 1550, when its author was thirty-two years old, having spent seventeen of them in these Indies."

—5—

Pedro de Cieza obviously made no great splash on his arrival at Seville, even though seventeen years absent from Spain. Many, far too many conquistadors sporting high-born Indian women and a profusion of golden ornaments had swaggered into Seville in the past decade for anyone to be excited by yet another returning from the Perus. One presumes that his betrothed, Isabel López, and her family were there, and that his own family came down from Llerena for the occasion—his aged father (his mother had died while he was

---

[31] The documents concerning Pedro de Cieza's marriage lie widely scattered in the *Archivo Nacional* in Lima, Peru, the Harkness Collection, Library of Congress, in Washington, and in the *Archivo General de Indias,* Seville. All are given by Miguel Marticorena in his paper on Pedro de Cieza (Seville, 1955).

in Peru), his brother Rodrigo, now a priest, along with a various assortment of Cazallas.

Henceforth Cieza was so thoroughly enmeshed in the varying aspects of his life—his forthcoming marriage and his plans to publish his histories—that he was not expected to pay much attention to the affairs current in Spain. He was in Llerena when the King-Prince Philip II rode through there, with a gay company of cavaliers, to escort his sister Juana to the borders of Portugal, at Badajoz, to marry the second son of King John. He had doubtlessly only a passing interest (not knowing then how much his own destiny would be bound up with it) of the rumors, then going around, that Philip II would marry Mary Tudor of England—to become a doubly crowned king.

At the beginning of August, 1551, Cieza was married to Isabel, and as the documents read, they took up their residence on the Calle de las Armas (now Calle Alfonso XII) in the district of San Vicente, within Seville. After all those years of privation in the Indies, all seemed promising. "Since it pleases us [Juan de Llerena and his wife, Maria Abreo] . . . we grant thee Pedro de Cieza de León . . . since by the grace of our Lord a marriage was made and arranged between Isabel López de León . . . which marriage was made and arranged with thyself in the province of Peru by Pedro López our son . . . and in order the better for thee to sustain the burden of marriage, we grant . . . together with our daughter . . . 3,500 ducats of gold . . . 2,000 ducats in cash as from today [this being August 11, 1551] and within eight days the rest . . . in bridal apparel, clothes, jewels, gems, and household furnishings and male and female slaves."

Pedro de Cieza responded, in another document, pledging in turn his own golden ducats to further "sustain the burden of marriage" and even through the dry and stilted phrasing of a scrivener's idiom one can feel the happiness of Cieza as he makes provision "for my wife and spouse and for the honor of her person and lineage and the sons and daughters that, God willing, by her we shall have."[32]

In the meanwhile Pedro de la Gasca, returned from Peru the pre-

[32] The ducat at that time was equivalent to two dollars, but had ten times the purchasing power. The dowry was equivalent to 1,315,500 Spanish *maravedís;* as an idea of its comparative worth, Francisco Pizarro was given only 750,000 *maravedís* annually by Queen Juana the Mad as his salary as governor of all Peru.

vious year, had seen all the gathered gold and silver safely through the treasury at Seville, where it "was checked piece by piece," then he hurried on to court "to kiss their Highness' hands." Charles V told him that "we will do all in our power to reward so signal a service," and so it was done; he was rewarded with the bishopric of Palencia, and was retained as the crown's private counselor in all things relating to Peru. It must therefore be presumed that Cieza communicated with him and doubtlessly visited his august person (La Gasca was also Conde de Pervia), where he was surrounded by the mementos of Peru, including the banners and flags of Gonzalo Pizarro which he had captured at the battle of Xaquixahuana.

lxvii

Pedro de Cieza's plans were ambitious. By 1552, an amanuensis had readied the *Parte Primera de la Crónica del Perú*[33] for the printer Martín Montesdoca in Seville. An artist under Cieza's direction had designed the first authentic illustrations pertaining to Peru for publication. In addition to this, Cieza had revised the other seven manuscript histories, having them copied by a scrivener on parchment. The whole was as he had planned it, an eight-volume history of the discovery, conquest, and civil wars of Peru, and the synopsis was given in its entirety. Prescott, who had no way of knowing, thought that the great work had never been completed: "He gave with curious minuteness the contents of several books of the projected history. But the First Part . . . was alone completed; and the author . . . died, without having covered *any portion* of the magnificent ground plan which he had thus confidently laid out. . . . the conception of a work at so early a period, on this philosophical plan [reminds one] of Malte-Brun in our own time," referring to the Danish-born geographer who wrote an encyclopedic geography of the world.

Cieza, it is obvious, was fully aware of all the problems that would arise when he attempted to publish, for to be printed, a book then had to have *"privilegio,"* that is, privilege, license showing that it had been examined and approved by the authorities, civil and ecclesiastical; all books had to run the gamut of the King's Council, the Holy Office of the Inquisition, the Council of the Indies, and, often, the royal board of trade—the *Casa de Contratación*—to be given light.

[33] "The First Part of the Chronicle of Perú, which Treats of the Demarcation of Its Provinces and the Description Thereof, of the Foundations of New Cities, of the Rites and Customs of the Indians. And other Strange Things worthy of Note, by Pedro de Cieza de León, citizen of Seville, 1553."

THE INCAS

To explain—most of us seem not to remember—Spain had only recently freed herself from Moslem domination at an incalculable cost in human lives and property in a war that had raged throughout the Peninsula for three hundred years. It had been one of the longest-sustained religious crusades in history, so that Spain's sense of holy mission was understandable; and despite the cynicism that often clothed many of their acts, religion was very real to the Spaniards. Thus every safeguard that they could devise was set up to thwart in any way or manner a deviation from their concept of a Christian life. Pedro de Cieza, as is seen from his life and acts, was a discerning man; he knew that to insure the publication of his histories, he must have a royal patron; if possible, the King himself. It is fully natural that Cieza would have sought out La Gasca when he was installed as Bishop of Palencia; this is almost certain even if at this writing there are no documents to support it. Although mayhap La Gasca was, as said, "modest and unpretending," and despite the fact that his bishopric fully assured him of heavenly immortality, still he was just as anxious as any other mortal to see his fame perpetuated on lowly earth. This is obvious, for during the same period as Cieza's visit, he was writing, as the Bishop of Palencia (August 23, 1552) to a friend and complaining about Gómara's *Historia de Indias,* published the previous year: "I am sure he would like the truth . . . he is somewhat misinformed. . . . I had already won over four-fifths of the people there and was put in a position to subdue the other fifth by force of arms, but as that would have meant bloodshed, unacceptable to my cloth, I endeavored to bring about the conversion as peacefully as possible." La Gasca had full interest to see that Pedro de Cieza published the first of the histories, which chronicled his triumphs in Peru over Gonzalo Pizarro.[34] That La Gasca gave him support and secured for him a personal audience with Phillip II can

[34] As seen by La Gasca's response to Gonzalo Oviedo y Valdes, the famous historian of the Indies, then living in Santo Domingo, from which a letter was sent dated January 3, 1550 (Puerto de Sto. Domingo, Isla Española) by Oviedo congratulating La Gasca upon the success of his "Caesarian venture" and requesting to be honored with your description of the glorious victory and death of the tyrant Gonzalo Pizarro," for he was then Charles V's official chronicler. La Gasca sent him the needed information, and he replied: "The news arrived in time to be inmortalized in the third volume . . . the first volume begins with the discovery by Columbus and the third closes with the triumphs of your Reverence." (Pizarro–La Gasca Papers, p. 517.) The whole of the history was not published, however, until recent date because of Las Casas' enmity.

be the only reasonable explanation of how Pedro de Cieza, of mean birth and without connections at court was able to gain audience.

In September, Philip the king-prince was at Toledo. The Spanish court, as peripatetic as wandering friars, voyaged all over Spain holding court in this and that kingdom. Here Cieza sought him out, crossing the famous bridge of Alcántara ("a work which I saw at Toledo when I came there in 1552 to present the first part of my chronicle to the Prince Don Felipe")—that bridge which had first been set up by the Romans, restored by the Arabs, and later rebuilt by the Spaniards—and then proceeding, he went by prearrangement to see Philip II.

Philip was then king of Spain in fact, if not in name. He was twenty-four years of age. The portrait made of him at that time by Titian shows him as he must have been, for Titian did not hide his unattractive features. He appears well knit, with an intelligent face and a look of inquiry about his eyes, but the protruding Hapsburg lip spoiled these otherwise good features and gave him the slack-jaw look of inbreeding, as one finds often in *dorftrottels* in isolated villages in the Tyrol. Philip was then neither gloomy nor introverted; he was an avid huntsman, fond of dancing, a patron of arts, and, in 1552, carrying on a spirited correspondence with Titian.

There is naturally no record of his audience with Pedro de Cieza, yet he either read or scanned the manuscript copy of the *"Primera Parte,"* for he gave sanction to the dedication and allowed the book his royal protection and copyright.

"Pedro de Cieza . . . I have been informed that thou hast dwelt in the provinces of Peru serving us with thy arms and horse and fortune . . . and that to serve us thou didst write and compile a book . . . and now thou hast requested that we grant thee leave to print same . . . now the said book having been seen and examined in the Council of the Emperor and King my Lord, we . . . have so agreed."

The copyright was for fifteen years, with rights to sell the book throughout Spain and the Americas; "And I further command," the royal grant read, "that during the lapse of said fifteen years no other person or persons . . . shall be so bold as to print this book, except thee, Pedro de Cieza." It was signed at Bonçon [Monçon de Aragón] on September 14, 1552.

On the fifteenth of March, 1553 the book was issued from the press of Martín de Montesdoca. The format was in folio; its title page with Renaissance borders is embellished with an impressive albeit ostentatious royal arms of Philip II. Now, at long last, after all the years of anxiety, Cieza could read on the title page, *"Fecha por Pedro d' Cieça de León, vezino de Sevilla."* It was the only contemporary edition printed in Spain, and it was not reprinted there until 1862. Through the extraordinary details given in Cieza's testament, we now know that the edition amounted to more than 500 copies, of which number Cieza still had 218 unsold copies in the hands of booksellers two years after publication.[35] The cost to the bookseller was four *reales,* three *cuartillos* the copy, an insignificant sum (in modern terms it would be forty cents)—and for this a folio-size book, printed on handmade paper and bound in vellum. That the *Primera Crónica* was very well received and thumbed through until copies were worn thin from use is proved by the scarcity of the first edition; it is of the utmost rarity.

lxx

Since Flanders was still under Spanish rule, Cieza then arranged for a second edition to be printed there, this time in an inexpensive smaller pocket-book size, with the original, although recut, illustrations. It appeared under the imprint of Martin Nucio, the same printer and publisher who, a year later, issued a competitive book by Agustín de Zárate which the King-Prince read on his way to England and urged him to publish.[36] Other editions of Cieza, attesting to the pop-

[35] In his testament he states: Furthermore, I declare that there are 130 books, belonging to me, of the chronicle which I wrote on the Indies, in the care of Juan de Espinoza, bookdealer and citizen of Medina del Campo . . . [in] Toledo another 30 books of the above-mentioned chronicle, which were sold by Juan Sánchez de Andrada . . . . Gutiérrez de los Ríos of Córdova has 8 books of the aforesaid chronicle . . . . Fulano de Vallalón, bookseller, who lives next to the Magdalena, has another 15 books . . . he should pay four *reales* and three *cuartillos* for each . . . . Rodrigo de Valles, bookseller, has another 8 books . . . . Furthermore, the printer Montesdoca owes me twenty-seven *reales* for other books."

[36] Agustín de Zárate arrived in Peru in 1544, after serving fifteen years as secretary of the Royal Council of Castile. He was to make an inspection of royal accounts, but he arrived in Peru at the height of the civil wars, and when Francisco de Carvajal threatened to hang him to the tallest tree in Lima if he discovered him writing anything, the poor man took his notes and left Peru almost within a year (June, 1545) of his arrival. He was able to gather much while there from Rodrigo Lozano, a citizen of Trujillo (whom Pedro de Cieza also knew), and from other fairly reliable informants. It was his intention after writing his *Historia* not only not to publish within the nine years recommended by Horace, but to extend it to ninety years so as not to embroil himself nor hurt living persons. However, he accompanied Philip to England, and Philip read the manuscript and urged upon him its immediate publication. Upon the boat's anchoring at Flanders, he made his way to Antwerp, quickly revised it so as

ularity of the book, were issued by printers in Antwerp. That Pedro de Cieza himself arranged the contracts and that the work was not pirated may be seen in his expectancy of revenue "from the Indies and Flanders."

The Italians, after 1555, took Pedro de Cieza to their heart and printed not less than seven editions within twenty years; the French and Germans, after their initial excitement over *"certaines nouvelles de l'isle du Perou,"* never issued, surprisingly enough, an edition of Cieza. The English managed an atrociously translated edition only after the passage of 150 years.[37]

lxxi

That he corrected the second edition is obvious on comparison of the various editions; and so having successfully braved the winds of doctrine in the first part of the *Chronicles of Peru,* he made ready the second volume: *La Segunda Parte de la Crónica del Perú que trata del Señorío de los Incas Yupanquis y de sus grandes hechos y Gobernación,* and even before this was submitted to the printer, he began the work on his other histories. At least one (now known as the *War* [or *Battle*] *of Quito*) he had prepared for the printer, since, when found, the manuscript, according to its discoverer, "bears a multitude of references, bookmarks, and notes at different places and in different manners, some in another light and in a later hand."[38] However, it advanced no further—death in various forms was at hand.

The year 1554 was a terrible one for Cieza. In the first months of 1553 he had attended, in great anguish, as one gathers from his own testament, the funeral of his bride, Isabel López de León. We know neither the precise date nor the precise cause of death, only that she died in 1553 and was laid in "the church of San Vicente of this city of Seville." One can see by the things that he later disposed of the luxuries which he lavished on his young bride, "the purple velvet

to dedicate it to Philip in his new capacity as "King of England," and had it issued on March 30, 1555, "At the house of Martin Nucio, at the place of the two storks," the same publisher who one year previously had issued the Flemish edition of Pedro de Cieza's book.

[37] "The Seventeen Years Travels of Peter de Cieza. Through the Mighty Kingdom of Peru and The large Provinces of Cartagena and Popayán in South America: From the City of Panama, on the Isthmus, to the Frontiers of Chile. Now first translated from the Spanish and Illustrated with a Map, and several Cuts. London: Printed in the Year MDCCIX."

[38] These discoveries of Pedro de Cieza's literary methods were first related by Marcos Jiménez de la Espada in his edition of Cieza's *Guerra de Quito* (Madrid, 1880), *cvii, cxiii.*

gown . . . with satin sleeves and gold braid . . . another net coif of small gold beads . . . a braid-trimmed skirt of crimson satin . . . the coffer in which I kept her jewels . . . and the slave 'Beatriz' which was hers. . . ."

Cieza himself became moribund soon afterward, and in his last months was so paralyzed that he was hardly able to sign his name. There is no indication of the disease which consumed him—it could have been any of several tropical infections which finally so possessed him that he could no longer "turn aside," as he once did, to look into the curiosities of life. It is well that his illusions sustained him up to the last, since, dying slowly, he was able to work at times on his histories, planning, while dying, for their eventual publication. He did not know then what Jean-Jacques Rousseau learned in his old age, "that ignorance is a necessary condition for human happiness" —Cieza had said too much too well in his books. The fever of the times and the fact that he sided so openly with the defender of the Indians—Las Casas—would undo all his heroic work of gathering the material for the first history of South America.

The times were not necessarily out of joint; the times were but the ordered sequence of events. Charles V, king of Spain and the Lands beyond the Seas, the one monarch who stubbornly opposed the spread of Islam into Europe and fought for a united Europe, maintaining the costly fiction of the Germanic Holy Roman Empire, had now reached fifty years of age, and the end. He had exhausted himself and the treasuries of Spain; all the golden flow from Mexico and Peru had gone into wars in attempt to bind Europe together. In 1554 he was planning to abdicate and retire to a monastery in Extremadura to prepare himself for death. Still, as the idea of physical perpetuity through the continuation of family was at the moment more important than his soul's immortality, he arranged for Philip's marriage so as to secure for him a greater crown than Empire.

On July 12, 1554, Prince Philip sailed from Coruña to England to wed Mary Tudor, daughter of Henry VIII. It was to be a fateful voyage. It was to bring England and Spain to war, create the atmosphere for the "Black Legend," and put back the intellectual clock in Spain; it was also to cause the total eclipse of Pedro de Cieza for a space of three hundred years.

It began as soon as Philip alighted on British soil. That he was invested with the Order of the Garter by the Earl of Arundel, that he was received as a king (for his father made him king of Milan so as to meet his bride, Mary, on equal terms)—all this ritualistic folderol did nothing to disguise the hostility of the people.

Philip at twenty-five years of age was a gay enough young man, he prided himself on his kindliness and clemency—his was one of the voices that made the humanitarian "New Laws" into decree—and he was capable of extraordinary concentration. He was also obstinate and self-willed, as a king to survive had then to be. Neither ambitious nor violent—with an absolute hatred of brawl and disturbance—he nonetheless sanctioned it when faith was involved; he regarded himself as the great protector of Catholicism. Even before the marriage there had been street brawls between the Spanish soldiers and the populace, and the authorities were hard put to keep down the public clamor and to hide from him the flurry of scurrilous pasquinades directed against the Church, himself, and Spain.

Mary Tudor and Philip were married on the twenty-fifth of July. They ruled England as joint sovereigns, a fact that Philip signalized when he wrote to the Bishop of Palencia, the well-remembered Pedro de la Gasca, and signed himself, "I, the King."

Religion had become the whoreson of politics. King Philip envisoned that through this marriage England would return to the mother church in Rome, and he stated his royal wishes in forceful Latin when he addressed Parliament. It was inevitable that a child would be sought from this marriage to unite both nations and people. It was just as inevitable that some of the people would react violently to both; lampoons appeared, pulpits thundered against the new look, and, above all, the implacable John Knox rolled out his theological cannons; the war of words was on. As also inevitable in this sort of business, there was attack and riposte, blood was spilled, treason was uttered, heads rolled, and Mary Tudor became "Bloody Mary"; there was now no turning back, from either side.

This is history only so far as it concerns the fate of Pedro de Cieza. Two days before the King married, Pedro de Cieza, on July 23, 1554, signed his last will and testament—and then died believing even as he took his last breath that he had provided for the publication of his next volume, that history which he had carried in manuscript for fifteen years: "I order that another book which I wrote which contains the chronicles of the Incas and all concerning the discovery and conquest of Peru, that if any one of my executors desires to print it, he take and benefit from the profits of the publication; if not, I order it to be sent, with an injunction that he print it, to the Bishop of Chiapas."

The "Bishop of Chiapas," whom Pedro de Cieza had met in Seville in 1552, was, of course, Bartolomé de las Casas. He was then residing at the Spanish court, wherefrom he still carried on an intense program for the "New Laws," of which he had been the prime mover. When Philip was prince, he listened to Las Casas as he detailed the crimes against the Indians and the disasters attending the encomiendas, those "commanderies of Indians" that had wiped out whole native populations, and he listened to accounts of the rapacious cruelty of both the conquistadors and colonists. While all this was admissible as evidence within the King's council chambers, it was not supposed to be noised abroad. Thus Las Casas compromised a generous cause by the very intensity he brought to it, for his charges were now repeated by Spain's enemies and even appeared in print while Philip was king of England. Because of these scurrilous broadsides with which the new king was belabored all the time he was in England, he naturally reacted violently to the implications contained in these libels. So the "Black Legend" was born, and the "hardening process" which would deny license to books that disseminated information about the New World began; Las Casas was going to bring down Cieza with his own decline and fall.

In 1555, Charles V abdicated. His son Philip II became king of Spain, while his brother Ferdinand acquired the empty title of emperor of the Holy Roman Empire; then Mary Tudor died, and her demise caused a worsening of ties between England and Spain. The Counter Reformation was in full stride. All the early frankness that characterized Spanish publications was gone. One by one, as new manuscripts were submitted to the Council of the Indies for license to publish, they were taken up and placed in security—many of them never came into light again for three hundred years, and then only because of the national shame evoked by the Spanish reaction to the affront to its honor, that William Prescott, an American, should have written the *History of the Conquest of Peru* out of the documents they had sealed up for centuries.

The fate of Cieza was tied up in the "hardening process" and the attitudes contained in the incipient Counter Reformation. Also, there was his tactical error in suggesting that the second volume of his Inca history be sent to Las Casas "with an injunction to print it." The manuscripts were seized by the Inquisition with this as an excuse (for either his executors did not "desire to print it" or were denied license), and after the manuscript books had wandered from one hand to the other, Andrés Gasco, Inquisitor in 1563, sent them on to the Council of Indies.[39]

Cieza thought to arrange for their publication and still cause no hurt. Of those books which formed the civil wars, he ordered that publication be delayed for fifteen years: "I command as I wrote a book or rather three books [in reality five] on the civil wars of Peru, all written and embellished by hand on parchment, which if now printed might cause some scandal and some people might resent what is contained therein. . . . I command that my executors take the said three books and reports (all of which are in my desk) and move the said letters and other writings that may be there and take the said three books and reports . . . seal them and place another two small locks on the said desk and before a Public Notary place it in the Convent of Las Cuevas . . . until fifteen years after my death."[40]

lxxv

---

[39] When ordered by royal command to return the manuscripts, Andrés Gasco used the classic form of Spanish dissimulation: "I obeyed, but I did not comply." "From the King: Licenciado Andrés Gasco, Inquisitor in the city of Seville, I am informed that you have two books written by the hand of one Pedro de Cieza, citizen of that city, that deal with matters of Peru . . . that have not been seen or examined or granted the necessary authority for distribution, and because it suits us that said books be brought to our Council of the Indies, as soon as you have perused this, I demand that you send said books with all diligence and speed to our aforementioned Council of Indies, so that once [they are] seen and examined in same, we may make convenient provision for them. Done in Monçón de Aragón on the twenty-ninth day of November of the year 1563, I the King." (See Miguel de Marticorena's article [Madrid, 1955], 18.)

[40] The fate of Pedro de Cieza's histories of the civil wars is explained and his humanism is illustrated by this excerpt from his testament: "Furthermore, I command that the following be done: as I wrote a book, or rather three books, on the civil wars of Peru, all written and embellished by hand on parchment, which if printed now might cause some scandal and some people might resent what is contained therein and the things that took place only recently in those wars, it is my wish that my executors take the three books and reports, all of which are in my desk, and remove the said letters and other writings that may be in this desk, leaving only the aforesaid three books and reports and anything else pertaining to them, and that they close and seal this [desk] and place another two small locks on this desk, and before a Notary Public take the locked desk to the monastery of Las Cuevas, or any other monastery my executors think fit, and once [it is] deposited there, the keys should remain in the possession of my executors, one key for each, until fifteen years after my death,

In vain did Cieza's brother, a priest who held the curacy of Castilleja de la Cuesta beg the council for the return of the manuscripts: "My brother [he petitioned in 1578], after having served many years in Peru and undergone signal sacrifices, wrote by order of La Gasca ... all that took place during the discovery of same and in the wars that there were, and having these books in his possession, they were taken from him and brought here [Council of the Indies] and having come to ask for them, and for reward for his services, he died so doing, and left as heir Rodrigo de Cieza; in consideration of this, the latter requests that these books be returned, since he was deprived of them, they being his and in his possession."

lxxvi

It was not until 1596, when Antonio de Herrera de Tordesillas, who had never seen the Americas in any form, was named historiographer royal, to compile in manner "pleasing to the King" a history of the discovery and conquest of the Americas, that Pedro de Cieza was resurrected; "In order to write the history of the Indies more effectively," Herrera stated, ". . . I must have for consultation that which Pedro de Cieza, chronicler of those parts, wrote at the order of President Gasca . . . and which was approved by the royal offices of Lima." And so he asked to see the *"dos cuerpos"* (i.e., bound manuscripts) of Cieza that are in the cases of His Majesty."[41]

---

during which time no one is to look inside; and later, by order of my executors or any one of them living, or if none are living, by order of the prelate of the monastery where the desk is, the books be given to some expert to see and correct and to remove from the said work what he thinks superfluous, without adding anything to what has been written; and as regards what still has to be written, in accordance with the reports which are in the desk, he may proceed as he thinks fit, stating the point to which he found it written and where he himself began to write, and in this manner he can print it, protecting the honor and fame of all, so that no one is hurt or defamed, and he may benefit from the profits of the publication; if one of my executors wishes to give it to a certain person, he may do so; and it is my wish that the said monastery, on taking the said desk and books for deposit, give a receipt or deed as my executors think fit." (See Last Will and Testament of Pedro de Cieza in the Appendix to this book.)

[41] Antonio de Herrera, a literary hack, was named in 1596 official historian of Spain, and wrote the collection known in full as *Historia General de los Hechos de los Castellanos en las islas y Tierra Firme del Mar Océano* (9 vols., Madrid, 1601–15). This history has been so severely condemned by his own countrymen, including none other than Marcos Jiménez de la Espada, that one need only quote the indictment: "No historian of the Indies, however, went as far as Antonio de Herrera in appropriating the work of others. . . . he dared to bury in his *Décadas* a whole chronicle [Cieza's], a model of its kind, and without the name of a brave and honorable soldier. . . . The picturesque geographical description was published under the title of *La Primera Parte de la Crónica del Peru* in Seville in the year 1553; the rest is usurped

"In a handbook that left the Royal Chambers and by command of King Philip II of glorious memory, Antonio Herrera was given [orders] to write the history of the Indies, the same as was written by P° de Cieça, chronicler of those parts by command of President Gasca, and has received the approval of the Royal Chancellry of the City of Kings."

The *"dos cuerpos"* of Cieza—this being no less than seven of his unpublished histories and possibly the lost "Book of Foundations"— was plagiarized in its entirety, often word for word, by the well-placed Antonio de Herrera.

In Roman law a "plagiarist," in the proper sense of the word, was a furtive person, kidnaper of children, or one who debauched another's slaves; figuratively, he was a thief of ideas. To Pierre Bayle, a contemporary of Antonio de Herrera, a "plagiarist" was, for his *Dictionnaire historique et critique,* published in 1697, one who carried off the furniture and its very sweepings, "who stole grain, straw, chaff, dust, and all"—in short, a writer without imagination, taste, or discernment. Such was William Prescott's judgment of Herrera's history, "a tasteless arrangement . . . the thread of interest being perpetually snapped . . . so that the reader is exhausted and his mind perplexed."

So disappeared Pedro de Cieza into the maw of a devouring anonymity. Those who wanted original material borrowed from Cieza until the manuscripts were completely castrated; ofttimes authorship was ascribed to another or lost in the unfathomed depths of the repository of El Escorial. The fact that an American lawyer who personally knew neither Spain, Mexico, or Peru should sing the praises of Cieza and lament that his other histories should be unwritten or lost provided the impetus that forced these manuscripts out of hiding. It was so humiliating for Spanish scholars that soon

with such cleverness or good luck that up to the beginning of the present century only a few bibliophiles knew." Herrera, as a sort of apology for his plagiarism, wrote: "This Pedro de Cieza is the one who wrote the history of the provinces of Quito and Popayán, with much punctiliousness, although (contrary to what one should expect of princes) he had less luck than others in compensation for his work." (See Jiménez de la Espada's edition of Cieza's *Guerra de Quito* [Madrid, 1880], *ix, x, xiii;* Miguel Marticorena, "Cieza de León en Sevilla y su Muerte en 1554," p. 22 and footnotes; and William H. Prescott's caustic and good critical judgments on Antonio de Herrera in his *Conquest of Mexico,* 308–309 and notes; and, for a contrary opinion, Ticknor's *History of Spanish Literature,* III, 153.)

many were engaged in burrowing for these histories which had been buried in oblivion. One of the finest Spanish scholars of them all, Marcos Jiménez de la Espada, found in the Escorial the second part of the *Crónica* of Cieza, a bad sixteenth-century copy, with its two opening chapters gone, its third chapter mutilated, and the book opening in the middle of a sentence. It was published in Madrid in 1880.[42] His enthusiasm fired by what he found, Jiménez de la Espada searched further, found a fragment of the *War of Quito,* which he promptly published, and followed it with two others, *Chupas* and *Salinas.* The other two "Huarina" and "Xaquixahuana," are still listed as missing, but with the third unpublished volume of Pedro de Cieza's history now having been found under mysterious circumstances— that part which he announced in the introduction of his first as "the third part in which I shall deal with the discovery and conquests of this kingdom of Peru and of the great tenacity of . . . Francisco Pizarro and the many trials the Spaniards underwent when thirteen of them [the men of Gallo] discovered it . . . and how they entered Peru and won it with 160 Spaniards, taking Atahualpa prisoner" (and yet still not fully published)—it is fully possible that the morass which is Spain's libraries may yield up from the quagmire of the past the other three missing manuscripts of Pedro de Cieza de León.[43]

lxxviii

[42] Edited and published as *Segunda Parte de la Crónica del Perú* by Marcos Jiménez de la Espada (Madrid, 1880), based upon a mutilated manuscript copy of Cieza found in the library of the royal monastery of San Lorenzo del Escorial. The whole title of the manuscript read, "Chronicle of the Succession and Government of the Incas, natural lords that were of the provinces of Peru, and Other Things relating to that Kingdom for the Illustrious lord Don Juan Sarmiento, president of the Royal Council of the Indies." This led Prescott, who used the volume, to attribute it to Juan Sarmiento, who had been president of the Royal Council of the Indies. Not knowing that he was in reality praising Pedro de Cieza, Prescott spoke of "prominent authorities on whom I have relied in this Introductory portion . . . Juan de Sarmiento . . . I have been able to collect no information beyond what is afforded by his own writings." So all the praise that Prescott gives to Juan de Sarmiento should have been, we now know, for Pedro de Cieza. (See notes on Sarmiento, p. 81 of the Modern Library edition of *The Conquest of Peru.*) Even with the superb industry which characterized Marcos Jiménez de la Espada, he did not find anything on the life of Cieza, and he lamented, "Unfortunately, the first of the chroniclers of Peru, and perhaps of the Indies, is in the same situation as the majority of our literary celebrities of the sixteenth century: he is known only through his writing." Now, all has been found; we know more about Pedro de Cieza than all the others. Jiménez de la Espada's lament has been silenced.

[43] The third and long lost book of Cieza's history as planned and announced by him in the first pages of the *Primera Crónica*—"The Discovery and Conquest of Peru by Pizarro and the Rebellion of the Indians"—has been discovered under circumstances which have not been revealed by Rafael Loredo of Lima, Peru. Under the title of *La Tercera parte de la Crónica de Cieza de León,* he has been publishing in tantalizing

At least for the here and now and after four hundred years, here are the two books which were marked as his *Chronicles of the Incas.*

"I have brought together," Cieza wrote in 1553, "and compiled this history of what I saw and experienced and from reliable information I received from persons whose word could be relied on.

"For what I write here is the truth . . . and the difficulties of land, mountains, and rivers . . . intolerable hungers and trials have never stood in the way of my two callings: that of following my standard and my captain without abate. . . .

"Much of what I have written I saw with my own eyes, being present, and I traveled many lands and provinces the better to see it, and that which I did not see, I strove to inform myself of from persons, Spaniards or Indians, of complete credibility.

"Traveling hither and yon . . . I saw strange and wonderful things that exist in the New World of the Indies and there came over me a great desire to write certain of them. . . .

"And so [in this book] I appeal to the judgment of learned and benevolent men, asking them to regard this work of mine with equity.

chapters this important "Third Part" for several years in *Mercurio Peruano.* Beginning in August, 1946: "Capítulos de la Tercera Parte de la Crónica de Cieza de León referente al Descubrimiento y Conquista del Perú: *La Tercera Parte de la Crónica de Pedro de Cieza de León* (Caps. 1–15, Año XXI, Vol. XXVII, No. 233); "Algunos Capítulos de la Tercera Part de la Crónica de Pedro de Cieza de León" (Caps. 16–21. Año XXVI, Vol. XXXII, No. 289); "El Tercer Viaje de Pizarro" (Caps. 22–23, Año, XXX, Vol. XXXVI, No. 340); "Nuevos Capítulos de la Tercera Parte de la Crónica del Perú de Pedro de Cieza de León" Caps. 34–41, Año XXXI, Vol. XXXVII, No. 347, pp. 409, 440, 144, 159, 453, 474, 75, 95). The last is May, 1958, Año XXXII, Vol. XXXVIII, No. 361, pp. 247–68. It is regrettable that this cannot be fully used.

Dr. Raúl Porras Barrenechea has impatiently written that "Loredo has hitherto abstained from giving any indication regarding the whereabouts of the Chronicle he discovered, the characteristics of the manuscript, the extension of same, the number of chapters it contains, and the events covered by this 'Third Part' of Cieza's. In his presentation Loredo mentions the existence of three copies of this part of the *Crónica del Perú:* one in the possession of Rosenbach & Co., in New York; another in the hands of a 'Spanish Duke'; and another existing in a center of American studies in Spain. This last—which seems to be Loredo's source—would be the copy that, as is known, Jiménez de la Espada obtained from the original manuscript belonging to D. José Sancho Rayón and which was used repeatedly by the famous Spanish Americanist. On the other hand, Loredo, as an enthusiastic cultivator of the history of the civil wars and especially the insurrection of Gonzalo Pizarro, has followed with fervor and admiration the footsteps of Jiménez de la Espada and has burrowed deeply into his papers and notes, kept in the *Consejo Superior de Investigaciones Ciéntificas de Madrid.* It is almost certain, then, that this is the text that serves Loredo for his enigmatic publications. Jiménez de la Espada said that Sancho Rayón's manuscript, which he used, was a 'contemporary and trustworthy copy—but extremely incorrect.' The copy used by Loredo presents the same features: it is full of salient errors . . . ."

"And if this history is not written with the polish which learning gives to letters, nor with the necessary pomp, it is at least full of truth. . . .

"It is my belief that other men might have concluded this undertaking more to the taste of the readers, more learned, I do not doubt, but bearing in mind my intention, they will take from it what I could give, for in any case . . . I deserve gratitude.

"What I ask is that, in payment for my work, even though this writing is devoid of rhetoric, it be kindly regarded, for I feel it goes hand in hand with truth. . . .

"This was begun in the city of Cartago [Nueva Granada] in the district of Popayán, in the year 1541, and concluded in Lima, City of the Kings, in the Kingdom of Peru, on the eighteenth of September, when its author was thirty-two years old, having spent seventeen of them in these Indies."

Signed,
Pedro de Cieza de León.

THE INCAS

of Pedro de Cieza de León

Wherein is stated the aim of this work and its divisions 3

HAVING LEFT Spain, where I was born and reared, at so tender an age that I had hardly rounded out thirteen years, and having spent in the Indies of the Ocean-Sea more than seventeen, many of them in conquests and discoveries and others in establishing settlements and in traveling hither and yon, and as I saw the strange and wonderful things that exist in this New World of the Indies, there came to me a great desire to write certain of them, those which I had seen with my own eyes, and also what I had heard from highly trustworthy persons. But when I considered my small learning, I cast this desire from me, holding it vain, because it has been the province of great and learned minds to write histories, lending them luster with their noble, wise pens, and for the unlearned, even to think of such a thing was folly. For that reason, time elapsed without my drawing on my scant powers until God, favoring me with grace, aroused in me once more what I had forgotten. And taking heart, with mounting confidence, I determined to devote a part of my life to writing history. And I was moved to this by the following reasons:

The first, because I had taken notice wherever I went that nobody concerned himself with writing aught of what was happening. And time so destroys the memory of things that only by clues and inference can the future ages know what really took place.

The second, because considering that we and these Indians all have our origin in our common parents, it is just that the world should know how so great a multitude as these Indians were brought into the lap of the Church by the efforts of the Spaniards, an undertaking so great that no other nation of all the universe could have accomplished it.

And also that it may be known in days to come how greatly the crown of Castile was increased. And how, under its king and lord, the rich and widespread kingdoms of New Spain and Peru were settled and other islands and vast provinces discovered.

And so I appeal to the judgment of learned and benevolent men, asking them to regard this work of mine with equity, for they know that the maliciousness and backbiting of the ignorant and unlearned is very great, and they are never at a loss for refutals and objections. For which reason many, fearing the poisoned envy of these scorpions, prefer to be looked upon as cowards rather than valiantly let their works see the light.

4

But neither from fear of one or the other shall I desist from carrying out my intention, setting more store by the favor of the few and the wise than by the harm that may come to me from the many and the vain.

I also write this work so that those who see in it the great services which many noble knights and youths rendered to the royal crown of Castile may be encouraged and spurred on to imitate them. And also so that seeing how not a few dared to commit treason, tyranny, robbery, and other crimes, they may learn from their example and the notorious punishments which they received to serve their kings and natural liege lords loyally and well.

For these reasons which I have set forth, determined in my endeavor, I set about the present work, which, for its better understanding, I have divided into four parts, arranged as follows:

1. *Crónica 1553:* This first part treats of the boundaries and division of the provinces of Peru, both by land and by sea, and of their longitude and latitude; the description of all of them; the founding of the new cities by the Spaniards; who were their founders; the dates of their settlement; the ancient rites and customs of the native Indians, and other things strange and different from our own worthy of remark.[1]

In the second part I will deal with the rule of the Incas Yupanqui, the ancient kings of Peru, and of their great deeds and government; their number and the names they bore; the proud and sumptuous temples they built; the remarkable highways which they constructed, and other great things which were found in this kingdom. In this book, too, an account will be given of what these Indians tell of the Flood and how the Incas magnify their origins.[2]

---

[1] *The Primera Parte* . . . , the only book published in his lifetime. Printed in 1553, in Seville, in an edition totaling at least 500 copies. Translated into English three times, 1709, 1864, and 1958.

In the third part[3] I shall deal with the discovery and conquests of this kingdom of Peru and with the great tenacity of the Marquis Don Francisco Pizarro, and the many trials the Spaniards underwent when thirteen of them, with the Marquis himself, discovered it. And after the aforesaid Don Francisco Pizarro had been appointed governor by His Majesty, how he entered Peru and won it with 160 Spaniards, taking Atahualpa prisoner. And this third part will also deal with the arrival of the Adelantado Don Pedro de Alvarado, and the agreements that were made between him and Don Francisco Pizarro. It will also tell of the noteworthy events that took place in different parts of this kingdom, and the uprising and rebellion of the Indians, and the reasons that moved them to this. It deals with the cruel and relentless war the Indians waged against the Spaniards who were in the great city of Cuzco, and the death of certain Spanish captains and Indians; and the end of this third part is the return from Chile of the Adelantado Don Diego de Almagro, and his entry into the city of Cuzco by force of arms, while Captain Hernando Pizarro, a knight of the Order of Santiago, was serving there as high justice.

5

The fourth part is more extensive than the three preceding, and deals with weightier matters. It is divided into five books, which I entitle *The Civil Wars of Peru,* wherein are shown rare things such as have never occurred in any part of the world among so few people and of the same nation.

The first book of the *Civil Wars* is that of the war of Las Salinas.[4] It deals with the capture of Captain Hernando Pizarro by the Adelantado Don Diego de Almagro, and how the latter made himself governor of the city of Cuzco, and the causes of the war that broke out between the Governors Pizarro and Almagro; the bargaining and agreements which took place between them until it was decided to put the question in the hands of an arbitrator, the oaths they swore, the hearings of the two governors that were held, and the royal instructions and letters of His Majesty which they both put forward; the decision that was handed down, and how Don Diego de Almagro

---

[2] *The Segunda Parte . . . ,* edited by Marcos Jiménez de la Espada (Madrid, 1880); English editions, 1883, 1958.

[3] *The Tercera Parte . . . ,* discovered and edited by Rafael Loredo. Being published in *Mercurio Peruano,* Lima, since 1946. Not fully published.

[4] *The Civil Wars: Las Salinas,* discovered and edited by Marcos Jiménez de la Espada (Madrid, 1882); English translation by Hakluyt Society, 1923.

released Hernando Pizarro from the prison in which he had confined him; and the return of the *adelantado* to Cuzco, where with great cruelty and greater enmity battle was joined in Las Salinas, which lies half a league from Cuzco. And it relates the descent of Captain Lorenzo de Aldana, as general of Governor Don Francisco Pizarro, to the provinces of Quito and Popayán; and the discoveries made by Captains Gonzalo Pizarro, Pedro de Candia, Alonso de Alvarado, Peranzúrez, and others. I conclude with the voyage of Hernando Pizarro to Spain.[5]

The second book is called *The Battle of Chupas*. It will have to do with certain discoveries and conquests, and the conspiracy entered into in the City of the Kings by the men of Chile (as those were called who had supported the Adelantado Don Diego de Almagro before he was killed) to kill the Marquis Don Francisco Pizarro in the manner they did; and how Don Diego de Almagro, the son of the Governor, had himself proclaimed governor throughout the greater part of the kingdom, and how Captain Alonso de Alvarado took up arms against him in Chachapoyas, where he was captain and high justice of His Majesty by appointment of the Marquis Pizarro; and Perálvarez Holgin and Gómez de Tordoya, with others, in Cuzco. And of the arrival of Master Cristóbal Vaca de Castro as governor; of the dissensions that arose among the men of Chile until, after the captains had killed off one another, the fierce battle of Chupas took place, near Huamanga, whence Governor Vaca de Castro went to Cuzco and cut off the head of Don Diego the Younger, with which I conclude this second book.

The third book, which I call *The Civil War of Quito*,[6] continues the two previous, and its contents will be very entertaining and deal with sundry events and great matters. It tells of the new laws promulgated in Spain, and the disturbances that took place in Peru, the juntas and councils, until Gonzalo Pizarro was received in the city of Cuzco as envoy and captain-general; and what happened in the City of the Kings while these storms were going on, until the arrest of the Viceroy by the city council, and his departure by sea; and of the

[5] *The Civil Wars: The Battle of Chupas,* discovered and edited by Marcos Jiménez de la Espada (Madrid, 1881); English translation by Hakluyt Society, 1918.

[6] *The Civil Wars: The Battle of Quito,* discovered and edited by Marcos Jiménez de la Espada (Madrid, 1877); English translation by Hakluyt Society, 1913.

entry into the City of the Kings of Gonzalo Pizarro, where he was acclaimed governor, and how he pursued the Viceroy, and the other episodes between them until the Viceroy was defeated and killed in the campaign of Añaquito. In this book I also give an account of the shifts that took place in Cuzco and Charcas and other places; and the encounters of Captain Diego Centeno, supporting the King, and **7** Alonso de Toro and Francisco de Carvajal, supporting Pizarro, until that loyal man, Diego de Centeno, was forced to go into hiding, and Lope de Mendoza, his master of troop, was killed in the action at Pecona. And what took place between the Captains Pedro de Hinojosa, Juan de Illanes, Melchior Verdugo, and the others who were in Terra Firma.

And of the death Governor Belalcázar meted out to Marshal Don Jorge Robledo in the town of Pozo; and how the Emperor, our King, using his great clemency and benignity, sent a pardon, with the behest that all should submit to his royal orders; and of the naming of Master Pedro de la Gasca as chief justice, and his arrival in Terra Firma and of the proclamations and methods he used to win over the captains there to the King's service; and of the return of Gonzalo Pizarro to the City of the Kings, and the cruelties executed by him and his captains; and of the general assembly that was called to determine who should go as legates to Spain; and the surrender of the fleet to the Chief Justice. And with this I shall make an end to what is dealt with in this book.

In the fourth book, which I entitle *The War of Huarina*,[7] I deal with the reappearance of Captain Diego Centeno, and how with the few he was able to assemble he entered the city of Cuzco and put it at the service of His Majesty; and how at the same time, as decided by the Chief Justice and captains, Lorenzo de Aldana set out from Panama, and arrived at the port of the Kings with other captains, and what they did; and how many, deserting Gonzalo Pizarro, went over to the service of the King. I shall also give an account of what took place between Captains Diego Centeno and Alonso de Mendoza until together they gave battle to Gonzalo Pizarro on the field of Huarina, where Diego Centeno was defeated and many of his captains and men killed and taken prisoner; and of what Gonzalo Pizarro ordered and did until he entered the city of Cuzco.

[7] *The Civil Wars: The Battle of Huarina.* Lost.

The fifth book, which is that of the war of Xaquixahuana,[8] deals with Chief Justice Pedro de la Gasca's arrival in the valley of Jauja, and the preparations and plans for war that he made after knowledge of Diego Centeno's rout, of his departure from this valley and arrival in that of Xaquixahuana, where Gonzalo Pizarro with his captains and men joined battle with him, in which the Chief Justice, and the King's supporters, came off victorious, and Gonzalo Pizarro and his followers and partisans were defeated and brought to justice in this very valley. And how the Chief Justice La Gasca arrived in Cuzco and had the tyrants publicly denounced as traitors, and withdrew to the town known as Guaynarima, where he allotted the greater part of the provinces of this kingdom to such as seemed best to him. And from there he went to the City of Kings, where he established the Royal Tribunal which exists there.

These books, which represent about a fourth part, being concluded, I make two commentaries: one of the things that occurred in the kingdom of Peru from the founding of the Tribunal until the Chief Justice left it; the second, from his arrival in Terra Firma and the death which the Contreras gave to the Bishop of Nicaragua, and how with treasonable intent they entered Panama and robbed great quantities of gold and silver, and of the battle the inhabitants of Panama fought with them near the city, where most of them were taken prisoner or killed, and others brought to justice, and how the treasure was recovered. I conclude with the uprisings that took place in Cuzco and the expedition of Marshal Alonso de Alvarado, under orders of the members of the tribunal, to put them down; and of the entry into this kingdom of that illustrious and prudent gentleman, Don Antonio Mendoza, to serve as viceroy.

And if this history is not written with the polish which learning gives to letters, not with the necessary pomp, it is at least full of truth and each receives his just due briefly, and ill deeds are reproved with moderation.

It is my belief that other men might have concluded this undertaking more to the taste of the readers, being more learned, I do not doubt; but bearing in mind my intention, they will take from it what I could give, for, in any case, I deserve gratitude. Diodorus Siculus, of an older time, wrote that without doubt men owe much to writers,

[8] *The Civil Wars: The Battle of Xaquixahuana.* Lost.

for thanks to their work, men's deeds live for the ages. And thus Cicero called writing the witness of time, the teacher of life, the light of truth.

What I only ask is that, in payment for my work, even though this writing is devoid of rhetoric, it be kindly regarded, for, that I feel, it goes hand in hand with truth. Thus I submit it to the judgment of 9 the wise and virtuous, and beg of others that they content themselves merely with reading it.

TO THE VERY NOBLE AND PUISSANT LORD, DON
PHILIP, PRINCE OF THE SPAINS, ETC., OUR KING

MOST NOBLE and mighty Lord: As not only praiseworthy feats of many
and very brave men, but countless things deserving of eternal memory
of great and varied regions, have remained in the dark night of for-
getfulness for a lack of writers to recount them and historians to describe them, I myself having gone out to the New World of the Indies
where having spent most of my years in wars and discoveries and the
settling of cities . . . I decided to assume this undertaking of setting
down the matters of the great and memorable kingdom of Peru; to
which land I traveled overland from the province of Cartagena,
wherein, as in that of Popayán, I spent many years.

And so after having served Your Majesty in that final war which
was concluded against the rebellious tyrant [Gonzalo Pizarro] and
giving much thought to the great wealth and the admirable things
contained in these provinces and the varied episodes that have occurred in the past as in the present . . . I decided to take up my quill
to set them down. I thus carried out my desire to render Your Highness some signal service and so that my purpose should be made
known . . . even though considering the scant powers of my ability,
I trust that you shall judge my efforts by the measure of my desire
and rather more, admire the intention with which I offer this book
to Your Highness, which deals with that great kingdom of Peru . . .
I was not unaware . . . that to relate the admirable things that have
existed and exist in this kingdom of Peru would be a task worthy . . .
of the great writers whom the world has known . . . even they would
find the task an arduous one. For who could recount the great and
diverse things to be found in it, the lofty mountains, the deep valleys
where the discovery and conquest were carried out, the many and
great rivers, of such mighty waters; the variety of provinces, so different in nature; the nations and peoples, each with their own strange
customs, rites, and ceremonies; the many birds and animals, trees and
fish, so different and so unknown? And aside from this, who could
recount the unheard of trials which such a small number of Spaniards

underwent in so vast an area? Who could imagine or set down the amazing episodes that have taken place in the wars and discovery of 1,600 leagues of territory, the hunger, thirst, deaths, fears, and fatigue? There is so much to say of all this that it would weary any writer to set it down. For that reason, from the most important of all this, puissant Lord, I have brought together and compiled this history of what I saw and experienced, and from reliable information I received from persons whose word could be relied on. And I would not have the temerity to submit it to the adverse judgment of the world if I did not have the hope that Your Highness would deign to lend it luster, shield and defend it so that it may venture forth freely; for there have been many writers who, with this fear, seek out princes of great estate to whom to dedicate their works, and of certain of them no one can affirm that he has seen what they treat of, for they are wholly fantastic and a thing that never was. What I write here is the truth, and matters of importance, useful, entertaining, and that have occurred in our own time, and addressed to the greatest and most powerful prince in the world, which is Your Highness. It seems temerity on the part of a man of so few letters to attempt what others more learned have not undertaken, especially being so occupied in matters of war; for often when the other soldiers were resting, I wearied myself writing. But neither this, nor the difficulties of land, mountains, and rivers of which I have spoken, intolerable hungers and trials have ever stood in the way of my two callings, those of writing and following my standard and my captain without abate. The fact that this work has been written with such toil and is addressed to Your Highness would seem to me to suffice for its readers to forgive me the faults they may think to find in it. And if they do not, it is enough for me to have set down the truth, for this is what I have most sought. Much of what I have written I saw with my own eyes, being present, and I traveled many lands and provinces the better to see it; and that which I did not see, I strove to inform myself of from persons of complete credibility, Spaniards and Indians. May it please God Almighty, since it was His will that Your Highness should be the master of so great and rich a kingdom as that of Peru, that you may reign for many and happy years and your realm be increased by many other kingdoms and dominions.

12 WHEREBY on thy behalf, Pedro de Cieza, citizen of the city of Seville, I have been informed that thou hast long dwelt in the provinces of Peru, serving us with thy arms and horse and fortune during the wars and conquests and discoveries that took place during the time of thy residence in said provinces; and that to better serve us thou didst write and compile a book dealing with the description of said provinces of Peru and the founding of cities and towns therewith and rites and customs of the native Indians of said provinces, in which thou hast spent much time, experiencing great hardships, likewise traveling through said provinces the better to effect the aforementioned description and compiling and writing the aforementioned book. Thou hast requested that we grant thee leave to print same: provided that during the lapse of twenty years no other person but thyself or whomsoever thou shouldst designate might print same; or as my mercy may decree. And I, taking heed of the aforesaid, and said book having been seen and examined in the Council of the Emperor and King my Lord, bidding thee well and in my mercy, have so agreed.

In consequence I herewith grant thee, Pedro de Cieza, or whomsoever thou shouldst designate, leave and faculty to print the aforementioned book during the lapse of fifteen years,[1] which shall commence and be counted as from the date of this my decree forward. And all volumes that thou shouldst so print, thou mayest sell in all of our kingdoms and domains, provided that after printing and before sale, they be brought to the Council: so as to ascertain the price for which they should be sold. And I command and enjoin that during the lapse of said fifteen years no other person or persons of these our kingdoms or domains shall be so bold as to print the aforementioned book, nor sell same, nor bring to sell, from or outside these

---

[1] Whether permission was granted or not, three Flanders editions of this Chronicle made their appearance in 1554; since Antwerp was then under Spanish rule, we may assume that it was subject to the King's pleasure or copyright of fifteen years. It is fully possible that they were legally printed, since in his testament Pedro de Cieza writes of "what [money] may come from the Indies and *Flanders.*"

kingdoms, excepting thyself the aforesaid Pedro de Cieza or whomsoever thou mayest designate. Under penalty that any other person or persons that print or sell the aforementioned book, or may bring same from abroad, these not being those which thou hast had printed, shall lose all that they have printed and have in their possession, as herein stated. And shall besides incur a fine of fifty thousand *maravedís*. Said fine to be divided, half for the coffers of His Majesty and the other half for thyself, the aforesaid Pedro de Cieza. And I command that members of the Council of His Majesty, presidents and judges of his high courts and chancelries, mayors, constables of his house and court, and chancelries and other justices and judges of all cities, villages, and places of these kingdoms and domains, those who are now in office and those who shall henceforward be in office, shall maintain and enforce and make others maintain and enforce this my decree and contents herewith: and that they shall not act against nor disregard or consent to the disregard of the tenor of same, at any time nor in any manner whatsoever, during the aforementioned lapse of fifteen years: under penalty of my chastisement and ten thousand *maravedís* for the coffers and treasury of His Majesty, to each one who should so proceed to the contrary.

Dated in Bonçon [Monçon de Aragón] on the fourteenth day of the month of September of the year one thousand, five hundred and fifty-two.

I, THE PRINCE
By command of His Highness
Juan Vásquez

PART I

CHAPTER I (XXXVI)*

Which contains the description and boundaries of
the kingdom of Peru as it runs from the city of Quito
to the town of Plata, a distance of more than
seven hundred leagues.

THE TIME has come to give my quill to the great things that are to be recounted of Peru.

But before I tell of the founding of [Quito], it would be well to indicate the extent of the kingdom of the Incas, which is some seven hundred leagues in length[1] and one hundred leagues in width, in some places more, in others less.

I do not intend to speak here of that which the Lord-Incas ruled, which was over 1,200 leagues; I shall merely state what is understood by Peru, which runs from Quito to the town of [La] Plata, from one boundary to another.

And to make all this clearer, I would say that this land of Peru consists of three ranges or barren stretches unfit for human habitation. One of these is the range of the Andes Mountains, covered with dense woods, where the land is so poor that, except beyond the mountains, there are no inhabitants and never were. The other is the plateau running the length of this range of the Andes which is intensely cold and whose peaks are covered with deep snow which never stops falling. Nor can people live in these sierras on account of the snow and cold and also because the land produces nothing as it is buffeted by snows and winds which blow continuously. The other range, as I call it, is the sands which stretch from Tumbes to beyond Tarapacá, where all there is to be seen are deserts of sand baked by the sun, where there is neither water nor grass, nor trees, not any living thing

---

* *Note to the Reader:* In fully integrating the two Chronicles of Peru into one, the editor has placed the original numbers from the Chronicles after the new series of chapters. The cryptic notation of (ii:VI) refers to the Second Chronicle and its chapter; that not carrying the book numeral is, naturally, the First Chronicle.

[1] A Spanish league then equaled about three miles, or as far as a horse or mule could walk in one hour.

except birds which, thanks to their wings, can go anywhere. Though the kingdom is as long as I have said, there are great uninhabited regions such as I have described. The land that is inhabited and where people live is the following: in many places in the Andes there are gaps which form openings and passes, making fairly broad valleys, so broad that there are wide plains among the sierras, and although snow falls, it stays on the heights. As the valleys are protected, they are not punished by the winds, nor does the snow reach them; on the contrary, the land is so productive that everything planted there grows well, and there are trees and many birds and animals are raised. As the land is so fertile, it is all well settled by the natives.

18

They build their well-laid-out villages of stone, with thatched roofs, and live healthy and free. Thus, in the openings and plains of the highlands of the Andes and the sierra, there are large settlements where there were and are many people, because through these valleys run rivers of excellent water which flow into the Southern Sea. And as these rivers enter the sands I have mentioned and flow through them, the moisture makes it possible to raise many trees and there are beautiful plains, some two and three leagues wide, where carob trees grow in abundance even though there is no water near by. Wherever there are groves of trees, the soil is not sandy, but very fertile and productive. These valleys were formerly thickly settled; there are still Indians, though not so many as there once were, not nearly. And as it never rained in these plains and sand wastes of Peru, they do not build covered houses like those of the highlands, but handsome open terraces, or large dwellings of adobes with their rooms and stone floors; to protect themselves from the sun, they stretch mats overhead. They do it in this way in our own days, and the Spaniards use no other roof on their houses than these mud-stiffened mats. As for their fields, they make conduits leading from the rivers that water these valleys, so well built and so carefully planned that all the land is watered and planted, and nothing is lost. These irrigation ditches are very green and gay, lined with orchards of fruit trees of Spain and those native to the country. And at all seasons in these valleys fine crops of wheat and corn and all that is sown can be harvested. So that although I have described Peru as being three desert and uninhabited mountain ranges, by the grace of God there are these valleys and rivers I have mentioned; if it were not for them, it would be impossible for people to live there, which is the reason the natives could be so easily conquered and why they serve without revolting, because if they did so, they would all perish of hunger and cold. For (as I have remarked) aside from the lands they occupy, the rest is uninhabitable, all snow-covered sierras and lofty, rude mountains. The contour of this kingdom is, as I have said, length, 700 leagues, running north to south, and, if we count the territory ruled by the Inca kings, 1,200 leagues of straight road, north to south by the meridian. At its widest point from east to west it is a little better than 100 leagues, and at others from 40 to 60, a little less, a little more. This length and breadth refers to the length and breadth of the sierras and mountains that run through all this land of Peru, as I have explained. And that long range called the Andes at some points lies forty leagues from the Southern Sea, and at others, sixty, in some places nearer, in others farther. As it is so high, and its greatest height is near the Southern Sea, the rivers are small because the watershed is short.

The slopes and declivities of the other highland which runs the length of this land open out in plains as they approach the sea, at three leagues in some places, and up to eighteen in others. The temper and climate of the plains is hot rather than cold, varying with the season, inasmuch as they lie almost at sea level. The hottest season is when the sun has passed overhead and enters the Tropic of Capricorn, which is December 21, returning toward the equator. In spite of the fact that in the uplands there are regions and provinces that are mild, it is the opposite of the plains, being cool rather than hot. This that I have said refers to the general nature of these provinces, which I shall later describe in more detail.

CHAPTER 2 (XXXVII)

Of the villages to be found between the town of Pasto and the city of Quito.

It would be well [now] to tell what lies along the way [between Pasto, the northern boundary of the Lord-Incas] until one reaches the city of Quito.

Leaving the town of Pasto, one proceeds until reaching the chieftaincy or settlement of those called *Funes;*[1] by this same route one arrives at another some three leagues (nine miles) off, known as *Iles,* and three leagues [nine miles] more brings one within sight of the tampu [tambo] lodgings of Gualmatán; on this same road lies the town of Ipiales, three leagues [nine miles] from Gualmatán.

20

Throughout this region little corn is raised, almost none, because the land is cold and the seed of the corn delicate; but there is an abundance of potatoes, quinoa, and other roots which the natives plant. Proceeding from Ipiales, one comes to a small province called Huaca, and before reaching it, one sees the famous highway of the Incas, as famous in these parts as that which Hannibal built across the Alps when he marched into Italy. And it is worthy of higher esteem, both because of the lodgings and depots to be found all along it as well as by reason of the difficulty of its construction over such rough and barren sierras, which make it an astounding thing to see. One also comes to a river near which the Inca kings in olden times had a fortress from which they made war on the Pastos and set out to conquer them. There is a bridge over this river which is natural but seems man-made, a high, thick rock with a hole in the middle through which the river pours, and over it go all who wish to cross. In the language of the Incas this bridge is called *Rumichaca,*[2] which in ours means "bridge of stone." Near this bridge is a hot spring in which it is impossible to keep the hand long because of the heat of the water that flows from it. There are other springs, too, and the water of the river and the climate are so cold that they are difficult to endure. Close to this bridge the Inca kings built another fortress, and there they posted loyal guards to see that their own people did not return to

[1] Cieza here describes tambo (Quechua, *tampu*) settlements along the Royal Road of the Incas (see map). Funes (9,800 feet altitude) lies twenty-two miles south of Pasto near the Telles River, which flows into the Amazon tributaries. Iles, at 11,500 feet altitude and still extant, is a settlement on the highway, as suggested by Cieza. Gualmatán follows at the same altitude until the road drops down to the valley of Ipiales, which, now in Colombia, marks the frontier with Ecuador. (See Pedro Maldonado, *Carta de la Provincia de Quito* [Madrid, 1750].)

[2] Rumichaca, a natural bridge over a river which bore the name of Angasmayo, now the Guiatara River, which debouches into the Pacific Ocean at Tumaco. It is so named in Maldonado's map (n. 1 above), and the river served then as frontier between the governments of Quito and Popayán. Humboldt surveyed it in 1802, when he took observations at "Tulcan, village à l'este du grand Nevado de Chiles et à une lieue et demie [a league and a half] au sud des ruines d'un château des Incas *près du rocher de Rumichaca*" (*Recueil d'Observations Astronomiques*, I, 307).

Cuzco or Quito, for many felt that the conquest of the territory of the Pastos they were carrying out was a waste of time.

From the small province of Huaca[3] one proceeds until reaching Tuza, which is the last village of the Pastos, to the right of which run the mountains that overlook the Freshwater Sea, and to the left, the peaks that overlook the Southern Sea. Farther on there is a small hill on which stands a fortress the Incas used to have, with its moat, and, as those of the Indians go, it must have been strong. Proceeding from the village of Tuza and this fortress, one comes to the Mira River, which is a warm stream, and along it are many fruits and melons of good quality, and rabbits, doves, and partridges, and a great amount of wheat and barley is harvested, as well as corn and many other things, for it is very fertile. From the Mira River one descends to the large and sumptuous lodgings of Caranqui. Before reaching them, one can see the lake called Yahuar-cocha, which in our speech means "sea of blood," where, before the Spaniards entered Peru, the Lord-Inca Huayna Capac (d. 1527), because of provocation given him by the natives of Caranqui and other neighboring villages, ordered more than twenty thousand men killed and thrown into this lake, according to the account of the Indians themselves. The dead were so numerous that it looked like a lake of blood, and from this it received the name or meaning I have told.

Farther on are the lodgings of Caranqui, where some claim Atahualpa, son of Huayna Capac, was born because his mother was a native of this village. This, however, is not true, for I made careful inquiry, and he was born in Cuzco, and the rest is nonsense. These lodgings of the Caranqui are in a small square; inside is a beautifully built stone pool, and the palaces and houses of the Incas are also made of fine great stones skillfully joined, without mortar, which is a sight to see. In olden times there was a temple of the sun, and in it lived more than two hundred beautiful virgins dedicated to its service, who took a vow of chastity, and if they broke it, they were cruelly punished. Those who committed adultery (which was considered a great

[3] Huaca, at 9,800 feet altitude, was presumably an Inca tambo, a way-station on the road, with Indians living close in attendance. It is still extant. Tuza, which lay west of it across the river, is at the base of large mountain peaks. The "Freshwater Sea" was the early name for the Amazon River. These villages were in the confines of the Pastos. In Incaic times they occupied both sides of what is now the Ecuadorian-Colombian frontier and extended as far south as the Mira River.

sacrilege) were hanged or buried alive. These virgins were watched over with great care, and there were a number of priests to perform the sacrifices called for by their religion. This house of the sun was held in great veneration in the time of the Incas, and it was guarded and revered, being filled with great vessels of gold and silver and other treasures, which cannot be easily enumerated. Even the walls were covered with sheets of gold and silver, and although it has now fallen into ruins, it can still be seen what a great thing it used to be. In these lodgings of Caranqui the Incas had their ordinary garrisons with their captains, which were stationed there in times of war and peace to deal with possible revolts.[4]

22

CHAPTER 3 (XXXIX)

Of the remaining villages and tambos to be found from Caranqui to Quito.

IN THE preceding chapter I have told of the authority and great power which the Incas, kings of Cuzco, held over all Peru, and it would be well, having made mention of this, that I should proceed.

From the royal lodgings of Caranqui, along the famous road of the Incas, one comes to the settlement of Otavalo, which was neither very rich nor important, nor poor, either, and on both sides of it there are large settlements of Indians.[1]

[4] The Caranqui [also Cara or Imbaya] occupied what is now the province of Imbabura, Ecuador, extending southward into the territory of Quito: it lies close to the colonial-modern city of Ibarra. There was a sun temple there, a house for the Chosen Women (Aclla-huasi), and other structures, and they were still to be seen as late as 1692. By 1798 they had disappeared. Today some of the walls form part of the parochial church. According to Cara myth-history, the Caranqui were supposed to have arrived in boats from the north, landing at the Bahía de Caranqui at Esmeraldas. Led by their chieftain (scyri), they ascended the Esmeraldas River, defeated the primitive tribes about Quito, and settled in their traditional area about Imbabura. They are believed to have been related to the Colorado and Cayapas Indians.

The settlements of the Caranqui were large: their houses were of wattle and daub with straw thatch; their dress was Andean, their gods were of wood and stone, their agriculture followed the Andean pattern, they used coca leaves, and their chiefs were inherited direct on patrilinear lines.

The Incas defeated them, their chieftain Cacha was killed in battle, and his daughter Paccha given to Huayna Capac as a concubine, from which union, it was held, was born Atahualpa. (See Victor W. von Hagen, Tsatchela Indians of Western Ecuador, Museum of the American Indian, Indian Notes, No. 51; and Juan de Velasco, Historia del Reino de Quito.)

There is bitter enmity between those of Caranqui and those of Otavalo, because most of them say that, when the news reached this region of Quito (within whose boundaries these Indians live) of the entrance of the Spaniards in the kingdom and the imprisonment of Atahualpa, after their first fright and wonder and amazement over what they heard about the horses and the speed with which they traveled—believing the men who rode them and the horses were one and the same thing—the fame of the Spaniards aroused great excitement in these people. And they awaited their arrival, believing that inasmuch as they had been powerful enough to overthrow the Inca, their ruler, they would be able to subdue all of them. It is said that at this time the chief of Caranqui [Cacha] had in his lodgings a vast treasure, his own and that of the Incas. And the lord of Otavalo, who must have been very shrewd, astutely realizing that at such times it is well to hide away treasures and things of value, for everything was in a state of confusion, and, as the saying goes, "There's good fishing in troubled waters," sent for many of his Indians and headmen, and chose and appointed from among them those he believed most capable and fleet-footed. He then ordered them to attire themselves in shirts and long blankets, and take slender wands, all the same length, and mount the largest of their llamas and station themselves on the hilltops and peaks where they could be seen by the people of Caranqui. Meanwhile, he with a good number of Indians and some of the women, feigning great fear, arrived at the village of Caranqui, telling how they were fleeing from the fury of the Spaniards who had attacked their villages on horseback, and to escape their cruelty, they had abandoned their treasures and possessions.

According to the story, this news sowed great panic, and was believed, because the Indians on the llamas could be seen on the peaks and hillsides, and as they were far off, what the lord of Otavalo said

23

1 Pedro de Cieza de León: "Those to the west of the town are Poritaco, Collaguazo, of the Huancas and Cayambes, and close to the great Marañón River are the Quixos, in scattered settlements among high mountains. Gonzalo Pizarro came through here on his expedition in search of cinnamon, with a fine force of Spaniards and abundant supplies; but in spite of all this, they had a very bad time and suffered greatly from hunger. In the fourth part of this work I shall give a complete account of this expedition and tell how it happened that the Great River was discovered, and how Captain Orellana sailed down it to the Ocean-Sea, and his voyage to Spain, where His Majesty appointed him governor and *adelantado* of the lands he had discovered. To the east lie the farming lands of Cotocoyambe and the mountains of Yumbo, and many settlements, as well as some that have not been completely discovered [explored?]."

was held to be true, and they all lost their heads and began to run. Otavalo, pretending to do the same, lagged behind with his people, and returned to the houses of the Indians of Caranqui, and stole all the treasures he found, which was no small amount, and returned to his village. A few days later the trick was discovered.

24

Otavalo and his people kept what they had stolen, according to many of the Indians of these regions, and the enmity between them continues.[2]

After the settlement of Otavalo, called after this lord, come those of Cochasqui, and to reach them one crosses a snow-covered pass, and a league before reaching them, the land is so cold that life is difficult.[3] From Cochasqui the road leads to Guailla-bamba, four leagues from Quito, where as the land is so low-lying and almost under the equator, it is hot; but not so much so that it is not thickly settled, and everything grows there that man needs for his existence. We who have traveled through these regions know what lies below the line of the equator, although certain writers of antiquity (as I have said) held the land to be uninhabitable. Below it there is a winter and a summer season, and many people live there, and what is sowed yields abundantly, especially wheat and barley.

Along the roads between these settlements there are various rivers, all of which have bridges, and they are well made, and there are great buildings and many things to see which, for the sake of brevity, I omit.[4] . . .

[2] The Otavalo Indians, south of Caranqui, were Cara-speaking peoples. A royal tambo was there in the times of the Incas. The village is famed, even now, for its weavings, and the Otavalo Indians in distinctive dress are often seen traveling far beyond the confines of Ecuador.

[3] The late great German archaeologist Max Uhle found remains of Incaic buildings at Cochasqui.

[4] Pedro de Cieza de León: "It is four leagues from Guailla-bamba to the city of Quito, in the space of which there are various plantations and farms which the Spaniards have for their cattle, before reaching the field of Añaquito. Here, in the year 1546, in the month of January, the Viceroy Blasco Núñez Vela came with a force of Spaniards to put down the rebellion of those who were defending tyranny. And Gonzalo Pizarro came forth from the city of Quito, where, under false colors, he had assumed the government of the kingdom and entitled himself governor, accompanied by most of the nobility of all Peru, and joined battle with the Viceroy, in which the ill-starred Viceroy was killed, together with many valiant men and knights, who, for their loyalty and desire to serve His Majesty, fell there. This I shall relate more at length in the fourth part of this work, which is where I tell of the cruel civil wars that took place in Peru among the Spaniards themselves, which will be sorrowful to hear, and

CHAPTER 4 (XXXVIII)

Which deals with who these Lord-Incas were and their dominions in Peru.

As IN this part I shall have to make frequent reference to the Incas 25
and give an account of their many lodgings and other noteworthy things, it seems fitting to say something of them at this point, so that the reader will know who these lords were, and not be unaware of their importance nor confuse them.

On many occasions I asked the inhabitants of these provinces what they knew of what went on before the Incas ruled them, and in reply they said that they all lived without order, and that many of them went naked, like savages, without having houses or other dwellings except caves, of which we see many in the mountains and on the hillsides, from which they came out to eat what they could find in the fields. Others built fortresses, which they call *pucarás,* in the hills, from which they sallied forth, howling in strange tongues, to fight one another over the lands they planted, or for other reasons, and many were killed, and the victors carried off such booty as they could find and the women of the vanquished, with all of which they returned to the hilltops where they had their strongholds, and there made sacrifices to the gods they worshiped, pouring out before the stones and idols quantities of human blood and [the blood] of llamas. They were all uncivilized, recognizing no overlord except the captains who led them to war. If any of them went clothed, it was in scant attire, and not like the garments they now wear. The fillets or bands they wear on their head to identify themselves were like those they now use, they say.

From what I gathered from the accounts of the Indians of Cuzco, it would seem that in olden times there was great disorder in this kingdom we call Peru, and that the natives were stupid and brutish beyond belief. They say they were like animals, and that many ate

soon after this field of Añaquito one comes to the city of Quito." (*The Civil Wars: The Battle of Quito.*)

The Guailla-bamba River, the largest tributary of the Esmeraldas, has hollowed out a deep canyon in the central plateau. Humboldt in 1802 found it "neuf cents mètres de profoundeur et . . . une chaleur étouffante." At 2,000 meters and under the equator it can be very hot; thus it was densely populated. Four Inca suspension bridges crossed it at various places.

human flesh, and others took their daughters and mothers to wife, and committed other even graver sins, and had great traffic with the devil, whom they served and held in great esteem. Aside from this they had strongholds and fortresses in the mountains and hills, and on the least pretext, they sallied forth from them to make war on one another, and killed and took prisoner as many as they could. In spite of the fact that they were given over to these sins and worked these evils, they also say that some of them were religiously inclined, and for that reason in many parts of this kingdom they built great temples, where they prayed, performing their rites and superstitions before big idols, and the devil appeared to them and was worshiped. And while the people of this kingdom were living in this way, great tyrants arose in the provinces of the Colla and in the valleys of the Yungas and elsewhere, who carried on war against one another, and committed many killings and thefts, and they all suffered great calamities. Many fortresses and castles were destroyed, but the struggle between them went on, at which the devil, the enemy of mankind, rejoiced to see so many souls lost.

Manco Capac founded the city of Cuzco and gave it laws which he put into effect, and he and his descendants were called Incas, which means or signifies kings or great lords. They became so powerful that they conquered and ruled from Pasto to Chile, and to the south the Maule River saw their banners, and to the north, the Angasmayo, and these rivers were the boundaries of their empire, which was so large that the distance between these two limits was more than 1,200 leagues. And they built great fortresses and strongholds, and stationed captains and governors in all the provinces. They did great things, and governed so well that few in the world excel them. They were very keen of understanding, and kept careful accounts without writing, for none has been found in these parts of the Indies. They instilled good customs in all their subjects, and ordered them to clothe themselves and to go shod in *ojotas* [*usutas*], which is a kind of sandal. They gave much importance to the immortality of the soul and other secrets of nature. They believed that there was a Creator of all things, and the sun was their sovereign god, to whom they erected great temples. Led astray by the devil, they worshiped trees and stones, like the Gentiles. In the principal temples they had a great number of beautiful virgins, like those in Rome in the temple of Vesta, and these were ruled by almost the same statutes. For their armies they selected brave captains, and the most loyal they could find. They were very astute at converting their enemies into friends without war, and those who revolted were punished with great severity and no little cruelty.

27

CHAPTER 5 (ii: v)

Of what these natives tell of Tici-Viracocha, and the belief some held that one of the Apostles passed through this land.

BEFORE THE Incas came to reign in these kingdoms or were known there, these Indians tell a thing that far exceeds all else they say. They state that a long time went by in which they did not see the sun, and that they suffered great hardship from this lack, and that they made great prayers and vows to those they held to be their gods, imploring of them the light that had failed. When things stood like this, there emerged from the island of Titicaca, which lies in the great lake of the Colla, the sun in its splendor, at which all rejoiced. And after this had occurred, they say that out of the regions of the south there came and appeared among them a white man, large of stature, whose air and person aroused great respect and veneration. And this man whom they saw in this guise had great powers, making plains of the hills, and of the plains, high mountains, and bringing forth springs in the living rock. And when they saw his power, they called him the Maker of all things, their Beginning, Father of the sun, for aside from these, they say he did other even greater things, for he called into being men and animals, and, in a word, that great benefits came to them from his hand. And this man, so the Indians say who told me this which they had heard from their forefathers, who, in turn, had heard it in old songs that had come down to them, took his way to the north, working and doing these wonders, by the route of the uplands, and they never saw him again. They say that in many places he instructed people how they should live, and spoke to them lovingly and meekly, exhorting them to be good and not to do one another harm or injury, but rather to love one another, and use charity toward all.

For the most part he is called Tici-Viracocha, although in the province of the Colla they called him Tyapaca, and in other parts of it, Arnauan. Temples were built to him in many places, where statues in his likeness were erected before which they performed sacrifices. The huge statues in the town of Tiahuanacu are believed to be of those times, and although from what has been transmitted from the past they relate this that I have told of Tici-Viracocha, they know nothing more about him, nor that he ever returned to any part of this kingdom.

In addition to this they say that after some time had elapsed another man similar to the one described was seen, whose name they do not state, and that they heard for a fact from their forebears that wherever he went he healed the sick and restored their sight to the blind with only the words he spoke, and for these kind and helpful deeds he was greatly beloved. And in this manner, working great things with his words, he came to the province of the Canas, where, close to a village called Cacha, over which Captain Bartolomé de Terrazas holds an encomienda,[1] the natives rose up without consideration and advanced on him with the intention of stoning him. Suiting their acts to their thought, as they drew near, they saw him kneeling, with his hands raised to heaven as though imploring divine aid against the danger that threatened. These Indians go on to say that at that very moment a great fire appeared in the sky, so that they thought they should all be consumed. Filled with fear and trembling, they crowded toward him whom they wanted to kill, and with loud cries they begged him to have mercy and save them, for they recognized that this punishment had been sent them for the sin they had committed in wanting to stone him. Then they saw that when he ordered the fire to cease, it went out, but the flames had so scorched and consumed the stones that they served as witnesses that this which has been set down took place, for as a result of having been burned, they are so light that even a big one can be picked up as though it were of cork. And they further relate that, leaving that place, he went until he came to the shore of the sea, where, spreading his cloak, he moved on it over the waves, and never again appeared nor did they see him. And because of the manner of his departure they gave him

[1] It is known that this Captain Terrazas did hold the *encomienda* of Cacha. In the "Regulations for Tambos," written in Cuzco, May 31, 1543, appears this statement: "From the said tambo of Compapata one goes next to Tambo de Cacha, which is served by the Indians of [Captain Bartolomé de] Terrazas."

28

the name of Viracocha, which means "foam of the sea." After this
had happened, a temple was built in this village of Cacha, on the other
side of a river that flows beside it to the west, where a great stone
idol was set up in a somewhat narrow niche; this niche is not as large
and deep as those in Tiahuanacu built in memory of Tici-Viracocha,[2]
nor is the form of attire the same as those. Some gold in jewels was
found near by. 29

When I was passing through that province I went to see this idol,
for the Spaniards claim and insist that it might have been some apostle.
I even heard many of them say that it had a rosary in its hands, which
is nonsense, unless I am blind, for though I looked at it carefully, I
saw nothing of the sort, nor anything except that its hands were on
its hips, with arms akimbo, and at the waist there were marks which
seemed to indicate that the clothes he wore fastened with buttons.
If this one, or the former, was one of the glorious apostles who in
their preaching came to these regions, Almighty God alone can say.
As for me, I am of the opinion that if he were one of the apostles, his
teachings, with God's aid, would have had an effect on these peoples,
who are simple and devoid of malice, and there would be some evidence of it.

I inquired of the cacique or lord of the natives of Cacha, an Indian
of goodly appearance and reason, by name Don Juan, who had become a Christian, and who accompanied me to show me that antiquity, in memory of what god they had erected that temple, and he
answered that in memory of Tici-Viracocha. And as we are on the
subject of this name of Viracocha, I wish to disabuse the reader in

[2] Tici-Viracocha, or Kon-Tiki, as he is now popularly and mistakenly known, was
the Incas' creator-god. He created both natural and supernatural beings, and according to one of the three Spaniards who saw Cuzco before its rape, Viracocha was represented as man, in an effigy of solid gold, with his right arm raised "as in command."
He generally lived in the sky, but did appear to the people in time of grave crisis. Like
the Mexican god Quetzalcóatl he was a culture-hero, and was thought to have taught
all peoples the arts of civilization. When he reached the coast of Manta in Ecuador
(0°57′south), he is supposed to have set off across the ocean walking on the water.
This mytho-poetic figure bears no resemblance to the popular "Kon-Tiki" of the raft
and the theory as expounded by Thor Heyerdahl (1950). Heyerdahl has confused the
Viracocha (d. 1440) who was the Lord-Inca when the Chancas tribes attacked Cuzco
with the mythical battles which took place about Titicaca in the mythical period. Viracocha is mentioned by all the chroniclers, yet none agree on the origin of the name or
what it meant. The prefix "Kon," first put there by Betanzos, is mentioned by no
other and has no meaning. If the myth has substance, there must be some connection
between Quetzalcóatl (Mexico), Botchia (Colombia), and Viracocha (Peru). (See
Leonardo Villar, *Lexicología Keshua Uiracocha* [Lima, 1887].)

regard to the general belief that the natives gave the Spaniards the name Viracocha, which is tantamount to sea foam.[3]

And now I shall relate what I have been able to gather of the origins of the Incas.

CHAPTER 6 (ii: VI)

Of how certain men and women appeared in Paccaric-Tampu (the "origin-tambo") and what it is told that they did when they went forth from there.

I TOOK UPON MYSELF the task of describing what I could gather concerning the Incas and the methods and order of their governance, for

[3] Pedro de Cieza de León: "As far as the name is concerned, it is true, for *vira* is the word for foam, and *cocha*, sea; thus, as it seemed to them that they had come over it, they had given them that name. But this is an erroneous interpretation, according to the account I heard in Cuzco. They say that after Atahualpa had been taken prisoner by the Spaniards in the province of Cajamarca (Caxamarca), as there had been great wars between the two brothers Huascar Inca, the sole heir to the empire, and Atahualpa, and many battles had been waged by the captains of the one against those of the other until at the ford of Cotabamba in the Apurímac River, the Lord-Inca Huascar was taken prisoner and cruelly dealt with by Calicuchima, and in addition Quizquiz had wreaked great harm on Cuzco and, as is common knowledge, killed thirty of Huascar's brothers, and done other cruelties to those who supported him and had not looked with favor on Atahualpa. And in the course of these violent dissensions, Atahualpa, as I tell, was taken prisoner and had promised Pizarro that as ransom he would give him a household of gold, and Martín Bueno, Zárate, and Moguer went to Cuzco to fetch it, for the greatest part of it was in the sacred temple of Curicancha. As these Spaniards reached Cuzco at the time that Huascar's followers were suffering the aforesaid calamity, when they learned of Atahualpa's capture, they rejoiced, as can be imagined, and then, with earnest entreaty, they implored the help of the Spaniards against Atahualpa, their enemy, saying they had been sent by the hand of their mighty god, Tici-Viracocha, and that they were his sons, and for this reason they called and gave them the name of Viracocha. And they gave orders to the high priest and all the other ministrants of the temple that the sacred women were to remain in it, and Quizquiz turned over to them all the gold and silver. But as the insolence of the Spaniards has been so great, and they have shown so little regard for the honor and pride of these people in return for the welcome they gave them and the love with which they served them, they violated some of the virgins, and treated the men with contempt. This was why the Indians, because of this, and seeing the lack of reverence they showed for their sun, and how without shame or fear of God they ravished their *mamaconas,* which they held to be a tremendous sacrilege, later said that these people were not sons of God, but worse than *Supais,* which is the name of the devil, although to carry out Atahualpa's behest, the captains and officials of the city let them depart without doing them any harm, and afterwards sent the treasure. And the name of Viracocha has remained until this day which, as I have said, was given them for the reasons I have stated and not because it means sea foam."

my own recreation and to flee from the vices sloth engenders. As I have no other account or record aside from that they give, if anyone has the skill to set down this material more accurately than I, he should do it, though I spare no effort to achieve clarity in what I write, and, the better to come by the truth, I went to Cuzco at the time Captain Juan de Saavedra was chief magistrate there, where I brought together Cayu Tupac,[1] the one living descendant of [the Lord-Inca] Huayna Capac, and other *Orejones* who looked upon themselves as the nobility. And through the best interpreters to be found I asked these Incas what people they were and of what nation.

It would seem that the early Incas, to magnify their origins, proclaimed in their days that when all the peoples in these regions were living in brutish fashion, killing one another and given over to their vices, there appeared at a spot known as Paccaric-Tampu, not far from the city of Cuzco,[2] three men and three women. As far as can be gathered, Paccaric-Tampu means something like "house of production" or "house of origin." The men who appeared there, according to their account, were Ayar Oco, Ayar Cachi Awga, and Ayar Manco;[3] the names of the women were Mama Huaco, Mama [Ipi] Cora, and Mama Rahua. Some of the Indians give these names differently, and more of them, but I accept what they tell and hold to be true, for they know it better than any of the others. Thus they say that they appeared attired in long blankets and a kind of shirt, without collar or sleeves, of the finest wool of many different colors which they call *tucapu,* which in our language means "king's robes." And that one of these men carried in his hand a sling of gold holding a stone, and that the women were as richly dressed as they and brought many vessels of gold. They go on to say that they brought many vessels of gold, and that one of the brothers, he who was called Ayar Oco, spoke with his other brothers about beginning the great things they had

---

[1] Captain Juan de Saavedra was an old conquistador and was then in fact corregidor of Cuzco.

[2] Paccaric-Tampu (the "origin-tambo") lies eighteen miles east of Cuzco. The tambo is still extant, near to a hill in which there are caves (*tampu t'Oqo*—the tambo hole) out of which their myths said the first Incas "emerged" in order to enter the Cuzco valley to begin their empire.

[3] For a historical analysis of the conflicting myths of the four brothers "Ayar," see John H. Rowe, "Inca Culture at the Time of the Spanish Conquest," in *Handbook of South American Indians* (ed. by Julian H. Steward), II, 317–18. This publication is referred to hereafter as *Handbook.*

been called to do, for their presumption was so great that they aspired to make themselves the sole rulers of the earth. They decided to build a new settlement on that spot, to which they gave the name Pacaric-Tampu; and this was quickly accomplished, for they had the help of the natives of the region in this work. And as time went by, they brought to that place a great quantity of pure gold and jewels, and other valuable things, of which it is believed that Hernando Pizarro and Don Diego de Almagro the Younger acquired a large part.

Getting back to the story, they say that one of the three, he whose name was Ayar Cachi, was so brave and strong that with the sling he brought, dealing blows or hurling stones, he leveled the hills, and at times when he shot straight up, the stones almost attained the clouds. To the other two brothers this seemed an affront, for they felt themselves humiliated at not being able to match his feats. And so, galled by envy, they begged him with fair words, which were full of guile, to return to the cave where they had their treasures and bring them a goblet of gold they had forgotten, and to beg the sun, their father, to prosper them so they could rule the earth. Ayar Cachi, unaware of the deceit in what his brothers asked, went joyfully to do their bidding, and no sooner was he in the cave than the other two buried him under such a weight of stones that he was nevermore seen. When this was done, they tell that the earth shook in such a manner that many mountains fell down upon the valleys.

This is what the chieftains tell of the origin of the Incas, for as they were so proud and boastful they wanted it believed that they had appeared in this manner and were children of the sun. For this reason, afterwards, when the Indians extolled them with high praise, they called them *Ancha hatun apu, intip-churi,* which in our language means, "Oh, mighty lord, son of the sun."

What I myself think may be believed of this they allege is that just as in Hatun-colla [about Lake Titicaca] a leader named Zapana arose, and other brave captains in other places, these Incas who appeared must have been three brave, intrepid brothers whose thoughts soared high, natives of some village of these regions, or come from beyond the Andes Mountains. Finding the circumstances propitious, they conquered and won the power they held. Aside from this, it might even be that Ayar Cachi and the others were wizards who had

32

a pact with the devil to enable them to do what they did. At any rate, this is all we can get out of them regarding the matter.

After Ayar Cachi was left in the cave, the other two brothers decided, with some other people who had joined them, to build another settlement, to which they gave the name of Tampu Quiru, which in our language means something like "teeth of a dwelling" or "palace." From this it can be deduced that these settlements were not large, nor anything but small fortresses. And they spent some time in that place, already remorseful at having cast away their brother Ayar Cachi, who is also said to have been called Huana-cauri.[4]

CHAPTER 7 (ii: VII)

How the two brothers when they were in Tampu Quiru saw the one that they had lured into the cave emerge with wings of feathers, who told them to go and found the great city of Cuzco and they departed from Tampu Quiru.

THE BIG-EARED CHIEFTAINS[1] say that after the two Incas had settled in Tampu Quiru, before much time had elapsed and when they thought they would never again see Ayar Cachi, they saw him come flying through the air on great wings of colored feathers, and with the fear the sight of him aroused in them, they tried to run away. But he quickly dispelled that fear, saying: "Do not be afraid or troubled; I come only that the empire of the Incas shall begin to be known. Therefore leave, leave this settlement which you have built, and go farther down until you come to a valley where you will then found Cuzco, which is what will be of worth, for these are but mean hovels, and that will be the great city where a sumptuous temple will be built which will be so served, honored, and attended that it will be there

---

[4] Huana-cauri was one of the magical *huacas* of the Incas; it lay close to Cuzco. A curiously shaped upright stone was believed by them to have been one of Manco Capac's brothers who had turned himself into stone. It was visited by sons of the ruling class during puberty rites.

[1] The Big-Ears were called *Orejones* by the Spaniards—a literal translation. Members of the ruling class were allowed to use very large earplugs; their soubriquet was *Pako-yoq*, "earplug men."

the sun will be most honored. And as I shall always pray to God for you and help so that you may quickly achieve great power, in a near-by hill I shall remain in the shape and form you now see, and it shall always be sanctified and reverenced by you and your descendants, and the name you shall give it is Huana-cauri. In payment of the good services you have received from me, I beg that you will always worship me as God, and erect altars to me there where sacrifices will be performed. And if you do this, you will have my aid in war, and the sign you will display from now on to be esteemed, honored, and feared is that you pierce your ears in the manner you now see me." And when he said this, it seemed to them that they saw him with golden earrings, about a digit in circumference.

34

The brothers, dumbfounded by what they had seen, stood speechless, without saying a word. Finally when their confusion had abated, they answered that they were happy to do as he ordered, and then with all the speed they could they went to the hill called Huana-cauri, which from that time until now has been held sacred. At the peak of it they saw Ayar Cachi once more—who undoubtedly must have been some devil, if this they tell has any truth in it, who, God so permitting, under those lying appearances made them understand his wish, which was that they should worship and make sacrifices to him—and he spoke to them again, telling them that it was fitting that those who were to be the sovereign lords should assume the fringe or crown of the empire, and that they should know how at the time they did this the youths were to be invested knights and considered nobles. The brothers replied that they had already said his orders would be carried out in everything, and in sign of obedience, their hands joined and heads lowered, they made him the *mocha*, that is to say, reverence. And because the Big-Ears say that from this time comes the custom of assuming the fringe and being invested knights, I am setting it down here, so there will be no need to repeat it again. This may be taken as a pleasant and trustworthy account, inasmuch as in Cuzco Manco Inca assumed the fringe or crown of empire, and there are many Spaniards still alive who witnessed this ceremony, and I have heard many of them tell of it. The Indians say that in the days of their bygone kings this was done with more solemnity and preparation, and a gathering of peoples and wealth so great as cannot be enumerated.

It would seem that these lords gave out this order so they could assume the fringe or crown, and they say that Ayar Cachi on that very hill of Huana-cauri attired himself in this manner: he who is to be the Inca one day puts on a black shirt, without a collar, with red designs on it, and on his head a tawny braid twisted in a certain way, and, covered with a long, tawny blanket, he must leave his dwelling and go into the field and gather a sheaf of straw, and he must employ the whole day bringing it in, without eating or drinking, for he must fast; and the mother and sisters of the one who is to be the Inca must spin with all the speed they may, for in that same day they must spin and weave four garments for this same ceremony, and they must fast without eating or drinking while they are at this task. One of these suits must be a tawny shirt and white mantle; the other an all-white shirt and mantle, and the other blue, with fringes and cords. These suits must be put on by him who is to be Inca, and he must fast the appointed time, which is a month, and this fast is called *zaziy* [i.e., *sasi*], and is carried out in a room of the royal palace without sight of fire or having intercourse with woman; and during those days of the fast the women of his family must occupy themselves in preparing with their own hands a great supply of their chicha, which is wine made of corn, and they must go richly garbed. When the time of the fast has come to an end, he who is to be the ruler comes out, carrying in his hands a halberd of silver and gold, and goes to the home of some aged kinsman to have his hair cut. Then, attired in one of those suits, they leave Cuzco, where the ceremony is to be held, and go to the hill of Huana-cauri, where, as we said, the brothers were, and after certain rites and sacrifices they return to where the wine has been made ready and drink of it. Then the Inca sets out for a hill known as Anaguar, and at the foot of it he starts running so they will see how fleet he is and that he will be brave in war, and then he descends it, bringing a flock of wool tied to a halberd as token that when he is fighting his enemies he will endeavor to bring back their hair and heads. When this was done, they went to the aforesaid hill of Huana-cauri to gather tall-standing straw, and the one who was to be king carried a great sheaf of it, made of gold and very fine and matched, and with it he went to another hill called Yahuira, where he put on another of the aforesaid suits, and on his head braids or a fillet which they call *pillaca*, which is like a crown, below which

35

hang earrings of gold, and over it he wore a bonnet of feathers sewed like a diadem, which they call *puruchucu,*[2] and to the halberd was tied a long gold strand which touched the ground, and upon his breast he wore a moon of gold. Thus attired, in the presence of all those who had congregated there, he killed a llama, whose blood and flesh was handed about to all the principal guests, to be eaten raw, thus signifying that if they were not brave, their enemies would eat their flesh as they had eaten that of the llama that was killed. And there they swore a solemn oath after their custom, by the sun, to uphold the order of chivalry and die defending Cuzco, if it were necessary. Then they pierced their ears, putting in rings that were a digit in circumference.

When this was done, they put on masks of fierce pumas and returned with a great tumult to the square of Cuzco, which was completely encircled by a great cable of gold held up by posts of silver and gold. In the middle of this square they danced and held a great celebration after their fashion, and those who were to be knighted went masked with the puma heads I have spoken of in token that they would be as brave and fierce as those animals. When the dances were concluded, they became knights, and were known as Big-Ears, and enjoyed special privileges and many liberties, and were eligible, if chosen, to assume the crown, that is to say, the fringe. When this was conferred upon the one who was to be the ruler of the empire, still greater celebrations were held, and a great number of people assembled, and the emperor-to-be first took his own sister to wife, so the royal succession might not come through lowly lineage, and performed the great *zaziy,* which is the fast. While all these things were taking place, for during the time the lord was engaged in the

[2] Puruchucu (*puruhá,* "feather"; chuccu, "headgear") was a feather headdress worn by the nobles. Each tribe had a distinct headdress and these were not allowed to be changed. Such a headdress was called *"chuccu."*

The Puruhá tribes for whom Riobamba was the chief city, were distributed in the Andes between Chimborazo and Quito. It was a densely populated area, so great that Cieza says he does not name all the villages "to avoid prolixity." The language is lost, and it has been suggested by a comparison of place names that it is related to Cañari, a language spoken by a group of that name who bordered south of the Puruhás, which makes sense; also that it is related to Mochica, the language of the well-known coastal empire in Peru (A.D. 400–800), which makes no sense at all. Puruhá houses were of wattle and daub, thatched with grass; the men wore the typical poncho; their long hair was braided in a circle about the head and held with a cabuya-fiber sling (Quechua, *llautu*); this marked the Puruhás. Chiefs were polyandrous; mere man, monogamous. Volcanoes, of which there are many in Ecuador, played a great part in their cosmogony. (See Murra, "The Historic Tribes of Ecuador," *Handbook,* III, 796–98.)

sacrifices and fasts he took no part in private affairs or those of government, it was the law among the Incas that when one of them died and the crown or fringe was conferred on another, he could select among the noblemen of the realm one ripe in judgment and of great authority to govern the entire empire of the Incas, like the ruler himself, during those days. Such a one was allowed to have a guard and be addressed with reverence. When this was done and the blessings had been given in the temple of Curicancha, the new ruler received the fringe, which was heavy and hung from the *llautu* he wore on his head, falling almost to the eyes, and was accepted and revered as sovereign. To the celebration there came the principal chieftains to be found in the more than five leagues they ruled, and a vast treasure of gold and silver was brought to Cuzco, and precious stones, and feathers, the great cable of gold encircling it all, and the magnificent image of the sun which, so the Indians state as a fact, weighed over four thousand quintals of gold. And if the fringe was not conferred in Cuzco, they looked upon the one who called himself the Inca with contempt, whose rule was not accepted, and for this reason the Lord-Inca Atahualpa is not numbered among the kings, albeit he was so brave and killed so many people, and was obeyed by so many nations out of fear.

37

To return to those who were in the hill of Huana-cauri, after Ayar Cachi had told them what they were to do to be knighted, the Indians say that, looking at his brother Ayar Manco, he told him to go with the two women to the valley he had named, where he must found Cuzco at once, without neglecting to come and make sacrifices to that spot, as he had told him earlier. And when he had told him this, he and the other brother turned into two figures of stone in the likeness of men. When Ayar Manco saw this, he took his wives and came to where Cuzco now stands to found the city, naming and calling himself thenceforth Manco Capac, which means king and rich lord.

How, after Manco Capac saw that his brothers had been turned to stone, he came to a valley where he found certain peoples and founded and built the ancient and vastly rich city of Cuzco, which became the capital of the whole empire of the Incas.

38

I HAVE LAUGHED often to myself at what I have written [of the fables of] these Indians, yet I have set down what they told me, omitting many things and not adding a single one.

When Manco Capac saw what had happened to his brothers, and came to the valley where the city of Cuzco now stands, raising his eyes to heaven, he humbly prayed the sun to be propitious and help him with the new city he wanted to build, and then, turning his eyes toward the hill of Huana-cauri, he asked the same thing of his brother, whom he already looked upon and revered as a god. After observing the flight of the birds and the conjunction of the stars, and other auspices, he was filled with confidence, feeling sure that the new settlement would flourish, and he would be known as its founder and the sire of all the Incas who would reign in it. Thus, in the name of Tici-Viracocha and the sun and his other gods, he founded the new city, the origin and beginning of which was a little stone house covered with thatch which Manco Capac and his wives built, to which they gave the name Curicancha, which means "enclosure of gold," and this is the site where afterwards that so famous and rich temple of the sun was erected, which is now a monastery of the friars of the Dominican Order.

And it is believed certain that at the time this was being done by the Lord-Inca Manco Capac, there were many Indians in the region of Cuzco; but as he did them no harm or mischief, they did not interfere with his remaining in their land, but rather were pleased with him. Thus Manco Capac occupied himself in the building of the aforesaid house, and he was devoted to his religion and the cult of his gods, and was of proud bearing and had an air of great authority.

One of his wives was barren, and was never got with child; by the other he had three sons and a daughter. The eldest son was called

Sinchi Roca and the daughter Ocllo; of the names of the other two they tell and relate nothing. He married the eldest son to his sister, and taught them what they must do to be loved by the natives and not hated, and other great things. When the founder of Cuzco, the Lord-Inca Manco Capac, had married off his children and attracted certain peoples to his service with love and gentle words, thus aggran- dizing the house of Curicancha, after living many years, he died when he was very old, and his obsequies were performed with all ceremony, and a statue of him was made and he was worshiped as a child of the sun.

And because all these things were great and worth recalling, and so realms ruled by sages and great men may learn from this and be filled with admiration, bearing in mind that it was among a barbarous people without writing that this we know to be a fact was found, both the governing and the bringing of lands and nations under their rule, for under one monarchy they obeyed a single ruler who alone was the sovereign and entitled to reign in the empire the Incas held which had a coast line of more than 1,200 leagues.

Those who read this should know first that of all the Incas, who were eleven,[1] three stood out head and shoulders above the rest in the rule of their kingdom, whom the Inca nobility can never praise enough. These did not resemble one another in their traits as much as in intelligence. They were Huayna Capac [d. 1527], Topa Inca Yupanqui [d. 1492], his father, and Pachacuti [d. 1471], father of the one and grandfather of the other. To be sure, it may be assumed that as these were more recent, and the kingdom is full of Indians who knew Topa Inca Yupanqui, and accompanied him in his wars, and heard from their fathers what the Inca Yupanqui did during his reign, their achievements, seen almost at first hand, are more vividly recalled, whereas much of what took place under their forebears has been forgotten. Although to bear such things in mind, and so the memory of them might not be lost, they had a marvellous device, considering that they had no writing,[2] for as I have stated in

1 By which Cieza means the number of Lord-Incas who reigned during the life of the empire. His figure of eleven tallies with modern research if one excepts the last two half-brothers, Huascar and Atahualpa, who fought, as explained, a civil war for possession of the empire.

2 Cieza has been borne out by archaeological research. Neither the Incas nor those cultures which had preceded them by two thousand years had writing. The closest to

the first part of this history, no writing has been discovered in all this kingdom, nor even in this entire world of the Indies.

CHAPTER 9 (ii: x)

Of how the Lord-Inca, after assuming the royal fringe, married his sister, the Coya, which is the name of the queen, and how he was allowed to take many wives, although, of them all, the Coya was the only legitimate one, and the most important.

I HAVE RELATED in the foregoing chapters how those who were to be nobles were created knights, and also the ceremonies that accompanied the coronation of the Inca as king, assuming the crown which is the fringe [*llautu*][1] that falls to their eyes. It was ordered by them that he who was to be the Lord-Inca should take his sister, the legitimate daughter of his father and mother, to wife, so that the succession to the kingdom should be confined to the royal line, for it seemed to them that in this way, even if the woman in question, the sister of the Lord-Inca, were unchaste and, knowing another man, should become with child by him, the child who was born would be descended from her and not from an alien woman. For they also took into consideration the fact that even though the Inca married a woman of noble lineage, she might do the same and conceive adulterously, and if she were not found out, the child would be held to be the offspring of her lawful lord and husband. For these reasons, or because those who instituted it thought them advisable, it was the law of the Incas that he who was chosen among all as Lord Inca should take

writing was the quipu (see Chapter 53 below), which was, of course, not writing but a mnemonic system to aid the memory. Cieza is wrong about writing not being present "in this entire world of the Indies." The Aztecs had a glyphic language, as did the Mayas. (See Sylvanus G. Morley, *The Ancient Maya* [Stanford, 1946], 259ff.; and Victor W. von Hagen, *The Aztec and Maya Papermakers* [New York, 1943].)

[1] A *llautu* (sling) was worn by most Andean Indians. Their long hair was bound with *llautus* (or braids); the headband of the Lord-Inca was such a band, an inch wide, wrapped about many times until in some cases it formed a sort of turban. When a noble was declared Lord-Inca, red tassels adorned it, hanging in front of the eyes, and a yellow-tinted woolen pompom was also added to it. (See John Rowe, "Inca Culture," *Handbook*, II, 235.)

his sister to wife, who was known as *Coya*,[2] which is the word for queen, by which all called her, just as when a king of Spain marries a princess who has her own name, when she enters the kingdom she is called queen, so those of Cuzco were known as Coya. And if it so happened that he who was to become Lord-Inca had no sister, he was permitted to marry the woman of highest rank there was, that she might be considered the principal among all his wives, for there was no one of these lords who did not have more than seven hundred women for the service of his house and with whom to take his pleasure. Thus all of them had many children by these women who were their wives or concubines, and they were well treated by him and held in high regard by the natives. When the Lord-Inca was in residence in his palace, or wherever he went, they were guarded and watched over by the doorkeepers and *camayocs,* which is the name of the guards. And if any of them had knowledge of a man, she was put to death and he received the same penalty. When the sons of these Lord-Incas had by these women were grown, they bestowed upon them lands and estates which they call *chacaras,* and from the storehouses they were provided with clothing and other things for their needs. They did not, however, give them authority, for, in the event of any disturbance in the kingdom, they did not want them to attempt to seize power on the grounds that they were sons of the Lord-Inca. Thus none of them was put in command of a province, although when they went out on wars and conquests, many of them were captains and favored above the rest of the troops. And the successor to the kingdom treated them with consideration, although if they plotted any uprising, they were cruelly punished. None of them might speak to the Lord-Inca, even his own brother, without first putting on his shoulders some light burden and coming into his presence barefooted, like everyone else in the kingdom.

Now let us continue with what we have begun.

2 The Lord-Inca's wife after 1450 was his full sister, who was called "Coya." The nobles of this society were polyandrous; a harem of wives provided the ruler with an enormous number of progeny who formed the royal *ayllu.* The *ayllu* was the basic social unit; a clan of extended families living in a determined area formed an *ayllu.* Everyone was born into it, and in time it could extend into a *marca* or village or even a city, like Cuzco. Normally, Indians were born, matured, and were buried in their own *ayllu;* only those transferred to other regions by superior orders or meeting their end in battle failed in this fundamental loyalty.

CHAPTER 10 (XL)

Of the site of the city of Quito; its founding, and who was its founder.

42 THE CITY of San Francisco de Quito lies in the northern part of the last province of the kingdom of Peru. The size of this province (which runs from east to west) is about seventy leagues in length and twenty-five or thirty wide. It is situated on the site of old edifices which the Incas had ordered built there in the time of their rule, and they had been added to and beautified by Huayna Capac [d. 1527] and the great Topa Inca [Tupac Yupanqui, d. 1492], his father. The natives gave to these royal structures the name of Quito, and for that reason the city bears the same name as that of the ancient citadel. The climate is healthy, cold rather than warm. The city has little view of the countryside, or almost none, because it is situated on a small plain like a hollow formed by the high surrounding sierras, which lie to the northwest of the city. The site and the hollow are so small that it is believed that in the future it will be difficult for the city to grow, which could be made a stronghold if necessary. For neighbors it has the cities of Puerto Viejo and Guayaquil, which lie 60 and 80 leagues to the west, and to the south there are the cities of Loja and San Miguel, the one 130 leagues distant, the other 80. To the east are the mountains and the source of the river which in the Ocean-Sea is called the Freshwater Sea,[1] which is the closest to the Marañón.

This city of Quito lies some seven leagues below the equator. The surrounding land looks sterile, but as a matter of fact it is very fertile, for all manner of livestock flourishes there, as do breadstuffs and other foods, fruits, and fowl. The lay of the land is very pleasant, and it closely resembles that of Spain in vegetation and climate, for summer begins around the months of March and April and lasts until November, and although it is cold, the land becomes no more barren than in Spain.

Large crops of wheat and barley[2] are harvested on the lowlands, and the supply of food in the environs of this city is abundant. In

[1] The Ocean-Sea was the Spanish term for the Atlantic; the Freshwater Sea was the Amazon and took its name from the fact that the volume of water coming from the river was so great that it converted the Atlantic on the coast of Brazil, at its debouchment, into a fresh-water sea.

time most of the products of our Spain will be grown here, for they
are already beginning to raise some. The natives in general are more
docile and better disposed and freer from vices than any of those
previously described, and even than those to be found in most of
Peru, as I have been able to see and judge. Some may be of a different
opinion, but if they had seen and observed both, as I have done, I
feel sure they would agree with me. They are people of medium
stature, fine husbandmen, and they lived in keeping with the ways
established by the Lord-Incas, except that they were not, and are not,
as shrewd as these were, for they were conquered by them and received at their hands the standards by which they now live, for in
olden times they were like their neighbors, poorly dressed and un-
skilled at building.[3]

43

There are many warm valleys where fruit trees and vegetables are
cultivated and produce in abundance most of the year. Grapes will
grow in these valleys, although, as they have just been planted, one
can only express the hope that they will do well, and nothing more.
Orange and lime trees grow to a great size, and the vegetables of
Spain which are raised are especially fine, and all the most important
ones needed for human food. There is also a kind of spice which we
call cinnamon[4] that they bring from the mountains that lie to the

[2] Wheat and barley, naturally not native to the Americas, were first planted in
Quito about 1540 by Fray Jadôco Ricke, a Franciscan from Ghent.

[3] The Quitos had hereditary chiefs (*scyris*), a patriarchal line of descent, and were
monogamous. The pre-Inca history of Ecuador is imperfectly known, mostly on account
of the Inca methods of conquest, which were to make a selective manipulation of
history (see Victor W. von Hagen, *Realm of the Incas*, 24). Before the Inca conquest,
about 1450, Ecuador was broken up into a series of tribes, many of them in intramural
combat. The Panzaleo tribe (called Quito) lived where the capital of Ecuador now is;
the Incas established their northern capital there, and it became the axis of the famous
Quito-Cuzco highway. (See John Murra, "The Historic Tribes of Ecuador," *Handbook*, III.)

[4] The search for the spiceries brought about the discovery of the Americas, and the
hope was always present in the new discoveries that spices could be found. Cinnamon
brought about the discovery of the Amazon, although it was not real or useful cinnamon
that they found, as Gonzalo Pizarro, who led the famous journey, wrote to his king
in a letter dated from Tomebamba, September 3, 1542: ". . . I started off with more
than 200 men on foot and horse (also 4,000 Indians who went joyfully) . . . and
after seventy days during which we endured great hardships . . . we found the trees
which bear cinnamon, which is in the form of flower buds . . . the leaf has the flavor
also but not the bark. It is . . . a commodity by which Your Majesty cannot be
rendered service." What Pizarro had found was a species of Lauraceae, of which the
dried calyx (with a flavor reminiscent of cloves and cinnamon) alone was used as
spice. (See José Medina, *The Discovery of the Amazon*.)

east. It is a fruit or kind of flower that grows on large trees, and there is nothing in Spain to compare it with except that ornament or bud of the oak tree, the acorn, only this is of a tawny color, verging on black, and thicker and more hollow. It has a very pleasant flavor, as good as cinnamon, but it cannot be used except in powdered form, for if one employs it like cinnamon in cooking, it loses its properties and even its taste. It has been found to be of warm and cordial properties, and the natives gather it and use it when they are ill; it is especially good for affections of the stomach and bowels, and they mix it with their drinks.

44

They raise a great deal of cotton, which they use for their clothing and to pay their tribute. In the environs of this city of Quito there were great flocks of the animals we called sheep, but which are more closely akin to the camel.[5] Farther on I shall deal with this animal, and its shape, and the characteristics of these sheep and rams they call llamas "of Peru." There are also many deer and an amazing number of rabbits, partridges, turtledoves, pigeons, and other game. Of the native foodstuffs there are two which, aside from corn, are the main staples of the Indians' diet: the potato, which is like the truffle, and when cooked is as soft inside as boiled chestnuts; it has neither skin nor pit, any more than the truffle, for it is also borne underground. Its foliage looks exactly like that of the poppy. There is another very good food they call *quinoa,* which has a leaf like the Moorish chard; the plant grows almost to a man's height, and produces tiny seeds, some white, some red, of which they make drinks and which they also eat boiled, as we do rice.

There are many other roots and seeds besides these, but now that they know the value and utility of wheat and barley, many of the natives around this city of Quito plant them both, and eat them and make drinks of the barley. As I said above, all these Indians are good husbandmen, although the provinces differ from one another, as I shall tell when I reach them, and it is the women who till the fields and care for the plantings and the harvests, and the husbands spin and weave and occupy themselves in making clothing and other women's work, which they must have learned from the Incas. For I have seen among the Indians of the time of the Incas in the villages

[5] The llamas, alpacas, vicuñas, and guanacos (huanacos) are members of a distinct group of Camelidae (see Chapter 28 below).

near Cuzco that while the women were plowing, the men were weaving and preparing their arms and clothing and doing things more appropriate to women than to men.

In the time of the Incas there was a highway, built by man's hands and labor, which left this city and extended all the way to Cuzco, and from there another began as large and magnificent as this which went to the province of Chile, which is more than 1,200 leagues from Quito. On these highways every three or four leagues there were very fine and well-built lodgings or palaces of the ruler, richly furnished. 45

CHAPTER 11 (ii: LVII)

How Topa Inca sent out from Quito to learn how his orders were being carried out.

AFTER THE Lord-Inca [Topa Inca] Tupac Yupanqui had made himself master of the territory as far as Quito, ... and ... certifying himself that what he had ordained was being carried out and put into effect, he ordered that those among his men whom he considered the wisest should be borne in hammocks by the natives, some to one place, some to another, observing and informing themselves about the order that was being established in the new provinces, and to talk with the governors and collectors of tribute, and see how they were behaving toward the natives. To certain of the provinces we call Puerto Viejo [Ecuador] he sent his *Orejones* to talk with them and urge them to ally themselves with him as the others did, and to explain to them how they should sow, and serve, and dress, and worship the sun, and give them knowledge of their good ways of living and polity. It is told that in payment for the good they planned to do, they were killed, and that Topa Inca sent certain of his captains with troops to punish them; but when they learned of this, so many of these barbarians joined forces that they killed and defeated those who were sent against them, which caused the Inca great sorrow. But as he had great undertakings in the making and it was necessary for him to return to Cuzco, he did not go in person to punish them for what they had done.

In Quito he received reports of how well all that he had disposed was being done, and the care his delegates showed in teaching those people their duties, and how well they treated them, and how happy the natives were, doing all they were ordered to do. From many of the lords of the country there came emissaries every day bringing gifts, and his court was filled with nobles, and his palaces with vessels and goblets of gold and silver and other great treasures. In the morning he took his repast, and from noon until late in the day he gave audience, accompanied by his guard, to whoever wished to talk with him. He then spent the rest of the day until it was night drinking, when he dined by the light of wood, for they used neither tallow nor wax, although they had plenty of both.

He left in Quito as his captain-general and chief steward, an old Big-Eared chieftain, of whom they all say that he was very wise and brave and of handsome bearing, by name Chalco Mayta, and he gave him permission to travel in a litter and eat off gold plate, and other privileges which he esteemed highly. He enjoined upon him that every moon he was to dispatch a messenger bearing detailed news of all that occurred, and of how things were in the land, and of the crops, and the growth of the llama herds, and all the other things they all notified him of, such as the number of the poor, those who had died and been born during the year, and all I have previously told of which the Lord-Incas in Cuzco were notified. Despite the great distance from Quito to Cuzco, which is more than that from Seville to Rome, far more, the road was as busy as that from Seville to Triana, which is the most that can be said.[1]

CHAPTER 12 (ii: LXVI)

Of how Huayna Capac set out from Quito, sending ahead certain of his captains who returned fleeing from the enemy, and the steps he took.

When Huayna Capac [the son of Topa Inca] was in Quito with

---

[1] The distance from Quito to Cuzco is 1,230 miles. The road from Seville to Triana was part of the Via Argenta, the silver road which ran from Salamanca through Mérida to Seville. The Roman road over which Cieza traveled as a boy was begun in A.D. 24 by Tiberius (Salamanca-Mérida) and continuously repaired until it was rebuilt in A.D. 214 by Caracalla and extended to Seville.

all his captains and old soldiers who accompanied him, it is told as a
fact that he ordered certain of his captains to set out with troops to
subdue certain nations who had never wished to accept his friendship. These, knowing of his presence in Quito, and with misgivings,
had prepared themselves and sought the aid of their neighbors and
kinfolk to resist him who was coming against them. They had built 47
forts and stockades and had made many weapons of the sort they use.
When his captains set out, Huayna Capac followed them to attack
another neighboring land, which must have been in the region we
call Quito. As his captains and troops proceeded toward those they
held in contempt, thinking to make themselves easily masters of their
fields and lands, they pushed on fast; but things turned out differently
from what they had thought. For on the way a force fell upon them
so resolutely, with loud whoops and shrieks, that many were killed
and captured, and they were completely routed and forced to turn
back, fleeing as fast as they could, with the victorious enemy in pursuit, killing and capturing as many as they could.

Some of the most fleet-footed covered the ground with great speed
until they reached the Inca, to whom alone they recounted the misfortune they had suffered, which irked him not a little. But with
great shrewdness, he performed an act worthy of a great man, which
was to order those who had returned to keep silent and tell no one
what he already knew, and to go back to the road and tell all those
who came back defeated that on the first hill they reached they should
form themselves in a squadron as soon as they saw him, without fear
of dying, if that was to be their fate, for he, with fresh troops, would
fall upon the enemy and avenge them, and with this they set out
again. He revealed no dismay, for he was aware of the fact that if
the news became known, all would join forces and fall upon him,
and he would find himself in greater difficulty. Thus, with dissimulation, he told them to make ready, for he planned to attack certain
people whom they would see when they reached them. Leaving his
litter, he marched at the head of his army and traveled for a day and
a half, and those who came fleeing, who were many, seeing their own
people coming toward them, reluctantly halted on a hillside, and the
enemy who were pursuing them began to attack, and killed many.
But Huayna Capac fell upon them from three sides, and they were
not a little dismayed to find themselves encircled, and to see that those

they had considered vanquished yet managed to regroup and fight. The struggle was so bitter that the fields were covered with the dead, and when they tried to flee, they found themselves cut off, and few escaped alive, except for the prisoners, of whom they took many. All about, everything was in confusion, those who had thought to kill and defeat the Inca being dead or prisoners. And when the outcome was known, they rested, all content.

48

Huayna Capac recovered those of his men who were alive, and those who were dead he had buried with due honors, according to their heathen fashion, for they all recognize the immortality of the soul. There were also set up on the site of the battle statues and markers of stone to commemorate what had occurred there, and Huayna Capac sent word of all this to Cuzco, regrouped his men, and marched on to beyond Caranqui.

Those of Otavalo, Cayambe, Cochasqui, Pifo, and other peoples [north of Quito] had made an alliance among themselves not to allow themselves to be dominated by the Inca, but to die rather than lose their freedom and allow fortresses to be built in their lands, or be found to carry gifts as tribute to Cuzco, a land so distant as they had heard. Having agreed on all this and taken their measures, they awaited the Inca, who they knew was approaching to make war on them. The Inca and his army came as far as this region, and there he ordered stockades and fortresses, which they call *pucarás,* built for his troops and servitors. He sent messengers to these peoples, with great gifts, urging them not to fight him, for he wanted only peace with honorable conditions, and that they would always find help in him, as they had in his father, and that he wished to take nothing from them, but to give them of what he brought. But these gentle words had little effect, for the answer they made him was that he should depart from their land at once, and if he did not, they would drive him out by force. Thus, in battle formation they marched toward the Inca, who, in great anger, had put his army in the field, and the enemy fell upon him with such fury that it is said if it had not been for the protection of the fortress he had built, they would have broken through and completely routed him. Realizing the danger that threatened, he retired as best he could to the fortress, with all who had not been left on the field or prisoners of the enemy.

"Huarco, famous in this kingdom for its valley large and broad. They fought [with Chuquimancu, their chieftain] against the Inca warriors, as the natives did not want to become their vassals." It took the Incas fifty or more years to subdue the massive hilltop fortress of Chuquimancu, lord of the valleys of Huarco (now Cañete and Mala). *(Robert Shippee photo)*

"The villages had parts that were like a fortress made of stone, and from a distance, they seem to be towers of Spain." The ruins of the storehouses of Hatun-Jauja located on a high, bald hill.

"On a hill north of Cuzco is the fortress [Sacsahuamán]. The living rock was excavated for the foundations, and for this reason it was so strong that it will last as long as the world exists. By my calculations it was 330 paces long. The main gate was a thing to behold." "Indians" emerging from one of the sally points of Sacsahuamán in an enactment of its fall to the Spaniards in 1536.

"The temple to the sun was large and finely built, made of stones laid one upon the other with great skill. To enter, there were two stone stairways which by my count had thirty steps each." The sun temple at Vilcashuamán; it has two doorways and thirty stone steps.

"There was a shrine, all of a single stone so large that it was eleven feet long, with two seats cut out for them. They say that this stone used to be covered with gold." The stone seat found on top of the sun temple at Vilcas-huamán.

"There was a temple there built in honor of their god Viracocha, whom they called creator." One section of the Temple of Viracocha still stands, the center wall in the hamlet of Racchi.

"From this river of Apurímac one continues to the lodgings of Lima-tambo [Rimac-tampu]." The remains of the famous "speaking river" tambo, the royal lodgings on the way south to Cuzco.

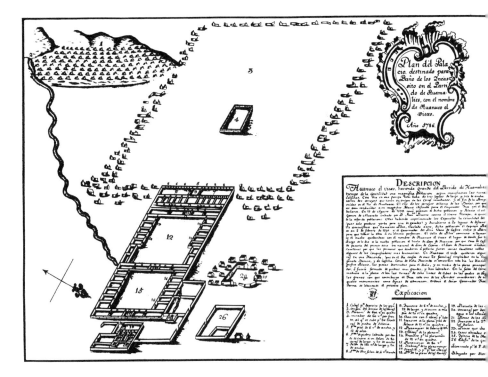

"In what is known as Huánuco the old there was an admirably built palace and beside it the temple to the sun. It was so important in the times of the Incas that there were always thirty thousand people to serve it." The ruins of Huánuco as mapped for the first time by Sierra in 1786.

How, assembling all his forces, Huayna Capac gave battle to his enemies and defeated them, and the great cruelty with which he treated them. **49**

WHEN THOSE people saw how they had managed to drive the Inca into his fortress, and had killed many of the *Orejones* of Cuzco, they were greatly content, and making such a din with their shouting that they could not hear one another, and beating drums, they sang and drank, and sent messengers throughout the land telling how they had the Inca and his army besieged. There were many who believed it and rejoiced, and even came to aid their friends.

Huayna Capac's fortress was well provisioned, and he had sent word to the governors of Quito that they were to come with part of the forces under their command. He was highly incensed because the enemy would not lay down their arms. He tried repeatedly, with embassies he sent them and gifts, to win them over, but it was useless. The Inca strengthened his army, and the enemy did the same, unswerving in their determination to fall upon the Inca and defeat him or die in the attempt. Putting their plan into action, they broke through two of the fortress walls, and if it had not been for the fact that there were other walls encircling a hill, they would undoubtedly have been victorious. But as their custom is to build a stockade with two gates, and beyond that another, there would be seven or eight redoubts on a hillside, so that if one was lost, they could retire to the next. The Inca and his troops took refuge in the strongest point of the hill, from which after a few days he came forth and with great valor met the enemy.

It is told that when his reinforcements arrived, he came to grips with the enemy, and the fighting was so fierce that for a time the outcome was in doubt; but in the end those of Cuzco with great skill managed to kill a large number of the enemy, and the survivors fled. So enraged was he with them that to punish them for having taken up arms to defend their land and not be brought under his rule, the Lord-Inca ordered his men to seek out all of them that they could find, which they did with great diligence, and captured all, few being able to make their escape. Then, beside a lake there, in his presence, he ordered that their throats be cut and their bodies thrown into the lake. So many were killed that the water changed color and turned into a pool of blood. When this cruelty and evil had been wrought, Huayna Capac ordered the sons of the dead brought before him, and looking at them, he said, "*Campa mana, pucula tucuy huambracuna,*" which means, "You will not make war on me because now you are all children." And from that time on, these people were known as the Huambra-cunas, and they were very brave, and the lake received the name it still bears today, which is Yahuar-cocha, meaning "lake of blood." *Mitimaes*[1] and governors were sent to the settlements of the Huambra-cunas, as in other regions.

After he had reorganized his troops, the Inca proceeded northward, his fame enhanced by the victory he had won, and went exploring as far as the Angasmayo River,[2] which was the boundary of his empire. And he learned from the natives that farther on there were many peoples, and that they all went naked without the least shame, and that all, all of them ate human flesh, and he built several strongholds in the region of the Pastos. He sent word to their headmen that they were to pay him tribute, and they replied that they had nothing to give him. Whereupon, to bring them to reason, he ordered that every house in the land, every so many moons, must give him in tribute a large quill of lice. At first they laughed at his order; but afterwards, however lousy they were, they found they could not fill so many quills. So they tended the flocks the Inca had ordered left with them, and paid with those that were born, and of the foods and tubers grown in their lands. And for certain reasons Huayna Capac returned to Quito, and ordered that there should be a temple to the sun in Caranqui, and a garrison with *mitimaes,* and a captain-general, as well as a governor, to make those lands a frontier and to guard them.

---

[1] *Mitimaes* were Quechua colonists (see Chapter 16 below).

[2] The Angasmayo (Ancas-mayu; *mayu* means "river"), fifty kilometers, beyond the present locality of Pasto (Colombia), 1°14' north, the northern limits of the Inca empire, placed on it by the last great Inca, Huayna Capac. It lies close to Mamendoy Valley, of the Mayo River. Humboldt, in December, 1801, making his leisurely trip down the backbone of the Andes, saw there the remains of the most northern tambo of the Incas; its altitude as recorded by him, 2,096 meters.

Of how the Lord-Inca Huayna Capac returned to Quito and learned of the Spaniards who had reached the coast, and his death.

THAT SAME YEAR Francisco Pizarro with thirteen Spaniards was moving along this coast, and word of them had been brought to Huayna Capac in Quito. He was told of the attire they wore, what their ship was like, and that they were bearded and white and spoke little, and were not as given to drinking as they were, and other things they had been able to learn. Desirous of seeing such people, it is told that he ordered one of the two men[1] they said had remained behind to be brought to him, the others having already returned with their captain to the island of Gorgona, where they had left some of the Spaniards and the Indians, men and women, whom they had with them, as we shall relate in the proper place. Certain of these Indians tell that after the departure of the Spaniards these two were killed, which greatly angered Huayna Capac. Others say that he dreamed they were bringing them, and when the news of his death was brought to those coming with them, they killed them. Others say they died. We are of the

---

[1] These were two of the famous thirteen men of the Isle of Gallo, who remained behind on the Gallo Isle (from a distance its fringed hills look like the crest of a cock [gallo]). They were the original conquistadors; their names: Pedro Alcon, Antonio de Carrión, Domingo de Soraluce (also Soria Luca), Pedro de Candia, Martín de Paz, Alonso Briceño, García de Jaren (or Jerez), Juan de la Torre, Francisco de Villafuerte, Nicolás de Rivera el Viejo, Alonso de Molina, Francisco de Cuellar, Cristóbal de Peralta.

In the capitulation—i.e., the contract of Francisco Pizarro with his queen, Juana the Mad (signed 1530)—these thirteen were especially mentioned: those who were *hidalgos* (that is, sons-of-somebody—they knew at least one of their grandfathers) were made Knights of the Golden Spur; those *villeins* who did not know their parents were declared hidalgos—that is, henceforth they knew the names of their parents. Two of the thirteen elected to remain behind in Tumbes and the Inca empire in June, 1527. They were charged by Pizarro, who sailed away with the others, taking with him several Indians, llamas, and gold (one of the Indians was to return to become the infamous Felipillo who was to be the interpreter of the conquest), to learn about the Incas. The two who remained, Alonso de Molina and Gines, a Negro, disappeared into history. On Pizarro's return, he found them missing. Some said they were brought to Huayna Capac, then in Tomebamba in the Ecuadorian Andes, not more than three days' walking distance from Tumbes; others say they were killed. They doubtless brought some disease—measles, scarlet fever, or smallpox—which caused a great plague. Alonso de Molina was made the hero of a baroque novel entitled *The Incas, or the Destruction of the Empire of Peru*, by Jean François Marmontel (1723–99), French dramatist, contributor to the *Encyclopédie*.

opinion that the Indians killed them shortly after they came into their territory.

Thus, when Huayna Capac was in Quito, with his cohorts and the lords of the land, monarch of such a kingdom, for he ruled from the Angasmayo River to the Maule, a distance of over 1,200 leagues, and possessed of such wealth that he had ordered brought to Quito more than five hundred loads of gold and some thousand of silver, and many jewels and fine raiment, feared by all his subjects, for if any of them ventured to overstep himself, justice followed swiftly, they say that a great plague of smallpox broke out,[2] so severe that more than 200,000 died of it, for it spread to all parts of the kingdom. The Inca was stricken by it, and notwithstanding all that has been recounted, he could not escape death, for such was not the will of God. And when he felt the disease upon him, he ordered great sacrifices made for his recovery throughout the land, and in all the shrines and temples of the sun; but as he grew worse, he called up his captains and kinsmen, and discussed certain matters with them, among which, so it is told, he said that he knew that the men they had seen in a ship would return in greater strength and would win the land. This may be a fable, and if he said it, perhaps it came from the lips of the devil, as one who knew the Spaniards would attempt to come back and rule. Others of these same ones tell that, realizing the vastness of the lands wherein dwelled the Quillacingas and Popayaneses, and that this was too much for one person to rule, he said that from Quito to those regions should be the domain of Atahualpa, his son, whom he loved dearly because he had always accompanied him on his campaign, and that the rest should be ruled and reigned over by Huascar, the sole heir to the kingdom. There are other Indians who state that he did not divide the kingdom, but, on the contrary, told those with him that they well knew how pleased he was that, when his span was run, his son Huascar should rule after him, who was also the son of Chincha Ocllo, his sister, at which all those of Cuzco were

[2] Cieza says "smallpox," but there is no certainty about it. There is a legend (given by Juan de Santacruz Pachacuti Yamqui Salcamaygua in *Relación de antiguedades deste Reyno del Pirú*, written in 1596 but only published in 1879) which tells of a pestilence that came when Huayna Capac was campaigning about Guayaquil (Ecuador). He had a vision of a half-million men—ghosts—arrayed as if to attack him. He hurried back to Quito; the pestilence, riding on the backs of the Apocalypse, followed him; he, too, died of it in 1527.

very happy. Even though he had other sons of great worth,[3] he did not choose to give them aught of the much he left, but that it should all form a single inheritance, as he had received it from his father, and he had every hope that his wishes would be observed, and what his heart desired carried out, even though the heir was only a youth; and he begged them to love him and see that he did good, and until he had come of age to govern, that his uncle Colla Tupac should be his mentor. And when he had said this, he died.

53

The mourning for Huayna Capac's death was such that the lamentations and shrieks rose to the skies, causing the birds to fall to the ground. The news traveled far and wide, and nowhere did it not evoke great sorrow. In Quito it is said they wept for him ten days together; from there he was borne to the Cañaris, where they mourned him for a whole moon, and his body was escorted to Cuzco by many chieftains, the roads lined with men and women weeping and shrieking. In Cuzco the mourning was even greater, and sacrifices were performed in the temples, and his burial was carried out in keeping with their customs, believing his soul was in heaven. They killed more than four thousand souls, what with wives, pages, and other servants, to lay in the tomb with him, and treasures, jewels, and fine raiment. There can be no doubt that what they buried with him was a vast sum. They do not say where or how he is buried, but all agree that his tomb was built in Cuzco. Certain Indians have told me that he was buried in the Angasmayo River, the stream having been deflected from its course to build the tomb; this I do not believe, but that he was buried in Cuzco. . . .

I have spent more time in relating the peculiarities of Quito than is my custom in the cities earlier described, and this has been because (as I have already said) this is the first city of Peru by this approach, and because it was always held in high regard, and it still is one of the best of Peru. To conclude, I will say that it was founded and settled by Captain Sebastián Belalcázar.[4]

[3] Among those sons were Nanque Yupanqui, Tupac Inca, Huanca Auqui, Tupac Hualpa, Titu, Huaman Hualpa, Manco Inca, Huascar, Cusi Hualpa, Paullu Tupac Yupanqui, Conono, and Atahualpa.

[4] Sebastián, called "de Belalcázar" after the village in which he was born (since he did not know his parents), came early to the New World, about 1515. Like most, he cut his conquistador's teeth in Darién (Panama). He made the conquest of Quito

Of the settlements met with on leaving Quito until reaching the royal lodgings of Tomebamba [Tumipampa], and of certain of the customs of the natives.

54

FROM THE CITY of San Francisco de Quito to the palaces of Tomebamba is a distance of fifty-three leagues. Upon leaving it by the route I have spoken of, one comes to a village called Panzaleo. The natives here differ somewhat from their neighbors, especially in their headbands, for that is the way the different tribes of Indians are known and the provinces from which they come.

These, and all those of this kingdom, in more than 1,200 leagues, speak the common language of the Incas, which is that used in Cuzco. And this language was in general use because the Inca rulers so ordered, and it was law throughout their kingdom, and they punished parents who failed to teach it to their children when they were small. But in spite of the fact that they all spoke the language of Cuzco, they had their own as well, that which their forefathers had used. Thus, for example, the people of Panzaleo had a different language from those of Caranqui and Otavalo. They resemble those I described in the preceding chapter in aspect and disposition. They wear shirts without sleeves or collar, with an opening at the sides for the arms and another at the top for the head, and blankets of wool, and some of cotton. The attire of the chiefs is of fine quality and of many and perfectly woven colors. For footgear they wear sandals made of a root or plant they call *cabuya*,[1] which puts out large fronds which yield white fibers, like hemp, very strong and useful, and from these they make their sandals, and these serve them for shoes, and on their heads they wear their head-bands. Some of the women dress after the fashion of Cuzco, very handsomely, with a long blanket that covers them from neck

in 1533, moved northward following the scent of El Dorado and the Golden Man (see Victor W. von Hagen, "The Golden Man," *Natural History Magazine*, September, 1952). He was wounded in 1540 in the war at Añaquito between the newly arrived viceroy and Gonzalo Pizarro. He died in the fortress of Cartagena (Colombia—Nueva Granada) in 1550, the same year that Pedro de Cieza de León quit Peru and the New World for Spain.

[1] *Cabuya* is a Furcraea, a related genus of the Agave, the common fleshy-leafed century plant; the leaves or pads are spiny-margined and sharp-pointed. When dried and combed, they yield fiber, as sisal hemp.

to feet, with only the arms exposed. At the waist they cinch it with a beautiful woven belt they call *chumpi,* like a fine-quality riata, but a little wider. Then over this they wear another thin blanket, called a *líquida* [*lliclla*] which hangs from their shoulders to their feet. They fasten these blankets with large pins of silver or gold, wider at one end, which they call *tupus.* Around their heads they, too, wear a band 55
which is very pretty indeed, called a *vincha* [*uncha*] and on their feet sandals. The style of dress of the women of Cuzco is the best and handsomest and richest that has been seen so far in all the Indies. They arrange their hair with great care and it is very long. Elsewhere I shall speak more at length of this attire of the *pallas,* or ladies of Cuzco.

Another road runs toward the rising of the sun which leads to other settlements called Quixo, which are inhabited by Indians having the same ways and customs as the aforementioned.

Three leagues before reaching Panzaleo[2] are the houses and villages of Mulahalo, where, although it is now small because the natives have diminished in number, in olden times there were lodgings for the Incas or their captains when they came that way, with great storehouses of supplies for the men of war. To the right of this village of Mulahalo, there is a volcano or fiery crater which the Indians say once erupted and spouted out a great shower of stones and ash which destroyed a part of these villages within the range of the eruption. Some tell that before the eruption hellish visions were seen and fearful cries were heard. What the Indians tell of this volcano would seem to be true, for at the time that the Adelantado Don Pedro de Alvarado,

[2] Pedro de Cieza de León: "Between this village of Panzaleo and the city of Quito there are several settlements on either hand situated in the hills. To the west lies the valley of Uchillo and Langazi, where, as the climate is very temperate, many of the things I described in the chapter on the founding of Quito are produced, and the inhabitants are friends and allies. Throughout these lands the natives do not eat one another, nor are they as wicked as some of those of the provinces I have described. In olden times they had great temples dedicated to different gods, as they themselves tell. After they came under the rule of the Incas, they made their sacrifices to the sun, which they worshiped as a god.

"From here a road leads to the mountains of Yumbo, where there are a number of settlements whose inhabitants are not as industrious as those around Quito, nor as tractable, but, on the contrary, mean and insolent, as a result of their living in territory difficult of access and because they make an easy living from their lands, which are warm and fertile. They, too, worship the sun, and their customs and ways are similar to those of their neighbors, because, like them, they were conquered by the great Topa Inca and Huayna Capac, his son."

once governor of the province of Guatemala, entered Peru with his fleet, and left by these provinces of Quito, it seemed that it was raining ashes for several days, so the Spaniards who accompanied him asserted. And it must have been that one of these fiery craters, of which there are many in those sierras, blew up, because of the great deposits of brimstone there must be there.

56

A little beyond Mulahalo is the village and lodgings known as Tacunga[3] [Llacta-cunga], which were as important as those of Quito. Those buildings, though now in ruins, reveal their one-time grandeur, for in certain walls of these buildings it can be plainly seen where golden llamas were incrusted, and other splendors carved on the walls. This magnificence was especially to be found in the apartment reserved for the Lord-Incas, and in the temple of the sun where the sacrifices and rites were carried out, which is also where the virgins dedicated to the service of the temple lived (as I have already related), who were called *mamaconas*. Although in the towns we have passed there were residences and depots, there was, in the time of the Incas, no royal lodging or temple like those here, nor anywhere along the way until reaching Tomebamba, as I shall point out in this history. The Inca kings had a high steward stationed in this village who was in charge of collecting the tribute of the neighboring provinces and storing it here, where there was also a great number of *mitimaes*.

The Incas had the seat of their empire in the city of Cuzco, where the laws were given and the captains set out to make war, and this city was more than six hundred leagues from Quito, and even farther from Chile. Inasmuch as all this length of territory was inhabited by barbarous peoples, some of whom were very warlike, in order more easily to insure and keep their power and tranquillity, the following policy had been put into force from the time of Inca Pachacuti [d. 1471], father of the great Topa Inca [d. 1492] and grandfather of Huayna Capac. As soon as one of these large provinces was con-

---

[3] Tacunga, properly *Llacta-cunga,* approximately forty miles south of Quito, near the active volcano of Cotopaxi. The Inca ruins of Callo were close to Llacta-cunga, erected by Tupac Yupanqui and Huayna Capac after the conquest of Quito (c. 1475). Alexander von Humboldt, in *Views of Nature,* has given the only description of the edifice on the Royal Road (between Quito and Cuzco). The building formed a square, the sides of which were thirty-five yards long; four great trapezoidal doors were distinguished (in 1801). There were eight apartments, the walls nearly five yards high and one yard in thickness. There were eighteen niches (the leitmotif of Inca architecture) "distributed," said Humboldt, "with the greatest symmetry."

quered, ten or twelve thousand of the men and their wives, or six thousand, or the number decided upon, were ordered to leave and remove themselves from it. These were transferred to another town or province of the same climate and nature as that which they left; if they came from a cold climate, they were taken to a cold climate, and if from a warm climate, to a warm, and these were called *mitimaes,* 57 which means Indians come from one land to another. They were given land to work and sites on which to build their homes. And these *mitimaes* were ordered by the Incas to be always obedient to what their governors and captains ordered, so that if the natives should rebel, and they supported the governor, the natives would be punished and reduced to the service of the Incas. Likewise, if the *mitimaes* stirred up disorder, they were put down by the natives. In this way these rulers had their empire assured against revolts and the provinces well supplied with food, for most of the people, as I have said, had been moved from one land to another. And they had another device to keep the natives from hating them, and this was that they never divested the natural chieftains of their power. If it so happened that one of them committed a crime or in some way deserved to be stripped of his power, it was vested in his sons or brothers, and all were ordered to obey them.

And to return to the subject, in these important lodgings of Tacunga there were these Indians whom they call *mitimaes* who carried out all the steward of the Inca ordered them to do. Surrounding these lodgings on either side are the villages and plantations of the chiefs and headmen, who have no shortage of foodstuffs.[4]

They all go dressed in their blankets and shirts, well made and handsome, and others not so good, depending on each one's means. The women are as well dressed as those of Mulahalo, and nearly all of them talk that same language. Their houses are all of stone, covered with thatch; some are large and others small, depending on the

---

[4] Pedro de Cieza de León: "At the time of the last battle in Peru, which was in the valley of Xaquixahuana, where Gonzalo Pizarro was killed, not quite two hundred of us Spaniards set out from the territory of Popayán with the Adelantado Don Sebastián de Belalcázar to support the cause of His Majesty against the tyrants. And some of us came to this town, because we did not all travel together, and they supplied us with food and other things we needed so generously and so willingly that I do not know where they could do it better. In one place they had large numbers of rabbits, and in another, pigs, and in another, hens, and llamas and fowls; and in similar fashion they supplied all who came that way."

rank and fortune of the owner. The chiefs and captains have many wives, but one of them is the principal one, and the succession goes to her son. They worship the sun, and when the chiefs die, they dig deep graves in the hills or fields in which they lay them with their jewels of gold and silver, their arms, clothing, and living women, and not the ugliest, and a supply of food. This burial custom, which is almost general throughout the Indies, is the work of the devil, who makes them believe that in this way they will go to the kingdom that he has prepared for them. They make great mourning for the dead, and the women who do not kill themselves, and the female servants, cut off their hair and weep for days on end; and in addition to weeping most of the day and night when they die, they mourn for a whole year. They drink like the others, and they eat their principal meal in the morning on the ground, without giving much thought to tablecloths, and after eating their corn and meat or fish, they spend the day drinking their chicha or wine which they ferment from corn, always going around with the cup in their hand. They spend much time in their *areitos* or songs, men and women holding hands and circling to the sound of a drum, relating in their songs and dirges things of the past, and always drinking until they are completely drunk. And being out of their senses, some of them take the women they want, and carrying them off to a house, satisfy their lust with them. They do not consider this a foul thing, for they do not grasp the reason for shame, nor give much esteem to honor or the opinion of the world, because their one object is to eat what they produce with the labor of their hands.

They believe in the immortality of the soul, so it seems to us, and they recognize that there is a Creator of all things, for, contemplating the vastness of the heavens and the movement of the sun and the moon and the other wonders, they hold that there is a Maker of all these things. They do great reverence to the sun and look upon it as a god; the priests are holy men and respected and esteemed by all, wherever they are.

There are other customs and things I would have to tell about these Indians; but as most of them observe and hold them, I shall deal with them all as I traverse their provinces. So I conclude this chapter by saying that these of Tacunga employ for arms palm lances and javelins and darts and slings. They are dark, like the others I have described; the women very affectionate, and some of them good-looking. There are still many *mitimaes* of those that existed in the days when the Incas ruled the provinces of their kingdom.

CHAPTER 16 (ii: XXII)

Where the mitimaes *were sent, and the classes there were of them, and how the Incas esteemed them.*

THE INDIANS known as *mitimaes,* for in Peru they tell so many things of them, were so honored and valued by the Incas that they considered them, after the *Orejones,* the highest nobility of the provinces. I mention this because in the *History,*[1] so called, of the Indies, the author has stated that these *mitimaes* were slaves of Huayna Capac. This is an error into which all those fall who write from hearsay or from books, without having seen the land they describe to know if what they say is the truth.

In most of the provinces of Peru, or in all of them, there were and are *mitimaes,*[2] and, as I have heard, there were three manners or classes of them, which contributed greatly to the upkeep and conservation of the kingdom, and even to its settlement. Once the reader knows how and in what way these *mitimaes* were distributed, and

1 The *"History"* is the *Hispanic Victrix: Primera y Segunda Parte de la Historia General de las Indias,* by Francisco López de Gómara, published in Medina del Campo in 1553.

2 *Mitimaes,* from the Quechua *mitima* (plural, *mita-ḳona*), were those persons who formed the transplanted populations, a system perfected by the later Incas in order to govern newly conquered territory. *Mitimaes* were of three kinds: military (to hold outposts), political (to insure allegiance of a newly conquered land), and economic and cultural, occupying thinly populated districts so as to bring the Incaic way of life and methods and to increase the use of the Quechua language. Each colony of transplanted populations, under their own chieftain, retained their distinctive headdress. Populations were shifted on a gigantic scale, and the *mita-ḳona* were a deciding factor in the spread of the Incaic system. There was hardly a valley, wrote one of the early chroniclers, that did not have its *mita-ḳona* population. Cuzco was filled with them, making it truly a cosmopolitan capital. When their missions were finished, they returned to the land of their birth, where they received women and other honors from the Lord-Inca. The Romans, as empire builders, used the same system in Italy; colonies of Roman citizens were planted and the Roman army of occupation in foreign lands can be thought of in the same tenor as the Peruvian *mitimaes;* these legions conquered the land, built bridges and roads, and remained there to the *Pax Romana.* When their service was complete, they were given a diploma and tax-free land by the emperor.

what they did and were for, he will realize how the Incas successfully governed so many lands and provinces as they ruled.

Mitimaes is the name given to those who are transferred from one land to another. The first class or kind of *mitimaes* the Incas ordered established was that after they had conquered some province or recently brought it under their rule, to hold it safely, and to teach the natives and inhabitants how they were to serve and comport themselves, and so they would quickly apprehend the other things their vassals of long standing knew and understood, and be peaceful and quiet and not always plotting revolt—and if, by chance, they attempted it, there would be those to prevent it—they transferred from such provinces the number of people it seemed to them convenient to move. These were ordered to settle in another region of climate and nature similar to that they were leaving, if cold, cold, if warm, warm, where they were given as much and as many lands, fields, and houses as they had left. And from the lands and provinces which had been peaceful and friendly for a long time, and had shown their disposition to serve him, the Inca ordered an equal number or more to pass over to the newly won lands and settle among the Indians that had been subdued, where they took charge of the aforementioned matters, and brought them to a knowledge of order and polity. Thus, the former departing, and the latter entering, and with the governors and representatives appointed, everything would be safe, as we have explained in the preceding chapter.

As the Incas were aware of how reluctant peoples are to leave their native land and the surroundings they know, in order that they should cheerfully accept this exile, they treated these people with special consideration; to many they gave arm bands of gold and of silver, and clothing of wool, and feathers, and women, and they enjoyed other privileges. And among them there were spies who were always listening to what the natives talked about and planned, and this they reported to the Lord-Inca's official, or went quickly to Cuzco to inform the Inca. In this way, all was quiet, and the *mitimaes* feared the natives, and the natives feared the *mitimaes,* and all occupied themselves only in obeying and serving. If among the one or the others there were mutinies or conspiracies or plotting, they were severely punished, for some of the Incas were vengeful and mercilessly meted out punishments of great cruelty.

60

Some of the *mitimaes* were assigned for the foregoing purpose; many of them were llama-herders and custodians of the flocks of the Inca and the sun; others were tailors; others, silversmiths; others, stonecutters and farmers; and others designed and carved statues; in a word, whatever the Inca wished and demanded of them. And *mitimaes* were also ordered to go from the villages to the highlands of the Andes to sow corn and raise cocoa and care for the fruit trees, and supply what was needed in settlements where because of the cold and snow such things could not be planted or raised.

The second thing for which the *mitimaes* were used was that, as the Indians along the frontier of the Andes, such as the Chunchos, Moxos, and Chiriguanos,[3] most of whom had their lands on the eastern slope of the mountains, are barbarous and warlike people, many of whom eat human flesh, and who often went out to make war on the natives of this side and ravaged their fields and towns, taking prisoner as many of them as they could; to remedy this, captaincies and regular garrisons were established in many places where some *Orejones* were stationed. And so that no tribe should be in a position to make war or quickly organize a rebellion or conspiracy, they assigned as soldiers of these captaincies *mitimaes* from such regions and provinces as seemed best, who were taken to those places where they had fortresses, *pucarás,* to defend themselves, if necessary. And these soldiers were provided with rations, corn and other articles of food supplied by those of the vicinity as their tribute and tax, and the pay they received was that from time to time they were given woolen clothing and feathers, or arm bands of gold and silver to those who had displayed the most bravery. They were also given women from among the many who were kept in each province in the name of the Inca. And as most of these were beautiful, they prized and cherished them greatly. Aside from this, they gave them things of lesser value, which the governors of the provinces had the duty of providing, for they had authority and power over the captains from

3 The Chunchos, who live in the eastern *montaña* of Peru; the Moxos (Mojos), the inhabitants of a large province in the humid hot lands east of mountainous Bolivia; and the Chiriguanos, who lived on the humid *montaña* sloping into the Amazon from the Bolivian Andes. An attack in 1522 from this area by Chiriguanos allied with the Guaranis was led by Alejo García, a Spaniard captured by the Indians and promoted to captain. He was the first white man to see the outposts of the Inca empire, five years before the 1527 landing of Francisco Pizarro at Tumbes. (Alfred Métraux, "Tribes of the Eastern Slopes of the Bolivian Andes," *Handbook,* III, 465ff.)

whom these *mitimaes* took their orders. In addition to the aforementioned regions, there were fortresses of this sort on the frontiers of the Chachapoyas and Bracamoros, and in Quito, and in Caranqui, which is beyond Quito to the north, close to the province known as Popayán, and in other places they thought necessary, such as Chile, and in the plains and hills.

The other use of the *mitimaes* was stranger, for albeit these described were great, it is nothing unusual to station captains and garrisons along a frontier, for it has frequently been done. What they did was that if, perchance, they had conquered territory in the highlands or plains or on a slope suitable for plowing and sowing, which was fertile and had a good climate, and was empty of people, they quickly ordered that from near-by provinces that had the same climate as these, for the good of the health, enough people come in to settle it, and to these lands were given, and flocks, and all the provisions they needed until they could harvest what they planted. These new settlers were treated so well, and the Lord-Inca put such diligence into the matter, that in a short time the lands were settled and under cultivation so that it was a pleasure to see. After this manner many valleys of the plains and villages of the highlands were settled, some of which the Incas saw for themselves, and others about which they received reports. For a number of years no tribute was exacted of these new settlers, but on the contrary, they were given women, coca, and food so that they would carry out the work of settlement with better will.

Thus, in the days of the Incas there was very little arable land in these kingdoms that was not under cultivation, and all as thickly settled, as the first Spaniards who entered this realm can testify. To be sure, it is a sad thing to reflect that these idol-worshiping Incas should have had such wisdom in knowing how to govern and preserve these far-flung lands, and that we, Christians, have destroyed so many kingdoms. For wherever the Spaniards have passed, conquering and discovering, it is as though a fire had gone, destroying everything in its path.

It should be pointed out that the city of Cuzco, too, was full of foreign tribesmen, all according to plan, and being of so many different origins they did not join forces to rebel or for anything that was not in the Lord-Inca's service. Even today there are in Cuzco,

Chachapoyas Indians and Çañaris, and those of other regions who are the descendants of those who were brought there.

It may be taken as certain with regard to the *mitimaes* that they have been used since the times of Pachacuti, he who established the posts, and was the first to enlarge the temple of Curicancha, as will be told when the time comes. Some Indians say that the *mitimaes* were first instituted in the days of Viracocha Inca, the father of Pachacuti. Whoever wishes to believe this may do so; I have informed myself so thoroughly on the matter that I repeat, it was the invention of Pachacuti.

63

CHAPTER 17 (XLII)

Of the settlements between Tacunga and Riobamba.

AFTER LEAVING Tacunga by the highway leading to the great city of Cuzco, one comes to the settlements of Muli-ambato, of which I need say nothing except that the Indians who live there belong to the same nation and have the same customs as those of Tacunga. There were ordinary lodgings there and storehouses of the supplies ordered by the representatives of the Incas, and they obeyed the high steward who was in Tacunga. For this place was held in the highest regard by the Lord-Incas, like Quito and Tomebamba, Cajamarca, Jauja, and Vilcas and Paria, and others which were like capitals of a kingdom of the head of a diocese, where the captains and governors resided who were empowered to mete out justice and raise armies if war was threatened or a tyrant attempted to seize power. Nevertheless, they took no decision without notifying the Lord-Incas, and for this purpose they had things so well organized that in a week the news was carried by messenger from Quito to Cuzco. For this, every half-league they had a small house, where two Indians always resided with their wives, and as soon as the news to be relayed reached them, one of them set out on the run and did not stop for half a league, and before he arrived at the next house, he shouted out what had happened and was to be said. As soon as this was heard by the other, he ran another half-league so swiftly that, the country being as rough and broken as it is, neither horses nor mules could travel more swiftly.

Inasmuch as in my book on the Lord-Incas (which, God willing, will come out after this one)[1] I deal at length with these posts, I shall say no more here, for I mentioned it only to make it clear to the reader and so he will understand.

64 From Muli-ambato[2] one proceeds to the Ambato River, where there are lodgings for the same purpose as those described. Three leagues farther on come the sumptuous lodgings of Mocha, so many and so large that I was amazed. Now that the Lord-Incas have lost their power, all the palaces and dwellings and other marvels they possessed have fallen into ruin and in their present state only their general outlines can be seen, and remnants of the buildings. But as they were of beautiful stone and finely constructed, they will endure for time and ages without wholly disappearing.

Around Mocha there are some Indian settlements. These people all go clothed, men and women, and their customs and language are like those we have seen.

To the west lie the settlements of the Indians called Sichos, and to the east, the Pillaros. In both there is an abundance of food, as the land is very fertile. There are great herds of deer, and llamas, and many rabbits and partridges, turtledoves, and other game. In addition, throughout all these settlements the Spaniards have great herds of cattle which prosper because of the excellent pasturelands, and many goats which do well there because they find plenty to eat, and pigs which are better than most of those in other parts of the Indies, and fine hams and bacon are cured like those of Sierra Morena.[3]

Leaving Mocha, one comes to the lodgings of Riobamba, which are no less impressive than those of Mocha. They are situated in the province of the Puruhás in beautiful fair fields, whose climate, vegetation,

[1] God apparently was *not* willing. The first Chronicle was published in 1553 with considerable success, judged by the number of editions in which it was issued. The second disappeared, presumably with the death of the author in 1554. It was used extensively by every chronicler who followed Cieza. It was found in the library of The Escorial—an imperfect copy of the end of the sixteenth century—and was rescued from oblivion by the Spanish historian Marcos Jiménez de la Espada. So, in Madrid, in 1880, God became willing after 330 years to allow light to be shed on "*La Crónica del Peru,* Newly Written (1550) by Pedro de Cieza de León, a citizen of Sevilla."

[2] The royal Inca Quito-Cuzco highway passed through Muli-ambato (or Molle-ambato), now merely Ambato, crossed the river by means of a suspension bridge located at the town of Pelileo; Mocha occupies the same site now as then—it was a royal tambo with a residence reserved for the Lord-Inca Huayna Capac.

[3] Sierra Morena were the mountains about the birthplace of Cieza, Llerena. It was famous for its smoked hams.

flowers, and other features resemble those of Spain, as is testified by all who have been there.

CHAPTER 18 (XLIII)

Which deals with the remaining Indian settlements before reaching the city of Tomebamba.

I HAVE MENTIONED the fact that these lodgings of Riobamba are in the province of the Puruhás, which is one of the well-settled regions about the city of Quito, and good people; they go clothed, they and their women. Their customs resemble those of their neighbors, and for identification they wear their special headband, and most of them have very long hair, which they plait tight, as do the women. They worship the sun; those they select as most fitted for the purpose talk with the devil, and they had, and it would seem, still have, other rites and vices, like those of the Incas, by whom they were conquered. When the chiefs die, they dig them a deep, square grave, in the field they choose, where they lay them with their arms and treasure, if they possess it. Some of these graves are dug in the house where the deceased dwelt; they do as the natives of these regions generally do, which is to put in the tomb most of the man's wives. And they do this because, as I have heard from Indians who have a reputation for truth, at times, God permitting it because of their sins and idolatry, the devil deludes them into believing that they see those long since dead walking about their lands adorned with what they were buried with and accompanied by the women who were put alive into the tomb. Seeing this, it seems to them that where the souls go, gold and women are necessary, and they put them in, as I have related. The reason for this, and also for the son of the sister and not the brother inheriting the power, I shall tell farther on.

There are many villages throughout this province of the Puruhás which I do not mention to avoid being prolix. To the west of Rio-bamba[1] there are other settlements in the mountain which borders

---

[1] Riobamba (Lira-pampa), situated more or less in the same location as the colonial-modern city of Ecuador, under the shadows of the giant snow-covered extinct volcano Chimborazo (6,272 meters high), was the chief city of the Puruhá tribe. In Inca times

upon the sources of the Marañón River and the sierra called Tungura-
hua, where there are also many villages. All of these hold to the same
customs as these other Indians, and they all go clothed, and their
houses are of stone. They were conquered by the Lord-Incas and their
captains, and they speak the common language of Cuzco, although
they had and have their own. To the west there is another snow-
covered sierra, known as Urcolazo [Chimborazo], where there are
few inhabitants, Skirting this sierra runs the road leading to the city
of Santiago, called Guayaquil.

66

Leaving the city of Riobamba, one comes to the settlements called
Cayambi [Columbe]. Here the land is all level and very cold; after
these come the lodgings or dwellings of Teocaxas [Tiocajas], situated
on wide, barren, chill plains where the battle of Teocaxas took place between the Indians of the region and Captain Sebastián de Belalcázar.[2]

Three leagues farther on are the important lodgings of *Tiquizambi,*
to the right [west] of which lie Guayaquil and its mountains, and to
the left Pomallacta and Quizna and Macas, together with other regions, until one comes to those known as Río Grande. Beyond these,
in the lowlands, are the dwellings of Chan-Chan, which, as they lie
in the hot country, are called by the natives *Yungas,* which means
"hot country." As it never snows or is very cold here, trees and other
things thrive which are not to be found in cold climates. For this
reason all those living in hot or warm valleys or regions are called

it had a sun temple, a house for the Chosen Women (*Aclla-huasi*), and a royal tambo
for the Lord-Incas, and it ranked with Quito in importance; so much so that after
Sebastián de Belalcázar had routed the Inca forces in 1534, he thought of founding
the capital of the newly conquered territory at Riobamba.

[2] Columbe was a stop on the road beyond the frigid tarn of Colta; the site was
located at the headwaters of the Guamote River. The Tambo de Guamote (not mentioned by Cieza) was the next way-station. Humboldt was there in July, 1802: "Tambo
de Guamote, tambo ou caravansérai dans une valle l'entrée des hautes savannes de
Tiocaxas. . . ." Both ancient villages are now towns on the modern automobile and
railroad route in Ecuador. Teocajas, located on a high knob or *"nudo de Tiocajas"* of the
cordillera, was also a tambo stop.

When the Incas under Pachacuti (the name by which Inca Yupanqui is commonly
known) were making the first conquest of the north, they forced the Cañari, recently
conquered, to erect a fortress there to protect the newly conquered land from the
Puruhás.

Tiquizambi (Ticsán or Tixán on modern maps), the next way stop southward after
crossing the high *páramos* at 12,000 feet elevation, was on a different watershed; here
all rivers flowed into the Pacific. Ruins of Ticsán were seen by Padre Velasco in 1789
and in modern times by Jijón y Caamaño.

Yungas, as they are known today and will be, even though centuries elapse.

From these lodgings to the sumptuous palaces of Tomebamba, is a distance of nearly twenty leagues, the territory between being broken every two or three leagues with lodgings and depots.[3] Among these there are two main ones, Cañari-bamba and Hatun-cañari, from which the natives and their province take their name, both being known as Cañaris. To the right and left of the highway I am traveling there are not a few settlements and provinces, which I do not mention because the natives of them, having been conquered and ruled by the Lord-Incas, observed the customs of those I have been describing, and spoke the common language of Cuzco, and they and their women went clothed. In their marriage customs and the inheritance of power they observed the same rule as those I have mentioned in the foregoing chapters, as well as in putting food in the graves and prolonged mourning, and burying living women with the dead. All held the sun to be the chief god; all believed that there is a Maker of all created things who, in the language of Cuzco, they call Tici-Viracocha. But in spite of this belief, in olden times they worshiped trees and stones and the moon and other things imposed upon them by the devil, our enemy, with whom those designated for that purpose spoke, and they obeyed him in many things. . . .

All along this route there are small rivers, some medium-sized, some larger, all of very fine water, and some of them are spanned by bridges. In bygone times, before the Spaniards conquered this kingdom,

3 These lodgings not mentioned by Cieza de León were Pomallacta [Pama-llacta] at the present town of Achupallas; there are remains of a tambo. The temple of the sun was incorporated into the masonry of the parish church. Next in line was Sinazahuán; Humboldt crossed the heights of "Cerro de Sitzán . . . dangereux pour les voyageurs," and the tambo was the most elevated point on the Alto de Picches (3,774 meters). The next phase of the Inca road passed over the highest point in Ecuador (anciently Cañar), the Ladera de Cadlud, over the hail-swept heights at an average of 4,529 meters; this to reach the place of Paredones de Incas, the ruins of a tambo and the palace of Topa Inca (1471–93) near the grand Llano de Pullal (4,732 meters). Hence one dropped down to Cañar through to 3,022 meters and the Tambo de Burgay; thence southward twenty miles to Tomebamba, now Cuenca, the third-ranking city in Ecuador. From this point to the southwest one reached Cañar [Hatun-cañar], where (close to the Hacienda Turcha) was the far-famed Inca-pirca built by Huayna Capac, the conquerer of the Cañari and father of Atahualpa. This is the only sizable Inca ruin extant in all of Ecuador. It was examined by the French *Académie des Sciences* expedition in 1735 and again by Humboldt in 1802.

there were throughout these sierras and countryside great numbers of llamas, and even guanacos and vicuñas. But the Spaniards killed them off so fast that there are almost none left. Neither wolves nor other ravenous animals have been found in these regions, aside from the jaguars I mentioned in the mountains of Buenaventura, and a few small panthers and bears. In the ravines and forests one sometimes sees snakes, and everywhere foxes, opossum, and such other wild animals as are to be found here; also many partridges, pigeons, turtledoves, and deer, and in the vicinity of Quito, rabbits abound and in the forests, a few tapirs.[4]

68

CHAPTER 19 (XLIV)

Of the grandeur of the palaces in the city of Tomebamba in the province of the Cañari.

IN PLACES in this book I have mentioned the great power the Lord-Incas of Peru possessed, their worth, and how in the more than 1,200 leagues of coast they ruled they had their representatives and governors, and many lodgings and great storehouses filled with all necessary supplies. This was to provide for their soldiers, for in one of these depots there were lances, and in another, darts, and in others, sandals, and in others, the different arms they employed. Likewise, certain depots were filled with fine clothing, others, with coarser garments, and others, with food and every kind of victuals. When the lord was lodged in his dwellings and his soldiers garrisoned there, nothing, from the most important to the most trifling, but could be provided. And if in the adjacent territory there were quarrels or thefts, these were at once severely punished, for the Lord-Incas employed such justice that they did not fail to order punishment executed even if the culprit was their own son. And in spite of this foresight and that there were so many storehouses and lodging places (the kingdom was full of them) every ten or twenty leagues, more

4 The panther is the puma (*Felis concolor*); there is but a single bear (*Ursidae*) from South America, the spectacled bear (*ucumari*), distributed in the high Andean slopes from Venezuela to and beyond Bolivia. There are two species of tapirs, one (*Tapirus Americanus*) that is confined to the tropical lands, and the hairy tapir (*Tapirus roulini*), thickly haired, that is found in the Andes as high as 13,000 feet.

or less, throughout the extent of their provinces, there were sumptuous palaces for the Lord-Incas, and temples to the sun where the priests and the virgins—the *mamaconas*—lived, and where there were larger storehouses than the usual. Here the governor resided, and the Inca's officers, together with *mitimaes* and other serving people. And when they were not at war, and the Lord-Inca was not traveling through those regions, they collected the tributes from the land of which they were in charge, and ordered the storehouses filled and the supplies renewed whenever they judged necessary, and did other mighty things. For, as I have said, this was like a capital or head of a diocese. These palaces were a grand thing; when one of the Lord-Incas died, his successor did not abandon or destroy them, but, on the contrary, improved and added to them; for each built his own palace, leaving that of his predecessor adorned and standing as he had left it.

These famous lodgings of Tomebamba, which, as I have said, were situated in the province of the Cañari,[1] were among the finest and richest to be found in all Peru, and the buildings the largest and best. Whatever the Indians said about these residences fell short of reality, to judge by the remains.

To the west of them lies the province of the Huancavilcas, which neighbors on the city of Guayaquil and Puerto Viejo, and to the east, the great Marañón River with its mountains and some settlements.

The lodgings of Tomebamba are situated at the joining of two

[1] The Cañari occupied most of the highlands between Peru and the Puruhá tribes to the north. They were allied to the jungle tribes both east and west, particularly with the Jívaro (Shuara) head-shrinking tribes of Ecuador's Upper Amazonia. They were, as all other Andean people, agriculturists; their houses were round or oval, built of posts, wattle, and daub, with thatched roofs. The chieftain's houses were rectangular, and later (1450) built of stone in the Incaic manner. Their dress was Andean; the men wore their hair long, braided on top and held by a wooden or wickerwork hoop. This headdress was peculiar to them and identified them in battle or when away from Cañar. They were excellent gold craftsmen; their goldwork is superb. Gold was obtained from the highly aurific rivers of Upper Amazonia, by means of trade with the Jívaros. The sixteenth-century European goldsmiths were amazed at the dexterity of their craft. The rulers were polygamous; common man, monogamous. Intertribal marriages were encouraged in order to build up a confederation to oppose the Incas advancing up from Peru. Topa Inca after 1471 began the conquest of the Cañari, and after 1493 Huayna Capac consolidated the northern conquests and added to the luster of Tomebamba. After his death and the advent of the civil war, the Cañari sided with Huascar and captured Atahualpa at Tomebamba, but he escaped and in revenge ravaged the Cañari tribe. After the death of Atahualpa, the Cañari became willing auxiliaries to the Spaniards, helped them defend Cuzco against the attack by Manco Inca and were instrumental in recapturing the *pucará* of Sacsahuamán (1536) which broke the siege of Cuzco.

small rivers in a plain having a circumference of over twelve leagues. It is a chilly land, abounding in game such as deer, rabbits, partridges, turtledoves, and other birds. The temple of the sun was of stones put together with the subtlest skill, some of them large, black, and rough, and others that seemed of jasper. Some of the Indians claimed that most of the stones used in the construction of these lodgings and the temple of the sun had been brought all the way from the city of Cuzco by order of the Lord-Inca Huayna Capac and his father, the great Topa Inca, pulled with great cables. If this is true, it is a remarkable thing, considering the size and number of the stones, and the distance. The fronts of many of the buildings are beautiful and highly decorative, some of them set with precious stones and emeralds, and, inside, the walls of the temple of the sun and the palaces of the Lord-Incas were covered with sheets of the finest gold and incrusted with many statues, all of this metal. The roof of these buildings was of thatch, so well laid that barring a fire, it would last for ages.[2] Inside the dwellings there were sheaves of golden straw, and on the walls carved figures of the same rich metal, and birds, and many other things. In addition to this, it was said that there was a great sum of treasure in jugs and pots and other receptacles, and many rich blankets covered with silver and beadwork. Whatever I say, I cannot give an idea of the wealth the Incas possessed in these royal palaces, in which they took great pride, where many silversmiths were kept busy making the things I have described and many others. The woolen clothing in the storehouses was so numerous and so fine that if it had been kept and not lost, it would be worth a fortune. The virgins [Ñustas] dedicated to the service of the temple numbered more than two hundred, and were very beautiful, chosen from among the Cañari and the region of the district governed by the high steward of the Incas, who lived in these dwellings. They and the priests were well supplied by those in charge of the maintenance of the temple, at whose gate there were gate-keepers (some of whom were said to be eunuchs), whose duty it was to watch over the *mamaconas,* as the virgins living in the temple were called. Besides the temple and the palaces of the Lord-Incas there were a great number of dwellings where the soldiers were garrisoned,

2 Tomebamba has suffered the insults of time. The site on the outskirts of Cuenca (Ecuador) is known, and that is all. Max Uhle in 1922 made detailed excavations there and published *Las Ruinas de Tomebamba.*

and still greater storehouses filled with the provisions I have described, however much was used. For the stewards kept careful account after their fashion of all that entered and all that was given out, and the will of the Lord-Inca was observed in all things. The natives of this province, known as the Cañari, are well built and of goodly countenance. They wear their hair very long and coil it around their head, so by it and a round crown of wood, as fine as sieve wire, they can be recognized as Cañari wherever they go, and this is their identification.

As all these Indians are dark and given to shouting, and resemble one another so much (as those of us who have dealings with them today can see), to avoid difficulties and so they could understand one another, for except when certain of the *Orejones* went about visiting the provinces, none of them spoke anything but their native tongue, even though it was a law that they must all know the language of Cuzco, and the same thing happened in the camps, as it does everywhere, for it is evident that if the Emperor Charles V has an army in Italy made up of Spaniards, Germans, Burgundians, Flemings, and Italians, those of each nation will speak their own language, throughout all this kingdom they all wore special insignia on their head to distinguish themselves one from the other. If they were Yungas, they went muffled like gypsies; if Collas, they wore caps shaped like mortars, of wool; if Canas, they wore larger caps, and much broader. The Cañari wore a kind of narrow wooden crown like the rim of a sieve; the Huancas, strands that fell below their chin, and their hair braided; the Canchis, broad black or red bands over their forehead. Thus all of them could be recognized by their insignia, which was such a good and clear system that even if there were five hundred thousand men together, they could be clearly told from each other. Even today in a gathering of people we can say at once, these are from this place, those from that, and, as I say, this was how they recognized one another.

Their women, too, take great pride in their long hair, and wear it coiled about their head, by which they are known, like their husbands. Their clothing is of wool and cotton, and they wear the sandals I have described, on their feet. Some of the women are beautiful, and not a little lascivious, and fond of the Spaniards. They are hard workers, for it is the women who till and plant the fields and harvest the crops, while their husbands for the most part stay indoors spin-

THE INCAS

ning and weaving and preparing their arms and clothing and caring
for their faces, and other feminine occupations. And when an army
of Spaniards passes through their province (in those days the Indians
were obliged to carry the Spaniards' luggage), many of them sent
their daughters and wives while they stayed at home. I saw this at
the time we went to join Master La Gasca, president of His Majesty's
Council, when they gave us a number of women to carry our luggage.

72

Some of the Indians claim that they do this because of the scarcity
of men and the abundance of women, the result of the cruelty with
which Atahualpa proceeded against the natives of this province when
he invaded it after having killed and defeated the commander of the
army of Huascar, his brother, by name Atoco, in Ambato. They tell
how, in spite of the fact that men and boys came out bearing green
branches and palm leaves to implore mercy, with irate countenance
and great severity he ordered his men and captains to kill them all,
and a great number of men and boys were slaughtered, as I shall
relate in the third part of this history. Those now alive say that there
are fifteen women to each man, and as they are so numerous they
do this work, and anything else their fathers or husbands order.

The houses of the Cañari are small and built of stone, straw-
thatched. The land is fertile and abounds in food and game. They
worship the sun like the others we have seen. The chieftains marry
as many women as they wish who please them, but one is the principal
wife. And before they marry they make a great feast at which, after
they have eaten and drunk their fill, they do certain things as is their
custom. The son of the principal wife inherits the rule, even though
the chieftain has many sons by his other wives. The dead are laid in
tombs, as their neighbors do, together with living women and their
prized possessions. Their arms and customs are like those we have
seen. Some of them are great soothsayers and warlords; but they do
not indulge in the abominable sin and other idolatries, though they
did revere the devil with whom those chosen for the purpose communicated. Now the chiefs are Christians and the most important of
them (when I passed through Tomebamba in 1547) was called Don
Fernando. . . .

And they tell that when Huayna Capac was there, the news was
brought to him of the arrival of the Spaniards in his territory, at the

time that Don Francisco Pizarro reached the coast with the ship in which he and his thirteen companions were traveling, who were the first discoverers of Peru, and even that he said that after his days, strange people like those in the ship would rule in his kingdom. He probably said this prompted by the devil, just as he foretold that the Spaniards would return to the land in great force. And I heard from many old, wise Indians that the question of building certain palaces in this place played a considerable part in the differences that arose between Huascar and Atahualpa. 73

In conclusion I would say that these lodgings of Tomebamba were a remarkable thing. Today all is cast down and in ruins, but still it can be seen how great they were.

Great events took place in the time of the Incas' reign in these palaces of Tomebamba and many armies assembled there for weighty matters. When the Lord-Inca died, the first thing his heir did, after assuming the royal fringe, or crown of the kingdom, was to send governors to Quito and to this Tomebamba, to take possession in his name, ordering that golden palaces should be built immediately for him, such as his forebears had had. The *Orejones* of Cuzco (who are the wisest and most noble of the kingdom) relate that Pachacuti, father of the great Topa Inca, who was the founder of the temple, preferred to live in these palaces rather than anywhere else, and they say the same of his son, Topa Inca.

I could extend myself on this conquest of Quito carried out by Topa Inca,[3] but there is so much to say about other things that I cannot go into this as fully as I should like, and must limit myself to stating it summarily, inasmuch as what is already known everywhere will suffice to comprehend it. For the expedition made ready by the Lord-Inca, which was to depart from the city of Cuzco without knowing whither it was bound nor where the war was to be fought, more than two hundred thousand men had been assembled with such a supply of baggage and provisions that it covered the countryside. By the posts the governors of the provinces were notified that supplies and munitions and arms were to be brought from all

[3] This part which refers to the conquests of Topa Inca is taken from the second Chronicle, "Of how Topa Inca set out from Cuzco and subdued all the lands as far as Quito, and the great feats he accomplished" (Chapter LVI), in order to give the history continuity.

districts to the highway of Chinchay-suyu[4] which was being built not far removed from the one his father had ordered constructed, nor so close that the two were one. This highway was large and fine, laid out with the planning and care that have been described, and everywhere there were provisions for the multitude of people that went in his armies, who lacked for nothing, and for this reason none of his men ventured to touch even an ear of corn of the countryside, and if he did, he paid for it with his life. The natives acted as porters and performed other personal services, but only up to a fixed limit; and as they did this willingly, and such exactitude and fairness was observed, they did not find it burdensome.

Having left behind in Cuzco garrisons of the *mitimaes* and a governor chosen from among his most loyal friends, he set forth with his uncle Capac Yupanqui as captain-general and chief adviser, not the one who made war on those of Jauja, for he, so they tell, hanged himself because of a certain resentment. When the Inca left Cuzco, he proceeded as far as Vilcas, where he spent several days observing with satisfaction the temple and lodgings that had been built there, and he gave orders that silversmiths were to employ themselves fashioning goblets and other articles and jewels for the temple and his royal dwelling of Vilcas.

He went to Jauja, where the Huancas received him ceremoniously, and he sent messengers in all directions to let it be known that he sought the friendship of all, without intention of doing them harm or making war on them, and that, therefore, as they knew that the Incas of Cuzco did not exercise tyranny nor oppress those who were their confederates and vassals, but in return for the service and homage received, did them great good, they should send their emissaries to arrange a peace with him. In Bombón they had learned of the great force with which the Inca had come, and as they had heard of the great clemency he exercised, they went to do him reverence, and those of Yauyos did the same, and those of Apurímac, and many others, all of whom he received graciously, giving some of them women, and others coca, and others blankets and shirts, and attiring himself in the costume of the province where he happened to be, which was the thing that pleased them most.

---

[4] Chinchay-suyu, which included all the land to the north of Cuzco toward Quito, was one of the "four sections of the world."

In the provinces which lie between Jauja and Cajamarca they tell that several wars and skirmishes took place, and he ordered large stockades and fortifications built to defend themselves against the natives, and with his skillful arts he subdued them without shedding much blood, and did the same with those of Cajamarca. Everywhere he left governors and representatives and posts, to be sure of receiving news, and he never departed from any of the large provinces without first ordering lodging and a temple to the sun built, and bringing in *mitimaes*. Aside from this, they tell that he entered Huánuco and ordered a palace built there as fair as we see it today, and proceeding to the lands of the Chachapoyas, he made such fierce war against them that in a short time they were completely undone; but he addressed such words to them that they offered themselves to him of their own accord. In Cajamarca he left many people from Cuzco to instruct the natives as to how they should dress, and the tribute they should pay, and, above all, how they should worship and reverence the sun.

Nearly everywhere they called him father, and he gave stern orders that no one was to do any damage to the lands through which they passed, nor violence to any man or woman, and whoever did so was immediately to suffer the death penalty. He urged those whom he subdued to build their settlements close and in orderly fashion, and not to make war on one another, nor to eat each other, nor to commit other sins against the laws of nature.

He entered the land of the Bracamoros, but hastily left it, for that hilly region is bad country; it also gave him great trouble to subdue the Paltas, and those of Huancabamba, Cajas, Ayabaca, and its confines, for those are strong, warlike people, and he carried on war with them for five moons; but at last they sued for peace, and he granted it to them on the same terms as the others. Peace was arranged as of today, and tomorrow the province was filled with *mitimaes,* and governors, without removing the native chieftains, and storehouses were built and filled with supplies and all the other things ordered brought to them, and a highway was built and the customary posts established along it.

From these regions Topa Inca proceeded until he reached the lands of the Cañari, with whom he also had his encounters and clashes, but the same thing happened to them as to the others, and they became his vassals, and he ordered more than fifteen thousand men with their women and their headmen to come to Cuzco and remain in the city as hostages, and all was done as he ordered. There are those who say that this transfer of the Cañari to Cuzco took place in the time of Huayna Capac. At Tomebamba he ordered large and sumptuous buildings constructed. In the first part of my work I described these buildings and their magnificence. From there he sent different embassies to many lands of the region urging them to come to see him, and many, eschewing war, offered themselves to his service. Against those who refused he sent captains and troops, making them do by force what the others did of their own will.

After establishing order in the land of the Cañari, he went to Tiquizambi, Cayambi, the Puruaes, and many other regions, where they tell of such a multitude of things that it is difficult to believe them, and of the wisdom he displayed to make himself the ruler of such vast kingdoms. In Tacunga he fought a hard war with the natives, and concerted peace with them after they had been vanquished, and ordered so many and such splendid buildings constructed there that they outdo those of Cuzco. He wanted to spend some time in Tacunga so his men could rest; and almost daily messages arrived from Cuzco concerning the state of affairs there, and from other parts, too, came runners bringing news and information of the great things being done by the governors in the administration of the lands. News reached him of a certain disturbance that had arisen in Cuzco among the *Orejones* themselves, which had caused some trouble, and which he feared might take a more serious turn; but shortly afterward there came another dispatch to the effect that everything was quiet and in order, and that the governor of the city had severely punished those responsible for the disturbance.

From Tacunga he proceeded until he reached what we call Quito, where the city of San Francisco del Quito is founded, and as he found the land good, as good as that of Cuzco, he founded a settlement there, which he called Quito, and peopled it with *mitimaes,* and ordered great moats and buildings and storehouses constructed there, saying, "Cuzco will be the head and defense of my kingdom to one end, and Quito at the other." He invested the governor of Quito with great powers, and throughout the region he appointed his delegates and representatives. He ordered that a garrison be established in Caranqui to maintain peace and in the event of war, and he brought people in from other lands, and transferred the natives of these parts to other places. Everywhere they came to worship the sun and take over the customs of the Incas, to such a degree that it seemed that all had been born in Cuzco, and they loved and revered him so much that they called him Father of All, good Inca, the lover and the arm of justice. They tell that his son Huayna Capac was born in the province of the Cañari, and that great celebrations were held. All the natives of the provinces that the great Topa Inca had brought under his rule with the goodly zeal that he employed built their settlements in fitting places, and constructed lodgings along the highways; they learned the general tongue of Cuzco, and the laws which they were to observe. The buildings at Tomebamba were erected by artisans who came from Cuzco and taught the others their craft; and in similar fashion all the other things the Lord-Inca ordered were done.

There Huayna Capac enjoyed himself greatly, for that was said to be his birthplace, and he found great storehouses and lodgings built there, and abundant supplies, and he sent out embassies inviting those of the neighboring lands to come and visit him, and from many places ambassadors came bringing gifts.

According to my information, he was so incensed because of an attempted revolt on the part of certain peoples in the vicinity of Cuzco that, after having had the heads of all the ringleaders cut off, he expressly ordered that the Indians of these regions should transport from Cuzco the amount of stone he specified to build fine lodgings in Tomebamba and that in obedience to his order they hauled them there with cables. And Huayna Capac often remarked that to keep the people of those kingdoms well in hand it was a good thing, when they had nothing else to do or busy themselves with, to make them move a mountain from one spot to another. He even ordered stone and tiles brought from Cuzco for the buildings of Quito, where they are still to be seen in the buildings where they were used.

From Tomebamba, Huayna Capac set out and passed through the land of the Puruhá, resting several days at Riobamba, and his troops rested in Mocha and Tacunga, and drank to their content of the liquor that had been specially brewed for them and brought in from all sides. There he was greeted and visited by many chieftains and captains of the region, and he sent *Orejones* of his kinsmen to the coast of the Llanos and into the highlands to examine the accounts of the *quipus-camayocs,* who are the accountants, as to the contents of the storehouses, and to learn how those he had named governors were conducting themselves toward the natives, and if the Temples of the Sun were well tended, and the shrines that had been established everywhere. He sent his messengers to Cuzco to see how things were going there and whether all he had ordered was being fulfilled. Not a day went by that posts did not arrive, not one or a few, but many, from Cuzco, the Colla, Chile, and all his kingdom.

78

And I heard from many old, wise Indians that the question of building certain palaces in this place was the cause of the differences that arose between Huascar and Atahualpa.

CHAPTER 20 (ii: LXIX)

Of the lineage and attributes of Huascar and Atahualpa.

THE EMPIRE of the Incas was so at peace when Huayna Capac died that in all that vast territory not one person ventured to make a move to provoke war or withhold obedience, because of fear of both Huayna Capac and the *mitimaes* he had established, which were the main strength. But just as after the death of Alexander in Babylon many of his vassals and captains made themselves kings and ruled great lands, so on the death of Huayna Capac [in 1527] dissensions and wars arose between the two brothers; and on the heels of this came the Spaniards. Many of these *mitimaes* became chieftains, for as the natives had been killed in the wars and conflicts, they won the favor of the people who accepted them in their stead.

I could recount at length the qualities of these powerful lords, but I shall observe brevity for those reasons I have set forth on other occasions. Huascar was the son of Huayna Capac, as was Atahualpa. Huascar was the younger, Atahualpa, the elder. Huascar was the son of the Coya, the sister of his father; Atahualpa was the son of a woman of Quilaca, by name Tupac Palla. Both of them were born in Cuzco,[1] not in Quito, as some have said and even written, without

---

[1] It is not certain that Atahualpa was born in Cuzco. Various cities within the Inca empire have been suggested as his birthplace; all historians seem to be in agreement that it was in the north, either at Tomebamba or elsewhere in what is now Ecuador.

knowing the facts. This is borne out by the fact that Huayna Capac was engaged in the conquest of Quito and those lands for some twelve years, and Atahualpa was over thirty when he died. As for being the Lady of Quito, which is what they tell of his mother, there was no such thing, for the Incas themselves were kings and lords of Quito. Huascar was born in Cuzco, and Atahualpa was four or five years older than he. This is the truth, and so I believe it. Huascar was beloved in Cuzco and throughout the kingdom as the lawful heir; Atahualpa was loved by the old captains of his father and the soldiers, because he went to the wars with him as a child, and because Huayna Capac had so loved him during his lifetime, allowing him to eat nothing except what he left on his plate. Huascar was clement and pious; Atahualpa, ruthless and vengeful; both were generous, but Atahualpa was a man of greater determination and endeavor, while Huascar was the more presumptuous and courageous. The one aspired to be the sole master and rule without an equal; the other made up his mind to rule, and to accomplish this, he broke the law which the Incas had established in this matter, which was that only the eldest son of the Inca and his sister could be Lord-Inca, even though he had others who were older by other wives and concubines. Huascar wanted to have the army of his father on his side; Atahualpa suffered because he was not near Cuzco so he could perform his fast in that city and emerge with the fringe to be acclaimed Lord-Inca by all.

CHAPTER 21 (ii: LXX)

Of how the Lord-Inca Huascar was raised to the throne in Cuzco on the death of his father.

AFTER HUAYNA CAPAC had died and the mourning and lamentations for him had been carried out, as has been told, although there were in Cuzco more than forty of his sons, none of them attempted to forswear the obedience due Huascar, to whom they knew the kingdom belonged. And although it was known that Huayna Capac had ordered that his uncle should rule, those were not lacking who ad-

---

It is believed that Atahualpa never had seen Cuzco, although this seems highly improbable, as he traveled much with his father, Huayna Capac.

vised Huascar to assume the fringe publicly and rule all the kingdom. And as most of the native lords of the provinces had come to Cuzco for the obsequies of Huayna Capac, the feast of his coronation could be splendid and quickly known and accepted, and so he determined upon it. Leaving the government of the city to the one his father had designated, he withdrew to carry out the fast as custom required. He came out adorned with the fringe, and great feasts were held, and the cable of gold was brought out in the square, and the statues of the Incas, as they did on such occasions, and several days were spent in drinking and dancing. When these were ended, word went out to all the provinces and orders of what the new Lord-Inca wished to have done, and certain of the *Orejones* were sent to Quito to bring back his father's wives and servitors.

80

Atahualpa learned how Huascar had assumed the fringe and expected all to render him obedience. The captains of Huayna Capac had not departed from Quito and its confines, and secret conferences were held among them as to whether the thing to do would not be to seize the lands of Quito without going to Cuzco at the summons of Huascar, for that was a fair land where they were all as well off as in Cuzco. Some of them did not hold with this, saying that it was not lawful to deny recognition of the great Inca, for he was the lord of all. But Illa Tupac was not loyal to Huascar, as Huayna Capac had enjoined upon him and he had promised, for they say that he carried on secret conversations with Atahualpa, who, of all the sons of Huayna Capac, was the one who showed most determination and valor, either as the result of his own ambition and the support he found, or because his father had decreed (if this was true) that he should govern Quito and its environs. Atahualpa talked with the captains, Calicuchima, Aclahualpa, Rumiñahui, Quizquiz, Zopozopanqui, and many others, asking them if they would help and support him to become the Inca of those regions as his brother was of Cuzco. And they and Illa Tupac, traitor to his liege Lord-Inca Huascar, for having been named regent until he should come of age, he betrayed him and went over to Atahualpa, who was now accepted as Lord-Inca by all the army, and the wives of his father were handed over to him, and he took them for himself, which gave him great standing among these peoples, and the service of his household and all his other possessions, so that he might use them as he wished.

There are some who tell that certain of the sons of Huayna Capac, brothers of Huascar and Atahualpa, and other *Orejones* fled to Cuzco to carry word of all this to Huascar; and when he and the old *Orejones* of Cuzco learned what Atahualpa had done, they considered that he had done evil, and had gone against their gods and the orders and statutes of the past Lord-Incas. They said they would not suffer or tolerate that the bastard should bear the name of Inca, but would punish him for what he had carried out with the help of the captains and troops of his father. Accordingly, Huascar ordered preparations to be made everywhere, and arms got ready, and the storehouses stocked with the necessary supplies, for he was setting out to make war on the traitors, unless each and every one recognized him as Lord-Inca. He sent ambassadors to the Cañari to strengthen them in their friendship, and it is said that he sent to Atahualpa himself one of his chieftains to warn him not to proceed with his plan, for it was so evil, and to speak to Colla Tupac, his uncle, and advise him to come where he was. When all this had been done, he named as captain general one of the leading men of Cuzco, by name Atoco.

81

CHAPTER 22 (ii: LXXI)

Of how the struggle between Huascar and Atahualpa began and the great battles that were fought between them.

IT BECAME KNOWN throughout all the kingdom of Peru that Huascar was the Inca, and as such he ruled and had his guard and sent out *Orejones* to the capitals of the provinces to take the needed measures. He was of such good intelligence and so cherished his people that, during the time he reigned, he was greatly beloved by all. According to what the Indians say, he was about twenty-five years old when he began his reign. After he had appointed Atoco as his commander, he ordered him to gather the troops he deemed necessary in the places through which he passed, *mitimaes* and natives, and to proceed to Quito to put down the revolt his brother was attempting, and to hold that land for him.

These Indians tell things in many different ways. But I always follow the best opinion, that of the oldest and best informed of them, who are nobles, for what the common folk tell cannot be considered the truth just because they say it. Thus, some say that Atahualpa, when he had resolved not only to deny obedience to his brother, who was now Lord-Inca, but even to take for himself the kingdom by any means he could, and as he was supported by the captains and soldiers of his father, came to the Cañari, where he talked with the native lords and the *mitimaes,* alleging, with pretexts he invented, that his desire was not to do harm to his brother for his own advantage only, but to have them all as friends and kinsmen and to make of Quito another Cuzco in which all could rejoice; and inasmuch as he was so well disposed, to make sure they felt the same way toward him, they should allow him to build himself lodgings and rest houses in Tomebamba, where he, as Lord-Inca, could take his pleasure with his women, as his father and grandfather had done. He said other things in this same vein which were not as joyfully received as he had thought, for the messenger of Huascar had arrived, and had told the Cañari and *mitimaes* that Huascar expected them to honor their pledges of friendship and not to oppose his fortune, and for this he sought the help of the sun and his gods, and that they should not allow the Cañari to be party to the evil intent his brother had set afoot, and they wept with longing to see Huascar, and raising their hands, they pledged that they would keep faith with him.

This being their frame of mind, Atahualpa was unable to do anything with them; on the contrary, it is said that the Cañari with the captain and *mitimaes* seized Atahualpa, with the intention of taking him to Huascar. They had put him in a room of the lodging, but he managed to escape and got to Quito, where he gave out that with the help of God he had turned himself into a snake to evade his enemies, and that all should prepare for open war, for that was the best plan. Other Indians tell as the truth that Captain Atoco and his men came to the Cañari, where Atahualpa was, and that it was he who seized him, and he made his escape, as has been told. I myself believe, though it may have happened differently, that it was Atoco who took Atahualpa prisoner, and, greatly chagrined at his escape, with all the troops he could raise among the Cañari, he set out for Quito, sending messengers everywhere to strengthen the governors and *mitimaes* in their support of Huascar. It is told as a fact that Atahualpa managed to escape by making a hole with an *oca,* which is a crowbar, which a woman, Quella, gave him, while the guard of the lodging were in their cups from much drinking, and with all haste he managed to reach Quito, as has been told, without being overtaken by his enemies, who would have given a great deal to get their hands on him again.

CHAPTER 23 (ii: LXXII)

Of how Atahualpa marched from Quito with his army and captains, and the battle he fought with Atoco in the settlements of Ambato.

As THE POSTS along the highway were so numerous, nothing could occur in any part of the kingdom that was not known, but, on the contrary, became common knowledge everywhere. When it was learned that Atahualpa had made his escape and was in Quito assembling an army, it instantly became apparent that there would be war, and this resulted in divisions, pacts, and ideas that boded no good. Huascar, in his sphere, had the obedience of all, and there was none who did not hope that he would emerge from the conflict with victory and honor. Atahualpa had on his side the captains and army, and many of the native lords and *mitimaes* of the provinces and regions of that area. They say that in Quito he swiftly sent out troops, swearing by the oaths they use that he would inflict condign punishment on the Cañari for the affront he had received from them. When he learned that Atoco was moving toward him with his cohorts, which were said to exceed forty *huarangas,* that is to say, forty thousand, he quickly went to meet him.

Atoco came marching so that Atahualpa would have no opportunity to call up the troops of the provinces, and when he learned that he [Atahualpa] was advancing, he spoke to his men, reminding them that the honor of their Lord-Inca Huascar was in their hands, and that they should stint no effort to punish the insolence of Atahualpa. To strengthen his cause, he sent him, so they say, messengers admonishing him to be satisfied with what he had done, and not to set off a conflagration throughout the kingdom, and to recognize the Lord-

Inca Huascar, which would be the wisest course. And although these messengers were the greatest of the *Orejones,* it is said that he laughed at Atoco's message, and with threats and great savagery ordered them put to death, and proceeded in his rich litter, which was borne on the shoulders of his most important counselors and closest associates.

84

It is said that he put the conduct of the war in the hands of his captain-general, Calicuchima,[1] and two other captains, by name Quizquiz and Ucumari, and as Atoco moved forward with his army, they met near the town of Ambato, where, after their manner, they joined battle, which was hard fought. Calicuchima, having seized a hill, at the suitable moment attacked with a force of full five thousand men, and falling on those who were weary, pressed them so hard that after most of them were killed, the survivors fled in terror, hotly pursued, and many of them were taken prisoner, among them Atoco. Those who have informed me concerning this say that he was tied to a post and secretly put to death with great cruelty, and from his skull Calicuchima made himself a drinking bowl, set in gold. The most accepted opinion, and which I believe to be true, is that the losses on both sides in this battle amounted to fifteen or sixteen thousand, and most of the prisoners that were taken were put to death without mercy by Atahualpa's orders. I have been through this town, and have seen the battlefield; probably even more died than they tell.

With this victory Atahualpa's fame grew, and the news of it spread through the kingdom, and those who supported his cause called him Inca, and he said that he intended to assume the fringe in Tomebamba, although, if this was not done in Cuzco, it was held ineffective and worthless. He ordered the wounded to be cured; issued commands like a Lord-Inca, and as such he was obeyed, and he set out from Tomebamba.

[1] Calicuchima was one of the great Inca generals. He defeated Atoco and the faction of Huascar at the battle near Ambato, captured him, killed him, and made a drinking cup out of his skull. When Atahualpa was captured by the Spaniards, he came attended by a numerous retinue, borne in a palanquin, and when he faced Atahualpa, he groveled before him as the lowest of the Indians. This much impressed the Spaniards; he was burned at the stake by Francisco Pizarro in 1534. Quizquiz, another of the famous generals, retreated after the death of Atahualpa into Ecuador with a large body of troops. Sebastián de Belalcázar pursued him and defeated him in sight of Riobamba.

CHAPTER 24 (ii: LXXIII)

How Huascar dispatched captains and troops against his enemy [Atahualpa] once more, and how Atahualpa came to Tomebamba, and the great cruelty with which he acted there, and what took place between him and Huascar's captains.

ONLY A SHORT TIME elapsed before the news of the defeat and destruction of Captain Atoco's army in the town of Ambato became known not only in Cuzco, but everywhere, and Huascar was dismayed and disheartened over the outcome of the affair. But his advisers urged him not to abandon Cuzco, but to send out a new army and captains. There was great mourning for the dead, and sacrifices were made in temples and shrines, after their usage, and Huascar sent out an appeal to many of the native lords of Colla, the Canchis, Canas, Chancas, Caranquis, and those of Condesuyo, and many from Chinchay-suyu. When they had all come before him, he spoke to them of what his brother was doing, and asked them to behave toward him as friends and comrades. Those present replied in keeping with his desires, for they were deeply bound by the rite and custom that none should be recognized as Inca except the one who had assumed the fringe in Cuzco, which Huascar had done some time before, and the kingdom held him to be the rightful heir. As it was necessary to take immediate steps to proceed with the war in which he was engaged, according to certain of the *Orejones,* he appointed one of his brothers, Huanca Auqui, as captain-general, though there are those who say that the choice fell on a son of Ilaquito. With him he named as captains other important men of his people, namely Ahuapanti, Urco Huaranca, and Inca Roca. These set out from Cuzco with the force they were able to muster, and were joined by many of the native lords and *mitimaes,* and wherever Huanca Auqui went, he took the men he wished and everything else needful for the conduct of war, and proceeded as swiftly as he could in search of Atahualpa who, after defeating and killing Atoco, as has been hold, directed his march toward Tomebamba, accompanied by his captains and many men of importance who had come to ingratiate themselves with him, seeing that he was the conqueror.

The Cañari were fearful of Atahualpa, because they had failed to carry out his orders, and had had a hand in his imprisonment; they mistrusted that he planned them injury, for they knew he was vengeful and bloodthirsty. When he approached their main settlements, according to many Indians I talked with, to placate his wrath they sent out a company of children and another of men of all ages to meet his litter, in which he came with great pomp, bearing green branches and palm fronds, to implore his favor and friendship for the settlement, without remembering past offenses, and they besought him with such outcries and humility that it would have moved a heart of stone. But it made little impression on cruel Atahualpa, for it is told that he ordered his captains and men to kill all those who had come to meet him, and this was done, with the exception of only a few children and the vestals of the temple, whom, in honor of his god, the sun, he spared.

After this he ordered certain persons of the province put to death, set up a captain and steward by his own hand, and having brought together all the rich men of the district, he assumed the fringe and took the title of Inca in Tomebamba, although, as I have said, this was worthless, as the ceremony had not been performed in Cuzco. But his strength was in his troops, and for him might made right. I have heard from certain Indians that Atahualpa assumed the fringe in Tomebamba before he was made prisoner or Atoco had set out from Cuzco, and that Huascar learned of it and took the steps he did. But I think what was earlier said is more likely.

Huanca Auqui proceeded by forced marches, for he hoped to reach the Cañari before Atahualpa worked the harm he did. Some of the men who had escaped from the battle of Ambato joined him. They all tell that he had a force of more than eighty thousand soldiers, and Atahualpa had more or less the same number when he set out from Tomebamba, saying that he would not stop until he reached Cuzco. But in the province of the Paltas, near Cajabamba, the two armies met, and after each captain had harangued and heartened his men, battle was joined. It is said that Atahualpa did not participate in it, but watched from a small hill. God so willing, despite the fact that in Huascar's army there were many *Orejones* and captains who, for them, were skilled in war, and albeit Huanca Auqui behaved as a good and loyal servant of the Lord-Inca, Atahualpa won the victory, slaying many of his adversaries, so many that it is said that more than thirty-five thousand were killed on both sides, and many were wounded.

The enemy pursued them, killing, taking prisoner, and sacking the camps. Atahualpa was so happy that he said his gods had fought on his side. As the Spaniards had already entered the kingdom some time before,[1] and Atahualpa had word of this, for this reason he did not proceed in person to Cuzco.

87

CHAPTER 25 (LVI)

Of the settlements of Indians between Tomebamba and the city of Loja, and of the founding of the latter.

LEAVING TOMEBAMBA by the great highway leading to the city of Cuzco, one crosses the entire province of the Cañari until reaching Cañari-bamba and other lodgings farther on. Everywhere there are settlements to be seen and a mountain which lies to the east, whose slope is peopled, and which descends toward the Marañón River. Once out of the boundary limits of these Cañari, one comes to the province of the Paltas,[1] where there are lodgings known today as

---

[1] The Spaniards made their first contact with the Incas at Tumbes in 1527 (see page 51). The second coming of the Spaniards to Tumbes was on May 13, 1532; 130 foot soldiers and 40 cavalry entered Cajamarca on "Friday the 15th of November, 1532, and at the hour of vespers." The next day towards dusk (Atahualpa thought that the horses were powerless at night) the Incas moved into the Spanish ambush. (See von Hagen, *Realm of the Incas,* 219–23.)

---

[1] Cieza does not detail this route; however, the first tambo stop south of Tomebamba was Cumbe on the *páramo* of Sarar; then Nabon on the heights overlooking the Leonguaicu River; Oña followed, which was reached after crossing the *páramo* of Alpachaca (*chaca* means "bridge," and there are many suspension bridges along the route); at the height of 11,000 feet, Humboldt in the month of July, 1802, could glimpse the Pacific Ocean sixty miles away on a line with the Isle of Puná in the Gulf of Guayaquil. Saragaru, the next tambo stop, was an important center of the Palta tribe. Saragaru [possibly "Las Piedras" of Cieza] has remains of fortresses at Paquishapa, confirming the statement of Cieza that "this province of the Paltas was considered important." The Royal Road of the Incas then continued down over the Alto de Pullal, reaching first Tambo Blanco [Las Ventas], "where," as Cieza states, "the highway

Las Piedras, because there were many and fine-quality stones to be seen there, which the Lord-Incas in the days of their rule had sent to their stewards or representatives, for as this province of the Paltas was considered important, these lodgings were built fine and spacious, and the stone of which they were built was very skillfully cut and joined.

88

To the west of these lodgings lies the city of Puerto Viejo, to the east, the provinces of Bracamoros, where there are great wastelands and many rivers, some of which are large and swift flowing. There is great hope that twenty or thirty days' journey inland rich and fertile land will be discovered; and there are high mountains, some of them very difficult and fearsome. The Indians go naked, and are less intelligent than those of Peru: they were never conquered by the Lord-Incas.

It is well known among many of the natives of these regions that Huayna Capac entered the land we call Bracamoros,[2] and emerged fleeing the fury of those who dwelt there, who had joined forces and assembled to defend themselves against their aggressor. Aside from the *Orejones* of Cuzco, this is so stated by the lords of Chincha, and some of the leading men of Colla and Jauja. They are all in agreement that when Huayna Capac was completing the pacification of those lands through which his father had passed and had subdued, he learned that in Bracamoros there were many men and women possessed of fertile lands, and well inland there was a lake and many rivers beside which there were large settlements. Eager to discover and bring them under his rule, with the troops he judged necessary and with little baggage, he gave marching orders, leaving the bulk

---

meets the Catu-mayu River." The next stop, an important one, was the royal tambo of Loja [Zarza].

The Paltas occupied southern Ecuador and part of Peru; they centered about Loja on the headwaters of the Zamora River which leads into the Upper Amazon. They were newcomers to the mountains; their language was understandable to the Jívaros, the head-hunting Shuaras who occupied the forests immediately below them. They adopted mountain agriculture and dress, and their dwellings were of the same structure as all other pre-Inca structures in Ecuador. *Palta* is Quechua for avocado. (See Humboldt, *Receuil d'Observations Astronomiques,* 311–12; and Martín de Morúa, "Historia de Origen y Genealogía . . . Incas del Perú."

[2] This part of Huayna Capac's military disaster while attacking the head-hunters of the Amazon is taken from the second Chronicle, Chapter LXIV, "How Huayna Capac entered Bracamoros [in the Upper Amazon] and was obliged to flee, and the other things that happened to him until he reached Quito."

of his army in the royal lodgings under the command of his captain-general. They made their way through the land they entered with difficulty, for after crossing the range of snow-covered peaks, they came to the Andes, where they encountered swift-flowing rivers and heavy rains. All this did not, however, prevent the Inca from reaching the fortresses where the natives from many regions were awaiting him, and they received him uncovering their private parts and mocking him for coming. Battle was joined, and so many of the barbarians had come together, most of them naked, without clothing of any sort, so it is said, that the Inca decided to retire, and did so without having won anything in that land. When the natives saw this, they so harried him that by forced marches, at times engaging them, at times sending gifts, he managed to escape from them and returned in flight to his kingdom, swearing that he would avenge himself on those "long tails," to whom he gave this name because some of them wore such long loincloths that they hung down to their legs. For these Indians of the provinces of the Bracamoros resemble those in most of their habits and in having the same inclinations. It is said that they are very brave and warlike, and even the *Orejones* of Cuzco admit that Huayna Capac fled from their fury. Captain Pedro de Vergara spent several years exploring and conquering the region, and he made some settlements there.

From the province of the Cañari to the city of Loja (which is also known as Zarza) they calculate seventeen leagues. The road is rough all the way; there are a number of swamps. In between lies the province of the Paltas, as I have said.

After leaving the lodgings of Las Piedras, one comes to a range of mountains, not very high, though very cold, which extends for a little more than ten leagues, at the end of which there is another lodging place, by name Tambo Blanco, where the highway meets the Cata-mayu River.

To the right, close to this same river, the city of Loja is situated.

On either side of this city of Loja there are many and very large villages, and the natives of them observe and hold almost the same customs as their neighbors. For identification they wear their fillets or headbands. They have the same religious rites as the others, worshiping the sun as god, and other more common things. They recognize a Creator of all things like the others, and with regard to the immortality of the soul, all understood that there was more to man than the mortal body. When the chieftains died, misled by the devil like most of these other Indians, they laid them in large tombs, accompanied by living women and their prized possessions.

90 And even the poor Indians gave much thought to the adornment of their graves. But now that some of them have come to understand how little their ancient vanities boot them, they no longer put women into the grave with the dead, nor shed human blood, nor pay so much attention to the matter of burial. On the contrary, they laugh at those who still do it, and abjure what their forebears esteemed so highly. As a result, they not only do not waste time in preparing these solemn graves, but, on the contrary, when they feel that death is approaching, they order themselves buried in small, unpretentious graves like the Spaniards. In hidden and remote spots of the settlements and roads where the Spaniards live and travel, and in the high hills or among snow-covered rocks they order their bodies laid, wrapped in fine garments and large, bright blankets, with all the gold they possess. And while their souls wander in darkness, they mourn them for many days, and with the consent of those to whom the matter has been entrusted, several women are killed to keep them company, and much food and drink is laid with them.

Most of the settlements under the jurisdiction of Loja were ruled by the Incas, who had their capital in Cuzco, a city made illustrious by them and which was always the head of all the provinces. And despite the fact that many of these Indians had little reason, through their contact with the Incas they left many of their barbarous ways and acquired more polity.

The climate of these provinces is pleasant and healthy; the valleys and river banks are more temperate than the highlands. In the settled parts of the highlands the land is good, too, cold rather than warm, and the deserts and mountains and snow-covered rocks are extremely cold. There are many guanacos and vicuñas, which resemble the llamas, and many partridges, some a little smaller than hens and others larger than turtledoves. The valleys and river bottoms are thickly wooded, and there are many trees of the native fruits, and the Spaniards have now planted vines and figs, oranges, and other trees of Spain. Around this city of Loja there are great droves of swine of Spanish stock, and goats and other livestock, for there is good pasturage and rivers everywhere which descend from the mountains and their waters are very delicate. There is hope of finding in the environs of this city rich mines of gold and silver, and some have already been discovered. The Indians, now that they are safe against the ravages of war and have peace, and are masters of their person and lands, raise many chickens of Spanish stock, and capons, pigeons, and other things that have been introduced. Vegetables grow very well in this new city and its environs. Some of the natives of the provinces under its jurisdiction are of medium stature, others not. They all go clothed in shirts and blankets, and their women the same. In the heart of the forest beyond it, the natives say there is a great settlement and several large rivers, and that the people are rich in gold, in spite of the fact that they all, men and women, go naked, for the land must be hotter than Peru and because the Incas did not bring them under their rule.[3]

The site of Loja[4] is the best and most suitable that could have been chosen in this region of the province. The *repartimientos* of Indians held by its inhabitants were first assigned to those who were residents of Quito and San Miguel. This city was founded because the Spaniards who traveled by the highway to reach Quito and other places were in danger from the Indians of Carrochamba and Chaparra.

Following the same highway [of the Lord-Incas in] the mountains, one comes to the provinces of Calva and Ayabaca, to the east of which lie the heaths and mountains of the Andes, and to the west, the [Yungas] . . . of which I shall speak later.[5]

In the province of Cajas[6] there were great lodgings and storehouses

---

3 Pedro Cieza de León: "Captain Alonso de Mercadillo, with a force of Spaniards, went out this year of 1550 to investigate this report, which is considered important."

4 Loja was founded close to the Incaic royal tambo at Cusi-pampa. The buildings and road (the Royal Road between Quito and Cuzco) were still there in 1560 when Pedro Salinas Loyola traveled there: ". . . ancient buildings here and elsewhere along the whole 'camino real'; the good roads are those which the Indians made . . . among the noteworthy in the world." Loja became famous later, after 1631, when quinine was brought from the mountains to the Countess of Chinchón, who was dying of malaria in Lima. Loja is close to the frontier with modern Peru. (See Salinas Loyola, *Relación y Descripción de la ciudad de Loja* [1571 RGI], III, 205; and Victor Wolfgang von Hagen, *Ecuador and the Galápagos Islands*, 90–102 ["A Tree Grows in Loja"].)

5 This section begins at the second paragraph of Chapter LVIII of Cieza's original Chronicle (1553).

6 Cajas (the modern town of this name is quite near to the Inca ruins) is famed in the Spanish conquest since Hernando de Soto set off with forty soldiers at the beginning of the conquest on a lateral road that connected Zaran on the coast with

built at the order of the Incas and the governor, where there was a number of *mitimaes,* whose duty it was to collect the contributions. Leaving Cajas, one travels until one reaches the province of Huancabamba,[7] where there were larger buildings than in Calva, because the Incas had fortifications there, and among them there was a fortress which I saw, now in ruins and useless like all the rest. Here in Huancabamba there was a temple of the sun with many women. From all these regions they came to worship in this temple and bring their offerings; the virgins and attendants who resided in it were held in high esteem and reverence, and the rulers of all these provinces brought their contributions here, unless ordered to send them to Cuzco. Beyond Huancabamba there are other lodgings and peoples.

92

In bygone times certain of these Indians warred and were at strife with the others, as they themselves tell, and killed one another over trifles, seizing the women, and they even say they went naked and that some of them ate human flesh, resembling in this and in other things the natives of the province of Popayán. When they were conquered and came under the rule of the Lord-Incas, they left off

---

the royal mountain road. In June, 1532, De Soto and his myrmidons entered "a village surrounded by mountains." Here they saw the first evidences of the grandeur of the empire that they had come to conquer, "fine edifices and a fortress built entirely of cut stone . . . and also the royal road . . . so broad that six men on horseback could ride abreast." The ruins of Cajas are still extant, as well as those at Ayabaca to the north. Humboldt saw them in August, 1802: "grand village Peruvién . . . à deux lieues au sud des ruines intéressantes du palais de l'Inca à Suquhu-bamba." (Humboldt, *Recueil d'Observations Astronomiques;* and von Hagen, *Highway of the Sun,* 276–93 [Chapter XVI, "A Great City Called Tumpiz"].)

[7] Huancabamba, visited by Hernando de Soto after the Cajas adventure, who found it "larger than Cajas with better buildings and a fortress built entirely of stone"; it was one day's journey from Cajas along the royal road. It had in addition to the fortress a sun temple and an *Aclla-huasi*—house of the Chosen Women. It was an important region before the Inca conquest; the name itself is Quechua, meaning "valley-of-the-field guardian." Little is known of this tribe in pre-Inca times except that its influence extended down into the jungles about the Marañón; von Hagen, with the Inca Highway Expedition, in 1954 found evidences of the road that had been built by the Huancas and enlarged by the Incas to exploit the jungles about Jaén (see map). However, the Incas were repulsed by the people called Aguarunas (water-people). They were (and still are) head-hunters, sharing the same culture and language as the Shuara tribes of Ecuador. The Jívaros [Shuaras] are scattered over a vast territory approximating 25,000 square miles; language, appearance, beliefs, and customs are closely interrelated; those on the Marañón called Aguarunas are actually Huambizas.

After the conquest of northern Peru, including Huancabamba, the Inca ordered a lateral road to extend down to the Marañón, from which the conquered people obtained gold, feathers, and wood. Topa Inca began the assault some time after 1470. The army met with disaster, as Cieza gathered from firsthand information.

many of these customs and adopted the polity and reasonable procedure they now employ, which is more than some of us admit. And they laid out their settlements in different fashion. They wear clothing made of wool of their flocks, which is of fine quality and useful for that purpose, and they no longer eat human flesh, holding it, on the contrary, to be a great sin, and they abominate those who do so. 93 And despite the fact that they are all inhabitants of these provinces which border on those of Puerto Viejo and Guayaquil, they did not indulge in the abominable sin of sodomy, for I gathered from them that they considered it beastly, and held anyone guilty of it benighted and deceived by the devil. They tell that before the natives of these regions were subdued by the Inca Pachacuti, and his son, Topa Inca, who was the father of Huayna Capac and grandfather of Atahualpa, they resisted so stoutly and so stubbornly that, rather than lose their freedom, many thousands of them died, with a considerable number of the *Orejones* of Cuzco. But they were so hard pressed that certain captains, to prevent their complete extermination, swore fealty to the Incas in the name of all.

The men of these regions are dark, of goodly aspect; they and their women go dressed in the fashion they learned from the Incas, their former rulers. In certain districts they wear their hair overly long; in others, short; and in some places, tightly braided. If any hairs of the beard grow, they cut them off, and throughout all the lands that I traveled, only exceptionally did I ever see a bearded Indian. They all understand the common language of Cuzco, in spite of which they employ their own tongue, as I have related. There used to be an abundance of llamas; now there are few as a result of the wanton killing by Spaniards. Their clothing is made of the wool of these llamas, and of that of the vicuñas, which is better and finer, and of the guanacos, which are found in the mountains and uninhabited regions. Those who cannot afford garments of wool use cotton. In the valleys and bottomlands of the settled regions there are many rivers and brooks, and certain springs whose water is good and palatable. Everywhere there are stock-raising farms, and plantations of the produce and roots I have mentioned. Their old temples, commonly known as *huacas,* are all cast down and profaned, and the idols broken, the devil driven from these places. . . . In truth, we Spaniards should be eternally grateful to Our Lord for this.

*Which tells how beyond the province of Huancabamba
lies that of Cajamarca and others that are
large and thickly settled.*

94

RESUMING THIS ROUTE [on the Inca highway], I would say that from Huancabamba to the province of Cajamarca[1] is something like fifty leagues, more or less. This province was famous because of the imprisonment of Atahualpa, and was known throughout the kingdom because of its size and wealth. The natives of Cajamarca tell that they were held in high regard by their neighbors before the Incas brought them under their rule, and that they had their temples and places of worship in the high places of the hills, and that although they went clothed, their attire was not so fine as it was afterwards and is now. Some of the Indians tell that the first to conquer them was the Inca Pachacuti; others, that it was not until the reign of his son, Topa Inca. Whichever it was, it seems to be an established fact that before he made himself master of Cajamarca, he lost many of his troops in battle, and it was by artfulness and gentle words rather than by force that he achieved his conquest. The native rulers of this province were well obeyed by these Indians, and had many wives. One was the principal wife, whose son, if she had one, succeeded to power. And when he died, they observed the same customs as those of the rulers and caciques we have described, burying with him his treasures and wives, with great and prolonged mourning. Their temples and places of worship were greatly venerated, and sacrifices were made of the blood of lambs and llamas, and they say that the priests of these temples talked with the devil. And when they observed their feasts, a great multitude of people assembled in the clean, well-swept squares, where they performed dances with no small quantity of their wine, brewed from corn and other roots, con-

[1] Cajamarca was "held in high regard, especially by the coastal kingdom of Chimor [Chimú], a rival empire of the Incas that had an alliance with Cajamarca [*Cassamarca* means "town in a ravine"]." In 1461 the Inca general Capac Yupanqui appeared at the boundaries of Cajamarca; his forces were vigorously opposed by the chieftain Cusimancu and the fighting was heavy, reinforcements being sent up to the mountains by the coastal Chimús. Eventually Cajamarca was subdued; later the Incas outflanked the kingdom of Chimor and brought about its collapse. (See John H. Rowe, "The Kingdom of Chimor," *Acta Americana*, Vol. VI [1948].)

sumed. They all went dressed in blankets and fine shirts, and about their heads, as a distinguishing insignia, they wore bands, and others, narrow strips like ribands.

After this province of Cajamarca had been won and conquered by the Incas, it is said that they prized it highly and ordered their palaces built there, and erected a temple for the service of the sun, a very splendid one, and many storehouses. And the virgins attached to the temple did nothing but spin and weave clothing fine beyond compare, to which they gave colors so beautiful it would be hard to equal them in most of the world. There was great wealth in this temple for its upkeep. On certain days the devil was seen by his ministers, who talked with him and told him their affairs. In this province of Cajamarca there were many *mitimaes,* and they all obeyed the head steward whose duty is was to provision and command the area and districts to which he was assigned. For, although everywhere and in most of the settlements there were great storehouses and lodgings, it was here that the accounts were rendered, as this was the capital of the neighboring provinces and of many of the valleys of the plains. And they say that in spite of the fact that there were those temples and shrines I have described in the settlements and valleys of the plains, and many others, they came from far and wide to worship the sun and perform sacrifices in this temple.

There were many things to see in the palaces of the Incas, especially fine baths in which the lords and nobles bathed when they lodged there. This province has suffered a great decline after the death of Huayna Capac, the native Lord-Inca of these kingdoms who died the very year and season that the Marquis Don Francisco Pizarro and his thirteen companions,[2] God so willing, were privileged to discover this rich kingdom. When the news of his death reached Cuzco, his eldest son and universal heir, Huascar, son of his legitimate wife, the Coya, as the queen and principal wife is called, assumed the fringe and crown of the whole empire and sent messengers everywhere to inform all that because of the end and death of his father they were to accept and obey him as sole lord. But as in the conquest of Quito the great captains—*Orejones*—who were famous among their own people, had fought with Huayna Capac, they talked of establishing a new Cuzco in Quito and the provinces that lie to the north, as a

[2] See note 1, Chapter 14 for a list of the thirteen men of Gallo.

95

kingdom divided and separate from that of Cuzco, and setting up as Lord-Inca Atahualpa, a noble, intelligent, and astute youth, greatly beloved by all the soldiers and old captains because he had gone out from the city of Cuzco with his father while still a mere boy, and had spent much time with his army. And many Indians even say that Huayna Capac himself, before his death, realizing that the kingdom he was leaving was so large and had over a thousand leagues of coast line and that in the region of the Quillacingas and Popayáns there were great lands, decided to leave him as ruler of the region of Quito and its conquests. Be that as it may, when Atahualpa and his supporters received word that Huascar expected them to render him fealty, they took up arms. Though it is said that first, by a stratagem of Captain Atoco, Atahualpa was taken prisoner in the province of Tomebamba and, so it is said, made his escape with the help of a woman, and when he reached Quito he assembled troops and fought a fierce battle with Captain Atoco in which the latter was killed and Huascar's army routed, as I tell at greater length in the *third* part of this work[3] which is where I deal with the discovery and conquest of this kingdom. . . .

Atahualpa was always victorious; he reached the province of Cajamarca with his army (which is why I deal with this episode here) where he confirmed what he had already heard about the new people who had entered his kingdom, and that they were close by. And believing that he could easily take them prisoner and make them his slaves, he sent Captain Calicuchima with a great army against Cuzco with orders to capture or kill his enemy. After ordering this, he remained in Cajamarca, and the Governor Don Francisco Pizarro arrived, and after the events and incidents earlier described, there came the encounter between the forces of Atahualpa and the Spaniards, who numbered no more than 160, in which many Indians died and Atahualpa was taken prisoner. With these conflicts and the long sojourn of the Spaniards in Cajamarca, it was left in such shape that it can be judged only by its reputation, for beyond question it suffered great harm. Later it was somewhat restored, but as there has never been a lack of war and disasters, it is not and never again will it be

[3] The Third Part of this work—*La Tercera Parte de la Crónica del Perú*—has been found and is now being edited by Rafael Loredo (see Editor's Introduction, p. lxxiv).

what it was. All the edifices of the Incas and the storehouses were, like the rest, destroyed and ruined.

This province of Cajamarca is fertile in extreme, for wheat does as well here as in Sicily, and cattle thrive, and there is an abundance of corn and other edible roots, and all the fruits I have mentioned in other places. In addition there are falcons and many partridges, pigeons, doves, and other game. The Indians are well mannered, peaceable, and by and large they have certain good habits which makes life easy for them; they give small thought to honors and thus are not ambitious to seek them. They lodge the Spaniards who pass through their province and feed them well, without harming or ill-treating them, even if they are traveling alone. The Spaniards who have spent time among these Indians of Cajamarca praise them highly for these and other things. They are very skilled at digging irrigation ditches and building houses, cultivating the land, and raising cattle, and they work gold and silver expertly. And with their hands they weave as good tapestry as in Flanders from the wool of their flocks, and so fine that it seems of silk rather than of wool. The women are loving and some of them beautiful. Many of them dress like the *pallas* of Cuzco. Their temples and burial places are now destroyed and their idols broken. Many of them have accepted Christianity and there are always priests and friars among them teaching them the precepts of our holy Catholic faith. In the confine of this province of Cajamarca there are always rich mines.[4]

97

CHAPTER 27 (LXXVIII)

Of the founding of the city of [Chachapoyas], city of Frontera, who was its founder, and certain of the customs of the Indians of its region.

BEFORE REACHING the province of Cajamarca, one comes to a road

---

[4] Humboldt has left us in his charming *Views of Nature* a very interesting picture of the Cajamarca of 1802, his visit to Atahualpa's ransom room, and his meeting with Astopilca, said to have been a direct descendant of that unfortunate Inca. See also W. B. Stevenson, *A Historical and Descriptive Narrative of Twenty Years' Residence in South America* (3 vols., London, 1825).

that was also ordered built by the Lord-Incas, which leads to the provinces of the Chachapoyas. . . .[1]

When Huayna Capac arrived at Cajamarca, he remained there several days to rest from his march, and ordered his troops lodged on the outskirts of the country, and to eat of what was in the storehouses. Then with the number of troops he thought advisable, he entered the land of the Huancachupachos, and fought a hard war with them, for the natives had not been entirely satisfied and submissive under his father; but he was so strong that he conquered and subdued them, and appointed governors and captains, and named native lords to rule the lands, those he judged best fitted, for they, from olden times, had recognized no other lords than those who, being the most powerful, arose to lead them in war, and made peace when they wished. Among the Chachapoyas, Huayna Capac met great resistance, so much that twice he had to make a hasty retreat to the fortresses he had built for defense. But with reinforcements that were brought him he marched upon the Chachapoyas once more and inflicted such a defeat on them that they sued for peace, and laid down their arms. The Inca granted them favorable terms and ordered many of them to take up their residence in Cuzco, where their descendants still live; he took many women because they are handsome and comely and very white; he set up garrisons of *mitimaes* as soldiers, to guard the frontier. He appointed a governor in the capital of the region; he supplied them with what they most used; he punished many of the headmen because they had made war on him; and when all this was done, he returned to Cajamarca, whence he continued his trip, and brought the provinces of Cajas, Ayahuaca, Huancabamba, and others which neighbor on them into order.

And so, after they came under the rule of the Inca, many of them were ordered to Cuzco, where they were given lands to cultivate and sites for their houses not far from a hill close to the city called Car-

[1] Chachapoyas (2,328 meters) lies west of the Marañón above the Uctubamba River; the jungles of the Amazon lie to the north and west of it. The whole area is filled with the ruins of a culture which existed before and contemporaneous with that of the Incas. The remains are massive and interesting. (See Henry and Paule Reichlen, "Recherches Archéologiques dans les Andes du Haut Uctubamba," *Jour. de la Soc. des Américanistes*, Vol. XXXIV [1950], 219–46). The tribes were called Chacha, Huanca, Chillao, and Cascayunca before they were conquered by and incorporated into the Inca state. Chachapoyas is also reached by another road, a stone road over three hundred miles in length originating in Huánuco.

menga. And as the upland provinces that bordered on the Chachapoyas were not wholly pacified, the Incas ordered them and certain of the *Orejones* of Cuzco to establish a frontier garrison as a safeguard. For this reason they had great provision of all the arms they employ to be ready for any contingency. These Chachapoyas Indians are the whitest and most attractive I have seen anywhere I have been in the Indies, and their women were so beautiful that many of them were chosen to be wives of the Incas and vestals of the temples. Even today we see that the women of this lineage who are left are extremely beautiful, as they are very white and many of them very gracefully proportioned. They and their men wear woolen clothing and a headband by which they are known wherever they go. After they were subdued by the Incas, they assumed their laws and customs, by which they lived, and worshiped the sun and other gods.

Alonso de Alvarado entered the settlements of this province of the Chachapoyas . . . and after he had conquered the province and brought the Indians under the authority of His Majesty, he founded and settled the city of Frontera at a spot known as Levanto,[2] a place strong in natural defenses. It was graded with pick and shovel to build the city, though a few days later it was moved to another province called Huancas, which is considered a more healthful region. The Chachapoyas Indians and these Huancas serve the residents of this city to whom they have been assigned, and the same thing happens in the province of Cascayunga and other settlements whose names I omit because they are not important. Throughout all these provinces there were great lodgings and storehouses of the Incas. The settlements are very healthy, and in some of them there are rich gold mines. The natives all go clothed, as do their women. In olden times they had temples and made sacrifice to those they held to be gods, and they had large flocks of llamas. They made fine and highly prized clothing for the Incas, and they still make excellent garments, and tapestry so fine and handsome that it is greatly esteemed for its quality. In many of the aforesaid provinces under the jurisdiction of this city there are groves and an abundant yield of the products I have mentioned on other occasions, and as the land is fertile, wheat and barley do well, as is the case with the vines and figs and other fruit trees that have been brought from Spain.

[2] Levanto is still extant with the ruins of both native and Spanish architecture.

In their customs, ceremonies, burials, and sacrifices, what has been told of the others holds true, for they, too, buried their dead in large graves, accompanied by their wives and wealth. The Spaniards have their plantations around the city, with their cattle and crops, and harvest wheat in abundance, and the vegetables of Spain yield well. To the east of this city runs the range of the Andes; to the west lies the Southern Sea. And beyond the hills and forests of the Andes run the Moyobamba and other large rivers, and there are settlements of less civilized people than these I have been describing. It is considered to be a fact that these provinces of the interior are inhabited by the descendants of the famous chieftain Ancoallo [Hanco-Huallu],[3] who, because of the cruelty with which he was treated by the captains of the Inca, driving him out of his country, left with those of the Chancha who wanted to go with him, as I shall tell in the second part. And there are reports of a famous lake where it is said these settlements are situated.

In the year 1550 there came to the city of Frontera [Chachapoyas] (at the time the noble knight Gómez de Alvarado was mayor) more than two hundred Indians, who told that a large number of them had left the land where they had lived some years before and had traversed many regions and provinces where they made such cruel war against them that they had all died except those I have mentioned. They told that to the east lay great lands, thickly populated, some of them very rich in gold and silver. These Indians, and the rest who died, had set out in search of lands where they could settle, so I was told. Captain Gómez de Alvarado and Captain Juan Pérez de Guevara and others have tried to secure permission to search for and conquer the land, and many soldiers are awaiting the arrival of the viceroy to follow the captain who receives the authorization to make the discovery.

The city of Frontera [Chachapoyas] was founded and settled by Captain Alonso de Alvarado in the name of His Majesty . . . in the year 1536.

[3] "The famous chieftain, Hanco-Huallu," was the leader of the Chancas, that tribe that once had the audacity to attack Cuzco itself. For greater detail, see pp. 130ff. and 228 below.

100

Of what is worth relating from Cajamarca to the valley of Jauja and of the village of Huamachuco, which borders on Cajamarca.

HUAMACHUCO, another large province about eleven leagues beyond Cajamarca, was in ancient times thickly settled. Before reaching it, about halfway, there is a very quiet, pleasant valley, which, as it is sheltered by the sierras, is warm of climate. Through it runs a beautiful river,[1] along whose banks wheat is raised in abundance, and grapes, figs, oranges, lemons, and many other fruits brought from Spain. In olden days on the lowlands and plains of this great valley there were lodgings for the rulers and many fields whose crops were for them and the temple of the sun. The province of Huamachuco resembles that of Cajamarca and the Indians speak the same language and use the same dress, and imitate one another in their religion and rites, as well as in clothing and headbands. There used to be great lords in this province, of Huamachuco, who, so they tell, were highly respected by the Incas.[2]

In the best part of the province there is a great field where the tambos [Viracocha-tambo], or royal palaces, stood, among which there are two that are twenty-two feet wide and about one hundred

[1] "A very quiet, pleasant valley . . . a beautiful river" is the Pampa-runi, through which runs the Crisnejas River (made up of the confluence of the Cajamarca and Condebamba streams). The altitude is 6,500 feet and an Inca bridge crossed this river. There were thermal baths here also, as at Cajamarca.

[2] Huamachuco is on a direct line with Chan-Chan (the capital of Chimor) on the coast, and lies at 12,200 feet. It was the center of one of the larger tribes of an Andean area which was divided into an almost unbelievable number of small political units. There are vast pre-Inca ruins, which, although studied, are unassigned as to definite period or culture except the general term "Andean archaic." Because of the Inca system of complete absorption of conquered tribes and their selective manipulation of remembered history, so as to appear to be culture bearers, names and customs of most of these pre-Inca regions, such as Huamachuco, have disappeared. Before 1473, when the Incas began their *drang nach norden,* the "good Prince Huamachucu," according to Garcilaso de la Vega, asked Topa Inca to enter his lands peacefully. The Incas did, took over, commanded a field called Viracocha-pampa, and there built sun temples, royal palaces, and tambos, and connected it with roads to Cuzco. Hernando Pizarro entered the city in January, 1553, making his gold-gathering and iconoclastic anabasis to Pachacamac from Cajamarca, and he pronounced it "large and well situated in a valley surrounded by mountains." (See T. D. McCown, *Pre-Incaic Huamachuco,* and Francisco de Xeres, *Verdadera Relación de la Conquista del Perú.*")

feet long, all of stone, and trimmed with long, thick beams covered with straw, which they employ very skillfully. With the past disturbances and wars, many of the people of this province have disappeared. Its climate is good, cool rather than warm, and it produces abundant food and other things needful for human life. Before the Spaniards entered this kingdom, there were in the lands of this province of Huamachuco many flocks of llamas, and in the highlands and unsettled regions a still greater number of wild flocks, called guanacos and vicuñas, which resemble the domesticated llama.

102

In the valleys of the plains, and other warm regions, the natives plant cotton and make their clothing of it, so they lack for nothing, inasmuch as cotton clothing is suitable for these lands.

In many parts of the highlands, such as the province of Colla, and among the Soras and Charcas of the city of [La] Plata [i.e., Potosí in Bolivia], and in other valleys, no trees grow nor does cotton mature even if it is planted. And if it were not by trading, it would be impossible for all the natives to have clothing. Thus, the author of all good, God, made to grow in these regions such numbers of these llamas we call sheep that, if the Spaniards with their wars had not almost exterminated them, there would be no tale of the number of them to be found everywhere. But, as I have said, the wars the Spaniards waged against one another were like a plague for the Indians and the [llama] flocks. The natives call the females *llamas* and the males *urcos*. Some of them are white, some black, and others brown. Some of them are the size of small donkeys, with long legs and broad bellies; their body and neck resemble that of a camel; the head is long, like that of the sheep of Spain. The meat is excellent if the animals are fat, and the lambs are better and more flavorful than those of Spain. They are very tame and make no noise. The llamas can carry loads of two or three arrobas easily and when they can no longer work, there is no loss, for the meat is good. In the Colla [Lake Titicaca region] it is a pleasure to see the Indians set out with these llamas and their plows, and come back in the afternoon with loads of wood. They feed on grass. When they are tired, they lie down like camels and groan. There is another species of this animal called guanaco, similar in form and shape, but larger, which are wild, and one sees great flocks of them in the mountains, and they go leaping along so swiftly that the dog that can overtake them has to be very fast indeed.

In addition to these there is still another variety of them, known as vicuñas. These are even swifter than the guanacos, though smaller; they live in the uninhabited regions eating the grass God makes to grow there. The wool of these vicuñas is so fine that it surpasses that of the Merinos [sheep] of Spain. I do not know if it could be used for [our form of woven] cloth, but I can say that the garments they used to make of it for the rulers of this land were a beautiful thing. The meat of these vicuñas and guanacos is a little gamey. There is another kind of domestic animal they call *paco* [alpaca]. They are very ugly and woolly, and resemble llamas or sheep, except that they are smaller. When they are young, they are very much like the lambs of Spain. These bear young only once a year.[3]

103

The Incas had in this province, so I have been informed, a royal forest where the natives were forbidden, under penalty of death, to enter and kill any of these wild sheep, of which there were many, and pumas, bears, foxes, and deer.

These Indians of Huamachuco are very domesticated, and have nearly always been closely allied with the Spaniards. In bygone days they had their religions and superstitions, and worshiped certain stones the size of eggs, and others still larger, of different colors, which they had in their temples or shrines in high places and the snowy sierras. When they came under the Incas, they worshiped the sun and became more refined in both their behavior and their personal habits. They used to offer up the blood of llamas and lambs in their sacrifices, skinning them alive without cutting their throats, and then they quickly tore out their hearts and entrails to observe portents and witcheries, for some of them were augurs (as I understood and learned) and watched the movements of comets.

From this province of Huamachuco a highway of the Incas runs to Conchucos and at Bombón it joins another as large as itself. They

[3] These four species of llamoids are related to the proto-cameloid, dominant types of primitive camels, which appeared in the Eocene epoch; it is believed that these, found mostly about what is now Nebraska, evolved into "camel" and "vicuña" faunal readjustments through migration. The vicuña and guanaco, both wild species, were the original types; the llama is a hybrid (as is the alpaca, which is only a fur-bearing species; it is not used for cargo). The llamas, vicuñas, and allied species do not have, as the camel, the hump, sternal knee, or hock callouses; whereas the camel grows to a weight of 2,200 pounds, the llama never surpasses 500. Both llama and camel have a social symbiosis with man. (See von Hagen, *Realm of the Incas*, 80–82; and Raymond M. Gilmore, "Fauna and Ethnozoology of South America," *Handbook*, VI, 429–54.)

say one of these was built at the orders of Topa Inca and the other
by Huayna Capac, his son.

CHAPTER 29 (ii: XVI)

*How and in what manner the royal hunts were carried
on by the Lord-Incas of Peru.*

WHEN THE Lord-Inca decided to organize a royal hunt, the number
killed and taken was amazing; there were days when over thirty
thousand head were taken. But when the Lord-Inca did it for pleasure
and went out only for that, his tents were set up where he indicated;
even in the highest mountains these flocks were always to be found
in the abundance we have noted. There, fifty or sixty thousand people
having gathered, or a hundred thousand if it was so ordered, they
encircled the thickets and fields and with the noise of their shouts
and cries the animals came down from the hills to the level ground,
where, little by little, the men closed ranks until they could join
hands, and in the circle formed by their bodies the game was brought
together and penned in, and the Lord-Inca watched from the post
he chose to see the kill; and other Indians entered with a thing they
call *ayllos* [bolas] which are to throw and entangle the feet, and
others with sticks and clubs, and began to catch and kill them. A
great number of animals were rounded up, among them many guanacos, which are a little larger than small donkeys, with long necks
like camels, that would try to escape, spitting saliva from their mouth
in the men's faces, and breaking through wherever they could with
great bounds. It is said that it is terrifying to hear the noise the
Indians make when they try to catch them, and the uproar of the
animals trying to escape, which can be heard a long distance from
where it takes place. And if the Lord-Inca wished to kill a piece of
game without entering the circle, he did it as he wished.

Many days were spent in these royal hunts, and after a large quantity had been killed, the inspectors were sent for to take all the wool
to the storehouses or temples of the sun so the *mamaconas* could
make attire for the Lord-Inca which was so fine that it seemed silken
serge, and its colors could not have been more perfect. The meat

that was left was eaten by those who were with the Lord-Inca, and part of it was dried in the sun to be put in the storehouses for the fighting men.

CHAPTER 30 (LXXXII)

Of how the Incas ordered the storehouses kept well provisioned, as they were, for their troops.

PROCEEDING FROM this province of Huamachuco by the highway of the Incas, one comes to the province of the Conchucos, two short days' journey from Huamachuco, and midway between them there were lodgings and storehouses for the Lord-Incas to stay when they were traveling.[1] For it was their custom when they were making a progress through any part of this great kingdom to travel with great pomp and fine style, in keeping with their habits, for except when it was to the state's interest, they did not travel more than four leagues a day. And so there would be adequate supplies for their men, every four leagues there were lodgings and storehouses abundantly supplied with everything to be found in these regions. Even in the uninhabited areas and deserts there had to be these lodgings and storehouses, and the representatives or stewards who lived in the capital of the provinces took great care to see that the natives kept these inns or lodgings [tambos] well supplied. And so certain of them would not give more than others, and all should make their contribution, they kept the accounts by a method of knots, which they call *quipus,* and in this way, after the troops had passed by, they could check and see that there had been no fraud. And although to us it may seem strange and awkward, it is a fine way of counting, as I shall explain in the second part. So, although it was only a two days' journey from Huamachuco to the Conchucos, there were these store-

[1] At Mollebamba. There are ruins of the tambo there called Castillo Grande. Here one branch bifurcated down to Corongo and entered the Callejón de Huaylas, for this was the route of Hernando Pizarro; this led to the coast at Paramonga fortress, where it connected with the coastal road (see map). That road which Cieza describes branched eastward and entered Conchucos. It was a royal tambo, with lodgings for the Inca and his governors. The whole region is high, above 13,000 feet; "it is rough country and the Corongos and Pallasca Indians were very warlike; it cost much effort to subdue them," writes one chronicler.

houses and lodgings in two places. And all the roads in this region were very well tended, and where the mountains were too rough, they built them on the hillsides, with terraces and flagged stairways, and so strong that they endure and will endure as they are for many ages.

Among the Conchucos there is no lack of lodgings and the other things we have seen among the peoples already described, and the natives are of medium stature. They and their women go clothed, with their ribands or insignia about their heads. It is said that the Indians of this province were warlike, and the Incas had trouble subduing them, although some of the Incas always tried to win the people over with kindly acts and friendly words. These Indians have killed Spaniards on several occasions, so many that the Marquis Don Francisco Pizarro sent Captain Francisco de Chávez[2] out with a force of Spaniards, and the war they made on them was fierce and horrible, for certain of the Spaniards tell that a great number of the Indians were burned and impaled. The fact of the matter is that during that time, or shortly before, there came the general uprising in most of the provinces, and the Indians in the region between Cuzco and Quito killed with great cruelty over seven hundred Spaniards, those they could take alive and carry away as prisoners. God save us from the fury of the Indians, which is something to be feared when they can give vent to it. They said they were fighting for their freedom and to save themselves from the harsh treatment they suffered; and the Spaniards, to remain in possession of their lands and Indians. In this province of the Conchucos there have always been rich gold and silver mines.

Sixteen leagues beyond lies the province of Piscobamba,[3] where there was also an inn or lodgings for the rulers, made of stone, wide

[2] Francisco de Chávez was an old conquistador, and was involved in the civil wars. He was one of those who protested at the judicial murder of Atahualpa; captured later by the Indians, he was treated well and released. He was killed with Francisco Pizarro in Lima.

[3] Piscobamba was reached (and still is in places) by a spectacularly built Inca road, with ascending stone steps, retaining walls, and drainage system; it moves between the towering snow-capped peaks of the Cordillera Blanca and the deep canyon of the Marañón River at an average altitude of 14,000 to 15,000 feet. Piscobamba, near the Yanamayu River, had a suspension bridge which Hernando Pizarro crossed in April, 1534, with his golden loot from Pachacamac, "two bridges built next to each other . . . with suspension cables waist-thick made of cabuya."

and very long. The Indians of Piscobamba go dressed like the others, and wear on their heads a kind of skein of red wool. In their customs they resemble their neighbors, and they are held to be intelligent and very domesticated, well intentioned and friendly to the Spaniards. The lands where their settlements are situated are fertile and bounteous, and yield abundantly the food and supplies they all plant. Beyond lies the province of Huaraz, eight leagues from Piscobamba over rough mountains, and it is a sight to see the highway, how well built and laid out it is, and how wide and level it runs over the slopes and mountains, parts of it being dug through the living rock to make landings and stairways. These Indians, too, were of medium stature, and they are hard workers and miners of silver, and in the past they paid tribute to the Lord-Incas in this metal. Among the old lodgings there is a large fortress or ancient monument, which is in the shape of a rectangle, 140 feet long and greater in width, and in many parts of it there are human figures and faces, all wonderfully represented. Some of the Indians say that the Incas ordered this fortress built to commemorate some victory they had won, and as a stronghold for their allies. Others say, and it is generally believed, that it was not this, but that in olden times, long before the Incas reigned, there lived in these regions men like giants, as large as the figures sculptured in stone reveal, and that with time and the fierce wars carried on against them by those who are now the rulers of these lands, they died off and disappeared, without leaving any trace of themselves except the stones and structures I have mentioned.

Beyond this province comes that of Pincos [Pachacoto?], near which runs the river Santa, where piles have been sunk to lay the bridge they built to cross it. The natives here are of goodly stature, and, for Indians, they are fine looking. Farther on is the large and sumptuous lodging of Huánuco, the principal seat of all the provinces between it and Cajamarca.

107

CHAPTER 31 (LXXX)

Of the site of this city [Huánuco], the fertility of its countryside, and the customs of the natives, and of a beautiful lodging or palace in Huánuco el Viejo constructed by the Incas.

108

THE SITE of this [new] city of León de Huánuco[1] is good and held to be very salubrious, and praised for its temperate nights and mornings. Because of its good climate people there live healthy. Wheat is produced there in abundance, and corn. There are vineyards, and figs, oranges, citrons, lemons, and other fruits that have been brought from Spain, as well as the native products, and all the vegetables of Spain. In addition there are large banana groves, so it is a good city, and it is believed it will grow better each day. In the country many

[1] Pedro de Cieza de León: "In connection with the founding of the city of León de Huánuco, it should be pointed out that when the Marquis Don Francisco Pizarro founded on the plains and sands the rich City of the Kings, all the provinces that at the time were subordinate to this city served it, and the residents of the City of the Kings held encomienda over the caciques. And as Illatope the tyrant, with his kin and other Indian vassals, was making war on the natives of this province and devastating the settlements, and there were too many *repartimientos,* and many of the conquistadors had had no Indians assigned to them, the Marquis wished to do away with such handicaps, and satisfy them, giving Indians also to some of the Spaniards who had followed Don Diego de Almagro, whom he was trying to win over, contenting them all for they had worked for and served His Majesty, and give them certain benefits from the land. And in spite of the fact that the council of the City of the Kings tried by complaints and in other ways to prevent what he was doing against the interests of his government, the Marquis appointed as his representative Captain Gómez de Alvarado, the brother of the Adelantado Don Pedro de Alvarado, and sent him to found a city in the provinces called Huánuco. Thus Gómez de Alvarado set out, and after certain incidents with the natives, founded the city of León de Huánuco, at the spot he judged most suitable, to which he afterwards gave the name of republic, setting forth the standards he judged advisable for its government. When this had been done, and a number of years had elapsed, the new city was abandoned because of the uprising of the natives throughout the kingdom. A few years later, Pedro Barroso rebuilt the city, and finally, with powers from Master Cristóbal Vaca de Castro, after the cruel battle of Chupas, Pedro de Puelles went to take charge there, and the city was permanently settled, because Juan de Varagas and others had captured the tyrant Illatope. So although what I have set down took place, I can say that the founder was Gómez de Alvarado, for he gave the city its name, and if it was abandoned, it was of necessity and not choice, and he held it so the Spanish settlers could return to their homes. The city was founded and settled in the name of His Majesty, with authorization of the Marquis Don Francisco Pizarro, governor and captain-general of this kingdom, in the year of Our Lord 1539."—Chapter LXXIX [1553], "Which deals with the founding of the [new] city of León de Huánuco and who its founder was."

cows, goats, mares, and other livestock are raised, and it abounds in partridge, turtledoves, pigeons, and other fowl, and falcons to hunt them. In the woods there are some pumas, and bears, and other animals, and highways run through most of the settlements under the jurisdiction of this city and there were well-furnished storehouses and lodgings of the Incas.

In what is known as Huánuco [The Old] there was an admirably built royal palace, made of very large stones artfully joined. This palace or lodging was the capital of the provinces bordering on the Andes, and beside it there was a temple to the sun with many vestals and priests. It was so important in the times of the Incas that there were always over thirty thousand Indians to serve it. The stewards of the Incas were in charge of collecting the regular tributes, and the region served this palace. When the Lord-Incas ordered the headmen of these provinces to appear at the court of Cuzco, they did so. They tell that many of these tribes were brave and strong, and that before the Incas brought them under their rule many and cruel battles were fought between them, and that in most places the villages were scattered and so remote that there were no relations between them except when they met for their gatherings and feasts. On the hilltops they built their strong places and fortresses[2] from which they made war

[2] León de Huánuco (settled in 1539) is on the upper reaches of the Huallaga River, an Amazon tributary under 5,000 feet altitude. Huánuco el Viejo is fifty miles east on an elevation 12,156 feet above sea level. The ruins of Huánuco, located in the old province of Huamalíes, are immense (see detailed plan); the plaza alone, which holds over eight buildings, of which one, "El Castillo," has been often figured, the great square measures 675 feet x 950 feet and is approached by three flights of steps; it is surrounded on all sides by buildings. The over-all measurement of Huánuco is 2,100 feet x 1,900 feet; the structures number more than a thousand. It is fully possible that the inhabitants numbered the "30,000" given by Cieza.

Huánuco was inhabited by other Andean tribes, namely the Yachas, before its conquest by Topa Inca after 1470; it is fully probable that the buildings, which have many non-Inca architectural features, embody some of the structures of this conquered tribe. A massive report, written in 1562 by Iñigo Ortiz de Zúñiga, for the Viceroy to determine why the Indians, living under encomienda to Gómez Arias Dávila—a grant given to him by La Gasca—were not producing the amount of tribute for His Majesty's government that they had in the time of Inca rule, is now ready for publication by the editor.

Huánuco was first seen by the party of Hernando Pizarro on the last day of March, 1534, as they returned through it on the way to Cajamarca with the gold from Pachacamac for the ransom of Atahualpa; "we reached Guaneso [Huánuco] . . . over a road the greater part of which was paved on account of the snow . . . this town is large . . . it is situated in a valley, being three miles in circuit."

The editor is not fully certain that Pedro de Cieza visited Huánuco personally; he

on one another at the slightest pretext. And their temples were located in convenient places for their sacrifices and rites; . . . [yet] beneath their general blindness, they believed in the immortality of the soul. These Indians are intelligent, and they show it in their answers to questions put to them. The native chieftains of these people were never laid in their graves alone, but accompanied by living women, the most beautiful of them, as was the case with the others. And when these chieftains were dead and their soul had departed their body, these women buried with them in those great vaults which are their tombs await the fearful hour of death to go and join the dead man. They consider it a great good fortune and blessing to leave this world together with their husband or lord, thinking that afterwards they will serve him as they did on earth. And for this reason they believe that the woman who died quickly would the sooner find herself in the other life with her lord or husband. This custom has its root in what I have described on other occasions, which is that they see (so they say) the devil in the fields and lands, pretending to be the dead man, accompanied by his wives and the other things that were put into the tomb with him. Among these Indians there were those who were augurs, and studied the stars.

Ruled by the Incas, these people observed the rites and customs of their overlords, and built orderly settlements, and in each there were storehouses and royal lodgings, and they went better attired, and spoke the general language of Cuzco, in keeping with the law and edicts of the Lord-Incas, who ordered that all their subjects should know and speak it.

The Conchucos and the great province of Huaylas, Tarma, and Bombón [Pumpu], and other villages, some large, some small, serve this new city of León de Huánuco, and they are all rich in provisions, and there are many savory, nourishing tubers for food. In olden times there were innumerable flocks of llamas, but the wars have so decimated them that of the many they once were, so few now remain that if the natives did not tend them carefully to have wool for their

did not say he saw it all, only that for things he did not see, he obtained information from those whose judgment he could trust: "this history of what I saw and experienced, and from reliable information I received from persons whose word could be relied on." However, his information was exact. (See von Hagen, *Highway of the Sun* [Chapter XI, "The Road to Chachapoyas"]; and C. R. Enock, *Andes and the Amazon* [London, 1907], 229–336.)

110

clothing, they would have a hard time. The houses of these Indians, and even those of the others, are of stone with a thatch roof. All wear ribands and insignia about their heads for identification. Even though evil has had great power over them, I have never heard that they were guilty of the abominable sin of sodomy. To be sure, as happens everywhere, there are bad among them; but if the practices of these are known, they are despised and looked down on as effeminate, and they treat them almost like women, as I have written.

In many parts of this region great lodes of silver have been found, and if they work them, they can mine a great deal.[3]

CHAPTER 32 (LXXXIII)

Of the lake of Bombón [Pumpu], of Chinchay-cocha, which is presumed to be the source of the great La Plata River.

THE LAY OF this province of Bombón [Pumpu] makes it strong, and this is the reason why its inhabitants were very warlike. Before the Incas could dominate them, they had great difficulties and many battles, until finally (according to many of the older Indians) they won them over to their rule by gifts and promises. In the territory of these Indians there is a lake over ten leagues in circumference. This land of Bombón is very level and extremely cold, and the mountains are some distance from the lake [of Chinchay-cocha].[1] The

[3] That there were "great lodes of silver" was proved true when in 1569 an Indian named Aari Capcha found, while herding his llamas, that when he built a fire against a rock to keep out the cold of the *puna,* the melted rock had turned into a silver ingot. Thus were the Cerro de Pasco mines discovered, which between 1630 and 1898 produced $565,000,000 worth of silver ore.

[1] Chinchay-suyu was one of the four directions, the term given by the Incas to all that Andean area north of Cuzco, until reaching Quito. The lake (now Laguna de Junín), the second largest, is thirty-six miles long and lies at 12,940 feet. The Chinchays, (we do not know what they were called before being incorporated into the Inca realm) defended themselves from fortified islands erected offshore. Huayna Capac, who finally defeated them, is said to have brought balsas all the way from Tumbes to reach and defeat them. The Incas built a large city, complete with sun temple and royal tambo; they raised a suspension bridge to cross the Mantaro River which drains the lake. It was an important hub of communications; out of the plaza went three roads (see map), and Hernando Pizarro passed through there on March 11, 1533, taking the lateral at Huaura on the coast, that joins with the Royal Road in the Andes (Huaura,

villages of the Indians are situated around it, with great moats and fortifications they built. They owned many herds of llamas, and although a great number of their animals were eaten and destroyed in the wars, as may be supposed, they still have some, and in the hills and uninhabited parts of their territory great herds of the wild ones are to be seen. Little corn is raised here because of the cold climate, but they do not lack for roots and other foodstuffs. There are certain islands and rocks in this lake where in times of war the Indians took refuge and were safe from their enemies. It is believed that the water which flows out of this mere or lake is the source of the famous La Plata River,[2] because by the time it reaches the valley of Jauja it is a large stream, and later it is joined by the Parcos, Vilcas, Abancay, Apurímac, and Yucay; and flowing westward, it crosses many lands, from which it emerges, receiving as tributaries many other large rivers of which we know nothing, until it reaches Paraguay, where the Spaniards who first discovered La Plata are. I am of the opinion, from what I have heard about this great river, that it must rise in two or three arms, or perhaps more, like the Marañón, the Santa Marta, and the Darién, and others in these lands. Be that as it may, we in the kingdom of Peru believe its source to be this lake of Bombón [Pumpu], into which the water of the snow in the mountains and sierras flows when the sun melts it, and it must be no small amount.

Ten leagues beyond Bombón lies the province of Tarma, whose natives were no less warlike than the natives of Bombón. Its climate is better, which is why corn and wheat yield well there, as do the other native products found in these lands. In bygone days there were great lodgings and storehouses of the Lord-Incas in Tarma. The natives, and their women, wear garments made of the wool of their flocks, and worship the sun, which they call *mocha*. When one of them marries, they all come together, drinking their wine, to see the groom and his bride, and kissing each other on the cheeks, the mar-

112

Guranga, Aillón, and Chincha) and on "Wednesday 11th March . . . reached Pombo [Pumpu or Bombón] . . . and the Lords of Pombo came out to meet him . . . . a river flows out of the lake to the village of Pombo."

[2] This river, now called the Mantaro, does not, naturally, flow into the Plate, the river of commerce of Paraguay and Argentina. Cieza's mistake is natural enough, for the Mantaro flows southeast until it reaches Mayoc, thirteen degrees south latitude, where it makes a radical bend, like a fishhook, twists, and joins the Apurímac River, which is the source of the Ucayali, one of the great tributaries of the Amazon.

riage is sealed. And when the chieftains die, they are buried in the same manner as those we have already seen, and the wives who are left shear their hair and put on black hoods, and daub their faces with a black mixture they make, and they must wear these signs of widowhood for a year. After this time, as I understand it, and not before, they may marry if they want to. During the year the Indians have communal feasts, and the fast days appointed by them are carefully observed during which they neither eat meat or salt, nor know their wives. And they ask the one among them who is considered most religious or closest to the gods to fast for a whole year for the health of all. When this has been done, at the time of the corn harvesting they all assemble and pass several days and nights eating and drinking. They are free of the sin of sodomy; so much so that they have an old, witty proverb which is to the effect that in olden times there must have been in the province of Huaylas some given to this grave sin. This was considered so foul by the neighboring Indians that to shame and insult them they used, referring to this, a phrase that has not yet disappeared, *"Asta Huaylas,"* which in our language means, "May the men of Huaylas run after you."

113

Following the highway of the Incas, from Tarma[3] one comes to the large beautiful valley of Jauja, which was one of the finest things in Peru.

CHAPTER 33 (LXXXIV)

Which deals with the valley of Jauja and its natives, and how great it was in other days.

THROUGH THIS valley of Jauja there runs a river [the Mantaro] which, as I said in the chapter on Bombón [Pumpu], is the headwaters of La Plata River. This valley is about fourteen leagues long, and four or five wide, more and less. It was all so thickly settled that when the Spaniards entered it, they say, and it is believed true, there were over thirty thousand Indians. Now I doubt that there are ten thou-

[3] Tarma (tambo), "in bygone days were great lodgings," and remains of royal tambo fortifications, storehouses, and a small *pucará* are still to be seen. They are above the modern town of the same name, off the ancient Royal Road. The French traveler Charles Wiener (*Perou et Bolivia,* 234–35) left fairly accurate drawings of it.

sand. They were divided into three groups, although they all were known, and still are, as Huancas. They say that this arrangement was made in the time of Huayna Capac, or his father, who divided the lands and the boundaries. Thus, one part is called Jauja, from which the valley takes its name, and the other, Marca-villca, whose chieftain was called Huacara-pora, and the third was known as Llacsa-pallanca, and its chieftain Alaya. In all these regions there were great lodgings of the Incas, although the most important ones were at the head of the valley, in the part known as Jauja, because there was a great wall there where there were strong, finely built lodgings of stone,[1] and a house of the sun virgins, and a very rich temple, and many storehouses filled with everything to be found. Aside from this, there were many silversmiths who made goblets and vessels of silver and gold for the service of the Incas and the adorning of the temple. More than eight thousand Indians were on hand for the service of the temple and the palaces of the ruler. All the buildings were of stone. The roofs of the houses and lodgings were of thick beams, covered with long thatch. Before these Huancas were conquered by the Incas, fierce battles took place, as will be told in the second part. The women of the sun were guarded with great care, and if any of them knew a man, she was punished with great severity.

These Indians tell a very amusing thing, and that is that they claim they descend from a certain man (whose name I cannot recall) and a woman called Urochombe, who emerged from a fountain known as Marca-villca. And the two of them procreated so zealously that the Huancas descend from them. To commemorate this, their forebears built a great high wall, and alongside it a temple to which, as something very important, they came to worship. These Huanca Indians know that there is a Maker of all things, whom they call Tici-Viracocha. They believed in the immortality of the soul. They flayed the prisoners they captured in war and stuffed their skins with ashes, and of some they made drums. The villages had parts that were like

---

[1] Some melancholy fragments of this ancient Jauja (Hatun-xauxa) still exist and enough to make a plan of what the place was like in Incaic times. Still to be seen are the storage chambers that appeared to Cieza to look like "towers of Spain." Remains of the suspension bridge which spanned the turbulent Mantaro River can be seen resting next to fragments of a colonial bridge. This bridge led to the lateral road, famed for its ruggedness in conquistadors' memories, that went down to the coast and Pachacamac. Cieza rode over it as described in the introduction to this volume.

a fortress made of stone, resembling small towers, broad at the base and tapering at the top, and from a distance they seem towers of Spain. All of them were wild in olden times, and made war on one another. But later on, when they came under the rule of the Incas, they became more industrious and raised llamas in great number. They adopted longer clothing than that which they had worn. As insignia they use a headband of wool four fingers wide. They fought with slings and darts and some with lances.

In olden times, beside the fountain I have mentioned, they built a temple which they called Huari-vilca. I saw it, and near by stood three or four trees called *molles,* like big walnuts. They look upon these as sacred, and beside them is a seat for the lords who came there to make sacrifice, and from it steppingstones led to a fence within which the temple stood. Here I should like to tell of the *molle* tree, because of its great utility. In the plains and valleys of Peru there are great forests, and in the fastnesses of the Andes, too, where trees of many varieties and properties grow, few or none of which resemble those of Spain. Some of them, such as the alligator pear, cassia, caimito, and guava, bear fruit such as I have mentioned in other parts of this narration. The rest are thornbushes and briars, or sparse thickets, and certain very large *ceibas,*[2] in which, and in the hollow of other trees, bees store honey of excellent flavor. In most of the settled areas one sees certain trees, large and small, which they call *molles.* The leaf is very small and the smell is like that of fennel, and the bark of this tree is so valuable that if a person is suffering from pains and swelling in the legs, if they are washed several times in an infusion made by boiling the bark in water, the pain and swelling disappear. The little twigs are very good for cleaning the teeth. From a small fruit the tree bears they make wine, or a very good beverage, and vinegar, and excellent syrup by crushing the amount they wish of this fruit in a vessel of water, and boiling it until it has partly evaporated, and it turns into wine or vinegar or syrup, depending on the length of the cooking. The Indians prize these trees highly.

[2] *Molle* is the pepper tree of Peru (*Schinus molle*). It was planted along roads and in towns. The spread of the Inca state helped to diffuse the tree throughout the Andes; it was used for making strong chicha, for medicinal and embalming purposes. The alligator pear (*Persea Americana*) is *palta* in Quechua; the caimito is the star apple (*Chrysophyllum caimito*); guava—of the jelly—grows from bush height to trees of thirty feet (*Psidium guajava*); *ceba* is ceiba, the immense-trunked, spined *Ceiba Erianthos,* which yields silky cotton.

At the doorway [to Jauja] there were gatekeepers to guard the entrance, and a stone stairway led to the aforementioned fountain, where there is a great old wall in the form of a triangle. Near these buildings there was a flat place where they say the devil used to be, whom they worshiped, and he spoke with certain of them at that spot.

Aside from this, these Indians tell another thing: that they heard from their forebears that once upon a time a great multitude of devils suddenly appeared in the region who did great harm to the inhabitants, terrifying them with their sight. This being the situation, there arose in the sky five suns, which with their appearance and brilliance so dismayed the devils that they fled with great howls and groans. And the devil Huari-vilca, who was in the aforementioned spot, was never again seen, and all the place where he had been was burned and charred. And as the Incas ruled this land and were lords of this valley, although they ordered a temple to the sun as large and important built there as elsewhere, they did not give over making offerings and sacrifices in the one to Huari-vilca. All, the one and the other, are now fallen down and in ruins, and grown over with briars and weeds. For when the governor, Don Francisco Pizarro, entered this valley, the Indians say that Bishop Fray Vicente de Valverde smashed the figures of the idols, and from then on the devil was never again heard in that place. I went to see this building and the aforesaid temple, and Don Cristóbal, the son of the late lord, Alaya, went with me, and showed me this antiquity. He and the other lords of the valley have become Christians, and there are two priests and a friar in charge of teaching the matters of our holy Catholic faith. This valley of Jauja is encircled by snow-covered sierras; it consists mainly of valleys where the Huancas have their planted fields. The capital of the kingdom was situated in this valley before it was settled in the place where it now stands, and they found there large amounts of gold and silver.[3]

[3] Jauja was settled as Santa Fé de Hatun Xauxa. It was the first Spanish capital of Peru. When Francisco Pizarro stopped there on his way to Cuzco, he decided to found his capital there "in the city of Xauxa, the twenty and ninth day of the month of November, 1534, the very noble lords Juan Mogrovejo de Quiñones and Sebastián de Torres were chosen mayors; for aldermen, García de Salcedo, Alonso Riquelme, Rodrigo de Mazuelas, Juan de Barrios, Gregorio de Sotello, and Diego Maldonado." The scrivener was Captain Gerónimo de Aliaga.

*Of how the Inca Yupanqui sent Lloque Yupanqui
to the valley of Jauja to endeavor to win over to his
rule the Huancas and Yauyos and others of
the nations of those parts.*

MY INFORMANTS told me that as the Lord-Inca Yupanqui felt himself so powerful, he issued another call to arms, because he wanted to undertake another war [on the Huancas at Jauja] more important than the preceding ones. In compliance with his mandate, many chieftains answered with a great number of troops equipped with the arms they employ, which are slings, axes, clubs, *ayllos,* darts, and some lances. When they had assembled, he ordered banquets and feasts given for them, and to delight them, he appeared every day in different garb or attire, that of the nation he wished to honor that day, and the next he put on another, such as those invited to the banquet or drinking feast wore. With all this their hearts were merry beyond power to describe. When the great dances were held the square of Cuzco was roped off with a cable [*huascar*] of gold which he had ordered made of the stores of that metal which the regions paid as tribute, whose size I have already told, and an even greater display of statues and relics.[1]

And when they had made merry for the days Inca Yupanqui had appointed, he spoke to them and told them that he wanted them to go to the Huancas and the Yauyos, their neighbors, and endeavor to persuade them to accept his friendship and service without war, and, if this were not possible, if they had to fight them, to see that they conquered them and obliged them to do so. They all replied that they would do his bidding cheerfully. The captains of each nation were appointed, and over them all Lloque Yupanqui was made general, and together with him, as his adviser, Tupac Yupanqui. After he outlined to them what they were to do, they set out from Cuzco and marched to the province of Andahuaylas, where they were well

---

[1] The word *huascar* meant "cable." This chain of gold was actually a rope cable, immensely long and fringed with red wool at either end. It was plaited with gold, beaten thin, and strung on to the rope cable. It was supposed to have been thrown into Lake Urcos, south of Cuzco. Huascar was also the name of the last Inca.

received by the Chancas, and there they were joined by one captain with a force of soldiers of that province, to serve the Inca in war.

From Andahuaylas they went on to Vilcas, the site of the lodgings and temples to the sun that the Lord-Inca Yupanqui had ordered built, and they spoke in the kindliest terms to those who had executed these works. From Vilcas they proceeded to the villages of Huamanga, Azángaro, Parcos, Picoy, and Acos,[2] and others, all of which had pledged obedience to the Inca, and supplied food and the other products of their villages, and built the highway they were ordered to construct, long and very wide.

Those of the valley of Jauja, when they learned of the approach of the enemy, were smitten with fear and sought the aid of their kinfolk and friends, and in their temple of Huari-vilca they made great sacrifices to the devil who made reply there. When their allies arrived, as they were many, for it is said that there were more than forty thousand men where now I doubt that there are twelve thousand, the captains of the Inca took up their positions on the rim of the valley, and endeavored without war to win the good will of the Huancas and their consent to go to Cuzco and recognize the Lord-Inca as their lord, and so they notified them by messengers. But as this was of no avail, they met on the field, and a great battle took place in which it is said that many on both sides lost their lives, but that victory went to those of Cuzco. And as Lloque Yupanqui was a man of great prudence, he did not allow any harm to be done the valley and forbade all looting, and ordered the prisoners released, until the Huancas, cognizant of the favor and clemency which he had used toward them after they were conquered, came to speak with him and promised to live henceforth in keeping with the laws of the Lord-Incas of Cuzco, and pay tribute of what their valley yielded, and moving their settlements down from the mountainsides, they planted them, without dividing them up until the Lord-Inca Huayna Capac assigned to each his holding, and messengers were dispatched.

---

[2] All these villages were tambos on the Royal Road dividing at Marcavilca (Marcavalle). One side of the road goes over the high, bald mountains bordering the river and canyon of the Mantaro.

CHAPTER 35 (LXXXV)

Which tells of the road from Jauja to the city of Huamanga [Ayacucho], and of what is worth noting on this route.

BY MY CALCULATIONS, it is thirty leagues from this valley of Jauja to the city of Victoria de Huamanga [Ayacucho]. One follows the Inca highway until on a group of hills rising above the valley some very old buildings, all in ruins and fallen down, are to be seen. Continuing by this route, one reaches the village of Acos, situated alongside a marsh overgrown with rushes, where there were lodgings and storehouses of the Incas, as in the other villages of their kingdoms. The natives of Acos are some distance from the highway, settled in craggy sierras lying to the east. I have nothing to tell of them except that they go dressed in woolen clothing and their houses and villages are of stone, thatched with straw, like the others. From Acos there is a road leading to the lodging of Picoy, and it follows a bluff and then descends hillsides on which, although they are rough and this would seem to make the road difficult, it is so well laid out and broad that it is almost like walking on level ground. It descends to the river that runs through Jauja, which has its bridge, and the crossing is known as Angoyaco. Beside this bridge there are white cliffs from which flows a spring of salt water. At this pass of Angoyaco there used to be buildings of the Incas, and a stone enclosure in which to bathe in the waters that came out warm and agreeable for bathing. All the Lord-Incas set great store by this, and even the other Indians of these regions were in the habit, and still are, of washing and bathing every day, they and their women. The part where the river runs forms a kind of small valley where there are many *molle* trees, and other fruit trees and groves. Past this, one comes to the village of Picoy, first crossing another small river, where there is also a bridge, because in winter it is very turbulent. Leaving Picoy, one comes to the lodgings of Parcos, which were built on the crest of a sierra. The Indians live in large, craggy, high sierras which lie to either side of these lodgings, some of which still stand, where the Spaniards who come and go by these roads take shelter.

Before reaching this village of Parcos, in a small barren spot there is a place called Pucará (which in our language means a stronghold), where in olden times, so the Indians tell, there were palaces of the Incas and a temple to the sun. Many Indians brought their regular tributes to Pucará, turning them over to the steward who was in charge of the storehouses and of collecting these tributes. There are a multitude of stones in this place, cropping out and scattered in such a way that from the distance it truly looks like a turreted city or castle, from which it would seem that the Indians had given it a fitting name. Among these cliffs or crags there is one alongside a small stream, as large as it is astonishing to see, in size and thickness the strongest that can be imagined. I saw it, and slept on it one night, and it seemed to me it must have been over two hundred fathoms high, and more than two hundred feet in circumference at its summit. If it were on some exposed frontier, a fortress could easily be built there that would be impregnable. There is another remarkable thing about this great rock; there are so many hollows in it that more than one hundred men and some horses can take shelter under it. In this, as in other things, our God shows his might and foresight, for all these roads are full of caves where men and beasts can take shelter from rain and snow.

The natives of this region have their settlements in great sierras, as I have said. The summits of most of them are covered with snow nearly all the time. They plant their crops in sheltered spots, like valleys, which open out in the mountains. In many of them are great lodes of silver.

From Parcos the highway descends a mountainside until it comes to a river by the same name as the lodgings, where there is a bridge set upon large stone piles.[1] After this river of Parcos comes the lodging of Azángaro, which is a *repartimiento* that belongs to Diego Gavilán,[2] from which, by the highway, one comes to the city of San Juan de la Victoria de Huamanga [Ayacucho].

[1] Pedro de Cieza de León: "It was in this sierra of Parcos that the battle between the Indians and Captain Mogrovejo de Quiñones took place, and where Gonzalo Pizarro ordered Captain Gaspar Rodríguez de Camporedondo killed, as will be told in later books." (*The Battle of Salinas,* Chapter XI.)

[2] All of these tambos and ancient villages mentioned by Cieza have been confirmed by the editor, who as leader of the Inca Highway Expedition passed through them all during the year 1953. To reach the Mantaro, this turbulent river, one first goes to Acos (Acos-tambo), now a flourishing little village; at Angoyaco, at the river canyon.

CHAPTER 36 (LXXXVI)

Which deals with the reason for the founding of the city of Huamanga.

AFTER THE bitter war that was fought in Cuzco [1536] between the Indians and Spaniards, when Manco Inca II was defeated and unable to recapture the city of Cuzco, he decided to withdraw to the provinces of Viticos [Vilcas] which lay in the heart of the backlands, beyond the Andes Mountains, though first he was harried by [Spaniards] who liberated Captain Ruy Díaz whom the Inca had captured some days before. Many of the *Orejones* of Cuzco, who were The nobility of that city, chose to follow Manco Inca II. So when Manco Inca II reached Viticos with a vast quantity of treasure, removed from many of the places where he had it hidden, and his wives and court, they chose as their seat the palace that seemed to them the strongest, from which they often sallied forth in all directions to stir up many regions that were at peace, trying to do all the harm they could to the Spaniards, whom they looked upon as cruel enemies, for they had occupied their kingdom and forced them to leave their native land and live in exile. These and other things were proclaimed by Manco Inca II and his followers when they went out to pillage and wreak the harm I have mentioned. And as no city of the Spaniards had been built in these provinces, the Indians of some having been assigned to residents of the city of Cuzco, and of others to that of Lima, for this reason Manco Inca II's Indians could easily do great harm to the Spaniards and their allies, and in fact they killed and robbed many. The matter became so serious that

there are still the "white cliffs" produced by sulphurous streams and the remains of the suspension bridges; "there were two," noted Pedro Sancho, scrivener to Pizarro, ". . . one for the nobles and the other for the common people." On the other side (west) there are the remains of the royal tambo. Picoy, above the river, has the ruins of the tambo whose chief was "Tomeyaguata," and they can still be seen. The site of Paucará, over 8,500 feet altitude, is very rugged and mountain-bound, filled with caves and ruins of a fortress. Next in line to confirm Cieza is Parcos(-tambo), whose Indians in his time were held in encomienda by Francisco Balboa and Vasco Suárez. The bridge which crossed the river Huarpa has long since disappeared, although part of its stone pillars can be seen; across it, near the present flourishing commercial town of Huanta, are the ruins of the tambo Azángaro. Diego Gavilán did hold the place in encomienda, as is confirmed by the "Regulations for Tambos" issued from Cuzco, May 31, 1543.

the Marquis Don Francisco Pizarro dispatched captains against them. At his orders they proceeded from Cuzco against them, and he sent Captain Villadiego with a force of Spaniards to search out the land, for word had come that Manco Inca II was not far from where they were. And despite the fact that they had no horses (which is the main instrument of war against these Indians), trusting to their own strength and eager to measure forces with the Inca because they thought he would come accompanied by his wives and a part of his treasure and belongings, they ascended a high sierra, and when they reached the top they were all so exhausted that Manco Inca II, with a little better than eighty Indians, fell upon the Spaniards (having had word of their approach), who were twenty-eight or thirty, and killed Captain Villadiego and all the others, save two or three who managed to escape with the help of friendly Indians, who brought them to the factor, who greatly lamented what had happened. When the Marquis Don Francisco Pizarro learned of this, he swiftly set out from Cuzco with his troops in pursuit of Manco Inca II. He was unable to overtake him, however, for he withdrew to this stronghold of Viticos with the heads of the Spaniards, until Captain Gonzalo Pizarro attacked him in force and demolished many of his breastworks and captured several bridges. And as the harm and mischief done by the rebellious Indians was great, Francisco Pizarro, after conferring with a number of citizens and crown officials who were with him, decided to found a city of Spaniards between Cuzco and Lima to guard the road for travelers and merchants, which was called San Juan de la Frontera.[1] All the settlements and provinces in this region from the Andes to the Southern Sea were under the jurisdiction of Cuzco and Lima, and the Indians were assigned to residents of these two cities. But when the governor, Don Francisco Pizarro, decided to found this city, he ordered the former and the latter to take up their residence in this city; otherwise they would lose their rights to the Indians of that area.

[1] Pedro de Cieza de León: "Until Master Cristóbal Vaca de Castro, his successor in the government of the kingdom, changed it to Victoria in commemoration of the victory he won against the men of Chile on the bluffs of Chupas."

CHAPTER 37 (LXXXVII)

Of the founding of the city of Huamanga and who its founder was.

WHEN THE Marquis Don Francisco Pizarro decided to establish this city in this province, he founded it not where it is now, but in an Andean village known as Huamanga [close to the highway of the Inca], which was why the city took this same name, situated close to the long, high range of the Andes. There he left Captain Francisco de Cárdenas as his lieutenant. Later on, for various reasons, it was moved to its present site, which is on a plain close to a range of small sierras to the south, despite the fact that the settlers preferred another plain half a league from this, but it had to be given up because of lack of water. Near the city runs a small stream of very good water, which supplies the city, where the largest and best houses in all Peru have been built, all of stone, brick, and tile, with great turrets, so there is no lack of dwellings. The square is level and large. The city is very salubrious, for neither sun, wind, or night air are harmful, nor is it damp or hot, but, on the contrary, enjoys an excellent climate. The Spaniards have built their haciendas where they have their cattle, in the valleys and along the rivers in the neighborhood of the city.

The largest of those streams is called the Viñaque,[1] where there are some large and very old buildings which, judging by the state of ruin and decay into which they have fallen, must have been there for many ages. When I asked the Indians of the vicinity who had built that antiquity, they replied that other bearded, white people like ourselves, who, long before the Incas reigned, they say came to these parts and took up their abode there. This and other ancient

123

1 Viñaque, now called Huari, is a large pre-Inca archaeological site, close to Ayacucho, one of the vexing problems of archaeology, since potsherds of many cultures are found there and the various stone monuments, figures, immense stone graves, etc., are like nothing else in the region. The closest resemblance in the stone monuments is to classic Tiahuanacu in Bolivia. Cieza, archaeologists agree, was quite right in saying that the style of this great ruined site was not Inca, and the observation does him great credit. Not taken in by the local folklore, he later observes, when in Tiahuanacu, that the style does resemble that of Viñaque (see page 284 below). (See also John H. Rowe, Donald Collier, and Gordon R. Willey, "Reconnaissance Notes on the Site of Huari, near Ayacucho, Peru," *American Antiquity*, Vol. XVI, No. 2 [October, 1950].)

buildings in this kingdom seem to me not of the sort the Incas built or ordered built, for this building was square, and those of the Incas, long and narrow. And it is also said that certain letters were found inscribed on a stone of this building. I neither affirm nor deny that in bygone days people of such intelligence and judgment might have come here and done these things and others we do not see. Along this Viñaque River, and others in the vicinity of the city, wheat does well, and from it they make bread as fine and good as the best of Andalucía. Vines have been planted, and it is believed that in time there will be large vineyards,[2] and the other products of Spain that they plant will flourish. Of the native fruits, there is an abundance, and very good, and so many pigeons as I have seen nowhere else in the Indies. In the summer there is some shortage of pasture for the horses; but with the services of the Indians the lack is not felt. It should be pointed out that in no season of the year do the horses or other animals eat hay, nor is that which is cut here used for anything, for the cattle do not eat it either, but only the grass of the fields. The roads leading from the city are good, although in many places there are so many thorns and briars that those traveling on foot or by horses must go carefully.

124

This city of San Juan de la Victoria de Huamanga [Ayacucho] was founded and settled by . . . Francisco Pizarro, governor of Peru, on the ninth of January, 1539.

CHAPTER 38 (LXXXVIII)

Concerning certain facts about the natives of this city [Ayacucho].

MANY INDIANS were assigned to the residents of Huamanga; they are now very numerous [even though] many of them succumbed in the wars. Most of them were *mitimaes,* who, as I have said, were Indians transferred from certain regions to others, the doing of the Lord-Incas. Some of them were *Orejones,* although not of the lead-

---

[2] This proved to be true. Cuttings of these vines were taken down to the coast at Ica, where in time they grew into the wine industry; pisco, a grape brandy made in Ica, is shipped from the port of Pisco.

ing families of Cuzco. To the east of this city runs the great range of the Andes, and to the west, the coast and the Southern Sea. I have already mentioned the Indian settlements along the highway; the others have fertile farmlands, abundant herds of llamas, and they all go clothed. They[1] had their shrines and oracles in secret places where they performed their sacrifices and vain rites. Their burials were like those of the others, burying with the dead certain women and the things they had most esteemed. When they came under the domination of the Incas, they worshiped the sun and governed themselves by their laws and customs. Formerly they were indomitable and so warlike that the Incas had great trouble conquering them. So much trouble, indeed, that they say that during the reign of Pachacuti, after he had defeated the Soras and Rucanas, provinces where the people were sturdy, and which also came under the jurisdiction of this city, a large force of Indians fortified themselves on a high cliff, and there were bitter fights before they were conquered, as will be told in its place. For, rather than give up their freedom and become slaves of the tyrant, they paid no heed to the hunger they underwent and the repeated attacks they suffered. Whereupon Pachacuti, ambitious to dominate them and eager not to suffer in his reputation, besieged them and put them to great hardship for over two years, until finally, after holding out as long as they could, they surrendered to him. At the time that Gonzalo Pizarro rose in his rebellion,[2] out of fear of his captains and desirous of serving His Majesty's cause, the leading inhabitants of this city of Ayacucho raised the Royal Standard and entrenched themselves on this cliff,[3] and they saw there, as I have heard from certain of them, traces of what these Indians tell.

All these Indians wear the insignia by which their ancestors were recognized, and some of them were much given to auguries and were

1 "They" were called Tanquihua, the original inhabitants of Ayacucho. They had their own language, but apparently spoke both Quechua and Aymara, and their cultural level seemed as high until the coming of the Inca. The Soras lived to the south on the left bank of the Pampas River. They had four thousand tribute payers after the Inca conquest and were allied to the Rucanas (Quechua, "finger"), who lived in the area known as Andamarka, close to the Soras. They were the litter bearers for the Inca and wore a special, light-blue livery.

2 See the Editor's Introduction for events leading to the rebellion of Gonzalo Pizarro.

3 The cliff is called Pillucho, an immense upthrust of soil; this mountain lies about five miles from Vilcas-huamán. It is full of deposits and houses, and below it lies the Vishongo River.

great soothsayers, boasting that they could read the future, which was pure nonsense, [just] as [it is] now when they try to prophesy or foretell what no human can know or forecast, for God alone knows the future.

126

<h2 style="text-align:center">CHAPTER 39 (LXXXIX)</h2>

Of the great lodgings there once were in the province of Vilcas [-huamán], which lies beyond that of Ayacucho.

FROM THE CITY of Ayacucho to that of Cuzco is 60 leagues, or 180 miles thereabouts. Along this road are the bluffs and plains of Chupas;[1] farther on, keeping to the Inca highway, one comes to the edifices of Vilcas, eleven leagues from Ayacucho, which, according to the natives, was the midpoint of the kingdom and rule of the Incas.[2] For they state that it is the same distance from Quito to Vilcas as from Vilcas to Chile, the limits of their empire. Certain Spaniards who have traveled the road from one end to the other say the same. It was Pachacuti who ordered these lodgings to be built, according to the Indians, and his successors enlarged what he had done. The temple to the sun was large and finely built. Where the buildings are, there is a plain on the highest point of a sierra, which was always carefully tended. To one side of this plain, toward the rising sun, there was a shrine for the Lord-Incas, of stone, from which small terraces emerged, about six feet wide, where other enclosures came

[1] Pedro de Cieza de León: "And the site of the battle between Governor Vaca de Castro and Diego de Almagro the Younger, as bitter and fiercely contested as I shall tell when I come to it." (That is, the battle of Chupas; see *The Civil Wars: The Battle of Chupas.*)

The battle was fought on a fairly level area of ground, near Ayacucho, on Saturday, September 16, 1542. Cieza vividly describes it (p. 270, Hakluyt Society translation), although he was not a participant. More than 240 men were killed and three times as many wounded out of a combined force of 1,200. The battle marked the appearance of Francisco de Carvajal, the witty cutthroat who became general to Pizarro's later rebellion, and it also marked the death of one of the "thirteen of Gallo," Pedro de Candia.

[2] It was considered the geographical center of the Inca empire, but calculating geographically, the distance from Pasto to Cuzco is 1,230 miles and that from Cuzco to Talca (in Chile and the terminus of the Inca road) is 1,885 miles.

together, and at the center there was a bench where the Lord-Inca sat to pray, all of a single stone so large that it was eleven feet long and seven feet wide, with two seats cut for the aforesaid purpose. They say this stone used to be covered with jewels of gold and precious stones to adorn this place they so venerated and esteemed, and on another stone, not small, now in the middle of this square, like a baptismal font, was where they sacrificed animals and young children (so they say), whose blood was offered up to the gods. On these terraces the Spaniards have found some of the treasure that was buried there.

127

Behind this shrine stand the palaces of Topa Inca and other large buildings, and many storehouses where arms and fine clothing were kept, together with the other articles of tribute paid by the Indians and provinces which came within the jurisdiction of Vilcas, which, as I have said before, was like a capital of the kingdom. Close to a small sierra there were and are over seven hundred houses in which the corn and other provisions for the troops patrolling the kingdom were stored. In the middle of the great square there was another bench, like that of a theater, where the Lord-Inca sat to watch the dances and lay feasts. The temple of the sun, which was made of stones laid one upon the other with great skill, had two main doorways. To enter them, there were two stone stairways which, by my count, had thirty steps each. Inside this temple there were rooms for the priests and for those who watched over the vestals, the *mamaconas,* who observed their vows faithfully, with no other duties than those mentioned in other parts of this account. The *Orejones* and other Indians tell that the image of the sun was of enormous value, and that there was great treasure both in the temple and buried, and that these palaces had at their service over forty thousand Indians, serving in turn, each of the headmen sending his quota according to the orders of the governor, who was the surrogate of the Lord-Inca, and solely to guard the gates there were forty gatekeepers. What can be seen are the foundations of the buildings, and the walls and enclosures of the shrines, the stones I have mentioned, and the temple with its stairways, even though it has fallen into ruins and is overgrown with grass and the storehouses have fallen down. In a word, it was once what it no longer is, and by what it is, we can judge what it was.

Among some of the first Spanish conquistadors there are those who saw this building intact and in all its perfection, and I have heard of it from their own lips.

The *Orejones* relate extraordinary things of this Pachacuti [who conquered Vilcas].[3]

128

As this Inca was so eager to have in his power those who had taken refuge on the rock, he proceeded with his troops until he came to the Vilcas River. Many of those of the region, when they knew that he had arrived, came to see him and do him homage, and make a pact of friendship with him, and at his behest they began to build lodgings and large buildings in what we now call Vilcas, builders of Cuzco remaining there to draw up the plans and teach them how to lay the stones and masonry work of the buildings. When he finally came to the Pillucho rock, he tried in every reasonable way to win over to friendship those who had entrenched themselves there, sending them emissaries, but they laughed at his offers and hurled many stones down against them. The Inca, seeing their determination, made up his mind not to leave until he had punished them. News was brought to him how the captains he had sent to the province of Cuntisuyu had fought various battles with those of that region and had conquered them, and brought most of the provinces under his dominion. And so that those of the Colla would not think themselves safe, knowing how brave Hastu Huallaca, the lord of Andahuaylas was, he dispatched him with his brother Tupac Huasco against the Colla, to endeavor to bring the natives under his rule. They replied that they would do as he bid, and set out at once for their lands, whence they would come to Cuzco bringing the troops they were able to raise.

Those on the rock remained steadfast in their determination to defend themselves, and the Inca besieged them, and great things took place on both sides, for the siege lasted a long time. But finally, their supplies exhausted, they were forced to surrender and agree to submit

[3] Pedro de Cieza de León: "And of Topa Inca his son, and Huayna Capac his grandson, for these were the bravest of all. Those who read of these events may rest assured that I omit rather than exaggerate in what I relate, and in order to be able to give a trustworthy account, I tell nothing but what I have heard from those Indians. As for myself, I believe all this and more from the vestiges and traces the footprints of these Lord-Incas have left, and from their vast powers, of which what I write is nothing compared to what took place, the memory of which will endure in Peru as long as there are native people there." (ii:XLVIII.)

to Cuzco, like the others, and pay tribute and send troops. With this submission they found favor with the Inca, who, it is said, promised to do them no harm, but on the contrary to see that they were provided with food and other things and returned to their lands. Others tell that he killed them all, without sparing a single one. I myself believe the first, though in both cases I know only what these Indians tell.

When this had been brought to an end, they say that people came from many regions to offer themselves to the Inca, and that he graciously received all who came. He then departed for Cuzco, and found on the route many lodgings that had been built, and that nearly everywhere the natives had come out of the hills and established orderly settlements as he had bidden. . . .

From here the highway proceeds to Uranmarca,[4] seven leagues toward Cuzco. Through its confines runs the broad river known as the Vilcas [Pampas] from its proximity to these dwellings. From one side of the river to the other there are two high rows of stone piles, stout and deeply buried, on which to lay the bridge, which is made of twisted withes, like well ropes for drawing up water with a pulley. The bridges made in this way are so strong that horses can gallop over them as though they were crossing the bridge of Alcántara or Córdoba.[5] This bridge when I crossed it was seventy-six feet long. The source of the river is in the province of the Soras which is very rich and fertile and inhabited by warlike people. They and the Rucanas speak the same language and dress in woolen clothing. They once had great flocks, and there are rich mines of gold and silver in their province. The Incas held the Soras and Rucanas in such high regard that these provinces were their antechambers, and the sons of the chieftains lived at the court in Cuzco. There are lodgings of Uranmarca, which is a settlement of *mitimaes,* for the the wild llamas. Returning to the main highway, one comes to the lodgings of Uran-marca, which is a settlement of *mitimaes,* for the natives, in the wars of the Incas, were nearly all killed off.

---

[4] Uranmarca is reached by a three-thousand-foot climb from the Pampas, or Vilcas, River over parts of a road, still Inca. Ruins of the tambo can be seen.

[5] Pedro Sancho, the conquistador scrivener who passed over it in 1534, said that it was 360 Spanish feet long and wide enough for two horses to pass abreast on it.

CHAPTER 40 (XC)

Of the province of Andahuaylas and what is to be found there until reaching the valley of Xaquixahuana.

130

WHEN I FIRST·came to this province, its lord was an Indian chieftain called Huasco and the natives were known as Chancas. They went clothed in blankets and shirts of wool. In times gone by they were so brave (it is said) that they not only won lands and domains, but were so strong that they besieged the city of Cuzco and great battles were fought between them and those of the city, until in the end the bravery of Topa Inca defeated them. Hanco-Huallu,[1] so renowned in these regions for his valor, was a native of this province. It is told of him that, unable to endure the rule of the Incas and the tyranny of their captains, after having performed great feats in the region of Tarma and Bombón, he pushed into the remote fast-

---

[1] Hanco-Huallu and the Chancas are of the greatest interest to Inca history. The tribes, divided into distinct *ayllus* or lineages—Hancohuallas, Hatunsullas, Uranmarcas, Vilcas, Yquichanos, Morochucos, Tacmanas, Quinuallas, and Pocras—appear to have been originally centered about Huanta, although they contend they originated at Choclococha, "lake of the fresh corn," north of Vilcas. They were warlike, turbulent, and indomitable, claiming descent from a puma; on great festive days they dressed in puma skins. Between the dates of 1350 and 1400 the Chancas moved south and broke the power of the Quechuas, that tribe that gave name and language to the Incas. The Quechuas, "warm-valley" people, centered between Abancay and Curahuasi, the latter village being the key to the road which led to the great Apurímac River and the famous bridge that hung across it. The Chancas were now ready to take on the Incas. They delayed their attack until the Inca Viracocha was an old man; then in 1437 they crossed that river, moved on to Cuzco, invaded the city, and tried to take it by storm. Cuzco was defended fiercely by the second son of the Inca, who forced his father to give up the leadership of the realm; he called himself then Pachacuti Inca, "earth-shaker." The Inca army pushed back the Chancas and defeated them on the plains of Xaquixahuana (see map), south of the Anta marshes. Many of the leaders of the Chancas were then flayed and their skins stuffed with ichu grass and set "in a sort of museum," where Cieza saw them, close to the spot of their defeat. Pachacuti then tried to incorporate the Chancas into his army; and Hanco-Huallu, who survived Inca vengeance, and the Chanca contingent helped to conquer Tarma, and they moved farther north beyond the bounds set by the Inca. An Inca general named Capac Yupanqui, in charge of the operations, got on badly with the Chancas. Suddenly, and without warning, Hanco-Huallu and his entire army escaped with their wives at Huánuco and entered the eastern *jalcas* and jungles of the Marañón. The Inca general was executed for allowing him to escape. Later the Incas built an immense military road to get at the escaped Chancas. All this is told by the editor, who explored the road, in *Highway of the Sun,* Chapter XI, "The Road to Chachapoyas."

ness of the mountains and settled on the shores of a lake, so they also tell, which lies below the Moyobamba River.

According to the Chancas, as the Indians who came from their province of Andahuaylas with Captain Hanco-Huallu had performed great feats in these wars, jealous of them, and with an old grudge they bore Captain Hanco-Huallu from the time of the siege of Cuzco, they planned to kill them. Thus, they sent for them, and when many of them had come, together with their captain, they grasped what they had in mind, and with their arms they defended themselves against those of Cuzco and although some of them were killed, the others, with the help and valor of Hanco-Huallu managed to escape. He complained to his gods of the wickedness and ingratitude of the *Orejones,* swearing that rather than see or follow them again, he would take his people into voluntary exile. And so with the women in the van, he set out and traversed the provinces of Chachapoyas and Huánuco, and having crossed the Andes Mountains, they wandered through those sierras until, as they also relate, they came to a great lake, which I believe must be the site of the tale they tell of El Dorado, where they built their settlements and have multiplied greatly. And the Indians tell remarkable things of that land and of Captain Hanco-Huallu.

After what has been told was accomplished, the captains of the Inca returned to the valley of Jauja, where great gifts had been brought and many women to be taken to Cuzco, and those of Tarma did the same. News of everything was sent to Cuzco, and when the Inca heard it he was highly pleased by the success of his captains, though he gave signs that he regretted what they had done to Hanco-Huallu. But it is believed that this was feigned, for there are those who say that the captains did what they did at his orders. And as Huasco and the other Chancas had gone to make war on the province of the Colla, and had won victories over various settlements, the Inca became fearful that when they learned of what had happened to Hanco-Huallu, they might turn against him and betray him, and he sent them messengers telling them to return to his side at once, ordering that no one was to inform them of what had happened, under penalty of death.

When the Chancas received the message of the Inca, they immediately returned to Cuzco, and when they arrived, the Inca spoke to them with falsely affectionate words, concealing the treachery with which Captain Hanco-Huallu had been treated, and in his words greatly deploring it. When the Chancas learned of it, their feeling of affront was great, but seeing how little they could do to avenge it, they swallowed their injury and asked permission of the Inca to return to their province. When this was granted, they departed, after their chieftain had been given the privilege of sitting upon the stool set with gold, and other marks of honor.

When I asked these Chancas what ideas they had about themselves, and where they came from, they told another fairy story or fable like those of Jauja, saying that their forefathers appeared and emerged from a little lake called Choclococha, from which they went forth conquering until they came to a place they named Chuquibamba, where they settled. And after some years had passed, they fought with the Quechuas, an ancient tribe that ruled this province of Andahuaylas, which they conquered and where they have remained as rulers to the present day. The lake from which they emerged was sacred to them, and their principal shrine where they worshiped and made sacrifice. Their burials were like those of the others, and they believed in the immortality of the soul, which they call *xongo,* which is also the word for heart. They buried with their lords living women and treasure and clothing. They had set days, and probably still have, to celebrate their feasts, and places to hold their dances. As there have been priests in this province uninterruptedly, teaching the Indians, some of them have become Christians, especially the younger ones. Captain Diego Maldonado[2] has always held an encomienda over them. They all wear their hair long and finely plaited, tied with woolen strings that fall below their chins. Their houses are of stone. In the center of the province there were great lodgings and storehouses for the rulers. In olden times there were many Indians in this province of Andahuaylas, but the wars have reduced their number as in the rest of this kingdom. It is very long, and there are quantities of domestic flocks, and the wild ones are innumerable. It is well supplied with food and wheat is raised, and in the warm valleys there are many fruit trees. We spent many days there with President [of the *audiencia* of Peru] La Gasca when he set out to put down the

---

[2] Surnamed "the Rich," an old conquistador whose biography appears in note 2, Chapter 74 below.

rebellion of Gonzalo Pizarro, and these Indians suffered much from the importunity of the Spaniards, and were of great service to them. That good Indian, the lord of this valley, Huasco, handled the matter of provisions with great care.

From this province of Andahuaylas one comes to the Abancay River, which is nine leagues toward Cuzco, and this great river has its strong piles or stone pillars,[3] over which the bridge goes, as in the case of the other rivers. Where it runs, the sierras form a small, wooded valley where fruit and other food grow abundantly. Not far from this river there were lodgings [Cochacajas] and storehouses as in the other small villages, but they were not very important.

[3] In the course of these "nine leagues" before reaching the Abancay is the tambo of Condorhuasi, near the lake of Pacucha; Pincos follows there; the road then mounts the canyon to the pre-Inca ruins of Curamba, which have been noted continuously since 1534. The ruins, consisting of a sun temple and various other dwellings and storehouses, stand on an elevation of approximately 12,500 feet and are grouped about a rectangular plaza which has been leveled. The temple, a truncated-pyramid type, has a stone stairway. The importance of Curamba is that it was one of the Inca centers of wind ovens for smelting gold, silver, and copper ore. At the highest part of the crest, overlooking Curamba, are numerous oval-shaped wind ovens eight feet in diameter with walls two feet thick; the mouths of the tunnels face northeast in the direction of the winds from the Amazon. The ovens were called *huayra* and doubtlessly the place was named Huayra-pampa, the "plain of the wind ovens," since Pedro Sancho in 1534 called it "Airabamba," which is close enough. This is one of the few Inca manufacturing centers that have been found. As the primitive bellows of the Indians could not manually produce sufficient heat to melt metals (gold melting point, 1,063° C.; silver, 1,420° C.; and copper, 1,083° C.), the strong winds produced sufficient draft to obtain the needed temperatures. During the Spanish conquest a number of large silver ingots were found at Andahuaylas which came from Curamba. At Curamba four roads left the plaza in four directions: to the east, the Abra de Curamba; west, Abra de Huancarama, with egress to the Royal Road of the Incas. The south road led to the province of the Rucanas (and may well have been the Inca lateral to the coast), while the north road went in the direction of the Vilcabamba massif where Manco II after 1536 established his neo-Inca state; at least, there is an Inca road that goes in that direction and a large unexplored ruin, Winaysono, stands as a fortress along the way leading to the remarkable stone city of Choqque-quirau, northeast of the Apurímac River.

Cochacajas was a large tambo stop inhabited by Indians whose task it was to keep in repair the suspension bridge that crossed the Pachachaca (*chaca* means "bridge"). Pedro Pizarro described it as a village situated on a high mountain near a lake; the tambo took its name from the lake (*cocha*) on which it is located. The Inca road, leading down to the river in steps about three miles in length, still can be seen in certain sections; at the bridge there are "strong stone towers for the bridge." Cochacajas was destroyed by the Spaniards during the civil war; its great importance is that close to it or at Curamba, the traveler took off along the lateral road that led to Nazca and the coastal road, along the Pacific Coast.

Of the Apurímac River and the valley of Xaquixahuana,
and the road that goes through it, and of other
things, until reaching the city of Cuzco.

134

PROCEEDING ALONG the road, eight leagues from Abancay, one comes to the Apurímac River, which is the largest crossed between here and Cajamarca, traveling southward. The road is well laid out along the slopes and mountains, and those who built it must have had a hard time breaking the rocks and leveling the ground, especially where it descends to the river, and the road is so rough and steep that some of the horses loaded with silver and gold have fallen into the river, where it was impossible to rescue them. There are two great platforms on which to lay the [Apurímac] bridge.[1] When I returned to the City of Kings after we had defeated Gonzalo Pizarro, some of us soldiers crossed the river without the bridge, for it had been destroyed, each of us in a basket, pulling ourselves along with a rope tied to the piles from one bank to the others, over fifty fathoms. It is a fearful thing to see the risks the men who go out to the Indies undergo. Once across this river, one sees where the lodgings of the Incas were, and where they had an oracle, and the devil gave answers through the trunk of a tree, so the Indians say, beside which they buried gold and performed their sacrifices. From this river of Apurímac one continues until coming to the lodgings of Lima-

[1]The bridge was called the *Huaca-chaca*, the "holy bridge," and represented one of the Incas' greatest engineering feats. Cieza believed it was built during the reign of Inca Roca (c. 1350). After Pachacuti defeated the Chancas, the tambo of Curahuasi (still to be seen in utter ruin close to the modern village of the same name) was designated as protector of the bridge. The inhabitant's work-service tax (*mit'a*) was for its upkeep, which the village performed for the life of the bridge, i.e., up until 1890. The road, upon coming to the Apurímac Canyon, passed through a long tunnel; a flight of steps brought one to the platform from which the suspension bridge hung. It stretched 250 feet across, mounted on cabuya cables as thick as a man's body (they were renewed every two years) and hung suspended 125 feet above the roaring Apurímac. Close to it was the shrine "with thick beams," wrote Pedro Sancho, ". . . with a girdle of gold bound around it . . . idols occupied the entire room, coated with human blood and golden robes . . . through the largest one the demon of the river used to speak to the Indians." The American diplomat-archaeologist E. G. Squier crossed it in 1864 and left us its best description; it is also the setting of the novel, *The Bridge of San Luis Rey*. (See von Hagen, *Highway of the Sun*, Chapter VIII, "Apurímac: The Bridge of the Great Speaker.")

tambo, and crossing the sierra of Vilca-conga one comes to the valley of Xaquixahuana,[2] which is level-lying, between the mountain ranges. There were in this valley sumptuous, rich palaces where the rulers of Cuzco used to come to take their pleasure and recreation. It was here that the Governor Don Francisco Pizarro ordered Atahualpa's captain-general, Calicuchima, burned at the stake. It is five leagues from this valley to the city of Cuzco, and the great highway runs through it. The water of a river that rises near this valley forms a deep bog which would be very difficult to cross without a broad and solid highway such as the Incas ordered built,[3] with walls on either side that will last for a long time. Leaving the highway, the way leads over knolls and slopes until coming to the city of Cuzco.

In former times all this valley was densely populated and full of cultivated fields, so many of them and so large that it was a pleasure to see, laid out as they were with broad terraces, from which ran others, with space between to plant the corn and other products they raised. This is the way they were built, clinging to the sides of the mountains. Many of these fields are planted to wheat, for it does well. And there are in them many herds belonging to the Spaniards residing in the ancient city of Cuzco. It is situated between hills in the form and manner set forth in the next chapter.

135

CHAPTER 42 (ii:xv)

Of how the buildings for the Lord-Incas were constructed, and the highways to travel through the kingdom [of Peru].

ONE OF THE things that most took my attention when I was observing and setting down the things of this kingdom was how and in

[2] Xaquixahuana has many fames; here the Chancas were defeated after their attack on Cuzco and the bodies of their chieftains flayed and stuffed and set up as a warning to those who would attack the Inca. Here in 1534 Pizarro defeated the last sizable opposition before moving on to Cuzco. It was here also that Pedro de Cieza served as a soldier with La Gasca in 1548 (and where he lost part of his manuscript), and there Gonzalo Pizarro and Carvajal met their end.

[3] This is the famous causeway of Anta, ten kilometers long, one meter elevation from the morass, and seven meters wide. (See von Hagen, *Highway of the Sun*, Chapter VIII; and Heinrich Ubbelohde Doering, *Auf den Königstrassen der Inka*, 95–96.)

what way the great, splendid highways we see throughout it could be built, and the number of men that must have been required, and what tools and instruments they used to level the mountains and cut through the rock to make them as broad and good as they are. For it seems to me that if the Emperor were to desire another highway built like the one from Quito to Cuzco, or that which goes from Cuzco to Chile, truly I do not believe he could do it, with all his power and the men at his disposal, unless he followed the method the Incas employed. For if it were a question of a road fifty leagues long, or a hundred, or two hundred, we can assume that, however rough the land, it would not be too difficult, working hard, to do it. But these were so long, one of them more than 1,100 leagues, over mountains so rough and dismaying that in certain places one could not see bottom, and some of the sierras so sheer and barren that the road had to be cut through the living rock to keep it level and the right width. All this they did with fire and picks. In other places the incline was so steep and rough that they built steps from the bottom to ascend to the top, with platforms every so often so that the people could rest. In other places there were piles of snow, and this was the most dangerous, and not just in one spot but in many, and not just a little, for there are no words to describe or tell what they were like when we saw them. And through these drifts and where there were forests of trees and turf, they built them smooth and paved with stone, if this was necessary.

Let those who read this book and have been in Peru recall the road which goes from Lima to Jauja over the craggy sierras of Hua-rochirí,[1] and the snow-covered peaks of Pariacaca, and say whether what they saw is more than I describe. Let them also recall the slope that runs down to the Apurímac River, and how the road crosses the sierras of the Paltas, Cajas, and Ayabacas, and other regions of this kingdom, where it is some fifteen feet wide, more or less. In the time of the Lord-Incas it was clean, without a stone or blade of grass, for they were always looking after it; and in the near-by settlements there were great palaces and lodgings for the soldiers, and in the

---

[1] The Jauja road went through Huarochirí and hence down to the Pacific Coast to meet the coastal road at Pachacamac. Cieza rode over this astounding road; parts of it are still to be seen. (See Editor's Introduction, p. xlvi, and José de Acosta's experiences on that same road, in *The Naturall and Morall Historie of the East and West Indies*, 294.)

snowy deserts and open country there were lodgings where they could take refuge from the cold and the rain. In many places, as, for example, in the Colla and other spots, there were road markers like those of Spain, only larger and better made. These are known as *topos,* and each of them represents a league and a half by Castile measure.[2]

Having described how these roads ran and how good they were, I shall tell how easily they were built by these people, without the work occasioning death or undue hardship. When a Lord-Inca had decided on the building of one of these famous highways, no great provisioning or levies or anything else was needed except for the Lord-Inca to say, let this be done. The inspectors then went through the provinces, laying out the route and assigning Indians from one end to the other to the building of the road. In this way, from one boundary of the province to the other, at its expense and with its Indians, it was built as laid out, in a short time; and the others did the same, and, if necessary, a great stretch of the road was built at the same time, or all of it. When they came to the barren places, the Indians of the lands nearest by came with victuals and tools to do the work, and all was done with little effort and joyfully, because they were not oppressed in any way, nor did the Incas put overseers to watch them.

Aside from these, great fine highways were built, like that which runs through the valley of Xaquixahuana, and comes out of the city of Cuzco and goes by the town of Muhina. There were many of these highways all over the kingdom, both in the highlands and the plains. Of all, four are considered the main highways, and they are those which start from the city of Cuzco, at the square, like a crossroads, and go to the different provinces of the kingdom. As these monarchs held such a high opinion of themselves, when they set out on one of these roads, the royal person with the necessary guard took one, and the rest of the people another. So great was their pride that when one of them died, his heir, if he had to travel to a distant place, built his road larger and broader than that of his predecessor, but this was only if this Lord-Inca set out on some conquest, or [performed] some act so noteworthy that it could be said the road built for him was longer. This can be clearly seen, for there are three or four roads

[2] Approximately four and one-half miles.

near Vilcas,[3] and once I got lost on one, thinking it was the one now in use. One of these is called the road of Pachacuti, the other that of Topa Inca, and the one now in use and which will always be used is the one ordered built by Huayna Capac, which runs near the Angasmayo River to the north [in Colombia], and to the south, well beyond what we now call Chile, which roads are so long that there is a distance of more than 1,200 leagues from one end to the other.[4]

138

Huayna Capac ordered this highway built, larger and wider than that his father had made, as far as Quito, where he planned to go, and that the regular lodgings and storehouses and posts be transferred to it. So that all these lands might know that this was his will, messengers set out to notify them, and then *Orejones* to see that it was fulfilled, and the finest road to be seen in the world was built, and the longest, for it started in Cuzco and went to Quito, and joined that which led to Chile. In the memory of people I doubt there is record of another highway comparable to this, running through deep valleys and over high mountains, through piles of snow, quagmires, living rock, along turbulent rivers; in some places it ran smooth and paved, carefully laid out; in others over sierras, cut through the rock, with walls skirting the rivers, and steps and rests through the snow; everywhere it was clean-swept and kept free of rubbish, with lodgings, storehouses, temples to the sun, and posts along the way. Oh, can anything comparable be said of Alexander, or of any of the mighty kings who ruled the world, that they built such a road, or provided the supplies to be found on this one! The road built by the Romans that runs through Spain and the others we read of were as nothing in comparison to this. And it was built in the shortest space of time imaginable, for the Incas took longer to order it than their people in carrying it out.

---

[3] They are three roads: (1) the Quito road, (2) the Cuzco road, and (3) the Soras road which connects with the Cochacajas-Nazca lateral which leads to the coast.

[4] The distance of the Royal Road from Angasmayo (Colombia) to the Maule River in Chile is 3,250 miles; the coastal road beginning at Tumbes extends 2,520 miles to Chile. There were many other radials and laterals which totaled more than 10,000 miles of all-weather roads. The coastal road had a uniform width of twenty-four feet; the mountain road varied, depending on terrain, from fifteen to twenty-four feet; the laterals which joined coastal and Andean roads were of varying widths, three to ten feet, since they were built into canyon walls.

How the posts [O'kla-cuna] were established in this kingdom.

THE KINGDOM of Peru was so vast that, if the Lord-Inca happened 139 to be at one end of his territory, he had to be informed of what was going on at the other by a messenger, who, if he had to make the trip alone, however much he traveled each day, by the time he had covered the thousand leagues it would be too late to do what needed to be done or make the necessary decisions. For this reason, and the better to rule the provinces, the Incas devised a system of posts which was the best that could be thought of or imagined, and this was the invention of Pachacuti, the son of Viracocha Inca, father of Topa Inca, according to the songs of the Indians, which the *Orejones* confirm. Not only did Pachacuti invent these posts, but he did other great things, as we shall relate. Thus, from the time of his reign along all the highways every half-league, more or less, there were little houses well built of wood and straw, and in the mountains they were built along the hillsides and cliffs, so the roads were full of these little houses every so often, as has been said above. And in each of them two Indians were to be stationed, with supplies, and these Indians were to be drawn from the neighboring settlements, and were not to be there permanently, but replaced from time to time by others. This was so carefully observed that all that was necessary was to order it, and it never failed during all the time the Incas reigned.

Each province took care to supply the posts which came within its confines, whether in the wastelands and snow-covered highlands or near the highway. And when word had to be sent to the Lord-Inca in Cuzco or anywhere else of something that had happened or was required for his service, a runner set out from Quito or Tomebamba, or Chile, or Caranqui, or any other part of the kingdom, whether plains or mountains, and at full speed ran that half-league without stopping, for the Indians selected for these posts must have been the swiftest and most agile of all. And when he came near the other post he began to call to the one in it, saying to him, "Set out at once, and go to such and such a place, and tell that this and that has happened, or that this governor begs to inform the Inca. . . ." And as soon as the one who was there heard this, he set out at full speed, and the one who had come went into the little house to rest and eat and drink of what was always kept there, and the other did the same when he reached the next post.

Thus in a short time the news had been carried three hundred leagues, and five hundred, and eight hundred, of what had happened or was needed and should be ordered. And those who carried these messages observed such secrecy on their mission that neither plea nor threat could make them reveal the news they were bearing, even though the message had already been passed on to the next messenger. It is a known fact that over such roads, through rough sierras and perilous mountains, snow-covered peaks, and rocky wastes overgrown with every kind of briar and thorn, neither swift horses nor mules could carry the news with more speed than these messengers on foot. For they are very swift, and one of them could cover more ground in a day than a messenger on horse or mule in three; I do not mean to say a single Indian, but by the system they used, which was for each to travel half a league.[1] And never, because of a storm or anything else that might happen, was any post deserted, but the Indians I have mentioned were always there, and never left until others had come to take their place.

In this manner the rulers were notified of all that happened in their kingdom and realm, and took the measures the situation called for. Nowhere in the world does one read that such an invention existed, although I do know that when Xerxes the Great was defeated, the news was carried in this way, by runners, in a short time. There is no doubt that this organization of the posts was very important in Peru, and it can be seen from this how good was the government of its rulers. Even today in many parts of the uplands, alongside the highways, certain of these post houses can still be seen, and they bear out the truth of what is said. I have seen certain *topos* which are, as I said earlier, like boundary markers, except that these here are large and better made, and by them they counted the leagues, and the distance between each was a league and a half by the measure of Castile.

---

[1] The editor has made an empirical attempt to determine if such a relay capable of running 240 miles within twenty-four hours is possible. It is. (See von Hagen, *Highway of the Sun*, 153–54.)

PART II

CHAPTER 44 (XCII)

Of the manner and fashion in which the city of Cuzco
is built, and the four highways that lead from it, and
the great buildings it had, and who was the founder.

THE CITY of Cuzco is laid out on rough terrain, surrounded by mountains on all sides, between two small brooks, one of which runs through the middle of it, because it has been settled to both sides. To the east there is a valley which begins at the city itself, so the waters of the brooks that run through the city flow out of it westward. Because of the cold climate of this valley there are no fruit-bearing trees except a few *molles*. To the north of the city, on the hill closest to it, there is a fortress [Sacsahuamán],[1] which by reason of its size and strength was once a mighty building, and it still is, even though the greater part of it is in ruins. But the powerful foundations still stand, and the main pillars. To the east and north lie the provinces of Anti-suyu, which are the dense forests and mountains of the Andes, and the largest part of Chinchay-suyu, which includes the regions in the direction of Quito. To the south lie the provinces of the Colla and Cunti-suyu, of which the Colla lies between the east wind and the austral, or that which navigators call the south, and Cunti-suyu south-southwest. One part of this city is known as Hanan-Cuzco and the other as Hurin-Cuzco, where the principal nobility and the old families lived. In another section stands Karmenka Hill,[2] where at inter-

[1] The fortress of Sacsahuamán, overlooking Cuzco on the Anti-suyu (or jungle) road, was without doubt one of the most gigantic single structures ever built by the American Indian. It was begun by the Inca Pachacuti sometime after 1440, when he undertook to build Cuzco after the attack by the Canchas (see Chapter 46 below). It was more than eighty years in the building and, according to native historians who still used the quipu, more than 20,000 workmen were engaged in the work. It was completed about 1520 in the reign of the Inca Huayna Capac, not many years before the arrival of the Spaniards. (See *Guide to the Ruins of Sacsahuamán*, by Victor W. von Hagen.)

[2] Karmenka, a section of Cuzco which stood on the hill that marked the beginning of the long Chinchay-suyu road had a gateway called *Huaca-puncu*, the "holy gate," the first shrine at which the Indian traveler on this road made his devotions "so that the Inca road would not collapse or be destroyed," writes Pedro de Cieza. At the

144

vals there are small towers which they used to study the movement of the sun, to which they attached great importance. Midway between the hills, where most of the inhabitants resided, there was a good-sized square [*Huayḳa-pata*] which they say was a swamp or lake in olden times, and which the founders of the city filled in with stones and mortar and made as it now is. From this square four highways emerge; the one called Chinchay-suyu leads to the plains and the highlands as far as the provinces of Quito and Pasto; the second, known as Cunti-suyu, is the highway to the provinces under the jurisdiction of this city and Arequipa. The third, by name Anti-suyu, leads to the provinces on the slopes of the Andes and various settlements beyond the mountains. The last of these highways, called Colla-suyu, is the route to Chile. Thus, just as in Spain the early inhabitants divided it all into provinces, so these Indians, to keep track of their wide-flung possessions, used the method of highways. The [Huata-nay] river that flows through this city is spanned by bridges.

Nowhere in this kingdom of Peru was there a city with the air of nobility that Cuzco possessed, which (as I have said repeatedly) was the capital of the empire of the Incas and their royal seat. Compared with it, the other provinces of the Indies are mere settlements. And such towns as there are lack design, order, or polity to commend them, whereas Cuzco had distinction to a degree, so those who founded it must have been people of great worth. There were large streets, except that they were narrow, and the houses made all of stone so skillfully joined that it was evident how old the edifices were, for the huge stones were very well set. The other houses were all of wood, thatch, or adobe, for we saw no trace of tile, brick, or mortar. In many parts of this city there were splendid buildings of the Lord-Incas where the heir to the throne held his festivities. There, too, was the imposing temple to the sun, which they called *Curicancha*,[3] which was among the richest in gold and silver to be found anywhere in the world.

It is well known among the Indians that this temple [of Curi-

place where this Karmenka stood, a church, Santa Ana, was erected from the beautifully cut stone of the holy gate.

[3] Curicancha (the "golden enclosure"), temple of the sun, was, it has been affirmed by archaeology, the oldest, wealthiest, and most sacred of Inca shrines. For a full historical and architectural description of it, see John H. Rowe, *An Introduction to the Archaeology of Cuzco*, Peabody Museum *Publications*, Vol. XXVII, No. 2.

"It is five leagues from this valley of Anta to the city of Cuzco, and the great highway runs through it. The water of a river that rises near the valley forms a deep bog which would be very difficult to cross without a broad and solid highway such as the Lord-Incas ordered built." The ancient causeway of Anta still is used and the bogs are still there.

"Eight leagues from Abancay one comes to the Apurímac River, the largest crossed between here and Cajamarca. There are two great platforms on which to lay the bridge." The "bridge of the great speaker" from an engraving in E. G. Squier's *Peru*.

"Some of the mountains so sheer and barren that the road had to be cut through the living rock"—like this main road through Pisac.

"And in other places the incline [of the highway] was so steep and rough that they built steps from the bottom to ascend to the top, with platforms every once in a while where people could rest."

"I doubt there is record of another highway comparable to this running through deep valleys, over high mountains, through piles of snow, quagmire, living rock, and across turbulent rivers." A stone Inca bridge beyond the mountains of Macusani.

"They used, as they went by the way, to cast stones on the highways, on the hills and tops of mountains, and these are called *apachetas*. These are piles of stones which are built up at every mountain pass; they carry the stone for a little way before arriving, [then] deposit the stone on the *apacheta* and leave their tiredness behind." A massive *apacheta* on the Macusani Inca road.

"The Incas devised a series of posts along all the highways every half-league. And in each of them two Indians *(chasquis)* were stationed, and when a message had to be sent out to Cuzco or anywhere else, a runner set out and at full speed ran half a league without stopping and passed the message to the next, who set out at full speed. Thus in a short time the news could be carried a thousand miles." A modern *"chasqui"* making a test run over the Royal Road of the Incas near Tarma.

"The great coastal highway which the Incas ordered built across the desert; although in many places this road is now ruined and destroyed, it still reveals what a splendid thing it was." The Inca coastal road going through the desert near Saña.

cancha] is as old as the city of Cuzco itself; however, the Inca Yupanqui [Pachacuti], son of Viracocha Inca, added to its riches and left it as it was when the Spaniards entered Peru. Most of its treasures were taken to Cajamarca for the ransom of Atahualpa, as we shall tell when the time comes. And the *Orejones* relate that after the conclusion of the dubious war between the inhabitants of Cuzco and the Chancas, who are now the lords of the province of Andahuaylas, in the victory he won over them Pachacuti achieved such widespread renown and esteem that from all sides chieftains came to render him fealty, and the provinces brought him great tribute of gold and silver, for in those days there were great mines and richest lodes. Seeing himself so opulent and powerful, he decided to ennoble the house of the sun, which in their language they call Indehuaxi and to which they gave the name of Curicancha, as well—which means "fenced with gold"—and endow it with riches. And that all who see or read this may know how rich the temple of Cuzco was, and the prowess of those who built it and did such great things in it, I shall give an account of it as I saw it and what I heard from many of the first Spaniards, who had it from the three[4] who went to Cajamarca and saw it, although what the Indians tell is so complete and so true that no other proof is needed.

145

This temple had a circumference of over four hundred feet, and was all surrounded by a strong wall. The whole building was of fine quarried stone, all matched and joined, and some of the stones were very large and beautiful. No mortar on earth or lime was employed in it, only the pitch which they used in their buildings, and the stones are so well cut that there is no sign of cement or joinings. In all Spain I have seen nothing that can compare with these walls and the laying of the stones except the tower known as the Calahorra, the bridge of Córdoba, and a building I saw in Toledo when I went to present the

---

[4] Martín Bueno, Francisco de Zárate, and Pedro de Moguer were sent in March, 1533, by Francisco Pizarro from Cajamarca to hurry up the flow of gold from Cuzco, but they, carried as gods in golden litters, behaved in so forward a manner that the Inca officials loaded them with gold and returned them to Cajamarca. They were perhaps the only Christians to see Cuzco before its fall. Hernando de Soto—the same De Soto who met with death and glory on the Mississippi River—was sent with one Pedro del Barco to Cuzco, although this is disputed by one of Peru's foremost scholars (see Raúl Porras Barrenechea, *Las Primeras Crónicas de la Conquista del Perú*). The whole episode is related by Garcilaso de la Vega in *Comentarios Reales de los Incas* (Part II), I, chap. 31.

First Part of my Chronicle to the Prince, Don Philip,[5] which is the hospital built at the orders of the Archbishop of Toledo, Tavera. Although these buildings somewhat resemble those I have mentioned, they are finer, that is to say, as regards the walls and the cutting and laying of the stones, and the fence was plumb and very well laid. The stone seems to me blackish and rough and of excellent quality. It had many gates, and the gateways finely carved; halfway up the wall ran a stripe of gold two handspans wide and four fingers thick. The gateway and doors were covered with sheets of this metal. Inside there were four buildings, not very large, fashioned in the same way, and the walls inside and out were covered with gold, and the beams, too, and the roof was of thatch. There were two benches against that wall, which the rising sun fell upon, and the stones were very skillfully perforated, and the openings set with precious stones and emeralds. These benches were for the Lord-Incas, and if anyone else sat there, he was sentenced to death.

146

There were guards at the doors of these houses whose duty it was to watch over the virgins, many of whom were daughters of the leading nobles, the most beautiful and comely that could be found. They remained in the temples until they were old, and if any of them knew a man, she was killed or buried alive, and he suffered the same fate. These women were called *mamaconas;*[6] they did nothing but weave and dye woolen garments for the service of the temple and make chicha, which is the wine they drink, of which they always had great vessels.

In one of these houses, which was the richest, there was an image of the sun, of great size, made of gold, beautifully wrought and set with many precious stones. It [this house] also held some of the statues of the Incas who had reigned in Cuzco, with a vast store of treasure.

Around this temple there were many small dwellings of Indians

[5] Apparently Pedro de Cieza de León was brought to Philip, prince of Spain (1527–98), just before his ascension to the throne. This was in the last months of 1552. Cieza's *Primera Crónica del Perú* (First Chronicle) is dedicated to the Prince, who became Philip II, king of Spain, Sicily, and Naples.

[6] They were chosen as young girls, for their beauty and perfection, and sent to the houses of the Chosen Women, where, under the guidance of the *mamaconas* ("mothers"), they learned fine weaving, cooking, and attendance on the sun temples. Some of the *mamaconas* were sworn to perpetual chastity and served the "Sun"; others prepared food and drink for the Inca; some became his concubines. The Chosen Women were selected at the age of ten; they were considered fortunate.

who were assigned to its service, and there was a fence inside which they put the white lambs and the children and men to be sacrificed. There was a garden in which the earth was lumps of fine gold, and it was cunningly planted with stalks of corn that were of gold—stalk, leaves, and ears. These were so well planted that no matter how hard the wind blew it could not uproot them. Aside from this, there were more than twenty sheep of gold with their lambs, and the shepherds who guarded them, with their slings and staffs, all of this metal. There were many tubs of gold and silver and emeralds, and goblets, pots, and every kind of vessel all of fine gold. On the other walls there were carved and painted other still greater things. In a word, it was one of the richest temples in the whole world.

147

The high priest, called Vilaoma [Villac-umu],[7] dwelt in the temple, and aided by the priests, performed the ordinary sacrifices with great ceremony, in keeping with their custom. The general feasts were attended by the Inca to witness the sacrifices, and these were carried out with great celebration. Within the house and temple there were more than thirty bins [made] of silver in which they stored the corn, and the contributions of many provinces were assigned to this temple. On certain days the devil appeared to the priests, and made them vain answers of the sort that he gave.

Many other things could be told of this temple which I omit because it seems to me that what has been said suffices for an understanding of what a great thing it was. For I make no mention of the silverwork, beads, golden feathers, and other things which, if I were to describe them, would not be believed. And, as I have said, there are Spaniards still alive who saw most of this, which was taken to Cajamarca for the ransom of Atahualpa, but the Indians hid much, and it is buried and lost. Although all the Incas had contributed to the aggrandizement of this temple, in the days of Pachacuti he so enhanced it that when he died and Topa Inca, his son, ruled the kingdom, it was in this state of perfection.

Most of the city was settled by *mitimaes,* and the great laws and statutes had been enacted, after the Inca custom, which were obeyed by all, both as refers to their vain observances and temples as well as their government. It was the richest city in all the Indies, as far as we can gather, for the treasures assembled for the glory of the Incas

7 See note 2, Chapter 57 below.

had been collected there for many years, and none of the gold and silver brought into it could be removed, under penalty of death. Sons of all the provincial chieftains came to live at this court with their pomp and service. There were numbers of silversmiths and goldsmiths who worked for the Incas. In the main temple there lived a high priest called Vilaoma. Today there are very good, turreted houses, covered with tiles. Although this city is cold, it is very healthy, and the best provisioned in the whole kingdom, and the largest, where the most Spaniards hold an encomienda of Indians. It was founded and settled by Manco Capac, the first of the Inca lords. And after ten Incas had succeeded him in the rule,[8] it was rebuilt and refounded by Francisco Pizarro, governor and captain-general of these kingdoms, in the name of the Emperor Charles V . . . in the month of October of 1534.

As this was the main and most important city of this kingdom, at certain times of the year the Indians of the provinces came there, some to construct buildings, others to clean the streets and districts, and [to do] anything else they were ordered. Near to it, on either hand, there are many buildings which were lodgings and storehouses, all of the design and structure of the others throughout the kingdom, although some are larger, some smaller, some stouter, than others.

As these Incas were so rich and powerful, some of these buildings were gilded, and others were adorned with plates of gold. Their forebears considered a hill near this city, which they called Huana-cauri, sacred, and there, it is said, they made sacrifice of human blood and of many llamas. And as this city was full of strange and foreign peoples, for there were Indians from Chile, Pasto, and Cañari, Chachapoyas, Huancas, Collas, and all the other tribes to be found in the provinces we have described, each of them was established in the place and district set aside for them by the governors of the city. They observed the customs of their own people and dressed after the fashion of their own land, so that if there were a hundred thousand men, they could be easily recognized by the insignia they wore about their heads. Some of these outlanders buried their dead on high hills, others in their houses, and others in their fields, with living women

---

[8] According to modern researchers, there were thirteen historical Incas, ending with Atahualpa (who was never actually "crowned" as Inca, but served as such). (See Rowe, "Inca Culture at the Time of the Spanish Conquest," *Handbook*, II, 202–203.)

and the things they had prized most, as has been told before, and much food. And the Incas (as I can gather) did not prohibit any of these things, provided they all worshiped the sun, which they called Mocha, and did it homage. In many parts of this city there are large buildings under the ground, and in the bowels of it even today paving stones and pipes are found, and an occasional jewel and piece of gold of that which they buried. Without doubt there must be great treasures buried in the area of this city, of which those now living have no knowledge. As so many people lived there, and the devil held such sway over them, with the permission of God, that there were many wizards, augurs, and idolators. Nor is the city wholly free of such relics, especially as refers to witchcraft. Near this city there are many temperate valleys where there are orchards and gardens, both of which flourish, and much of the produce is brought to the city to be sold. Abundant wheat is now harvested, from which bread is made. In these places to which I refer many oranges and other fruit trees of Spain are raised, as well as the native ones. In the river which runs through the city there are mills, and four leagues away one can see the quarries from which they dug the stone for their buildings, an impressive sight. Aside from the foregoing, many fowl and capons are raised in Cuzco, as good and fat as those of Granada, and in the plains and valleys there are herds of cows and goats and other livestock, both that of Spain and the native. Although there are no orchards in this city, the vegetables of Spain do very well.

CHAPTER 45 (ii: XXVIII)

Which deals with the other temples which, aside from this, were considered the most important, and their names.

MANY WERE THE temples in this kingdom of Peru, and some of them were held to be very old, for they had been founded before, long before, the Incas reigned, both in the uplands of the mountains and in the . . . plains. During the reign of the Incas many others were built where they performed their sacrifices and observed their feasts. Inasmuch as to list one by one the temples to be found in each province would be long and prolix, I have decided to put down only those which were considered most eminent and noteworthy. Thus, after the temple of Curicancha, the second most important place of worship of the Incas was the hill of Guanacaure [Huana-cauri],[1] which is within sight of the city, and was often visited and honored by them because of what was told by some about the brother of the first Inca having turned to stone at that place at the time they emerged from Pacaritambo [Paccaric-Tampu],[2] as I related in the beginning. In olden days there was in this hill a shrine, and around it was buried a great wealth of treasure, and on certain days women and men were sacrificed, who, before they were sacrificed, were made to believe by the priests that they would go to serve that god whom they adored, there in the glory that their folly painted. The sacrificial victims being persuaded of this, the men decked themselves out in their finest attire, clothing of rich wool, headbands of gold, breastplates of gold, bracelets of gold, and sandals with cords of gold. After listening to the lying exhortation of the priests, they were given much of their chicha to drink in goblets of gold, and the sacrifice was solemnized with songs, relating how, to serve their gods, they were giving up their lives in this way, considering themselves happy to receive death on that spot. When all this had been chanted, they were strangled by the priests, and on their backs was hung a knapsack of gold and a pitcher of the same metal [placed] in their hands, and they were buried near the shrine in their graves. And these were regarded among them as canonized saints, believing beyond the shadow of a doubt that they were in heaven serving their Huana-cauri. The women who were sacrificed likewise went bravely attired in their fine colored

150

1 Huana-cauri was one of the most sacred of Inca shrines. Situated about eight miles southeast of Cuzco on a hill, it is connected with the legend of Cuzco's founding by the first Inca, Manco Capac, and was reputed to be one of Manco Capac's brothers, turned to stone. The monolith was of medium size, spindle-shaped, and stood on top of the hill. Many of the puberty ceremonies of the Incas were held there. The site has now all but disappeared. (See Rowe, *An Introduction to the Archaeology of Cuzco*.)

2 Paccaric-Tampu is one of the most controversial sites in the Incas' legendary history, mostly because it has been given prominent place in Hiram Bingham's last book, *The Lost City of the Incas* (New York, 1948), wherein he tried to identify Machu Picchu with this "origin place" of the Incas. The site of the ruins is located twenty miles, more or less, southwest of Cuzco on the Cunti-suyu road toward the Pacific. Its excavation corresponds very well with the description of it given by the Inca legends. (See *Revista Sec. Arq. del Cuzco* [Cuzco, 1946].)

clothing and feathers, and their pins of gold, and their spoons and bowls and plates, all of gold. And thus decked out, after they had drunk deep, they were strangled and buried, believing, they and those who killed them, that they were going to serve their devil or Huana-cauri. Great dances were held and there was singing when these sacrifices were celebrated. This idol where the shrine was had its farms, laborers, flocks, and virgins, and priests who made use of most of these things.

The third oracle and temple of the Incas was that of Vilcanota, famous throughout these kingdoms, [that] . . . spoke through the mouth of the false priests who were there at the services of the idols. This temple of Vilcanota was a little more than twenty leagues from Cuzco, near the village of Chungara, and it was held in great veneration and esteem, and many gifts and presents were brought to it, by both the Incas and chieftains, as well as by rich men who came to make sacrifices. It had its priests, virgins, and lands, and nearly every year offerings were made in this temple of *capaccocha*,[3] which I shall later describe. Great credence was given to the replies, and at times great sacrifices were made.

The fourth temple the Incas and natives of the provinces esteemed and frequented was that of Ancocagua, where, too, there was an ancient oracle held in high regard. It lies alongside the province of Hatuncana, and at times they came devoutly from many regions to listen to the vain replies of this devil. There were great treasures in it, for the Incas and all the others brought them there. And it is said. that aside from the many animals sacrificed to this devil, whom they held to be a god, they did the same with Indians, men and women, just as I have related of Huana-cauri. And that there was all the treasure reported in this temple is believed to be true, for more than three years after the Spaniards had won Cuzco, and the priests and caciques had taken away the great treasures all these temples possessed, I heard that a Spaniard by the name of Diego Rodríguez Elemosin got from this temple over thirty thousand gold pesos; aside from this, still more has been found, and it is said that there is a vast sum of silver and gold buried in places nobody knows of, unless it be God, and it will never be found unless it is discovered by chance.

In addition to these temples, there was another as venerated and

3 A ritual for human sacrifice. See Chapter 60 below.

frequented, or even more so, which was known as Coropuna,[4] in the province of Cunti-suyu, on a lofty hill that was always covered with snow, in winter as well as summer. The Incas of Peru and the leading nobles visited this temple, making gifts and offerings as to those already described; and it is held to be a fact that of the gifts and *capaccocha* made to this temple there are many loads of gold and silver and jewels buried in places nobody knows of, and the Indians hid another great sum which was for the service of the idol and the priests and *mamaconas,* of which there were also many in the temple. And as the snow is so deep, they cannot climb to the summit, nor have they been able to discover where these great treasures are. This temple had many flocks and farms and Indians to serve it, and *mamaconas.* There were always people from many places in it, and the devil talked here more freely than in the aforementioned shrines, because he continually gave a thousand answers, not periodically, as in the others. Even today, for some secret reason of God, it is told that devils appear visibly around that region, and that the Indians see them and take great fright therefrom. I have even heard from the Spaniards that they have seen them, in the shape of Indians, appear and disappear in the twinkling of an eye.

Aside from these temples, there was that of Aperahua [Apurímac],[5] where from the trunk of a tree the oracle gave answer, and close by it a quantity of gold was found; and that of Pachacamac,[6] which is of the Yungas, and many others, in the region of Anti-suyu [eastern jungle *montaña*], in that of Chinchay-suyu and Oma-suyu, and other parts of this kingdom, of which I could make further relation. In those not so venerated they did not shed human blood nor kill people, but offered only gold and silver. To the shrines they held in less esteem, which were like hermitages, they brought beads and feathers and other trifles of slight value. I say this because the idea we Span-

[4] In Cunti-suyu in the *puna,* about 5,000 meters high, close to the flamingo lake of Parinacochas, for which see Chapter 65.

[5] This shrine was located on the north bank of the Apurímac River, close to the famous swinging bridge. Here was an idol, lodged in a painted hut and set up in a thick beam, thicker than a fat man, wrote Pedro Sancho in his *Relación* (trans. by P. A. Means; New York, Cortés Society, 1926): "The idol had a girdle of gold bound around it and soldered so as to resemble lace, and on the front of it two large golden teats like a woman . . . . Through this largest idol they say it was the demon of the river who used to speak (*apurímac*) to them."

[6] Pachacamac (near Lima), the greatest of Peru's *huacas.* (See Chapters 82 and 116 below.)

iards have that they sacrificed human beings in all their temples is false, and what I say is the truth as I was able to understand it, without omitting or adding anything except what I could gather and consider true.

CHAPTER 46 (ii: li)

Of how the royal house of the sun was founded on a hill that overlooks Cuzco to the north, which the Spaniards usually refer to as the Fortress, and of its remarkable construction and the size of the stones employed.

THE CITY OF Cuzco is built in a valley, on slopes and hills, as has been related, and from the buildings themselves there run wide walls of a sort, within which they plant their crops, and they abut evenly one upon the other, so all was terraced, which made the city stronger, even though its natural setting made it so; for this reason the Incas chose it among all the territory they possessed. And as the power of the Incas was increasing, and Pachacuti had such great ambitions, in spite of the fact that he had already beautified and enriched the temple of the sun called Curicancha, and had built other large edifices, he decided [c. 1439] to build a house of the sun[1] which should surpass everything done until then, and that it should house everything imaginable, such as gold and silver, precious stones, fine garments, arms of all the types they used, materials of war, sandals, shields, feathers, skins of animals and birds, coca, bags of wool, a thousand kinds of jewels; in a word, everything anyone had ever heard of was in it. This work was conceived on such a vast scale that even if the monarchy had lasted until now, it would not have been completed.

He ordered twenty thousand men sent in from the provinces, and that the villages supply them with the necessary food, and if one of them took sick, that another should be sent in his place and he could

[1] This actually was the fortress of Sacsahuamán. (See note 1, Chapter 44, for description.)

return to his home. These Indians were not permanently engaged in this work, but only for a limited time, and then others came and they left, so the work did not become onerous. Four thousand of them quarried and cut the stones; six thousand hauled them with great cables of leather and hemp; the others dug the ditch and laid the foundations, while still others cut poles and beams for the timbers. So that they would be contented, these people lived in separate groups, each with those of his own region, near the site where the building was to be erected. Even today most of the walls of the houses they occupied can still be seen. Overseers went around watching what they did, and masters who were highly skilled in their work. Thus, on a hill to the north of the city, at its highest point, slightly more than a bow-shot distance, this fortress was built which the natives called the "House of the Sun," and we the "Fortress."

The living rock was excavated for the foundations, and for this reason it was so strong that it will last as long as the world exists. By my calculations, it was 330 feet long and 200 wide. It had many walls that were so strong that no artillery is powerful enough to break them down. The main gate was a thing to behold, so beautifully was it built, and the walls so aligned that one did not project beyond the other. There are stones of such size and magnificence in these walls that it baffles the mind to think how they could be brought up and set in place, and who could have cut them, for they had so few tools. Some of these stones are about twelve feet wide and over twenty long; others are as thick as an ox, and all so exactly set that a coin could not be inserted between them. I went to see this building twice, once with Tomás Vásquez,[2] conquistador, and the other with Hernando de Guzmán,[3] who was at the siege, and Juan de la Playa;[4] and those of you who read this may rest assured that what I am telling is not a patch on what I saw. And as I went about observing, I saw close to

[2] Tomás Vásquez, called by Garcilaso de la Vega *"conquistador de los primeros,"* "one of the first," had his house close to the Inca chronicler in Cuzco, in the Cusipata section. He fought in the battle of Chupas and signed the report on the "Regulations for Tambos" (Cuzco, 1543).

[3] Not to be confused with the *pícaro* Alonso Enríquez de Guzmán who wrote his Benvenuto Cellini–like memoirs of his adventures during the conquest (*Life and Acts of Don Alonso Enríquez de Guzmán*). This Guzmán was never mentioned again. The "siege" was the investment of Sacsahuamán and Cuzco by forces of Manco II in 1536. It is vividly and accurately described by Prescott in his *Conquest of Peru*.

[4] Juan de la Playa (the name variously spelled in various editions) is unknown.

this fortress a stone which I measured, and it was 270 handspans of mine in circumference, and so high that it seemed to have originated there. All the Indians tell that this stone got tired at that spot, and that they were never able to move it from there. The fact is that if there were not signs on the stone itself that it had been quarried, I would not believe, no matter what they told me, that human hands could have brought it there, where it will remain as proof of what the builders of so vast a construction were, for the Spaniards have already done so much damage and left it in such a state that I hate to think of the responsibility of those who have governed in allowing so extraordinary a thing to have been destroyed and cast down, without giving thought to future times and events and how much better it would be to have it standing and cared for.

155

There were many apartments in this stronghold: some, one above the other, these small; and others, on different floors, these large; and two towers, one larger than the other, broad and so well designed that I cannot praise them enough, so fine were they and the stones so well cut and laid, and they say there are even larger buildings underground. They also recount other things which I am not setting down because I am not sure of them.

This fortress had been begun in the days of Pachacuti; his son Topa Inca and Huayna Capac and Huascar [d. 1532] added greatly to it, and even though today it is still a remarkable sight, it was once far more.[5] When the Spaniards entered Cuzco, the Indians of Quizquiz removed great treasures from it, and the Spaniards still found some, and it is believed that there is still a great deal buried around it. The remains of this fortress and that of Huarco[6] should be preserved in memory of the greatness of this land, and even for the sake of having

[5] It is now deduced that the *pucará* of Sacsahuamán was begun by the Inca Pachacuti some time after 1440—after Cuzco was almost totally destroyed in the battle against the Chancas tribe. The building was directed by professional architects, whose names are remembered at two of three entrances to the fortress. More than 20,000 *mit'a* labor Indians were involved for the sixty-eight years of its building, and, according to the records of the "rememberers" who consulted the quipu strings, it was finished in 1508 in the time of the last great Inca, Huayna Capac. (See von Hagen, *Guide to the Ruins of Sacsahuamán.*)

[6] Huarco is in the valley of Cañete—named after the second viceroy of Peru. The extensive ruins are known today by the name Incahuasi (a term which means no more than the "Inca's house"); it was the most ambitious of the Inca's coastal cities and was called, according to Pedro de Cieza, "New Cuzco." (See Chapters 117 and 118 below.)

these two fortresses there, which were found already built at so little cost. And with this, I shall return to my subject.

CHAPTER 47 (ii: xiv)

*Of the great wealth the Incas possessed and held,
and how sons of the nobles were always ordered to
be at their court.*

IN VIEW of the great wealth we have seen in these regions, we can well believe that what the Incas were said to possess is true. I am of the opinion, as I have said many times, that there is no kingdom in the world so rich in precious ores, for every day great lodes are discovered, both of gold and of silver. And as gold is washed from the rivers in many of the provinces, and silver is found in the mountains, and it all went to a single Inca, he could hold and possess so much wealth. It amazed me that the whole city of Cuzco and its temples were not of solid gold. For what impoverishes princes and keeps them stripped of money is war, as we have a patent example in what the Emperor [Charles V] has expended for this purpose from the year he was crowned until now.[1] Possessing more silver and gold than any king of Spain from Don Rodrigo to himself, none of them was as hard up as His Majesty, and if he had no wars and remained in Spain, with the nation's revenues and what has come from the Indies, all Spain could be as full of treasure as was Peru in the days of its Incas.

I make this comparison to point out that had all the Incas spent only on their own adornment and for the beautifying of the temples and the service of their palaces and lodgings, for the provinces provided all the men, arms, and supplies needed for war, and if they paid any of the *mitimaes* in gold for their services in some war they considered difficult, it was little and could be taken from the mines in a

[1] Charles V (Charles I to the Spaniards) was the son of Queen Juana the Mad and Archduke Philip the Fair. Born in 1500, his consuming interest was to become Holy Roman Emperor. His wars with France, within Italy, and in the Lowlands kept the imperial treasury constantly strained. His struggles with Turks and the Barbaresques evaporated the whole of his golden patrimony from the American conquests, and he was forced to borrow money from the German bankers, the Fuggers and Welsers.

single day. As they esteemed silver and gold so highly, they ordered it mined in many parts of the provinces in great quantity, in the way and manner I shall describe.

Accumulating such a fortune, and with the heir being obliged to leave the possessions of his predecessor untouched, that is to say, his house, his household, and his statue, the treasure piled up over many years, so that all the service of the king's house, even water jars and kitchen utensils, was of gold and silver; and not only in a single place, but in many, especially the capitals of the provinces, where there were many gold and silversmiths engaged in the manufacture of these objects. In their palaces and lodgings there were bars of these metals, and their garments were covered with ornaments of silver, and emeralds and turquoise, and other precious stones of great value. And for their wives there was even greater luxury in their adornment and for their personal service, and their litters were all encrusted with silver and gold and jewels. Aside from this, they had a vast quantity of ingots of gold, and unwrought silver, and tiny beads, and many other and large vessels for their drinking feasts, and for their sacrifices still more of these treasures. And as they observed and held to that custom of burying treasure with the dead, it is easy to believe that in the obsequies and burials of these Incas incredible quantities of it were placed in the graves. Even their drums and chairs[2] and musical instruments and arms were of this metal. And to glorify their state, as though all this I have described were not enough, it was a law that none of the gold or silver brought into Cuzco could be removed, under penalty of death, which was immediately carried out against any who contravened it. With this law, and so much coming in and none going out, there was such an amount that if, when the Spaniards entered, they had behaved differently and had not so quickly displayed their cruelty by putting Atahualpa to death, I do not know how many ships would have been needed to carry to Spain the vast treasures lost in the bowels of the earth, where they will remain, for those who buried them are now dead.

As these Incas held themselves in such high esteem, they ordered that all year long sons of the lords of all the provinces of the kingdom should reside in their court to learn the manners of it and see its

157

---

[2] This was the golden stool (*osño*); only the Inca and his governing blood-relatives were permitted it.

majesty, and understand how the Inca should be served and obeyed when they came into the rule of their fiefdoms. When those of certain provinces departed, their place was taken by those from others. As a result of this system, the court was always very splendid and full, for, aside from these, the Inca was always surrounded by many nobles of the *Orejones* and elder men of wisdom [*amauta-cuna*] with whom he consulted what should be planned and ordered.

CHAPTER 48 (ii: XVII)

Which deals with the manner in which the Incas carried out their conquests, and how in many places they made arid lands fertile, and the way in which they accomplished this.

ONE OF the things most to be envied these rulers is how well they knew to conquer such vast lands and, with their forethought, bring them to the flourishing state in which the Spaniards found them when they discovered this new kingdom. Proof of this is the many times I recall hearing these same Spaniards say, when we were in some indomitable region outside these kingdoms, "Take my word for it, if the Incas had been here it would have been a different story." In a word, the Incas did not make their conquests any way just for the sake of being served and collecting tribute. In this respect they were far ahead of us, for with the order they introduced the people throve and multiplied, and arid regions were made fertile and bountiful, in the ways and goodly manner that will be told.

They always tried to do things by fair means and not by foul at the beginning; afterward, certain of the Incas meted out severe punishments in many places, but they all tell that they first used great benevolence and friendliness to win these people over to their service. They set out from Cuzco with their men and weapons, and traveled in careful manner until they were close to the place they were going and planned to conquer. There they carefully sized up the situation to learn the strength of the enemy, the support they might have, and from what direction help might come, and by what road. When they had so informed themselves, they tried in every possible way to prevent them from receiving succor, either by rich gifts or by blocking the way. Aside from this, they built fortifications on hills or slopes with high, long stockades, each with its own gate, so that if one were lost, they could retire to the next, and so on to the topmost. And they sent out scouts of their confederates to spy out the land and learn the paths and find out whether they were waiting for them, and where the most food was. And when they knew the route by which the enemy was approaching and the force in which they were coming, they sent ahead messengers to say that the Inca wanted them to be his kin and allies, and, therefore, to come out to welcome him and receive him in their province with good cheer and light heart, and swear him fealty as the others had done. And so they would do this willingly, he sent gifts to the native rulers.

In this way, and with other good methods they employed, they entered many lands without war, and the soldiers who accompanied the Inca were ordered to do no damage or harm, or robbery or violence. If there was a shortage of food in the province, he ordered supplies brought in from other regions so that those newly won to his service would not find his rule and acquaintance irksome, and that knowing and hating him would be one. If in any of these provinces there were no flocks, he instantly ordered that they be given thousands of head, ordering that they tend them well so that they would multiply and supply them with wool for their clothing, and not to venture to kill or eat any of the young during the years and time he fixed. And if there were flocks, but they lacked some other thing, he did the same. If they were living in hills and wooded places, he made them understand with courteous words that they should build their villages and houses in the level parts of the sierras and hillsides; and as many of them were not skilled in the cultivation of the land, he had them taught how they should do it, urging them to build irrigation canals and water their fields from them.

They knew how to provide for everything so well that when one of the Incas entered a province in friendship, in a little while it seemed a different place and the natives obeyed him, agreeing that his representatives should dwell there, and also the *mitimaes*. In many others, where they entered by war and force of arms, they ordered that the crops and houses of the enemy be spared, the Inca saying, "These will soon be ours like those we already possess." As this was known to all, they tried to make the war as mild as possible even though fierce battles were waged in many places, because, in spite of everything, the inhabitants of them wanted to preserve their ancient liberty and not give up their customs and religion for others that were alien. But in the end the Incas always came out victorious, and when they had vanquished the others, they did not do them further harm, but released those they had taken prisoner, if there were any, and restored the booty, and put them back in possession of their property and rule, exhorting them not to be foolish and try to compete with his royal majesty nor abandon his friendship, but to be his friends as their neighbors were. And saying this, he gave them a number of beautiful women and fine pieces of wool or gold.

160

With these gifts and kindly words he won the good will of all to such a degree that those who had fled to the mountains returned to their homes, and all laid down their arms, and the one who most often had sight of the Inca was considered blessed and happy.

They never deprived the native chieftains of their rule. They were all ordered to worship the sun as God, but they were not prohibited from observing their own religions and customs. However, they were ordered to be ruled by the laws and customs which prevailed in Cuzco, and all were to speak the general language.

And when the Inca had appointed a governor with a garrison of soldiers, he went on, and if the provinces were large, he at once ordered a temple built to the sun and women assigned to it as in the others, and palaces built for the Inca, and the amount of tribute to be paid fixed, without ever making this burdensome or offending the people in any way, but guiding them in the ways of their polity, and teaching them to wear long clothing and live in their settlements in orderly manner. And if they lacked for anything, they were provided with it, and taught how to plant and cultivate. So well was this done that we know of many places where there had been no flocks that had them in abundance from the time the Incas subdued them, and others where there had been no corn that later had more than they could use. Those who had lived like savages, poorly clad and barefoot, after they acknowledged this ruler wore shirts and ribbons and blankets, and their women likewise, and other good things; so much so that there will always be memory of all this. In the Collao

and other regions they ordered *mitimaes*[1] to go to the highlands of
the Andes to plant corn and coca and other fruits and roots, the
necessary number from all the settlements. And these and their wives
always lived in the place where they planted their crops, and harvested so much of what I have described that there was no lack, for
these regions produced so much that there was no village, however
small, that did not receive something from these *mitimaes*. Farther
on we shall tell of the different kinds of *mitimaes* there were, and
what the different ones did and engaged in.

161

CHAPTER 49 (ii: XVIII)

Which deals with the manner in which the provinces
were taxed, and the equitable fashion in
which this was done.

AS IN THE previous chapter I described the way in which the Incas
carried out their conquests, in this it would be well to tell how the
different nations were taxed, and how the returns of this taxation
were handled in Cuzco. For as is well known to all, not a single
village of the highlands or the plains failed to pay the tribute levied
on it by those who were in charge of these matters. There were even
provinces where, when the natives alleged that they were unable to
pay their tribute, the Inca ordered that each inhabitant should be
obliged to turn in every four months a large quill full of live lice,
which was the Inca's way of teaching and accustoming them to pay
tribute. We know that for a time they paid their tax in lice until, after
they had been given flocks and had raised them, and made clothing,
they were able to pay tribute henceforth.

According to the *Orejones* of Cuzco and the other native rulers of
the land, the system of taxing was said to be this: the ruling monarch
sent out from the city of Cuzco certain of the most important officials
of his household on a visit of inspection over one of the four highways
that lead out of the city, which, as I have said, are those of Chinchay-
suyu, which crosses the provinces as far as Quito, including all the
land lying to the north; Cunti-suyu, which includes the regions and

[1] For a full discussion of the *mitimaes,* see Chapter 16 above.

provinces neighboring on the Southern Sea and many of those of the
highlands; Colla-suyu, which runs through all the provinces lying to
the south as far as Chile; and, finally, Anti-suyu, which is the route
to the lands of the Andes Mountains, including the slopes and flanks
of these.

162

Therefore, when the Lord-Inca wished to learn what all the provinces between Cuzco and Chile, such a vast extension, were to contribute, he sent out, as I have said, persons who enjoyed his confidence,
who went from village to village observing the attire of the natives
and their state of prosperity, and the fertility of the land, and whether
they had flocks, or metals, or stores of food, or the other things which
they valued and prized. After they had made a careful survey, they
returned to report to the Inca about all this. He then called a general
assembly of the principal men of the kingdom, and when the chieftains of the different provinces that were to be taxed had gathered,
he addressed them with affectionate words, saying that inasmuch as
they accepted him as sole sovereign and monarch of so many and
such great lands, they would agree, without being distressed thereby,
to give him the tribute due his royal person, which he wanted to be
moderate and so unvexing that they could easily pay it. And when
he had been answered to his satisfaction, certain of the *Orejones* set
out with the native lords to fix the tribute they were to pay. In some
regions this was more than that now paid to the Spaniards, but the
system the Incas employed was so good that the people did not feel
it, and prospered; but with the disorder and greed of the Spaniards
the number of the people has fallen off to such a degree that most of
them have disappeared, and they will be wiped out completely as a
result of the covetousness and greed of most, or all of us here, unless
God in His mercy remedies the situation, putting an end to the wars[1]

1 The "wars" were, of course, the civil wars which began in 1536 between those
partners in the conquest of Peru, Almagro the Blinkard and Francisco Pizarro. Almagro
was defeated at the battle of Salinas in 1537 and was garroted by the victorious Pizarros.
("He died," wrote Cieza, "at the age of sixty-three . . . a man of short stature with
ugly features but of great courage . . . he was of such humble origin that it may
be said of him that his lineage began and ended with himself.") Francisco Pizarro
was in turn assassinated by Almagro's men in 1541, and this brought on further
anarchy, which distant Spain tried to quiet by sending out a representative of the
Crown with the "New Laws": these favoring the Indians brought on a complete
revolt by Gonzalo Pizarro, brother of the conquistador, who was urged by some
to marry an Inca *coya* (queen) and proclaim himself "king of Peru." The battles,
which were many and sanguinary, did not end until the final defeat of Pizarro at

which can rightfully be considered the scourge of His justice, and the taxation is carried out with moderation so that the Indians can be free and masters of their person and property, without other taxes or tributes than the levy on each settlement. I shall go into this later on in more detail.

On these visits of the envoys of the Incas to the provinces, as soon as they arrived they could tell from the quipus[2] the number of people, men and women, old folks and children, and gold or silver miners, and they ordered that so many thousand Indians be put to work in the mines, to dig the amount of those metals that had been set to be turned over to the inspectors assigned for that purpose. And as during the time the Indians appointed to work the mines were doing this they could not cultivate their fields, the Incas ordered those from other provinces to come and plant the crops at the proper season in lieu of tribute, so that they [the fields] would not lie fallow. If the province was a large one, it furnished Indians both to mine the metals and to sow and work the land. If one of the Indians working in the mines got sick, he was allowed to return home at once, and another came to take his place; but none was assigned to the mines unless he was married so that his wives could look after his food and drink, and, aside from this, it was seen to it that they were supplied with food in abundance. With this way of doing things, none of them considered it hard work even if they spent their whole life in the mines, and none of them died from overwork. Besides, they were permitted to stop work several days in the month for their feasts and recreation; and the same Indians were not continuously in the mines, but every so often they were sent away and others came in their place.

So well had the Incas organized this that the amount of gold and silver mined throughout the kingdom was so great that there must have been years when they took out over fifty thousand arrobas of silver, and over fifteen thousand of gold, and all this metal was for their use. These metals were brought to the capital of each province, and the same system of mining and delivering them prevailed

163

Xaquixahuana in 1548. These civil wars killed more Indians and Spaniards and destroyed more of the evidences of Inca culture than the years of the conquest. Cieza relates it all in his books: *The War of Quito*, *The War of Salinas*, *The War of Chupas*, and the lost manuscript, *The War of Huarina*. (See the Hakluyt Society publications, vols. LVI, XLII, and XXXI.)

[2] String-knot mnemonic devices. See Chapter 53 below for details.

throughout the kingdom. If in certain regions there were no metals to be mined, so that all should contribute their share, they set tribute of small things, and of women and children who left their villages without any sorrow, for if a man had only one son or daughter, they did not take the child, but if he had three or four, they took one in payment of his service.

Other regions paid as many thousand loads of corn as there were houses in it, which was done at every harvest, and was credited to the province. In other areas they similarly supplied as many loads of *chuño*[3] as the others of corn, and others *quinoa,* and others tubers. Some places gave as many blankets as there were married Indians in it, and others as many shirts as there were people. Others were obliged to supply so many thousand loads of lances, and others, slings and *ayllos,*[4] and the other arms they use. Certain provinces were ordered to contribute so many thousand Indians to go to Cuzco to work on the public buildings of the city and those of the Incas, supplying them with the necessary food. Others contributed cables to haul stones; others, coca. In this way all the provinces and regions of Peru, from the smallest to the most important, paid tribute to the Incas, and all this was accomplished in such orderly fashion that neither did the natives fail to pay what they owed and were assessed, nor did those who collected these tributes venture to take one grain of corn in excess. And all the food and articles necessary for making war which were contributed were expended on the soldiers or the regular garrisons that were established in different parts of the kingdom for its defense. When there was no war, most of this was eaten and consumed by the poor, for when the Incas were in Cuzco they had their *hatun-conas,* which is the name for a bondsman, and in

---

[3] Essentially dehydrated potatoes. To prepare it, the Indians used their worst agricultural enemy, frost. *Chuño* properly made cannot be injured by either frost or damp. Potatoes are spread out, allowed to freeze, then trod upon to squeeze out all moisture; the process is repeated day upon day until the *chuño* is white and dry. It is of two kinds, *tunta* and *moray. Chuño* was used for thickening of soups. No precise period can be ascribed to its "invention," but it pre-dates the Incas by at least two thousand years. (See Redcliffe E. Salaman, *The History and Social Influence of the Potato.*)

[4] *Ayllos,* which the Spaniards called *bola(s),* is a sling, used to entangle the feet of warriors or animals. It consisted of two weights of stone varying in size from that of a pullet's egg to that of an orange. The weights were wrapped in rawhide and attached to the sling. It was used (and still is in Argentina by Gauchos) with extreme accuracy.

such number that they sufficed to work their lands and care for their houses and sow the necessary food supplies, aside from that which was always brought for their table from the different regions, many lambs and fowls and fish, and corn, coca, tubers, and all the fruits they raise. And there was such order in these tributes which the natives paid and the Incas were so powerful that they never had a war break out again. 165

To know how and in what way the tributes were paid and the other taxes collected, each *huata,* which is the word for year, they sent out certain *Orejones* as supervisory magistrates, for they had no authority beyond visiting the provinces and notifying the inhabitants that if any of them had a complaint, he should state it, so that the one who had done him a wrong could be punished. And when the complaints were heard, if there were any, or it was learned that somewhere a debt was pending, they returned to Cuzco, from which another set out with authority to punish the culprits. In addition to this, there was another important provision, which was that from time to time the headmen of the provinces appeared on the day appointed for each nation to speak to bring to the knowledge of the Inca the state of the province and the shortage or abundance that existed in it, and whether the tribute was too large or too small, and whether they could pay it or not. After which they were sent away satisfied, for the Inca rulers were certain they were not lying but telling the truth. For if there was any attempt at deceit, stern punishment followed and the tribute was increased. Of the women given by the provinces, some of them were brought to Cuzco to become the possession of the Lord-Incas, and some of them were sent to the temple of the sun.

CHAPTER 50 (ii: xx)

Of how there were governors assigned to all the provinces, and how the Incas went out to visit them, and their coat of arms was serpents around a staff.

IT IS TOLD for a fact of the rulers of this kingdom that in the days of their rule they had their representatives in the capitals of all the provinces, such as Vilcas, Jauja, Bombón, Cajamarca, Huancabamba,

Tomebamba, Llactacunga, Quito, Caranqui, and to the south of Cuzco, Hatuncana, Hatuncolla, Ayaviri,[1] Chuquiabo, Chucuito, Paria, and the others as far as Chile, for in all these places there were larger and finer lodgings than in most of the other cities of this great kingdom, and many storehouses. They served as the head of the provinces or regions, and from every so many leagues around the tributes were brought to one of these capitals, and from so many others, to another. This was so well organized that there was not a village that did not know where it was to send its tribute. In all these capitals the Incas had temples of the sun, mints, and many silversmiths who did nothing but work rich pieces of gold or fair vessels of silver; large garrisons were stationed there, and, as I have said, a steward or representative who was in command of them all, to whom an accounting of everything that was brought in was made, and who, in turn, had to give one of all that was issued. And these governors could in no way interfere with the jurisdiction of another who held a similar post, but within his own, if there were any disorder or disturbance, he had authority to punish it[s perpetrators], especially if it were in the nature of a conspiracy or a rebellion, or failure to obey the Inca, for full power resided in these governors. And if the Incas had not had the foresight to appoint them and to establish the *mitimaes,* the natives would have often revolted and shaken off the royal rule; but with the many troops and the abundance of provisions, they could not effect this unless they had all plotted such treason or rebellion together. This happened rarely, for these governors who were named were of complete trust, all of them *Orejones,* and most of them had their holdings, or *chacaras,* in the neighborhood of Cuzco, and their homes and kinfolk. If one of them did not show sufficient capacity for his duties, he was removed and another put in his place.

When one of them came to Cuzco on private business or to see the Inca, he left a lieutenant in his place, not one who aspired to the post, but one he knew would faithfully carry out what he was ordered to do and what was best for the service of the Inca. And if one of these governors or delegates died while in office, the natives at once sent word to the Inca how and of what he had died, and even transported the body by the post road if this seemed to them advisable. The tribute paid by each of these districts where the capital was situated, and

1 See the map of Inca roads and sites for the precise locality of these ancient cities.

that turned over by the natives, whether gold, silver, clothing, arms, and all else they gave, was entered in the accounts of the [*quipu-*] *camayocs,* who kept the quipus and did everything ordered by the governor in the matter of finding the soldiers or supplying whomever the Inca ordered, or making delivery to Cuzco; but when they came from the city of Cuzco to go over the accounts, or they were ordered to go to Cuzco to give an accounting, the accountants themselves gave it by the quipus, or went to give it where there could be no fraud, but everything had to come out right. Few years went by in which an accounting of all these things was not made.

These governors had great authority and were empowered to raise armies and call up soldiers if there was some sudden disturbance or uprising, or if a foreign people came from anywhere to make war, and they were honored and favored by the ruler. And when the Spaniards entered, many of them remained with permanent command in certain of the provinces. I know some of them, and their power was so established that their sons inherited the property of others.

When the Incas set out to visit their kingdom, it is told that they traveled with great pomp, riding in rich litters set upon smooth, long poles of the finest wood and adorned with gold and silver. Over the litter rose two high arches of gold set with precious stones and long curtains hung from all sides of the litter in such a way as to cover it all; if the one who was riding in it did not so wish, he could not be seen, nor were the curtains raised except when he got in or out. To give him air and for him to see the road, there were holes made in the curtains. Everything about these litters was luxurious, and on some the sun and moon were carved, and on others great serpents intertwined around a kind of staff—this was their insigne or coat of arms. These litters were borne on the shoulders of the highest and most important lords of the realm, and the one most often chosen was considered the most honored and favored.

Around the litter and alongside it came the Inca's guard with the archers and halberdiers, and behind an equal number of lancers with their captains, and along the road and over the road itself went faithful runners seeing what there might be and giving word of the coming of the Inca. So many people came to see his passing that all the hills and slopes seemed covered with them, and all called down blessings upon him, screeching and howling as they do, calling out:

"Ancha hatun apu, intip-chari, canqui zapallapu tucuy parcha ocampa uyau sullull," which in our language means, "Most great and mighty lord, son of the sun, thou alone art our lord, may the entire world hearken unto you." Aside from this, they said other praises, so that little was lacking for them to worship him as God.

168   All along the road went Indians, cleaning it so that neither a blade of grass nor a pebble was to be seen, for all was cleaned and swept. He [the Inca] traveled four leagues each day, or as much as he wished; he stopped wherever he liked to inquire into the state of his kingdom; he willingly listened to those who came to him with complaints, righting wrongs and punishing those who had committed an injustice. Those who accompanied him never got out of hand or departed from the route. The natives supplied whatever was needed, and, aside from this, the storehouses were so well provided that there was more than enough of all that was needed. Wherever he went, many men, women, and children came forward to serve in whatever might be asked of them; and the baggage was carried by people of one town to another, where they laid it down and others took it up; and as it was only for one day, or at most two, it was not burdensome nor was anyone vexed thereby. In this manner the Inca traveled through his kingdom for the time he liked, seeing with his own eyes what was taking place and ordering what he thought necessary, all great and important things, and when this was done, he returned to Cuzco, the principal city of his entire empire.

CHAPTER 51 (ii: XXIV)

How the Incas ordered the natives to build well-planned villages, and divided up the land that might give rise to dispute, and how they ordered that all were to speak the language [Quechua] of Cuzco.

LONG AGO, before the Incas reigned, it is well known that the natives of Peru did not have established villages as they now have, but fortified strongholds which they called *pucarás,* from which they went out to make war on one another, and for this reason they were always on guard and lived uneasy and with great hardships. When the Incas came to rule them, as this fashion and manner of living seemed bad to them, they ordered them, sometimes with flattery, other times with threats, and always with gifts they made them, to give up living like savages and behave like people of reason, establishing their villages with the houses beside one another on the plains and hillsides in keeping with the lay of the land. Thus these Indians, leaving the *pucarás* they had first had, constructed their villages in comely fashion, both in the valleys of the savannah and in the highlands and plains of the Colla. And so there should be no ill feeling about the fields and holdings, the Incas themselves divided the lands, apportioning what each was to have, and boundaries were set up so that those living and those yet to be born would recognize them. Naturally, this is what the Indians say today,[1] and I was told of this in Jauja, where they say that one of the Incas divided up among them the valleys and fields they now hold, after which manner they remained and will remain. And in many of the villages in the highlands there ran irrigation ditches drawn from the rivers with great skill and ingenuity on the part of those who built them; and all the villages, wherever they might be, had lodgings and storehouses for the Incas, as has often been said.

169

Realizing how difficult it would be to travel the great distances of their land where every league and at every turn a different language was spoken, and how bothersome it would be to have to employ interpreters to understand them, these rulers, as the best measure, ordered and decreed, with severe punishment for failure to obey, that all the natives of their empire should know and understand the language of Cuzco, both they and their women. This was so strictly enforced that an infant had not yet left its mother's breast before they began to teach it the language it had to know. And although at the beginning

[1]Cieza was skeptical of this simplification of Andean history, i.e., that before the advent of the Incas there was a cultural void throughout the area. He was the first to recognize the distinct cultures which had preceded the Incas. The Incas after their conquest used what has been described as a "selective manipulation of remembered history": local traditions were allowed to lapse and lay unremembered, leaving a hiatus between legendary man and those innumerable cultures which had preceded the Inca culture (Chavín, Paracas, Mochica, Tiahuanacu, Chimú, etc.). The Incas evolved as the culture-bearers of South America. Everything or almost everything was antecedent to the Incas. They arrived late. They were organizers rather than originators. (See von Hagen, *Realm of the Incas*.)

this was difficult and many stubbornly refused to learn any language but their own, the Incas were so forceful that they accomplished what they had proposed, and all had to do their bidding. This was carried out so faithfully that in the space of a few years a single tongue was known and used in an extension of more than 1,200 leagues; yet, even though this language was employed, they all spoke their own [languages], which were so numerous that if I were to list them it would not be credited.

When a captain set out from Cuzco, or one of the *Orejones* went to check the accounts or make a report, or act as judge, or on some errand with which he had been entrusted, wherever he went he spoke no other language than that of Cuzco [i.e., Quechua], nor did those of the different provinces to him. It is a very good tongue,[2] succinct, easily grasped, and rich in words and so clear that in the few days I gave to it, I knew enough to ask many things wherever I went. The word for man in this language is *runa;* woman, *huarmi;* father, *yaya;* brother, *huayqui;* sister, *nana;* the moon, *quilla,* which is also the word for month; year, *huata;* day, *pinche;* night, *tuta;* the head is called *uma,* and the ears, *rinri;* the eyes, *ñaui;* the nose, *senkka;* the teeth, *quiru;* the arms, *rillra;* and the legs, *chaqui.*

I include these words in this chronicle only because I now see that with regard to the ancient language of Spain, there are differences of opinion, and some say one thing, and some another. In times to come, God alone knows what things may happen; therefore, in case something should occur to bury or cause to be forgotten this language which was so widespread and used by so many people, there will be no doubt about which was the first or general, or where it came from, or whatever else may be sought to know. It was a great advantage

2 Quechua was the dominant Inca language in the Andes, because the conquering Incas insisted that all must speak it in addition to their own tribal tongues. Quechua was originally spoken by a tribe of that name (as has been pointed out before, it means "warm valley people"), close to the warmer regions of the Apurímac River, some distance from Cuzco; they were a large and dominant tribe while the Incas were still struggling to find themselves about Cuzco. But they were attacked by powerful neighbors, overwhelmed, and so fell easily into the pattern of Inca expansion. It is not known what language (perhaps a related one) the Incas spoke before this, but after 1438 Pachacuti Inca made Quechua the official language and it gradually superseded all others in the Andes. It remains a living language: it is spoken by millions of Indians and whites alike in Peru; a dialect is used in Ecuador; and there are variants of it in Colombia, Chile, and Argentina. As a language, Quechua has marked characteristics: its closest related tongue, morphologically, is Aymara (which centers about Lake Titicaca and it is spoken exclusively in Bolivia).

for the Spaniards that there was this language, for with it they could go everywhere, and in some places it is already [i.e., 1549] disappearing.

CHAPTER 52 (ii: XXVI)

Of how the Incas had advisers and ministers of justice, and the record they kept of time.

As THE CITY of Cuzco was the most important in all Peru, and the Incas lived there most of the time, they had with them in the city many of the leading men of the country, the most intelligent and informed of all, as their advisers.[1] For all agree that before they undertook anything of importance, they discussed it with these counselors [*amauta-cuna*], and submitted their opinion to that of the majority. And for the administration of the city, and that the highways should be safe and nowhere should offenses or thefts be committed, from among the most highly esteemed of them he [the Inca] appointed those whose duty it was to punish wrongdoers, and to this end they were always traveling about the country. The Incas took such care to see that justice was meted out that nobody ventured to commit a felony or theft. This was to deal with thieves, ravishers of women, or conspirators against the Inca; however, there were many provinces that warred on one another, and the Incas were not wholly able to prevent this.

By the river [Huatanay] that runs through Cuzco justice was executed on those who were caught or brought in as prisoners from some other place. There they had their heads cut off, or were put to death in some other manner which they chose. Mutiny and conspiracy were

[1] The Lord-Incas tried to make these offices hereditary, occupied by men who were blood-relatives of the Inca; since he had many concubines he had many such to draw upon. Rulers came from the Inca class (related by blood) or the *curaca* class (Incas by privilege), the latter consisting of men who had by sheer ability raised themselves to position. These, since they pierced their ears, making a hole so large that an egg could pass through it, and were always bedecked with very large earplugs, were called by Cieza and others *Orejones;* they were in effect the nobility. Each quarter of the Inca world (there were four) was administered by an *apu* (governor.) These governors lived in Cuzco and formed the council of which Cieza speaks. The four quarters were then split up into provinces (*wamañ*), each with its own *t'oqrikoq* (governor), "he who sees all." (See Rowe, "Inca Culture before the Spanish Conquest," *Handbook*, II, 261–64.)

severely punished, and, above all, those who were thieves and known as such; even their wives and children were despised and considered to be tarred with the same brush.

These Indians were very learned in natural phenomena, such as the movement of the sun and the moon; certain of them said that there were four great heavens, and they all believe that the residence and seat of the great God, Creator of the world, is in the heavens. I asked them many times if they understood that the world would come to an end, and they laughed; in regard to this they know little, and what they do know is what God permits the devil to tell them. The world in its totality they call *Pacha[c]*, and they know the revolutions the sun makes, and the waxing and waning of the moon. They counted the year, by this, and it consists of twelve months, by their calculations. They had a number of small towers,[2] of which there are many on the hills of Cuzco, now in a state of neglect, so that they could tell by the shadow the sun cast when to plant, and other things they gathered from this. And these Indians scanned the heavens with great care, watching for portents, which also had to do with the fact that they were great soothsayers. When they see a shooting star, they make a great outcry, and consult earnestly with one another.

172

CHAPTER 53 (ii: XII)

Of how they had chroniclers to keep record of their deeds, and the use of the quipus, and what we see of them now.

WE HAVE WRITTEN how it was ordered by the Incas that the statues be brought out at their feasts, and how they selected from the wisest among their men those who should tell what the life of their kings had been and how they had conducted themselves in the rule of their kingdoms, for the purpose I have stated. It should also be known that, aside from this, it was the custom among them, and a rule carefully observed, for each of them to choose during his reign three or four

---

[2] The stone towers are mentioned by Garcilaso de la Vega (Book I, Chap. xxii) as stone pillars "que fueron ocho torres que labraron al oriente y otros ocho al poniente de la ciudad del Cuzco." They were erected to ascertain the time of the equinoxes for the principal festivals.

old men of their nation, skilled and gifted for that purpose, whom they ordered to recall all that had happened in the province during the time of their reign, whether prosperous or adverse, and to make and arrange songs so that thereby it might be known in the future what had taken place in the past.[1] Such songs could not be sung or proclaimed outside the presence of the Inca, and those who were to carry out this behest were ordered to say nothing referring to the Inca during his lifetime, but after he was dead, they said to his successor almost in these words: "Oh, mighty and powerful Inca, may the Sun and Moon, the Earth, the hills and trees, the stones and your forefathers guard you from misfortune and make you prosperous, happy, and blessed among all who have been born. Know that the things that happened to your predecessor were these." And saying this, with their eyes on the ground and heads hanging, with great humility they gave an account and report of all they knew, which they could do very well, for there were many among them of great memory, subtle wit, and lively intelligence, and abounding in knowledge, as those of us who are here and hear them can bear witness. After they said this, when the Inca had heard them, he sent for other of his old Indians whom he ordered to learn the songs the others bore in their memory, and to prepare new ones of what took place during the time of his reign, what was spent, what the provinces contributed, and put all this down in the quipus, so that after his death, when his successor reigned, what had been given and contributed would be known. And except on days of great celebration, or on the occasion of mourning and lament for the death of a brother or son of the Inca, for on such days it was permitted to relate their grandeur and their origin and birth, at no other time was it permitted to deal with this, for it had been forbidden by their lords, and if they did so, they were severely punished.

[The Indians] had a method of knowing how the tributes of food

1 These were in effect bards; this manner of "remembered history" appears in other, unrelated cultures. The Druids were court bards called *ollamhs,* their function not to guide and protect their king, "but merely to celebrate his temporal power." Richard Coeur de Lion employed a *versificator regis* to chant rhymed chronicles, epitaphs, and the like. The Welsh bards found, as did many other people, that "regular verse was a wonderful aid to memory and since vellum was prohibitively dear," writes Robert Graves in *The Crowning Privilege* (New York, 1956), "they recorded their chronicles, their treatises in geography, husbandry . . . in mnemonic rhyme" (p. 98). Those numbered more than nine hundred such.

supplies should be levied on the provinces when the Lord-Inca came through with his army, or was visiting the kingdom; or, when nothing of this sort was taking place, what came into the storehouses and what was issued to the subjects, so nobody could be unduly burdened, that was so good and clever that it surpasses the *carastes* used by the Mexicans for their accounts and dealings. This involved the quipus, which are long strands of knotted strings, and those who were the accountants and understood the meaning of these knots could reckon by them expenditures or other things that had taken place many years before. By these knots they counted from one to ten and from ten to a hundred, and from a hundred to a thousand. On one of these strands there is the account of one thing, and on the other of another, in such a way that what to us is a strange, meaningless account is clear to them. In the capital of each province there were accountants whom they called *quipu-camayocs,* and by these knots they kept the account of the tribute to be paid by the natives of that district in silver, gold, clothing, flocks, down to wood and other more insignificant things, and by these same quipus at the end of a year, or ten, or twenty years, they gave a report to the one whose duty it was to check the account so exact that not even a pair of sandals was missing.

174

I was dubious about this accounting, and even though I was assured that it was so done, I considered it for the most part a fable. But when I was in the province of Jauja, in what they call Marcavillca, I asked the cacique Huacara-pora to explain the system to me in such a way that I could understand it and make sure that it was exact and dependable. Whereupon he sent his servants to fetch the quipus, and as this man is of goodly understanding and reason, for all he is an Indian, he readily satisfied my request. He told me, so that I would better understand, that I should observe that all he had given to the Spaniards from the time of the entry of Governor Francisco Pizarro in the valley [1533] was recorded there without a single omission; and in this I saw the account of the gold, silver, and clothing that had been given, the llamas and other things, and I was amazed thereby. And there is another thing which I firmly believe: the wars, cruelties, pillaging, and tyranny of the Spaniards have been such that if these Indians had not been so accustomed to order and providence they would all have perished and been wiped out. But being very prudent and sensible, and trained by such wise princes, they all decided that if an army of Spaniards passed through any of the provinces, unless the harm was irreparable, such as destroying the crops and robbing the houses and doing other still greater damage, as all the regions along the highway by which our men passed had their accountants, these would give out all the supplies the people 175 could furnish so as to avoid the destruction of everything, and thus they were provided. And after they had passed through, the chieftains came together with the keepers of the quipus, and if one had expended more than another, those who had given less made up the difference, so they were all on an equal footing.

In each valley there is still this system of accounting, and there are always in the storehouses as many accountants as there are lords, and every four months they cast up their accounts in the manner described. Thanks to this system, they have been able to survive such cruel strife, and if God were pleased to bring it completely to an end, with the good treatment they have lately received and the order and justice that exists, they would revive and multiply, and in some fashion this kingdom might become again what it once was, though I fear this will be late or never. The fact is that I have seen villages, and large ones, which with a single time that the Christian Spaniards had passed through, looked as though they had been razed by fire. And as the people were not so reasonable, they did not aid one another, and fell victims to hunger and disease, for there is little charity among them, and it's each for himself, and that is the end of it.

This orderly system in Peru is the work of the Lord-Incas who ruled it and in every way brought it so high, as those of us here see from this and other greater things. With this, let us proceed.

CHAPTER 54 (CXIV)

Of how the Indians of this kingdom were master silversmiths and builders, and the splendid dyes they gave their fine cloth.

FROM THE ACCOUNTS of these Indians they give us to understand that in olden times they lacked the order and government they had after they came under the rule of the Incas, and have now. There is no disputing the fact that when one sees the fine handicraft they have produced, it arouses the admiration of all who have knowledge of it. The most amazing thing is how few tools and instruments they have for their work, and how easily they produce things of finest quality. At the time the Spaniards conquered this kingdom, articles of gold, clay, and silver were discovered, the parts joined one to the other as though they had been created that way. The most amazing examples of silverwork, statuettes, and other larger things were seen, which I do not describe because I have not seen them. It is enough for me to state that I have seen dinner services made with the use of pieces of copper and two or three stones, so finely worked, and the goblets, platters, and candelabra all embossed with leaves and designs, that master workmen would have their work cut out for them to do as well with all the instruments and tools they have. Aside from the articles of silver, many of them make medallions, chains, and other things of gold. And little boys, who if you saw them you would not think knew how to talk yet, understand how to do these things. Not much of this work is done now in comparison with the large, rich pieces made in the days of the Incas; the tiny, uniform little beads they make show what great silversmiths there were in this kingdom, and many were sent by the Incas to the most important parts of it.

As for laying foundations, making strong buildings, they do this very well; it was they who built the houses and dwellings of the Spaniards, and they made the bricks and tiles, and laid large, heavy stones, putting them together so skillfully that it is hard to see the joinings. They also make statues and other larger things, and in many places it is clear that they have carved them with no other tools than stones and their great wit. In the building of irrigation canals, I doubt that there has ever been a people or nation in the world who constructed and conducted them over such rough and difficult terrain, as I have set forth at length in foregoing chapters.

For the weaving of their blankets they have small looms, and in olden times, when the Lord-Incas ruled this kingdom, in the capitals of the provinces they had great numbers of women, known as *mamaconas,* who were dedicated to the service of the gods in the sacred temples of the sun, who did nothing but weave the finest clothing for the Incas from the wool of the vicuñas. The quality of this clothing has been seen in Spain from samples that were taken there after this kingdom was conquered. The clothing of these Incas was shirts of this wool, some of them adorned with gold embroidery, others with emeralds and precious stones, and others with feathers; some were plain. For these garments they had such perfect dyes—red, blue, yellow, black, and other colors—that they truly excel those of Spain.

177

CHAPTER 55 (XIX)

Of how the Incas of Cuzco ordered that a yearly record be kept of all those who were born and died throughout their realm, and how all worked and none suffered from poverty, thanks to the storehouses.

THE *Orejones* OF Cuzco who supplied me with information are in agreement that in olden times, in the days of the Lord-Incas, all the villages and provinces of Peru were notified that a report should be given to the rulers and their representatives each year of the men and women who had died, and all who had been born, for this was necessary for the levying of the tributes as well as to know how many were available for war and those who could assume the defense of the villages. This was an easy matter, for each province at the end of the year had a list by the knots of the quipus of all the people who had died there during the year, as well as of those who had been born. At the beginning of the new year they came to Cuzco, bringing their quipus, which told how many births there had been during the year, and how many deaths. This was reported with all truth and accuracy, without any fraud or deceit. In this way the Inca and the governors knew which of the Indians were poor, the women who had been widowed, whether they were able to pay their taxes, and how many men they could count on in the event of war, and many other things they considered highly important.

As this kingdom was so vast, as I have repeatedly mentioned, in each of the many provinces there were many storehouses filled with supplies and other needful things; thus, in times of war, wherever the armies went they draw upon the contents of these storehouses, without ever touching the supplies of their confederates or laying a finger on what they had in their settlements. And when there was no war, all this stock of supplies and food was divided up among the poor and the widows. These poor were the aged, or the lame, crippled, or paralyzed, or those afflicted with some other diseases; if they were in good health, they received nothing. Then the storehouses were filled up once more with the tributes paid the Inca. If there came a lean year, the storehouses were opened and the provinces were lent what they needed in the way of supplies; then, in a year of abundance, they paid back all they had received. Even though the tributes paid to the Inca were used only for the aforesaid purposes, they were employed to advantage, for in this way their kingdom was opulent and well supplied.

178

No one who was lazy or tried to live by the work of others was tolerated; everyone had to work. Thus on certain days each lord went to his lands and took the plow in hand and cultivated the earth, and did other things. Even the Incas themselves did this to set an example, for everybody was to know that there should be nobody so rich that, on this account, he might disdain or affront the poor. And under their system there was none such in all the kingdom, for, if he had his health, he worked and lacked for nothing; and if he was ill, he received what he needed from the storehouses. And no rich man could deck himself out in more finery than the poor, or wear different clothing, except the rulers and headmen, who, to maintain their dignity, were allowed great freedom and privilege, as well as the *Orejones,* who held a place apart among all the peoples.

CHAPTER 56 (ii: xxv)

Of how the Incas were free of the abominable sin [sodomy] and of the other vices displayed by other princes of the world.

In this kingdom of Peru it is notorious among all the natives that in certain settlements in the vicinity of Puerto Viejo [Ecuador] the abominable sin of sodomy was practiced, and also in other lands there were no doubt evil-doers, just as in the rest of the world. I must point out a great virtue of these Incas, for being such absolute rulers who had to account to nobody for what they did, nor was there any among their subjects powerful enough to demand it, and though they spent their nights and days sporting with their women and in other pastimes, yet never was it said of any of them that they were guilty of the aforesaid sin, but, on the contrary, they despised those who used it, looking down on them as vile and contemptible for glorying in such filth. Not only did they themselves not indulge in this, but they did not even allow anyone whom they knew to practice it to enter their homes or palaces. Aside from this, it seems to me that I heard it said that if it came to their knowledge that anyone had committed this sin, he was so severely punished that he was pointed out and known to all.[1] There is no doubt of this, but rather it is to be fully credited that this vice was to be found in none of them, neither among the *Orejones* nor among many other nations. And most of those who have written about the Indians, accusing them in general of this sin and stating that they were all sodomites, have exaggerated, and should retract what they have said, for with this they have condemned so many nations and peoples who are far freer of this than I can state. For, aside from Puerto Viejo [in coastal Ecuador], in all Peru sinners of this kind were not to be found, except as happens in every place, that there was one, or six, or eight, or ten, and these secretly practiced this vice. As for those who served as priests in the temples, with whom it is known that on feast days the headmen had carnal knowledge, they did not think they were doing wrong or committing a sin, but did this as a sacrifice prompted by the devil. It might even be that the Incas were unaware that such a thing was done in the temples; and even though they overlooked certain things, it was so they would not be disliked, and they may have felt that it was enough for them to order that the sun and their other gods be worshiped everywhere, without taking measures to

179

---

[1] That sodomy was practiced in Peru, Cieza himself confirms (see Chapter 107), but he is correct as regards the Incas. The whole of the north coast people (that is, those under the influence of the Chimú empire), were much addicted to sodomy. The Incas regarded it as an abomination and tried vainly to stamp it out, sometimes liquidating whole families and clans. (See Rowe, "The Kingdom of Chimor," *Acta Americana*, Vol. VI, Nos. 1 and 2 [1948], 49.)

forbid ancient religions and customs, which, to those born in them, it is like death to deprive them of them.

We have also been informed that in olden times, before the Incas reigned, in many provinces the men lived like savages, making war on one another and eating each other, as they still do in the province of Arma[2] and certain adjoining parts. But when the Incas came to rule, as they were people of high reason and had saintly and just customs and laws, not only did they not eat such flesh, which has been and is greatly esteemed by some, but they devoted themselves to doing away with this custom among those with whom they dealt, and so effectively did they accomplish this that in a short time it was forgotten and wholly cast aside, and throughout their realm, which was so vast, human flesh has not been eaten for many years. Those who have come after them reveal the notable benefit they received from the Incas in that they do not imitate their forebears in eating this viand, sacrificing men and children.

It is told by many—perhaps by one of those writers who rushes headlong to take up his pen—that there were feast days when they killed a thousand or two thousand children, and even more Indians. These and other things are the testimony we Spaniards raise against these Indians, endeavoring by these things we tell of them to hide our own shortcomings and justify the ill treatment they have suffered at our hands. I am not saying that they did not make sacrifices, and that they did not kill men and children at such sacrifices; but it was not as is told, not by a long shot. They did sacrifice animals and llamas of their flocks, but many fewer human beings than I had thought, many less, as I shall relate when the time comes.

Thus I have it from the old *Orejones* that these Incas were free of this sin, and that they did not engage in other evil habits such as eating human flesh, nor glory in their vices, nor were they headstrong and reckless, but, on the contrary, they corrected their faults. And if God had permitted that they have persons animated by Christian zeal, and not by greed, to teach them fully the precepts of our holy faith, they were people in whom it could easily have been inculcated, as we see from what is being done now that there is order. But let us leave what has been done to God, for He knows the reason;

[2] Arma, close to modern Cali in Colombia, where Cieza (see Editor's Introduction, xl–xli) had an *"encomenderia"* of Indians.

180

and for what is to be done henceforth, let us implore Him to give us His grace so that we may pay back to these people something of the great debt we owe them, who did us so little harm to have been harassed by us, with Peru and the rest of the Indies so many leagues from Spain, and so many seas between.

181

CHAPTER 57 (ii: xxx)

Of the celebrations and sacrifices made at the great and solemn feast known as Hátun Raimi.

DURING THE YEAR the Incas held many feasts[1] at which great sacrifices were performed in keeping with their custom, and to describe them all in detail would require a volume for that purpose alone. Moreover, they have little bearing on what we are relating, and it is better not to attempt to tell of the foolishness and witchcraft done at them, for various reasons. I shall describe only the feast of Hátun Raimi because it is very famous. It was observed in many provinces, and was the principal feast of all the year and that in which the Incas took most pleasure and made the most sacrifices. This feast was celebrated at the end of August when they had harvested their corn, potatoes, *quinoa, oca,* and the other seeds they plant. They call this feast, as I have said, Hátun Raimi, which in our tongue means "very solemn feast," because at it thanks and praises were given to the great god, maker of heaven and earth, whom they called, as I have repeatedly said, Tici-Viracocha, and to the sun, the moon, and their other gods,

---

[1] A comparison of the Inca calendar with the Gregorian calendar follows (from Luis E. Valcárcel, "The Andean Calendar," *Handbook,* II, 471–76):

Gregorian Months	Peruvian Months	Translation
December	Kapaj Raymi	The principal festival
January	Juchuy Pokoy	The small ripening
February	Jatun Pokoy	The great ripening
March	Paukar Waray	The garment of flowers
April	Ayriway	Dance of the young maize
May	Aymuray	Song of the harvest
June	Inti Raymi	Festival of the Sun
July	Anta Situwa	Earthly purification
August	Kapaj Situwa	General purification
September	Koya Raymi	Festival of the Queen
October	Uma Raymi	Festival of the Water
November	Ayamark'a	Procession of the Dead

for having given them a good year of harvests for their maintenance. And to celebrate this feast with greater devotion and solemnity, it is said that they fasted for ten or twelve days, refraining from eating much and sleeping with their women, and drinking chicha only in the morning, which is when they eat, and then during the day taking only water, and no hot pepper, or keeping anything in their mouth, and other proscriptions which they observe in such fasts. When this has been done, they brought from Cuzco large numbers of lambs, llamas, pigeons, guinea pigs, and other birds and animals which were killed as sacrifice. After having cut the throat of many of the llamas, they anointed the statues and figures of their gods or devils with the blood, and the doors of the temples and shrines, where they hung the entrails; and after a time the soothsayers and oracles examined the lights of the animals for signs, as the Gentiles did, foretelling whatever came into their heads, to which much credence was given.

When the sacrifice had been made, the high priest and the other priests went to the temple of the sun, and after having sung their cursed psalms, they ordered the *mamaconas* to come forth richly attired and with a great quantity of that chicha which they considered sacred, serving it in goblets of gold from the tubs of silver, of which there were many in the temple.

After having eaten and drunk repeatedly, and all being drunk, including the Inca and the high priest, joyful and warmed by the liquor, a little after midday the men assembled and began singing in a loud voice the songs and ballads which had been composed by their forebears, the burden of all being their gratitude to their gods and promises to return the benefits received. They also had many drums of gold, some of them set with precious stones, which were played by the women, who together with the sacred *mamaconas* took part in the singing.

In the middle of the plaza they had erected, so they tell, a great theater with tiers, covered with cloth of feathers thick with beads of gold, and great blankets of their finest wool, embroidered in gold and jewels. At the top of this throne they placed the figure of their Tici-Viracocha, large and richly adorned, who, as they held him to be the supreme god, author of all creation, they seated at the top and gave the most eminent place. And all the priests were around him, and the Inca with the nobles and common people went to make obeisance before him, removing their sandals, barefoot, with all humility. Bending their backs and puffing out their cheeks, they blew their breath toward him, making the *mocha,* which is like paying obeisance.

Below this throne there was the image of the sun, which I do not venture to tell what it was made of, and that of the moon, and other statues of gods carved in wood and stone. And the reader may be sure, for we firmly believe it, that in neither Jerusalem, Rome, nor Persia, nor anywhere else in the world, did any republic or king ever bring together in one place such wealth of gold and silver and precious stones as in this plaza of Cuzco when these feasts and others of the same sort were celebrated. The statues of the dead Incas, their kings, were brought out, each with the service and pomp of gold and silver he had possessed, that is to say, those who during their lifetime had been good and valiant, compassionate toward the Indians, generous in conferring benefits upon them, forgiving injuries done them. In their blindness they canonized these as saints, and honored their bones without understanding that their souls were burning in hell, and thinking they were in heaven. And the same thing happened with certain of the *Orejones* or those of other nations who for some heathenish reason they also called saints. They call this way of canonizing *illapa,* which means "body of him who was good in life," and in another sense *illapa* means thunder or lightning; thus the Indians call artillery fire *illapa* because of the noise it makes.

Thus the Inca and the high priest and the courtiers of Cuzco and many people who had come from the neighboring regions, after enthroning their gods, made them obeisance and laid before them many little idols of gold, and llamas of gold, and figures of women, all small, and many other jewels. This feast of Hátun Raimi lasted fifteen or twenty days, during which there were great *taquis,* or drinking feasts, and other celebrations such as they employed. When it was over and the ceremonies concluded, the statues of the idols were returned to their temples, and those of the dead Incas to their houses.

The high priest [Villac-umu][2] held that post for life, and he was

[2] The high priest was the Villac-umu ("soothsayer who speaks"): *villac,* "one who speaks"; *umu,* "sorcerer." He was the supreme pontiff. According to most chroniclers, the holder of this lofty office was related by blood to the Inca and, as Cieza avers, held his post for life.

183

married, and so revered that he competed in authority with the Inca, and he had power over all the shrines and temples, and appointed and removed priests. The Inca and he often played at their games, and these priests were of noble lineage and powerful families, and this dignity was never conferred on men of low, obscure origin, however great their merits. All those who lived in Cuzco were called nobles, and were known as Hurin-Cuzcos and Hanan-Cuzcos, as were their descendants, even though they dwelled in other places. I recall that when I was in Cuzco last year, 1550, in the month of August, after they had harvested their crops, the Indians and their wives entered the city making a great noise, carrying their plows in their hands, and straw and corn, to hold a feast that was only singing and relating how in the past they used to celebrate their harvest. The *apus* and priests do not permit these Gentile[3] feasts to be held in public, as they used to be, nor would they allow them to be held secretly if they knew about it; but as there are so many thousands of Indians who have become Christians, it seems credible that, where they cannot be seen, they do what they like. The image of Tici-Viracocha and that of the sun and the moon, and the great cable of gold,[4] and other known objects have not been found, nor is there an Indian or Spaniard who knows or can guess where they are; but much as this is, it is little compared with what is buried in Cuzco and the shrines and other places of this great kingdom.[5]

184

[3] The Indians were always called Gentiles. Originally the Latin *gentilis,* "of the same clan or race," was used by the Romans to refer to a Jew, Christian, or other non-Roman. The Spaniards, after the conquest of the Moslems, applied the term "Gentiles" to them. The Jews used the term *goyim* for sects other than their own, and the Spaniards, making it *gentes* or *gentiles,* gave this name to all who were neither Jew nor Christian. Thus the Indians became "Gentiles."

[4] The so-called "golden chain" was not a chain at all, but precisely what the chroniclers said it was, a "cable," made of plaited maguey fibers (the same from which the hanging-bridge cables were made). It was reputed to be six hundred feet in length, plaited with thinly beaten gold sheets, with red ornamental tassels at either end. It was called a *Muru urcu;* some insist that it was *huascar* (a name also held by the last Inca). It was supposed to have been thrown into the lake of Urcos, seventy-five miles south of Cuzco. It was used in a dance in the sixteenth month of Camay: both sexes grasped the heavy gold-plaited cable and performed a dance with it in front of the Inca. After the dance it was left in the great plaza coiled up like a gigantic serpent.

"The Inca . . . caused to be made a great woollen chain of many colours garnished [i.e., plated] with two red fringes at the end. It was 150 fathoms in length, more or less [one fathom is six feet].This was used in their public festivals." (Pedro Sarmiento de Gamboa, *History of the Incas* [written in 1572], 102.) (See also P. A. Means, *Ancient Civilizations of the Andes,* 383.)

CHAPTER 58 (ii: XIII)

How the sovereigns of Peru were greatly loved, on
the one hand, and at the same time feared by all
their subjects, and how no one, even though a great
lord of ancient lineage, dared to come before them
without bearing a load in token of obedience.

IT SHOULD BE carefully noted that as these Incas ruled over such
large provinces and such a length of territory, part of it so wild and
full of mountains and snow-covered peaks and deserts devoid of trees
or water, great prudence was needed to govern such a variety of peoples so different from one another in language, laws, and religion, and
keep them all satisfied and in peace and friendship. Thus, despite the
fact that the city of Cuzco was the capital of their empire, as we
have remarked on many occasions, they had as their representatives
and governors the wisest, most experienced, and bravest that could
be found, and none so young that he was not in the final third of
his years. As they were faithful to the ruler, and none of them dared
rebel, and they were supported by the *mitimaes,* none of the natives,
however powerful, ventured to initiate any revolt, and if any so
attempted, the town where it took place was punished, and the insti-
gators taken prisoner to Cuzco. As a result, the Incas were so feared
that when they made a progress through the kingdom if they permitted one of the curtains of the litter in which they traveled to be
raised so they might be seen by their vassals, such an outcry arose that
the birds in their flight fell to the ground and could be picked up in
the hand. All feared them so much that within the shadow their
person cast none dared speak an evil word. And not only this, for
it is a fact that if any of their captains or servants went to visit some
part of the kingdom on business, they came to meet him on the way
with rich presents, not venturing, even if he came alone, to fail to
comply in every way with his orders.

So great was their fear of their princes in this vast extent of terri-

---

[5] The image of the sun in solid gold plate—its exact size is not known—was found
by the Spaniards in the year 1572 when they captured the Inca Tupac Amaru in the
neo-Inca kingdom in Vilcabamba; it was brought back by Captain García de Loyola.

tory that each village was as orderly and well governed as if the Inca himself were there to punish those who did the contrary. This fear was the result of the rulers' worth and justice, for they knew that if they did evil, punishment would follow, no matter who the culprit was, and neither plea nor bribe could stay it. The Incas always treated those under their rule well, not countenancing that they should suffer offense or be overtaxed or outraged in other ways; in addition, for many of those who dwelt in arid provinces where their forefathers had lived penuriously, they ordered that the land should be made fertile and fruitful, providing them with such things as they needed; in others where they lacked clothing because they had no flocks, they ordered them liberally supplied. In a word, just as these Incas knew how to make themselves served by their subjects and receive tribute from them, just so they knew how to preserve their lands and turn them from uncouth to civilized, and from impoverished to bountiful. With these good deeds, and the fact that the Inca always gave the chieftains women and rich presents, they gained the good will of all, and were so beloved that I remember seeing with my own eyes old Indians who, when they came within sight of Cuzco, stood looking at the city and making a great outcry that afterwards turned to tears of sadness, contemplating the present and recalling the past, when for so many years they had had rulers of their own in that city who knew how to win them to their service and friendship in a different way from that of the Spaniards.

It was the custom and an inviolable law among these lords of Cuzco, to the greater grandeur and respect of the royal dignity, that when one of them was in his palace or traveling with his soldiers or without them, no one, not even the greatest and most powerful lords of all the kingdom, might come to talk with him or enter his presence without first removing his shoes, which they call *usuta,* and putting a weight on his shoulders to enter the presence of the Inca.[1] It did not matter whether this weight was large or small, for it was only a

___

[1] "I remember," wrote Pedro Pizarro, cousin of The Conquistador and the only one who actually participated in the conquest to write his memoirs, "that the Lord of Huaylas once asked the Inca [for permission] to visit his estates and it was granted, the Inca giving him limited time in which to go and return. He took rather longer and when he came back (I was present) brought a gift of fruit and arrived in the Inca's presence. The Lord of Huaylas began to tremble in such a manner before the Inca that he was unable to remain on his feet." (*Relación del Descubrimiento y Conquista de los Reinos del Perú.*)

token of the reverence due to the Inca. Once in his presence, his back
turned to the face of the Inca, after a bow, which they call *mocha,*
he said what he had come for or listened to the order given him, and
when this was done, if he remained at the court for some days and
was a person of consequence, he did not enter with the weight again,
for those who came from the provinces were always with the Inca   187
in the banquets and other things that were done for them.

CHAPTER 59 (ii: xi)

*Of the custom the Incas had of commemorating in
their songs and with statues the Inca who had enlarged the kingdom or performed other acts worthy
of recall; and of the one who had been craven or
slothful, it was ordered that little mention be made.*

I LEARNED WHEN I was in Cuzco that it was the custom among the
Incas to mourn the Inca when he died with general and prolonged
weeping, and perform other great sacrifices according to their religion and custom. When this had been done, the elders of the people
discussed among themselves the life and habits of the dead Inca,
what he had done for the good of the republic, or what battles he
had won against the enemy. And after they had talked such matters
over among themselves, and others we do not wholly know, if the
late Inca had been so fortunate that he had left behind praiseworthy
fame, and by reason of his bravery and good rule deserved to live
forever in their memory, they would send for the great *quipu-camayocs,*[1] who kept the accounts and could tell the things that had
taken place in the kingdom, so that they should instruct others of
their own calling, selecting those possessing the best faculties and the
greatest flow of words, to relate in orderly manner each thing that
had taken place, as is done among us in ballads and lays. These men
occupy themselves in nothing but learning and composing such accounts in their language that they may be heard by all at marriage

[1] *Quipu-cayamocs,* those who read the quipu histories. For an explanation see
Chapter 53 above.

festivities and other joyful occasions they appoint for this purpose. Thus, knowing what should be told of the past at such celebrations in honor of the dead Incas, if the subject was war, in pleasing manner they recounted the many battles that took place in different parts of the kingdom. For every occasion they had their songs and ballads, which, when the moment came, they sang to lift up the hearts of the people hearing them and so they would know what had happened in bygone times without wholly forgetting it. These Indians who, by order of the Incas, knew these ballads were honored and favored by them, and they zealously taught them to their sons and the most gifted and learned men to be found throughout their provinces. In this way they learned such things from one another, so that even today they tell among themselves things that happened five hundred years ago as though it were only ten.

In keeping with this manner of not forgetting what had happened in the kingdom, when the Inca died, if he had been brave and had governed wisely, without losing any province of those his father had left him, nor behaved ignobly or been miserly, nor fallen into follies such as unwise princes insolently use, it was permitted and ordered by the Incas themselves that songs should be made extolling and praising them so that all who heard should admire their great feats and deeds, and these were not to be published and proclaimed everywhere, but only when there was a great gathering of people from all the kingdom for some purpose, and when the nobles came together with the Inca for their amusements and pastimes, or in their *taquis,* or drinking feasts. At such times those who knew the ballads, with loud voice, their eyes on the Inca, sang to him of what his forebears had done. And if there had been one among the Incas who was lazy, cowardly, given over to vices, and who took his pleasure rather than enlarging his power, they ordered that little mention be made of such, or almost none. They put such care in this that if any mention of them was made, it was only so their names and succession should not be forgotten, but about all else they were silent, singing only of those who had been good and brave. They held their memory in such esteem that when one of these mighty lords died, his son took for himself nothing but the crown, for it was a law among them that the wealth and royal possessions of him who had been Inca of Cuzco were not to belong to anyone else, nor should

188

his memory be lost. To this end they made a statue in the form they chose to give it, which they called by the name of the dead Inca. These statues were set up in the square of Cuzco when they held their celebrations, and around each statue of these Incas their wives and servants gathered, and they all came, setting out their food and drink there, for the devil probably spoke to them through those statues, as they were used for this purpose. Each statue had its buffoons, or jesters, who amused the people with merry words, and all the treasure the Inca had possessed when he was alive was in the custody of his servants and kinfolk, and was brought forth on such occasions with great display. In addition to this, they had their *chacaras,* which is the name they give their plantations, where they raised corn and other victuals to maintain the wives and all the other members of the family of these lords who had statues and memorials, even though they were already dead. And beyond doubt it was this custom that was in large part responsible for the vast treasures beheld by our own eyes in this kingdom. I have heard from Spanish conquistadors that when they were discovering the provinces of the kingdom, these statues still existed in Cuzco, which would seem to be true, for when shortly afterward Manco Inca Yupanqui [Manco Inca II] aspired to the royal fringe, they were brought out in the square of Cuzco before the Spaniards and Indians who were there at the time. To be sure, the Spaniards had already taken a great part of the treasure, and the rest was hidden and concealed in places which few or perhaps none know of.[2] As for their statues and other mighty things, there is no longer any memory except such as they preserve and tell in their ballads.

The Spaniards who were in Cuzco in the year 1550 will recall what they saw done at the ceremonies in honor of Paullu Inca's anniversary,[3] albeit he had become a Christian, and they can deduce what

189

[2] Many of the royal mummies were found after Cieza wrote this in 1550. As related by Garcilaso de la Vega (Book V, chap. cxxix), three mummies of the Lord-Incas were discovered: Viracocha (d. 1440), Topa Inca Yupanqui (d. 1492), and the last of the great Incas, Huayna Capac (d. 1527). The gold-plated mummies were found with some of the mummified wives in a perfect state of preservation. Later they were borne through the streets of Lima and given a Christian burial (so as to preserve the amenities) in the courtyard of San Andrés, in the year 1572.

[3] Paullu was a son of Huayna Capac (d. 1527); he was the younger brother of Huascar (who fought the civil war with Atahualpa and was killed in 1533 by him) and of Manco Inca II, who, after being "crowned" Inca by Francisco Pizarro in 1534, escaped

there must have been in the reigns of bygone Incas before they lost
their power.

CHAPTER 60 (ii: XXIX)

Of how the capaccocha, *which means the gifts and
offerings they brought to their idols, was performed,
and how prevalent it was among the Incas.*

THIS IS A FIT POINT at which to explain the *capaccocha,*[1] so it will
be understood, for it all had to do with the service of the aforesaid
temples and others. From information received from old Indians who
are still alive and saw how this took place, I shall set down what I
understand to be the truth about it. Thus they say that it was the
custom of the Incas of Cuzco to have all the statues and figures of
the idols in the *huacas,*[2] which were the temples where they wor-

---

from Spanish hands and put Cuzco under a siege that lasted five months, until it was
broken by the arrival of other Spaniards from Chile. He escaped to a prearranged
inaccessible area within Vilcabamba. Paullu refused to take part in the Inca uprising.
He accompanied Diego Almagro to Chile on that ill-fated expedition in 1535; he also
sided with Diego's son at the battle of Chupas, for which he earned the enmity of
the Pizarro faction. In 1543 he was baptized under the name of Cristóbal and took
up residence in the Inca palace of Manco Capac at Colkam-pata (under the shadows
of Sacsahuamán fortress) and in the section known as Lower (Hurin-) Cuzco, and
there built a church, which is called San Cristóbal. He seems to have been both respected by the Spaniards and beloved by the Indians, which apparently shows that
one can walk the social tightrope. He died in the odor of sanctity in 1549; his son was
made a Knight of Santiago and lived in Spain.

[1] Cieza does not explain *capaccocha,* nor is the custom of human sacrifice much
referred to, even by those who would denigrate the Incas and their customs. A great
many types of sacrifices were made; human sacrifice was the most awe inspiring and
only used in dire need—when famine, war, or pestilence threatened them. "Capaccocha," according to Sarmiento de Gamboa (*History of the Incas,* 56), "is the immo-
lation of two male and two female infants before the idol of *Huanacauri* . . . and the
time when Incas were armed as Knights." Again it is said by the same chronicler that
when Topa Inca (d. 1492) and Huayna Capac were nominated as Inca, ". . . they
made their sacrifices and offered Capac-cocha to that diety [of the sun]." All this,
however, explains nothing."

[2] The word *huaca* appears often in Cieza; it is repeated with amazing frequency
in any discussion about the Incas, principally because almost everything was *huaca.*
In itself it means "shrine," but it has not been satisfactorily explained by the Indians
whether the supernatural being or element which resided in the *huaca* had an existence
apart from it; the "thing" was also *huaca.* Physically, as one will readily see upon
disembarking in Lima, a *huaca* is an adobe-constructed shrine, usually in the fields.
But there were other forms of *huaca,* so many that it is almost impossible to classify
them: crags, rivers, lakes, springs, shrines, mountains, caves—anything that might

shiped, brought into that city each year. They were transported with
great veneration by the priests and [*quipu-*]*camayocs,* which is the
name of the guardians. When they entered the city, they were received with great feasts and processions and lodged in places set aside
and appointed for that purpose. And people having assembled from
all parts of the city and even from most of the provinces, men and
women, the reigning monarch, accompanied by all the Incas and
Orejones, courtiers, and important men of the city, provided great
festivals and *taquis* [drinking bouts].

191

They encircled the entire square of Cuzco with a great cable of
gold, and inside it they placed all the treasure and precious stones
that can be imagined from what I have said of the wealth these Incas
possessed; after that was done, they went through the annual ceremony, which was that these statues and images and priests came
together and announced what was going to happen during the year,
whether there would be abundance or scarcity; whether the Inca
would have a long life, or might, perchance, die that year; if enemies
might be expected to invade the country from some side, or if some
of the pacified peoples would rebel. In a word, they were questioned
and questioned again concerning these things, and about others more
or less weighty which are not worth going into. For they asked if
there would be plague, if the flocks would suffer from blackleg, and
if they would multiply. And this was asked not all the oracles together, but one by one; and if the Incas did not do this every year,
they were troubled, and lived unhappy and fearful, and did not consider their lives safe.

And so, making the people joyful and giving their solemn banquets and drinking feasts, great *taquis,* and other celebrations such
as they use, completely different from ours, in which the Incas show
their splendor, and all the feasting is at their expense, where there
were vessels of silver and gold, and goblets and other things, for everything for the service of their table, even the cooking pots and utensils,
are of gold and silver, they ordered those appointed for this purpose,
among whom was the high priest, who attended these feasts with

inspire awe and suspense was *huaca;* the recently dead were *huaca.* "Huaca," says a
penetrating writer, "is the most persuasive, primitive, fundamental, and enduring religious idea of the Andean peoples; hardly less prevalent today than in the past is the
huaca which combines 'holy,' 'magic,' and 'charm' in a primordial synthesis in which
the conceptual differences of content have never been made analytically distinct."

great pomp and ceremony like the Inca himself, accompanied by the priests and *mamaconas,* to question each idol about these matters, who answered through the mouth of the priests assigned to his statue. These, who were good and drunk, invented what they saw would most please those who asked the questions, assisted by the devil who was in those statues. And when each idol had been questioned, as the priests were so astute in their guile, they asked for a pause before they replied, so their foolishness would be hearkened to with more devotion and belief. They said they wished to make their sacrifices pleasing to the mighty gods so that they would deign to answer what was to come. And so many head of llamas and lambs, guinea pigs, and birds were brought, the llamas and lambs alone numbering more than two thousand, and after cutting their throats and performing the diabolical exorcisms and vain rites they employed, they then uttered what they dreamed or feigned, or perhaps the devil told them. When they gave their answers, they were attentively observed to see what they said and how many of them agreed on each forecast or prophecy of good or evil; and the same thing occurred with all the other replies, to see who was telling the truth and could accurately predict what was to happen in the year in question.

When this had been done, the alms-gatherers of the Inca went gathering the offerings they called *capaccocha,* and after the alms of all had been collected, the idols were returned to the temples. And if at the end of the year it turned out that one of these dreamers had by chance made a prediction that came true, the Inca joyfully ordered him to become a member of his household.

The *capaccocha,* as I say, was the offering that was paid in lieu of tithes to the temples, consisting of many goblets of gold and silver and other vessels and precious stones, and loads of rich blankets, and many llamas. And those whose forecasts had been false and lying the next year received no offering, but on the contrary, suffered in their reputation. At the time this was done, great things took place in Cuzco, far more than I have written. Now [i.e., 1549] that the Royal Tribunal has been founded, and [Pedro de la] Gasca has returned to Spain,[3] among other matters dealt with in certain lawsuits

[3] Pedro de la Gasca returned to Spain in 1549, when his task of putting down the rebellion of Gonzalo Pizarro was completed. He left to rule Peru until the arrival of the first viceroy, Antonio de Mendoza, the judge who formed the Royal Tribunal.

192

mention was made of this *capaccocha;*[4] and this and all the rest we have set down was really done and observed. And now I shall tell of the great feast of Hátun Raimi.[5]

CHAPTER 61 (ii: XXXI)

Of Sinchi Roca, the second Inca, who reigned in Cuzco.[1]

Now THAT I have written as briefly as I could what I could gather of the government and customs of the Incas, I wish to go back and relate what took place between the time of [the first Inca] Manco Capac[2] down to Huascar [the last Inca]. Those responsible for what had been set down and the bravest of them all were the Inca Pachacuti, Topa Inca, his son, and Huayna Capac, his grandson. Part of the reason may be, too, as I have already stated that these were the most recent.

After the death of Manco Capac, when fitting mourning and obsequies had been performed, Sinchi Roca Inca assumed the fringe [*llautu*] or crown with the usual ceremonies; he enlarged the house of the sun, and endeavored to win over all the people he could with flattery and gifts, calling the new city by the name it already bore, Cuzco. Some of the natives of that city state that where the great square was located, which is the same place it now occupies, there was a small lake and bog which made it difficult to erect the large buildings they wished to begin to construct. When the Inca Sinchi Roca learned of this, with the aid of his allies and the inhabitants of the city, he went about draining that swamp, blocking it up with great stones and thick logs, filling it in where the water once stood until it was made as it is now. They even say that all the valley of

---

[4] Again, *capaccocha* (see note 1 above), and still no explanation of what it was. Nowhere does Cieza say that *capaccocha*—which means only "beautiful lake"—involved human sacrifice.

[5] See Chapter 57 above.

[1] Sinchi Roca is named by Fernando Montesinos (*Memorias Antiguas Historiales del Peru*, written about 1650) as the "fifth Inca." He calls him "sagacious" and says that he is one who fought the growing power of the wizards in the tribe. Archaeology and oral history do not support his list of the Incas.

[2] The first Inca, Manco Capac, the founder of the Capac-cuna tribes, called Inca, is given in Chapter 7 above.

Cuzco was unproductive and the land never yielded a good crop of what they planted; so from inland in the great range of the Andes they brought thousands of loads of dirt, which they spread over it, thus—if this is true—making the valley as fertile as we now see it.

This Inca had by his sister and wife many sons, the oldest of which was called Lloque Yupanqui. And when the neighboring peoples saw the good system employed by the new settlers of Cuzco, and how they won people over more by kindness and benevolence than by force of arms or harshness, certain captains and headmen came to talk with them, admiring the temple of Curicancha and the seemly manner in which things were done, and as a result many of the various regions made pacts of alliance with them. They go further and say that one of those who came to the city, a chieftain of the village of Zañu [Saña], not far from the city, entreated Sinchi Roca to deign to accept a very beautiful and comely daughter of his to be the wife of his son. This put the Inca in a difficult dilemma, for if he complied with the request, he would be going against what his father had established and ordered; and if he did not grant what this chieftain asked, he and the others would look upon them [the Incas] as heartless men, who had no thought but for themselves. After taking counsel with the *Orejones* and principal men of the city, it seemed to them all that he should accept the maiden and marry her to his son, for until they had more strength and power, they should not be guided in this case by what his father had ordered. So they say he replied to the father of the girl that he should bring her to be wed to his son, and the marriage was carried out with great solemnity after their custom and fashion, and in Cuzco she was called Coya. A daughter of the Inca, who was to have been the wife of her brother, was sent to the temple of Curicancha, to which priests had already been assigned and where sacrifices were made to the image of the sun and there were gatekeepers to guard the sacred virgins, as has been related. And when this marriage was sealed, the Indians tell that those of that tribe came together with the inhabitants of Cuzco, and, feasting and drinking, they pledged friendship and brotherhood and that all should be one. To celebrate this great pledge, sacrifices

---

3 Huana-cauri (see Chapter 6 above) is one of the celebrated Inca shrines in the Cuzco valley connected with the origins of the Incas. The sons of the nobility (*Orejones*) performed their ceremonies of putting on of the breechclout there.

were made on the hill of Huana-cauri[3] and in Tampu Quiru[4] and in the temple of Curicancha[5] itself. After this was done, more than four thousand youths gathered, and with ceremonies they had devised for this purpose, they were knighted and made nobles, and their ears were pierced and the earrings they use inserted.

After this and other things which we do not know occurred, the Inca Sinchi Roca,[6] full of years and leaving many sons and daughters, died, and was greatly mourned and wept for and buried with sumptuous obsequies, and his statue was preserved to commemorate the fact that he had been good, and it was believed that his soul rested in the heavens.

CHAPTER 62 (ii: XXXII)

Of the third Inca who reigned in Cuzco, Lloque Yupanqui.

AFTER THE DEATH of Sinchi Roca, his son, Lloque Yupanqui,[1] was received as Inca, after first having fasted the appointed days. And as by his divinations and thoughts great hopes were aroused that in the future the city of Cuzco would flourish, the new Inca began to ennoble it with new buildings, and requested of his father-in-law, so they tell, that he come with his allies and confederates to dwell in the city, where he would be honored and given that part of it which he chose. The lord or chieftain of Zañu did so, and he was given and assigned the westernmost part of the city, which, as it lay on slopes and hills, was called Hanan-Cuzco; on the level and lower part the

---

[4] Tampu Quiru (Tampu-quirao, "cradle of the Incas") is another shrine connected with the origin of the Incas: Manco Capac, the first Inca, begot a son by his sister, Mama Ocllo, there.

[5] Curicancha, the "golden enclosure," thought to have been the first formal building raised by the Incas when they took possession of the glebe of Cuzco. (See Chapter 8 above.)

[6] Sinchi Roca (i.e., "strong," "valiant"; pronounced *Sinchee Roq'ah*) is accepted by most authorities as the historical second Inca. If John Rowe's chronology of the Incas is accepted, that the Inca dynasty began about A.D. 1200, the second Inca, Sinchi Roca, would appear about A.D. 1250 in Andean cultural history.

[1] Lloque ("left-handed") Yupanqui ("to count"); in the second person singular of the verb "count," so that the name Lloque (*Yo-key*) Yupanqui, "you will count," meant doubtlessly that in the future "you will count as a great and virtuous Inca."

Inca remained with his household and neighbors. As by this time all were *Orejones,* which is the same as saying nobles, and nearly all of them had had a part in the founding of the new city, the people who lived in these two areas of the city, known as Hanan- [Upper] Cuzco and Hurin- [Lower] Cuzco, were always regarded as illustrious. Certain of the Indians even said that one Inca had to be one of these lineages, and the next of the other; but I do not believe this is true, nor is it other than as the *Orejones* relate, which I have already written. To either side of the city there were large districts in the hills, for it was laid out in the hills.

There is no notice that there was any important war during these times; on the contrary, those of Cuzco tell that, little by little, with the friendly arts they employed, they won over to their friendship many peoples dwelling in the vicinity of the city, and enlarged the temple of Curicancha, both in buildings and in riches. They were already mining silver and gold, of which large quantities were brought to the city to the *catu* or market there; and they put in the temples women who were never to depart, as has been told in other places.

Reigning in this manner in Cuzco, Lloque Yupanqui came to be very old, and his life span was almost run, and he had had no son by his wife. This greatly troubled the residents of the city, and they made great sacrifices and prayers to their gods, in Huana-cauri as well as in Curicancha and in Tampu Quiru. And it is told that from one of these oracles to which they went for vain answers they heard that the Inca would beget a son who would succeed him in the kingdom. From this they took great pleasure, and happy with this hope, they helped the old Inca aboard the Coya, and in a short time she knew beyond doubt that she was with child, and in due course she bore a son.[2]

Lloque Yupanqui died, first ordering that the fringe or crown of empire should be placed and kept in the temple of Curicancha until his son, who had been named Mayta Capac, was old enough to rule, and as governors he left two of his brothers, whose names I did not learn.

On his death the Inca [Lloque] Yupanqui was mourned by all the members of his household; and in many parts of the city, in keeping

[2] Lloque Yupanqui, in the version of Montesinos, had three sons by his first wife, the one called Mayta Capac, who was the third son, being named Inca on his death.

with their blindness, many women and youths were killed, thinking that they would go to serve him in heaven, where they were sure his soul was. Canonizing him like a saint, the elders of the city ordered a great statue made to be brought out on the occasion of their feasts. Truly the preparations made for the burial of one of these Incas were very great, and as a general thing he was mourned in all the provinces, and in many of them the women cut off their hair, binding their heads with hempen ropes; and at the end of the year they made such lamentation and heathenish sacrifices as can hardly be imagined. In this connection, those who were in Cuzco in the year 1550 saw what happened at the observation of the anniversary of Paullu;[3] most of the women of the city went to his house to see it; I was there, and it was really a thing to arouse admiration. And it should be understood that this was as nothing compared with the past. Now I shall tell of Mayta Capac.

197

CHAPTER 63 (ii: XXXIII)

Of Mayta Capac, fourth Inca, who reigned in Cuzco and what took place in the time of his rule.

AFTER THE EVENTS I have described, Mayta Capac was growing up, and after the customary ceremonies, his ears were pierced, and when he had reached manhood, in the presence of many people, both natives and foreigners, who had assembled for this purpose, he received the crown or fringe of the kingdom. As he had no sister whom he could marry, he took to wife a daughter of a lord or chieftain of the village of Oma, which lay some two leagues from Cuzco, whose name was Mama Cahua Pata.

There was a district near the city where a clan of people, known as Alcaviquiza [Alcavilcas],[1] lived who had never wanted to be on

3 Paullu Tupac Yupanqui lived after the conquest; a descendant of the Inca Huayna Capac (d. 1527), he managed somehow to please the conqueror and the conquered. (See note 3, Chapter 59.)

1 The precise spelling of the name of this tribe is as uncertain as the tribe itself. Girolamo Benzoni, who was in Peru at the same time as Cieza and who wrote a *History of the New World,* first published in Venice in 1572, said they were called "Alcaviya." According to Pedro Sarmiento de Gamboa, who wrote his *apologia* for the Spanish conquest under the title of *History of the Incas,* the Alcaquiza or "Alcabisa,"

friendly terms with those of Cuzco, and there was always bad feeling between them. It is said that once as a woman from Cuzco was going for water to certain springs near by, a boy from the other district came out and broke her jar and had words with her. The woman, screaming, returned to Cuzco, and as these Indians are so excitable, they immediately took up arms and set out against the others, who had also armed themselves when they heard the noise, and came to see how the matter was going to end. When the Inca and his men came near, they drew up in battle formation, having taken as an excuse this trifling episode between the woman and the boy to conquer those of that clan or wipe out the memory of them.

Those of Alcaviquiza understood this clearly, and, like the brave men they were, with great valor went into battle, which was the first that was fought in those times, and they fought one another for a long time, the incident having come about so suddenly that those of Alcaviquiza had had no time to seek allies or help. Although they fought bravely, they were conquered after nearly all had been killed, hardly fifty escaping with their lives. Whereupon Inca Mayta Capac, taking possession of the fields and property of the dead, after the custom of the conqueror, divided them up among the residents of Cuzco, and great feasts were held to celebrate the victory, all going to the shrines they held sacred.

The Incas tell no more of Mayta Capac except that he reigned in Cuzco for some years,[2] and when he was assembling men to set out for the place they call Cunti-suyu, he contracted an illness from which he died, leaving as his heir his eldest son, by name Capac Yupanqui.

as he called them (p. 40), were one of the original tribes of the Cuzco valley which were conquered and replaced by the intruding "Incas." "Manco Capac," he writes on page 59, "entered the houses and lands of the natives especially of the *Alcabizas,* condemned their [chief] to perpetual imprisonment . . . and forcing others to pay tribute."

[2] Mayta Capac is dismissed by the chronicler Fernando Montesinos (*Memorias Antiguas Historiales del Peru*), in this manner: "Nothing memorable is said of this Inca, who was the third, save that he had two sons. . . . His heir was Capac Yupanqui." Others, principally Garcilaso de la Vega, give Mayta Capac considerable martial history, marking him as conqueror of the provinces of Carabaya (east of Lake Titicaca) and other provinces to the south of Lake Titicaca. This account does not coincide with what we now know of Andean history. None of those who questioned the Indians then living (in 1550) are agreed about the name of his wife and whence she came.

Of the fifth Inca who reigned in Cuzco, Capac Yupanqui.

AFTER MAYTA CAPAC had died and his obsequies had been carried **199** out according to their rites and his statue placed in the temple, Capac Yupanqui assumed the fringe and his coronation was solemnized by great feasts. After the celebration, which consisted for the most part in drinking and singing, the Inca went to make sacrifice at the hill of Huana-cauri, accompanied by the high priest and the ministers of the temple, and many of the *Orejones* and residents of the city.

It had been learned in the province of Cunti-suyu that at the time the late Inca died, he was planning to set out to make war on them, and they had made ready, not to be taken unawares.[1] When a few days later they learned of his death and the trip Capac Yupanqui, his son, was making to perform sacrifice at the hill of Huana-cauri, they decided to make war on him, and take booty if victory favored them. Putting the thought into action, they set out from a village in that province, called Marca, and arrived at where the Inca had already come, who, having been informed of what was happening, was on the alert. Before many days had gone by, they joined battle, which lasted for a long time and in which all fought valiantly; but in the end those of Cunti-suyu were defeated and many of them killed. Therefore the sacrifice was performed even more joyfully, and various men and women were killed, in keeping with their blind superstition, and many llamas, from whose entrails they made their auguries. When these sacrifices were completed, the Inca returned to

---

[1] The Cunti-suyu quarter of the world lay east of Cuzco; loosely defined: lying between the Andes and the Pacific, extending as far south as what may now be called the border of Chile and north to the valley of Lima. The Cunti-suyu was composed of many tribes, many in a loose confederacy held together alone by their fear of the expanding Inca realm. It included the Chumpivilcas, who had their own language but used Quechua, and when conquered paid their *mit'a* tax by dancing at the Inca's court; the Cavanas, who spoke a corruption of Quechua and deformed their heads; the Rucanas, who when finally defeated became loyal vassals of the Incas and furnished their blue-clad litter-bearers to the Inca; the Soras, who had 4,000 tax-paying Indians for the Inca realm, who had their own language but understood Quechua as well as the Aymara spoken about Lake Titicaca—all the tribes grouped within that quarter of the Inca world which was known as the Cunti-suyu.

Cuzco, where great feasts and celebrations were held in honor of the victory he had obtained.

Those who had escaped from their enemies, as best they could made their way back to their province, where once more they set about assembling troops and seeking support, announcing that they would destroy the city of Cuzco or die in the attempt, wiping out the upstarts that had come there. And with great insolence, consumed by wrath, they made haste to gather arms, and had already divided up among themselves the virgins of the temple of Curicancha without having laid eyes on it. When they were arrayed for war, they set out for Huana-cauri, and from there to enter Cuzco. But Capac Yupanqui had received word of their movements, and had gathered together all the neighbors and confederates of Cuzco, and with the *Orejones* awaited the enemy until he knew they were approaching Cuzco. Then he went out to meet them, and they fought, and each captain urged on his own men. Even though those of Cunti-suyu fought to the limits of their strength, they were defeated again, with the death of more than six thousand of their men, and those who escaped fled to their lands.

Capac Yupanqui pursued them to their own territory, where he made such war on them that they came suing for peace, offering to recognize him as the Inca of Cuzco, as did the other people who were his friends. Capac Yupanqui forgave them, and showed them favor, and ordered his men to do them no harm and to steal nothing from those who were now their friends. And certain beautiful maidens were selected from that province to be taken to the temple of the sun in Cuzco. Capac Yupanqui spent some time in the region, urging the natives to live in orderly fashion, and not have their settlements among the heights and snow-covered mountains; and when what he had ordered had been done, he returned to his city.

This was being further ennobled every day, and the temple of Curicancha beautified. He ordered a dwelling built for himself that was the finest that had been constructed in Cuzco up to that time. It is told that by his legitimate wife, the Coya, he had sons who succeeded him in power; and as by now word had spread through all the provinces neighboring on Cuzco of how the Incas and the *Orejones* lived there, and the temple they had founded, and their intelligence and order, and how they went clothed and adorned, they were amazed at all this, and the news spread proclaiming these things.

When those who ruled the part that lay to the west of Cuzco and reached to where Andahuaylas now is heard of this, they sent ambassadors to Capac Yupanqui with great gifts and presents, begging him to accept them as friends and confederates; to which the Inca replied that he was pleased to do so, and gave them rich objects of gold and silver for those who had sent them. These messengers remained for several days in the city, where they were well treated and lodged, and it seemed to them that what they saw outdid what they had heard, and so they reported when they returned to their lands. Some of the *Orejones* of Cuzco state that the general language spoken in all the provinces was that used and spoken by these Quichoas [Quechuas],[2] who were considered very brave by their neighbors until the Chancas destroyed them.

After a long life Capac Yupanqui died at a very old age,[3] and after the mourning and days to honor him had passed, his son was accepted

201

[2] The Quechuas lived in a semitropical climate north of the great Apurímac River in the region of Curahuasi, which village for six hundred years kept in repair the famous suspension bridge that swung across the Apurímac. About the beginning of the fourteenth century they were doubtlessly one of the largest and most culturally advanced tribes in the central Andes; their language, "Quechua," became a lingua franca throughout the Andes. Later in this century they were attacked by a more primitive tribe, the Chancas, who were legended to have come from the region of Choclococha on the eastern side of the cordilleras. Utterly defeated, the Quechuas had the conquest road open for the Incas, who absorbed the remainder of them, fully adopted the Quechua tongue, and allowed the Incas—as Quechua-speaking people—to gain hegemony over all others of this speech. Since Quechua was then an adopted Inca language, it poses the question of just what precisely did the "Incas" speak before they used this language. The question has never been answered satisfactorily. Their language was first called "quichua" by Domingo de Santo Tomás, a friar who wrote the first Quechua grammar (Valladolid, Spain, 1560). A "Quichua," it was then pointed out, was an Indian who inhabited the temperate zone of the Andes; Garcilaso de la Vega said that the original "Quichuas inhabited the region of Abancay but they probably extended to the Apurímac." The word seems to be derived from *quehani* ("twist"), *quechuasca* ("twisted"), and *ichu* (the particular grass that grows in these regions and is used almost exclusively for roof thatch), so that the combined form of *Quechuasca-ichu* ("twisted grass") was shortened into *Quechua,* a word which gave both name and language to this Andean tribe who bordered the Incas.

[3] This fifth Inca is said (by Pedro Sarmiento de Gamboa, in his highly equivocal history) to have been the first to "make conquests beyond the valley of Cuzco"; those tribes of Cuyumarca, Ancasmarca (four leagues from Cuzco), and Ayamarca were made conquest; the chieftain of the last named gave his daughter, Curi-Hilpay, as *coya* (queen). Although Capac Yupanqui had other concubines, his Coya bore him a son, who, as Inca Roca, succeeded him as the Lord-Inca of the realm.

without any objection as realm leader, as his father had been; his name was Inca Roca Inca.

CHAPTER 65 (ii: xxxv)

Of the sixth Inca who reigned in Cuzco, and what
happened in his day, and the fable or story they tell
of the river that runs through the center
of the city of Cuzco.

ON THE DEATH of Capac Yupanqui, his son Roca Inca succeeded him, and, as was the custom, many people came to his coronation from many regions. These Indians tell that at the time this Inca's ears were pierced for the earrings the *Orejones* wear to this very day, one of them hurt him very much, and that with this annoyance he left the city and went to a very high near-by hill, called Chaca, where he sent for his wives and the Coya, his sister Micay Cuca, whom he had received as his wife during the life of his father, to keep him company. At this point they tell of a fabulous mystery that occurred. In those days no brook or river ran through the city, and this worked no little hardship, for when it was hot they went to bathe in the rivers that lay around the city, and even when it was not warm they bathed; and to supply the inhabitants with water there were small springs, which there still are. Now when the Inca was at this hill, withdrawing from his people, he began to pray to the great Tici-Viracocha,[1] and to Huana-cauri, and to the sun, and to the Incas, his father and grandfathers, to make known to him how and in what way, by human means, he could bring a river or canal of water to the city; and while he was praying, a great clap of thunder was heard which frightened all who were there, and the Inca himself, from the great fright he received, lowered his head until his left ear touched the ground, from which blood began to gush, and suddenly he heard a great rushing of water beneath that spot. When he perceived this wonder, he joyously ordered many Indians to come from the city, who quickly set about digging until they reached the stream

[1] For a full discussion of Tici-Viracocha, see Chapter 5 above.

of water which had made a channel through the bowels of the earth and was flowing without doing any good.

Proceeding with this tale, they go on to say that after they had dug deep and discovered the underground stream, they made great sacrifices to their gods, believing that it was by virtue of their godhead that they had received this blessing, and with great skill they conducted the water through the middle of the city, having first paved the ground with great stones and built fine walls with strong foundations along either side of the river, and, to cross it, stone bridges at intervals.

203

I have seen this river [the Huatanay], and it is true that it flows as they say, its source being in the direction of that hill.[2] Aside from this, I can only set down what they tell about it. It might well be that there was an underground stream whose water had never been seen or heard, and which was diverted to the city, as we now see. For in many parts of this great kingdom large and small rivers run beneath the surface of the earth, as all those who have traveled through the plains and mountains know. At present there are great rubbish heaps alongside the banks of this river, full of dung and filth, which was not the case in the days of the Incas, when it was very clean, the water running over the stones. At times the Incas went there to bathe with their women, and on various occasions Spaniards have found small gold ornaments or pins which they forgot or dropped while they were bathing.

After this had occurred, the Inca Roca, so they tell, went out of Cuzco to make sacrifices, trying with guile and friendly words to win over all the people he could. He proceeded to what they call Cunti-suyu, where, in the place called Pomatambo,[3] he fought a

[2] The Huatanay is one of the two streams (the other is the Tullumayu) which flow down from the hills back of the fortress Sacsahuamán. These, rising and falling with the season, caused the Inca's engineers to confine them by stone walls; the Huatanay, as it was the largest, was well and skillfully lined with fitted stone slabs. The name, it has been suggested, comes from the words *huata* ("year") and *ananay* (a sigh of weariness), which combined form means the yearly weariness of repairing the stone masonry from the year's onslaught of descending water.

[3] Pomatambo lies in the Cunti-suyu, midway between Cuzco and the Pacific Coast; it is dominated by the great shallow lake, *Parina* ("flamingo") *-cocha* ("lake"). Hiram Bingham, in his *Inca Land* (New York, 1922), gives a vivid description of Parina-cochas, 12,000 feet altitude, 170 kilometers west of Cuzco. The whole region is filled with Inca remains and is little known. It is fully possible that at this time (c. 1350) the Inca Roca pushed his western conquests down to the Pacific, constructing the lateral highway to the sea at Chala (parts of it well discernible still) and establishing the

battle with the natives of those regions, from which he emerged victorious and the lord of all, for, pardoning them and making liberal gifts, and telling them of his great achievements, they came to love him and offer themselves to his service, binding themselves to pay him tribute. After spending some time in Cunti-suyu and visiting the shrines and temples in those lands, he returned victorious to Cuzco, preceded by the nobles who protected his person with axes and halberds of gold.[4]

204

This Inca had many sons and not a single daughter. When he had ordered and disposed of matters of magnitude and great importance for the governing of the kingdom, he died, having first married his eldest son, by name Inca Yupanqui, to a lady of Alamarca who was called Mama Chiquia.

CHAPTER 66 (ii: XXXVI)

Of the seventh Inca, Yahuar-Huacac, who reigned in Cuzco.

ON THE DEATH of Inca Roca there came from Cunti-suyu, Vicos [Chumpivilcas], from Ayamarca and the other regions with which he

---

fishing villages that made it possible for the inhabitants of Cuzco to have fresh fish from the sea, as well as molluscs and seaweed (still an important item of diet and medicinally important for its high content of iodine). The bridge that crossed the river in Cuzco toward the west on the road that led to the Cunti-suyu and the coast was known as the Chaquill-chaca (the seaweed bridge).

[4] Inca Roca's rule extended to A.D. 1350 and beyond. Garcilaso de la Vega states that he was the one who ordered the bridging of the Apurímac with the longest suspension bridge in the realm (see von Hagen, *Highway of the Sun,* Chapter VIII). This could be true, since at that time they began to absorb the Quechuas, who lived beyond the Apurímac. All authorities seem to agree that he was the sixth Inca. One of the chroniclers called him "sagacious . . . endeavoring to enforce the laws of the Incas." Pedro Sarmiento de Gamboa states that "he gave himself up to pleasure and banquets" and that "he loved his children to the extent that he forgot his duties to his people." Another (Garcilaso) makes him a great conqueror; absorbing the Quechuas, making the first of a series of raids on the Chancas tribes, conqueror of Curamba (the ruin is still lying close to Pincos, south of Andahuaylas), and beginning the conquest of Vilcas (where later the great Inca center of Vilcas-huamán was built). All agreed that he married as his *coya* Mama Micay (Cieza calls her Chiquia, which is close enough), and that she bequeathed him many sons, of which the eldest, Titu Cusi Huallpa—known as Yahuar-Huacac ("bloody weeper")—was created seventh Inca.

made alliances and friendships, many people, both men and women, and great weeping was made for the dead Inca, and many of the women who had loved and served him during his life, in keeping with the general blindness of the Indians, hanged themselves by their own hair, and others killed themselves in other ways so their souls could quickly go to serve that of Inca Roca. And in his tomb, which was magnificent and sumptuous, they placed great treasures and a greater number of women and servants with victuals and fine attire.

None of the tombs of these Incas has been discovered,[1] but the only proof needed as to whether they were rich or not is to know that in ordinary graves as much as sixty thousand gold pesos, more and less, have been found. So what must they have put in those of these monarchs who possessed so much of this metal, and who considered it so important to leave this world rich and adorned?

A statue of Inca Roca was also made, and he was numbered among their gods, and his soul was believed to have gone to rest in heaven.

When the mourning and funerals were over, the new Inca[2] shut himself away to fast. And so no sedition or insurrection of the people might break out during his absence, he ordered one of the most prominent members of his family to represent him in public, whom he empowered to punish any who gave cause, and see that peace and order prevailed in the city until he came forth with the royal insigne of the fringe. They tell that this Inca was said to be of noble air, grave, and of commanding presence. He withdrew to the most secret parts of the palace, where he performed his fast. From time to time corn was brought to him, which was what he most ate, and he abstained from intercourse with women. When the appointed days were completed, he came out, and the people revealed their happiness at the sight of him. Great feasts and sacrifices were made, and when these were over, the Inca ordered much gold and silver to be brought from many places for the temple, and the stone they call the

[1] This proved not to be true. Inca Roca's *huaca* was found in the village of Rarapa in 1560 by Juan Polo de Ondegardo, a lawyer and official at Cuzco immediately following the conquest. He wrote exhaustive inquiries about the Inca religion and mode of government, and he was responsible for finding many of the mummies of the Incas.

[2] Inca Yupanqui is best known by the name his people gave him, Yahuar-Huacac, "the bloody weeper," because he always had bad eyes and they were so continually red that, by exaggeration, his people said that he wept blood, and for this reason they called him Yahuar-Huacac.

stone of war was made in Cuzco, large and set with gold and precious stones.[3]

CHAPTER 67 (ii: XXXVII)

206

Of how, when this Inca was preparing to set out to make war in the province of the Colla, there was an uprising in Cuzco, and how the Chancas defeated the Quechuas and won their territory from them.

WHEN YAHUAR-HUACAC was in Cuzco engaged in ennobling the city, he decided to go to Colla-suyu, which are the provinces which lie to the south of the city because word had been brought him that the descendants of [a chief named] Zapana, who was lord of the region of Hatuncolla, had become very powerful and were so haughty that they were assembling people to march against Cuzco, and he ordered his troops to make ready. And as Cuzco cannot endure peace long, the Indians say that when Yahuar-Huacac had brought together many men for the expedition he planned and was on the point of departing, certain captains of Cunti-suyu, with their soldiers, conspired to kill the Inca,[1] because if he returned from that expedition victorious, his fame would be such that he would want to make them all his vassals and servants. So, they tell, when the Inca was at one of his feasts, merry with the much wine they had drunk, one of those in the conspiracy approached him and raising his arm brought down a club on the royal head. The Inca, dazed but courageous, rose up, saying, "What have you done, traitor?" Those of Cunti-suyu had already killed many, and the Inca thought of taking refuge in the temple; but it was useless, for his enemies overtook him and killed him, and many of his wives.

[3] The "stone of war" which was set up in the great plaza of Huayka-pata is often mentioned by Cieza but seldom or almost never by other chroniclers. Captains seemed to have sworn fealty to the Inca on it, and they met there before proceeding with a conquest.

[1] The personal history of the Inca "The Bloody Weeper" is confused. Every chronicler seems to have had a different informant with different information. That the seventh Inca had numerous sons—all valiant warriors, who contended for the fringe or crown of their father—is agreed by all. The ruler was much troubled by his headstrong sons, and there were a number of attempts at assassination as the Inca aged and the time came for him to select a successor, there being no clear rule of descent.

The city was in such a tumult that the people could not hear one another. The priests had taken refuge in the temple, and the women of the city went howling, tearing their hair, horrified to see the Inca dead in his blood as though he were a commoner. Many of the inhabitants were trying to flee the city and the assassins were preparing to sack it when, so they tell, with mighty blasts of lightning and claps of thunder, so much rain fell from the sky that those of Cunti-suyu took fright and, without pursuing their purpose, turned back, satisfied with the harm they had done.

And these Indians relate that at this time the Quechuas were the rulers of the provinces called Andahuaylas, and that from beside a lake known as Choclococha there came forth an army under two captains, by name Guaraca and Uasco,[2] who came conquering everything in their path until they reached the aforesaid province. As the inhabitants had learned of their approach, they made ready for war, encouraging one another, saying that it would be just to give death to those who had come against them. Thus, leaving by a gate that opens in the direction of the Aymaraes,[3] the Chancas and their captains approached the oncoming forces, and they met and held parleys, but as they could reach no agreement, they joined battle. According to what is told, it was savagely fought and the victory was in doubt, but in the end the Quechuas were defeated and cruelly treated; all those the enemy could lay hands on were killed without sparing the young children nor the defenseless aged, and the women were taken as concubines. And after wreaking other harm, they made themselves the masters of that province, and to this day their descendants rule it. I have related this because farther on I shall have occasion to make mention of these Chancas.

To return to our story, when those of Cunti-suyu left Cuzco, the dead were removed from the city, and great sacrifices were made. And it is told for a fact that Yahuar-Huacac[4] did not receive the

---

[2] For this turbulent part of Inca history, see Chapters 34 and 64. Of the Quechuas and Chancas and the land they ruled, see Chapters 74 and 75.

[3] Aymaraes, in the Cunti-suyu quarter. It is now a province; Acobamba is its capital.

[4] Inca Yupanqui, the "bloody weeper," is here confused with his son, Viracocha. Much land about Cuzco in all of the directions was made conquest by him and consolidated into the Inca realm. Some chroniclers have it that he followed the advances of his father toward the Vilcas (now the Pampas) River and was responsible for the suspension bridge across it. Poma de Ayala (*El Primer Nueva Coronica* [*sic*]) states that the bridge across the Vilcas (Pampas), which joined the site of Vilcas-huamán to

burial honors of his ancestors, nor was a statue made of him, as of them, and he left no son.[5]

CHAPTER 68 (ii: XXXVIII)

Of how the Orejones *took counsel as to who should be the Inca, and what happened until Viracocha Inca assumed the fringe, who was the eighth Inca to rule.*

AFTER WHAT I have told took place, when due mourning had been made for the death of the Inca, the leading men of the city considered who should be chosen Inca and receive this dignity. There were different opinions on the matter; there were those who did not want a Lord-Inca, but that the city should be governed by those chosen for that purpose; others said it would be lost if it did not have a head.

The discussions were heated, and it was feared that it might end in strife, when, it is told, a woman stepped out of the ranks of the Hanan-Cuzcos and said: "What are you arguing about? Why don't you choose Viracocha Inca, for he well deserves it." When they heard her words, as these people are so unpredictable, they set down their goblets of chicha, and with all haste went for Viracocha Inca, the son of Inca Yupanqui, saying when they saw him that he should perform the customary fast and accept the fringe they wished to confer upon him. After thinking it over, Viracocha went in to fast, and put the city in charge of Roca Inca, his kinsman, and when the time came, emerged with the crown, royally attired, and solemn feasts were held in Cuzco which lasted for many days, and everyone was well pleased with the election of the new Inca.

There are those who say that this Inca was called Viracocha because he came from a different region, and his attire was different, and that in his features and appearance he looked like a Spaniard because he had a beard. They tell other things that it would be tedious

the village of Oran-marca, "was built by the Inca Yahuar-Huacaca." Cieza wrote that that "bridge is so strong that horses may pass over it," and "was 166 paces long." (See von Hagen, *Highway of the Sun,* Chapter IX.)

[5] An error; he left six sons, one of whom, Viracocha, was named eighth Inca.

"Near Desaguadero [the outlet of Lake Titicaca] in the time of the Incas there used to be guards to collect toll from those who crossed the [pontoon] bridge which was made of sheaves of oats [balsa] and constructed in such a way that men, horses, and all else could pass over it." This type of balsa boat was also used for navigation.

"In many of the villages of the highlands [they built terraces] and there ran irrigation ditches drawn from rivers, and with great skill and ingenuity on the part of those who built them." The agricultural terraces in the eastern section of Pisac, where houses, storerooms, and terraces remain intact.

"Four leagues from this city of Cuzco there is a valley called the Yucay, which is beautiful. There are large terraces which look like walls, rising one above the other; on [these] they plant what they eat." The terraces above Yucay close on to Pisac.

"The natives call them *llamas* — some of them are white, some black, others brown. Some of them are the size of a donkey with long legs and broad bellies."

"When the Lord-Inca decided to organize a royal hunt, fifty or sixty thousand people gathered, encircled the fields, and a great number of animals were rounded up, among them many *vicuñas,* with long necks like camels."

"The most extraordinary things to be seen here in the Colla are the *chullpas* — graves of the dead. They seem to me the most noteworthy thing about the Indians, for where they are to be buried constitutes their entire happiness." Burial *chullpas,* seen by Cieza, overlooking Lake Umayo; there are many of them, but all have been rifled of their dead.

"When the natives of the Colla died, they were buried in the *chullpas*." A stone entrance to one of the tombs; on it is carved figures of the wild *vizcacha*, relative of the chinchilla.

"And the houses made of stone so skillfully joined that it was evident how old the edifices were, for the huge stones were very well set." An example of Inca stonework, showing the skillful tying in of each huge worked stone to another.

"There are great stands of carob trees in this valley of Ica. One finds extensive woods of *guarango* and *algarrobo* impenetrable at many points. On the Nazca road there are five leagues of these woods so thick that the Inca highway is the only way to get through them, and one sees nothing but woods and sky."— Antonio Vásquez de Espinosa. This immense forest of algarrobos is on the Ica-Nazca road.

to relate. In Cuzco I asked Cayu Tupac Yupanqui[1] and others of the most illustrious men of the city to give me the account of the Incas that I am here relating, and they told me this was nonsense, and there was not a word of truth to it, for Virachoca Inca was born and reared in Cuzco, like his father and grandfathers, and that he was given the name of Virachoca as his first name, just as they all had one.

209

As soon as he was crowned, he married a lady of high rank, by name Runtu Caya, who was very beautiful. And when the celebration was over, he decided to set out and conquer various peoples in the vicinity of Cuzco who had refused to accept the friendship of the previous Inca, trusting to the strength of their fortresses. And with the troops he assembled, he set out from Cuzco in his rich litter, with a guard of the nobles, and proceeded toward a place called Calca,[2] where his messengers had been discourteously received. When they knew that the troops from Cuzco were close by, they armed themselves, took their positions on the heights of the hills in their fortresses and stockades, and from there they rolled down great rocks on the camps of the Incas to kill those they could reach. Their adversaries, however, scaled the mountains and, in spite of strong resistance, were able to take one of those fortresses. When the men of Calca saw the men of Cuzco inside their fortifications, they came out to a great square, where they fought hard, and the battle lasted from morning until noon, with many killed on both sides and more taken prisoner. But victory went to those of Cuzco.

The Inca was in his camp beside a river [Vilcanota], and when news of the victory was brought to him he rejoiced greatly. At this point his captains descended with the booty and prisoners. The Indians who had survived the battle, and other captains of Calca and its surrounding regions, seeing how badly their plan had turned out, decided that the only thing to do was to throw themselves on the mercy of the conqueror and sue for peace, accepting reasonable terms, as many others did. When they reached this decision, they emerged from among the mountains, shouting with loud voices, "Live forever, mighty Inca Viracocha, our sovereign." At the sound of the echo

---

[1] Cayu Tupac Yupanqui was in all probability the father of Andrés Tupac Yupanqui, the one who at the age of forty signed as one of the witnesses for the *ayllu* of Topa Inca (*History* of Sarmiento de Gamboa, p. 198).

[2] In the Vilcamayu (upper Urubamba valley) distant thirty miles from Cuzco.

their voices made, the men of Cuzco resumed their arms, but in a little while the vanquished were prostrate in the dust at the feet of Viracocha Inca, in which position, without arising, one of them who was held to be the wisest, lifting up his voice, began to speak: "Do not become overweening, O! Inca, with the victory God has given you, nor hold us in contempt because we have been vanquished, for it has been given to you and the Incas to rule peoples, and to us to defend with all our power the liberty we inherited from our forebears, and if this is denied us, to obey and receive with good spirit our subjection. Accordingly, order that no more people shall be killed or done harm, and dispose of us as you wish." And when the leading Indian had spoken these words, the others who were with him began to howl loudly, imploring clemency.

The Inca replied that if they had suffered harm, it had been the result of their own wrath, for they had not wished to believe his words or accept his friendship, which he regretted; he generously agreed to let them remain in the lands they possessed, as before, and in their fields, on condition that at the appointed time and in keeping with the laws they should make tribute to Cuzco of what their settlements produced, and that they should send men to the city at once to build him two palaces, one within it and the other in Caqui [Caquia-Xaquixahuana], where he might go to take his pleasure. They replied that this would be done, and the Inca ordered the captives released, without exception, and that their lands be restored to those who were now his allies. And so they would understand what was expected of them, and to avoid dissensions among them, he appointed a delegate of his to remain there, with ample powers, but without stripping the native ruler of his authority.

After which this which I have written took place, Inca Viracocha sent a messenger to summon those of Caitomarca, who were yond side a river in strongholds they had built, and who had never wanted to be friends with the Incas of Cuzco. When the messengers of Viracocha Inca arrived, they insulted him, and called the Inca mad if he thought they were going to submit to his rule so meekly.

Of how Viracocha Inca shot a fiery stone from his sling against Caitomarca, and how they did him reverence.

AFTER HE had sent the messenger Viracocha Inca ordered his men to break camp and set out for Caitomarca. On the way they came to a river [Vilcamayu] where he directed them to stop and rest. While they were there, the messenger arrived and told how the people of Caitomarca had mocked him and said they had not the least fear of the Incas. When Viracocha Inca heard this, he angrily mounted his litter, ordering his men to march swiftly. So they did until they came to the banks of a mighty, swift-flowing river, which I think must have been the Yucay.[1] There the Inca ordered his tents pitched, and made ready to attack the town of his enemies which lay across the river. But the river ran so swiftly that it was impossible to carry this out. Those of Caitomarca reached the opposite bank, from which they hurled many stones from their slings at the camp of the Inca, and from both sides came loud cries, for it is a strange custom among these people how little rest they give their mouths when they are fighting.

Two days the Inca camped beside that river, they tell, without being able to cross it, for there was no bridge, nor were those now employed in use before the time of the Incas, although some say they were, and some that they were not. So in order for Viracocha Inca to be able to cross the river, it is told that he ordered a small stone heated in a great fire, and when it was very hot, a mixture or substance was rubbed on it so that wherever it fell it would kindle a fire. Then he ordered it placed in a sling of cloth of gold with which, when he was so minded, he shot stones, and with mighty strength he hurled it against the village of Caitomarca. It chanced to fall on the eaves of a house thatched with straw that was very dry, and the flames it lighted crackled so loudly that, as it was night, all the Indians

---

[1] Yucay is the river which flows through the Yucay valley. Following a strange custom, the upper reaches of this river are called the Vilcamayu; about Pisac it is the Vilcanota; below it the river becomes the Urubamba, by which name it continues in foaming violence until it joins the tributaries of the Amazon.

ran to see the fire that had started in the house, asking one another how that had come about, and who had set fire to the house. Whereupon an old woman came out, who, they say, said: "Listen to what I tell you and what is for your own good. Do not think this house has been set afire by anyone here, but rather that it descended from heaven, for I saw a burning stone which fell from on high upon the house and left it as you see it."

When the leading men and rulers and elders of the village heard that, being, as they are, so given to augury and witchcraft, they believed that the stone had been sent by the hand of God to punish them for refusing to obey the Inca. So, instantly, without awaiting a response from the oracle or making sacrifice of any sort, they crossed the river in boats, bearing gifts to the Inca. And when they came into his presence, they begged for peace, offering him their persons and possessions, as did his allies.

After hearing what the men of Caitomarca had to say, Viracocha Inca answered them craftily, telling them that if they had not had the good sense to come that day, the next he had intended to fall upon them with great boats that he had ordered built. After this a pact was signed between those of Caitomarca and the Inca, who gave the captain or chieftain of that village one of his wives, who was from Cuzco and who was greatly esteemed and honored.

The fame of the Inca's deed spread through all the region, and many of the settlements, without ever seeing the arms of the men of Cuzco, sent him pledges of their allegiance by friends and allies of the Lord-Inca, who received great satisfaction from this, and spoke to all lovingly and gave proof of his great benevolence, providing those who were in need with all that he could supply. And as he saw that he could assemble a great army, he decided to call up men and go in person to Cunti-suyu.

Of how a tyrant rose in Cuzco, and the uprising that took place, and how certain of the mamaconas *were punished for having made evil use of their bodies against the mandates of their religion, and how Viracocha Inca returned to Cuzco.*

NEWS OF EVERYTHING that happened to Viracocha was borne to Cuzco, and when word reached the city of the war he was waging against those of Caitomarca, they say that a usurper arose, a brother of the late Inca Yupanqui, who had greatly resented the fact that the rule and sovereignty had been given to Viracocha Inca and not to him, and had been biding his time to try to seize power. This idea came to him because he found favor among certain of the *Orejones* of the Hurin-Cuzco lineage. With this new war the Inca was carrying on, it seemed to them that he would have his hands full to bring it to an end, and so they encouraged the one I have referred to, urging him, without further delay, to kill the governor who had been left in charge of the city and make himself master of it.

Capac, for this was his name, thirsting for power, assembled his supporters, and one day when most of the *Orejones* were in the temple of the sun, and with them Inca Roca, the governor Inca Viracocha had named, they took up arms, proclaiming the liberty of the people and that Viracocha Inca was not entitled to rule, and rushed on the lieutenant and killed him as well as many others, strewing the blood upon the altars where the sacred vessels and shrines and images of the sun stood. The *mamaconas* and priests came forth making a loud outcry, cursing the assassins and saying that so great a sin deserved a great punishment. A crowd of people came rushing from the city to see what was happening, and when they were informed, some, who approved what had been done, joined Capac. Others, lamenting it, took up arms, unwilling to countenance it. Thus, being divided, many were killed on both sides. The city was in such an uproar that the sound of their voices rent the air and they could neither hear nor make out what was said. Finally, the usurper prevailing, he seized the city, killing all the wives of the Inca, although the most important of them had accompanied him. Some of them managed to flee the city and finally reached Viracocha Inca. When he learned what had happened, restraining the indignation he felt, he ordered his troops to take the road to Cuzco.

To return to the tyrant Capac, once he had secured the city, he wished to appear in public with the fringe so that all would look upon him as Inca. But after the first impulse had passed, and that fury under which men, losing their heads, embark on great evils, the very ones who had urged him to rebel insulted and deserted him, mocking him for aspiring to the royal insigne, and went out to meet the rightful Inca, whom they begged to forgive them for what they had done.

Capac did not lack the courage to pursue his project, but chagrined to see how his supporters were deserting him and the sudden change of his fortunes, cursed those who had deceived him, and himself for trusting them; and in order not to have to see the Inca with his own eyes, he himself punished his crime, taking poison by which he died. His wives and children and other kinsmen imitated him in his death.

The news of all this was brought to the Inca's camp, and as soon as he reached the city and entered it, he went straight to the temple of the sun to make sacrifices. The bodies of Capac and the others who had died he ordered thrown into the fields to be devoured by the birds, and seeking out those who had shared in the treason, he condemned them to death.

When Viracocha Inca's allies and friends learned what had happened, they sent him many embassies with rich gifts and offerings, congratulating him and themselves, and he welcomed these embassies joyfully.

At this time, as the *Orejones* tell it, there were in the temple of the sun many virgins who were highly honored and respected, and occupied themselves only in such duties as I have mentioned in many parts of this history. According to their account, four of them made evil use of their bodies with certain of the gatekeepers whose duty it was to guard them, and when this was learned, they were seized, together with their partners in adultery, and the high priests ordered them all put to death.

The Inca had his heart set on the Cunti-suyu undertaking [conquest], but feeling himself old and weary, he gave it up. It was then that he ordered palaces built for himself in the valley of Xaquixa-huana[1] where he could take his pleasure; and as he had many sons, and realized that the eldest of them, by name Inca Urco, who in due course would inherit the rule of the kingdom, had bad habits and was given to vices and was very cowardly, he wished to deprive him of the succession and give it to a younger one, by name Inca Yupanqui.

215

CHAPTER 71 (ii: XLI)

Of how emissaries came to Cuzco from the tyrants
of the Colla, by name Sinchi Cari and Zapana, and of
the expedition of Viracocha Inca to the Colla.

MANY EPISODES and events took place among the natives of these provinces in these times; but as it is my habit to relate only what I believe to be true in the opinion of the people here and the relation I took down in Cuzco, I omit all of which I am poorly informed and do not clearly comprehend, and shall deal only with what I understand, as I have said many times. Thus, it is common knowledge among the *Orejones* that at this time there came to Cuzco emissaries from the province of Colla, for they say that during the reign of Inca Viracocha the ruler of Hatuncolla was a lord named Zapana. And as in the lake of Titicaca there were islands settled by people, in large boats he came to these islands, where he waged war on the inhabitants, and great battles were fought between him and them, from which Cari emerged the victor. But as he aspired to no other honor or power beyond robbing and destroying the villages, loaded with booty, without taking captives, he returned to Chucuito [on Lake Titicaca], which he had made his seat, and by his orders the villages of Hilave,

---

[1] "My Refuge" is the translation of Caquia-Xaquixahuana, where the old Inca Viracocha fled the frosts of Cuzco. Its precise location was in dispute, but ruins of an enormous palace, together with potsherds of the finest pottery, were found at traditional Xaquixahuana (near the modern village of Surite), which is in the valley of Anta, a quagmire fifteen miles northeast of Cuzco, across which the Incas had built a wide eight-mile-long causeway in the fourteenth century. Beyond this, on the Inca road, are the remains of "My Refuge." The ruins have never been studied. Many decisive battles were fought here (see Chapter 75 and note 2, Chapter 41). Archaeological history will be fully rewarded by the first one who digs below the surface there.

THE INCAS

Xulli [Juli], Zepita, Pumata [Pomata], and others had been settled.[1]
With the forces he could assemble, after having made great sacrifices
to his gods or devils, he determined to march against the province
of the Canas. When they learned of this, calling upon one another,
they went out to meet him, and a battle was fought in which the
Canas were defeated and many of them lost their lives. After Cari had
won this victory, he determined to proceed, and so doing, he came to
Lurocachi, where it is told that another battle took place with the
same Canas in which they suffered the same fortune as in the others.

With these victories Cari had become very haughty, and the news
had spread everywhere. When Zapana, the lord of Hatuncolla, learned
of it, he was envious of the other's good fortune, and ordered his allies
and vassals to assemble to go out to meet him and strip him of his
booty. But this meeting could not be kept so secret that Cari did not
learn of Zapana's design, and in orderly fashion he withdrew to Chucuito by a different route so that Zapana could not molest him. When
he reached his own territory, he called his leading men together so
that they would be ready for anything Zapana might attempt, his aim
being to destroy him so that there would be but one ruler in Colla.
Zapana had this same thought.

When it was learned through all this kingdom of the valor of the
Incas and their great power and the bravery of Viracocha Inca who
ruled in Cuzco, each of these two, hoping to win his friendship, sought
him out with emissaries whom they sent, each asking him to succor
him and oppose his enemy. These emissaries were dispatched to
Cuzco with fine gifts, and they reached the city at the time the Inca
was returning from the palaces or rest houses he had ordered built
in Xaquixahuana for his pleasure. When he learned the purpose of
their mission, he listened to them and ordered that they be lodged
in the city and their needs provided for. Then taking counsel with
the *Orejones* and the elders [*amauta-cuna*] in his confidence about
what he should do in regard to the embassies that had come from
Colla-suyu, it was decided to consult the oracles. This the priests do
before the idols, bowing low, resting their chin on their breast, and
puffing out their cheeks until they themselves look like fierce devils,

[1] All of these villages were given by the Viceroy of Peru to the administration of
the Jesuits in 1576. They built, with the Indians' aid, a concourse of beautiful churches,
still a delight to see. In Juli they set up a printing press as early as 1582.

216

and then they begin to talk in a loud, clear voice. There have been times when I, with my own eyes, have heard the Indians talking with the devil, and in the province of Cartagena. . . .

So, as the Inca wanted to learn the answer of the oracles, he sent those appointed for this purpose, and they say he was told that the thing for him to do was to go to Colla and seek the friendship of Cari.[2]   217
When he heard this, he ordered the messengers of Zapana to come before him, and told them to tell their lord that in a short time he would come from Cuzco to see the land of Colla, where they would meet and talk over their alliance. To those from Cari, it is said that he told them to tell him he was preparing to come to his help and support, and would soon be with him. After this had taken place, the Inca ordered troops to assemble and set out from Cuzco, leaving one of the most important members of his family as governor of the city.

CHAPTER 72 (ii: XLII)

Of how Viracocha Inca traveled through the provinces of the Canchis and Canas and proceeded until he entered the region of the Collas, and what took place between Cari and Zapana.

HAVING DECIDED on his expedition to Colla [-suyu], the Inca set out from the city of Cuzco with a large force, and passed through Muhina and the villages of Urcos and Quiquixana [Quispicancha]. When the Canchis learned of his approach, they determined to take up arms and prevent his passage through their land. When he heard of this, he sent messengers to advise them not to pursue this design, for he intended them no harm, but, on the contrary, wanted to have them as friends; and if their headmen and captains came to him in this spirit, he would let them drink from his own goblet. The Canchis answered the messengers that they were not of a mind to do as they were told,

---

[2] In the basin that surrounds Lake Titicaca, the two Aymara-speaking tribes of Lupaca and Colla (hence the name for the entire southern quarter or *suyu* of the Inca realm, "Colla-suyu"), were great rivals for power. Each tried to obtain Inca military support to attack the other. Viracocha Inca delighted to fish in the muddied waters; he tried to intervene, but the Lupacas won a great battle at Paucar-colla (today a village on the main road) before the Inca's troops arrived.

but to defend their territory against anyone who tried to enter it. Returning with the message, the emissaries found Viracocha Inca in Cangalla, and, enraged at the contempt with which the Canchis had treated his embassy, he quickened his march, and when he came to a village by name Compapata, beside a river which runs through it, he found the Canchis drawn up in fighting array. There battle was joined in which many on both sides lost their lives, and the Canchis were defeated, and those who could, fled, with the victors in hot pursuit, killing and taking prisoners. After a considerable time they returned with booty and many captives, both men and women.

218

Seeing what had happened, the Canchis from the entire province sent messengers to the Inca asking him to pardon them and receive them into his service; and as he wished for nothing else, he offered them his usual terms, which were that they should recognize the Incas of Cuzco as their sovereign lords, and be ruled by their laws and customs, paying tribute of what they had in their settlements, as the others did. After spending some days arranging these matters and making the Canchis understand that they were to build their villages in close and orderly manner and were not to fight or bear resentment, he proceeded.

A large force of the Canas had assembled in the village called Lurocachi, and when they learned how badly things had gone with the Canchis, and that the Inca did no harm to those who accepted his friendship, nor allowed any injury to be done to them, they decided to offer him their friendship. The Inca was approaching Lurocachi, and when he was informed of the decision of the Canas,[1] he was greatly pleased; and as the temple of Ancocagua[2] was in that territory, he sent splendid gifts to the idols and priests.

When the emissaries of the Canas arrived, they were graciously received by Inca Viracocha, and he told them that the headmen and elders of the Canas should gather near by, where, after he had spent several days in the temple of Vilcanota,[3] he would make haste to receive them. And he gave the messengers jewels and clothing of fine

[1] The Canas, who had their own language but spoke Quechua and also Aymara, lived on the upper Vilcanota River, divided from their traditional enemies, the Canchis, by the river. (See Markham's notes in his translation of Cieza, p. 356.)

[2] This temple is not mentioned in this form by any other chronicler.

[3] Perhaps the temple to Viracocha is meant here, parts of which still stand at a village called Racchi (see Chapter 45 above).

wool, and ordered his soldiers not to venture to enter the houses of the Canas, or steal any of their belongings, or do them harm of any sort, so they would not be swayed from their good intent and change their minds.

When the Canas received his answer, they ordered supplies of food to be placed along the roads and descended from their villages to serve the Inca who with such justice had ordered that they be offended in no way, and furnished him with llamas and *suvica* [*a'kla,* chicha], which is their wine. When he arrived at the main temple, they performed many sacrifices in accordance with their heathen ways, sacrificing many llamas. From there they proceeded to Ayaviri, where the Canas had prepared great stores of food, and the Inca addressed them with loving words, and established peace with them, as was his wont with others. The Canas, seeing the advantage of being governed by such wise and just laws, did not refuse to pay tribute or go to Cuzco in token of recognition.

After this Viracocha Inca made ready to set out for Colla[-suyu], where news had already arrived of all that he had done both with the Canchis and the Canas, and they were awaiting him in Chucuito [at the side of Lake Titicaca], as well as in Hatuncolla. Zapana, who had already learned how Cari had curried favor with Viracocha and was awaiting his coming, decided to go out to meet him and make war on him before the Inca could join him, so he should not become still more powerful. Cari, who must have been brave, marched with his men to a village known as Paucar-colla, and before it the two most powerful tyrants of the region met with a force said to have numbered 150,000. And they joined battle after their fashion, which it is said was bitterly fought and over 30,000 Indians were killed. It lasted for a long time, and Cari won the victory and Zapana and his men were defeated, many of them losing their lives. Zapana himself was killed in this battle.

Of how Cari returned to Chucuito, and the arrival of Viracocha Inca, and the peace they agreed upon.

AFTER ZAPANA was killed, Cari seized his camp and took everything that was there, and with this booty he returned to Chucuito, where he awaited the arrival of Viracocha Inca, ordering lodgings made ready and provided with supplies. On the way the Inca learned of the outcome of the war and Cari's victory, and even though in public he pretended to be pleased, he secretly regretted what had happened, for, with the two of them at odds, he thought he could easily make himself master of Colla, and he wanted to return without delay to Cuzco, lest some misfortune overtake him.

When he had come close to Chucuito, Cari and the most important among his people came out to receive him, and he was lodged and well served. Inasmuch as he wished to return quickly to Cuzco, he talked with Cari, addressing him in flattering words, telling him how pleased he had been by his good fortune and that he had come to help him wholeheartedly, and, so he would know that he would always be his friend, he wished to give him one of his daughters to wife. To this Cari replied that he was very old and very tired, and begged him to wed his daughter to some young man, for there were many from whom to choose, and to rest assured that he would always regard him as his master and friend, and would obey him in all he ordered and aid him in war and in other matters that might arise. Then, in the presence of the leading men who were there, Viracocha Inca ordered a great goblet of gold brought in and they sealed their friendship in this manner: They drank for a time of the wine the women had prepared, and then the Inca took up the goblet, and setting it on a smooth stone, said, "Let this be the sign, that this goblet remain here, and I shall not move it nor you touch it, in proof that what has been agreed on is true." Then kissing, they paid homage to the sun, and held a great drinking feast and dance to the sound of many instruments; and the priests, uttering certain words, carried the goblet to one of the main temples where such pledges between Incas and lords were kept. After spending several days in Chucuito, the Inca Viracocha returned to Cuzco, being well received and faithfully served wherever he went.

By this time many provinces were well ordered and the people wore better clothing and followed better customs and religions than formerly, being governed by the laws and customs of Cuzco. The son of Viracocha Inca, Inca Urco, had been named governor of the city, and it is told of him that he was very cowardly, lazy, with many vices and few virtues; but as he was the eldest, he would one day succeed his father as ruler.[1] The Inca, being aware of these things, was very anxious to deprive him of the succession and give it to Inca Yupanqui, his second-born, a youth of exceeding valor and upright habits, courageous, stout-hearted, and filled with high and noble ambitions. But the *Orejones* of the city did not want the laws broken and that which had been done and observed by order and statute of their forebears changed, and even though they knew the evil inclinations of Inca Urco, they wanted him and none other for Inca after the death of his father. I have gone into this at such length because those who informed me of this say that from [Lake] Urcos, Viracocha Inca sent his emissaries to the city [Cuzco] to discuss this matter, but was unable to accomplish what he wanted. When he entered Cuzco, he was received with great honors, and as he was now very old and tired, he decided to hand over the government of the kingdom to his son and transfer the *llautu* [i.e., crown] to him, and go off to the valleys of Yucay and Xaquixahuana to rest and take his pleasure. He notified those of the city of his determination, for he was unable to arrange for Pachacuti [his second son] to succeed him.

221

[1] The Incas had no clear line of succession; they were like the Romans in the latter days of the empire. The Roman Caesars invariably looked for a suitable successor, adopted, trained, and enthroned him. The Inca descended through the male line, but without fixed rule; i.e., the eldest son did not automatically inherit unless he proved himself worthy. The selection of the Inca-to-be was approved by the Inca's council of elders.

Of how the Inca Urco was received as supreme ruler
of all the kingdom and assumed the crown in Cuzco,
222   *and how the Chancas resolved to make*
war against Cuzco.

ALL THE NATIVES of these provinces, as well as the *Orejones,* laughed at the acts of this Inca Urco. Because of his pusillanimity they did not wish him to enjoy the reputation of having attained the dignity of the Inca realm, and so we see that when in their songs and ballads they tell of the Incas who ruled in Cuzco, they do not mention [this Inca Urco]. But I shall do this, for, after all, well or badly, with vices or virtues, he governed and ruled the kingdom for some time. Thus, after Viracocha Inca departed for the valley of Xaquixahuana, he sent the fringe to Cuzco so the elders could hand it over to the Inca Urco, saying that he had worked and done enough for the city of Cuzco, and that during the time left to him he intended to take his ease, for he was old and no more a warrior. When his desire was known, the Inca Urco withdrew to perform his fasts and other customary rites, and when he had concluded them, he came out with the crown and went to the temple of the sun to make his sacrifices, and his coronation was celebrated after their manner with great feasts and drunkenness.

The Inca Urco had married his sister in order to have a son who should succeed him. He was so vice-ridden and given to lusts and incontinence that, without respecting his sister Coya, he spent his time with women of low condition and concubines, who were the ones he liked best and enjoyed. It is even said that he corrupted some of the *mamaconas* who were in the temple, and he was so devoid of honor that he did not seek to be respected. He went about the city drinking, and when he had a couple of gallons of that liquor in him, he brought on vomiting and threw it up, and shamelessly uncovered himself and pissed out the chicha. To the *Orejones* [nobility] who had handsome wives, when he met them, he would say, "And how are my children?" —implying that he had lain with them and that the children they had were his and not their husbands'. He built no house or edifice; he was an enemy of arms; in a word, they say nothing good of him except that he was open-handed.

When a few days had elapsed after he had assumed the fringe, he decided to go and amuse himself in the pleasure houses the Incas had for their solace, leaving as his representative Pachacuti, who was the father of Topa Inca,[1] as will be told later on.

223

This being the state of affairs in Cuzco, the Chancas, who, as I previously related, had conquered the Quechuas and occupied the better part of the province of Andahuaylas, flushed with victory and hearing what was told of the grandeur of Cuzco and its wealth and the pomp of the Incas, decided to throw aside caution and press forward, winning by force of arms all they could. After making mighty prayers to their gods or devils, and leaving in Andabailes (which is what the Spaniards call Andahuaylas, and is the encomienda of Diego Maldonado the Rich[2]) men enough to defend it, with the army they had assembled, Hastu Huallaca [Hanco-Huallu] and a very brave brother of his, by name Omaguara, set out from their province with great confidence for Cuzco, and proceeded until they reached Curampa [Curamba],[3] where they pitched camp and worked great harm to the natives of the region. But as in those times many of the villages were high in the mountains and sierras, with great stockades which they call *pucarás,* they were unable to kill many, nor did they want prisoners, only to despoil the fields. And they left Cu-

[1] Inca Yupanqui took the name Pachacuti (1438); his son Topa Inca (who assumed the fringe about 1471) was a great conqueror.

[2] Diego Maldonado, born in Salamanca, was surnamed "the Rich" because of his incredibly good fortune during the conquest. He took part in the capture of Atahualpa, for which he reaped a cavalryman's part (7,760 gold doubloons and 362 marcos of silver). He was so fortunate in gambling that he won twice that amount with the dice. His fief, as Cieza says, included Andahuaylas (where he stumbled on bars of silver), and as one of the founders of Cuzco he took a big part of Hatun-cancha, the palace of Topa Inca. His life was like a picaresque novel. Needless to say, he died in the odor of sanctity in 1565.

[3] Curampa (present-day Curamba) is an isolated ruin on the Royal Road of the Incas between Pincos and Cochacajas, close to Andahuaylas. The ruins, very extensive, occupy a rectangular plaza, with a full view in all directions. The altitude is 10,125 feet. The most prominent feature of the site is a stepped pyramid, with the stone steps leading to the top still in good condition. The site is doubtlessly pre-Inca, although used and extended by the Incas. Its importance to the Incas was the smelting ovens, *huayras.* These are wind ovens, built so as to catch the strong trade winds that ceaselessly blow from the east. This was one of the centers of silver production.

rampa and proceeded to the lodging of Cochacassa [Cochacajas]⁴ and the Amancay [Abancay] River, laying waste all that they found, and drew near to Cuzco, where news of the approaching enemy had already reached the city. Even when old Viracocha learned of this, he was unmoved, and leaving the valley of Xaquixahuana, he went to the valley of Yucay with his wives and retinue. They say that Inca Urco laughed, giving little thought to what he should have considered highly important. But as Cuzco was destined to be aggrandized by Pachacuti and his descendants, it was he who by his virtue had to exorcise the fear of all, and not only did he defeat the Chancas, but subdued most of the nations in this kingdom, as I shall relate farther on.

224

Chapter 75 (ii: XLV)

Of how the Chancas reached the city of Cuzco and set up their camp there, and the fear that seized the inhabitants of the city, and the great valor of Pachacuti.

AFTER THE CHANCAS¹ had made sacrifices in Apurímac,² and had drawn near the city of Cuzco, their captain-general, or lord, Hastu Huallaca,³ told them to be mindful of the great enterprise they had undertaken, and to show themselves valiant and have no fright or fear

---

⁴ Cochacajas was the large tambo or royal way-station inhabited by Indians whose task it was to maintain the suspension bridge that crossed the Pachachaca River (*chaca*, "bridge"). It is now called the Abancay River. Pedro Pizzaro (*Relación*, 133) wrote: "Cochacajas is situated on a high mountain with a small plain where the town is, and a small lake on it is called cocha [Quechua for "lake"]. From this mountain and lake there is a slope down to the river and the bridge." Cochacajas was also a junction for the road which led to the coast and the valley of Nazca.

¹ The Chancas, after defeating the Quechuas, held the territory between the Apurímac River and Andahuaylas. They had been long at war with the Incas—they were both expanding, but held in check by a balance of strength. In 1437 the Chancas began their full-scale assault on Cuzco.

² On the left (northeast) bank of the river, an idol-oracle, described in Chapter 45.

³ Hastu Huallaca (Hanco-Huallu), the chieftain of the Chancas, had an amazing personal history. Although none of the chroniclers agree about the spelling of his name, all agree on the point of his extraordinary exploits. He escaped from the Incas, after the battle to be described, made a march of five hundred miles into strange territory to Moyobamba, and there set up a kingdom, which enraged the latter-day Incas. (See note 1, Chapter 40 above, for his history.)

of those who thought to frighten others by waggling the big ears they
had made themselves; and that if they conquered them, there would
be great booty and beautiful women with whom to take their pleasure.
His men joyfully replied that they would do their duty.

When the city of Cuzco received news of the army coming against
it, and that neither Viracocha Inca nor his son Inca Urco were in
the least concerned, the *Orejones* and other nobles were greatly dismayed. When they learned how near the enemy was, they made great
sacrifices according to their custom, and decided to beg Pachacuti
[who was Viracocha's second son] to take charge of the war, looking
to the safety of all. And one of the elders, speaking in the name of
all, spoke with him, and he answered that when his father had
wanted to give him the royal fringe, they had not consented, but had
said that the coward who was his brother should be Inca, and that
he had never aspired to assume the crown by tyranny or against the
will of the people. Now that they had seen that the Inca Urco was
not fitted to be Inca, let them do what was their duty for the public
weal, without thought to whether the ancient custom was broken
or not. The *Orejones* replied that, once the war was concluded, they
would take the measures required for the good of the realm. And it
is told that they sent emissaries all through the region saying that
all those who wished to become citizens of Cuzco would receive
lands in the valley and sites for their houses, and special privileges.
Thus they came from many places. When this had been done, Pachacuti [as general] went to the plaza where the stone of war was,[4]
wearing a puma skin on his head, to make it understood that he
would be as strong as that animal.

By this time the Chancas had [crossed the bridge and river of
Apurímac and had] reached the sierra of Vilcaconga,[5] and Pachacuti

225

[4] The stone of war, discussed in Chapter 66, was a bejeweled monolith which
stood in the Joy Square (Huayka-pata) of Cuzco. Captains made their war oaths
upon it.

[5] The sierra of Vilcaconga is a high pass (13,900 feet altitude) between the
ancient tambo of Apurímac (Rimac-tampu) and the valley of Anta on the Royal Road
of the Incas. It appears today on maps as the *Abra de Hillque* (Vilca). The immense
snow-covered mountain peak Salcantay, 20,000 feet altitude, can be seen scarcely less
than twelve kilometers to the north. A clash in the civil war between Atahualpa and
Huascar took place here, and in 1534 the Spaniards were ambushed. "And four days'
journey we came to a mountain range [Vilcaconga] *where they had an idol* which
was called Vilca-ninca, five leagues [seventeen miles] from Cuzco" (Miguel de Estete,
"Noticia del Peru" [written in 1535], ed by H. H. Urteaga and C. A. Romero, *Col.*

called up all the fighting men there were in the city with the intention of going out to meet them, naming as captains those who seemed to him the most valiant; but after further consultation, he decided to await them in the city.

226 The Chancas set up their camp near the hill of Karmenka,[6] which overlooks the city, and then pitched their tents. Along the approach to the gates of the city the men of Cuzco had dug deep holes filled with stones, and had covered them over artfully so that those coming that way would fall into them. When the women and children of Cuzco spied the enemy, they were greatly frightened and made a loud cry. The Inca Pachacuti sent messengers to Hastu Huallaca urging him to come to an agreement with him to avoid killing people. Hastu Huallaca treated the embassy with haughty disdain, and refused to accept anything but the fortune of war, although at the urging of his kinsmen and others he agreed to talk with the Inca, and so notified him.

The city (of Cuzco, as I said) is situated among hills in a naturally fortified spot, and the slopes and base of the mountains had been cleared, and in many places sharp spikes of [chonta] palm had been set which are as strong as iron and more harmful and poisonous.

The Inca and Hastu Huallaca held a talk, but, as they were all armed for war, the interview was useless, for they grew more irate with their own words, and finally came to blows with terrific whooping and uproar, because these people are very noisy in their fights, and we fear their shouting more than their deeds. They fought for a long time, but with night, the strife ceased, the Chancas bivouacked in their camp, with those of the city surrounding and guarding it on all sides so that the enemy could not enter, for neither Cuzco nor other places of these regions are walled.

When the call to arms was sounded, Hastu Huallaca encouraged his men, urging them to do their utmost, and the Inca Yupanqui did the same with the *Orejones* and the people inside the city. The Chancas bravely came out of their camp, determined to enter the city, and

---

Libr. Doc. Ref. Hist. Perú, 2d ser., Vol. VIII, 3–56 [Lima, 1924]). The Chancas stopped here to regroup their troops and in all possibility to consult the oracle of Vilca-ninca.

[6] Karmenka was the entrance to Cuzco from the north or Chinchay-suyu road, that road which ran all the way from Cuzco to Quito, an extent of 1,250 miles.

those of Cuzco determined to defend themselves; and the fight was resumed, and many were killed on both sides. But the bravery of Inca Pachacuti was so great that he triumphed over the Chancas, killing them all, so that only a few more than five hundred managed to escape, so they say, among these their captain Hastu Huallaca, who, with great difficulty, returned with them to his province. The Inca took great booty and many prisoners, men and women.

227

CHAPTER 76 (ii: XLVI)

Of how Pachacuti was received as Inca, and Urco deprived of the name of it, and the peace that was made with Hastu Huallaca.

AFTER DEFEATING the Chancas, the Inca Pachacuti entered Cuzco in great triumph and spoke with the leading *Orejones,* reminding them of how he had exerted himself for them, as they had seen, and the indifference his brother and father had displayed in the face of the enemy, and that therefore they should confer on him the crown and rule of the empire. The men of Cuzco, after discussing and pondering it with one another, both what Inca Yupanqui had said and all that Inca Urco had done, by unanimous consent of the people it was decided that the Inca Urco should nevermore enter Cuzco and that he be deprived of the fringe or crown, which should be given to Inca Pachacuti. And although when Inca Urco learned of this, he wanted to come to Cuzco to justify himself and showed great sorrow, complaining of his brother and those who had stripped him of the government of the kingdom, he was given no opportunity, nor did they fail to carry out what had been decided. There are those who say that the Coya, the wife of Inca Urco, who had no child by him, came to Cuzco, where she was taken to wife by her second brother, Inca Pachacuti, who, after the fast and other ceremonies, emerged with the fringe, and great celebrations were held in Cuzco, attended by people of many regions. And for all those who had died in battle defending his cause, the new Inca ordered a new burial, with the customary obsequies. As for the Chancas, he ordered a large house to serve as a tomb on the site of the battle, where, as a warning, the skin was flayed from the bodies of the dead and stuffed with ashes or straw so that they retained their human shape; they were left in a thousand different ways: some, with a drum protruding from their stomachs, and their hands in praying position; others, with a flute in their mouth. In this guise and others they remained until the Spaniards entered Cuzco. Peralonso Carrasco[1] and Juan de Pancorvo,[2] of the old conquistadors, told me of seeing these ash-stuffed skins, as did many others of those who entered Cuzco with Pizarro and Almagro.

The *Orejones* recount that at this time Cuzco had many inhabitants and its population was steadily growing, and from many regions messengers came to seek the favor of the new Inca, who replied to all with friendly words, and was eager to make war on what is known as Cunti-suyu. As he knew from experience how intrepid Hastu Huallaca,[3] the lord of Andahuaylas, was, he sought to win him to his service, and to this end, they relate that he sent messengers urging him to come with his brothers and friends to pay him a pleasure visit, and Hastu Huallaca, realizing that it would be to his interest to enjoy the friendship of Inca Yupanqui, went to Cuzco, where he was well received. And as troops were being called up, he decided to go to Cunti-suyu.

They tell that at this time Viracocha Inca died, and was buried with less pomp and honor than his forebears,[4] because in his old

1 Peralonso Carrasco, although not mentioned by any other chronicler as a participant in the conquest, was, as Cieza noted, an old conquistador. He is listed as holding the encomienda of Indians at the tambo of Pomacancha, south of Cuzco. He also held, with Juan de Pancorvo (mentioned above), the encomienda at the tambo of Abancay (now a city); his house in Cuzco was in the Cusi-pata plaza, next to that of Antonio Pereira. This, if it were needed, is confirmation of the places Cieza visited and the information he gleaned for his chronicles.

2 Juan de Pancorvo is often mentioned by the chroniclers as an old conquistador; he had a house in Cuzco, of which he was one of the founders, located on the western side of the Joy Square, Huayka-pata.

3 Garcilaso de la Vega calls him Hanco-huallu; Cieza in the first part of his chronicles calls him Anco Allo (which is similar enough); Sarmiento de Gamboa, Asto Huaraca. Whatever he was called, he could not endure the limited existence granted him by the Incas after his defeat; he escaped with the remnant of his tribe—the reported number of them varies—into the jungles of the Upper Amazon at Moyobamba. The Incas undertook a long campaign to reach him, building a stone road all the way from Huánuco to Chachapoyas, a distance of 450 miles, on the right (east) bank of the Marañón River. (See von Hagen, *Highway of the Sun*, chap. XI.)

4 The history of Inca Viracocha is confirmed from other chroniclers. He fled from Cuzco and took refuge in his palace called Caquia-Xaquixahuana, where he died, deprived of the honors usually given an Inca. Sarmiento de Gamboa (*History of the*

age he had deserted the city and had refused to return when it was at war with the Chancas. I relate nothing further of Inca Urco, because the Indians never refer to him except to laugh at him; so leaving him aside, I say that Pachacuti was the ninth Inca to reign in Cuzco.

CHAPTER 77 (ii: XLVII)

Of how the Inca Pachacuti set out from Cuzco, leaving Lloque Yupanqui as governor, and the things that took place.

AT THE CALL of Pachacuti, more than forty thousand men had gathered, whom he reviewed beside the stone of war, and appointed captains, and there were feasts and much drinking. When all was in order, he set out from Cuzco in a litter rich with gold and precious stones, surrounded by a guard with halberds, axes, and other arms. With him went the lords, and this Inca displayed more valor and authority than all his ancestors. He left in Cuzco, so they tell, his brother Lloque Yupanqui as governor. His Coya and other wives traveled in hammock-litters, and it is said they carried many loads of jewels and provisions. Ahead of him went road cleaners, who left not a blade of grass nor a stone, large or small [on the Royal Road].

When he reached the Apurímac River, he crossed by a bridge that had been built,[1] and proceeded until he came to the lodgings of Curahuasi. From the vicinity came many men and women and certain of the chieftains, and when they saw him, they were filled with amazement and cried out, "Great Lord, Son of the Sun, Monarch of all," and other magniloquent names. It is told that at this lodging he gave to a captain of the Chancas, by name Tupac Huasco, a princess [*palla*] of Cuzco as wife, and he held her in high regard.

Incas, 86) makes him "inventor of a type of weaving called *Viracocha tocapu,* a form of brocade." He was buried in this Caquia-Xaquixahuana. Now, whether this was the Caquia-Xaquixahuana that was a *pucará* (fortress) above Chalca in the Yucay valley (as John Rowe contends ["Inca Culture before the Spanish Conquest," *Handbook,* II, 204]), or whether it was the Xaquixahuana in the Anta valley, which ruins the editor of this chronicle studied, is yet to be determined. Gonzalo Pizarro discovered Viracocha's mummy "with a large sum of gold."

[1] The Huaca chaca ("Holy Bridge"); it was built, says Garcilaso, by Inca Roca in 1350. (See Chapter 41 above for details.)

After the Inca had crossed the Apuríma[c] and Cochacajas rivers,[2] as the natives of the region lived in their fortresses and had no settled villages, he ordered them to live in orderly fashion without evil ways or killing one another. Many rejoiced at hearing these words, and obeying his commands, things went well with them. The natives of Curampa[3] scoffed at this, and when Pachacuti learned that his warnings had been unavailing, he defeated them in battle, killing many and taking others prisoners. And as the land was good, he ordered one of his stewards to remain there and organize it and see that lodgings were built and a temple to the sun.

230

Having arranged all this with great prudence, the Inca set forth from there and proceeded until he came to the province of Andahuaylas, where he was solemnly received, and remained there some time considering whether he should go to conquer the natives of Huamanga, or Jauja, or the Soras and Rucanas. After due thought, however, and with the approbation of his advisers, he decided to go against the Soras.[4] And leaving that place, he traversed an uninhabited region which led to the Soras, who had had word of his coming and assembled troops to defend themselves.

The Inca Pachacuti had sent captains with troops to many regions to persuade the natives with all gentleness to enter his service, and he sent messengers to the Soras telling them not to take up arms against him, promising to treat them well and do them no hurt or ill. But they did not want peace at the price of slavery, and preferred to fight to defend their liberty. Thus a battle was fought which those

[2] Cochacajas was actually the tambo on the northeast side of the river, which was the Pachachaca (now the Abancay) River. (See Chapter 74 above.)

[3] Curampa, or Curamba, was, as Cieza suggested, rebuilt by Pachacuti Inca; this has been discussed in Chapter 74.

[4] The Soras united with the Rucana tribes of Indians living in the sparsely settled *punas* (above 13,000 feet altitude), southwest of the tribes of Andahuaylas. The region today is incorporated in the province of Aymaraes, and villages retain many of their original names, including "Soras." These two tribes had been at intermittent war with the Incas for centuries. Once conquered, the Rucanas were loyal vassals, and eighty of their number were chosen to carry the Inca's litter, as has been related. A lateral of the Royal Road left Vilcas-huamán (see Chapter 64) and connected with the Soras; this in turn joined the great lateral road Nazca-Soras-Cochacajas, which joined the Inca coastal road to the Royal Road in the cordilleras.

Soras was divided into three administrative sections. These Indians had their own language in Inca times, and there were four thousand taxpayers to Cuzco; Quechua and Aymara also seem to have been spoken. The province of Rucanas was divided into upper and lower and Andamarka. Although they had their own language, the Rucanas used Quechua as a lingua franca.

who have memory of it say was bitterly contested, and that there were many losses on both sides, but victory went to those of Cuzco. Those who escaped being killed or taken prisoner returned howling and lamenting to their village, and removing such of their possessions as they could, and their women, they abandoned it and took refuge, so it is told, on a high peak close to the Vilcas River,[5] where around the summit there were many caves and a spring of water. Many men and their women withdrew to this stronghold, providing themselves with all the supplies they could gather. And not only the Soras took refuge on this peak, but others from the region of Huamanga and the Vilcas River and other parts joined them, horrified at the thought that the Inca wished to make himself sole ruler of people.

After winning the battle, the victors collected the booty, and the Inca ordered that no harm be done to the prisoners, but, on the contrary, that they all be set free, and he sent a captain with troops to Cunti-suyu in the direction of Pumatampu.[6] When he entered the lands of the Soras and learned about the people withdrawing to the aforesaid peak, he was greatly incensed and decided to go and besiege them. Accordingly he ordered his captains with their troops to march against them.

CHAPTER 78 (ii: LII)

Of how the Inca Pachacuti set out from Cuzco for the Colla, and what happened to him.

As THESE Indians have no writing, and relate their past from the memory of it that has been preserved from one age to another in their ballads and quipus, they differ on many points, some saying one thing, and some another, and no human mind could put all this in order, but can only take from what they relate that which they

[5] The peak of Pillucho is located three miles from the center of Vilcas-huamán and overlooks the twisting waters of the Pampas (then the Vilcasmayu) River. Since the place was easily defended, the Soras gave a good account of themselves, but the Inca was incensed at the amount of time it took for the siege. Later it was made into storage depots and garrisons for the defense of Vilcas-huamán. The ruined site is still much in evidence.

[6] Pumatampu (or Pumapumpu, Pomatambo), which means the lodge of the puma, was located about the lake of Parinacochas, midway between Cuzco and the Pacific Coast.

themselves consider most true. I point this out for the benefit of those Spaniards in Peru who pride themselves on knowing many of the secrets of these people; I learned and informed myself about all they think they know and understand, and much more, and out of all this I have set down what they can see, and to do this I took the trouble they are fully aware of.

Thus, the *Orejones* relate that when Inca Yupanqui's [Pachacuti's] affairs were at this point, he determined to set out from Cuzco with a large army for the Colla and its environs. After appointing a governor of the city, he departed and proceeded until he came to the great settlement of Ayaviri,[1] where, they say, as the natives were unwilling to accept his proposals, he waited until he could fall on them by surprise, and killed all the inhabitants, men and women, and did the same with those of Copacopa. The destruction of Ayaviri was so great that nearly all perished, only a few remaining, who were appalled at such wickedness and ran like madmen about their fields, calling upon their forebears with loud howls and woe-stricken words. And as by this time the Inca had hit upon the splendid and useful system of the *mitimaes*,[2] when he saw the fair meadows and fields of Ayaviri and the beautiful river that runs by it, he ordered the necessary number of men from adjoining regions to come with their women and settle it. So it was done, and great lodgings were built for him, and a temple to the sun, and many storehouses and a mint,[3] with the result that through the introduction of the *mitimaes,* Ayaviri became more important than it had been before, and the Indians who have survived the wars and cruelty of the Spaniards are all transferred *mitimaes* and not natives, as I have told.

In addition to this, they tell other things. The Inca having sent

[1] Ayaviri, where the Royal Road of the Incas bifurcated to make a double-pronged way about Lake Titicaca. (See Chapter 89 below for Cieza's fuller description.)

[2] *Mitimaes* see Chapter 15 and note 2, Chapter 16) were Quechua-speaking colonists (*mita-kona*), sent out by the administration after the conquest of a new territory. By moving out unruly or politically suspect people and quartering it with Quechuas, who were bringers of Inca culture, this made the entire Inca realm a homogenous nation. It brought about rapid unification. They were of three kinds: political, economic, and military. The military *mita-kona* were sent out to man outposts, particularly in the Amazon, where the Incas were always under pressure; political, where the newly conquered peoples had to be indoctrinated and the Inca aims secured; economic, where the land was depopulated and where villages and communities were needed either to increase the agriculture or else to keep open communications and repair bridges.

[3] By "mint," since the Incas had no form of money, Cieza means a building where silver and gold were melted into ingots and stored.

certain of his captains with sufficient troops to make war on Anti-suyu, which comprises the settlements and regions in the uplands, they encountered snakes as large as thick logs which killed as many as they could, and the result was that these snakes waged war so well that, without seeing other enemies, few of those who had set out came back. This news greatly disturbed the Inca, and when he was in the midst of his tribulation, a witch came to him and said she would go and turn the aforesaid snakes silly and inoffensive so that they would never again harm anyone even if he sat on them. Gratefully the Inca accepted her offer, and ordered her, if she could do what she said, to carry it into effect. So she did, as they believe, but not I, because to me it seems nonsense. And after the snakes had been enchanted, the soldiers fell upon their enemies and subdued many of them by war, and won over others with exhortations and kindly words.

233

The Inca is said to have departed from Ayaviri by the highway known as Oma-suyu,[4] which had been built for his royal person, as broad and in the manner we see, and passed through the settlements of Oruro, Asillo, and Azángaro, where he had certain encounters with the natives; but so compelling were his words that with them and the gifts he bestowed, he won them to his friendship and service, and henceforward they were governed by the polity of all those who had a pact of friendship and alliance with the Incas, and they built their villages in orderly fashion on the level plains.

Proceeding, the Inca is said to have visited most of the settlements bordering on the great lake of Titicaca, and with his great skill he won them over to his service, attiring himself in each village in the garb used by the natives, which was the thing that pleased them most. He went out on the great lake of Titicaca, observed its islands, and ordered built on the largest of them a temple to the sun and palaces for himself and his descendants.[5] And having brought them under

[4] The Royal Road which bifurcated at Ayaviri was known under two general names: *Oma-suyu* was that part which went to the east of Lake Titicaca; *Urco-suyu*, that section which moved to the west of Lake Titicaca; later the roads joined into one below Oruro in what is now Bolivia.

[5] Remains of the temples of the sun are still to be seen on the Isle of the Sun, the largest of a group of islands, on the Bolivian side of Titicaca. E. G. Squier provided in 1867 the best reliable information up to that time with engravings taken from daguerreotypes (in *Peru*, 339ff.); and in a later century Adolph Bandelier, in *The Islands of Titicaca and Koati*.

his sovereignty, as well as the rest of the great region of Colla, he returned to the city of Cuzco in triumph, where, upon his entry, he ordered great celebrations after their fashion, and people came from most of the provinces to do him reverence and bring rich gifts; and their governors and representatives were zealous in carrying out all his orders.

234

CHAPTER 79 (ii: LIII)

Of how the Inca Pachacuti set out from Cuzco, and what he did.

THE FAME of the Inca Pachacuti spread over all the land in such a way that his great deeds were talked about everywhere. Many, without having seen a standard or captain of his, came to see him and offer themselves as vassals, affirming that his ancestors had descended from heaven, for they knew how to live with such order and honor. Inca Pachacuti, without laying aside his gravity, answered mildly that he wished to do no nation harm, but only that they should come and promise to obey him, for the sun so desired and ordered. And when he had called up an army again, he set out with it for what is known as Cunti-suyu, and subdued the Yanahuaras[1] and the Chumpivilcas,[2] and in certain provinces of this region of Cunti-suyu he fought fierce battles. But even though they warred against him, his courage and wisdom were so great that, after the death and suffering of many, they gave him obedience, accepting him as king, as did the others. After bringing order to the land, and naming native caciques, and ordering that no affront or harm be done to these subjects, he returned to Cuzco, first naming governors of the most important areas to teach the natives the order they were to employ, both in their manner of living as in serving him and building their villages, and in observing great justice in all they did, and that no one was to suffer injury, not even the poorest.

[1] Yanahuara, literally (Quechua) "black breechclout," comprised one of the *ayllus* or lineages of the Quechua tribe. Their traditional land was on the west side of the upper Apurímac, within the present province of Cotabamba.

[2] Also a Quechua-speaking people, who lived still farther up the Apurímac River, more or less on a direct line with Cuzco. They were famed as dancers.

They go on to say that when this was done, he rested but briefly in Cuzco, because he wished to go in person to the Andes [i.e., Antis—the eastern jungles], where he had sent his captains and scouts to spy out the land and report to him what the inhabitants were like. And as at his orders the whole kingdom was filled with storehouses, he ordered that the route he was to take be adequately supplied, and this was done. Then with his captains and troops he set out from Cuzco, where he left his governor to administer justice, and crossing the mountains and snow-covered uplands, he learned from his scouts what lay ahead, and of the great forests in the mountains, and that although they had come upon the huge serpents that live there, they did no harm, although they were horrified by their size and fierce aspect. 235

When the natives of those regions learned of the coming of the Inca to their land, as many of them had already been brought to his service by the hand of his captains, they came to do him reverence, bearing gifts of feathers of many birds and coca, which is the most abundant product of their lands, and he thanked them all profusely. Of the other Indians who inhabited these *montañas,* those who wished to become his vassals sent him messengers; those who were unwilling abandoned their villages and, with their women, took refuge in the mountain forests.

Inca Pachacuti had been informed that several days' journey to the east there was a large and thickly settled land. With this news, as he was eager to discover it, he pushed on. But as he had received word from Cuzco that there had been some disturbance in the city, when he reached a village called Marcapata, he returned with all haste to Cuzco, where he remained for some days.

When this occurred, so the Indians tell, as the province of the Colla is so large, and in those days there were so many people there and powerful native realms, having been informed that Inca Pachacuti had entered the Andes Mountains and believing he would either be killed there or return defeated, they all decided, from Vilcanota on, everywhere, in great secrecy to revolt and not be under the rule of the Incas, saying that it was pusillanimous for them, who had been left free by their forebears, and not slaves, and with so many and broad lands, to submit to the rule of a single master. And as they all detested the sway the Inca held over them, even though he had not offended or ill-used them, nor behaved tyrannically or committed abuses, when his governors and delegates were unsuspecting of what was taking place, they came together in Hatuncolla and in Chucuito, Cari, and Zapana, and Humalla, and the lord of Azángaro, and many others, and swore an oath, misled by their blindness, to carry out their plan and decision. And to seal the pact, they all drank out of a single goblet, and ordered it placed in a temple among their sacred objects, that it might bear witness to what has been told. Thereupon they immediately killed the governors and delegates who were in the province, and many [of the] *Orejones* who were with them, and throughout the kingdom the news of the revolt of the Colla ran, and the death the *Orejones* had suffered. When this became known, certain parts of the kingdom became restive, and revolts broke out in many places; but these were ineffectual because of the system of the *mitimaes,* and because the governors had been warned, and, above all, because of the great bravery of Topa Inca, who began to reign [c. A.D. 1471] at this time, as I shall relate.

236

CHAPTER 80 (ii: LIV)

Of how, when the Inca Pachacuti became very old,
he left the rule of the kingdom to his son Topa Inca.

IN PUBLIC Inca Yupanqui [Pachacuti] revealed no distress at the news of the revolt of the Colla; on the contrary, with great fortitude he ordered up troops to set out in person to punish them, sending his messengers to the Canas and Canchis to warn them to remain loyal to his friendship, and not to become emboldened by the defection of the Colla. It was his wish to set out immediately for Cuzco, but as by now he was very old and weary with the wars he had fought and the roads he had traveled, and so heavy with years and declined in powers that he felt unequal to the undertaking and even to carrying on the government of such a great kingdom, he sent for the high priest and the most important *Orejones* of the city and told them that he was now so old that his place was by the fireside and not in camp. And as they knew that what he was telling them was the truth, they should choose as Inca, Topa [Tupac] Inca Yupanqui, his son, a youth as brave as they had seen for themselves in the wars he had fought, and he should hand the fringe over to him so that he would be accepted as Inca by all and obeyed as such; and that he would take measures to punish those of the Colla for their rebellion, and for having slain the *Orejones* and delegates left there. Those whom he had summoned replied that all would be done as he ordered, and to order whatever he liked, for they would obey him in everything as they had always done. At the Colla and in the province of the Canchis and Canas he was received with rich gifts, and in what is known as Cacha[1] they had built him palaces after the fashion in which they construct them, very handsome.

When the Collas learned that Topa Inca was coming against them in such force, they sought the aid of their neighbors, and most of them gathered with the plan of meeting him in the field and doing battle with him. Advised of all this, Topa Inca, as he was so clement, even though he knew his advantage over the enemy, sent messengers to them from the Canas, their neighbors, to notify them that his desire was not to be at enmity with them nor to punish them for the evil they had done when they killed the governors and delegates of his father who had done them no harm, but that he asked them to lay down their arms and be obedient to him, for to be well governed and ruled, it was better to recognize a king, and one was preferable to many.

He sent this message by one of the *Orejones,* with gifts for the headmen of the Collas, but it availed nothing, nor did they wish his alliance, but, on the contrary, the assembly of troops that had been formed, whose captains were the chieftains of the different settlements, pressed forward until they were close to Topa Inca's

---

[1] At San Pedro (Cacha) are the famous ruins of the temple of Viracocha (see Chapter 89); the remains are those of one of the outstanding structures in the Inca realm; what remains of the center wall is more than three stories in height; the ground plan covers 330x87 feet. The ruins in Racchi village, twenty kilometers northeast of the market city of Sicuani, are on the main highway. As it carries the name of Viracocha, it is presumed to have been built by this Inca (see Chapter 68), but since he failed in the defense of Cuzco during the attack by the Chancas and his son Pachacuti took over the leadership and the Inca died without the usual demi-god honors, it is not possible to ascribe the ruins to Viracocha himself. The style of the ruins is late Inca. (See Squier, *Peru,* 405ff.; Bingham, *Inca Land,* 129–32; Means, *Ancient Civilizations of the Andes,* fig. 170.)

headquarters. As is told by all, in the village called Pucará,[2] they established themselves in a fortress they had built there, and when the Inca approached, they sallied forth with that whooping they always employ, and battle was joined, in which many on both sides lost their lives. The Collas were defeated, and many of them taken prisoner, both men and women, and there would have been more if the Inca had allowed stronger pursuit. To Cari, the lord of Chucuito, he spoke harshly, asking him if this was the way he kept the peace his grandfather Viracocha Inca had established, and saying that he did not intend to kill him but would send him to Cuzco, where he would be punished. Accordingly, he and other of the prisoners were sent to Cuzco under guard; and to commemorate the victory he had won over the Collas, he ordered great statues of stone to be erected on the spot, and a stretch of the sierra leveled, and other things which anyone who goes that way can see and observe, as I did, stopping there two days to see and understand it fully.

238

CHAPTER 81 (ii: LV)

Of how the Collas sued for peace, and the Inca granted their plea and returned to Cuzco.

THE COLLAS WHO MANAGED to escape alive from the battle were so fearful, it is told, that the men of Cuzco were hot on their heels that they fled with all the speed they could muster, and kept looking back from time to time to see what was not to be seen, for the Inca had forbidden it. Once they had crossed the Desaguadero,[1] the headmen gathered and took counsel with one another, and decided to sue the

---

[2] Pucará (fortress) is an immense Gibraltar-like massif (4,380 meters high) close to the Lake Titicaca basin. It is a natural stronghold, 1,200 feet above the valley and augmented in this battle by parapets, and is described further by Pedro de Cieza (in Chapter 35). The Incas, after their victory, rebuilt it as one of their most strategic *pucarás*. The padre Antonio Vásquez de Espinosa, traveling there in 1618, places it among one of "their marvelous works—there were great proud buildings [at Pucará] with many stone statues in the likeness of men and other creatures, very neatly worked" (*Compendium and Description of the West Indies*). (See also John H. Rowe, *Sitios Históricos en la Región de Pucará*.)

[1] The Desaguadero (its original indigenous name seems not to have been preserved) is the only drainage of Titicaca. It now marks the border of Peru and Bolivia. It was bridged by a pontoon bridge (see Chapter 95).

Inca for peace, promising that if he would receive them as his subjects, they would pay the tribute due from the moment of the revolt, and that forever henceforward they would be loyal. The wisest of them were dispatched on this mission, and they encountered Topa Inca as he was coming toward them. He heard out their embassy with kindly countenance, and replied in the words of a magnanimous victor that he deplored all that had happened because of their folly, and that, without hesitation, they should all come to Chucuito, where a peace would be drawn up which they would find advantageous. This was no sooner said than done.

239

Abundant supplies of food were made ready, and the lord Humalla went to meet them, and the Inca addressed him benignly, both him and the other chieftains and captains, and before the peace was pacted, it is said that there were great dances and drinking feasts, and when these were concluded, in the presence of all, he told them that he did not want them to be burdened by the payment of the tribute due him, for this was a large amount; but that inasmuch as they had revolted without justification or reason, he would maintain garrisons of soldiers whom they were to supply with provisions and women. To this they agreed, and then he ordered *mitimaes* from other regions brought in for that purpose, and at the same time he appointed governors and officials to collect the tributes. When this had been arranged, he said that so their misdeeds would never be forgotten, he intended to pass a law to the effect that no more than so many thousand men and women of their provinces could ever enter Cuzco, under penalty of death if they exceeded this number. This distressed them, but they acquiesced in it, as in everything else, and the fact is that if there were the appointed number of Collas in Cuzco, no more could enter until these had left, and even if they attempted to, it was impossible, for the gatekeepers and tax collectors and guards would not allow or permit it, and bribes were unknown among them, nor did they ever lie to their Inca or reveal any of his secrets, which is deserving of the highest praise.

Once the province of Colla was pacified and put in order, and the chieftains knew what they were supposed to do, the Inca returned to Cuzco, first sending his messengers to Cunti-suyu and the Andes, asking them to report to him on what was happening there, and whether his governors were abusing their power or the natives were

restless. Then, accompanied by many commoners and nobles, he returned to Cuzco, where he was received with great honors; and great
sacrifices were performed in the temple of the sun and by those who
were engaged in the construction of the great stronghold Pachacuti
had ordered to be built, and the Coya, his wife and sister, by name
Mama Ocllo, on her own initiative organized great feasts and dances.
And as Topa Inca was eager to set out on the highway of Chinchay-
suyu and subdue the provinces that lie beyond Tarma and Bombón,
he called up another great levy from all the provinces.

240

CHAPTER 82 (ii: LX)

*Of how Topa Inca set out once more from Cuzco
and went to the Colla and from there to Chile, and
won over and brought under his rule the peoples of
those lands, and of his death.*

[Topa Inca assembled in Cuzco an army of more than 200,000 men
and ordered arms and provisions to be sent ahead to Chinchay-suyu,
the road to the north.[1] In each province or *marca*, the Royal Road
was repaired and extended. His uncle, Capac Yupanqui, was made
chieftain of all the armies. Those he had previously conquered, the
Huancas, the Jauja valley, and those of Lake Chinchay, settled into
the Inca orbit, joined the expedition. In the land that lay between
the valleys of Jauja and Cajamarca—a distance of some four hundred
miles—he subdued, transplanted the populations, built roads, constructed *pucarás,* and opened communications. He began the construction of Huánuco, which, lying in the province of Huamalíes
at 12,150 feet altitude, became the greatest Inca city north of Cuzco.
Forty thousand people were said to have lived there. It was the garrison city from which the Inca marched his troops to conquer the
tribes on the east bank of the Marañón River, five hundred miles
northeast to Chachapoyas.

Far beyond Huánuco and Cajamarca he fought with the tribes of
Huancabamba, Cajas, and Ayavaca; east from Huancabamba he built

[1] A synopsis of Chapters LVI, LVII, LVIII, LIX of the second Chronicle of Peru,
which chapters are found in their proper geographical and historical sections in this
book.

a road reaching through the *montaña* to the Marañón River in order to find the source of placer gold which the Huancabambas got as trade from the jungle Indians. His troops clashed with the "water-people," the Aguarunas, a subtribe of the Shuara head-hunters; as Cieza recounts, he "returned flying, for it is an evil region covered with forest."

Topa Inca took more than five months to conquer and longer to **241** consolidate the victory about Huancabamba with the transplanted *mitimaes* and the establishment of roads, fortresses, and communications. He then entered what is now Ecuador, fought with the Paltas, entered the high *páramos* about Azuay, and fought long and hard with the redoubtable Cañari. The advance continued to Llactacunga, where, having again conquered, he "ordered edifices to be erected as grand as those of Cuzco."

Topa Inca then went on to Quito. After a short, decisive war, he "peopled it with *mitimaes,*" ordered the construction of Inca-style buildings, storehouses, and fortresses, saying "Cuzco must be the capital of one part of my great realm and Quito the other." Master builders were brought from Cuzco, engineers to further the consolidation into empire. At Tomebamba in the heartland of the Cañari, his son Huayna Capac, destined to be the last great Inca, was born.

Chalco Mayta, a venerable chieftain, was left as governor of Quito with the privileges of a vice-Inca; he was allowed to travel in a litter, eat off of gold service, and sit on the golden *osño* stool.

The Inca and his armies then set off toward the west for the subjection of the coastal provinces of Quito.

The Inca armies entered the hotlands, which they called the Yungas, made a peaceable conquest of the Huancavilcas (centered about the Guayas River on the plains about what is now Guayaquil), then by balsas and by land moved southward toward Tumbes.

Tumbes, or Tumpiz, was the demarcation line of desert and humid jungle and peopled by a tribe called the Tallanes. It was conquered. Large buildings, sun temples, administrative centers, and tambos were constructed. He rested, and then began the construction of the great coastal road "as may be seen" (Cieza writing in 1550) "from what now remains of it."

Topa Inca was now in the territory of the Chimú empire; these people were to the coast what the Incas were to the Andes. There was a prolonged struggle (see Chapter 113); the Incas, as usual, were the victors. They allowed the Chimús to retain their titles, sent some as hostages to Cuzco, and brought to Cuzco their gold and silver workers, the best in Peru. The Inca system, replete with roads, ad-

THE INCAS

ministrations, *mitimaes,* tribute (*mit'a* tax), *chasquis,* and food deposits, were imposed on the north coast. This took place about A. D. 1476.

The Incas, having broken the power of the Chimús at the source of their power at Chan-Chan (present-day Trujillo), went triumphant down the coast, improving or changing the cultural ways of the Chimús. At last they were in the Rimac valley (where modern Lima lies), and at the famous oracle of Pachacamac. This Pachacamac was one of the most revered shrines on the coast; intertribal wars ceased so that the Indians might make pilgrimages to the sacred *huaca.* Topa Inca did not attempt to interfere with it; he merely built additional structures (the temple of the sun for the *mamaconas* is Inca), adopted it into the Incaic pantheon of gods, organized it, and initiated the possessors of Pachacamac into the new order. That done, he returned to Cuzco by way of a new road he ordered built, which went from the shrine of Pachacamac up the Lurin valley to Huarochirí, crossing in steps the frigid snowbound altitudes of Pariacaca to Jauja, a distance of 175 kilometers, one of the most spectacular roads ever built by man.

After Topa Inca had been received in triumph at Cuzco, he began to plan the conquest of the Chinchas, who lived in the hot desert Yungas on the coast two hundred kilometers south of Pachacamac. The Chinchas, who had a reputation for warlike attitudes, had made raids up into the highlands and returned with booty. In the time of his father, Pachacuti Inca, the Inca governor of the Soras (east of Cuzco in the Cunti-suyu) had gone on a mission to the Chinchas to persuade them to accept the *pax Incaicum.* They refused. The Inca again assembled his army, moved to Cochacajas (on the Pachachaca River), and then began his descent to the coast. He passed through the country of the Soras and the Rucanas, and went along the lateral road which joined the Royal Road of the sierra to the coast. First he disposed of the Nazcas, then moved north along a road made for him to Ica, the next valley, which easily fell into the Inca maw; after Pisco, which was under the sway of the Chinchas, he faced 30,000 warriors. Again, as his father had done, but this time with a huge army to help persuade, he sent his emissaries to the lords of Chincha. "The Topa Inca became lord of Chincha," writes Cieza, "without fighting."

The Inca army then moved toward the next valley, that of the Huarcos (now called the Cañete valley). Neither the Inca's ambassadors nor the threat of his armies would change the attitude of the

Huarcos. They put their *pucarás* in readiness, sent their women and children to its protection, and faced the Inca's army.

But the summer heat was upon the desert; the Inca, old in years, grew ill and retired to Cuzco. Later he again assembled his *Orejones,* his captains, and their armies, and constructing a new road out of Jauja, ran it across the eastern cordilleras down the sides of the valley.[2] When he reached the borderlands of Huarco, he built a city, calling it "New Cuzco" (now known as Incahuasi). The war lasted three years. The chieftains, including the redoubtable Chuquimancu, surrendered and were butchered for their long display or resistance. A fortress was erected,[3] the valley was subdued, and he returned again to Cuzco.]

243

WHEN TOPA INCA HAD RETURNED to Cuzco with these great victories to his credit, he spent some time feasting and drinking and taking his pleasure with his wives and concubines, who were many, and with his children, among whom was Huayna Capac, who was to succeed him on the throne, and had turned out very brave and spirited. When the celebrations had come to an end, the great Topa Inca decided to go and look over Colla and make himself master of as many of the lands beyond as he could. For this he ordered up troops from all sides, and many tents made ready to camp in the desert places. And they began to arrive with their captains and were quartered around Cuzco, only those permitted by law entering the city, and all were provided with what they needed, the governors and sutlers of the city handling this diligently. And when all those who were to set out for war had gathered, sacrifices were made to their gods, in keeping with their blindness, the soothsayers consulting the oracles concerning the outcome of the war; and after a magnificent banquet for all, Topa Inca set out from Cuzco, leaving in the city his representative and his eldest son, Huayna Capac, and with great pomp and majesty he took the highway of Colla-suyu, visiting his

[2] See von Hagen, *Highway of the Sun,* 68–72.

[3] Hervay (or, as it is spelled on Peru's official map, Herbay) is little known. The site was at the mouth of the Cañete River (now the Herbay Bajo Hacienda). The ruins were visited by Sir Clements Markham in 1853. He reports that the site, in sections, was built on a steep hill. The architecture, resembling that of the late Inca period, differs from the coastal types. Even in Markham's time there was still evidence of beams, plaster, and remains of figures, seen by Pedro de Cieza in 1548. Portions of the fortress were made of stone, but these were removed by order of the Viceroy, Count of Monclova, in order to build the fortress castles of Callao at Lima.

garrisons and royal lodgings, and taking his pleasure in the settlements of the Chancas and Canchis.

When he came into Colla, he advanced as far as Chucuito [at Lake Titicaca], where the rulers of the land had gathered to celebrate a feast in his honor; and with the order he had established there was such an abundance of supplies that there was plenty for the 300,000 men who made up his army. Some of the lords of the Colla offered to go themselves with the Inca, and with those he chose, he went out on the lake of Titicaca, and praised those who had put up the buildings his father had ordered constructed for the excellence of their work. He performed great sacrifices in the temple, and bestowed rich gifts on the idol and the priests, as befitted the great lord he was. He then rejoined his men, and traveled all the way across the province of the Colla until he emerged from it. He sent his messengers to all the nations of the Charcas, Caranquis, and other peoples dwelling in those lands. Some of them came to give him allegiance, and others to make war on him, but, even though they fought him, his power was so great that he subdued them, displaying great clemency toward the vanquished, and toward those who had come of their own accord, much love. In Paria[4] he ordered large edifices built, and in other places as well. Beyond doubt Topa Inca must have done great things, many of which have been forgotten because of the lack of writing. I am summarily setting down some few of the many which we know to have happened, because we hear and see them, those of us who are here.

Proceeding triumphantly past the Charcas,[5] he crossed many lands and provinces and great wastes of snow until he came to what we call Chile, and he mastered and conquered all those lands, where it is said that he reached the Maule River. He erected some buildings in Chile, and as tribute he received from those regions many bars of gold. He set up governors and *mitimaes,* and after putting his conquest in order, returned to Cuzco.

To the east he sent wily *Orejones* disguised as traders to observe the lands there might be and the people who ruled them, and having disposed such matters, he returned to Cuzco, from which, it is told,

4 Paria was a late Inca *marca* located close to the area of the eastern cordillera, between what is now the modern Bolivian cities of Oruro and Sucre.

5 Charcas was located in the Bolivian cordillera south of Lake Titicaca; it was a Spanish *Audiencia de Charcas* in the eighteenth century.

he set out again in a short time, and with the troops he judged necessary, entered the Andes, and suffered great hardships because of the
dense forests, and conquered certain peoples of the region, and ordered many fields of coca planted, whose crop was to be taken to
Cuzco, whither he returned.

A short time later, they tell, he fell ill of a sickness that caused his
death, and after entrusting to his son the rule of the kingdom and
his wives and children, and saying other things, he died. Great mourning and deep sorrow were displayed for him from Quito to Chile,
and it is a moving thing to hear what the Indians tell of this.

Where, or in what place, he is buried they do not say.[6] They tell
that a large number of women and servitors and pages were killed
to be laid with him, and so much treasure and precious stones that
it must have amounted to more than a million. Even this figure is
probably less than it was, for there were private persons who were
buried with over a hundred thousand *castellanos*. Aside from the
many who were buried with him, many men and women in different
parts of the kingdom hanged themselves and were buried, and everywhere mourning went on for a whole year, and most of the women

---

[6] Topa Inca Yupanqui, according to Sarmiento de Gamboa, came into power very
young and was "frank, merciful in peace, cruel in war, a great man of indefatigable
industry and a notable builder." He is credited with the conquest of Chinchay-suyu,
Tomebamba (in Ecuador), where his son was born, the subjugation of the Huancavilcas, and when at Tumbes in Peru the conquest of some unidentified Pacific islands.
They were called Avachumbi and Ninachumbi, and some have tried to identify them
with the Galápagos Islands, six hundred miles westward in the Pacific. He arrived
back in Cuzco after an absence of six years "with the greatest and richest and most
solemn triumph" with which any Inca had ever been honored. After the death of the
reigning Inca Pachacuti, he penetrated the eastern Upper Amazon jungles—the Anti-
suyu—and there conquered four great tribes, given as the Opataris, Mano-suyu, Manaris
or Yanasimis ("black mouth"), and Chuncos. He descended the Tono River, penetrated as far as the Chiponauas, and sent one of his chieftains along a route called
Camata to the east "in the direction of the rising sun," until he came to a river called
Paytiti; there he set up the eastern frontier pillars of the Anti-suyu.

His next exploit was the final subjugation of the Colla-suyu tribes. He continued
southward into Chile as far as the Maule River (35° south). "He came to Coquimbo
(30° south) and to the banks of the Maule, where he set up his frontier columns,"
calling it Purumauca. Sarmiento credits him also with the beginning of the erection
of Sacsahuamán, that guarded Cuzco.

Topa Inca named his son Huayna Capac as his successor to the realm in the fateful
year of 1492. He came to power at the age of eighteen, and sired two legitimate sons,
sixty bastards, and thirty daughters by his concubines. His *huaca*, one of the most
sumptuous of all the Incas', was razed in 1531 by Calicuchima, general to Atahualpa
in the civil wars between the brothers for the realm of the Incas. The mummy was
burned; the ashes of Topa Inca Yupanqui's mummy were later found in Calis-puquiu.

cut off their hair, binding their heads with hempen ropes; and at the end of a year they did him his honors. What they say they used to do, I do not choose to set down, for they were heathenish things.

CHAPTER 83 (ii: LXI)

Of how Huayna Capac reigned in Cuzco, who was the twelfth Inca.

UPON THE DEATH of the great Inca, Topa [Tupac] Inca Yupanqui, his obsequies and burial were effected with great pomp, after the manner of his ancestors. The *Orejones* tell that there were those who plotted to recover their past liberty and throw off the rule of the Incas, and that, in fact, they would have succeeded in their attempt had it not been for the skill with which the governors of the Inca and the *mitimaes,* in those disturbed times when there was no Inca, managed to carry out what the deceased Inca had ordered. Huayna Capac did not overlook nor ignore the fact that he must display courage not to lose what his father had won with such great effort. He began his fast at once, and the governor of the city was faithful and loyal. Not that there were not certain disturbances among the Incas themselves, for some of the sons of Topa Inca, born of women who were not the Coya, wanted to claim the royal dignity for themselves; but the people, who supported Huayna Capac, would not consent to it, but prevented the attempt to punish them. When the fast had been concluded, Huayna Capac assumed the fringe, very handsome and richly attired, and performed the ceremonies of his forebears, after which he was given the title of Inca, and great shouts went up, saying, *"Huayna Capac Inca Zapalla tucuillacta uya,"* which means, "Huayna Capac alone is Inca; let all nations give ear to him."

Huayna Capac, according to many Indians who saw and knew him, was not large of stature, but strong and well built, of grave, goodly countenance, a man of few words and many deeds; he was stern, and unmerciful in his punishments. He wanted to be so feared that at night the Indians would dream of him. He ate as was the manner among them, and lived wanton of women, if the word can be so used. He listened to those who spoke to him fairly, and was

inclined to be credulous; flattery and adulation influenced him, for
there was no lack of this among them then, nor even today. He
listened to liars, and for this reason many innocents lost their lives.
Young men who succumbed to the temptations of the flesh, and
slept with his wives or concubines or with the women of the temple
of the sun, were given instant death, and the women, too. Those 247
who had a part in riots or uprisings were punished by being stripped
of their property, which was given to others; for other crimes the
punishment was only corporal. Many of these things his father had
overlooked, especially with regard to the women, and if a man was
caught with them, he said it was the young blood. The mother of
Huayna Capac, a great lady, the wife and sister of Topa Inca Yupanqui, by name Mama Ocllo, was said to have been a woman of great
prudence, and informed her son of many of the things she had seen
Topa Inca do; and as she loved him so much, she begged him not to
go to Quito or Chile until after her death. And they tell that to please
and obey her, he remained in Cuzco until she had died and was
buried with great pomp, much treasure, and fine clothing, some of
her ladies and servitors being placed in the tomb with her. Most of
the treasures of the dead Incas, and their lands, which are called
chacaras, were kept intact from the very first one, and none ventured to touch or spend any part of them, for they had no wars or
needs which required money. For this reason we believe that there
are great treasures lost in the depths of the earth, and will remain
there unless someone, building or doing some other thing, should by
chance stumble on part of the much that there is.

CHAPTER 84 (ii: LXII)

How Huayna Capac set out from Cuzco, and what he did.

HUAYNA CAPAC summoned to appear before him the principal native
lords of the provinces, and when his court was teeming with them,
he took to wife his sister, Chincha Ocllo, with great festivities omitting the customary mourning for the death of Topa Inca. When
these were concluded, he ordered some fifty thousand troops to ac-

company him in a progress through his kingdom. As he ordered it, so it was done; and he set out from Cuzco with more pomp and majesty than his father, for his litter was so rich, according to those who carried the Inca on their shoulders, that the many and large stones with which it was set were priceless, not to mention the gold of which it was made. And he went through the provinces of Xaqui-xahuana and Andahuaylas until he reached the Soras and Rucanas, where he dispatched embassies to many parts of the plains and highlands, and received a reply from all of them, with great presents and promises.

248

From these regions he returned to Cuzco, where he occupied himself in making great sacrifices to the sun and to those they held as greater gods, asking their favor in the undertaking he planned, and he made great gifts to the idols in the temples, and learned from the soothsayers, either through the words of the devils or because they invented it, that success would attend the ventures he planned and he would return to Cuzco with great honor and profit. When all this had been done, from many parts there came at his call armed troops with their captains, and they were lodged and provisioned by the city.

The construction of the fortress [Sacsahuamán] went on, none of those assigned to it missing a day's work. A great cable of gold was put around the square of Cuzco, and great dances and drinking feasts took place, and beside the stone of war captains and leaders were appointed, in keeping with the custom of the country; then, when they were drawn up, Huayna Capac addressed them in well-conceived words spoken in vehement tone, telling all to be loyal, those who accompanied him as well as those who remained behind. They answered that they would never deviate from his service, and he praised their answer and held out the hope that he would bestow munificent rewards. And when everything required for the campaign had been made ready, he set out from Cuzco with the army he had assembled, and by one of the great highways, as fine as it still is today, as all of us who see and use it know, he advanced toward Colla-suyu, displaying as he passed through the provinces slight esteem for the great services they rendered him, for it is told that he said everything was due the Inca. He inquired about the amount of tribute they paid and the resources of the province. He collected many women, the most beautiful to be found; some of them he kept for himself, and some he gave to his captains and counselors; others were sent to the temple of the sun to be kept there.

When he entered the Colla, they brought him reports of the great number of their flocks, and how many thousand loads of fine wool were sent annually to those who made clothing for his household. He went to the island of Titicaca, and ordered great sacrifices performed. In Chuquiabo [La Paz] he ordered Indians to work uninterruptedly under his inspectors mining gold in the manner and way described. Proceeding, he ordered that the Charcas [in the Bolivian Andes] and other nations as far as the Chinchas should extract bars of silver in large quantity, and take them to Cuzco at his expense, in the full amount; he transferred a number of *mitimaes* from one region to another, although they had been settled for only a short time; he ordered all to work and that none should be idle, because he said that where there were idlers they thought of nothing but provoking disturbances and corrupting the chastity of the women. Wherever he went he ordered lodgings and fortresses built, drawing up the designs with his own hand; he revised the boundaries of many provinces so that they would not seek to better them by force of arms. His troops, despite their number, were so well disciplined that they did not set foot outside their camps; wherever they went the natives provided for their needs so fully that more was left over than they used. In certain places he built baths; in others he established hunting preserves, and in the deserts he had large houses built. Wherever the Inca passed, he left behind such noteworthy accomplishments that their mere relation arouses wonder. Those guilty of misdemeanors were punished, nothing being overlooked, and he rewarded those who served him well.

After disposing these and other things, he moved on to the provinces now under the jurisdiction of the city of La Plata,[1] and dispatched captains with troops to the region of Tucumán[2] against the Chiriguanos;[3] but things did not go well with them, for they returned

[1] La Plata, in the Bolivian Andes, embraced that territory which included the famous silver mine of Potosí.

[2] Tucumán, in northwestern Argentina at the base of the eastern cordilleras, was the terminus of one branch of the Royal Road of the Incas.

[3] The Chiriguanos were Guarani tribes who in historic times migrated from Paraguay across the Chaco plains to settle in the foothills of the Andes on the upper Pilcomayo River. There, tribal boundaries in the west fronted the Chinchas, the Aymaraes, and to the northwest the Yamparas. In 1521–26 the Chiriguanos invaded the border-

in flight. In the other direction, toward the Southern Sea, he sent other troops to subdue the valleys and settlements which his father had not wholly conquered. He proceeded with the bulk of his army toward Chile, completing the conquest of the peoples on the way. He suffered great hardships in the deserts, and great snows fell upon them; they carried tents under which to protect themselves, and many servants, men and women. A road was built through all these snows, or was already built and well tended, with posts set up along it.

He reached what is known as Chile, where he spent more than a year, devoting himself to subduing those peoples and establishing order among them; he commanded them to furnish the amount of gold bars he ordered, *mitimaes* were settled there, and many of the people of Chile[4] were transferred to other regions. In some places he built strongholds and fortifications such as they use, known as *pucarás,* for the war he waged against certain of them. He penetrated much farther into the land than his father had, and he ordered monuments erected in many places as witness to his grandeur for future ages, and great statues.

When Chile had been pacified and the necessary measures taken, he appointed his representatives and governors, ordering them to advise the court of Cuzco of all that occurred in that province. He impressed upon them that they should execute justice, and in the event of any uprising or revolt they should kill all the conspirators, without leaving a single one alive.

lands of the Inca empire at lower Colla-suyu; present—and supposed to have been the leader of the raiding force—was a Spaniard, Alejo García, one of the captured sailors of the Solís armada. García was the first white man to enter Peru, and his presence (with white skin and beard) was conspicuously noted by the warriors of the Inca. The Chiriguanos got as far into Bolivia as the settlement of Sucre [Chuquisaca]. The raid was successful, although Alejo García was later dispatched by the Guarani. They became so much a threat to the Inca-established towns of the Charcas that the Inca Huayna Capac ordered his *mitimaes* to construct the *pucarás* of Savapata, Saigpuru, and Huancabamba in an attempt to halt the Chiriguano inroads. The ruins of these fortresses were still in evidence in 1915 and 1924. (Alfred Métraux, "Tribes of the Eastern Slopes of the Bolivian Andes," *Handbook,* III, 465ff.; and Erland Nordenskiöld, "Incallacta; Eine Befestigte und von Inca Tupac Yupanqui Angelegte Stadt," *Ymer. Tidskrift utg. af Svenska Sällskapet för Antropologi och Geografi* (Stockholm), Vol. XXXV, 169–85.)

4 Chile was known to the Incas as *Copiapó* (still the name of a large town 28° south latitude), and still farther south was the *marca* (province) of Coquimpu (the modern Coquimbo is a port on the Pacific at 30° south latitude). Chile was, in all probability, the name of an important chieftain at the time of the Diego de Almagro expedition in 1536.

He returned to Cuzco, where he was received with honors by the city, and the priests of the temple of Curicancha called down many blessings upon him, and he rejoiced the populace with the great feasts he ordered. And many sons were born to him, among whom was Atahualpa, according to the opinion of all the Indians of Cuzco, who say that his mother was called Tuta Palla, and was a native of Quilca, although there are those who claim she was of the Hurin-Cuzco [that is Lower Cuzco], and always, from the time he was a child, Atahualpa accompanied his father. He was older than Huascar.

251

[Huayna Capac rested in Cuzco after this Chile expedition, planning a visit to the northern frontiers of his realm. He ordered the Chinchay-suyu road to Quito broadened, "grander and wider than his father's road," and the extension of the tambos and *chasqui* stations along its entire length. "Accordingly," wrote Cieza, "the grandest road was constructed that there is in the world as well as the longest (3,250 miles)." Huayna Capac then set out with 200,000 warriors; he passed through Vilcas-huamán, Jauja, and so north to Cajamarca. From there he made war upon the Huancachupachos tribes, bringing them to submission, crossed the upper Marañón, and forced the Chachapoyas, who had been previously conquered, to accept an Inca-appointed governor; from that place he took "many women for they are beautiful and graceful and very white." He continued his northern journey.

At Huancabamba, which his father had previously conquered, he followed the road he had built, repairing it as he went along, east to the Marañón River. He built an outpost, Bracamoros, at the edge of the tribal territory of the people called Aguarunas, in reality a subtribe of the Shuaras (Jívaros) of Ecuador. The Inca forces came to great rivers; the war began; the savages came out to fight naked, and harassed by elements he did not understand, Huayna Capac beat a retreat.

Once again in the Andes, the Inca's real milieu, the expedition went on to Tomebamba (in Ecuador). A local uprising in Cuzco so angered him that he gave orders that the leaders should be killed and their warriors made to drag stones from Cuzco all the thousand-mile way to Tomebamba, his birthplace. "To keep the people of his realm under subjection he said was a good thing, and work was prescribed for 'good government' even if it meant forcing them to remove an entire mountain from one place to another."

At Tomebamba, he inspected the accounts of the *quipu-camayocs* to see if all was well ordered; then he went on the road built for him to Quito. From there he continued northward to the tribal seats of the Otavalos, Cayambes, and Cochasquis, where the tribes in confederation opposed him. The resistance so enraged Huayna Capac that upon emerging victorious, he ordered all of the chieftains beheaded at the Otavalo Lake. There was so much blood that it reddened the waters of the lake, and from that day grew its name of Yahuarcocha, "lake of blood."

The organization continued until he reached a plunging river (approximately on the present borders of Ecuador and Colombia), which had eaten its way through the rock, making a natural bridge. This was called Rumichaca ("stone bridge"), and the river, Angasmayo. This Huayna Capac marked as the northern limits of the realm of the Incas, and built a fortress at Pasto.

Huayna Capac was in Quito or Tomebamba when in 1527 messengers brought him notice of the arrival of a strange ship and bearded men at Tumbes. This was Francisco Pizarro and his "thirteen men of Gallo." He was well informed of their dress, skin coloring, and long black beards, and he was quick to deduce that they were similar to the white man, Alejo García, who earlier had led the Chiriguano raid at the southern frontier of the empire.

At this time a pestilence broke out in the Quito provinces—perhaps a form of pox brought by the white men, since they had touched along all the shores for upwards of five years before arriving in Tumbes in 1527. Two hundred thousand Indians were said to have died of it; Huayna Capac himself contracted it.

He had ordered that the two men left behind at Tumbes by Pizarro when he sailed away, that is, Alonso de Molina, a native of Ubeda, Spain, and Gines, a Negro, be brought to him. There are many versions of what happened to them; either they were killed when Huayna Capac died or they died during the various uprisings following the Inca's death.

The "official history of the Incas," that of Sarmiento de Gamboa, who questioned those of the Incas who still remembered in 1570, was that Huayna Capac first went into Chachapoyas, then on a gargantuan tour of 10,000 miles from Quito to Chile. It is agreed that he fought against the Chiriguanos, as told in footnote 3 above, and that he made successful war on the tribesmen north of Quito. He was married to Cusi Rimay Coya, and then his sister Araua Ocllo, by whom he had a son, Tupac Cusi Hualpa, who was called Huascar ("chain").

Huayna Capac, it is here averred, came down ill with a fever in Quito ("though others say it was smallpox or measles"). He died without naming a successor to the fringe—and this, among other things, brought about the civil war between Huascar and Atahualpa, his two contending sons. He died at eighty years of age, leaving more than fifty sons. His body was brought back to Cuzco, as Cieza believed;[5] his *huaca* was so well concealed in Cuzco that the conquistadors missed it, with all its golden loot. It was found in 1560 by Polo de Ondegardo, brought to Lima with other mummies, by order of the Viceroy, Marquis de Cañete, and buried in the churchyard of San Andrés. His image, a full life-size of gold, has never been found.][6]

253

CHAPTER 85 (XCIV)

Which deals with the valley of Yucay and the mighty lodgings of [Ollantay-] Tambo, and part of the province of Cunti-suyu.

SOME FOUR LEAGUES from this city of Cuzco there is a valley called the Yucay,[1] which is very beautiful, situated in the lee of the moun-

---

[5] See Chapter 115.

[6] Editor's synopsis.

[1] The Yucay is the most beautiful valley of Peru, and was held to be so by the Incas. The river begins from the melting glaciers of the Nudo de Vilcanota (5,486 meters high), northeast of the divide of La Raya, flows along warm, pleasant valleys, and through towns famous in Inca history: Sicuani, the temple of Viracocha at Cacha, Compapata, and the fortress of Quiquixana. At Pisac the canyon of the Vilcanota River is already deep and the valley of Yucay begins. It is seldom more than one mile in width, and the river is held to its banks by stone walls placed there by the Inca engineers. Below Pisac is the village of Yucay, one of the favorite retreats of the Incas, then Urubamba, and below it the fortress of Ollantay-Tambo. Immense, eternally snow-clad mountains rise high above the valley to heights of over 5,800 meters; beyond this point the river, now the Urubamba, is a plunging, wild stream; to the north is the massif of Vilcabamba, a wild, high, frigid plateau dominated by a score of snow-topped peaks.

At Ollantay-Tambo the Incas abandoned the river valley as a means of communication and used instead the valley east of the Urubamba canyon (the towns bear the names of the halting stations along the route of this road—Piri, Huambas-pampa; Pinassniyocc; Tasti-yocc to La Puerta, "the door"). Farther along, the road crossed a suspension bridge, turned east to Huayka-pata, then down again to the Urubamba to cross the bridge—a famous point of attack during the Spanish attempts on the neo-Inca kingdom of Manco II. On the left or southwest bank of the Urubamba, there was then a contains, so that with this protection it has a healthful, pleasant climate, neither too hot nor too cold. On the contrary, it is considered so excellent that the residents and authorities of Cuzco have considered very seriously transferring the city to it. But as their houses are so large they will not move it so as not to have to rebuild them, and also to preserve the antiquity of the city. . . . There is great hope that in this valley and that of Vilcas, and other similar ones, in time there will be goodly vineyards and orchards, and cool, delightful flower gardens. I mention this particularly of this valley because the Incas esteemed it highly, and came to it for their celebrations and feasts, especially Viracocha Inca, the grandfather of Topa [Tupac] Inca Yupanqui. All through it one sees remains of the many and large buildings there once were, especially those of [Ollantay-] Tambo,[2] which lies three leagues down the valley, between two great hills, beside a gulch through which a brook runs [Patacancha River]. And although the valley has the agreeable climate mentioned above, most of the year the mountains are white with the snow that falls on them. At this place the Incas had a great fortress, one of the strongest throughout their realms, built among rocks, so that a small force could defend it against many. Among these rocks there were several sheer cliffs, which made the spot impregnable, and below there are large terraces which look like walls, rising one above the other, on whose flat surface they plant the seeds of what they eat. Among these rocks there can still be seen figures of lions and other wild animals, and of men

254

---

stellation of Inca cities which were connected with a lateral road which entered Surite at the end of the Anta marshes. It surmounted the high canyons and continued along the high edge, two thousand feet above the roaring Urubamba, going through many terraced cities until it reached Machu Picchu.

2 Ollantay-Tambo, on the Urubamba, the royal administrative tambo of the eastern or Anti-suyu quarter of the realm, was built half a mile east of that river against the sides of the rising spurs of the eastern cordillera. It guarded the routes into the Amazon. Early in the fifteenth century it was ruled by chieftains, in all probability Laris, who disputed with Cuzco. It was conquered in 1440 by Pachacuti, and the Laris were made "Incas by privilege." The fortress, town, and tambo were begun about 1460, and the building was continued up until the time of the Spanish conquest (1534), and then afterwards by Manco II (1536–38). The tambo consists, first, of a town, where the people lived; a fortress or *pucará* immediately above it; walls—a rarity in Inca defense—and flights of stone steps which led to the *Inti-huatana* (hitching-place of the sun). The sides of the mountain were terraced. Opposite the fortress on the southwest wall of the canyon was a house for the *Ñustas* (sun maidens), complete with terraces and defenses. The site is vaguely associated with the eighteenth-century Quechua-written drama of *Ollantay*. (See Victor W. von Hagen, *Guide to the Ruins of Ollantay-tambo and Pisac.*)

with arms in their hands that look as though they were guarding the entrance, all skillfully carved.

The buildings were many, and they say there used to be in them, before the Spaniards conquered the kingdom, great treasures. What is certain is that the stones of these buildings are so large and so well matched and joined that many people and great skill were required to assemble them and put them where they are. Aside from this, it is told as true that in these buildings of [Ollantay-] Tambo or others having the same name (this is not the only place called Tambo), in a part of the royal palace or the temple of the sun, molten gold was used in place of mortar, together with the tar they employed, to join the stones. They say that Governor Don Francisco Pizarro collected a great deal of this before the Indians broke it up and carried it away, and some of the Spaniards say that Hernando Pizarro and Don Diego de Almagro the Younger carried away a quantity of gold from Paccaric Tampu. I do not doubt that this was the case when I recall the magnificent specimens exhibited in Seville which had been brought from Cajamarca, where the treasure Atahualpa promised the Spaniards was brought together, most of it coming from Cuzco.[3] And this was trifling compared with what was later divided up, which the Spaniards found for themselves; and more than all this was what the Indians carried off and buried in places nobody knows of. And if the fine clothing that was cast aside and destroyed had been kept, it would be worth so much that I do not venture to set a figure on it. To continue, the Indians known as the Chumpivilcas and the Ubinas, and Pomatambos, and many other tribes I am not naming, made up what they call Cunti-suyu. Some of them were warlike, and their settlements are high in the mountains. They owned innumerable herds of llamas. The houses are of stone and thatch. There were lodgings of the rulers in many places. The natives had their rites and customs like the others, and in their temples they sacrificed llamas and other objects, and it is said that the devil was seen in a temple they had in a certain place in this region of Cunti-suyu, and even in our times I have heard from certain Spaniards that our enemy and adversary still appears. In the rivers that run through the lands of the Aymaraes

255

[3] The treasure ransom of Atahualpa, brought to Seville by Hernando Pizarro, arrived in Seville on the *Santa María del Campo* on January 9, 1534. Cieza was then thirteen years of age; this so fired him that he left for the New World in the autumn of that same year.

large amounts of gold have been washed, and this happened when I was in Cuzco. In Pomatambo and in other parts of this kingdom fine tapestry is woven, for the wool of which it is made is of such excellent quality and the colors so good that it excels that of all the other kingdoms. There are many rivers in this province of Cunti-suyu; some of them are spanned by bridges of twisted withes, like those I have described. There are also many of the native fruits and many orchards. And deer and partridge, and good falcons to hunt them.

CHAPTER 86 (XCV)

Of the mountains of the Andes and their great forests, and the huge serpents to be found there, and the bad habits of the Indians who live in the remote regions of the mountains.

THIS CHAIN of mountains known as the Andes is believed to be one of the largest in the world. They run from the Strait of Magellan, as is borne out by those who have seen them, all through this king-dom of Peru, and cross more lands and provinces than can be enu-merated. They are full of high peaks, some of them covered with snow, and some of them volcanoes. These sierras and mountains are very difficult of access because they are so densely wooded and be-cause it rains there most of the time. The earth is so shaded that one must proceed with great care, for the roots of the trees jut out of the ground all along the mountainsides, and the hardest work is to clear a path for the horses.

It is told by the *Orejones* of Cuzco that Topa Inca crossed these mountains with a great army, and many of the peoples living there were hard to conquer and bring under his rule. On the flanks that slope toward the Southern Sea, the natives were of good intelligence, and they all went clothed, and were ruled by the laws and customs of the Incas. But of those on the side that slopes toward the other sea, to the east, it is a known fact that they are of less intelligence and understanding. They raise much coca, a plant highly prized by the Indians, as I shall relate in the next chapter.

As these mountains are so vast, it can well be believed, as they tell, that there are many animals to be found there, such as bears, jaguars, pumas, tapirs, wild pigs, and lynx, and many other kinds. Some of the Spaniards have seen serpents the size of logs, and they say of them that, despite their size and ferocious appearance, even if one sits on them they do no harm, nor do they attack anyone. In Cuzco, when I was talking about these serpents with the Indians, they told me something I shall set down here, because they assured me that it was indeed true. This was that in the time of the Inca Pachacuti, the son of Viracocha Inca, certain captains set out at his orders with a large army to visit these Andes and bring such of the Indians as they could under the rule of the Incas. And when they were deep in the mountains, these serpents killed most of the troops that had set out with the aforementioned captains, and the Inca took this great loss very much to heart. When it became known, an old witch told him to let her go to the Andes, and she would cast such a spell on the serpents that they would never again do harm. She received permission, and went to where the disaster had occurred; there, working her spells and saying certain words, she changed them from the fierce wild creatures they were to the harmless, inoffensive things they now are. This may be one of their fictions or fables; but the fact remains that these snakes, for all they are so large, do no harm.

These Andes, where the Incas had lodgings and palaces, were, in parts, thickly settled. The land is very fertile, and corn and yuca do well there, and other tubers they plant. There are many and delicious fruits, and most of the Spaniards living in Cuzco have already set out oranges, limes, figs, grapes, and other plants of Spain, aside from which there are large banana groves and delicious, fragrant pineapples. Deep in these mountains and forests they say there are people so uncivilized that they have neither houses nor clothing, but live like animals, killing birds and beasts with arrows for food, and recognize no lords or leaders, but live in groups in caves or hollow trees, some in one place, some in another. They also say that in most of these places (although I have not seen them) there are large monkeys that live in the trees, and that, at the instigation of the devil, who is always seeking ways to make men commit more and greater sins, these people cohabit with them; and they say that some of them bring forth monsters whose heads and private parts are like those of men, and the hands and feet like those of monkeys. They are, it is said, small of size and monstrously shaped, and covered with hair. In a word, they would seem to resemble (if it is true that they exist) their father, the devil. They even say that they cannot talk, but utter only squeals or frightening howls. I do not affirm this, but at the same time I know that many men of understanding and reason, who know that there is God, heaven, and hell, have left their wives and befouled themselves with mules, bitches, mares, and other animals, which it grieves me to state, so this [what they say of these animals] may be true.

258

When I was on my way to Charcas in the year 1549 to visit the provinces of that land, carrying with me letters from President La Gasca for all the mayors asking them to assist me in learning and finding out the most important things of these provinces, we tented one night—a hidalgo of Málaga, one López de Moncibay,[1] and I— and a Spaniard who was there told us that he had seen one of these monsters dead in the woods, and it was of the shape and appearance that was told. And Juan de Varagas,[2] a resident of the city of La Paz [Chuquiabo], told me that in Huánuco the Indians had heard the howls of these devils or monkeys. So there is knowledge that this sin has been committed by these benighted creatures. I have also heard for a fact that Francisco de Almendras,[3] who used to live in the city of [La] Plata [Chuquisaca], caught an Indian woman and a dog in this sin, and ordered the woman burned. And aside from this, I have heard from Lope de Mendieta[4] and Juan Ortíz de Zárate[5] and

---

[1] Inigo López de Moncibay was an *old* conquistador, one of the *regidores* of La Paz. He had first been a partisan of Gonzalo Pizarro, but seeing the direction of the political wind in 1547, he volunteered to deliver letters to Pedro de la Gasca, then encamped at Jauja. He went over to the King's cause, as La Gasca taunted Gonzalo Pizarro: ". . . he volunteered to deliver the letters . . . in order to escape your power." (La Gasca Papers, Henry E. Huntington Library Collection.)

[2] Juan de Varagas (or Vargas), "a veteran conquistador in these parts" (Cieza), a native of La Huguera, Spain, was involved in most of the conflicts of the civil wars. He was famed for having captured Illa Tupac, one of Manco Inca's captains, near the redoubt of Vilcabamba in 1544.

[3] Francisco de Almendras, a violent and active partisan of the Pizarros, was at the capture of Atahualpa, and on the eighteenth of June, 1533, received his share of the loot: 181 marcos of silver (*marco*=mark, one-half pound, valued at that time at 101,615 pesos) and 4,440 pesos of gold. He settled in Charcas, became regidor of Chuquisaca (afterwards Villa de la Plata and now Sucre, in Bolivia), executed enemies of Gonzalo Pizarro, and in turn was murdered—despite his plea that he be spared because of his large family—on June 16, 1545.

[4] Lope de Mendieta in Pedro de Cieza's time was one of the magistrates of Villa de

other residents of the city of La Plata that they heard from their Indians of a woman in the province of Aulaga [Lake Poopó] who gave birth to three or four monsters sired by a dog, which lived only a few days. May it please Our Lord God, though our transgressions are so many and so great, not to permit such horrendous and abominable sins.

259

CHAPTER 87 (XCVI)

How throughout most of the Indies the natives were given to the habit of chewing plants or roots, and of the highly prized plant, coca, which is raised in many parts of this kingdom.

EVERYWHERE that I have traveled in the Indies I have noticed that the natives find great pleasure in keeping roots, twigs, or plants in their mouth. In the vicinity of the city of Antiocha [Antioquia in Colombia] some of them chewed small coca leaves, and in the province of Arma, other plants, and in Quimbaya and Ancerma they cut slivers from a kind of small tree that is soft-wooded and always green, and keep them between their teeth all the time. In most of the tribes under the jurisdiction of the cities of Cali and Popayán they keep leaves of the small coca I have spoken of in their mouth, and dip out of little gourds they carry a mixture they prepare, which they put in their mouths and chew it all together, and do the same with a kind of earth that is like lime. All through Peru it was and is the custom to have this coca in the mouth, and they keep it there from morning until they go to sleep, without removing it. When I asked some of the Indians why they always had their mouths full of this plant (which they do not eat, but only keep between their teeth), they said that with it they do not feel hunger, and it gives them great

la Plata. He was a nephew of Diego de Zárate of the Board of Trade in Seville, fought at the battle of Chupas (1544) with the rank of captain, and later became magistrate of La Plata.

[5] Juan Ortiz de Zárate was the son of the Oidor (Judge) Zárate who came out from Spain to order the affairs of Peru. He took part in the murder-execution of Francisco de Almendras and later was a member of the City Council of La Plata.

vigor and strength.[1] I think it probably does something of the sort, though it seems to me a disgusting habit, and what might be expected of people like these Indians.

In the Andes this coca is planted from Huamanga to the city of Plata [Bolivia]. It grows on bushes which they carefully tend and cultivate for the leaves, which resemble those of myrtle. They dry them in the sun and then pack them in long, narrow baskets, which hold a little better than an arroba. This coca was so valuable in Peru in the years 1548, 1549, and 1551 that there has never been in the whole world a plant or root or any growing thing that bears and yields every year as this does, aside from spices, which are a different thing, that is so highly valued. In those years the *repartimientos,* that is to say, most of those of Cuzco, the city of La Paz [Bolivia], brought in an income of eighty thousand pesos, and sixty thousand, and forty thousand, and twenty thousand, some more, some less, all from this coca. Anyone holding an encomienda of Indians considered his main crop the number of baskets of coca he gathered.

This coca was taken to be sold at the mines of Potosí, and everyone began setting out bushes and gathering the leaves, so now this coca is not worth anything like what it used to be, but it is still valuable. There are those in Spain who became rich from this coca,[2] buying it up and reselling it and trading it in the *catus* or markets of the Indians.

260

---

[1] Coca (*q. cuca*) is as old as Peru. A South American shrub (*Erythroxylum coca*) whose delicate, tealike leaves yield cocaine, it has been and still is chewed by millions of Indians in the sierras (from Colombia to Argentina) and in the jungles. Coca is cultivated in the lush, rain-soaked *Montaña* on the eastern slopes of the Andes. Its cultivation and use predated the Incas by upwards of two thousand years. It has been found in graves of great antiquity, and the methods of use—including the bag for carrying the leaves and the lime-stick to hasten the breakdown of the leaf to release the minute quantities of cocaine—are all present.

So far as the Incas were concerned, its use seems to have been limited to the nobility, the priests (for divination), perhaps old people, and mayhap the *chasqui* couriers to aid their running in high altitudes. The Indians make a quid of the leaves, about the size of a walnut, which they hold in the sides of their cheeks; lime is added to it, quickening the process of leaf disintegration; the juice alone is swallowed. The average daily consumption of cocaine is minute, 300–400 mg. It seems to dull the senses, making the coca-chewer less hungry, cold, and thirsty. Its effects on the Indians over a period of time has been argued for four centuries; there is still no firm medical conclusion.

[2] "In trueth the trafficke of coca in Potosí doth yearely mount to above a halfe million of peeces [pesos] . . . for they use fifteene thousand baskets every yeare. It is a kind of merchandise, by which all their Markets and Faires are made with great expedition. The Indians esteeme it much and in the time of their Incas it was not lawfull for any of the common people to use this coca. . . . They say it gives them great courage, and is very pleasing unto them. Many grave men hold this as super-

Of the road by which one goes from Cuzco to the city of La Paz, and the settlements to be found until leaving the land of the Indians they call the Canchis.

FROM THE city of Cuzco to La Paz is some eighty leagues, and it should be said that before this city was settled, all the settlements and valleys now ascribed to this new city of La Paz fell within the territory of Cuzco. Thus, leaving Cuzco by the highway of Colla-suyu, one travels until reaching the passes of Muhina,[1] leaving the lodgings of Quiquixana[2] to the left. The road goes through this village after leaving Cuzco, and is a broad highway of thick stones. In Muhina there is a swamp full of bogs, over which the road is laid on stout foundations, the aforesaid highway. There were great buildings in Muhina, but they are now destroyed and fallen down. When the Governor Don Francisco Pizarro entered Cuzco with the Spaniards, they say they found near these buildings and in them a large amount of silver and gold, and even more of the fine, valuable clothing I have mentioned on other occasions. And I have heard some of the Spaniards say that there was at this place a stone statue of a man with a kind of long robe and beads in his hand, and other figures and statues. This was the grandeur of the Incas, the signs they wished to leave for the future. Some of them were idols which they worshiped. Beyond Muhina is the ancient town of Urcos, some six leagues from Cuzco. Along this road there is a very large, broad wall, along the top of which, according to the natives, ran pipes of water, laboriously

stition & a meere imagination: for my part, and to speak the truth I persuade not my self that it is an imagination; but contrariwise, I thinke it works and gives force and courage to the Indians. . . . They willingly imploy their money therein, and use it, as money: yet all these things were not inconvenient, were not the hazard of the trafficke thereof, wherein so many men are occupied. The Inguas used Coca as a delicate and royall thing, which they offered most in their sacrifices, burning it in honor of their idolls." (José de Acosta, *The Naturall and Morall Historie of the East and West Indies* [written c. 1570].)

[1] Muhina, situated on top of a flattened cliff that overlooks the bogs of the lake of Sucre, was once a large city. There was a way-stop here, as attested by the "Regulations for Tambos" (1543): "Tambo de Muhina . . . el dicho tambo está Quemado [burned]. . . ."

[2] Modern Quispicanchi. It was the first way-stop on the southern Colla-suyu road; it was held in fief by Alonso Riquelme, treasurer of the King of Spain, in the first conquest of Peru, and by Hernando Machicao later.

brought from some river and piped in with the forethought and care they used in building their irrigation ditches. There was a wide gate in this great wall[3] where there were gatekeepers who collected the taxes and tributes due the rulers, and stewards of the Incas to arrest and punish those who ventured to take silver and gold out of the city of Cuzco. In this region were the quarries [at Rumi-colca] from which they dug the stones they used in their buildings, which are a thing to see. Urcos is situated on a hill where there were lodgings for the rulers. From here to Quiquixana is three leagues, all over rough mountains; through them flows the Yucay [Vilcamayu] River, where there is a bridge built like those over similar rivers. Near by are the settlements of the Indians known as the Caviñas,[4] who, before they came under the rule of the Incas, wore their ears pierced, with that ornament they used in the opening, and these were the *Orejones*. Manco Capac, founder of the city of Cuzco, is said to have won them over by friendly methods. They go dressed in woolen clothing, most of them shave their head, and encircle it with a black braid. Their settlements are in the mountains, and their houses are of stone. In olden times they held a temple, which they called Auzancata, in great devotion, near which they say their forebears saw an idol or devil in their shape, clothed as they go, with whom they had their dealings, making sacrifices to it after their fashion. And these Indians tell that in olden times they firmly believed that the souls that departed the body went to a great lake which their silly superstition led them to believe was their place of origin, and from there they returned to the bodies of the newborn. Afterwards, when they came under the rule of the Incas, they became more civilized and sensible and wor-

---

[3] This wide gate is at Piqui-llacta (flea-town). Cieza is correct: this aqueduct once brought water to an immense pre-Inca city. A large number of buildings were laid out from a formal square (no potsherds of any form have been found there). It has occasioned much mystery since it was photographed from the air by the Shippee-Johnson expedition in 1931. However, the work of Ing. Emilio Harth-Terré suggested that these were storage chambers. Almost a duplicate of this type of storage complex is found in the Inca coastal ruins of Incahuasi, Cañete valley, which have also been studied by Ing. Harth-Terré. The aqueduct which brought water to Piqui-llacta from Lake Urcos is broken, but the fine wall of late Inca architecture, through which all had to pass to get to Cuzco, still stands; modern traffic funnels through it.

[4] The Caviñas were one of four federated communities of Aymara-speaking tribes of Ayaviris, Canas, Canchis, and Caviñas, which held, until they were finally conquered by the Incas in the early fifteenth century, the upper reaches of the Vilcamayu River.

shiped the sun, but without foregoing their devotion to their ancient temple.

Beyond this province come the Canchis,[5] domesticated Indians of sound reason, without malice, who were always good workers, especially at mining silver and gold, and who had large flocks of their llamas and rams. Their settlements are neither better nor worse than those of their neighbors, and their attire is the same. As insignia they wear black braids about their head which fall below their chin. They tell that in olden times they had great wars with Viracocha Inca and others of his predecessors, and that when they came under their rule, they were treated with great respect. The arms they used were darts and slings and a thing they call *ayllos,*[6] with which they caught their enemies. Their burial and religious customs were similar to those already described, and their graves were in high, rocky fields, where they laid their lords with certain of his wives and other servants. They are not given to honors or pomp, although some of the chieftains are arrogant toward their people and treat them inconsiderately. At certain times of the year, on appointed days, they hold their feasts. In the dwellings of the rulers there were plazas where they held their dances, and where the ruler ate and drank. They conversed with the devil like the others. Throughout the land of these Canchis wheat and corn is raised; partridge and condors are numerous, and in their homes these Indians have many chickens, and they catch much fish in the rivers, good and well flavored.

CHAPTER 89 (XCVIII)

Of the province of the Canas, and what they tell of Ayaviri, which, in the times of the Incas, was, so it would seem, a fine thing.

AFTER LEAVING the Canchis, one enters the province of the Canas,[1]

[5] The Canchis were tribesmen of the aforementioned confederation. If they fought with Viracocha Inca, the time of their absorption into the Inca realm would be about the year 1400.

[6] Cieza means *bolas,* described earlier as an entangling device, consisting of two to five stones or copper weights, connected by cords to a longer main cord. When thrown, it effectively tied up the arms and legs of an animal or man.

[1] The Canas were one of the four tribes which acted for centuries as a buffer between

another tribe, and their villages are known by these names: Hatuncana, Chicuana, Oruro, Cacha, and others I shall not mention. All the Indians go clothed, they and their women, and on their head they wear a kind of woolen cap, large, round, and high. Before the Incas ruled them, they had their settlements on fortified hills, from which they came down to make war; afterwards they settled on the plains, constructing their villages in orderly fashion. Like the Canchis, they, too, dig their graves on their lands, and observe and keep the same customs. In the region of these Canas there was a temple they called Ancocagua,[2] which is where they made their sacrifices in keeping with their blindness. In the village of Cacha there were great lodgings built by order of Topa Inca. Across a river is a small enclosure in which a quantity of gold was found, for they say there was a temple there in honor and commemoration of their god Tici-Viracocha, whom they called Creator, and in it was a stone idol the size of a man, with its raiment and a crown or tiara on its head. There are those who say this might be the figure of some apostle who came to this land. . . .

264

It is cold in all this region of the Canas, as in that of the Canchis, and it is well supplied with food and flocks. To the west lies the Southern Sea, and to the east the forests of the Andes. From the village of Sicuani, in this province of the Canas, to that of Ayaviri is some fifteen leagues, and in this stretch there are a number of villages of these Canas, and many plains, and broad bottomlands good for stock raising, although the excessive cold of this region is a handicap, and the grass that grows there is good only for the guanacos and vicuñas. In olden times (so they say) this village of Ayaviri was a great place,[3] and it still is, particularly because of the great tombs

---

the Incas and the Colla tribes about Lake Titicaca; they centered about the city of Sicuani (formerly Chicuana); their territory included Cacha, where the remains of what was the great temple of Viracocha stand.

[2] This Ancocagua has not been identified or mentioned in archaeological exploration. The "Regulations for Tambos" mentions that between the Andean tarn Urcos and Quiquixana there were villages called Ocongata and Bambachulla, of which the conquistadors Martín de Florencia and Gabriel de Rojas were proprietors. There seems to be no other record.

[3] The Ayaviris centered about a town which still bears their name. A river, also the Ayaviri, flows into Lake Titicaca. They were a very stubborn people, probably Aymara-speaking, related to the other tribes in the upper Vilcamayu country. They formed a sort of buffer state between the contending Incas to the south and the Collas

there, which are so numerous that they occupy more ground than the settlement. The Indians assert that the natives of this village of Ayaviri were of the lineage and race of the Canas, and that the Inca Pachacuti carried on a number of wars and battles with them in which, after being defeated by the Inca, they were so reduced in numbers that they had to surrender and become his slaves to keep from being completely wiped out. But as certain of the Incas must have been vengeful, they tell that after the Inca had treacherously and slyly killed many of the Indians of Copacopa and other settlements lying along the Andes, he did the same to the natives of Ayaviri, with the result that few or none of them were left alive, and those who managed to escape roamed the fields calling upon their ancestors, long departed, bewailing with piteous lamentations the disaster that had befallen them and their settlement. And as this village of Ayaviri lies in the center of a large region, and near by runs a fine river [Ayaviri], the Inca Yupanqui ordered great palaces built for him, which they did after their usage, as well as many storehouses along the slope of a small sierra, where they housed their tributes. And as the main and most important thing, he ordered a temple erected to the sun. When this had been done, as there was a shortage of the natives for the aforesaid reasons, the Inca Yupanqui ordered Indians (*mitimaes*) from the neighboring regions with their women to come there and take over the lands and establishments of the dead, and build the settlement large and orderly around the temples of the sun and the royal lodgings. And this village grew in size from that time

about Lake Titicaca, who fought for the hegemony of all Peru. They were finally subjugated, made "Incas by privilege," and helped to build the Inca administrative center at Ayaviri. At this point the Inca road branched off into two parts to move about Lake Titicaca. Another road (see map) also moved northeast toward the *montaña* jungles, going to Orurillo, shifting southwest to Asillo, where a branch road led to the rich placer gold region of Carabaya (see Chapter 94 for Cieza's commentary on this region).

The way-station of Chungara and the village of Ayaviri belonged to Francisco de Villacastin, says the "Regulations for Tambos": "Aqui se apartan los dos caminos a la redonda de la laguna (de Titicaca) que se llama omasuyu [western side], Hurcusuyu [eastern side]." Francisco de Villacastin, one of the first conquistadors, had a house in Hanan- (Upper) Cuzco, just below the fortress of Sacsahuamán. He married Doña Leonor Coya, one of the daughters of the Inca Huayna Capac, after she had first married *el conquistador* Juan Balsa. He arrived early in Panama, and before the conquest helped to open a road across the isthmus. But he played the wrong side. He sided with Gonzalo Pizarro, was imprisoned after his defeat at Xaquixahuana in 1548, and there he died. When Pedro de Cieza traveled to Ayaviri in 1549, this fief belonged to Juan de Pancorvo of Cuzco.

on until the Spaniards entered this kingdom, since when, with the wars and disasters that ensued, it has declined greatly, like all the others. I came there when it was held in encomienda by Juan de Pancorvo, a resident of Cuzco, and it was from the best interpreters that I learned this which I have written. Close to this village is a ruined temple, where they used to perform their sacrifices, and I was astonished by the many graves to be seen all around this village.

CHAPTER 90 (CXVII)

Stating certain things about the Indians that have been dealt with in this narration, and what happened to a priest with one of them in a village of this kingdom.

As THERE are people who say very harsh things of these Indians, comparing them to animals, saying that their habits and way of living are more like those of beasts than men, and that they are so evil that not only do they commit the abominable sin, but eat one another, and although in this chronicle of mine I have written something of this, and of other evils and abuses of which they are guilty, I want to make it clear that it is not my intention to say that this is true of all. On the contrary, it should be known that although in one province they eat human flesh and make human blood sacrifices, there are many others where they abhor this sin. And if in others they indulge in the sin against nature, in many they hold it to be a foul thing, and never commit it but, on the contrary, loathe it. Therefore, it would be unjust to condemn them all. And even these evils which they committed have the excuse that they lacked the light of our Holy Faith, and for that reason they were unaware of the wrong they were doing, like many other nations, especially the Gentiles in olden times, who, like these Indians, lacking the light of faith, made as many sacrifices as they did, and more. And if we consider the matter fairly, there are many who profess our law and have received the waters of baptism, who, led astray by the devil, commit grave sins every day. So if these Indians had the habits I have described, it was because there was no one to lead them in the paths of truth in bygone times. Now, those who hear the doctrine of the Holy Gospels know the darkness of perdition in which those walk who depart from them, and the devil, whose envy grows as he sees the harvest reaped by our Holy Faith, endeavors to deceive these people with fears and terrors. But he has little success, and each day it will be less, considering what our Lord God does at all times for the advancement of his blessed teachings.

267

Among other remarkable things I shall tell of one that took place in this province in a village called Lampaz [Lampa],[1] as it is set forth in the narrative given to me in the village of Azángaro, *repartimiento* of Antonio de Quiñones,[2] a resident of Cuzco, by a priest, telling what happened in the conversion of an Indian. I asked him to give it to me in his own handwriting, and omitting and adding nothing, this is what he said:

"I, Marcos Otazo, priest, resident of Valladolid, being in the village of Lampaz instructing the Indians in our Christian faith, in the year of 1547, the month of May, in the full of the moon, there came to me all the caciques and headmen to beg me most earnestly to give them permission to do what they were in the habit of doing at that season. I replied that I would have to be present, for if it was something not licit for our Holy Catholic faith, they were not to do it henceforth. They agreed to this, and they all went to their homes.

"And when it was, as I could judge, exactly noon, from different directions came the sound of the beating of many drums, played with a single stick, for that is their way of playing them, and then blankets were spread on the ground in the square, like carpets, for the caciques and headmen to sit on, all decked out and dressed in their best clothes, their hair hanging in a four-strand braid on each side, as is their custom. When they were seated, I saw a boy of about twelve advance toward each of the caciques; he was the handsomest and most agile of all, and richly dressed after their fashion, with his legs from the knee down covered with red tassels, and his arms the same, and on his body he wore many medals and ornaments of gold

[1] Lampa-pampa (3,898 meters high) is in the Titicaca drainage, thirty kilometers southwest of Pucará; it is today, as then, a center of mining and farming.

[2] Antonio de Quiñones, an early conquistador, had a house in Cusi-pata in Cuzco next to that of Garcilaso de la Vega, and married an Inca *coya* (princess) called Doña Beatriz.

and silver. In his right hand he carried a kind of arm like a halberd, and in his left, a big bag of wool in which they carry coca.

"On his left side came a girl of about ten, very pretty, dressed in the same fashion, except that she wore a long skirt, which the other women are not in the habit of wearing, and this was carried by an older Indian woman, very handsome and with an air of authority. Behind her came many other Indian women, like ladies-in-waiting, with great poise and breeding. And that girl carried in her right hand a beautiful woolen bag, covered with ornaments of gold and silver, and from her shoulders hung a small puma skin which completely covered her back. Behind these women there followed six Indians representing farmers, each with his plow on his shoulder, and on their heads diadems and feathers, very beautiful and of many colors. These were followed by six more, like helpers, with bags of potatoes, playing the drum, and in order they came to within a step of the cacique.

"The boy and girl I have described, and all the rest in turn, made him a deep bow, lowering their heads, and the cacique and headmen bowed in return. When this had been done to each cacique, for there were two of them, in the same order in which they had come the boy and the others moved backward without turning their faces, some twenty paces, in the order I have described. There the farmers sank their plows in the ground in a row, and hung from them those bags of potatoes, large and carefully selected; and when they had done this, playing their drums, they began a kind of dance without moving from where they were standing, on the tips of their toes, and from time to time they lifted the bags they had in their hands toward the sky. Only those I have mentioned did this, those who accompanied this boy and girl, and all the ladies-in-waiting; for the caciques and the other people, seated in order of rank, watched and listened in silence.

"When this was finished they sat down, and a yearling llama was brought in, uniform in color, without a single blemish, by other Indians who had gone for it. In front of the cacique, surrounded by so many Indians I could not see it, they stretched it out on the ground, and, still alive, removed all its entrails through one side, and gave them to the soothsayers, whom they call *huaca-camayocs*, who are like priests among us. And I observed that certain of the Indians quickly scooped up as much of the llama's blood as they could in their hands, and sprinkled it over the potatoes in the bags. At that moment a headman, who had turned Christian a few days before, as I shall tell, rushed forward shouting and calling them dogs and other things in their language, which I did not understand. And he went to the foot of a tall cross that stood in the middle of the square, where, shouting still louder, he fearlessly upbraided them for that diabolical rite. As a result of his reproaches and my warnings they went away frightened and confused, without concluding their sacrifice by which they foretell the crops and events of the entire year. There are others whom they call *homo,* whom they question concerning the future because they talk with the devil and carry with them his image, made of a hollow bone, and on this a carving in black wax, such as is found here.

"When I was in this village of Lampaz, one Maundy Thursday a servant of mine who slept in the church came to me in great fright, begging me to arise and go to baptize a cacique who was in the church kneeling before the images, all trembling and terrified; he told that the night before, Holy Wednesday, when he had been in a *huaca,* which is where they worship, he had seen a man dressed in white who asked him what he was doing there before that stone image, that he was to depart at once, and come to me to become a Christian. When daybreak came, I got up and recited my hours, and not believing what the boy had told me, I went to the church to say Mass, and there I found him, still on his knees. When he saw me, he threw himself at my feet, imploring me to make him a Christian, and I told him I would do so. I said Mass for the Christians who were there, and when it was over I baptized him, and he went off joyfully, shouting that he was now a Christian, and not wicked like the Indians. And without saying a word to anyone, he went to where his house stood and burned it down, and divided his wives and flocks among his brothers and relatives, and came to the church, where he was always preaching to the Indians what they should do to be saved, urging them to forswear their sins and vices. He did it with great fervor, like one who has been illuminated by the Holy Ghost, and he was always in the church or beside the cross. Many Indians became Christians at the persuasion of this new convert. He told that the man he saw when he was in the *huaca* or devil's temple was white and very beautiful, and that his garments gleamed."

The priests gave me this in writing. . . . The Indians are converted, and little by little are forsaking their rites . . . and if this has been slow, it is more because of neglect. . . . The real way to convert the Indians is by teaching and by upright behavior. . . .

270

CHAPTER 91 (XCIX)

Of the great territory of the Collas, and of the lay of the land where their villages are located, and how they used the mitimaes *to work for them.*

THE REGION of the Collas [about Lake Titicaca] is the largest of all Peru, and in my opinion the most thickly settled. It extends from Ayaviri as far as Caracollo. To the east lie the mountains of the Andes, to the west the promontories of the snow-capped sierras and their flanks, which descend to the Southern Sea. Aside from the territory occupied by their settlements and fields, there are great unsettled regions full of wild flocks [of llamas and alpacas]. The lands of the Colla are all level, and through them run many rivers of good water. In these plains there are beautiful broad meadows always thick with grass, and part of the time very green, though in summer they turn brown as in Spain. The winter begins, as I have written, in October and lasts until April. The days and nights are of almost equal length, and this is the coldest region of all Peru, aside from the high, snow-capped sierras, because of its elevation. It is so high that it is almost equal to the sierras. The fact of the matter is that if this land of the Colla were a low-lying valley like that of Jauja or Chuquiabo, where corn could be raised, it would be considered one of the best and richest of much of these Indies. It is very difficult to walk against the wind in these plains of the Colla; when there is no wind and the sun shines, it is a real pleasure to see these beautiful and thickly settled meadows. But as it is so cold, corn cannot grow nor any kind of tree; on the contrary, none of the many fruits produced in the other valleys can be raised here. The villages of the natives are close together, the houses one beside the other, not very large, all of stone, with roofs of thatch, which they all use instead of tile.

In olden times this region of the Collas was thickly settled, and there were large villages close together. Around them the Indians have their fields where they plant their crops. Their principal article of food is potatoes,[1] which are like truffles, as I have stated before in this relation, and they dry them in the sun and keep them from one harvest to the other. They call these dried potatoes *chuño*,[2] and among them they are highly esteemed and valued, for they have no irrigation system, as in many other parts of this kingdom, to water their fields. On the contrary, if there is a shortage of rainfall for their crops, they would go hungry if it were not for these dried potatoes. Many Spaniards became rich and went back to Spain prosperous just by selling this *chuño* in the mines of Potosí [of Bolivia]. They have another article of food called *oca*,[3] which is also useful, but even more so is a cereal they grow known as *quinoa,* which is small like rice.[4] When it is a good year, all the inhabitants of the Colla live happy and satisfied; but if it is a dry year and there is a shortage of rain, they undergo great hardships. But as these Lord-Incas, who ruled this empire were so wise and foresighted, they established customs and laws without which most of the people in their kingdom would have suffered great privations and hardships, as was the case before they came under their rule. I say this because among these Collas and in all the other valleys of Peru, which, being cold, were not as fertile and productive as the warm regions nor as well provided, they ordered that, as the great chain of the Andes borders on most of the settlements, a certain number of Indians, *mitimaes,* and their wives should go out from each of them to places designated by their caciques

---

[1] This is the first published account of the potato. Cieza saw it first in Colombia, observed it growing in the Peruvian coastal valleys, and made the first published account of it. The potato has a long and varied history. (See Salaman's *History and Social Influence of the Potato.*)

[2] The various types of dehydrated potatoes have been detailed earlier in notes to Chapter 49. The Quechua word for potato was *acsu.*

[3] The *oca,* also a tuber, is the botanists' *Oxalis tuberosa,* first classified by Linnaeus. It is sweet-potato shaped, with a pale red skin, white within. It is mealy, watery-sweet, and much liked by the Indians.

[4] Quinoa is a pseudo cereal, one of the buckwheats, among the hardiest growing in areas as high as 14,000 feet above sea level. It is an annual, reaching a height of four to six feet; the blossom is deep red, and the pod contains the *quinoa* grains, which, when boiled, taste something like rice.

and work the fields, where they planted what they could not raise where they lived, turning over the crops they gathered to their lords or captains. Now they are under an encomienda and raise and dry the valuable coca. So, even though in all the Colla no corn is planted or harvested, the native rulers do not lack for it nor those who care to obtain it in the manner described, for they are always bringing in loads of corn, coca, fruits of all kinds, and a great deal of honey.[5]

272

CHAPTER 92 (C)

What is told of these Collas, their origin and dress, and how they buried their dead.

MANY OF THESE Indians tell that they heard from their forebears that in remote times a great flood occurred as I [have already written] .... And they imply that the antiquity of their origins is very great,[1]

[5] Pedro de Cieza de León: "In the province of Charcas this honey is especially good. It is told of Francisco de Carvajal, Gonzalo Pizarro's master of troop who turned traitor, that he always ate this honey, and drank it as though it were water or wine, saying that it kept him very strong and healthy, and so he was when I saw him executed in the valley of Xaquixahuana, a fine figure of a man even though he was over eighty years old."

Francisco de Carvajal, the witty octogenarian *pícaro* who served Gonzalo Pizarro in the civil wars (1542–48) as master of the troop in Peru, was born in Arévalo, Old Castile. He had more than rudimentary education, and his cynical wit still comes out after all these years. He served as soldier with Charles V, was present at the battle of Ravenna (1527) and the sack of Rome (1527), and acquired enough ducats to come to America. He was sent from Mexico to Peru to aid Francisco Pizarro after the uprising of Manco Inca in 1536. He wished to leave Peru when the civil wars began, sensing catastrophe, but was hindered from doing so. At the final battle, in which Cieza participated as a soldier, he was captured and beheaded on April 10, 1548. He was then over eighty years of age.

[1] The Colla-suyu—the quarter of the south—comprised the Aymara-speaking rivals of the Incas. Their traditional land was about the Titicaca basin, at an altitude upwards of 12,000 feet, in a plateau alternating with rich soil and rock; corn grows badly there or not at all; *quinoa, oca,* and potatoes are the staples. A bleak, frigid land, where large herds of llamas and alpacas are domesticated, it seemingly was the last place from which one might expect a culture to develop. Yet here, twelve miles south of the eastern shore of Lake Titicaca (now in Bolivia), are the remains of Tiahuanacu, the most elaborate and the purest manifestation of this culture yet to be found. Presumably, as this is in the Colla-suyu and the people spoke then, as now, the Aymara language, the ancestors of the Collas in the centuries between A.D. 500 and 1000, were involved in the elaboration of this culture, which eventually invaded all Peru and left its cultural mark.

"Aymara" is the name given to the language spoken by those who then, as now,

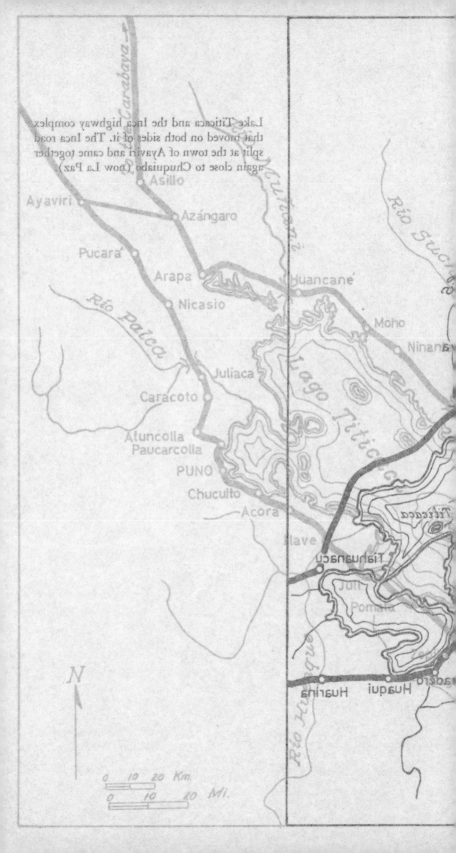

Lake Titicaca and the Inca highway complex that moved on both sides of it. The Inca road split at the town of Ayaviri and came together again close to Chuquiabo (now La Paz).

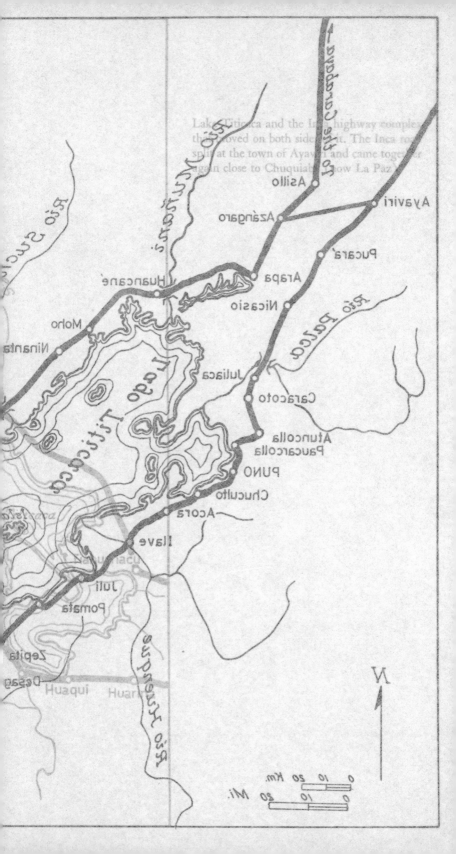

Lake Titicaca and the Inca highway complex that moved on both sides of it. The Inca road split at the town of Ayaviri and came together again close to Chuquiabo, now La Paz.

and in this connection they relate so many tales and fables, if they are that, that I shall not waste time setting them down. For some say that they emerged from a spring; others, from a rock; and others, from lakes. And this is all one can get out of them concerning their origin. They all agree that their forefathers lived with little order before the Incas ruled them, and that on the heights of the mountains they had their fortified settlements, from which they went forth to make war, and that they abounded in wicked customs. Afterwards they learned from the Incas what all who became their vassals learned, and built their villages as they now are. They go dressed in garments of wool, they and their women, who, although before they marry may be of loose habits, if after they have been handed over to their husband, they betray him, knowing another man, they are put to death. On their heads they wear a bonnet shaped like a mortar, made of wool, which they call *chullo;* their heads are very long and without nape, for from birth they bind them and shape them as they wish, as I have written. The women wear on their heads a hood very similar to that worn by monks. Many of these Colla Indians tell that before the rule of the Incas there were two great lords in their province, one called Zapana and the other Cari, and that they won many *pucarás,* which are their fortresses. And that one of them entered the lake of Titicaca, and found on the largest island of that body of water bearded white men with whom he fought until he had killed all of them. And they say more: that after this they waged great battles with the Canas and Canchis. And after having performed notable feats, these two tyrants or lords that had arisen in the Colla turned their arms against one another, vying for the friendship and favor of Viracocha Inca, reigning in Cuzco at that time, who concluded a peace with Cari in Chucuito, and was so adroit that without war he made himself ruler of many of these Collas. The headmen always

273

centered about the Titicaca basin. Actually it is not known what the original language was called; it is believed that the Aymaraes were only an insignificant tribe of the Colla and that their name was applied to it. Quechua and Aymara are related languages, although there are many differences in speech and vocabulary. It is not even known whether the Aymara-speaking people came from the south to fill the vacuum left by the Tiahuanaco peoples, who seem to have gradually become extinguished, or whether they are the remnants of that once great culture. They were, however, a formidable foe to the Incas. (See José Toribio Medina, *Bibliografía de las Lenguas Quechua y Aymará,* (Heye Foundation) Museum of the American Indian *Contributions,* Vol. VII, No. 7 [1930].)

go accompanied by a large retinue, and when they travel, they are borne in a litter and treated with the greatest respect by all their Indians. In the wastelands and secret places they have their *huacas,* or temples, where they pay homage to their gods, employing their vain superstitions, and those selected for this purpose converse with the devil in their shrines. The most extraordinary thing to be seen here in the Colla is, in my opinion, the graves [*chullpas*] of the dead.[2] When I went through, I stopped to set down what seemed to me the most noteworthy things about the Indians. And truly it amazes me to think how little store the living set by having large, fine houses, and the care with which they adorned the graves where they were to be buried, as though this constituted their entire happiness. Thus, all through the meadows and plains around the settlements were the tombs of these Indians, built like little four-sided towers, some of stone only, some of stone and earth, some wide, others narrow, according to their means or taste. Some of the roofs were covered with straw, others with large stone slabs, and it seems to me that the door of these tombs faced the rising sun.

274

When the natives of this Colla died, they were mourned with great lamentations for many days, the women carrying a staff in their hands and clasping one another, and all the relatives of the deceased brought whatever they could, llamas, corn, as well as other things; and before they buried the dead, they killed the llamas and laid the entrails in the square before their dwellings. During the days they mourned the dead before burying them, from the corn they owned or the relatives brought they made a great quantity of the wine they drink, and the more of this there was, the more they felt they were honoring the dead. After they had prepared their liquor and killed

[2] The *chullpas,* or towers of the dead, are found mostly (yet not wholly) in the back-lying hills of the Titicaca basin. These burial towers are either round or square, built of stone or adobe (often of both), and usually are scattered at random on or near hilltops. They were, as Cieza states, probably used for the burial of chieftains. The architecture of the *chullpas,* the engineering techniques of building with crescent-shaped stone, seems to be distinctly pre-Inca. In all probability they were erected before the Inca conquest of the Collas (1470), and it is not unlikely that the Inca masons learned advanced techniques in stone from the *chullpa*-builders rather than, as has been often assumed, the other way around. The origin of the word *chullpa* is unknown; it did not exist in the time of Cieza or he would have mentioned it; it means burial by means of a winding sheet or ichu grass, and extended thus to the stone burial towers; they, too, became *chullpas.* (See Marion H. Tschopik, *Some Notes on the Archaeology of the Department of Puno, Peru.*)

the llamas, they tell that they took the deceased to the fields where they had the grave. If it was a headman, the body was accompanied by most of the people of the village, and beside it they burned ten llamas, or twenty, or more or less, depending on who the deceased was. And they killed the women, children, and servants who were to be sent with him to serve him, in keeping with their superstitions. And all these, together with the llamas and certain household articles, were buried in the grave with his body, putting in also, as is their custom, several living persons. And after the dead person had received such burial, all those who had gone to do him honor returned to the house from which he had been taken, and there they ate the food that had been brought and drank the chicha that had been prepared, going out from time to time to the square built alongside the houses of the headmen, where they danced in a circle, as is their custom, wailing. And this lasted for several days, at the end of which they sent for the poorest Indians and gave them to eat and drink of what was left over. And if the deceased was a great lord, they say they did not bury him immediately upon dying, but kept him for several days, doing other foolish things which I do not set down. When this was done, they say that the women who had not been killed, and serving maids, went about the village in their hooded cloaks, some of them carrying the arms of the lord, others the ornament he wore on his head, and others his clothing. And finally bearing the stool on which he used to sit and other things, and moving to the sound of a drum played by a weeping Indian who walked ahead of them, they all uttered sad and dolorous words, and thus they went singing their dirges throughout the village, telling all the lord had done while he was alive, and other similar things. I recall that in the village of Nicasio,[3] when we were on our way to Charcas, one Diego de Uceda, a resident of the city of La Paz and I, we saw some women doing this I have described. And from the interpreters of the village we learned that they were saying what has been told in this chapter that they

275

[3] A village. An Aymara-speaking (Colla) center is still found in the same place, bearing the same name. It lies midway between Ayaviri and Juliaca on the modern highway, which lies more or less on top of the ancient road. It was held in fief by Francisco Maldonado until 1548. He had represented Gonzalo Pizarro at the court of Spain, petitioning for the cancellation of the hated "Ordinances" designed to end the holding of Indians by the conquistadors. He remained loyal to Gonzalo Pizarro and lost his head after the battle of Xaquixahuana in 1548.

do, and one of them who was there even said, "When these women finish mourning, they are going to get drunk, and some of them will kill themselves to go and bear the lord who has died company." In many other villages I have seen them mourn the dead for many days, and the women tie hempen ropes about their heads to show greater sorrow.

276

CHAPTER 93 (CI)

How these Indians observed their ceremonies and anniversary celebrations, and what their temples were once like.

As THESE PEOPLE set such importance by burying their dead as I have described in the preceding chapter, after the funeral the women and servants who were left cut off their hair and dressed themselves in their poorest clothes, with little attention to their person. And aside from this, to make their grief more apparent, they put hempen ropes about their heads, and spent a year in continual mourning if the deceased was a headman, kindling no fire in the house where he had died for several days. Misled by the devil like all the others, God so permitting, with his false arts he created in them the illusion that they saw certain of those who had died walking about their fields, adorned and dressed as they had been laid in the grave. And further to honor their dead, these Indians observed, and still do, anniversary celebrations, on which occasions they take certain plants and animals and kill them beside the grave, and burn the tallow of llamas. And when they have done this, they pour jugs of their liquor [chicha] into the grave, and with this they conclude this blind, vain superstition. As this nation of the Collas was so large, in olden times they had great temples and religious rites, venerating those who were their priests and talked with the devil. And they observed their feasts at the time of digging the potatoes, which is their principal food, killing of their animals for the necessary sacrifices.

These natives of the Colla, like all the others of the highlands, say that the creator of all things is called Tici-Viracocha, and they know that his throne is in the sky . . . they worship many gods. They employ a kind of ballad or chant in which they commemorate past events, without forgetting them, even though they have no writing. And among these natives of the Colla there are many of good reason who reveal it in the answers to the questions that are put to them. They reckon time and know certain of the movements of both the sun and the moon, which is how they keep track of the years, counting them by ten months. Thus I learned from them that the word for year is *huata,* and that for month and moon, *alespaquexe,* and for day, *auro.* When these people became vassals of the Inca, at his orders they built great temples, on the island of Titicaca, in Hatuncolla, and in other places. It is believed of them that they abhorred the abominable sin [i.e., sodomy], although it is said that certain of the rustics who guarded the llama-herds indulged in it secretly, and those whom they kept in the temples.

CHAPTER 94 (CII)

Of the antiquities of Pucará, and how they praise what Hatuncolla once was, and of the village called Azángaro, and other things here set forth.

CONCERNING THE Collas, I shall continue my travels on the highway, giving special mention to the villages to be found until reaching the city of La Paz [in Bolivia], which is situated in the valley of Chuquiabo, within the limits of this great region of the Collas.

Following the [Inca] highway, from Ayaviri one comes to Pucará, which means stronghold and is four leagues from Ayaviri. It is told by these Indians that in olden times there was a large population here in Pucará; now there is hardly a single Indian. I was there one day observing everything. Those living in the vicinity tell that Topa Inca during his reign [A.D. 1471–93] besieged these Indians for many days, and before he could subdue them, they fought so bravely that they killed many of his men. But as in the end they were defeated, the Inca, to commemorate his victory, ordered great stone statues made. If this was the case, I know it only by what they tell. What I saw at

THE INCAS

Pucará were great buildings in ruin and decay[1] and many statues of stone in the shape of human figures and other noteworthy things. From Pucará to Hatuncolla is a distance of fifteen leagues; halfway between them there are various villages such as Nicasio, Juliaca, and others. In olden times Hatuncolla was the most important place in the Colla, and the natives state that before the Incas conquered it, they were ruled by Zapana and certain of his descendants, who were so powerful that they took much booty in battle, which they distributed among their neighbors. Afterwards the Incas beautified this settlement with new buildings and many storehouses, where they ordered the tribute brought and stored, and a temple to the sun with a number of vestals and priests to serve it, and many *mitimaes* and troops to guard the province and insure that no tyrant would rise against him who was held to be the sovereign ruler. So it can be safely stated that Hatuncolla was a great thing, as its name indicates, for *hatun* means "great" in our language. Now all has disappeared, and most of the natives are gone, having been destroyed by war.

From Ayaviri, which we have left behind, another road emerges, called Oma-suyu, which runs along the other side of the great lake I shall describe later, and closer to the Andes Mountains. It was the route to the great settlements of Oruro and Asillo and Azángaro, and others not without importance. They were formerly considered very rich in both llamas and crops. When the Incas ruled this kingdom, in all these settlements they had many herds of their alpacas and llamas. In the vicinity of these settlements, in the forests of the sierra, is the famous, rich river of Carabaya,[2] from which in past years over 1,700,000 gold pesos of highest carat was washed; and much gold is

278

[1] Pucará has little or no remains of these buildings. The village squats below an almost perpendicular Gibraltar-like rock of reddish sandstone, which thrusts upwards to a height of over one thousand feet. (See Alfred Kidder II, "Some Early Sites in the Northern Lake Titicaca Basin," Peabody Museum *Papers*, Vol. XXVII, No. 1 [1943].)

[2] The rich river of the Carabaya was explored by the von Hagen expedition (1952–54), and its findings confirm what Cieza has here written about it. Beyond the town of Asillo, the Inca road ran on both sides of the Carabaya River, which flowed eastward toward the Amazon. The Inca road went through Macusani, then over passes higher than 15,000 feet. Remains of step roads are seen at many places. Seemingly uninhabitable slopes were terraced, and in the valleys where they washed placer gold from the Carabaya, remains of Inca villages were found. The Count of Chinchón (whose name was given to the genus *Chinchona*, quinine) was informed, "Carabaya, where they get out the richest gold in Peru." (See von Hagen, *Highway of the Sun*, 56–80; and Sir Clements Markham, *Travels in Peru and India* [London, 1862], chap. XII.)

still to be found in the river, but it is hard to take out and costs the lives of the Indians who pan it, for the spot is considered unhealthy. But the wealth of the river is great.

CHAPTER 95 (CIII)

Of the great lake in this vicinity of the Colla, how deep it is, and of the temple of Titicaca.

As THIS LAND of the Colla is so large (as I mentioned in the preceding chapters), there are, in addition to the settled areas, many deserts and snow-covered sierras, and fields thickly grown to grass which affords pasture for the herds to be seen everywhere. And in the middle of the province there is a lake [Titicaca], the largest and widest that has been seen in most of these Indies, and beside it are the other villages of the Colla. On large islands found in this lake they plant their crops and guard their most precious possessions, considering them to be safer than in the villages beside the roads.

As I pointed out, it is so cold in this province that not only are there no fruit orchards, but not even corn can be planted, for it does not bear for the same reason. In the rushes of this lake there are many birds of different kinds, and large ducks and other fowl, and two or three kinds of flavorful fish are caught there, though most of them are considered inedible. This lake is so large that it measures about eighty leagues in circumference,[1] and so deep that Captain Juan Ladrillero told me that when he sailed it in his brigantines, the soundings in some places were seventy and eighty fathoms, and more, and in places less. In this and in the waves that arise when the wind blows it would seem to be an arm of the sea. What I mean to say is that all this water is locked in that lake, and nobody knows where its source is, for even though many rivers and brooks empty into it, it seems to me that they alone would not account for its

---

[1] Padre Juan de Acosta, writing about 1590: "The most famous is that of Titicaca, which is in Peru in the province of the Colla. . . . containes neere fourscore leagues in compasse, into the which, there runnes ten or twelve great rivers. . . . The water is not altogether sower or salt, as that of the sea, but it is so thicke, as it cannote be drunke. . . . On the one and the other banke of this Lake, are the best habitations of Peru." (*The Naturall and Morall Historie of the East and West Indies*.)

volume, especially as the outlet from this lake drains into another smaller one known as Aulagas.[2] It might be that at the time of the Flood it was left with this water that we see, for, in my opinion, if it came from the sea, the water would be salt and not sweet, and moreover it is sixty leagues from the sea. And all this water drains into a deep river considered large for this region, called the Desaguadero, and empties into the other lake I have mentioned, the Aulagas. Another thing to be noted is that we see how the water of one lake enters the other, but not how it flows out, even though the whole lake of Aulagas has been carefully examined. In this connection I have heard from the Spaniards and the Indians that in certain of the valleys contiguous to the Southern Sea underground springs are frequently found which flow into the sea. And they are of the belief that it might be the water of these lakes, draining in different directions, making its way through the ground until reaching this common outlet, which is the sea.

280

The name of this great lake of the Colla is Titicaca [or Chucuito] from the temple that was built in the center of the lake. About this the natives had an idea that was pure superstition, and this is that they say their forebears asserted for a fact, like the other nonsense they tell, that for many days they were without light, and when they were all in darkness and gloom, there arose from this island of Titicaca the sun in all its splendor, for which reason they hold the island to be a hallowed spot, and the Incas built there the temple I have mentioned,[3] which was one of the most venerated, in honor of their sun, bringing to it vestals and priests and great treasure. Although the

[2] This is the first published description of Lake Titicaca. The two Spaniards (Diego de Agüero and Pedro Martínez de Moguer) first to see it in 1533 made a verbal report of its size and the number of Indian settlements about it. It is the largest lake "in the Indies," approximately eighty miles in length and forty in width. Geographically, Lake Titicaca is a basin formed by two ranges, east and west, of the cordilleras. It lies in the high (12,500 feet) *altiplano,* alternating between arid pampas and rich earth. Numerous rivers empty into Titicaca; it has only one outlet, the Desaguadero River, which flows out of the southwest corner and meanders into Bolivia to form another lake, Poopó (then Aulaga). (See Harry Tschopik, Jr., "The Aymará" *Handbook,* II, 501ff.)

[3] The temple of the sun is on Titicaca Island, the largest of several islands at the southern part of the lake. The ruins are still in a fair state of preservation. The Incas, as related in Chapter 5, traced their origin to this island; here Manco Capac, the first Inca, received his cultural mission from the sun god. The ruins are in the late Inca style (A.D. 1400–1500), and the structures doubtlessly were built at this time to give substance to the Inca origin legend. (See Squier, *Peru,* chap. XVII.)

Spaniards on different occasions have removed much of this, it is believed that most of it has not been discovered. And if these Indians were without light, as they say, it might have been caused by an eclipse of the sun.

CHAPTER 96 (CIV)

Continuing by this route, the settlements to be found until reaching Tiahuanacu.

To RETURN to where I left the road I am following in this narration, which was at Hatuncolla, from there one passes through Paucar-colla and other villages of this nation of the Collas until reaching Chucuito, which is the main and most complete settlement to be found in most of this great kingdom,[1] which was and is the capital of the Indians of His Majesty in their region. In olden days the Incas, too, considered Chucuito important, and it is one of the oldest of all I have described, according to the Indians' own account. Cari was the lord of this town and, for an Indian, he was a wise man. There are great lodgings there, and before they were dominated by the Incas, the lords of this settlement were very powerful. Two were held to be the most important, and their names were Cari and Humalla. It is now, as I have said, the capital of His Majesty's Indians, whose towns are Juli, Chilane, Acos, Pomata, and Zepita,[2] and in them there are chieftains who command many Indians. When I went through this region,

[1] Chucuito butts on a ridge which slopes into the lake (twenty kilometers south of Puno). It was the administrative center of the Lupaca-Aymara-speaking tribe, who were for some centuries at war with the Collas (the name which the Incas gave to the gigantic southern quarter of their world, Colla-suyo), whose capital was Hatuncolla. When the warriors under Inca Viracocha in 1430 began their conquest of the region, they allied themselves with the Lupacas. After the Incas had finally crushed all opposition in 1470–90, Inca *mitimaes* (colonists) were brought in and placed principally at Chucuito, which became the principal Inca administrative center in this part of the Colla; the remains of these structures, Ica-uyu and Kurin-uyu, are still to be seen.

[2] The most notable was Juli, with its four churches, reflecting the school of *mestizo* art; the earliest, San Juan, dating back to before 1590. A printing press was in operation at Juli in this century. In 1612, "Impressa en la Casa de la Compañía de Jesús del pueblo JULI," there was issued Bertonio's *Vocabulario de la Lengua Aymara. . . ."* The book was printed by a Christianized Indian named Francisco del Cato. (See José Toribio Medina, *Bibliografía de las Lenguas Quechua y Aymará;* and Harold E. Wethey, *Colonial Architecture and Sculpture in Peru* [Cambridge, Mass., 1949].)

the mayor was Ximon Pinto and the governor Don Gaspar, an Indian, very wise and of goodly reason. They are rich in llama herds, and in the islands and other places they have *mitimaes* to plant their coca and corn. In the aforementioned villages there are now well-built churches, most of them founded by Father Tomás de San Martín, a provincial of the Dominicans, and the children, and others who wish to, gather to hear the doctrine preached by friars and priests, and most of the headmen have become Christians. Near Zepita runs the Desaguadero, where, in the time of the Incas, there used to be guards to collect toll from those who crossed the bridge, which was made of sheaves of oats and constructed in such a way that men, horses, and all else could pass over it.[3]

Beyond these villages lies Huaqui, where there were lodgings of the Incas.

CHAPTER 97 (CV)

Of the town of Tiahuanacu and the large ancient buildings to be seen there.

TIAHUANACU IS not a very large town,[1] but it is famous for its great buildings which, without question, are a remarkable thing to behold.

[3] This was the famous pontoon bridge which crossed the 100-foot-wide river that drained Titicaca Lake. It was constructed on balsa-reed boat pontoons; the rush road was laid on top. It was fastened by ropes to two pillars on either side of the river. Since the balsas became water-logged, they were renewed every two years, but the bridge as bridge is pre-Inca. It endured up until 1867, when it was photographed by the American archaeologist E. G. Squier. In conquest times, one chronicler called it Chachamarca ("bridge place"), but in the "Regulations for Tambos" (1543), in which an itinerary was made of the road and the fiefs held by the conquistadors, it is called "Machaca"; it was owned by Francisco Pizarro.

[1] This is the first description of the archaeological site of Tiahuanacu. It lies on the Bolivian side of the Titicaca basin, twelve miles south of the lake. The land is bleak, windswept, bare, and frigid. Tiahuanacu is the most elaborate and purest manifestation of this culture yet found. The largest structure is a stepped pyramid, which was once stone faced. There is another ruin, Calasa-saya, measuring 445 by 225 feet (composed of stone uprights), the famous monolithic sun gate, and immense stone stelae. This site is believed to have been the origin of the Tiahuanacu style—highly stylized feline designs, abstract tiger eyes, and step designs, which are found widely scattered throughout the early coastal and highland cultures. Tiahuanacu was probably a religious center. It has been tentatively placed in Period IV (A.D. 1000–1300). (See Wendell Bennett, *Ancient Arts of the Andes*.)

Near the main dwellings is a man-made hill, built on great stone foundations. Beyond this hill there are two stone idols of human size and shape, with the features beautifully carved, so much so that they seem the work of great artists or masters. They are so large that they seem small giants, and they are wearing long robes, different from the attire of the natives of these provinces. They seem to have an ornament on their heads. Close by these stone statues there is another building, whose antiquity and this people's lack of writing is the reason there is no knowledge of who the people that built these great foundations and strongholds were, or how much time has gone by since then, for at present all one sees is a finely built wall which must have been constructed many ages ago. Some of the stones are very worn and wasted, and there are others so large that one wonders how human hands could have brought them to where they now stand. Many of these stones are carved in different ways, and some of them are in the form of human bodies, and these must have been their idols. Along the wall there are many underground hollows and cavities. In another spot farther to the west there are other still greater antiquities, for there are many large gates with jambs, thresholds, and door all of a single stone. What struck me most when I was observing and setting down these things was that from these huge gateways other still larger stones project on which they were set, some of which were as much as thirty feet wide, fifteen or more long, and six thick, and this and the door, jamb, and threshold were one single stone, which was a tremendous thing. When one considers the work, I cannot understand or fathom what kind of instruments or tools were used to work them, for it is evident that before these huge stones were dressed and brought to perfection, they must have been much larger to have been left as we see them. One can see that these buildings were never completed, for all there is of them are these gateways and other stones of incredible size, some of them which I saw, cut and prepared to go into the building. A great stone idol, which they probably worshiped, stands a short distance away in a small recess. It is even said that beside this idol a quantity of gold was found, and around this shrine there were a number of other stones, large and small, dressed and carved like those already mentioned.

There are other things to tell of Tiahuanacu which I omit to save time. In conclusion, I would say that I consider this the oldest antiquity in all Peru. It is believed that before the Incas reigned, long before, certain of these buildings existed, and I have heard Indians say that the Incas built their great edifices of Cuzco along the lines of the wall to be seen in this place. They even go further and say that the first Incas talked of setting up their court and capital here in Tiahuanacu. Another strange thing is that in much of this region neither rocks, quarries, nor stones are to be seen from which they could have brought the many we see, and no small number of people must have been needed to transport them. I asked the natives, in the presence of Juan Varagas (who holds an encomienda over them) if these buildings had been built in the time of the Incas, and they laughed at the question, repeating what I have said, that they were built before they reigned, but that they could not state or affirm who built them. However, they had heard from their forefathers that all that are there appeared overnight. Because of this, and because they also say that bearded men were seen on the island of Titicaca and that these people constructed the building of Viñaque, I say that it might have been that before the Incas ruled, there were people of parts in these kingdoms, come from no one knows where, who did these things, and who, being few and the natives many, perished in the wars. As these things are so obscured, we can give thanks that writing was invented, which perpetuates memory for many centuries and spreads the fame of things that have taken place throughout the universe, and we need not ignore what we want to know if we have the written record. As in the New World of the Indies no writing has been discovered, we must guess at many things.[2]

Some distance from these buildings are the lodgings of the Incas and the house where Manco Inca II, son of Huayna Capac, was born, and near them are two tombs of the native lords of this town, as tall as [they are] broad, square-cornered towers, with their doorways to the rising sun.

[2] Cieza doubtlessly means no writing was found in Peru. He knew from others that the Aztecs, Mayas, and other advanced Mexican cultures had a form of glyphic writing.

CHAPTER 98 (CVI)

Of the founding of the city known as Nuestra Señora de la Paz, who was its founder, and the road between it and the city of Plata.

AFTER TIAHUANACU, straight ahead, one comes to Viacha, seven leagues from Tiahuanacu. On the left are the towns of Cacayavire, Caquingora, Mallama, and others of the same sort. There seems to me no point in naming them one by one. Between them lies a plain beside another village called Huarina, which is where a battle took place between Diego Centeno and Gonzalo Pizarro.[1] To reach the city of La Paz, one turns off the Inca highway and enters the village of Laxa. A day's journey beyond it is the city, situated in the fold of a small valley between the mountains. The city was founded at the most suitable and level spot because of the abundance of water and wood to be found in this little valley, as well as because it is more temperate than the plains and meadows of the Colla. . . . La Paz will remain on the site where it was founded in the valley of Chuquiabo, where in former years a great amount of gold was mined from the rich lodes there. The Incas held this Chuquiabo in high esteem. Near it is the town of Oyune, where it is said that on the peak of a high snow-capped mountain there is a great treasure hidden in a temple the ancient people had, which cannot be found nor is it known where it was. This city of . . . La Paz was founded and settled by Captain Alonso de Mendoza in the name of His Majesty, the Emperor, when Pedro de la Gasca was president of this kingdom [of Peru] in . . . 1549.[2]

[1] Huarina, not far from Tiahuanacu, was the site of a battle—October, 1547—about which Cieza wrote in the lost manuscript, "The Wars of Huarina." Diego de Centeno, an enemy of Gonzalo Pizarro and a "King's man," mustered 1,000 men; Pizarro, only 400. La Gasca, who was sent by the King to put down the revolt of Pizarro, waited in Jauja for the news of the battle, which was finally conveyed in a letter dated December 27 from Lima by the defeated Diego de Centeno; 350 of his men had been killed in the space of an hour.

[2] The city of La Paz, founded on the site of the ancient site of Chuquiabo, was first called La Ciudad de Nuestra Señora de la Paz (now, shortened into La Paz, the capital of Bolivia) to mark the defeat of Gonzalo Pizarro. Alonso de Mendoza, a native of Garrovilla, Badajoz, and a member of Hernando Pizarro's party, fought in the battles of Las Salinas (1538) and Chupas (1542). He later joined Pedro de la Gasca, the King's envoy, and was at the final rout of the Pizarro forces at Xaquixahuana. He founded

To proceed in orderly fashion, I shall return from here to the [Inca] highway I left. Thus, from Viacha one comes to Hayo-Hayo, where there were great lodgings of the Incas. Beyond Hayo-Hayo is Siquisica, which is the limit of the province of the Collas, although there are other settlements to either side of these. From this village of Siquisica the route leads to the village of Caracollo, eleven leagues away, which is situated on meadowlands near the large province of Paria, which was highly prized by the Incas. The natives of the province of Paria go dressed like all the rest, and as head covering they wear a kind of small woolen cap. These rulers were well served by their Indians, and there were storehouses and royal dwellings for the Incas, and a temple to the sun. Now one sees many tall tombs in which they laid their dead. The villages of Indians subject to Paria, which are Caponota and many others, some are on the lake and some in other parts of the region. Beyond Paria lie the settlements of Pocoata, Macha, Caracara, Moromora, and near the Andes there are other provinces and great chieftains.

286

CHAPTER 99 (CVII)

Of the founding of the city of La Plata [in Bolivia], which is situated in the province of the Charcas.

THE NOBLE and loyal city of [La] Plata, a settlement of Spaniards in Charcas, situated at Chuquisaca,[1] is very famous in the kingdoms of Peru and in many parts of the world because of the great treasure that has gone from it to Spain in recent years. This city is in . . . a land of good climate, very suitable for the raising of fruit trees and the planting of wheat and barley, grapes, and other things.

Land brings very high prices at present because of the wealth that has been discovered in the mines of Potosí.[2] There are broad fields

the city of La Paz in 1549, and has been characterized as "one of the most distinguished warriors in Peru with whom neither Centeno nor Francisco de Carvajal could compare."

[1] La Plata, founded on the site of the Inca city of Chuquisaca, is today Sucre (after General José de Sucre, 1795–1830). It is the de jure capital of Bolivia and lies on the eastern slope of the cordilleras at 8,500 feet altitude.

[2] Potosí mines, of which Cieza published the first illustrations (Seville, 1553), were established in 1545 at the base of the richest ore mountains then known; even though

around it, and several rivers of good water run close by, and on the ranches of the Spaniards many cattle, mares, and goats are raised. Some of the residents of this city are among the richest and most prosperous of the Indies. In the years 1548 and 1549 there were *repartimientos,* like that of General Pedro de Hinojosa,[3] which yielded an income of one hundred thousand castellanos, and others eighty thousand, and some more. So the wealth in those times was very great. This city of Plata was founded and settled by Captain Peranzúres,[4]

at 13,780 feet altitude, they were the most fabulous source of silver in the world. The area had, in 1600, the greatest population in America, 160,000; then it declined rapidly after 1626, when its mines were flooded. The Jesuit, José de Acosta (writing in 1590), tells of Potosí's discovery: ". . . an Indian called Guanca, of the nation (tribe) of Chumbivilca, going one day to hunt for venison . . . beganne to runne uppe against the rocke, which at that time was covered . . . with certaine trees, they call Quinoa . . . he was forced to lay holde upon a branch, which issued from a veine of a silvermine . . . perceiving the hole or roote there of mettall the which hee knew to be very good, by the experience hee had of the mines of Pocro. He carried it to Pocro to trie by the Guayras [primitive blasting ovens heated by charcoal and fanned by the high east winds] and having thereby found the great riches and his happy fortune, he secretly digged and drew mettall out of this veine." Eventually he was discovered by a Spaniard named Villaroel, and by some miracle of justice, the Spaniard made the silver claim with the Indian. "So as the first discovery of the inregistering of the mines of Potozi was the 21. of April, in the yeare of our Lord one thousand five hundred and fortie five . . . by the saide Villaroel a Spaniard and Guanca an Indian." (*The Naturall and Morall Historie of the Indies,* Book 4, chap. 6.)

[3] Hinojosa was born in Trujillo, Spain, and came to Peru with Hernando Pizarro in 1534 after he had delivered Atahualpa's ransom to the King of Spain. He was in command of the Gonzalo Pizarro armada at Panama, designed to keep any of the "King's men" from moving in the Pacific, but the wily Pedro de la Gasca compelled him to give over the entire fleet. He was rewarded for his perfidy with a generalship of the King's forces; thus he participated in the final defeat of his liege and friend Gonzalo Pizarro in 1548.

[4] Peranzúres, a foreshortening of Pedro Anzures, an old conquistador "well versed in the art of war, a native of Sahagún," writes Cieza in his *War of Salinas,* was "respected, liked, and very liberal." It is he who sailed to Spain to explain the differences between Almagro and Pizarro—the partners in conquest—and to beg a royal ruling on the matter of their respective kingdoms; he left at the time of the uprising of Manco II in 1536 and "brought the news to the Emperor." The royal decrees brought back from Spain, dated January, 1537, were in vain; civil war broke out between Almagro and Pizarro, and Pedro Anzures, raised to a captaincy, fought at the battle of Salinas, where he helped to defeat Almagro. In September, 1538, he set off with what was then a huge army, of Spaniards and Indians, equipped himself at Ayaviri, took the Inca gold road into the Carabaya region, the rugged *montaña* east of the Titicaca basin, and plunging through mountain, jungle, and morass, moved up what was then the Tacaná River (probably the Beni in Bolivia). The forest Indians carried the general term of "Chunchos," which included many Arawakan-speaking tribes who had only vaguely felt the influence of the Incas. Garrisons, trading stations, and rudimentary roads seem to have been all that was found of the Inca civilization among them. (See Julian H. Steward, "Tribes of the Montaña," *Handbook,* III, 507ff.)

It was one of the horrendous epics in early Amazon exploration and is on a parallel

in the name of His Majesty, our emperor and king, at the time the Adelantado Don Francisco Pizarro was governor and captain-general of Peru, in the year 1538. Aside from the towns already mentioned, this city has under its jurisdiction Totora, Tapacari, Sipisipi, Cochabamba; the Caranquis, Quillancas, Chaiantas, Chaquis, and the Chichas, and many others, all very rich, and some, like the valley of Cochabamba, good for growing wheat and corn and raising cattle. Beyond this city lies the province of Tucuma [Tucumán, in Argentina], and the regions where Captain Felipe Gutiérrez and Diego de Rojas and Nicolás de Heredia went to explore, and where they discovered the Plata [River], and advanced farther to the south, where is the fortress built by Sebastian Cabot.[5] These regions were not wholly explored, for feeling ran so high among the men that they returned to Peru. Meeting Lope de Mendoza, Diego Centeno's master of troop, who was fleeing the fury of Carvajal, Gonzalo Pizarro's captain, they joined up with him. But divisions having arisen among them, they were defeated in a town called Cocona, by this same Carvajal who, with the speed that characterized him, took Nicolás de Heredia and Lope de Mendoza prisoner, and killed them and others. . . .

Beyond this is the province of Chile, of which Pedro de Valdivia[6] is governor, and other lands bordering on the strait known as that

---

with Pizarro's attempt to find "El Dorado." "The expedition caused the destruction of many natives; 7,000 of them perished . . . and they were reduced to such straits that they had to eat each other. . . . They also took the flower of the beautiful girls, few of whom escaped death in the forests. By the time they returned to Ayaviri, months later, 143 Spaniards had died of hunger or sickness, 4,000 Indians, men and women, 220 horses costing 600 pesos each [equivalent today of 5,000] had either died or had been eaten." (See Pedro de Cieza de León, *The War of Salinas*, Chapters LXXVI, LXXVII, LXXVIII, and appendix.)

[5] Sebastian Cabot, son of the English explorer John Cabot (1461–98), sailed in the service of Spain. Famous for his search for the Northwest Passage in 1508, he later sailed in 1526 from Spain under secret orders from Charles V to explore the Plate River; he spent many years in this and its tributary, the Paraná. (See H. Harrisse, *John Cabot, Discoverer of North America, and Sebastian, His Son* [1896].)

[6] Pedro de Valdivia, the conquistador of Chile. Born at Villanueva in Badajoz, he was a soldier in the Italian wars at an early age, then went to the Americas, arriving in Peru at the time of Manco II's uprising in 1536. He began his expedition to Chile in 1539 and founded the city of Santiago in 1541. He returned to Peru to aid Pedro de la Gasca's efforts to put down the revolt of Gonzalo Pizarro and organized the campaign of Xaquixahuana, close on to Cuzco, when defeat finally came to the last of the Pizarros. His own descriptions of the conquest of Chile, still unpublished in its entirety is one of the stirring pages of history. ("The La Gasca Documents, from Panama to Peru, a catalogue of the documents now at the Henry E. Huntington Library" [London, Maggs Bros. Catalog, 1925], 64.)

of Magallanes. Inasmuch as the affairs of Chile are important, and would call for special attention, what I have done is to set down what I have seen from Urabá [Colombia] to Potosí [Bolivia], which is close by this city, a distance (calculating it from the boundaries of Urabá to those of the city of [La] Plata) which I estimate at a good 1,200 leagues, as I have said. Therefore I shall not proceed further in this first part except to say of the Indians under the jurisdiction of the city of [La] Plata [Chuquisaca] that their customs and those of the others are all the same. When they were conquered by the Incas they built their cities in orderly manner, and they all go clothed, and their women, and worship the sun and other things, and had temples where they performed their sacrifices. . . .

PART III

CHAPTER 100 (LIII)

Of the founding of the city of Guayaquil[1] [and
Tumbes] and the death the natives inflicted on
certain captains of Huayna Capac.

I HAVE TOLD how in the days of Topa Inca [c. 1470], after he had
conquered and subdued the nations of the kingdom of Quito, show-

[1] Guayaquil, the present and principal port of Ecuador, lies on the upper reaches
of the Guayas River. At the time of the Inca conquest of what is now Ecuador and
during the fifteenth century, Guayaquil was the center of the Huancavilcas, whose
tribal territory lay along the Guayas and fronted the isle of Puná, and with whom
the Incas carried on perpetual wars. Cieza is the only important source of information
about the Ecuadorian coastal tribes: "The Indians and their women wear a kind of
apron to cover their privities. On their head they wear a kind of crown of small beads
which they call *chaquira* and some use them of silver and others of jaguar or panther
skin. The women's dress is a blanket from the waist down and another covering them
to the shoulders, and they wear their hair long. In some of these villages the caciques
stud or fill their teeth with gold. . . . when the chieftains died, they built a round
tomb with a vaulted roof, the entrance facing the sun, and buried them together with
living women in their arms and other things. . . ."
In a chapter (XLIX) entitled "Of the slight importance these Indians attach to the
virginity of their wives, and how they were guilty of the abominable sin of sodomy,"
Cieza de León writes ". . . and I have even heard some of them tell that before marriage the bride was deflowered and they sated their lusts with her." Of sodomy: "They
were religiously inclined [to it] and given to certain other vices" (LIV, 187). "In
spite of the fact that there were women in abundance and some of them beautiful,
most of them were given (so I have been assured) to the abominable vice of sodomy,
on which they greatly pride themselves."
Leadership in the Huancavilca tribe passed from father to son," . . . and if there
was none, passed to the son of the sister." It was the custom to pull out their teeth
as sacrifice "to honor their cursed gods" (Chapter LIII).
About 1450 the Incas began the conquest of Ecuador; their armies moved first
across the highlands conquering Quito; on the coast the Punás and the Huancavilcas
resisted the conquest for some time. Although the Inca conquest extended as far north
as Esmeraldas (close to the border of present-day Colombia), they regarded the natives
as not worth the problems of civilization.
The interesting phase of Cieza's narrative history of Inca penetration concerns the
roads built there; they are mentioned by no other chronicler. "There is no direct route
from Tomebamba to the coast except by way of the city of San Miguel de Piura, the
first settlement founded by the Spaniards in Peru." But farther on in the same chapter
he states that not very far from the city of Tomebamba (near Cuenca in Ecuador and
where Huayna Capac was believed to have been born) there is a province called
Chumbo. "The people were clothed typically in the highland dress and in its vicinity
there are important lodgings; fourteen leagues [approximately fifty miles] from this
province of Chumbo, all over rough and sometimes difficult roads, one reaches a

ing himself an excellent captain and winning great victories and trophies and destroying the strongholds of the natives so that nowhere should there be arms or soldiers except those stationed at his orders in the places he chose, he sent certain of his captains to explore the coast and the people settled there, and to endeavor with all kindness and friendship to win them to his service.

294

For the moment no steps were taken to punish as they deserved those who, betraying the peace, had killed those who trusted in their friendship, without suspecting the treachery of which they were to be the victims, for the Inca was in Cuzco, and his governors and representatives were busy looking after the territory which each of them governed. Time passed; Huayna Capac [1493] came to the throne and proved to be as courageous and brave as his father, and even more prudent and ambitious. Swiftly he set out from Cuzco accompanied by the principal men of the two most famous families of Cuzco . . . and after visiting the great temple of Pachacamac and the garrisons that had been established and were quartered in the provinces of Jauja and Cajamarca and other places among the inhabitants of the highlands as well as those of the fertile valleys of the plains, he came to the coast. At the port of Tumbes a fort had been built at his orders (even though certain Indians say this building was older). As the inhabitants of the island of Puná and the natives of Tumbes were at odds, it was easy for the Inca's captains to build this fortress . . . . As they were completing it, Huayna Capac arrived, who ordered a temple of the sun built near the fortress of Tumbes, and over two hundred virgins installed, the most beautiful to be found in the region, daughters of the headmen of the villages. And in this fortress (which before it fell into ruins was a fine sight), Huayna Capac appointed his captain or representative, with a large

river [the Alausi] which arises in the sierras about Cañar, and flows into the Yaguachi River, which in its turn connects with the Guayas five leagues above Guayaquil, a river where there are always Indians of the vicinity (Huancavilcas) who have balsawood rafts on which they take travelers over the river to a pongo called the 'Pass of Huayna Capac.' This lies, so they say, twelve leagues from the island of Puná." Later Huayna Capac, after a successful war upon Puná, took prisoners, ". . . and he ordered a highway built along the Guayaquil [Guayas] River, which is very large, a highway which, to judge by certain sections of it that remain, was a magnificent thing. But it was not finished nor done wholly as he wished. It is known as the Pass of Huayna Capac" (Chapter LIII). The Indian capital of the Huancavilcas became Santiago de Guayaquil in 1537 after it was founded for the third and last time by Captain Francisco de Orellana.

number of *mitimaes* and great deposits of valuable goods, and the food needed for those residing there and the soldiers who were passing through. And they even tell that they brought him a very fierce panther and jaguar, and he ordered that they be carefully guarded. These must have been the beasts to which they threw Captain Pedro de Candia[2] at the time Captain Francisco Pizarro and his thirteen companions (who were the discoverers of Peru) reached this land. And in this fortress of Tumbes there were a number of silversmiths who made vessels of gold and silver and all manner of jewels for the service and decoration of the temple, which they held sacrosanct, as well as for the use of the Inca himself, and who applied the wainscoting of silver to the walls of the temples and palaces. The women who were dedicated to the service of the temple did nothing but spin and weave the finest garments of wool, at which they were very skillful.

When Huayna Capac had made himself master of the province of Huancavilcas, and that of Tumbes and the surrounding regions, he sent word to Tumbala, the chieftain of Puná,[3] to come and do him homage, and after he had obeyed him, to pay him tribute of the

[2] Pedro de Candia, "the Greek," was born at Candia on the isle of Crete. He was one of the original "thirteen men of the Isle of Gallo," those who stood by Francisco Pizarro on the small island off of Tumaco (Colombia) waiting for succor and other ships so as to continue the search for the "Kingdom of Gold." In 1527, Pizarro's small galleon being anchored offshore at Tumbes, Pedro de Candia—an enormous, good-natured albeit dim-witted man—climbed into full armour, was rowed, then walked out of the water, carrying an arquebus. The Indians of Tumbes were utterly astonished at the apparition and loosed a jaguar and a puma on him. They were ineffectual; with good grace he shattered a board with his blunderbuss. He made a tour of the city, saw the temples and riches, and made the original report on Tumbes (now lost). He was the only white man to see it before it was destroyed in the war of contention between Atahualpa and Huascar. Pedro de Candia participated in the capture of Atahualpa, drew as his share of the ransom 407 marcos of silver (990 pesos of silver), and was involved in all of the civil wars. He shifted to the side of Almagro the Lad, and was killed by him at the battle of Chupas (1542) when treachery was suspected. His son, as enormous as his father, went to the School of Nobles in Cuzco with Garcilaso de la Vega, the "Inca" historian.

[3] Puná, an island which lies in the Guayas River estuary (2° 30′ south latitude) in the Gulf of Jambelim is low lying and tropical. Culturally and linguistically it was related to Huancavilcas. Fish, maize, and yuca were the staples of its inhabitants; they dressed as did the other coastal Indians. There were seven principal settlements on Puná, and evidence from some recent archaeological investigation suggests they were very advanced in building with stone. They had one principal cacique and were polygamous. They were known, feared, and respected as traders and pirates. War and commerce had so enriched Puná that all chroniclers were impressed with their prosperity. The friar Vicente de Valverde, who gave the signal for the seizure of Atahualpa Inca at Cajamarca, was captured and eaten by the Punás.

products of the island. When the chieftain of the island of Puná received the Inca's message, he was greatly troubled; for being chieftain and having received this honor from his forebears, he considered it a great misfortune to lose his liberty, a gift much prized by all the nations of the world, and accept a stranger as the single and universal master of his island, whom he knew he would not only have to serve with all his vassals, but allow to build strongholds and buildings there, and maintain and supply them at his expense, and even give into his service his daughters and most beautiful women, which was what he most regretted. But finally, having discussed with his headmen the feebleness of their power to resist that of the Inca, he decided that the safe thing to do would be to pledge their friendship even though with false intention. Whereupon Tumbala sent messengers to Huayna Capac with gifts and great promises, urging him to come to the island of Puná to take his pleasure there for a few days.[4] Having satisfied Huayna Capac with the humility

[4] If by pleasure Cieza de León was suggesting dalliance with the women in the harems of Tumbala, chieftain of Puná, it brings up the matter of the American origin of syphilis, a social disease which plagued the earlier conquistadors, then all the world. Cieza de León tells in Chapter LIV, "Of the islands of Puná and La Plata and the admirable root called sarsaparilla which is so salubrious for all ailments":

"The island of Puná, which lies near the port of Tumbes, is a little less than ten leagues in circumference. In olden times it was held in high esteem because its inhabitants, in addition to being great traders and having everything on their island needed for human sustenance, which in itself made them rich, were considered by their neighbors to be brave. In bygone epochs they carried on great wars and conflicts with the natives of Tumbes and other regions. And for trifling reasons they killed one another, stealing and robbing each other's wives and children. The great Topa Inca sent his ambassadors to this island asking the natives to be his friends and allies, and they, because of his fame and the great things they had heard of him, received his embassy, but did not ally themselves with him nor were they wholly subdued until the reign of Huayna Capac, although there are those who say they were brought under the rule of the Incas by the [Topa] Inca and that they revolted. . . .

"This island has great forests and woods and abounds in fruit. It produces quantities of corn, yuca, and other palatable roots, and there are many varieties of birds, parrots, macaws, wildcats, monkeys and foxes, panthers and snakes, and other animals. When a chieftain dies, he is mourned by his people, men and women, and buried with great ceremony, and his most prized possessions are put in the grave with him, and his arms, and some of his most beautiful wives, who, as is the custom in the greater part of these Indies, are placed alive in the grave to keep their husband company. They weep for many days, and the women left in his household cut off their hair, and even those who are closely related to him, and they go about with sad visages and perform rites in his honor. They were religiously inclined and given to certain vices. . . .

"Their temples were in dark, removed places, and the walls were adorned with fearsome paintings. Before the altar where the sacrifices were performed, they killed certain animals and birds, and, it is said, even Indian slaves or prisoners from other regions taken in war, and offered their blood to the cursed devil. . . .

with which they offered themselves for his service, Tumbala, with the headmen of the island, made sacrifices to their gods, asking the soothsayers to tell them what they must do not to come under the yoke of him whose ambition it was to be the ruler of all. It is told that they sent their messengers to many parts of Terra Firma to feel out the natives and to endeavor to persuade them to revolt against Huayna Capac, and by rising and taking up arms, to throw off the authority and rule of the Inca. This was done so secretly that it was known to few aside from the conspirators. While these conversations were being held, Huayna Capac came to the island of Puná, where he was fittingly received and lodged in the royal dwellings that had been swiftly ordered and prepared for him, where the *Orejones* met with the islanders, all making a show of frank, sincere friendship.

"There is a plant which grows abundantly on this island and around the city of Guayaquil called sarsaparilla, which is like a bush, whose shoots and branches are covered with a small leaf. The root of this plant is good for a number of ailments, especially for the pain which buboes, that pestilential disease, causes. Those who wish to rid themselves of this ailment should remain in a room where the air and cold will not reach them, physic themselves, take only a light diet, and drink the water in which these roots have been boiled for this purpose, which comes away clear, and is not unpleasant to taste or smell. Drinking this, without any other medication, the malady is purged so effectively that in a short time the person is healthier than he was before, and his flesh firmer and without scar or trace, as often happens with other cures. . .

"Many who had rotting flesh by simply drinking the water of these roots became well and had better color than before they were sick. Others, with advanced cases of buboes all over their body and whose breath was bad, were cured by drinking this water the necessary length of time. In a word, many who were swollen and others covered with sores have gone home well again. It is my belief that this is one of the best plants or roots in the world, and the most useful, as is apparent from the number of people it has cured. Sarsaparilla is found in many parts of the Indies, but it has been discovered that it is not as good or all-healing as that which grows on the island of Puná."

Of this sarsaparilla [*Similax medica*] and the "cure" the famous botanist Richard Spruce wrote (see Victor W. von Hagen, *South America Called Them*): "Piura [in Peru] is considered the sovereignest place on earth for the cure of 'rheumatic' (*lege* 'syphilitic') affections. Many wonderful cures are reported; but the treatment is rather severe. It is as follows: First, you pay the priest to say 'novenas'—that is, masses on nine consecutive days—on your behalf; on each of these days you drink copiously of a warm decoction of sarsaparilla towards midday, and then your friends take you outside the town and bury you up to the neck in the burning sand, shielding your head with a broad straw hat and an umbrella. There you perspire in such a way as to bring out all the mercury you may have taken, and to reduce your swollen joints to their proper dimensions. Now you may see the use of the masses, for if you survive the operation (which is not always), they serve to express your thankfulness; and if you die under it, you will need not only those nine masses, but several additional ones— for which you make due provision in your last will and testament—to secure the repose of your soul."

As many of those of the mainland longed to live as their forebears had done, and as foreign rule is always held irksome and that of one's own kind light and bearable, they plotted with those of the island of Puná to kill all who had come into their lands with the Inca. And it is related that at this time Huayna Capac sent certain of his captains with a number of fighting men to visit certain settlements of the mainland and see that certain things beneficial to his service were done, and he ordered the natives of the island to transport them by water in rafts, and land them beside a river where they would take the road they were to travel. Having ordered this and other things, Huayna Capac returned to Tumbes, or some other place near by, and when he had left the *Orejones* and the captains boarded the rafts, which were many and large, and as they were off-guard on the water, the natives slyly untied the ropes with which the poles of the raft were fastened together, and the poor *Orejones* fell into the water, where the natives, with weapons they had hidden upon them, killed them with great cruelty. Some killed, some drowned, all the *Orejones* perished, and nothing was left on the rafts except a few blankets and some of their jewels.

Great was the joy of the aggressors when they had done this, and they greeted one another and shouted gaily from raft to raft, thinking that by the feat they had just carried out, the Inca and his riches were in their power. Rejoicing in their success and victory, they took for themselves the treasures and ornaments of those from Cuzco. But things turned out very different from what they had thought, as I shall tell on the basis of their own accounts. After the *Orejones* on the rafts had been killed, the assassins swiftly returned home for another boat-load. And as the second group was ignorant of what had happened to their companions, an even larger number came aboard with their clothing, arms, and jewels, and at the same spot where they had killed the first, they killed these, without a single one escaping. Those who tried to save themselves by swimming were killed with savage, cruel blows; and if they dived under the water to escape their enemies and seek help from the fish who dwell in the sea, their efforts were vain, for the islanders were as good swimmers as the fish, as they spent most of their time in the water fishing, and they overtook them and there in the water killed and drowned them, so that the sea turned the color of blood, which was a pitiful thing to see. After the *Orejones* on the rafts had been killed, the islanders, with their fellow conspirators, returned to their island.

When the Lord-Inca Huayna Capac received the news of what had happened, it is told that he was filled with rage and sorrow to think that so many of his finest men should be without graves (the truth is that in most of the Indies more care and pains are given to the graves in which they are to lie after death than to adorning the houses where they live while alive). He called up his remaining troops, and made his plans to punish those wretches in such a manner that, even though they attempted to resist, it would avail them nothing, nor would they receive pardon, for the crime they had committed was so dastardly that his one thought was to punish them with all severity, rejecting clemency or mercy. Accordingly, many thousands of Indians were killed by various manners of death, and the leaders of the conspiracy impaled or drowned. After carrying out this great and fearful punishment, Huayna Capac ordered that in the songs sung on sad and mournful occasions, mention should be made of the foul deed which had been committed, which, with other episodes, they chant in their language like a kind of dirge. Then he ordered a highway built along the Guayaquil [Guayas] River, which is very large, a highway which, to judge by certain sections of it that remain, was a magnificent thing. But it was not finished nor done wholly as he wished. It is known as the Pass of Huayna Capac.

When the punishment had been carried out, and all were ordered to obey his governor in the fortress of Tumbes, and other dispositions taken, the Inca left that region. Other settlements and provinces lie within the region of this city of Guayaquil, of which I make no mention beyond the fact that in dress and customs they are similar to those we have seen, and the land is the same.

Continuing this narration [about Tumbes] to the founding of the city of San Miguel, and who its founder was.

300

As FOR THE ACCOUNT of the plains [*llanos*], they begin at the valley of Tumbes. A river [Tumbes] runs through them, which rises (as I said before) in the province of the Paltas[1] and empties into the Southern Sea. The province, settlements, and regions of these valleys of Tumbes are naturally arid and sterile, even though it sometimes rains in this valley and the water comes close to the city of San Miguel. For where it rains is in the regions that border upon the sierras, since in those that lie along the sea [coast] no rain falls. This valley of Tumbes was once thickly settled and cultivated, covered with fine, cool irrigation canals, channeled from the river, with which they watered their crops abundantly and harvested much corn and the other things needed for human consumption, and many delicious fruits. The ancient rulers, before they were subdued by the Incas,[2]

---

[1] The Tumbes River, as averred by Cieza de León, does rise in the Paltas' territory, flows westward through the Inca and later Spanish mines of Zaruma (in Ecuador), and so down to the Pacific and Tumbes; a road more or less paralleled this river direction connecting Tomebamba and the coast.

[2] "The great city called Tumpiz" was a contemporary account, written in 1536, by the *pícaro* Alonso Enríquez de Guzmán. In his memoirs, "The great city called Tumpiz is inhabited entirely by Indians and close to the shore is a great house belonging to the lord of the country with walls built of adobes like bricks, very beautifully painted with many colors and varnished. I never saw anything more beautiful. The roof is straw, also painted so that it looks more like gold. About a large temple was a garden with fruits and vegetables of the country imitated all in gold and silver. The women wore a dress large and broad like a morning gown, and the chieftains went dressed in mantles and shirts and wore a thing like a turban adorned with gold and silver beads which they call Chaquira. The country itself was a desert, but the Indians made it bloom by irrigation. They said they were the vassals of a great lord named Old Cuzco who lived in the mountains and that he had much gold and the people spent many days and nights at their drinking bouts and it is certainly marvellous the quantity of beer-chicha that these Indians drink."

Tumbes was originally inhabited by the Tallanes, who spoke a language related to Puná and Huancavilca (Guayaquil). They are famed for their lustrous black pottery and the very striking lip and nose ornaments. The Tallanes were first conquered by the kingdom of Chimor [Chimú] under Minchan-caman, about 1450, and then later in 1463 by the Incas, who absorbed them into the empire, making Tumbes the coastal terminal of the empire. Francisco Pizarro in 1527 left two of his men, Alonso de Molina and a Negro, Gines, with the Tallanes at Tumbes when he sailed to Spain

were more feared and obeyed by their subjects than any of those described, as they all state and recall, and they were served with great
ceremony. Their clothing consisted of a shirt and blanket, and they
wore a headdress which was a round affair made of wool, and sometimes of gold or silver or of small beads, which, as I have said, were
known as *chaquira*. These Indians were much given to their religion,
and performed great sacrifices . . . they are more self-indulgent and
comfort-loving than the mountain [dwelling Indians]. They are very
industrious in the cultivation of their fields, and carry heavy loads.
The fields are excellently cultivated, with much forethought, and
they are very orderly in their watering of them. They raise many
varieties of fruit and well-flavored roots. Corn is harvested twice a
year, it and beans, and broad beans yield abundantly when planted.
Their clothing is made of cotton, of which they gather as much as
they need in the valley. In addition, these Indians of Tumbes are great
fishermen, from which they receive great profit, for by this and the
other products they sell to the highland dwellers they have always
been rich. From this valley of Tumbes it is a two days' journey to
the valley of Solana,[3] which in ancient times was thickly settled, and
had lodgings and storehouses. The highway of the Incas runs through

to get his grant for conquest. Their fate is unknown; one tradition says that Huayna
Capac, who was on his death bed from a pestilence (probably measles or smallpox
brought by the white men exploring the Ecuadorian coast), sent for them, but he died
before they arrived and they were put to death; others say that they died in the wars
between Puná and Tumbes. They have entered history only by being present at the
Isle of Gallo and for the baroque romantic novel of the late eighteenth century by Jean
François Marmontel, *The Incas; or the Destruction of the Empire of Peru* (London,
1806). He makes Alonso de Molina the hero of the tragedy. It can be read as an index
to just what Europe thought then of the Incas, with all their romantic overtones, and
for its complement of errors. The romantic tradition still continues among French
authors writing about the Incas.

3 Sullana (Solana) is the first valley or oasis south of Tumbes. The precise route
of the Inca highway out of Tumbes south is not known despite the work of the von
Hagen expedition. Francisco de Xérez, the very literate secretary of Francisco Pizarro
who wrote the first report of the conquest in 1533, *Verdadera relación de la conquista
del Perú* (Seville, July, 1534), reported on their march inward where the soldiers used
the Inca road: "On the first day that [we] departed from Tumbes [May 16, 1532],
we arrived at a small village [this would be Rica Playa, less than twenty kilometers
from Tumbes near the banks of the Tumbes River, where there are vestiges of Inca
ruins]. . . . On the third day [fifty kilometers farther] we reached a village among
the hills [in the Cerro Tutumo, 998 meters above sea level, where semitropical
conditions prevail]. Here we rested for three days, and in three days more [that is,
seventy-five kilometers farther on] we came to the banks of a river [Chira] which
were well peopled. . . . the river is called Turicarami . . . [and] the village Puechio
[Poechos])."

these valleys between groves and cool, pleasant glades. From Solana one comes to Poechos, which is situated above the river also known as the Poechos, though some called it the Maicabilca [Mayca-huilca], because beyond this valley there was a chieftain or lord by that name. This valley was very thickly populated, and beyond doubt many were the people who dwelt there, to judge by the numerous and large buildings. These, though now in ruins,[4] bear out what was told of them, and the esteem in which the Incas held them, for in this valley they had their royal palaces and other lodgings and store-houses. Time and wars have so wasted all that the only thing to be seen in proof of what is told are the many and very large burial places of the dead, and how the many fields that lie in the valley were planted and cultivated by them when they were alive.

302

Two days' journey beyond Poechos lies the large, broad valley of Piura, where two or three rivers come together, which is why the valley is so broad, and this is where the city of San Miguel [de Piura] was founded and built. And despite the fact that this city is now held in little esteem as the *repartimientos* are small and poor, it is only fair that it should be honored and valued as the beginning of all that was done, and the site where the stout-hearted Spaniards established themselves before the great lord Atabaliba [Atahualpa] was taken prisoner by them. At first it was located on the site known as Tangarara, from which it was moved, because the location was unhealthy and the Spaniards contracted certain diseases, to where it is now situated, between two level valleys that are cool and full of shady groves near the city, and closer to one of the valleys than to the other, on a rough, arid spot to which, in spite of all efforts, they have been unable to bring water in conduits, as has been done in many other parts of the plains. According to those who have lived there, it is somewhat insalubrious, being especially bad for the eyes. This, I believe, is due to the wind and the great dusts of summer and the dampness of winter. They say that in olden times it did not rain

---

[4] Poechos (which name is still retained by a hacienda set upon the ruins) is in the upper Sullana valley on a bluff overlooking the Chira River. The dim outlines of the ruins and fortresses Cieza mentions are still to be seen, as well as the Inca Highway which moves through the coarse soil. (The river took its name from that of the cacique whose territory was lower down on the river, where the city of Sullana now stands.) Pizarro "set off down the river. On reaching a place where lived a chief named Lachira. . . ." (Francisco de Xérez, *Verdadera relación*.)

in this region, aside from an occasional mist; but in recent years heavy rains have fallen. The valley is similar to that of Tumbes. . . . This city of San Miguel was settled and founded by . . . Francisco Pizarro in the name of His Majesty, in the year 1533.

303

CHAPTER 102 (LIX)

Which deals with the differences of season in this kingdom of Peru, and the strange fact that no rain falls throughout the plains which lie along the Southern Sea.

BEFORE PROCEEDING, it seems well to me to discuss here the lack of rainfall. I should like to point out the fact that in the highlands the summer begins around April, and lasts through May, June, July, August, and September; and around October winter sets in, and lasts [through] November, December, January, February, and March, so there is little difference in the matter of seasons from our Spain. The fields wither when the time comes, the days and nights are nearly equal, and when the days grow somewhat longer, it is around the month of November. But in these plains along the Southern Sea it is just the opposite of what I have said, for when it is summer in the uplands, it is winter on the plains, for we see that the summer begins in October and lasts until April, and then winter sets in. Truly it is a remarkable thing,[1] this marked difference in the same land and a single kingdom, and what is even more extraordinary is that in certain areas one can come down to the plains wearing a raincape which is

[1] This seemed remarkable to José de Acosta also, this very astute Jesuit who traveled in Peru in 1590: "As at Lima and on the Plaines they find the . . . windes troublesome and unwholesome . . . yet it never raines . . . a wonder of Nature, never to raine upon that coast and ever to have one winde (from the south) without giving place to his contrary." (*The Naturall and Morall Historie of the East and West Indies,* Book III, chap. 3.) The climatic explanation of why rain generally does not fall on the coast of Peru and northern Chile is twofold: Geographically, the rain-laden southeast trades blowing across Brazil, strike the high cordilleras, and the rains fall into the Upper Amazon; the winds, pre-emptied of rain, tumble down on the Pacific Coast as cool, dry winds and reach the ocean again before they can be recharged with vapor. Meteorologically, the coast is cooled by the strong northern-moving Humboldt Current, as wide as 150 miles. The cold current (average 58°) lowers the temperature of the air that moves across it, and since its capacity for heat exceeds that of the air, rain almost never falls.

soaking wet, or, to put it more clearly, set out in the morning from lands where it is raining and before nightfall find oneself in regions where it is believed that it has never rained. For from the beginning of October no rain falls anywhere on the plains except for a light dew, which in many places hardly lays the dust. For this reason those who live there depend completely on irrigation, and cultivate only such lands as can be irrigated by the rivers, for throughout all the rest—because of its aridity—no grass grows, all being bare sand wastes and rocks, and the only thing that grows there are trees having very few leaves and bearing no fruit. Many kinds of thistles and thorn bushes grow, too, but in parts not even these, there being nothing but sand. What they call winter on the plains is only that there are very thick fogs, which look like clouds about to burst, and which let fall, as I have said, a rain so light that it hardly wets the dust. And it is strange that with the sky so heavy with clouds in this season of which I speak, the only rain that falls on the plains in these six months I have mentioned are these fine mists, and for days at a time the sun is hidden by these dense clouds. As the uplands are so high, and the plains and coast so low, it seems that the former hold the clouds without letting them reach the lowlands. Thus, in the rainy season it pours in the uplands, and none falls on the plains, where the heat is very great. And when the dews I have mentioned fall, it is in the season when it is clear in the uplands and does not rain there.

Another strange thing is that the wind blows from only one direction along this coast, from the south, and though elsewhere it is damp and brings rain, that is not the case here. And as it encounters no contrary wind, it blows uninterruptedly along the coast almost to Tumbes. From that point, as there are other winds from other directions of the heavens, it rains and there are high winds with heavy downpours. We can give no explanation of the foregoing; the fact remains that, as we see, from four degrees south latitude to beyond the Tropic of Capricorn this region is arid.

Another noteworthy thing is that below the line in these regions, some are hot and humid, others cold and humid. But this part is hot and dry, and once one emerges from it, it rains on all sides. This I can state because of what I have seen and observed; whoever can find the reasons for this should put them forward. I merely state what I have seen, nor do I understand more than I have said.

The northern part of the Inca empire, showing the complex of roads which bound what is now the frontier of Ecuador and Peru together. The road which passes from Chimbo to Guayaquil is conjectural and schematic, although fragments of it are known as the Pass of Huayna Capac. The heavy black lines are the two principal Inca highway systems going down coast and mountain. Note how the coastal road below San Miguel de Piura makes a wide detour; this was to avoid the Sechura desert.

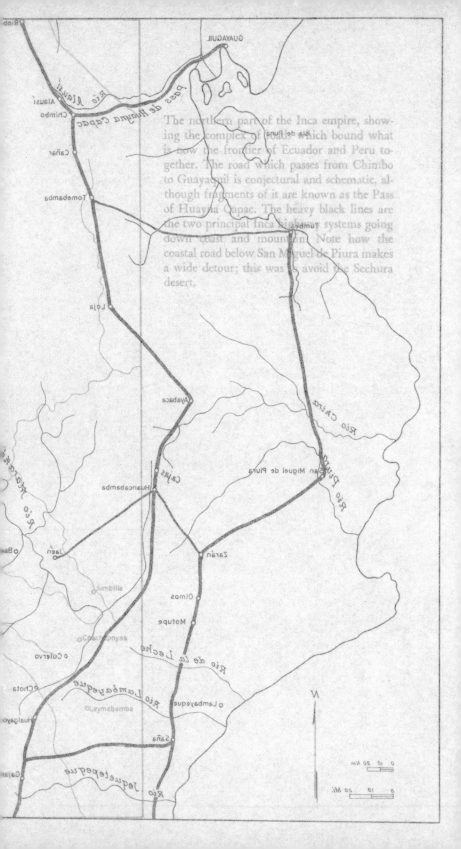

The northern part of the Inca empire, showing the complex of rivers which bound what is now the frontier of Ecuador and Peru together. The road which passes from Chimbo to Guayaquil is conjectural and schematic, although fragments of it are known as the Pass of Huayna Capac. The heavy black lines are the two principal Inca highway systems going down coast and mountain. Note how the coastal road below San Miguel de Piura makes a wide detour; this was to avoid the Sechura desert.

Of the road the Incas ordered built across these plains, along which there were lodgings and storehouses like those of the highland, and why these Indians were called Yungas.

AT THIS POINT I shall give an account of the great [coastal] highway which the Incas ordered built across them [the plains]. Although in many places this road is now ruined and destroyed, it still reveals what a splendid thing it was, and the power of those who ordered it built.

It was Huayna Capac [the Lord-Inca] and Topa Inca, his father, who first, according to the accounts of many of the Indians, descended to the coastal lands, visiting the valleys and provinces of the Yungas, although there are also those who say that the Inca Pachacuti, the grandfather of Huayna Capac and father of Topa Inca [was the Inca who] first saw the coast and crossed its plains. And in these valleys and [on the] coast the caciques and chieftains, at their command, built a road some fifteen feet wide, bordered by a mighty wall more than a fathom high.[1] Throughout its length this road was carefully tended, and ran beneath trees, and in many spots the fruit-laden boughs hung over the road, and all the trees were alive with many kinds of birds and parrots and other winged creatures. In each of these valleys there were large and fine lodgings for the Incas, and storehouses filled with supplies for their men of war, for they were so feared that they did not venture to scant their provisions. If anything was lacking, severe punishment followed, and, consequently, if any of the troops ventured to enter the fields or the houses of the Indians, even though the damage done was slight, he suffered the death penalty. Walls flanked this road on both sides; when the sand became so deep that it was impossible for the Indians to build a foundation

---

1 The coastal Inca highway is approximately twenty-four feet wide along its entire length. Although the road was carefully tended, as Cieza explains, and its walls, either of stone or adobe, were built on either side, it was not always bordered with trees, with the exception of the northern end, where there are dry forests and the road ran under trees, or when it passed through some valley oases. The length of the royal coastal road from Tumbes to Santiago, Chile, was 2,520 miles. (See von Hagen, *Highway of the Sun.*)

for them, to keep the traveler from losing his way and to proclaim the grandeur of the one who had ordered the road built, long poles of even length, like beams, were sunk at intervals. And just as care was taken to keep the road clean and repair the walls if they became worn and needed mending, so they were on the alert to replace any of the poles or piles in the sand if the wind blew them down. Beyond doubt this highway was a fine thing, though not as difficult as that of the uplands. There were certain fortresses and temples to the sun in these valleys, as I shall mention when the time comes.

And as in the course of this work I shall often have to refer to the Incas and also to the Yungas, I shall now explain to the reader what Yunga means, as I did earlier with regard to the Incas. Thus he should know that the towns and provinces of Peru are situated as I have stated, many of them in valleys formed by the Andes Mountains and the snow-covered highlands, and all the inhabitants of the uplands are called mountaineers, and those who live on the plains, Yungas. In many parts of the sierra where the rivers flow, as the sierras are very high, the plains are sheltered and temperate, so much so that in many places it is hot, as it is on these plains. The people who live there, even though they are in the sierra, are known as Yungas; and throughout Peru, when they allude to these warm, sheltered regions that lie among the sierras, they say, "It is Yunga," and the inhabitants have no other name, even though their settlements and regions have names. Thus those who live in the regions I have referred to, and those who dwell in these plains and coastal regions of Peru, are called Yungas because they live in hot country.

CHAPTER 104 (LXI)

Of how these Yungas received great service, and were given to their religions, and how there were certain families and tribes of them.

BEFORE I BEGIN enumerating the valleys of the plains and the foundation of the three cities, Trujillo, the City of the Kings [Lima], and Arequipa, I shall set down here certain matters bearing upon this, to avoid repeating what I saw, and what I learned from Fray Domingo de Santo Tomás,[1] of the Dominican Order, who is one of those who is well acquainted with the language and has spent much time among these Indians, instructing them in our holy Catholic faith. Consequently, on the basis of what I saw and apprehended in the time I spent in these valleys, and the information I received from Fray Domingo, I shall set forth what I know of these *llanos*.

In ancient times the native chieftains were greatly feared and obeyed by their subjects, and were served with great pomp, as was their custom, surrounding themselves with buffoons and dancers, who entertained them, and with others who continually made music and sang. They had many wives, selecting them from among the most beautiful; and each lord, in his valley, had his great dwellings, with many pillars of adobe, and great terraces and gateways, covered with mats, and surrounding this house was a wide square, where they performed their dances and *areitos*. And when the lord ate, a great multitude gathered who drank of his beverage that was brewed from corn or other roots. In these dwellings there were gatekeepers whose duty it was to guard the doors, and observe who came in and out, and all went attired in shirts of cotton and long blankets, and the women in the same fashion, except that the garment of the women was full and wide like a cape, with openings on the sides for the arms. Some of them made war on their neighbors, and there were regions where most of them never were able to learn the language of Cuzco. Although there were three or four different tribes among these Yungas, they all had the same rites and customs. They held banquets and drinking feasts which lasted for many days and nights; it is amazing how much beverage or chicha these Indians can drink, for the glass is never out of their hand. They used to lodge the Spaniards who passed by their dwellings, and treat them very kindly, and

---

[1] Friar Domingo de Santo Tomás, of the Dominican Order, was born in Seville about 1505; he was the author of the first Quechua grammar, published in 1560 in Valladolid. Present at the founding of San Miguel de Piura in 1553, he spent long years in the valleys of the Yungas: Chicama, Trujillo, Chancay, Aucallama, and Chincha. Much of his time was given to religious instruction of the coastal Indians and making a study of their language. He joined the forces of La Gasca (where Cieza de León first met him), and was present at the battle of Xaquixahuana. Simple, renowned, and humble, he retired to a convent in Lima and died there after 1567. His portrait is in the reception salon of the Rector of the Universidad de San Marcos in Lima. Such was Cieza de León's informant.

receive them with honors. They no longer do this, because after the Spaniards had broken the peace and engaged in war among themselves, the Indians came to detest them because of the cruel treatment they received at their hands, and also because some of those sent to govern them have acquainted them with acts of such villainy that they no longer pride themselves on their kindly treatment of travelers, who treat as servants certain of those who once were masters. This is the result and outcome of the behavior of those who have been sent to rule them, some of whom have held that the kind of service here was a bad thing, and that it was oppressive and troublesome to the natives to uphold them in their ancient customs, which, if they had them, would neither curtail their liberties nor even remove them from good polity or conversion. For, in truth, it is my belief that there have been few nations in the world that have had better government than the Incas. Leaving aside the government, I not only do not approve of anything, but, on the contrary, I grieve over the extortions and harsh treatment and violent deaths the Spaniards have caused among these Indians, motivated by their cruelty, without regard for the great nobility and virtue of these peoples, for most of these valleys are now almost deserted, when it is common knowledge how populated they were in the past.

308

CHAPTER 105 (LXII)

Of how the Indians of these valleys and others of these kingdoms believe that the soul departs from the body and does not die, and why they ordered their wives interred in their tombs.

IN THE COURSE of this history I have often alluded to the fact that in the greater part of this kingdom of Peru it is a very widespread custom generally observed by all the Indians to bury with the bodies of the dead all those possessions they most prized, and certain of their most beautiful and best-loved women. And it seems that this was the case throughout most of these Indies, . . . [for in the] Sinú[1] in

---

[1] The finding of all this gold in Colombia in the springtime of the New World's

the province of Cartagena, where I happened to be in the year 1535, there was found in a bare field, near a temple which had been built there in honor of this cursed demon, such a number of graves that it caused amazement, and some of them were so old that tall, thick trees had grown up in them. And they found over a million in these graves, aside from what the Indians looted from them and what was lost in the earth itself. In other places, too, great treasures have been found in graves, and will be found each day. It was not many years ago that Juan de la Torre,[2] one of Gonzalo Pizarro's captains, found in the valley of Ica, which is one of the valleys of these plains, one of these graves, and they say that what he took from it was worth over fifty thousand pesos. So the fact that they ordered these deep, magnificent tombs built, and adorned them with tiles and vaulted roof, into which they laid the dead man with all his possessions and women and servants and a great quantity of food, and not a few jars of chicha, which is the wine they drink, and his arms and ornaments, makes it apparent that they believed in the immortality of the soul and that there was more to man than his mortal body. Deceived by the devil, they carried out his behest, because he gave them to understand (so they say) that afterwards the dead would be resurrected in another place that he had prepared for them, where they would eat and drink their fill, as they did before they died. And so they would believe that what he told them was true, and not false and lying, at times when it was God's will to give him power and permit this, he would assume the shape of one of their leaders who was already dead, and show himself in the form and guise in which he walked this earth, well tended and adorned, and make them believe that he was in another pleasant, peaceable kingdom in the manner in which they saw him.

These Indians, blinded by the words and figments of the devil, be-

conquest whetted the appetite of Francisco Pizarro, who was one of them; this gave rise to a couplet:

It was a sad day for Perú
When they found gold in the Sinú.

2 Juan de la Torre, *El Mozo* (son of the father of the same name and one of the "thirteen men of Gallo," Knight of the Golden Spur and one of the founders of Arequipa), was a *pícaro* of different kidney from his father. Born on the isle of Hispañola in 1520, he attached himself to the side of Gonzalo Pizarro and his rebellion. He escaped from the battlefield in 1548, hid for four months in an Indian's hut in Cuzco, but was discovered and hanged in the same year by order of Pedro de la Gasca.

lieving these fictions, gave more thought to adorning their graves or tombs than to any other thing. And when the chief died, they put with him his treasures, living women and boys, and other persons who were good friends of his when he was alive. Thus, as can be seen from what I have said, it was the general belief among all these **310** Yunga Indians, and also the mountaineers of this kingdom of Peru, that the souls of the dead did not die, but lived forever, and came together with one another in the other world, where, as I said before, they believe that they take their pleasure and eat and drink, which is their chief delight. And firmly believing this, they buried with the dead their best-loved wives, and their closest vassals and servants, and their most prized possessions and arms and feathers, and other ornaments of their person. And many of their kinfolk, for whom there was no room in the tomb, dug holes in the fields and lands of the dead lord, or in those spots where he was most wont to sport and pleasure himself, and laid themselves in them, thinking that his soul would pass by those spots and take them along to serve him. There were even women who, to have more of a claim on him and so he would value their services more, fearing there would not be room for them in the tomb, hanged themselves by their own hair and killed themselves in this way. We believe all these things to be true because the tombs of the dead make it manifest, and because in many places they still hold and follow this cursed custom.

I have already told how in Puná and the region about Puerto Viejo they were guilty of the abominable sin [of sodomy]. Neither in these valleys nor in the highlands is there any evidence that they practiced it. It is my opinion that the same thing happened here as happens everywhere in the world: that there were some evil-doers. But if it became known, the [sodomist] suffered great scorn and was called a woman, and asked why he did not lay off the man's attire he wore. Now, in our days, as they have abandoned most of their rites, the devil no longer has sway or power, nor are there temples or oracles.

CHAPTER 106 (LXIII)

Of their burial rites and the mourning which attended the obsequies.

I RELATED . . . [all that] can be gathered from these Indians with regard to their belief in the immortality of the soul, and . . . it seems to me appropriate at this point to give an account of how they prepared their graves and laid the dead to rest in them. This varies greatly, for in some places they were deep; in others, high; and in others, flat; and each nation tried to find a different fashion for the graves of its dead. The fact is that although I have sought out and talked with learned and thoughtful men, I have been unable to discover with certainty the origin of these Indians, or their beginnings, to know whence they acquired this custom.[1]

In the vicinity of Cuzco they bury their dead seated on magnificent stools, which they call *duhos,* dressed and adorned with their best finery.

In the province of Jauja, which is a very important place in these kingdoms of Peru, they put them in a fresh llama-hide, and sew them in it, shaping on the outside face, nose, mouth, and all the rest, and in this fashion they keep them in their houses, and those who were chieftains and headmen are carried out at certain times of the year by their sons to their fields and villages in litters with great ceremonies, and sacrifices are made to them of llamas and even children and women.

In many other parts of the provinces through which I have passed they bury them in deep graves which are hollow inside, and in some, like those around the city of Antioquia, they make the graves large, and put so much dirt on them that they look like small hills. And through the door they leave in the grave they put in the dead, and the living women, and all the other things they lay in it. And in Sinú

---

[1] Pedro de Cieza de León: "In [another] part of this work, however, . . . I set down what I have been able to learn. To return to our subject, I would say that I have noted that these Indians have different customs in this matter of graves, for in the province of the Colla they erect them in fields, in rows, as big as towers [*chullpas*], some more, some less, and some handsomely constructed, of matched stones with doors opening to the rising sun, and beside them (as I shall also relate) they used to perform their sacrifices and burn certain things, and sprinkle the place with the blood of llamas or other animals."

many of the graves were flat and large, some square, some mounded in the shape of little hills.

In the province of Chincha in these plains they bury them lying on platforms or beds made of reeds.

312 In another of these same valleys, known as Lunahuaná [valley of Cañete], they bury them sitting up. In a word, in burying them lying down, or standing up, or seated, they vary from one another.

In many valleys of these plains, on emerging from the valley into the uplands of stones and sand, one finds great walls and divisions where each family has its allotted place to bury its dead, and for this purpose they have dug great hollows and cavities, each with its door, with all possible care. And it is a marvellous thing to behold the number of dead there are in those sand dunes and desert uplands; and separated one from the other, one sees a vast number of skeletons and their clothing, rotted and corroded by time. They call these places, which they hold sacred, *huacas,* which is a melancholy word, and many of them have been opened and, after the Spaniards conquered this kingdom, despoiled of great sums of gold and silver. For in these valleys it was the custom to bury with the dead his wealth and the things he most prized, and many women and servants of those who were closest to the lord when he was alive. And it was the custom in olden times to open the tombs and renew the clothing and food that had been buried in them.

And when the chieftains died, the headmen of the valley assembled and carried on great mourning, and many of the women cut their hair completely off, not leaving one. To the accompaniment of drums and flutes they marched around those places where the lord most frequently took his pleasure, singing sad songs to move the listeners to tears. And after they had mourned, they performed other sacrifices and ceremonies, carrying on their conversations with the devil. And when all this had been done, and some of the wives killed, they laid them in the grave with their treasures and abundant food, firmly believing that they were going where the devil had said. And they waited, and even now they generally do so, some four or five days or ten before putting them in the grave, depending on the rank of the dead man, because the more important the lord, the more honor they do him and the greater sorrow they profess, mourning him with loud groans and bewailing him with sorrowful music, relating in their songs all the things that had happened to the deceased while he was alive. If he was brave, they recount his feats in their dirges as they bear him along; and as they lay his body away, they burn certain of his jewels and garments beside him, and put others in with him. Many of these ceremonies are no longer used . . . because little by little these people are coming to know the error of their fore- 313 fathers, and how idle were these pomps and honors. For it is enough to bury the dead in a simple grave, as the Christians do, without attempting to take with themselves anything but good works, for all serves only to increase the power of the devil and lay more and more grievous weight on the soul descending to hell. But it is my belief that most of the older chieftains arrange to be buried in secret, hidden places, in the manner I have described, where the Spaniards can neither see or know of them. That they do this we know from what we are told by the younger people.

CHAPTER 107 (LXIV)

How the devil made the Indians of these regions believe that it was pleasing to the gods for them to have Indians as temple assistants so the chieftains could have carnal knowledge of them, thus committing the heinous sin of sodomy.

IN THE FIRST PART of this history I have described many customs and usages of these Indians, both those which I gathered for myself when I was traveling among them and those which I heard from certain friars and persons of standing who, it is my belief, under no circumstances would deviate from the truth of what they knew and had learned. . . . This was, that in certain parts of this great kingdom of Peru, not all, but only certain tribes in the vicinity of Puerto Viejo and the island of Puná indulged in the abominable sin [of sodomy]. I believe this was so, for the Inca lords were free from this, and the other native chieftains, too. . . . It is held to be certain that in the shrines and temples where conversation was held with [the devil], he let it be known that it was to his service for certain youths to be attached to the temples from childhood, so that at the time of sacrifices and solemn feasts, the chieftains and other men of rank could indulge in the cursed sin of sodomy. And so that all who read this may know how this diabolical ceremony still persisted among them, I shall set down an account of it which was given to me in the City of the Kings [Lima] by Father Fray Domingo de Santo Tomás, which I have in my possession, and runs as follows:

314

"It is true that as a general thing among the mountaineers and the Yungas the devil has introduced this vice under a kind of cloak of sanctity, and in each important temple or house of worship they have a man or two, or more, depending on the idol, who go dressed in women's attire from the time they are children, and speak like them, and in manner, dress, and everything else imitate women. With these, almost like a religious rite and ceremony, on feast [days] and holidays, they have carnal, foul intercourse, especially the chiefs and headmen. I know this because I have punished two, one of them of the Indians of the highlands, who was in a temple, which they call *huaca*, for this purpose, in the province of the Conchucos,[1] near the city of Huánuco, the other in the province of Chincha, where the Indians are subjects of His Majesty. And when I spoke to them of the evil they were doing, and upbraided them for the repulsiveness of the sin, they answered me that it was not their fault because from childhood they had been put there by the caciques to serve them in this cursed and abominable vice, and to act as priests and guard the temples of their idols. So what I deduced from this was that the devil held such sway in this land that, not satisfied with making them fall into so great sin, he made them believe that this vice was a kind of holiness and religion, to hold more power over them."

Fray Domingo gave me this in his own handwriting, and everyone knows how zealous he is of the truth. And I also recall that Diego de Gálvez, who is now secretary to His Majesty in the court of Spain, told me that when he and Peralonso Carrasco,[2] one of the old con-

---

1 The prevalence of sodomy, ceremonial and private, was well known. The Incas regarded it as an abominable vice, and in an attempt to stamp it out whole families were destroyed. Yet the coastal peoples remained much addicted to it, practicing it with both men and women. The evidence of this lies in coastal pottery, particularly in that of the Mochicas, where there was a strong and literal secular art. Here it is fully apparent. The number of distinct cases of pottery illustrating sodomy reaches into the hundreds.

2 The personal history of Pedro Alonso Carrasco, an old conquistador, and one of Cieza's best informants, is given in note 1, Chapter 76 above.

quistadores who resides in the city of Cuzco, were coming from the province of the Colla, they saw one or two of these Indians who had been put in the temples as Fray Domingo relates.

CHAPTER 108 (LXV)

Of the way of naming children in most of these provinces and the use of portents and auguries.

ONE THING I noticed while I was in these kingdoms of Peru was that in most of the provinces they had the custom of naming the children when they were fifteen or twenty days old, names which they used until they were ten or twelve years old, and then, or some earlier, they received other names. When this was to be done, on a certain day set for this purpose, most of the relatives and friends of the father assembled, and danced as was their custom, and drank, which is their favorite pastime; and when the celebration had come to an end, one of them, the oldest and most respected, cut the hair of the boy or girl who was to be named, and the nails which, with the hair, were carefully put away. The names they give them and which they use are names of towns and birds, or plants, or fish.[1] And I understand that this was what they did from the fact that I had an Indian named Urco, which means "ram," and another called Llama . . . and I have seen others called Piscos, which is the name of a bird. Some are very proud of bearing the name of their father or grandfather. The caciques and headmen pick names to their taste, and the best they can find, even though [the name] Atahualpa (the Inca the Spaniards seized in the province of Cajamarca) means something like "chicken," and that of his father, Huayna Capac, "rich youth." These Indians considered it an ill omen if a woman gave birth to twins, or if a child was born with some defect, such as six fingers, or something of the sort. And

---

1 "The child was not named until it was weaned. . . . The name giving was part of an elaborate ceremony, called *rutuchicoy*, 'hair cutting.' . . . *Inca* names referred to animals the qualities of which were admired, and to natural objects, places, or abstract qualities. A man might be named for his father or grandfather. . . . He might acquire a nickname such as 'weeper of blood,' stone-eye . . . [men might be called] tobacco . . . hawk . . . puma. . . . Women's names were . . . star . . . egg . . . gold . . . coca. (John H. Rowe, "Inca Culture before the Spanish Conquest," *Handbook*, III, 282, 284.)

if a woman brought forth twins, or a child with some defect, her husband and she took it very hard, and forswore pepper with their food, and chicha, which is the wine they drink, and did other things as is their custom and which they learned from their forebears.

316 These Indians also gave careful study to signs and portents. And if they see a shooting star they make a great outcry, and give much thought to the moon and planets, and many of them are augurs. When Atahualpa was taken prisoner in the province of Cajamarca, some Spaniards still alive who were with . . . Francisco Pizarro, who captured him, saw a green sign as thick as an arm and the length of a lancet descend from the midnight sky. And while the Spaniards were observing it, Atahualpa heard about it, and it is said that he asked them to let him out so that he could see it. And when he did, a great sadness came over him which lasted all the next day. And when the governor, Don Francisco Pizarro, asked him why he was so sad, he answered, "I have seen the sign in the sky, and when my father Huayna Capac died, a similar sign was seen." Fifteen days later Atahualpa was dead.

CHAPTER 109 (LXVI)

Of the fertility of the plains, and the many fruits and tubers they produce, and the excellent system of irrigation that is employed.

Now THAT I have related as briefly as possible certain facts pertinent to our design, I should like to go back and deal with the valleys, describing each of them, as I have done with the towns and provinces of the uplands, although first I should like to mention the fruits and food products they yield and the irrigation [systems] to be found there.

I may say that all the land of the valleys which is not sand is among the most fertile and productive to be found in the world, and the richest in produce of every sort, and the easiest to cultivate and be made to bear. I have told how it does not rain there, and such water as they have comes by irrigation from the rivers that flow from the sierras and empty into the Southern Sea. Throughout these valleys the Indians plant corn, which yields two crops a year, and in abundance. In certain places they plant yuca, which is used to make bread, and for beverages when they lack corn.[1] They raise many sweet potatoes whose flavor resembles that of chestnuts. They also raise potatoes, and a great many beans, and other edible roots. In all the valleys of these plains there grows one of the most unusual fruits I have ever seen, which they call cucumber,[2] of excellent flavor, and some of them very fragrant. Guava trees grow in profusion, and cassia, alligator pears, sour-sops, caimitos, and pineapples of the native variety. Around their houses one sees many dogs, different from those of Spain, about the size of terriers, which they call *chonos*.[3] They also raise many ducks, and in the woodlands of the valleys there grow carob beans, not as large as broad-bean pods. In some regions they make bread of these carob beans, and they like it. They dry many fruits and roots which are suitable for this purpose, as we do figs, raisins, and other fruits. In these valleys there are now large vineyards where they gather many grapes.[4] So far, no wine has been made, and for that reason I cannot say what it is like. I presume that, as the vines are irrigated, the wine would be thin. There are also groves of figs and pomegranates, and in some places quinces are already raised. But why do I go into all these details, when it is believed that all the products of Spain will flourish here? Wheat is

[1] Yuca (*Manihot esculenta*) is cultivated throughout the tropical Americas and is a parsnip-shaped tuber; the "bitter," which is poisonous with small quantities of prussic or hydrocyanic acid, is extracted in an ingenious manner by the Indians; this produces the tapioca of commerce. The "sweet" variety is eaten peeled and boiled, as any other vegetable. A beverage is made from it. (See "The Bitter Cassava Eaters," by Victor W. von Hagen, *Natural History Magazine* [March, 1949].)

[2] The true cucumber is not American in origin, although the gherkin (*Cucumis anguria*) is cultivated throughout the West Indies and tropical Americas and is indigenous.

[3] The native South American dog (*Canis ingae*) was barkless, of medium size, with pointed face, short legs, thick body, and a long tail curling tightly over the back; the Quechua word for it was *alqo*. It is believed that descendants of it exist in and about Cuzco (needless to say not now barkless). They were kept as pets and scavengers. The Mochicas (A.D. 400–1000) immortalized the dog in their pottery. Some tribes sacrificed dogs on occasion and even ate them; the Huanca tribe, which centered about Jauja in central Peru, were called contemptuously "dog-eaters" by the Incas.

[4] The grape vine was first brought to and planted in Ayacucho (1536), then brought down to Ica, on the coast and in direct line with Ayacucho, where a flourishing wine industry existed (and add to it pisco, the wine-brandy). Diego de Mora, one of the earlier conquistadors, who arrived in Peru with Almagro and was given the fief of the Chicama valley (hard on Trujillo), first planted the grape vine in that part of the coast.

harvested,[5] as those who have seen it can bear witness, and it is a beautiful sight to see the fields thick with stalks where there is no natural rainfall, and everything so green and lush that it looks like sweet basil. The yield of barley is like that of wheat; lemons, limes, oranges, citron, and grapefruit are produced in abundance, and there are large banana groves.[6] Aside from these, there grow in these valleys many other kinds of fruit which I do not mention because it seems to me that those I have listed suffice. As the rivers flow from the highlands through these valleys, and some of the latter are broad and all are cultivated, or were when they were thickly settled, they built irrigation ditches at intervals, and, strange though it seems, both in upland and low-lying regions and on the sides of the hills and the foothills descending to the valleys, and these were connected to others, running in different directions. All this makes it a pleasure to cross these valleys, because it is as though one were walking amidst gardens and cool groves. The Indians took and still take great care in bringing the water through these ditches. There have been occasions when I have stopped beside one of these canals, and before I have had time to pitch my tent, the ditch was dry and the water had been diverted elsewhere. For, as the rivers never dry up, the Indians can conduct the water where they will. There is always verdure along these ditches, and grass grows beside many of them, where the horses graze, and among the trees and bushes there is a multitude of birds, doves, wild turkey, pheasants, partridge, and also deer. Vermin, snakes, reptiles, wolves—there are none. At most there are foxes, so sly that however much care is taken, wherever the Indians or Spaniards live, they always steal something, and if they can find nothing better, the leather straps of the horses' girths or bridles. In many parts of these

---

5 Wheat, of course, came from Europe; Father Jodôco Ricke, of Ghent, planted the first wheat in South America at Quito, about 1538, from the grains which survived his dunking in the Atlantic, where French pirates had tossed him with no respect for his cloth.

6 Bananas and, of course, all their plantain relatives are not native to America. The first shoots from the Guinea Coast in Africa were brought to the West Indies or Panama by Tomás de Berlanga. Born in Spain, Bishop Berlanga, a Dominican, was sent to Peru to attempt to iron out the difficulties between Pizarro and Almagro; he discovered the Galápagos Islands (1535) by mistake, and historically he brought the first bananas. See von Hagen, *Ecuador and the Galápagos Islands;* and for the banana question, Emil Worth, *Zur Natur und Kulturgeschichte der Banane,* XIV, (Stuttgart, Menschen und Völkerkunde, Georg Buschan verlag, 1917.)

valleys there are great fields of sugarcane, and for this reason in places they make sugar and other products with the syrup. All these Yungas are good workers, and when they are carrying loads on their back, they go naked except for a little blanket not a handspan long, and even narrower, to cover their privities, and in this attire they trot along with their load.

319

To return to the irrigation system of these Indians, just as careful as they were in the watering of their lands, so they were, even more so, in their plantings. And now leaving this, I shall describe the [Inca highway] route that leads from the city of San Miguel to Trujillo.

CHAPTER 110 (LXVII)

Of the [Inca] road that lies between the city of San Miguel and Trujillo, and the intervening valleys.

IN THE FOREGOING chapters, having described the founding of the city of San Miguel [de Piura], the first Spanish settlement in Peru, I shall now tell what there is to be found between this and the city of Trujillo. From the one to the other is some sixty leagues [150 miles], more or less.

From San Miguel [de Piura] to the valley of Motupe is twenty-two leagues, all sand and hard going, especially the route now in use. In the area of these twenty-two leagues there are various little valleys, and although a number of rivers flow down from the sierra, they do not reach them because they are completely lost in the sand stretches, and serve no useful purpose.

To travel these twenty-two leagues, it is best to set out in the after-noon because, traveling by night, early in the morning one comes to pools where travelers can slake their thirst and continue their travels without feeling the sun too much. And they can take with them gourds of water, and wineskins for the road that lies ahead.

Once in the valley of Motupe, one comes to the highway of the Incas, wide and well constructed, as I have already related. The valley is broad and very fertile, and in spite of the fact that a good-sized river [Motupe] flows into it from the sierra, it disappears before reaching the sea. Carob[1] and other trees cover a large part of it, thanks to the moisture they find for their roots. And even though there are settlements of Indians in the lowest stretch of the valley, they get water from the deep wells they dig, and they all barter certain products for others, because they do not use money, nor has any coinage been discovered in these regions.

They tell that there were great lodgings for the Incas in these parts, and storehouses, and in the hills and sierras they had and still have their *huacas,* or burial sites. Since the late [civil] wars the population has declined, and the buildings and lodgings are neglected and abandoned, and the Indians live in small houses built after the fashion I have described in the foregoing chapters. In bygone days they trafficked with the inhabitants of the uplands, and there were great plantations of cotton in the valley, from which they wove their clothing.

Four leagues from Motupe lies the lovely, cool valley of Xayanca, some four leagues wide. Through it flows a bonny river from which they draw water to irrigate all that the Indians care to plant. In bygone times this valley was thickly settled, and in it were great lodgings and storehouses of the rulers, where their stewards resided, with the duties I have earlier described. The chiefs of this valley were venerated and respected by their subjects; even today this is true of those who have survived, and they are followed and served by their women and servants, and have their gatekeepers and guards. From this valley one proceeds to that of Tuqueme, which is also large, beautiful, and covered with groves and meadows, and despite the fact that its buildings are in ruins and falling to pieces, one can still see what it once was.

A day's journey farther on, one comes to another exceedingly beautiful valley, by name Cinto. The reader must realize that between one valley and another of these, and most of those still to be described, lie sand wastes and arid stretches of rocks where no living or growing

---

[1] Carob (from the Arabic *Kharrubah*) was the name for a North African evergreen caesalpiniaceous tree which yielded pods and seeds often ground into flour for St.-John's-bread. The arborescent vegetation of coastal Peru's desert is composed mostly of a mimosa, called by the Indians *huarango* and by the Spaniards (since it was similar to the Mediterranean species) "carob" and then "algarroba" (the botanists' *Prosopis limensis*). These forests of algarroba, scarcely grow higher than forty feet, are practically impossible to cut with an axe, and maintain moisture not by the depths of the roots of the plant, but by the massive network of roots covering an area of forty square yards to the tree. The pendulous, flattish yellow pods, six to eight inches long, yield flat seeds covered with a sweetish mucilaginous pith beloved by Indian children. It is one of the most common plants found in ancient kitchen middens.

thing is to be seen, neither grass nor tree, aside from a few birds flying over. And as the traveler trudges through all this sand and glimpses the valley (even though from afar), his heart rejoices, especially if he is traveling on foot and the sun is high and he is thirsty. It is not advisable for newcomers to the land to cross these plains unless they have experienced guides to take them across the land.

After this valley comes that of Collique, where there runs a river [Chancay] bearing the same name as the valley; and it is so large that it cannot be forded except when it is summer in the uplands and winter in the plains. Although the fact is that the natives are so skillful at channeling off the water that even when it is winter in the uplands there are times when they leave the bed of the river dry. This valley, too, is broad and covered with groves of trees like those we have seen. Most of the natives have disappeared as a result of the wars the Spaniards waged against each other. The evils and hardships these wars occasioned made an end of them.

CHAPTER III (LXVIII)

Pursuing the same [Inca] road described in the foregoing chapter until reaching the city of Trujillo.

CONTINUING FROM this valley of Collique, one reaches another known as Zañu [Saña],[1] similar in every way to the others. Farther on, one enters the valley of Pacasmayo, which is the most fertile and thickly settled of all those I have described, whose natives, before they were dominated by the Incas, were powerful and feared by their neighbors, and had great temples where they performed sacrifices to their gods. All is now in ruins. Among the rocks and stony hills there are many

---

1 This region between Motupe and Lambayeque had a distinct culture anterior to its conquest by the Chimor (Chimú) empire and later the Incas (1463). The largest lay-center of this culture was at Patapo (see map). It was the ancient Cinto, and is so referred to by Cieza and all the earliest chroniclers. In the Zañu valley there is on top of Cerro Corbacho an elaborate chain of stone structures, look-out stations, and garrisons, with intercommunication by extensive stone walls. The Inca highway over which Cieza de León traveled—and still to be seen—passes at the southwest foot of this fortress hill. The potsherd collections at Zaña corroborate oral history; Inca pottery fragments are found in abundance in the upper levels of the stone ruins, while Chimú, which came earlier, predominate at the base, freely mixed with the local cultural wares.

huacas, as the graves of these Indians are called. In most of these valleys there are priests or friars who occupy themselves in the conversion of the natives and teaching them their doctrine, forbidding them to follow their ancient religions and customs. Through this valley there runs a beautiful river [Zañu], from which they draw water for the many fine irrigation ditches with which the Indians water the fields they wish to plant, and they raise the roots and fruits already mentioned. The highway of the Incas runs through it, as through the other valleys, and in this one were great storehouses for their service. They tell a number of old tales about their ancestors, which as I consider them fables, I am not setting down. The deputies of the Incas collected their tributes in the storehouses which were built to house them, and from there they were taken to the capital of the provinces, the appointed place of residence of the captains-general, where the temples of the sun were.

In this valley of Pacasmayo cotton clothing is made in quantity, and cattle do well there, and swine and goats even better, and such other animals as they wish to raise, and the climate is very good. I went through it in the month of September of 1547 to join the other soldiers who set out from the district of Popayán to support the King's cause and put down the disturbance that had occurred and this valley seemed very pleasant to me, and I gave thanks to God for the freshness of it, with so many groves of trees and thickets filled with a thousand kinds of birds.

Continuing, one comes to that of Chicama, no less fertile and abundant than Pacasmayo in quality and richness, and in addition there are great plantations of sugarcane, from which they made such an excellent sugar and other products and conserves. There is a monastery of Santo Domingo which was founded by the Friar Domingo de Santo Tomás.

Four leagues on is the valley of Chimú, broad and very large, where the city of Trujillo is situated. Certain of the Indians relate that in olden times, before the Incas dominated them, there lived in this valley a powerful lord called Chimú,[2] the name the valley now bears,

[2] This was the fabulous kingdom of Chimor, called Chimú, famous for the gold it yielded to the conquering Incas and later to the Spanish conquistadors, and of great interest to archaeologists because of the spectacular pottery which the tombs have yielded and the impressive size of its capital, Chan-Chan. The kingdom of Chimor, contemporaneous with the Incas, was to the Peruvian northern coast what the Incas

who performed great feats and won many battles, and built buildings which, old as they are, clearly seem to have been a great thing.
When the Incas, lords of Cuzco, made themselves masters of these
plains, they held this valley of Chimú in high esteem, and ordered
built there great storehouses and houses where they could take their
pleasure, and the highway runs through it, with its walls. The
native chieftains of this valley were always highly regarded, and
believed to be rich. And it has been proved that this was true, for in
the tombs of their ancestors much gold and silver has been found.
At present there are few Indians, and their chiefs are not so respected,
and most of this valley has been divided up among the Spaniards who
settled the new city of Trujillo to build their houses and estates. The
port, as the reef of Trujillo is known, is not far from this valley, and
all along the coast much fish is caught for the use of the city and the
Indians themselves.

323

The city of Trujillo was founded in the valley of Chimú close to
a sizable, beautiful river, from which the Spaniards bring water in
irrigation ditches to water their vegetables and flower gardens, and
the water runs past all the houses of the city, and they are always
green and in flower. The site of this city of Trujillo is considered

were to the highlands—the dominant nation. In its most extended form, Chimor included all the valleys from Tumbes south to Rimac (Lima), a distance roughly of
six hundred miles, with a coastal depth of from twenty to one hundred miles. They were
inheritors of the Mochicas (200 B.C.–800 A.D.), acquiring from them their techniques of
pottery, weaving, and presumably basic social organization. The people of Chimor
spoke, presumably, a language called Mochica (see *Arte de la lengua yunga,* by Friar
Fernando de la Carrera, written in 1644, published by the Universidad Nacional de
Tucumán in 1939), a language that lingered on until the nineteenth century. The
empire of Chimor began to form in the thirteenth century, just about the time that
the Incas, about Cuzco, began their conquests. They continued from century to century
until all coastal cultures within the area indicated were made part of Chimor. Fearing
the Incas, who were already on the south coast, they built a series of fortifications and
made, in defense, an alliance with Cajamarca. Their capital was Chan-Chan (now lying
between the sea and Trujillo).

The clash between the Incas and the Chumús was inevitable; sometime after 1460
a large Inca army in force under the command of Capac Yupanqui (half-brother of
the Inca Pachacuti), moved into the territory of Cusmanco, lord of Cajamarca. He,
allied to the kingdom of Chimor, called for aid, and the battle for all of the Perus was
joined. Cajamarca soon fell, and was in time absorbed into the Inca system. Minchan-
caman, lord of the kingdom of Chimor, put up a bitter but, as it turned out, futile
resistance. The Incas prevailed, looted Chimor, carried off the lord as hostage, brought
their roads into the coastal system, and that was their end. But before the Incas could
thoroughly bring their own shrewd administration into action, the Spaniards were
upon them in 1533. (See Rowe, "The Kingdom of Chimor," *Acta Americana,* Vol.
VI, Nos. 1–2 (1948); and von Hagen, *The Realm of the Incas.*)

healthy, and it is surrounded on all sides by farms, which in Spain are known as *granjas* or *cortijos,* where the residents have their herds and acres. And as it is all irrigated, everywhere many vines have been planted, and pomegranates, and figs, and other fruits of Spain, and an abundance of wheat, and many orange groves, a beautiful sight when they are in bloom. There are also citron, grapefruit, limes, and lemons. There are many native fruits, and very good. Aside from this they raise many fowl, hens and capons. So it may be said that the Spaniards who live in this city are supplied with everything, given the abundance of the things described. And there is no lack of fish, for the sea is only half a league off.

324

The city is situated on a plain the valley forms among its groves and vegetation, near some rocky, arid sierras, and is well laid out and built, the streets being broad and the plaza large. The Indians of the highlands come down from their provinces to serve the Spaniards to whom they have been assigned, and they supply the city with the things they have in their villages. From here they load ships with cotton clothing made by the Indians to sell elsewhere. The city of Trujillo was founded and settled by . . . Francisco Pizarro, governor and captain-general of these kingdoms of Peru, in the name of . . . our king [Charles V], in the year . . . 1530 [-35].

CHAPTER 112 (LXX)

Of the remaining valleys and settlements to be found along the [coastal Inca] road until reaching the City of the Kings.

I WOULD SAY that from this city of Trujillo to that of [Lima, City of] the Kings is a distance of eighty leagues [240 miles], the whole road running through sand and valleys. After leaving Trujillo, one comes to the valley of Guañape, [within] seven leagues . . . and in bygone times it was no less famous among the natives because of the chicha made there than Madrigal or San Martín in Castile for the quality of their wine. In olden times this valley, too, was thickly settled, and there were great lords there whom the Incas treated well and respected after they had dominated them. The Indians who have survived the wars and past hardships work their lands like the others, bringing water from the river to irrigate the fields they plant, and it can be clearly seen that the Incas had storehouses and dwellings there. There is a good port in this valley of Guañape,[1] and many of the ships sailing this Southern Sea, bound for Peru from Panama, provision themselves in it.

One comes next to the valley of Santa, and before reaching it, one crosses a small valley having no river, but where there is a spring of good water from which the Indians and travelers drink. This must come from some river that runs underground. In bygone times the valley of Santa was very heavily populated, and there were great warriors and native lords there, so much so that at first they dared to measure their strength with the Incas, who, it is told, more by kindness and shrewdness than severity and force of arms, dominated them, and afterwards esteemed and respected them. They ordered great lodgings and many storehouses erected there, for this valley is one of the largest, and broader and longer than any we have seen so far. It is crossed by a large and turbulent river[2] [which drains the Callejón de Huaylas], and when it is winter in the sierra, it is so swollen that some Spaniards have been drowned trying to cross it. Now there are balsa rafts on which the Indians cross. There used to be many thousands of the natives, but now there are not more than four hundred left, a sad thing to consider.

[1] Guañape (pronounced Gwan-ya'pi) was an Inca administrative center, the first tambo south of Chan-Chan (Trujillo). It lay just north of the Virú valley near a protected bay. The Virú valley was subject in the years 1946–1948 to an intense coordinated study; it was found that near to it cultural man had appeared as early as 2500 B.C. He had then such food plants and techniques as appeared in the later advanced empire cultures. Valleys of the desert Peruvian coast are semi-isolated because of the hiatus of unliving land between each valley, but yet the tides of human culture drifted across the Virú: there were complex house patterns, enormous temples, fortresses, roads, and much indication of what would follow. In the centuries 500–900, elements of the Tiahuanacu empire, centered about Lake Titicaca, made a coastal invasion (A.D. 1000–1300), but that conquest, motivated by religious fervor, was not systematically organized, and the Tiahuanacus left behind little of social impress here in the Virú and elsewhere, only those unmistakable designs on pottery and cloth, the symbol of the cult of the "Weeping God." (See Gordon R. Willey, *Prehistoric Settlement Patterns in the Virú Valley, Peru*, Smithsonian Institution *Bulletin 155*.)

[2] The Santa River drains the great gorge of the Callejón de Huaylas. At its mouth, as it enters the sea during the rainy season in the cordilleras, it is as much as 1,800 yards across. For centuries the Incas maintained, and it was continued for additional centuries, a rope suspension bridge across the Santa, three miles from its mouth. It endured up until 1806, when it was destroyed. (See W. B. Stevenson, *A Historical and Descriptive Narrative of Twenty Years' Residence in South America* [London, 1825].)

The thing that struck me most when I crossed this valley was the multitude of graves to be seen, and throughout the sierras and scree of the upper regions of the valley there are many remote spots, laid out in their own fashion, all covered with bones of the dead. So the sights of this valley are the graves of the dead, and the fields they cultivated when they were alive. They used to dig great irrigation ditches from the river, with which they watered most of the valley, in high areas and on the hillsides. But now that there are so few Indians, as I have told, most of the fields are untended and grown up to thickets and brush, and so dense that there are places where one cannot get through.

The natives here go dressed in blankets and shirts, and the women the same. On their heads they wear a band or insigne. Fruits such as I have mentioned grow well in this valley, and the vegetables of Spain, and they catch fish in abundance. The coastwise ships always take on water from this river and supplies of these products. And as there are so many trees and so few people, such swarms of mosquitoes breed in the undergrowth that they cause great annoyance to those who cross or sleep in this valley, from which that of Huambacho is a two days' journey distant. All I have to say of it is that it is of the sort and manner of those we have seen, and had lodgings of the rulers, and that from the river that runs through it they drew water in ditches to irrigate the fields they planted.

From this valley I went in a day and a half to that of Huarmey, which in olden times also had many people. Now large numbers of swine, cows, and mares are raised there.

After this valley of Huarmey one comes to that of Paramonga, no less pleasant than the others, and I believe there are no Indians there at all to profit by its fertility. If by any chance any are left, they are in the passes of the sierra in the upper reaches of the valley, because all we saw were empty woods and thickets.

One thing to be seen in this valley is a handsome, well-designed fortress[3] in the manner of those who built it; and it is amazing to

[3] Paramonga, despite the insults of time and man, remains the best-preserved fortress on the entire Peruvian coast. It is built on a low hill within view of the sea and overlooking the swift-flowing Fortaleza River. Its outer walls, constructed of adobe bricks, are about nine hundred feet by six hundred; it commands a view of the road and has a view of the sea. Close to it is a complex of buildings never studied. It was painted and the plaster walls still carry the color, but the animals and birds seen by

see how they brought water in ditches to irrigate the highest part of it. The rooms and dwellings were very fine, and on the walls were painted many wild animals and birds, and it was all surrounded by strong, well-built walls. It is now all in ruins, and has been undermined in many spots by those searching for buried gold and silver. The only use of this citadel today is to bear witness to what it was. Two leagues from this valley lies the Huamán River, which in our Spanish tongue means "River of the Falcon," and it is commonly known as the Barranca. This valley is of the same nature as the others; and when it rains hard in the sierra, the aforementioned river becomes perilous, and people have been drowned trying to cross it. A day's journey off lies the Huaura valley, from which we shall proceed to that of Lima.

327

CHAPTER 113 (ii: LVIII)

Of how Topa Inca traveled through Los Llanos, and how most of the Yungas submitted to him.

WHEN TOPA INCA decided to go to the . . . Llanos to win over to his service and obedience those who dwelt there, he descended to Tumbes [as I said], where he was received with honors by the natives to

Cieza de León have long since vanished; but according to Proctor, a nineteenth-century English traveler, they were still visible then: he said they were "uncouth representations of birds and beasts." It is tradition that it was built by the Chimús under their chief Minchan-caman as a bastion of defense against the encroaching Incas. In all probability (although there is no immediate evidence of architectural alteration), it was taken over by the Incas after 1460 and made part of their own coastal defenses.

It was first seen by Europeans when Hernando Pizarro on the day of Epiphany, the fifth of January, 1533, set out "with twenty horse and a few arquebusiers" to traverse the Inca road from Cajamarca to the fabulous shrine of Pachacamac. Miguel de Astete, who served as scrivener to the expedition, wrote: ". . . marching along the banks of a river [Fortaleza], they stopped for the night at a village called Huaracanga [Huariconga]. . . . Next day they stopped at a large place called Parpunga [i.e., Paramonga]. It was a strong house with seven encircling walls painted in many devices both inside and outside with portals well built like those of Spain, with two [painted] jaguars at the principal doorway."

It will be noted that the lateral Inca road, which connected the coastal road with one of the main royal Andean roads, did not have its junction at the fortress of Paramonga; rather, ten kilometers southward at the part now named Tambo Viejo. The lateral road traveled along the south bank of the Fortaleza; Huariconga, mentioned by the Spaniards in 1533, is still to be seen.

whom Topa Inca showed great affection, and at once donned the attire they used to make them happier, and praised the decision of the chieftains to accept him as king without war. He promised to hold and esteem them as his own sons. Happy with his friendly words and the way in which he treated them, they accepted obedience in good faith, and agreed to the presence of governors and promised to construct buildings. There are [others] who say that Topa Inca by-passed this region without affirming his power there, which was done in the reign of Huayna Capac.

328

Departing from valley [to valley], the Inca proceeded along most of the coast, building as he went the grand and beautiful highway which we still see, and everywhere he was served and gifts were brought him, though it is said that in some places they resisted, but to no purpose, for in the end they became his vassals. He spent some time in these valleys, drinking and taking his pleasure, rejoicing in their pleasantness. At his orders great houses and temples were built. In the valley of Chimú . . . he fought [that] hard war with the lord [Minchan-caman] of that valley. Topa Inca, with his usual clemency, pardoned, ordering the survivors to devote themselves to tilling their fields and not to take up arms again against him or others. His delegate remained in Chimú, and most of these valleys bore their tribute to Cajamarca. As the [Chimús] were so skillful at working metals, many of them were taken to Cuzco and the capitals of the provinces, where they wrought jewelry, vessels, and goblets of gold and silver, and whatever else they were ordered. From Chimú the Inca went on, and in Paramonga he ordered a fortress built, which is still to be seen, though in ruins.

These Yungas are very self-indulgent, and their lords given to vices and festivities; they were carried on their vassals' shoulders, had many wives, and were rich in gold, silver, precious stones, clothing, and flocks. In those days they surrounded themselves with great pomp; ahead of them went jesters and wags; their houses were tended by doorkeepers; they followed many religions. Of their own accord they offered themselves to the Inca, while others took up arms against him, but in the end he made himself sovereign lord of them all. He did not deprive them of their liberties or old customs, provided they followed his, which, willingly or unwillingly, they had to observe. Skilled Indians remained with them to train them in what the Inca wanted them to know, and they took special care to see that they learned the common language. *Mitimaes* were brought in, posts established along the highways; each valley delivered a moderate amount of what its territory produced as tribute, without seeking it elsewhere; they were assured justice if they complied with their promises; if not, they suffered for it, and the Inca exacted the full measure of taxes. He did not remove any of the native chieftains, but many of the men of the valleys were transferred from one to another, and sent to other places for the work aforementioned.

329

The Inca traveled through the other valleys in the most orderly manner, never permitting any damage to the settlements or fields they traversed; and the natives brought abundant supplies to the storehouses and lodgings along the road. In this fashion he proceeded until he reached the valley of Pachacamac, where the oldest and most venerated temple of the Yungas was, which he was eager to see. When he came to that valley, it is said that he was very desirous of having there only a temple to the sun; but as that shrine was so venerated by the natives, he refrained, and contented himself with having a great temple to the sun built, with *mamaconas* and priests, so that the rites of his religion could be performed. Many Indians say that the Inca himself spoke with the devil that dwells in the idol of Pachacamac, and heard him say that he was the maker of the world, and other nonsense which it is not fitting I should set down, and that the Inca begged him to tell him with what service he would be most honored and happy, and he answered that with the sacrifice of much blood of humans and *llamas*.

After the foregoing, they state that great sacrifices were made in Pachacamac by Topa Inca, and great feasts were held, and when these had been concluded, he returned to Cuzco by a highway that had been built for him that comes out in the valley of Jauja and crosses the snow-covered sierra of Pariacaca,[1] and it is a sight to see how

---

[1] This is the Pachacamac-Huarochirí-Jauja lateral road which joined the coastal highway with that of the cordillera. It was the principal communication route between Jauja, the Inca garrison center in the Andes, and this important part of the coast. It began at the Lurín valley, proceeded east on the south bank of the river of the same name to Tambo Inga, crossed to the right or north bank of the river to take advantage of a solid rock wall, then moved through Chantay, Sisicaya, and so following the stream, evoluted southeast to the halfway stop of Huarochirí.

Cieza de León often mentions in his books on the civil wars the use of this large Inca center as an army depot: "Gonzalo Pizarro . . . and the others . . . arrived at

fine it is, and the stairs it has, and there it is even to this day to make
it possible to cross through those snows. Thus, visiting the provinces
of the highlands, and prescribing and ordering what was most advantageous for their good governance, he reached Cuzco, where he was
received with great feasts and dances, and in the temple great sacrifices were made in thanks for his victories.

CHAPTER 114 (LXXI)

Of how the City of the Kings [Lima] is situated, its founding, and who its founder was.

THE VALLEY of Lima is the largest and broadest of all those that have
been described between Tumbes and it.[1] As it was large, it was

---

Huarochirí. . . . a battle ensued with the Indians . . . who had gone to the upper
parts of the mountains where they had their principal dwellings." And later, "They
slept in the dwellings at Huarochirí" (p. 109, *War of Salinas*). And again, "Departing
from Lima they took the road to Huarochirí" (*War of Quito*). This place is ninety
kilometers in distance and the halfway mark. The next part of the journey is through
the rugged, snow-bound Pariacaca. The Inca road passes through this voiceless, frigid
land filled with small rivers, lakes, and snow, and always referred to by the conquistadors as the "snowy mountains of Pariacaca." The last ninety kilometers are over the
most difficult road in Peru, if not in the world. The Jesuit José de Acosta was caught
there, some time in the 1570's, on "the high mountains which they call Parriacaca,"
when he was seized with the onslaught of *soroche* (altitude sickness). "I was suddenly
surprised with so mortall and strange a pang . . . for having caste up meate, fleugme,
& choller, both yellow and greene; in the end I cast up blood. . . . I beheld one that
did beate himselfe against the earth, crying out for the rage and griefe which this
passage of Pariacaca hadde caused."
  The road emerges above (that is, north of) the present location of Jauja, where
there are the remains of an Inca bridge, as well as a colonial bridge that stood beside it.
  [1] The valley of Lima, watered by the Rimac, from which it takes its name, is, as
Cieza averred, the largest on the coast. Although the whole of the valley is thickly
studded with ruins, evidence of its once great population—the immense pre-Inca site
of Cajamarquilla (twenty kilometers from Lima up the Rimac valley), the site of the
shrine of Pachacamac, and many others—still its archaeology is imperfectly known;
the history of its people in the ebb and flow of history is one cultural blank. That it
was a bone of contention among the various coastal empire cultures can be seen in
the remains of immense adobe walls which tried to set boundaries to the fields of local
clans. The kingdom of Chimor did not extend down into the Rimac, although its
influence was felt. Chancay, a localized but vital center north of Ancón, had considerable
political power, and the fact that immense shrines (*huacas*) in the form of stepped
Pyramids are found all over the valley, culminating in the most gigantic of them all—
Pachacamac—suggests that it was a valley held sacrosanct by all along the coast. But
the Inca conquest, after 1450, completely obliterated all coastal names and traditions
in the Rimac valley, so that nothing remains. The names of cities and valleys on the

thickly populated. Now there are few of the native Indians because, as the city was settled in their lands and their fields and irrigation system taken over, some went to one valley and some to another. The few who happen to have remained have their fields and ditches to water what they plant. Don Francisco Pizarro, His Majesty's appointed governor, was in the city of Cuzco . . . [when he decided to] 331 descend to these plains and found a city in this valley. At that time neither Trujillo nor Arequipa nor Huamanga, nor the other cities later established, had been founded. And as the Governor Don Francisco Pizarro had the idea of establishing this settlement, after having surveyed the valley of Cangallo[2] and other places of this coast, one day as he was descending with a group of Spaniards to where the city now stands, it seemed to them a fit spot for their purpose, fulfilling the necessary conditions. And so the city was laid out and built on an open field of this valley, two short leagues from the sea. To the east of it rises a river [Rimac] which, when it is summer in the sierra, carries little water, and in winter increases in volume, and flows into the sea to the west. The city is so laid out that the sun never slants the river, but rises to the side of the city, which lies so close to the river that from the plaza a man with a good throwing arm can send a small stone into it. And the city cannot grow in that direction if the plaza is to remain in the center and not to one side. After Cuzco, this city is the largest in the whole kingdom of Peru, and the finest, and in it there are very good houses, some of them very handsome with their turrets and terraces, and the plaza is large, and the streets wide, and beside most of the houses run irrigation ditches which are a pleasure to see. With this water they irrigate their gardens and flowers, of which there are many, cool and delightful. The court and the royal chancellery are now located in this city,[3] and because of this and the fact that trade with all the kingdom of Terra Firma has its headquarters there, it is always full of people, and large, rich mer-

southern coast are Inca. We do not even know the original name of the great *huaca* which endured one thousand years before the advent of the Incas: "Pachacamac" is Quechua.

[2] Cangallo was the ancient name for the valley of Pisco. There is a large natural bay there and at one time it was seriously considered for the capital of Peru.

[3] Lima still preserves the sites of these structures; the Cathedral stands where the first pile was raised; the Presidential Palace occupies the space that once was Pizarro's house and then later the Viceregal Palace. Even the new city hall stands on the spot where the original one stood.

chants' establishments. The year I left this kingdom there were so many residents who had encomiendas of Indians, and they were so rich and prosperous, that their plantations were worth from 150,000 ducats to 80,000, 60,000, 50,000, some more, others less. In a word, I left most of them rich and prosperous. Ships often leave the port [Callao] of this city carrying 800,000 ducats apiece, and some over a million.

332

Above the city, to the east, stands a large, high hill [San Cristóbal] where a cross has been set up. Beyond the city, on either hand, there are many ranches and estates where the Spaniards have their cattle and dovecotes, and vineyards, and cool, pleasant gardens abounding in the native products, and fig trees, bananas, pomegranates, sugarcane, melons, oranges, limes, citron, grapefruit, and the vegetables that have been brought from Spain, all so good and fine flavored that there is no lack of anything, but, on the contrary, for his bounty one should give thanks to Almighty God, Our Lord, who made them to grow. And as a place to spend one's life, once an end has been made to the turmoils and disturbances and there are no more [civil] wars, it is truly one of the best lands in the world, for, as we see, there is neither famine nor plague, nor does it rain, nor does lightning strike, nor is thunder heard, and the sky is always clear and very beautiful. Other things could be said of it, but it seems to me that what I have mentioned suffices, so I shall conclude by saying that it was founded and settled by Francisco Pizarro, governor and captain-general of these kingdoms, in the name of the Emperor Charles V, in the year 1530 [1535].

CHAPTER 115 (ii: LXV)

Of how Huayna Capac traveled through the valleys of Los Llanos, and what he did.

CERTAIN OF [my informants] state that Huayna Capac returned to Cuzco from Quito by way of [the coastal valleys of] Los Llanos as far as Pachacamac, and others deny this, saying that he remained in Quito until his death [in 1527]. After making inquiry to try to arrive at the truth of the matter, I shall set down what I heard from some of the principal men who accompanied him in person during this war. They say that when he was in Quito, ambassadors came to him from many places to do him homage in the name of their lands; and that after having won over by peaceful methods the highland provinces, it seemed to him that it would be advisable to proceed to the provinces of Puerto Viejo and what we call Guayaquil, and to the 333 Yungas. After holding a council with his captains and advisers, they approved his idea, and advised him to carry it into effect. Many of his troops remained in Quito; he set out with the number he judged sufficient, and entered those lands where he had a few skirmishes with certain of the inhabitants, but, finally, all of them agreed to serve him, and he established governors and *mitimaes*.

[That] fierce war was going on between those of Puná and Tumbes [as I said], and the Inca had ordered the hostilities to cease, and that they prepare to receive him in Puná and make him gifts under a cloak of peace. But as soon as he had left, in conspiracy with the natives of the mainland, the Punás plotted to kill many of the *Orejones* and their captains. . . . But Huayna Capac got word of it, and did what I have told [in Chapter 100]; and after punishing them severely and ordering them to build the road, or mighty causeway, known as that of Huayna Capac, he returned to Tumbes and remained there, where buildings and a temple to the sun had been constructed. From all around they came with great humility to do him reverence. He went through the [coastal] valleys of Los Llanos, putting things in order, establishing the boundary limits and the waters [rights], ordering them not to make war, and doing what has been told in other places. And they tell of him that as he was crossing the fair valley of Chayanta, near Chimú, where the city of Trujillo is now situated, there was an old Indian in a field, and when he heard that the Lord-Inca was passing near by, he picked two or four cucumbers, and with dirt and all he took them to him saying, *"Ancha Hatun-pu Micucampa,"* which means, "Great Lord, eat this." And before all the lords and other people, the Inca accepted the cucumbers, and eating one of them said, in the hearing of all, to please the old man, *"Xuylluy, ancha mizqui cay,"* which in our language means, "In truth, this is very sweet." Which gave them all great pleasure.

Then proceeding, he ordered [all] those [tribes] of Chimú, and Guañape, Huarmey, Huaura, Lima, and the other valleys to do what he wanted done; and when he reached Pachacamac, he made great feasts and dances and drinking festivals.

... [And] Huayna Capac gave them, so it is told, more than a hundred arrobas of gold and a thousand of silver, and other jewels and emeralds, with which the temple of the sun and the ancient shrine of Pachacamac were still further adorned.

From here certain of the Indians say he went to Cuzco, and others that he returned to Quito. Be this as it may, and whether this took place on this occasion or earlier boots little; he visited all [the coastal valleys of] Los Llanos, and ordered built for him the great [coastal] highway which we see that they constructed, and we also know that in Chincha and other places in these valleys he built great lodgings and storehouses, and a temple to the sun. And when everything had been carried out and the whole kingdom pacified, he turned back to Quito, and proceeded north as far as the Angasmayo River.[1]

CHAPTER 116 (LXXII)

Of the valley of Pachacamac and the ancient temple that was there, and how it was revered by the Yungas.

LEAVING THE City of the Kings and proceeding [southward] along the same coast, four leagues off lies the valley of Pachacamac, famed among these Indians.[1] This valley is pleasant and fertile, and there stood there one of the most sumptuous temples to be found in these

[1] The Angasmayo (now in the Republic of Colombia), in the time of the Incas the territory of the Pastos, was the spot where Huayna Capac—at the place of Rumichaca, a natural stone bridge gouged out by the Angasmayo—set up, either actually or figuratively, the northern boundaries of the empire of the Incas.

[1] The Inca coastal road, on its way southward toward Pachacamac, passed into the suburb of Lima, Chorrillos (once greatly populated), to the base of a large Gibraltar-like rock, Morro Solar; at its base lay Arma-Tambo (Purification Tambo), where those making the hegira to holy Pachacamac bathed before going on five miles to the *huaca* itself. A small rivulet, the Río Surco, branching off from the Rimac River, flowed down to it. The ruins of Arma-Tambo, despite centuries of destruction, are still extant. This was the original way-stop of the Rimac. It was first visited by Hernando Pizarro in January, 1533, with his expedition of "twenty horse and a few arquebusiers." Wrote the scrivener: "They crossed a great river [Rimac] by a ford and marched along a road with a wall on each side, passing the night at a place [Arma-Tambo] belonging to the town [of Pachacamac], and at a distance of a league and a half [five miles] from it. The next day was Sunday, thirtieth of January and . . . he reached Pachacamac."

regions. They say of it that, despite the fact that the Inca lords built many [temples], aside from those of Cuzco, and glorified and embellished them with riches, there was none to compare with this of Pachacamac, which was built upon a small, man-made hill of adobes and earth, and on its summit stood the temple which began at the foot, and had many gates, which, like the walls, were adorned with figures of wild animals. Inside, where the idol stood,[2] were the priests who feigned great sanctimoniousness. And when they performed their sacrifices before the people, they kept their faces toward the door of the temple and their backs to the figure of the idol, with their eyes on the ground and all trembling and overcome, according to certain Indians still alive today, so that it could almost be compared to what one reads of the priests of Apollo when the [Greek] Gentiles sought their vain oracles. And they say more: that before the figure of this devil they sacrificed many animals, and human blood of persons they killed; and that on the occasion of their most solemn feasts they made

[2] Hernando Pizarro, on January 30, 1533, was the first and last to see "the idol." He had been sent down, on the orders of the captured Atahualpa, to pry out the gold from the Pachacamac sanctuary. Hernando Pizarro insisted on seeing the idol, ". . . he went." "It was [wrote his scrivener] in a good house, well painted, in a very dark chamber with a close, fetid smell. Here there was a very dirty idol made of wood, and they say that this is their god who created them [Pacha-camac = creator god] . . . and it was held in high veneration." "The *Capitán* [Hernando Pizarro] ordered the vault in which the idol was to be pulled down and the idol to be broken."

Although the idol had a Quechua name, "Pachacamac," it was of wood and therefore belonged to a coastal culture. We have no idea of the antiquity of the site. It is assumed that the original ancient *huaca* was enlarged and given content by the invaders of Tiahuanacu (A.D. 1000–1300) since many of the artifacts found there bear the Tiahuanacan imprint. These "Viracocha-worshipers" of the highlands might have deliberately colonized Pachacamac as a center from which their religious and political influence could be used up and down the coast. Pachacamac, with its immense stepped pyramid and its lesser *huacas,* houses, and streets, traditionally is believed to have been built by a chieftain named Cuis-mancu, whose domains began at the northern edge of those of Chimú (at the Huamán valley, close to modern Barranca), and continued southward to the Lurin valley. At least this is the vague empire's chief claim to fame: That Cuis-mancu built the temples of Pachacamac; time, about A.D. 1300. The fame of Pachacamac was such that local wars were suspended so that people could make a pilgrimage there; it was as colorful as the hegira to Mecca. It was visited by the tribes of the highlands, and, as Pizarro inquired, as far north "as the town of Catamez [Atacames, in northern Ecuador], for all the people of this coast serve this mosque with gold and silver and offer a certain tribute every year."

The Inca Pachacuti, the same who had saved Cuzco and rebuilt it, made the Inca conquest of Pachacamac about 1450. Pachacamac was too holy to destroy; so, like the Romans, they admitted the time-honored deity (Irma) into their own pantheon, but they added stone baths, built a temple for the Chosen Women, and adjusted it into the Inca scheme of things. It had been under the rule of the Incas, then, about eighty years when the Spaniards came to it on that thirtieth day of January, 1533.

utterances which were believed and held to be true. In the terraces and foundations of this temple great sums of gold and silver were buried. The priests were greatly venerated, and the lords and caciques obeyed them in many things that they ordered. And it is told that beside the temple there were many and spacious lodgings for those who came there in pilgrimage, and no one was deemed worthy nor allowed to be buried in its vicinity except the lords or priests or pilgrims who came bearing gifts to the temple. When the great yearly feasts were celebrated, many people assembled, carrying on their diversions to the sound of the musical instruments they possessed. And as the Incas, powerful lords that they were, made themselves the masters of the kingdom and came to this valley of Pachacamac, and, as was their custom in all the lands they conquered, they ordered temples and shrines built to the sun. And when they saw the splendor of this temple, and how old it was, and the sway it held over all the people of the surrounding lands, and the devotion they paid it, holding that it would be very difficult to do away with this, they agreed with the native lords and the ministers of their god or devil that this temple of Pachacamac should remain with the authority and cult it possessed, provided they built another temple to the sun which should take precedence. And when the temple to the sun had been built, as the Incas ordered, they filled it with riches and put many virgins in it. The devil Pachacamac, highly pleased with this arrangement, they say revealed his satisfaction in his replies, for the one and the other served his ends, and the souls of the misguided remained fast in his power. . . .

The name of this devil meant "maker of the world," for *camac* means "maker," and *pachac,* "world." And when the Governor Don Francisco Pizarro (because God so willed it) took Atahualpa prisoner in the province of Cajamarca, as he had heard about this temple and the riches it contained, he sent Captain Hernando Pizarro, his brother, with a force of Spaniards, to this valley to remove all the gold from that cursed temple, and return to Cajamarca. And although Captain Hernando Pizarro made his way to Pachacamac with all possible speed, it is common knowledge among the Indians that the headmen and priests of the temple carried away more than four hundred loads of gold which was never seen again, nor do the Indians alive today

PARTE PRIMERA

Dela chronica del Peru. Que tracta la demarca=
cion de sus prouincias: la descripcion dellas. Las
fundaciones de las nueuas ciudades. Los ritos y
costumbres de los indios. Y otras cosas estrañas
dignas de ser sabidas. Fecha por Pedro d̄ Cieça
de Leon vezino de Seuilla.

1553.

¶ Con priuillegio Real.

Title page of the first edition of Cieza's *Chronicle of Peru* (Seville, 1553).

"Certain of the *Orejones* [Big-eared chieftains] went about visiting the provinces." Curacas, with ears extended for ornaments, talking to the common Indians. From Cieza's own illustrations in the 1553 edition of his *Chronicle*.

"Cuzco was founded and settled by Manco Capac, the first of the Inca lords. And after ten Incas had succeeded him in the rule, it was rebuilt and refounded by Francisco Pizarro in the month of October, 1534." An illustration taken from Cieza's own edition (Seville, 1553) showing an Inca, possibly symbolizing Manco Capac, adorned with the royal fringe *(llautu)* or crown, gesturing toward Cuzco to Francisco Pizarro.

"The wealth that has been discovered in the mines of Potosí." Cieza's own illustration, the first ever made of the famous Cerro de Potosí, that appears in the 1553 edition.

"There is a lake — Titicaca — the largest and widest I have seen in the Andes; it measures eighty leagues in circumference." First seen by Europeans in 1553, Titicaca lies 12,500 feet above sea level and is approximately eighty miles in length; although many rivers enter it, it has but a single outlet.

La Gran Ciudad . . . real de los reyes Incas. The city of Cuzco, as drawn by Poma de Ayala about 1590, showing the good-sized square of Huayka-pata and Cusi-pata (Joy Square).

La Chronica

DEL PERV, NVEVA.

MENTE ESCRITA, POR

Pedro de Cieça de Leon,

vezino de Se-

uilla.

EN ANVERS

En casa de Martin Nucio,

M. D. LIIII.

Con preuilegio Imperial.

Title page of Cieza's *Chronicle* published in Antwerp by Martin Nucio, 1554.

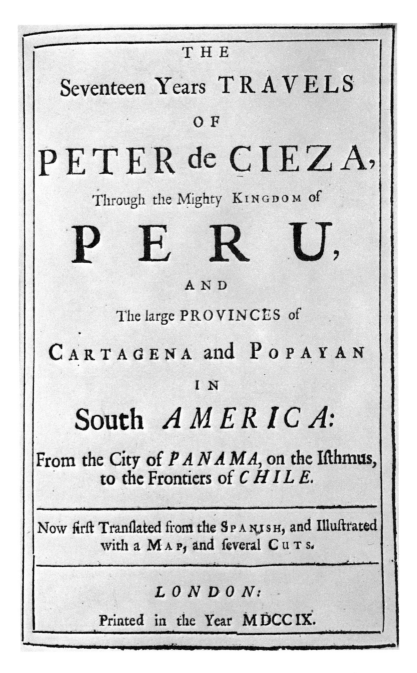

THE
Seventeen Years TRAVELS
OF
PETER de CIEZA,
Through the Mighty KINGDOM of
PERU,
AND
The large PROVINCES of
CARTAGENA and POPAYAN
IN
South AMERICA:
From the City of *PANAMA*, on the Ifthmus,
to the Frontiers of *CHILE*.

Now firft Tranflated from the SPANISH, and Illuftrated
with a MAP, and feveral CUTS.

LONDON:
Printed in the Year MDCCIX.

Title page of the first English edition of Cieza's *Chronicle*, 1709.

know where it is. Notwithstanding, Hernando Pizarro (who, as I have said, was the first Spanish captain to enter the temple) found considerable gold and silver. Later on, Captain Rodrigo Orgoñez and Francisco de Godoy and others found a great quantity of gold and silver in the burial sites, and it is believed and held certain that there is much more. But as no one knows where it is buried, unless it 337 is stumbled on by chance it will be lost. From the moment Hernando Pizarro and the other Spaniards entered this temple the devil was defeated and his power destroyed, and the idols in it cast down, and the buildings and the temple to the sun were lost, and most of the Indians have disappeared, so that there are very few left.

This [Lurin] valley is as lush and full of vegetation as those which border upon it, and in the fields much cattle and other livestock and mares are raised, which breed a number of good horses.

CHAPTER 117 (LXXIII)

Of the valleys that lie between Pachacamac and the fortress of Huarco, and of a remarkable thing done in this valley.

FROM THIS valley of Pachacamac, where the aforementioned temple was, one proceeds to that of Chilca, remarkable for a very strange thing, which is that neither does water fall from the sky, nor does river or brook run through it, and yet most of the valley is covered with cornfields and plantations of other roots and fruit trees. It is an amazing thing to hear what they do in this valley. To provide the needed humidity, the Indians dig wide, deep holes in which they sow and plant the things I have described, and with the dew and dampness God makes them to grow. But the seed of the corn in no wise sprout nor yield if they did not put with each a head or two of the sardines they take in their nets. Thus, when they plant the corn, they lay them with the grain in the hole, and in this way it comes up and bears abundantly. Truly it is a remarkable thing never before seen that in a land where it never rains and the only water is a light dew, people can live well. The water those of this valley drink comes from big, deep wells. In this vicinity of the sea they catch so many sardines that they supply these Indians with food and what they need for their plantings. There were storehouses here and lodgings of the Incas, where they could stop when they were visiting the provinces of their kingdom. Three leagues beyond Chilca lies the valley of Mala,[1] [and] through . . . [it] flows a very good river flanked by thick woods and groves.

338

Beyond this valley, a little more than five leagues, lies that of Huarco,[2] famous in this kingdom, large and broad and covered with groves of fruit trees. The number of fragrant, flavorful guavas is great, and that of cassias, still larger. Wheat and corn do well, and everything else they plant, both the native products as well as the trees of Spain. Aside from these there are many pigeons, doves, and other varieties of birds. And the groves and thickets of the valley are very shady, and beneath them run the irrigation ditches. The inhabitants of this valley say that in olden times there were many people in this valley, and they fought with those of the sierra and with other rulers of the plains. And as the Incas [warriors] came conquering and making themselves masters of all they surveyed, since the natives did not want to become their vassals, for their forefathers had left them free, they displayed such bravery that they carried on war, with no less courage than determination, for more than four years, during which noteworthy events occurred on both sides, as the *Orejones* of Cuzco and these people tell, as set forth in the second part. And as the struggle went on in spite of the fact that the Inca returned to Cuzco during the summers because of the heat while his troops con-

[1] Mala is known as the place where the dispute between Francisco Pizarro and Diego de Almagro over the spoils of the Inca empire first broke out into violence. A suspension bridge of coiled-rope cables hung across the river at Mala, and close to it near the canebrakes that lined the stream was the tambo, way-station, of the road. It was composed of two stories (Cieza, *War of Salinas,* 143), an unusual feature. An uncertain peace was signed between the two conquistadors there on the fifteenth of January, 1537, "in the tambo or building of Mala" (*ibid.,* 152).

[2] Huarco (now the Cañete valley) was in 1450 the capital of a multi-valleyed kingdom which was at the time of the Inca conquest ruled by a fierce chieftain called Chuquimancu—lord of the valleys of Chilca, Mala, Runahuanac (now Lunahuaná), and Huarco; who was, a historian tells us, "treated as king . . . exacted homage from all these tribes though they were not his vassals." Rich and abundant, these valleys were much sought after by neighboring kingdoms, and so in defense two of the greatest coastal fortresses were built there: one on the hill close to the Ungara Hacienda in the center of the valley, the other at Herbay, overlooking the sea, a few hundred meters from where the Cañete River debouches into the sea. The defense of Chuquimancu was long and costly for the Incas, as Cieza relates in a following chapter.

tinued the war, which was long drawn out, and the Inca was determined to bring it to an end, he came down with the *Orejones* of
Cuzco and built a new city, to which he gave the name of New
Cuzco,³ the same as his main seat. They also tell that he ordered that
the districts of the city and the hills should have the same names as
those of Cuzco. During this time, after the men of Huarco and their
allies had done their utmost, they were conquered and brought under
the yoke of the tyrant Inca, who had no other right to the lands he had
acquired than the fortune of war. And as this had favored him, he
returned with his army to Cuzco, and the name of the new city he
had built was lost. Nevertheless, to celebrate his victory, he ordered
built on a high hill of the valley the most beautiful and ornate citadel
to be found in the whole kingdom of Peru, set upon great square
blocks of stone, and with very fine gates and entrance ways, and large
patios. From the top of this royal edifice a stone stairway descends
to the sea.⁴ The waves beat against the structure with such force and

339

³ This "New Cuzco" is now known as Incahuasi, anciently Runahuanac; it is situated
fifteen miles up the valley, four hundred meters back from the river in a dry valley.
It is the largest Inca-built site on the coast, and covers at the very least five square miles.
Houses of the Chosen Women are perched on the sides of precipitous cliffs (as at
Ollantay-Tambo); there is an immense complex of ceremonial residences; a keystone-
shaped plaza six hundred feet long, with remains of an altar in its center; a gigantic
storage center with 248 one-foot-square cubicles, arranged with the precision of bee-
hive cells, with drying yards for the corn, beans, and peppers stored there. This enormous site has had little or no attention from archaeologists.

⁴ This *is* Herbay, situated on a steep hill, one hundred meters from the mouth of
the Cañete River on the Herbay Bajo Hacienda. It was first visited and described by
Sir Clements Markham in 1853. The ruins are divided into two parts, one section
overhanging the sea. The walls were made of adobe; the doorways were fifteen feet
high; remains of the roof-beams were still to be seen. The second section of the ruin
consists of a large court, with nine rooms replete with wall niches. The whole area
was covered with the remains of walls and other structures. It was again visited in
1863 by Squier, the American archaeologist who left in his *Peru* two ground plans
of Herbay; it was then locally known as the "Palace of the Inca King." He, too, thought
the building exceedingly well made and "remarkable for the numerous flights of well-
laid steps."

Apparently the top portions were made of stone—suggesting that the Incas on their
conquest of the Huarco valley had remodeled the ancient building. León de Pinelo
in the seventeenth century says that "It was a castle of stone, situated on an elevation
washed by the sea." And that it had an idol famous in the land, known as Rimac
("speaker"). The Viceroy of Peru in 1595, the same Marqués de Cañete after whom the
valley was renamed, was so impressed by the ruins that he appointed a guard of six
soldiers as a perpetual watch so that the inhabitants of the valley would not dislodge
the stones. But as payment for the guard was not carried through, they left, and the
demolition of the fortress oracle began by the people of the valley. "The ruin," that
author sadly wrote, "reflects disgracefully on our intelligence, which requires that this
work should be restored and preserved." (See Squier, *Peru,* 82–85; Sir Clements

fury that one wonders how it could be built so strong and handsome. In its day this fortress was adorned with paintings, and there used to be great treasure of the Incas there. In all this mighty building, which is as large as I have said, and the stones are of great size, there is no mortar or any sign of how the stones have been fitted together, and they are so close that it is hard to see the joining. When this building was being erected, they say that after they had laid open the hill with their picks and tools, they covered the cavities they had dug with big slabs and stones, and with these foundations the structure was so strong. And, without question, to be the work of these Indians, it is deserving of all praise, and arouses the admiration of all who see it. Although it is now deserted and in ruins, it is evident that it was once as they say. Where this fortress stood, and in the remains of that of Cuzco, it seems to me it should be forbidden, under severe penalties, for the Spaniards or the Indians to continue their destruction, for these two buildings seem the strongest in Peru, and the most noteworthy, and in time they might even prove useful.

340

CHAPTER 118 (ii: LIX)

How Topa Inca set out once more from Cuzco, and the hard war he fought with those of Huarco, and how, after he had conquered them, he returned to Cuzco.

IN THE PAST the province of Chincha was a great thing in this kingdom of Peru, and thickly settled, so much so that before this time we are telling about, they had gone forth with their captains and come to the Colla [around Lake Titicaca], whence, having taken much booty, they returned to their provinces. They had always been greatly respected by their neighbors, and feared. It is told that the father of Topa Inca sent a captain, by name Capac Inca, from the province of the Soras [in the Cunti-suyu division], with troops, to endeavor to win over the people of Chincha to his friendship; but

Markham, *Cuzco: A Journey to the Ancient Capital of Peru,* 29–32; and E. W. Middendorf, *Peru* (3 vols., Berlin, 1893–95), I, 138, with sketch.)

although they went and attempted it, it was of no avail, for they took up arms and prepared to defend themselves so stoutly that the *Orejones* withdrew as best they could. They had never laid eyes on a captain of the Incas until Topa Inca conquered them, according to their own account; I know of no more of this than what they tell themselves. 341

To return to our story, when Topa Inca had returned to Cuzco [in 1470], as has been told, after having rested and taken his pleasure for the time he saw fit, he once more called up troops, with the object of consolidating his power over the Indians of [the coastal valleys of] Los Llanos. His orders were obeyed, and in a short time there appeared in Cuzco the captains of the provinces with the troops they were to bring, and after having put the city in order, and done the other things incumbent upon the Inca, he set out from Cuzco and descended [down] to Los Llanos by the Huaytará road.[1] When they learned of his approach, many awaited him to swear allegiance to him, and many with the determination to fight him and endeavor to keep their freedom. In the valley of Nazca there was a great army prepared to fight.

When Topa Inca arrived, embassies were sent and conversations held, and although there were certain skirmishes and clashes, they accepted the basic conditions the Inca laid down, which were that they should build fortresses and admit *mitimaes,* and pay the tribute

[1] The Huaytará was the lateral road which, connecting the royal roads with the coastal road, originated at Vilcas-huamán, moved straight west across the unpopulated *puna* above 13,000 feet, through the snow-bound *tambos* of Hatunsulla, Tinoco, Inca-huasi, and then Huaytará. In 1537, as Cieza de León records in his *War of Salinas* (p. 179), Diego de Almagro took this road on his way to Cuzco, "where there was much snow. . . . They went on without their tents to protect them from the heavy falls of snow . . . [and] for a long time facing the icy winds, they were attacked by giddiness [*soroche*]. . . . It was only by a lucky chance they were not all frozen to death." At Huaytará there are superb Inca structures still extant; the local church, San Juan Bautista, is constructed over part of the walls; the stones were cut of porphyry in the best polygonal Inca manner and stone niches are well preserved.

Canals, baths, and burial places are found about Huaytará. It was strategic and commanded the heights of the upper reaches of the Pisco valley; it was also a junction place for another Inca lateral road that went southwest to Ica. The Inca road went through Huaytará, down the escarpment of the cordilleras, and followed the left or north bank of the Pisco (then Cangalla) River. On the route are the well-preserved ruins of Tambo Colorado, an Inca garrison and royal halting place; but the tambo of the road was farther down at Huamay. This connected it with the coastal road, which then moved across the protecting mountains southward to the next valley and site of Ica.

asked of them. From here the Inca proceeded to the valley of Ica, where he encountered more resistance than in that of Nazca; but employing his customary prudence, without war he converted the enemies into friends, and they submitted as the others had done. In Chincha, waiting to see if the Inca was going to enter their valley, there were over thirty thousand men equipped for war, and they hoped their neighbors would assist them. When Topa Inca learned of this, he sent messengers bearing fine gifts for the chieftains and captains and leading men, instructing his emissaries to make them generous offers in his name and to assure them that he did not want war, but peace and brotherhood, and other things of this sort. Those of Chincha listened to the Inca's offers, accepted his gifts, and some of the headmen went to him with the products of the valley, and talked with him and discussed the matter of friendship, with the result that peace was agreed upon, and those of Chincha laid down their arms and received Topa Inca, who then went on to [the chief city of] Chincha. This is told by the Indians of Chincha themselves, and the *Orejones* of Cuzco; I have heard a different version from Indians of other provinces, for, as they tell it, there was a great war; however, I am of the opinion that he became the ruler of Chincha without it.

When the Inca reached that valley and saw it so large and beautiful, he was well pleased. He praised the customs of the natives, and with affectionate words urged them to adopt those of Cuzco which they considered suitable, and they satisfied and obeyed him in everything. After giving orders as to what was to be done, he set out for Ica, whence he continued to what they call Huarco, for he had been advised that their intention was to make war on him, and this was the case, for the natives of these valleys, despising their neighbors because they had been so easily cowed and, for no good reason, had handed over the possession of their lands to a strange king, gathered resolutely, having built forts and strongholds in suitable spots near the sea, where they had placed their wives and children. The Inca advanced with his troops in orderly fashion, and sent them emissaries, at times with gifts, at times with threats and menaces, but they did not wish to suffer the fate of their neighbors and recognize foreigners, so combat was joined between them, after the custom of these lands, and great things took place. As summer was coming on and it grew very hot, the Inca's men suffered greatly, for which reason he decided to withdraw. And those of Huarco went out in their valley, harvested their crops, and planted their fields once more, and prepared arms so that if the troops of Cuzco attacked again, they would find them ready.

Topa Inca returned to Cuzco, and as men are so inconstant, when it was seen that those of Huarco had achieved their purpose, many of the others grew restive, and some of them revolted and refused to obey the Inca. These were the natives of this same coast. All this came to the Lord-Inca's knowledge, and he employed the remainder of that summer calling up troops and sending out *Orejones* to all parts of the kingdom to visit the provinces, and he determined to win possession of Huarco at all costs. When autumn came and the summer heat had abated, with all the troops he could assemble he descended to [the coastal] Los Llanos and sent his ambassadors through the valleys, reproaching the people for their disloyalty in venturing to rise against him and warning them to be faithful to their alliance, for, if they were not, he could assure them that the war he would wage against them would be a cruel one. When he reached the head of the valley of Huarco, on the slopes of the sierra, he ordered his men to found a city, to which he gave the name of New Cuzco [now Incahuasi], the same as his capital, and the streets and hills and plazas bore the same names as those of the real one. He said that until Huarco was won and the natives were his subjects, he would remain in this new city, and that a garrison would always be stationed there. After all he had ordered in this connection had been done, he moved with his troops to where the enemy had taken up positions, and surrounded them. So firm were they in their determination that they would listen to no talk of parley, so war ensued, which they say lasted for three years, during the summers of which the Inca went to Cuzco, always leaving a garrison to harry the enemy in the New Cuzco he had built.

Thus, one group wished to be the masters and the other unwilling to be slaves, each pursued his intent; but finally at the end of the three years, the Huarcos were becoming weakened, and as the Inca knew it, he sent them emissaries once more to tell them that they all ought to be friends and comrades, and that all he wanted was to wed his sons to their daughters, and base all confederation on equality, and other artful things, for it seemed to Topa Inca that they deserved severe punishment for having caused him so much trouble. Those of Huarco, fearing that they could not hold out much longer, and [believing] that under the terms the Inca offered they would enjoy peace and rest, acceded to his demands. This they should never have done, for, leaving their stronghold, the leading men went to do him reverence, and without a moment's hesitation he ordered his troops to kill all of them, and with great cruelty they carried out his command and killed all the nobles and most honorable men there present, and also carried out the sentence against those who were not. They killed many, as the descendants of the victims state, and the huge piles of bones bear witness, for that which they tell of this is what has been set down.

When this had been done, the Inca ordered a fine fortress built, as I have described in the first part. Peace having been restored to the valley, and *mitimaes* and a governor sent there, after receiving the embassies the Yungas and many of the mountain folk sent him, he ordered the New Cuzco he had built razed, and with all his army he returned to the city of Cuzco, where he was received with great rejoicing, and great sacrifices were performed in his honor in the temple and shrines, and the people made merry with feasts and drinking and solemn *taquis*.

CHAPTER 119 (LXXIV)

*Of the great province of Chincha and how highly
it was esteemed in olden times.*

BEYOND THE fortress of Huarco, a little better than two leagues, lies a good-sized river known as the Lunahuaná [now the Cañete], and the valley it forms, through which it flows, is of the sort we have seen. Six leagues [twenty miles] from this Lunahuaná River is the large beautiful valley of Chincha,[1] so famous (as I said before)

---

[1] Chincha is a compact triangular valley, with a twenty-mile base on the sea; it is one of the most fertile and prosperous of the coast. The great center of Chincha was near the sea and is still mouldering extant, known as Tambo de Mora. It was evidently a stepped pyramid around which a court was built; it measures 400 by 500 feet, and the structures about it, even though ruined, suggest the vastness of the center. It was

throughout Peru and formerly so feared by the rest of the inhabitants. It is believed that this must have been so, for we know that when Francisco Pizarro and his thirteen companions discovered the coast of this kingdom, everywhere they were told to go to Chincha, which was the largest and best of all. And believing this to be true, although without knowing the secrets of the country, in articles drawn up with 345 the king he requested that the boundaries of his territory be from Tempulla, or the Santiago River, to this valley of Chincha. As for the origin of these Indians of Chincha, and whence they came to settle in this valley, they tell that a large number of them set out in times gone by under the banner of a valiant captain of their own who was zealous in the service of their religions, and that, thanks to his able leadership, he reached this valley of Chincha with all his people, where they found many people, all of them so small of stature that the tallest measured little more than two cubits. And as the former showed themselves brave and the natives cowardly and timid, they captured and won their lands. They also say that all the natives who were left gradually died out, and that the ancestors of those now alive saw their bones in graves and they were as small as reputed.

So as these Indians remained as masters of the valley and it was so cool and fertile, it is told that they built well-ordered settlements. And they say more: that out of a rock came the voice of an oracle, and all held this to be a sacred spot, and they called it Chincha and Camac. And they always performed sacrifices there, and the devil talked with the older men, trying to deceive them as he did with the others. Now the principal caciques of this valley, as well as many other Indians, have become Christians, and a monastery of our glorious Santo Domingo has been founded there.

Returning to our narration, it is said that these Indians waxed so powerful and so numerous that most of those of the neighboring

the sanctuary of the local god, called Chinchay-camac by its Inca conquerors. The early chroniclers learned that the great lord of Chincha was called Huabia-rucana, "whose house [in 1558] is still extant and whose kinfolk and hereditary properties are known." The inclusion of the term *rucana* in his name is indicative of the Chincha oral history that they once conquered the highland peoples and brought back much booty; the Rucanas were a people living in the high *punas,* between the coast and Cuzco. The valley is filled with roads and lined with stately adobe walls. (See *"Relación . . . valle de Chincha . . . ,"* dated Chincha, February 22, 1558, and written by Friar Cristóbal de Castro and Friar Diego de Ortega Morejón, in *Colección de documentos inéditos para la historia de España,* [Madrid, 1877], L, 206–20.)

valleys sought their alliance and friendship, to their profit and honor. And when they found themselves so powerful, while the first Incas were engaged in the founding of Cuzco, they decided to set out with armed forces and seize the provinces of the sierras. As it is told, they carried out their plan, and wrought great damage to the Soras and Rucanas, and reached the large province of the Colla. There, after winning many victories and taking much booty, they returned to their valley, where they and their descendants flourished, given over to their pleasures and pastimes with many women, following and observing the rites and customs of the others. And the inhabitants of this valley were so numerous that many Spaniards say that when it was conquered by the Marquis [Pizarro] and themselves, there were in this kingdom more than twenty-five thousand men, and I doubt that there are now five thousand, so many have been the inroads and hardships they have suffered. Their kingdom was always safe and prosperous until the valiant Topa Inca Yupanqui extended his rule to the greater part of this kingdom. In the reign of Topa Inca Yupanqui, father of Huayna Capac, they say they were finally brought under his sway, and from that time forward they accepted the laws of their Inca masters, and the settlements of the valley were governed by these laws, and large and sumptuous dwellings were built for the Lord-Incas, and great storehouses filled with supplies and provisions for war. And although the Incas did not strip the caciques and headmen of their power, they sent out their representative or high steward to the valley, and ordered the worship of the sun, which was their God, and, accordingly, a temple to the sun was built in this valley. The same number of virgins as assigned to the other temples was sent there, and ministers of the temple to observe the feasts and perform the sacrifices. But despite this important temple to the sun, the natives of Chincha did not give up worship in their ancient temple of Chinchay-camac. The Lord Incas also sent their *mitimaes* to this great valley, and ordered that during certain months of the year the nobles of the court of Cuzco should reside there, and in most of the wars of Huayna Capac the lord of Chincha took part, who is still alive, and a man of great intelligence and good understanding, considering that he is an Indian.

This valley was one of the largest of all Peru, and it is a beautiful sight to see its groves and irrigation ditches, and the fruits that abound in it, and the fragrant, delicious cucumbers, not like those of Spain, although they resemble them in shape, for these are yellow when peeled, and so appetizing that a man has to eat many to satisfy himself. In the woods the fowl and birds mentioned elsewhere are to be found. Very few of the native llamas remain, because in the civil wars between the Spaniards they finished off most of the many there were. This valley [now] produces large amounts of wheat, and the vines that have been planted do well, and the other things brought from Spain.

347

There was an enormous number of graves in this valley in the hills and wastelands. Many of them were opened by the Spaniards, and they removed large sums of gold. These Indians had great dances, and the lords displayed much pomp and circumstance, and were well served by their vassals. As the Incas ruled them, they took over many of their customs, and used their same attire, imitating them in different things that they ordered, like the sole masters they were. The diminishment of the people of this great valley is the result of the long civil wars that were fought in Peru [between the contending Spaniards], and having taken many of them (as is common knowledge) to serve as bearers.

CHAPTER 120 (LXXV)

Of [Chincha] and the other valleys before reaching the province of Tarapacá.

FROM THE lovely valley of Chincha, across plains and sand, one comes to the cool valley of Ica,[1] which was no less extensive and settled than

1 The "lovely valley of Ica," an oasis in the Peruvian desert, was twenty-five kilometers in a direct line on the old Inca highway from the tambo of Humay, close to Tambo Colorado in the Pisco valley; by the new coastal highway it is seventy-five kilometers. Ica was one of the centers of the Ica-Nazca culture that flourished in its first phase between A.D. 400 and 1000, and later in a different form until 1450, when it was finally eclipsed by and then absorbed into the Inca empire. At the time of the Inca conquest the chieftain's name was Aranbilca, as reported in 1558; the center of the culture was located at Tacaracá in the Pampa de Tate, Ica, where there are still extensive remains of pyramids and where the Incas constructed their own administrative center. Ica is known for its fine pottery, ceremonial leeboards designed under the coastal Tiahuanacan influence, and mummies of varied forms.

Little is known of the architecture of these Ica-Nazca cultures; the only site appar-

the others. A river runs through it which, in certain months of the year when it is summer in the sierra, is so low that the inhabitants of the valley suffer a lack of water. In the time of its prosperity, before it was conquered by the Spaniards, when it enjoyed the rule of the Incas, in addition to the ditches with which they watered the valley, they had one larger than all the others which had been artfully brought from the heights of the sierras, so that it made no drain on the river. Now, when they have a shortage of water, the big irrigation canal having been destroyed, they dig cisterns along the river and the water collects in them, and they use it for drinking and dig little ditches out of them to water their crops. In this valley of Ica there were great lords in olden times who were greatly feared and obeyed. The Incas ordered palaces and storehouses built there, and the custom of the land was that which I have described of the others we have seen. Thus they buried their dead with living women and great treasures. There are great stands of carob trees in this valley and many groves of fruit such as I have described, and deer, pigeons, doves, and other game; many colts and cows are bred. From this valley one travels to within sight of the lovely valleys and rivers of the Nazca valley.[2] These, too, were thickly settled in times gone by, and the rivers watered the fields of the valleys in the form and manner already stated. The cruelty of the late civil wars (as is known to all) consumed all these poor Indians. Certain Spaniards whose word can be trusted told me that the greatest harm these Indians suffered was caused by the contention between the two governors, Pizarro and

---

ently undisturbed (by the Incas) is a large site discovered by the von Hagen expedition (1952–1954) in the dry desert hills of Huayuri (the next southern tambo stop south of Ica in the rugged mountains, one kilometer from the Huayuri Hacienda, at 1,500 feet altitude.

[2] These were known to the conquistadors as the valleys of La Nazca (there are five: Santa Cruz, Palpa, Ingenio, Nazca, Apoloma); a tangled web of rivers, perennial and occasional, like the fingers on a hand; verdant valleys compressed between deserts as dry as old bones which have known no rain of consequence in five thousand years. This is the arena of the famed Nazca culture, known for its weavings and pottery of the purest coastal Tiahuanacu style—the fine pottery embellished with figures of non-representational art—and for the strange and bewildering "Nazca Lines"—a maze of rectangles, circles, animals, fish, and insects, of enormous size, that have been traced in the desert on the Pampa Colorada between the valley of Ingenio and Nazca. Little or nothing in the matter of appearance, dress, or custom has come down to us, and until William D. Strong undertook extensive surveys of the area, little had been known of Nazca architecture. (See W. D. Strong, "Paracas, Nazca, and Tiahuanacoid Culture Relationships in South Coastal Perú," *American Antiquity,* Vol. XXII [April, 1957].)

Almagro, over the boundaries and limits of their territories, which cost so dear, as the reader will see when the time comes (and he reads my histories of these wars).

In the main valley of these of Nazca (also known as Caxamalca)[3] there were great buildings and many storehouses erected by order of the Incas. As for the natives, all I have to say is that they, too, tell 349 that their forefathers were brave, as these people go, and esteemed by the Lord-Incas of Cuzco. I have heard that the Spaniards found considerable treasure in their graves and tombs. As these valleys are so fertile, great fields of sugarcane have been planted in one of them, from which they make sugar in abundance and other products which are sold in the cities of this kingdom. Through all these valleys and those already passed runs the fine, beautiful highway of the Incas, and in certain spots in the sand desert there are signs to mark the route. Proceeding from these valleys of Nazca one comes to that of Acari, and beyond this lie Ocoña and Camaná and Quilca, where there are large rivers.[4] And although now there are few natives, in the past there were as many as everywhere in these plains. But with the wars and calamities that have occurred, their number has diminished to what we now see. Aside from this, the valleys are rich and fertile, very good for cattle raising.

Beyond this valley of Quilca, which is the port of the city of Arequipa, lie the valleys of Chuli and Tambopalla and Ilo. Farther on are the rich valleys of Tarapacá. Along the coast, in the vicinity of these valleys, there are islands inhabited by birds. The natives visit

---

[3] At Nazca, called Caxamalca by the Incas, these conquerors placed their administrative center. As Paredones, it still stands to offer mute testimony to what it once was. It guarded the great lateral road, that bound the coast to the Andean highlands. This road, parts of which can still be seen, began at Nazca, moved across the towering cordilleras into the country of the Soras and Rucanas and keeping to the left (north) bank of the Pachachaca River, made the junction of the Royal Road of the Andes at Cochacajas, where there was both tambo and rope suspension bridge.

[4] At Quilca (16° 45′ south latitude) the Inca highway turned mountainward, following the way of the Sihuas River for seventy-five kilometers to the tambo (now marked Tambillo on the maps), thence it turned southward again, moved across the Pampa de Sihuas, a dry desert at 5,000 feet altitude on average, to the next valley of Vitor, where once again it turned toward the Andes until it arrived at Arequipa, which, although a relatively unimportant center under Inca rule, was nevertheless a junction point for: (a) roads going to Chile (followed by Diego de Almagro in 1536); (b) the Arequipa–Cailloma–Hatun-cana–Pomacancha–Quiquixana–Cuzco route ("Regulations for Tambos," written at Cuzco, May 31, 1543). In all probability the Inca highway did not go directly down to the coastal deserts of Mollendo, but kept to the heights and from there moved in its various indicated directions.

them in balsa rafts, and from the peaks of the rocks they bring back the droppings [guano] of the birds to fertilize their cornfields and gardens, and this greatly enriches the ground and increases its yield, even if it was once barren. And if they fail to use this manure, they gather little corn, and they could not feed themselves if the birds that gather on these rocks of the islands did not leave this, which when collected is highly prized, and they sell it as a valuable thing to others.

350

To go into further details about these valleys before reaching Tarapacá seems to me unnecessary, for I have set down the most important and pertinent of what I saw and could gather. I shall, therefore, conclude by saying that there are few of the natives left, and that in olden times there were in these valleys [tambo] lodgings and storehouses like those in the plains and sand wastes. And part of the tribute they paid to the Lord-Incas was taken to Cuzco, another to Hatuncolla, another to Vilcas-huamán, and some to Cajamarca, for the strength of the Incas and the capitals of the provinces were, in the main, in the highlands.

It is a fact that in the valleys of Tarapacá there are large and rich mines of very white and gleaming silver. Beyond them, according to those who have traveled through those lands, there are a number of deserts until one reaches the boundaries of the territory of Chile. All along this coast they catch fish, some of it good, and the Indians made fishing boats of great sheafs of oat straw or sealskin, for there are so many of these animals in some places that it is a sight to see them roar when they come together.

CHAPTER 121 (LXXVI)

Of the founding of the city of Arequipa, how it was founded, and who was its founder.

FROM LIMA, the City of the Kings, it is 120 leagues to Arequipa. This city is situated and built in the valley of Quilca, fourteen leagues from the sea, in the best and coolest spot suitable for that purpose. And the location and climate of this city are so good that it is reputed the healthiest and the pleasantest in which to live. Excellent wheat is raised there from which they make very good and tasty bread. Its boundaries are from the valley of Acari to beyond that of Tarapacá, and certain villages of the province of Cunti-suyu are under its jurisdiction, and some of the Spaniards residing in it have encomiendas over the natives of these settlements. The Hubinas and Chiquiguanitas and Quimistacas and Collaguas are among the tribes under the authority of this city, who were once very numerous and owned great herds of llamas. The war between the Spaniards did away with most of them and their llamas. The Indians of the highlands of these regions worshiped the sun and buried their headmen in large graves, like the others. All of them go attired in shirts and blankets. Through most of these regions there ran the old Inca highways, built for the Lord-Incas, and there were storehouses and lodgings, and all paid tribute of what they harvested and raised on their lands. This city of Arequipa, being so close to a seaport, is well supplied with the products and merchandise brought out from Spain, and the major part of the precious metals mined in Charcas [Bolivia] is brought to it, where they are loaded on the ships which most of the time ply between the port of Quilca and Lima, the City of the Kings.

351

Some of the Indians and the Spaniards say that in the vicinity of Acari, well out to sea, there are various large, rich islands from which it is told that they brought much gold to traffic with the natives of this coast. In the year 1550 when I left Peru, the judges of the Royal Tribunal had authorized Captain Gómez de Solís to discover these islands. It is believed that they are rich, if they exist.

As for the founding of Arequipa, all I have to say is that it was first established in another spot, and for good reasons transferred to where it now is. Near by is a volcano [El Misti], and some of the people are afraid it might erupt and do damage. At times there are strong earthquakes in this city. It was founded and settled by . . . Francisco Pizarro, in the name of His Majesty, in the year . . . 1535. . . .

. . . And with this I make end to this first [and second] parts of my Histories to the glory of Almighty God . . . "Up to this point [I have written] all that I wished to write of the Incas and that which I had recounted to me in Cuzco. If anyone can do this more accurately and in greater detail [than I have done in the First and Second Chronicles], the road lies open to him, for it is one which is not overcrowded.

When I undertook to do this thing I believed it beyond my literary powers, although to have done what I have done, God alone knows how much I worked at it.

Most of what I have written was seen by Dr. [Melchor] Bravo de Saravia and the Master Hernando de Santillán, judges of the Royal Tribunal of Lima, City of the Kings.

I commenced writing in the city of Cartago, in the district of Popayán, in the year 1541, and concluded [these histories] in Lima, City of the Kings, in the Kingdom of Peru on the eighteenth of September, 1550; the author then being thirty-two years of age and having spent seventeen of them in these Indies.

MARRIAGE CONTRACT

between Pedro de Cieza de León and Pedro López
for the wedding of his sister Isabel.

KNOW YE ALL who might see this contract how I, Pedro de Cieza de León, being in this City of Kings of New Castile, provinces of Peru, state that as I am bound for the kingdoms of Spain, I have contracted with you, Pedro López, merchant, here present, that should I arrive safely at the city of Seville, I will wed, in accordance with the laws of the Holy Church, Isabel López, your sister [daughter of Juan de Llerena and María de Abreu, her parents], who is of approximately twenty years of age; consequently, by this I hereby grant and agree that I shall go to the kingdoms of Spain, to the city of Seville, and there I shall wed as aforesaid, the above-mentioned Isabel López; and I promise and bind myself to give and will give on wedding the said Isabel López, by letter of dowry, 2,000 crowns of the currency circulating in said city of Seville; and I Pedro López hereby present to all that is said above, grant and agree hereby and bind myself, that as soon as you, the aforesaid Pedro de Cieza, shall arrive at the said city of Seville, Spain, my father, on your wedding the said Isabel López, my sister, will give you together with her, 4,000 crowns of the currency circulating in the said city of Seville; Juan de Llerena and María de Abreu, my parents, on whose behalf I bind myself to the above, will do this, and give you the said Isabel López as wife, for you to wed as aforesaid; should they not comply and not deliver to you the said 4,000 crowns, I bind myself to give you the said 4,000 crowns, guaranteed by my person and property, when you wed my sister; should they be demanded of me once the wedding has taken place, not otherwise; and I, the said Pedro de Cieza, state that should the said 4,000 crowns be delivered to myself, with the 2,000 that I am bound to give as dowry, making 6,000 in all, I will make out a letter of endowment before a Notary, to the said Isabel López, your sister; and both of us, as far as each is concerned, promise so to do, and that the agreement hereby entered into shall not fail to be carried out on account of any of us or the said Juan de Llerena and María de Abreu his wife, under penalty that whosoever should fail to comply and go against same shall incur a fine of 1,000 crowns, which amount it is our wish and will that, without legal action whatsoever, be delivered to that one of us who obeys, agrees, and complies with this contract, and we wish that by this letter, this penalty be executed and its payment demanded, or it shall mean we do not wish this contract to be valid and firm, and because we shall carry it out, as aforesaid, we bind our person and property, furniture and lands, present and future wherever they may be, and by this contract we grant power to any justice, mayors, and judges of His Majesty, of any towns and jurisdictions, to which we submit with our persons and property, renouncing our rights, jurisdiction, and residence, and should the law *sit convenerit, de juridicione omnium judicum,* in order that with all the force of right and law we be compelled to carry out, respect, and comply and pay, as if all the aforesaid were commanded by the definite sentence of a competent justice and agreed to by all and each of us, for which we renounce to any and every law, right, letter and grant, sentence, aid and remedy that might be employed in our favor and against this agreement, that they may not avail in trial or otherwise, and especially the law that maintains that a general renunciation of laws is not valid. In testimony of which we grant this deed and its contents before the Public Notary and witnesses. Drawn up in the aforesaid City of Kings on the nineteenth day of the month of August of the year of our Lord Jesus 1550; witnesses present being Alonso de Illezcas and Diego de Illezcas and Julián de Abiñón, merchant, citizens, and residents of this city, and the parties herewith, whom I, the Notary, affirm I am cognizant of, affixed their names to this Register.

354

SIGNED: *Pedro de Cieza de León.*
Pedro López.
Before myself, *Simón de Alzate,* Notary Public.

MARGINAL NOTE: We request that one or two or more copies be made of this deed, as each party may demand.

Seville, Tuesday the eleventh of August, 1551.　　355

IN THE NAME of the Lord, amen, whosoever might see this letter know how I, Juan de Llerena, and I, María de Abreu, his wife, citizens of this most noble and most loyal city of Seville in the district of San Vicente in the Calle de las Armas; I, the aforesaid María de Abreu, with license and faculty, pleasure and consent of the aforesaid Juan de Llerena, my husband, here present, from whom I request and demand [authority] to do and grant what is herein contained; and I, the aforesaid Juan de Llerena, here present, grant, give, and concede the said license that you request for this object to you, my aforesaid wife, since it pleases me and I consent to same, both jointly and separately, renouncing . . . and the benefit of the division and all other laws and rights pertaining to those who undertake joint obligations; we grant to you, Pedro de Cieza de León, legitimate son of Lope de León and Leonor de Cazalla, his wife, deceased, citizen that he is, your aforesaid father, of the Villa de Llerena, here present, and we state that, since by the grace of our Lord a marriage was arranged between Isabel López de León, our legitimate daughter, and yourself, the aforesaid Pedro de Cieza, which marriage was arranged with yourself in the province of Peru by Pedro López, our son, and our will has been, and is, that it shall take place, and to better enable you to sustain the burden of matrimony we grant and promise and bind ourselves to give you, together with out aforesaid daughter, as dowry and in marriage and as her endowment and for her, for sustaining said marriage, 3,500 ducats of gold of 375 *maravedís* each, of the currency now in use, which sum we promise and bind ourselves to give you and pay you here in Seville, in peace and safety, with no quarrel or argument whatsoever, 2,000 ducats in cash, as from today, on which this letter is drawn up and granted, until within the next eight days or before, or later, or when you should wish to receive same, and the 1,500 remaining in bridal apparel, clothes, jewels, gems, and household furnishings and male and female slaves and in cash to that amount, as from today to within one year from today. And you shall take a house for which [*page torn, words missing*] and thus pay and comply by this letter with any judges, here in this aforesaid city of Seville or elsewhere, wherever and before whomsoever this letter should be shown, so that lacking our presence, nor being called to

356

trial, we can be seized and made to deliver and be executed on our person and property, on each of our pieces of furniture and property wherever commanded, and they may be sold and auctioned immediately, without delay, since from the *maravedís* they be worth, you will be paid and receive the above-mentioned 3,500 ducats hereby offered, and at the time stated; and I renounce all appeal, supplication, injury, or invalidity and any law or right that might be to our favor and those rights which state that a general renunciation is not valid, as if this were contained in judgment by a competent justice and definite sentence passed and approved by the litigant parties; and to comply as aforesaid, we bind ourselves, each and every one of us, and all our present and future property, and I, and the aforementioned María de Abreu, renounce the laws of the Emperors Justiniano and Veliano that exist in favor and succor of women, since the Notary Public has called our attention to same; and I, the aforesaid Pedro de Cieza, here present, receive from you the aforesaid Juan de Llerena and María de Abreu, his wife, my parents-in-law, this promise that you are party to with the aforesaid Isabel López de León, your daughter, of the 3,500 ducats of gold, to be paid in the terms and grants herein contained, and since at the time of the arranging of this wedding between myself and the aforesaid Pedro López your son, the latter agreed that you would give me, together with your daughter, as dowry, 4,000 gold crowns, respecting which there exists a deed drawn up before Simón de Alzate, Notary Public and in service to His Majesty, in the City of Kings of the province of Peru on the nineteenth of August, 1550, I hereby relieve your son Pedro and his property of this compromise, in view of the present one you now grant me, and am well content with the aforesaid 3,500 ducats and consider the previous deed as void, and have no cause for action against him, and I promise not to demand anything else whatever and I pledge to this effect my person and present and future property.

This document being drawn up in Seville in the house of the aforesaid Juan de Llerena and María de Abreu, his wife, on Tuesday the eleventh of August in the year of the Lord 1551, and the said Juan de Llerena and Pedro de Cieza signed their names, and as María de Abreu stated she could not sign her name, at her request the witnesses present, Francisco de Paredes and Alonso Rodríguez, Notaries of Seville, did so for her.

357

Pedro de Cieza.
Juan de Llerena.
Alonso de Cazalla, Notary Public of Seville.
Francisco de Paredes, Notary of Seville, as witness.
Alonso Rodríguez.
(Signatures and rubrics)

358 *of Pedro de Cieza de León.*

IN THE NAME of God, Amen, and of the Holy Virgin, whosoever sees
this letter and testament and last will know how I, Pedro de Cieza
de León, citizen of this city of Seville in the parish of San Vicente,
being ill in body and healthy in mind and completely sane as to the
judgment and understanding that God deigned to bestow upon me
and believing and holding with all that the Holy Catholic Church
commands and holds and wishing to live and die, as I state, in that
Holy Faith and not withdraw from it, and fearing death, which is
a natural thing, and wishing to do that which any good Christian
should do, I make out, and am fully conscious of making and ordering, this my last will and testament in the following manner, invoking
divine aid.

First, I commend my soul to God, who created and redeemed it
by His precious blood, and my body to the earth whence it came,
and I direct that should death befall me from this illness which I
have, my body be interred in the Church of San Vicente of this city
of Seville in the grave where my wife was interred, and I command
that the obsequies and funeral rites and interment and all the rest
that should be done during rites of mass for the dead be said according to and in the manner agreed upon by my executors, as much in
the saying of masses as in other things.

I direct that on the day of my burial six beggars of my executors'
choosing be clothed and that they be given coats, breeches, shoes,
and shirts; to each a dress of wool and linen according to what my
executors decide.

I direct that there be said on my behalf five hundred masses, which
I request my executors to distribute and have said in the parochial
churches and monasteries in this city and outside of it, in the order
and manner they think fit, dividing them where they think best, and
to be said as soon as possible, for which I commission them freely

and generally so that nobody can prevent this, and the usual alms should be given for each mass.

I request that on each Friday, when two years have passed from the day of my death, there be said a Passion Mass for my soul in the Colegio de Santo Tomás of this city, by the monks of the said college, who are to be paid the usual alms.

359

Furthermore, I request that there be said another fifty masses for the souls in purgatory where my executors think best.

Furthermore, I request that there be said fifty masses for the soul of my wife; and for the soul of my mother, twenty masses; and for the soul of a saintly sister of my mother, ten masses; and for another sister of mine who died, ten masses; and for an Indian woman called Ana, eight masses, all where my executors shall ordain.

Furthermore, I request another ten masses to be said for the souls of the Indian men and women in purgatory who came from the lands and places where I traveled in the Indies.

Furthermore, I direct that at the end of a year another three hundred masses be said for the souls of the persons [as] I thus command, as much for the sake of a good deed as for other reasons which I do not recall, all of which I ordain, and it is my wish that my executors have these masses said where they think best, as has been stated above.

Furthermore, I direct that every Sunday and on the feast days of the Apostles and of Our Lady and of the Magdalen and of St. Catherine and St. Elizabeth and St. Joseph falling during the year after my death, masses be said on each of these days at the altar which is next to the tomb where my said wife is buried, and where I order that I be buried myself; the masses should be said with responses over the tomb, and I order and charge Juan de Llerena, my father-in-law, to contribute an offering.

Furthermore, I direct that one ducat be given to each of the monks who reside and are in the said Colegio of Santo Tomás, who are ordained priests, so that they remember to pray to God for my soul.

Furthermore, I direct that the children of the Christian doctrine be given alms of six ducats and the nuns of the Concepción which is by San Miguel and the repentant nuns of the monastery of the Name of Jesus another six ducats.

Furthermore, I direct that at a monastery of nuns which is in

Llerena called Our Lady of Succor, my executors spend and have paid from my estate up to the sum of two hundred ducats to enlarge the church and do what is necessary to it, in accordance with the wishes of the nuns there as to how it should be enlarged, and this I order to be done on the condition that the said nuns undertake to make each year and forevermore a feast at the Conception of Our Lady, with masses and sung vespers for my soul, on the proper day of the Conception and on the eighth day thereafter, and an agreement should be entered into with the said nuns in the manner my executors see fit.

Furthermore I direct that six beds be given to two or three hospitals of the said city of Llerena, to be distributed as my executors think fit, each of which should have two benches and a frame and one mattress and two sheets and one pillow and one woolen blanket.

Furthermore, I direct that another twenty-four beds of the type mentioned above, with a straw matting each, be given: six to the Hospital del Amor de Dios, six to the Hospital de las Buvas, another six to the Hospital de los Desamparados, and six to the hospital which is by the iron foundries facing the *alholí* of the Bishop of Escalas.

Furthermore, I direct that the purple velvet gown which is in my house, with satin sleeves and gold braid, which belonged to my wife, be given to the statue of Our Lady which is in the Monastery of the Concepción of the town of Llerena, and I also give to this statue a net coif with small gold beads, which is to be handed over on the condition that it is not to be taken apart or anything pertaining to it sold, but used and worn out by the said statue, for this is my wish and the nuns and members of the monastery must conform to it, and an indenture should be made to this effect.

Furthermore, I direct that another gown which belonged to my wife, of plain hazel-colored taffeta, with its sleeves and bodice, be given to another statue of Our Lady which is in the monastery of Los Remedios in the town of Llerena.

Furthermore, I direct that a braid-trimmed shirt of crimson satin which also belonged to my wife be given to another statue of Our Lady which is in the church of St. Anton in the town of Trigueros, for it to be dressed, and also a headdress and coif from among the best that were left by my wife.

Furthermore, I direct that a shirt of black velvet which belonged to my wife be given to the statue of Our Lady of Consolation of Trigueros.

Furthermore, I direct that some tablecloths which I have in my house, not the damask ones, be given to churches chosen by my executors, provided always that some be given to the Church of San Vicente, and a face towel to San Vicente of this city, the rest to be distributed where my executors wish; they shall give the face towels there might be and the small hand towels for the service of the altars, and I especially order that for the service of the altar which is next to the tomb where masses are to be sung, two small hand towels I have, embroidered in black, which are in a coffer where I keep the jewels, be given.

Furthermore, I direct that from my estate and that of my wife, especially from the dowry I sent her, there be taken 1,100 ducats and that in equal halves of 550 they be given as I state below to Juan de Llerena, my father-in-law, so that from them he recover what he has spent for the soul of my wife, and with the remainder he buy perpetual offering, or temporary or permanent, or whatever he thinks is best and should be done, and what is thus purchased should be adjudicated; and I as from now thus adjudicate this so that from the interest therefrom there be said and sung a chaplaincy in the said Church of San Vicente of this city at the said altar which is near the tomb where my wife is buried and where I wish to be buried, in which chaplaincy there shall be said every month the masses which the income shall purchase as the aforementioned Juan de Llerena sees fit; and he should obtain an assessment by making inquiries from some scientific and conscientious person as to the amount he should take out from the above income to be given to the building of the said Church of San Vicente, so as to provide for the adornment and candles and wine and hosts and everything else that is necessary to serve and sing the masses, of which I made and institute as patron the said Juan de Llerena, my father-in-law, and he may name the chaplain he wishes for the masses; and when his life is ending, he, the aforementioned patron, Juan de Llerena, shall name whom he wishes, and this one shall name another and another and another forevermore, and if any succeeding patron or the said Juan de Llerena should die without naming a succeeding patron, then the patronage shall be given to the eldest son of such a patron who should he die without naming a successor, and whosoever should succeed to the patronage may thus name whom he wishes as patron successively, as stated above, and these patrons shall name the successive chaplains when it is necessary to have a chaplain for the masses, which the prelate shall provide to this effect, and who shall not meddle nor try to nominate another chaplain, except the one whom the patron names, and he shall choose and confer license upon him so that he may officiate and sing the masses and place another in his stead to officiate and sing the masses, of which two-thirds are for my soul and for the soul of my wife and the other third for the persons to whom she or I are indebted for good deeds or other obligations.

362

Furthermore, I declare that I received as marriage dowry with my wife, Isabel López de León, daughter of Juan de Llerena and María de Abreu, his wife, my father- and mother-in-law, 3,500 gold ducats, which amount to 1,312,500 *maravedís,* which Juan de Llerena truly paid me and passed from his possession into mine, and I command that this be paid and handed over to him from the best there is of my estate; and regarding the dowry I sent my wife, the aforesaid Juan de Llerena and I have discussed this and it is agreeable to him to receive the 550 ducats which I wish to have taken from my estate, in lieu of the said dowry, for the chaplaincy I have founded, and I command that if Juan de Llerena wishes as part of the dowry mentioned a slave called Beatriz whom he gave me for 100 ducats, he take her for the same 100 ducats for which he sold her.

Furthermore, I state that if some amount should appear over and above the assets which I placed into the joint matrimonial account and after defraying the above-mentioned dowry, half of this should be given to the said Juan de Llerena, my father-in-law, as it belongs to him.

Furthermore, I state that there have been accounts kept between myself and Juan de Llerena, my father-in-law, after I came from the Indies, and he and I were in my house before Alonso López, his brother, and Lope de Llerena, his nephew, and by these accounts I owe eighty and some thousand *maravedís* he lent me, according to what appears in his books and the closing of these accounts which we at that time carried out, to which I submit, and later he has given me more *maravedís* and continues to give me what I need; I direct that what he thus gave me and what he has since given me and all he might give or spend for me be paid out of my estate, on account of which he has received from Alonso García Cartero, in the first quarter of this year of 1554, from the income which the Señor Conde de Palma is obliged to pay each year, and the said Alonso García collects for me, and this has been given to the aforesaid Juan de Llerena and I direct that no account be demanded or investigation made of anything, either by my heirs or by any other persons, from the said Juan de Llerena, beyond that which he affirms, as I wish his word to be trusted.

Furthermore, I state that I was entrusted with and am obliged to repay 300 ducats that certain Indians whom I knew gave me to invest, which I did not, and as they are dead and in no way can restitution be made to them, to ease my conscience and because they were not Christians and lived badly, I command that these 300 ducats be given as charity to three very poor sisters I have, Beatriz de Cazalla, Leonor de Cieza, and María Álvarez, 100 ducats to each, as they are very needy.

Furthermore, I declare that I owe ten ducats to Manuel de Campo, native of Valverde, and since I do not know whether he is alive or has left heirs, I direct that if within two years he or some heir of his is not found, some good be done for his soul, as my executors see fit.

Furthermore, I direct that since I and the priest Francisco de Frias and Pedro de Velasco were guarantors to Captain Pedro de Ayala de Castro on behalf of Jorge de Robledo, for 243 *castellanos* and as I must pay this and Juan de Llerena, my father-in-law, is obliged to pay this for me and should be empowered to collect from the said Frias and Pedro de Velasco the part which they should pay of the guarantee; when the said Francisco de Frias pays his share, there should be discounted from it 30 ducats and he should pay the rest, and I declare that of this guarantee there is owing to the said Pedro de Ayala de Castro 71,000-odd *maravedís,* and Juan de Llerena, my father-in-law, is under the obligation to pay this, and later he must be repaid from my estate.

Furthermore, I declare that Captain Alvaro de Mendoza, citizen of Cartagena de las Indias, owes me 120 *castellanos,* the receipt for which is in Quito in the care of Juan de Cobo, and I command that my heirs collect this, discounting from it 15 *castellanos.*

Furthermore, I direct that the silver candlesticks I have in my house be given to the Church of Santa María in Llerena on account of an obligation I have.

Furthermore, to each church, hermitage, and monastery of Llerena, those inside the city as well as those outside the walls, half a ducat should be given, as charity and for obligations I have towards them.

Furthermore, I declare that I owe to Pedro López de Abreu, my brother-in-law, 100 *castellanos* which he lent me, and if I have not paid this, it should be paid out of my estate; and I also declare that the said Pedro López should receive another 80 *castellanos* he sent, and should Juan de Llerena not have paid this, he should; and if by chance the aforesaid Pedro López has been paid from my property he holds there, then it should be returned to my heirs.

Furthermore, I declare that I owe Alonso de Cazalla, in Panama, 100 *castellanos* which he gave me for a certain business that was not carried out, and as he has not been paid, he must receive this out of my estate.

I declare that I owe to Don Juan Toscano, dean of the Reyes [i.e., Lima], four *castellanos,* which I order to be paid to him out of my estate.

I declare that I owe to García Martínez de la Torre, who was a citizen of Cali, thirteen and one-half pesos of gold, of which Antonio Redondo, citizen of Cali, was executor; I order that they be paid to him or to his heirs.

Furthermore, I declare that I owe to Juan Martín, who was a servant of Jorge de Robledo and is in Cartago, nine and one-half pesos, which I direct be paid to him.

Furthermore, I declare that I owe to Pedro Alonso Carrasco, citizen of Cuzco, 30 ducats which he gave me for a certain business that could not be effected; I order that they be paid to him.

I state that I had an account with Robledo and the executors demanded from me 70 *castellanos* and as I paid these to Pedro de Ayala for account of the said Robledo, should they come to ask for something, nothing is owing to them, since I have paid for him, and have also paid other accounts; I owe him nothing.

Furthermore, I direct that there be paid to Diego Mexía, son-in-law of Judge Vanegas, three *escudos* which he lent me at the Azores, coming from the Indies.

Furthermore, I direct that there be paid to Lope de Llerena what he states and accounts for as given to my father for food.

I state and declare that my possessions are listed in an inventory I made at the time of the death of my wife, which is signed with my name and is in the care of my father-in-law.

Furthermore, I declare that there are 130 books, belonging to me, of the chronicle which I wrote on the Indies, in the care of Juan de Espinoza, bookdealer and citizen of Medina del Campo, of which he should give account and pay their value and he should receive a discount of 45 *reales* for two blankets he sent me.

Furthermore, I declare that I sent to Toledo another 30 books of the above-mentioned chronicle, which were sold by Juan Sánchez de Andrada, who should render an account and pay the money.

Furthermore, I declare that Diego Gutiérrez de los Ríos of Córdova, has eight books of the aforesaid chronicle, for which he should be charged.

Furthermore, Fulano de Villalón, bookseller, who lives next to the Magdalena, has another 15 books of the said chronicle; he should pay four *reales* and three *cuartillos* for each or return the books, and should be paid the value of the *Geografía* de Enziso which he sold me.

Furthermore, Rodrigo de Valles, bookseller, has another 8 books and I owe him for 20 sheets of paper.

Furthermore, the printer Montesdoca owes me 27 *reales* for other books; I order that this be collected from him.

Furthermore, I state that I sold to Juan Canalla a hundred or more books for 500 *reales,* of which he has paid me 170 *reales;* I order that he be pardoned 130 *reales* as he is poor, and the remainder be collected from a house which is mortgaged to the debt, of which transaction there exists a deed drawn before Cazalla, Notary Public, stating that 100 *reales* shall be paid this coming July; and once this is collected, I wish that it be given as charity to Our Lady of the Valley of Seville, which is in the monastery of monks near the Puerta del Onzario.

Furthermore, I declare that Hernando de Alfaro owes me 30 *reales* which I lent him; I order that they be collected and given as charity to the poor of the parish of San Vicente.

Furthermore, I declare that Plazencia owes me 60 *ducats,* the receipt for which Lope de Llerena has; I order this to be collected, and 25 ducats given as charity to the hospital chosen by my executors, and I say it should be the Hospital de Santa Brígida of Trigueros, and could be used to make beds for the poor.

Furthermore, I direct that as the administrators of the Hospital of the Cardenal, from whom I have in perpetuity this house where I live, lent me 40,000 *maravedís* to help with the expenses that I undertook, which they ordered to be discounted from the income I paid, at the rate of 10,000 *maravedís* a year, and since last year they discounted 10,000 *maravedís,* and this year they will discount from the said income another 10,000 *maravedís,* I wish that the balance of 20,000 *maravedís* which the hospital still owes me should not be demanded and I give this as charity to this hospital of theirs.

Furthermore, I command that the following be done: as I wrote a book, or rather three books, on the civil wars of Peru, all written and embellished by hand on parchment, which if printed now might cause some scandal and some people might resent what is contained therein and the things that took place only recently in those wars, it is my wish that my executors take the three books and reports, all of which are in my desk, and remove the said letters and other writings that may be in this desk, leaving only the aforesaid three books and reports and anything else pertaining to them, and that they close and seal this [desk] and place another two small locks on this desk, and before a Notary Public take the locked desk to the monastery of Las Cuevas, or any other monastery my executors think fit, and once [it is] deposited there, the keys should remain in the possession of my executors, one key for each, until fifteen years after my death, during which time no one is to look inside; and later by order of my executors or any one of them living, or if none are living, by order of the prelate of the monastery where the desk is, the books be given to some expert to see and correct and to remove from the said work what he thinks superfluous, without adding anything to what has been written; and as regards what still has to be written, in accordance with the reports which are in the desk, he may proceed as he thinks fit, stating the point to which he found it written and where he himself began to write, and in this manner he can print it, protecting the honor and fame of all, so that no one is hurt or defamed, and he may benefit from the profits of the publication; if one of my executors wishes to give it to a certain person, he may do so; and it is my wish that the said monastery, on taking the said desk and books for deposit, give a receipt or deed, as my executors think fit.

Furthermore, I order that regarding another book I wrote, which contains the chronicle of the Incas and all concerning the discovery and conquest of Peru, if one of my executors should desire to print it, he take it and benefit from the profits of the publication; and if none should wish to do this, I order it to be sent to the Bishop of Chiapas at the court, with the injunction that he print it.

I direct that my servant Juan be paid what is owing to him for his services, and in addition that he be given one of two capes I have of sheared black cloth and the shoes I have on which are open, and one of my two caps and a linen doublet and shirt.

Furthermore, I wish to make my peace with the Commissary of the Crusade, and if I have not done so before my death, I direct that my executors do so for me with all speed and diligence, as I went on the discovery of some parts of the Indies and found myself with warring people at many critical moments on these discoveries, and [there were] personal wars and damages committed when I was with soldiers against the Indians and their towns and haciendas, both offending as defending, of which damages I have not either reason or recollection to make restitution, and for this and for the security of my conscience and to rid myself of scruples I may have therefrom, I pray and entreat my executors to make such peace, if I have not done so.

Furthermore, when this will and testament is complied with and the directions contained therein carried out, it is my wish and command that the remainder of my estate be distributed in the following manner: although my father Lope de León is alive and according to law I cannot deprive him of more than one third of my estate as he is the ascendant heir, I have his permission and faculty, which he granted me and agreed to before Rodrigo Garzón, Notary Public of the town of Llerena, to will all my estate in the manner I wish and dispose of it and order and give it to whom I wish during my lifetime or at my death, with the only condition that I should leave him a certain sum of *maravedís* as income for life for his sustenance, as is stated in the said deed to which I refer. I could comply and leave him just that and dispose of all the rest without breaking the said permission or deed, only using it when necessary and leaving it in force, but I state that I give and bequeath the remainder of my estate to my father, Lope de León, as my universal heir, with the charge and condition that this remainder of the estate be used for the purchase of an annuity in the said town of Llerena by the hand of Rodrigo de Cieza, my brother, who shall receive and collect the income or order someone to do so, and my father shall be sustained according to what his age and person require; and what is left shall be distributed by him and by my other sisters and his sisters, who are Beatriz de Cazalla and Leonor de Cieza and María Álvarez, in equal parts, and after the death of my father it is my wish that all my referred-to estate, which they will inherit by his death, be given half to my sister María Álvarez for her marriage and the other half be divided into equal thirds, one-third for Rodrigo de Cieza and two-thirds to the other two sisters, Beatriz de Cazalla and Leonor de Cieza; and with this charge I appoint my father as heir, and in no other manner, and if he does not accept this charge, I furthermore direct that the 15,000 *maravedís* mentioned in the aforesaid deed be given to him for his sustenance and the rest of the estate should be distributed among my said brothers according to and in the manner mentioned above, and if any one of them contests this and does not accept, for the same reason it is my wish that they shall not have any part of the estate nor enjoy any of the inheritance, and that their share be given to the poor, as chosen by my executors, and the holder of my estate shall hand over the said estate and inheritance to my heir or to any other persons according to what I state above, who accepts this clause and is bound to comply as herein stated, and a deed should be signed, and it should not be granted in any other manner, and to insure compliance, if a lawsuit should result, all that is necessary shall be spent out of my estate.

Furthermore, I direct that all my possessions, including the furniture that is in my house and the income paid me by the Conde de Palma, and what should come from the Indies and Flanders, shall without exception become the possession of Juan de Llerena, my father-in-law, and he shall keep same in order to carry out the requests expressed in this my will, and when all is paid and complied with, the remainder shall be handed over in the manner described in the clause previous to this; and while this is being done, my father should be given the necessary sustenance from the residue, and this should be in the hands of the aforesaid Juan de Llerena until the arrival of that from the Indies and Flanders, so that all can be placed together and my directions carried out.

Furthermore, I state that Antonio Pimentel, citizen of the town of Arma, owes me ten pesos which I lent him in Lima, and Juan Ruiz de Norena, citizen of the same town, another thirteen which I also lent him; I direct that this be collected from them. 369

Furthermore, if a bill for ten or eleven *castellanos* which I think I owe to a certain Juan Cota, citizen of Moguer, should appear, I order that the bill be accepted and paid from my estate.

And in order to comply with the contents of this my will and so that everything contained herein be done, I name as my executors the aforementioned Juan de Llerena, my father-in-law, and the aforesaid Rodrigo de Cieza, my brother, and Dr. Rodrigo de Ribera, priest, to each of whom I give as complete authority as I myself possess, to enter into and take from my estate the amounts and portions necessary to comply with and pay for everything in this my will and all herein contained, as stated, and I pray and request them to do so, to comply and undertake all this for the discharge of my conscience and the compliance of my soul; and I pray and ask as a favor of the said Juan de Llerena, for the love we had for each other, that he take of his money if no other be available, so as to comply with diligence and speed with the things pertaining to my soul and the chaplaincy and all else, as soon as possible; and since this is my last and definitive will and I wish it to be carried out and complied with, I revoke and annul and consider any other wills, commands, or codicils I might have made up to date, null and void, and this one I wish to remain legal and final forever, to which effect I sign with my name on the twenty-third day of June in the year MDLIIII, these ten sheets written on both sides, except for this last page with the date which is slightly blank and lined, and each face is signed with my name, and I order it to be sealed before Alonso de Cazalla, Notary Public of Seville.

Pedro de Cieza de León (rubric).

Furthermore, having exercised this power to clear my conscience, my executors are to receive and take from my estate 50,000 *maravedís,* which they are to disburse as marriage settlement on two poor orphan girls, and if there be any of my lineage, they should be preferred to others; if not, those whom they may choose.

Furthermore, that which should be forthcoming from my books that were sent to Honduras by myself to be sold should be given to the Church of Santa Catalina of Llerena to be expended as my executors think fit.

370

Furthermore, I direct that Dr. Ribera, for him to pray to God on my behalf, be given one small gilded silver salt-cellar which I have that I brought from the court and the satin hooded cloak I had made for mourning and ten yards of linen, for him to pray to God for me in his orisons. Furthermore, I direct that the proceeds of the carmine hoopskirt that went to the Indies be dedicated to increase the chaplaincy I have established.

Furthermore, I command that from the monies to be collected from Plazencia, after removing what has been ordered and what is to be spent, and from the books sent to Santo Domingo, there be brought two ducats of income, sufficient to be given to the Church of San Vicente of this city, so that they make a feast for me each year on the day of Santa Catalina, with all solemnity, with ministers, sermon, and organ, for the good of my soul and that of my wife, and what is left should be given to the poor at the choice of my executors, notwithstanding the aforesaid, which has been written on ten sheets and which is valid and my last will and I sign it with my name on the XXIII day of June of the year one thousand, five hundred and fifty-four.

Pedro de Cieza de León (rubric).[1]

[1] From "Cieza de León en Sevilla y su Muerte en 1554. Documentos," by Miguel Marticorena Estrada (Seville, 1955).

First Part of the Chronicles of Peru

Editions in Spanish

Parte primera de la Chronica del Peru. Que tracta de la Demarcación
de sus Provincias, La Descripción dellas, Las Fundaciones de las
nuevas ciudades, los ritos y costumbres de los indios y otras cosas
estrañas dignas de ser sabidas.

Folio ix hojas (preliminares y cxxxiv hojas con el texto de la obra).
Con grabados de madera en el texto.

Imprenta: Casa de Martín de Montesdoca.

Sevilla, 1553.

La Chronica del Peru, Nuevamente escrita, por Pedro de Cieça de
León, vezino de Sevilla.

Imprenta: Casa de Martin Nucio.

Anvers, 1554.

Parte prima de la Chronica del Peru, que tracta la demarcación de
sus provincias, la descripción dellas, las fundaciones de las nuevas
ciudades, los ritos y costumbres delos Indios, y otras cosas estrañas
dignas de ser sabidas.

Imprenta: Casa de Juan Steelsio.

Anvers, 1554.

Parte primera de la Chronica del Peru, que tracta la demarcación de
sus provincias, la descripción dellas, las fundaciones de las nuevas
ciudades, los ritos y costumbres delos Indios, y otras cosas estrañas
dignas de ser sabidas.

Imprenta: Juan Bellero.

Anvers, 1554.

La Crónica del Perú.

Edit. por Enrique de Vedia en "Biblioteca de autores españoles . . . ,"

Tomo XXVI.
 "Historiadores primitivos de Indias," Tomo II.
 Madrid, 1862.

La Crónica del Perú.
372 Colección "Los grandes viajes clásicos," Tomo XXIV. With 3 maps.
 Imprenta: Calpe.
 Madrid, 1922.

La Crónica General del Perú, Tomo I.
 Anotada y concordada con las crónicas de Indias por Horacio H.
 Urteaga. "Historiadores clásicos del Perú," Tomo VII.
 Imprenta: Librería e Imprenta Gil.
 Lima, 1924.

La Crónica del Perú.
 Colección "Viajes clásicos." With 3 maps.
 Imprenta: Espasa-Calpe S.A.
 Madrid, 1941.

La Crónica del Perú.
 Colección Austral.
 Imprenta: Espasa Calpe Argentina S.A.
 Buenos Aires, 1945.

La Crónica del Perú.
 Forms part of the book, *Crónicas de la Conquista del Perú* (944 pp.).
 Imprenta: Editorial Nueva España S.A.
 Mexico, 1946.

Translations in Italian

La prima parte de la cronica del grandissimo regno del Peru che parla
de la demarcatione, de la sue provintie, la descrittione d'esse, le fun-
dationi de le nuove citta, li ritti & costumi de l'Indiani, & altre cose
strane degne di esser sapute.
 Trad. per Agustino de Cravaliz.
 541 pp.
 Printed by: Valerio . . . Luigi Dorici fratelli.
 Roma, 1555.

La prima parte dell'istorie del Peru, dove si tratta l'ordine delle Provincie, delle Citta muove in quel Paese edificate, i riti et costumi de gli Indiani, con molte cose notabile, & degne, que vengano a notitia.

Printed by: Andrea Arivabene.

Venetia, 1556.

La prima parte dell'istorie del Peru, dove si tratta l'ordine delle Provincie, delle Citta nuove in quel Paese edificate, i riti & costumi de gli Indiani, con molte cose notabile, & degne, che vengana a notitia.

Printed by: Giordano Ziletti.

Venetia, 1557.

Cronica del gran regno del Peru, con la descrittione di tutte le provincie, e costumi, e riti, con le nuove citta edificate, & altre strane & maravigliose notitie.

Trad. Agostino di Cravaliz.

Printed by: Francesco Lorenzini da Turino.

Venetia, 1560.

La Prima parte dell'Historie del Peru. Dove si tratta l'ordine delle Provincie, delle Citta nuove in quel Paese edificate, i riti, & costumi de gli Indiani, con molte cose notabili, et degne di consideratione.

Printed by: Giordano Ziletti.

Venetia, 1560.

Historia, over cronica del gran regno del Peru, con la descrittione di tutte le Provincie, e costumi, e riti, & con le nuove Citta edificate, & altre strane e maravigliose notitie.

Printed by: Giovanni Bonadio.

Venetia, 1564.

Cronica del Gran Regno del Peru, con la descrittione di tutte le Provincie, costumi, e riti. Con le nuove citta edificate, & altre strane & maravigliose notitie.

Printed by: Camillo Franceschini.

Venetia, 1576.

Translations in English

The Seventeen Years Travels of Peter de Cieza, Through the Mighty Kingdom of Peru, and the large Provinces of Cartagena and Popayan in South America: From the City of Panama, on the Isthmus, to the Frontiers of Chile.
374
> Translated by Captain John Stevens.
> With engravings, 1 map, 1 plan.
> London, 1709.
> (Contains only 94 chapters of the 119 of the First Part.)

The travels of Pedro Cieza de Leon, A.D. 1532–50, from the Gulf of the Darien to the City of La Plata, contained in the first part of his Chronicle of Peru.
> Translated by Cl. R. Markham.
> *Works* issued by the Hakluyt Society, Vol. XXXIII.
> London, 1864.

Second Part of the Chronicles of Peru

Editions in Spanish

[La segunda parte de la crónica del Perú que trata del señorío de los Incas Yupanquis y de sus grandes hechos y gobernación. MS in the Biblioteca del Escorial, Códice Lj5. (Chapters I and II and the first part of Chapter III are missing.)]

Relación de los Ingas (first impression).
> Edit. Manuel González de la Rosa.
> 255 pp.
> *Printed by:* Ballantyne, Hanson & Co.
> London, 1873.
> (Deposited in the Trübner Library.)

The copy which existed in the Preussische Stattsbibliothek of Berlin before World War II is probably the only one which remained of the edition published in 1886 and never put in circulation. Concerning this edition there was a controversy between González de la Rosa and M. Jiménez de la Espada. R. Vargas Ugarte, *Historia del Peru, Fuentes* (2d ed., 1945), p. 22. There is a reproduction of the first chapter of the second part by M. González de la Rosa, in the *Revista Peruana* (Lima), Vol. II (1879).

Segunda parte de la Crónica del Perú, que trata del Señorío de los Incas Yupanquis y de sus grandes hechos y gobernación.
    Edited, with introduction and notes, by Marcos Jiménez de la Espada.
    "Biblioteca Hispano-Ultramarina," Vol. V.
    Printed by: Manuel Gines Hernández.
    Madrid, 1880.

Del Señorío de los Incas.
    Introduction and notes by Alberto Mario Salas; also notes by M. Jiménez de la Espada.
    Printed by: Ediciones Argentinas Solar.
    Buenos Aires, 1943.

Translations into English

The second part of the Chronicle of Peru, 1532–50.
    Translation, with introduction and notes, by Cl. R. Markham.
    Works issued by the Hakluyt Society, Vol. LXVIII.
    London, 1883.

Part III of the Chronicles of Peru

[This part, which concerns the conquest of Peru, was used extensively by A. Herrera de Tordesillas in his *Década,* V.]

La tercera parte de la Crónica de Piedro de Cieza de León.
    (15 chapters, which constitute only a fraction of Part III.)
    First reproduction by Rafael Loredo, *Mercurio Peruano,* Año XXI, Vol. XXVII, No. 233, pp. 411–40.
    Lima, August, 1946.

THE INCAS

Part IV of the Chronicles of Peru

Divided into 5 books:
Book I: *Guerra de las Salinas.*
Book II: *Guerra de Chupas.*
Book III: *Guerra de Quito.*
Book IV: *Guerra de Huarina.* Lost.
Book V: *Guerra de Xaquixahuana.* Lost (or perhaps this last book was never written).

Guerra de Chupas. Guerras Civiles del Perú.
   "Colección de Documentos Inéditos para la Historia de España," Vol. LXXVII.
   Madrid, 1881.

Tercer libro de las guerras civiles del Perú el cual se llama la Guerra de Quito.
   "Historiadores de Indias," Vol. II.
   "Nueva Biblioteca de Autores Españoles."
   Edit. M. Serrano y Sanz.
   Madrid, 1909.

Translations (English)

The War of Las Salinas.
   Hakluyt Society.
   London, 1923.

The War of Chupas.
   Hakluyt Society.
   London, 1918.

The War of Quito.
   Hakluyt Society.
   London, 1913.

[Attention is called to the fact that Cieza seems never to have been translated into French or German.]

Acosta, José de. *The Naturall and Morall Historie of the East and* *West Indies.* London, 1604.

Bandelier, Adolph. *The Islands of Titicaca and Koati.* New York, 1910.

Bennett, Wendell C. *Ancient Arts of the Andes.* New York, 1954.

Benzoni, Girolamo. *History of the New World.* Trans. by W. H. Smyth. London, 1857.

Bertrand, Louis, and Sir Charles Petrie. *The History of Spain.* New York, 1934.

Betanzos, Juan de. *Suma y Narración de los Incas.* Ed. by Marcos Jiménez de la Espada. *Biblioteca Hispano-Ultramarina.* Madrid, 1880.

Cieza de León, Pedro de. *Crónica del Perú.* Seville, 1553.

———. *Crónica del Perú.* Antwerp, 1554.

———. *The Travels of Peter de Cieza* . . . . Ed. by Clements Markham. London, 1864.

———. *The War of Quito and Inca Documents.* Ed. by Clements Markham. Hakluyt Society, 2d. ser., No. XXXI. London, 1913.

———. *The War of Las Salinas.* Ed. by Clements Markham. Hakluyt Society, 2d. ser., No. LIV. London, 1923.

———. *The War of Chupas.* Ed. by Clements Markham. Hakluyt Society, 2d. ser., No. XLII. London, 1917.

Doering, H. *Auf den Königsstrassen der Inka.* Berlin, 1941.

Enríquez de Guzmán. *The Life and Acts of Don Alonso Enríquez de Guzmán.* Ed. by Clements Markham. Hakluyt Society, *Work No. 29.* London, 1862.

Hagen, Victor W. von. *Ecuador and the Galápagos Islands.* Norman, 1949.

———. *Guide to the Ruins of Ollantay-tambo.* Lima, 1958.

———. *Guide to the Ruins of Sacsahuamán.* New York, 1949.

———. *Highway of the Sun.* New York, 1955.

———. *Realm of the Incas.* New York, 1957.

———. *South America Called Them.* New York, 1945.

————. *Tsatchela Indians of Western Ecuador*. Museum of the American Indian, *Indian Notes No. 51*. New York, 1939.

Haring, C. H. *The Spanish Empire in America*. New York, 1947.

Humboldt, Alexander von. *Views of Nature*. London, 1858.

————, and Aimée Bonpland. *Recueil d'observations de zoologie et d'anatomie comparé*. 2 vols. Paris, 1811.

Kidder, Alfred, II. *Some Early Sites in the Northern Titicaca Basin*. Peabody Museum *Report*, Vol. XXVII, No. 1. Cambridge, Mass., 1943.

La Vega, Garcilaso de. *Comentarios Reales de los Incas*. 5 vols. Buenos Aires, 1945.

McCown, Theodore D. *Pre-Incaic Huamachuco*. University of California *Publications in American Archaeology and Ethnology*, Vol. XXXIX, No. 4 [1945].

Madariaga, Salvador de. *Christopher Columbus*. New York, 1940.

————. *Hernán Cortés*. New York, 1941.

Markham, Sir Clements. *Cuzco: A Journey to the Ancient Capital of Peru . . . and Lima . . . .* London, 1856.

————. "On the Geographical Positions of the Tribes Which Formed the Empire of the Yncas," *Journal* of the Royal Geographical Society (London), Vol. XLI (1871), 281–338.

———— (ed.). *Reports on the Discovery of Peru* (Francisco de Xérez, Miguel de Estete, Hernando Pizarro, Pedro Sancho). *Publications* of the Hakluyt Society. London, 1872.

Marticorena Estrada, Miguel. "Cieza de León en Sevilla y su Muerte en 1554," Documentos, *Anuario de Estudios Americanos* (Seville), Separata del Tomo XII (1955).

Means, Philip Ainsworth. *Ancient Civilizations of the Andes*. New York, 1931.

Medina, José Toribio. *The Discovery of the Amazon According to the Account of the Friar Gaspar de Carvajal . . . ,* as published with an introduction by J. T. Medina. Trans. by T. Lee and ed. by W. C. Heaton. American Geographic Society *Special Publication No. 17*. New York, 1934.

Métraux, Alfred. "Études sur la civilisation des Indiens Chiriguano," *Revista del Instituto de Etnología de la Universidad Nacional de Tucumán* (Argentina), Vol. I (1930), 295–494.

Monge, Carlos. *Acclimatization in the Andes.* Tr. by Donald F. Brown. Baltimore, 1948.

Montesinos, Fernando. *Memorias Antiguas Historiales del Peru.* Ed. by P. A. Means. Hakluyt Society, 2d. ser., No. XLVIII. London, 1920.

Morúa, Martín de. *Historia del Orígen y Genealogía Real de los Reyes Incas del Perú, de sus hechos, costumbres, trajes, y manera de gobierno.* Ed. by H. H. Urteaga and C. A. Romero. *Colección de Libros y Documentos Referentes a la Historia del Perú* (Lima), 2d. ser., Vol. IV, pp. 1–253; Vol. V, pp. 1–72 (1922–25). 379

Murra, John. "Tribes of Ecuador," in Steward (ed.), *Handbook of South American Indians* (*q.v.*), II, 785–821.

Nordenskiöld, Erland. "The Secret of the Peruvian Quipus," *Comparative Ethnographical Studies* (Gothenburg), Vol. VIII (1925).

Ocampo, Capt. Baltasar de. *The Execution of the Inca Tupac Amaru.* Ed. by Sir Clements Markham. Hakluyt Society, 2d. ser., Vol. XXII. London, 1907.

Pizarro, Pedro. *Relación del Descubrimiento y Conquista de los Reinos del Perú* . . . . Buenos Aires, 1944.

Pizarro–La Gasca Papers: From Panamá to Perú, a catalogue of the documents now at the Henry E. Huntington Library (San Marino, Calif.). London, Maggs Bros., 1925.

Pogo, Alexander (ed.). "The Anonymous *La Conquista del Perú,*" *Proceedings* of the American Academy of Arts and Sciences, Vol. LXIV (1930), No. 8.

Poma de Ayala, Felipe Huamán. *El Primer Nueva Coronica* [*sic*] *y Buen Gobierno.* Ed. by Ing. Arthur Posnansky. La Paz, 1944.

Porras Barrenechea, Raúl. *Las Primeras Crónicas de la Conquista del Perú.* Madrid, 1949.

———. *Las Relaciones Primitivas de la Conquista del Perú.* Paris, 1937.

———. *Una Relación Inédita de la Conquista del Perú.* Madrid, 1940.

Reichlen, Henry and Paule. "Recherches Archeologiques dans les Andes du Haut Uctubamba," *Journal de la Société Americanistes* (Paris), new ser., Vol. XXXIX (1950), 219–46.

Rowe, John H. "Inca Culture at the Time of the Spanish Conquest," in Steward (ed.), *Handbook of South American Indians* (*q.v.*), II, 183–330.

———. *An Introduction to the Archaeology of Cuzco.* Peabody Museum, Harvard University, *Report No. 2.* Cambridge, Mass., 1944.

———. "The Kingdom of Chimor," *Acta Americana* (Mexico), Vol. VI (1948), Nos. 1 and 2.

380 ———. *Sitios Históricos en la Región de Pucará, Puno.* Cuzco. 1942.

———, Donald Collier, and Gordon R. Willey. "Reconnaissance Notes on the Site of Huari, Near Ayacucho, Perú," *American Antiquity,* Vol. XVI (1950), No. 2.

Salaman, Redcliffe N. *The History and Social Influence of the Potato.* Cambridge, Eng., 1949.

Santa Clara, Pedro Gutiérrez de. *Historia de las Guerras Civiles del Perú.* 4 vols. Madrid, 1904–10.

Santistéban Ochoa, Julián. *Los Cronistas del Perú.* Cuzco, 1946.

Sarmiento de Gamboa, Pedro. *History of the Incas.* Ed. by Sir Clements Markham. Hakluyt Society, 2d. ser., Vol. XXII. London, 1907.

Spruce, Richard. *Notes of a Botanist on the Amazon and Andes.* 2 vols. London, 1908.

Squier, E. G. *Peru: Incidents of Travel and Explorations in the Land of the Incas.* New York, 1877.

Steward, Julian H. (ed.). *Handbook of South American Indians.* 6 vols. Washington, D.C., 1946–.

Tschopik, Marion H. *Some Notes on the Archaeology of the Department of Puno, Peru.* Papers of the Peabody Museum, Harvard University, Vol. XXVII, No. 3. Cambridge, Mass., 1946.

Uhle, Max. *Las Ruinas de Tomebamba.* Quito, 1927.

Urteaga, Horacio H., and Carlos A. Romero. *Fundación Española del Cuzco y Ordenanzas para su Gobierno.* Lima, 1926.

Vaca de Castro, Cristóbal. "Ordenanzas de Tambos," ed. by C. A. Romero, *Revista Histórica* (Lima), Vol. III (1909), No. 4, 427–92.

Vásquez de Espinoza, Antonio. "Compendium and Description of the West Indies," Smithsonian *Miscellaneous Collections,* Vol. CVIII (1942).

Velasco, Juan López de. *Historia del Reino de Quito en la América Meridional.* 3 vols. Quito, 1841–44.

Wiener, Charles. *Perou et Bolivie: Recit de Voyage.* Paris, 1880.

Willey, Gordon R. "Prehistoric Settlement Patterns in the Virú Valley, Peru," Smithsonian Institution *Bulletin No. 155* (1953).

Xérez, Francisco de. *Verdadera Relación de la Conquista del Perú.* Ed. by Alexander Pogo. *Papers* of the Bibliographical Society of America, Vol. XXX, Part I (1936).

383

Chucuito: 219, 244; impórtance of, 281 & n.
Chullpas (houses of the dead): lv, 274ff., 311n.; *see also* tombs
Chumpivilcas (Indians): 199n., 234, 255
Chunchos (Indians): 61 & n., 287n.
Chuño (dried potatoes): 164 & n., 271 & n.
Chupas, battle of: xlvii, 126n.
Chuquiabo (La Paz): 249, 285; *see also* La Paz
Chuquimancu (chieftain): 338n.
Chuquisaca: 286; *see also* La Plata
Cieza de León, Pedro de: birth, xxvii, xxix; religious beliefs, xxxi; arrival in New World, xxxv–vii; impressions of Peru, xxxvii–viii; marriage of, lxiv–v; return to Seville, lxv; reasons for writing Chronicles, xl–li; character of, xli–lii, lix–x; contemporary historians of, liiin.; *repartimiento* of, xliv & n.; "Cronista de Indias," liv; as human geographer, lvii; as historian, lvii; style of, lvii–viii; feeling for Indians, lviii–ix; marriage contract, lxvi; methods of research, lxii–xiii; gets license to publish, lxvii–viii; last years of, lxxii; death of, lxxiii; on publication of manuscripts, lxxiii–iv; visits Andean provinces, 258
Cieza de León, Pedro de, works of: evaluation of, xxv, xxvii–ix, xxxviii–ix, xlii–iii, lix; plagiarism of, xxvi–vii; list of published, xxviii n.; "Book of Foundations," lxiv & n.; plan of projected histories, lxvii, 4ff.; *First Chronicle,* lxiii, lxvii, lxix–xi, lxx–xxi; *Second Chronicle,* lxxi, lxxviii–x & n., 64n.; "War (Battle) of Quito," lxxi; reasons for not being printed, lxxvff.; on civil wars, lxxv n., lxxviii; publication of, lxxviii–ix & n.
Cinnamon: *see* spices

Cinto: valley, 320–21; ancient, 231n.
Civil wars in Peru, Spanish: xxxix–x, xlvi ff.; 162 & n., 348–49
Civil wars, Inca (Huascar *vs.* Atahualpa): 78, 81ff., 95ff.
Climate: 303 & n., 304
Cloth, vicuña: 103
Clothing, native: 57, 70; of Panzaleo, 54–55; women's, 54–55; Puruhás, 65; of Cañaris, 69n.; differences in, 71; of Loja, 89; of Huancabamba, 93; of Cajamarca, 95; of Chachapoyas, 99; of Conchucos, 106; of the Huancas, 115; quality of, 177; of the Caviñas, 262; of the Canas, 264; of the Collas, 273; of Paria, 286; of Ecuadorian coastal tribes, 293n.; of Tumbes, 300n., 301; of the Yungas, 307; for sale, 324; in Santa valley, 326
Coat of arms (Inca): 167
Coca: use of, xxvii, 259–60, 272; described, lv, 260
Cochacajas: 133 & n., 224 & n., 230 & n.
Colla (province): description, 270ff.
Colla(s) (Indians): 217n.; revolt against Pachacuti, 235ff.; peace with Topa Inca, 238–39; customs of, 272ff.; mourning rites, 274–76
Collaguas (Indians): 351
Colla-suyu (quarter of the South): 162; Viracocha's expedition to, 217ff.; description of, 272n.
Collique valley: 321
Columbe (Cayambi): 66 & n.
Communications: 63–64, 139–40
Conchucos (Indians): 105, 110; character of, 106; sodomy among, 314
Condorhuasi tambo: 133n.
Conversos: xxxi
Copacopa: 265
Copiapó: *see* Chile
Corn: 44
Coropuna temple: 152

385

387

Index

Maldonado, Diego ("the Rich"): lxi, 132, 223 & n.

Maldonado, Francisco: 275n.

Mamaconas (temple virgins): 56, 70, 182; make clothing for Inca, 104; duties of, 146; punished, 214

Mama Ocllo (wife of Pachacuti): 247

Mamendoy valley: 50n.

Manco Capac, first Inca: founds Cuzco, 26, 30, 37, 38–40; deeds of, 38–39

Manco Capac II (Manco Inca II): war with Spaniards, 121; leads uprising against Spaniards, 189n., 284

Manco Inca: *see* Manco Capac

Mantaro River (miscalled "La Plata" by Cieza): source, 112, 113

Marañón River: 66, 87

Marca-villca (Marca-valle): 114, 118

Marriage customs: Cañari, 72; Tarma, 112–13; *see also* polygamy

Mayta Capac, fourth Inca: accomplishments of, 197–98

Medicines and treatment: 115, 296–97 & n.

Mendieta, Lope de: 258 & n.

Mendoza, Alonso de: 285

Mendoza, Antonio de: sketch of, lxiii n.

Mendoza, Lope de: 288

Minchan-caman, chieftain of Chimor: 300 n., 323n., 328

Mita-ḳona: see mitimaes

Mitimaes: defined, 56–57, 147; system of, 59, 232 & n.; classes of, 59n., 60ff.; rewards to, 60

Mocha: 64

Mochicas Indians: 323n.; sodomy among, 314n.

Mochica language: 323

Mogrovejo de Quiñones: 120n.

Moguer, Pedro Martínez de: lxn., 30, 145n., 280

Molina, Alonso de (of the "thirteen"): 51n., 252, 300n.

Molle trees: 115 & n.

Mollebamba: 105

Monkeys: 257–58

Mosquitoes: 326

Motupe valley: 319

Moxos (Indians): 61 & n.

Muhina: 261

Mulahala: 55–56

Muli-ambato: 63

Mummies of Incas: 189n.

Names: method of giving, 315–16

Nazca, valley of: 342; description and history of, 348 & n.; as Inca administrative center, 349 & n.

New Cuzco (Incahuasi): 339 & n., 343

"New Laws": xliv, xlvii, 162; reasons for enactment of, lix

Nicasio: 275 & n.

Núñez Vela, Blasco (first viceroy to Peru): xlvii, 24n.

Oca: 271

Ogoñez, Rodrigo: 337

Ollantay-Tambo: description and history of, 253n., 254 & n.

Oma-suyu (highway): 233, 278

Orejones (Big-Ears): 162, 165, 236; explanation of name, 33n.; creation of, 36; complaints about, 131; disturbance among, 76; choose Viracocha as Inca, 208; subjects of treachery at Puná, 297ff.

Oruro: 233, 278

Otavalo (Indians): 23–24

Paccaric-Tampu ("origin tambo"): 30ff., 150 & n., 255

Pacasmayo valley: 322

Pachacamac, temple of: description of, l, 242, 329, 334–37

Pachacuti (Inca Yupanqui), tenth Inca (d. 1471): 39, 94, 221; institutes *mitimae* system, 56; conquest of Jauja, 117–18; con-

389

390

quers Huamanga, 125; conquest of Vilcas, 128–29; contends with Hastu Huallaca, 130n., 131; establishes highway posts, 139; orders building of Sacsahuamán, 143n., 153, 155; builds temple of sun in Cuzco, 145; takes charge of realm, 225; defeats Chancas, 226–27; becomes Inca, 227; achievements as Inca, 228–36; Colla revolt against, 235ff.; relinquishes fringe, 236–37; conquers Canas, 265; conquest of Pachacamac, 335

Palomino, Capt.: in civil wars, li

Paltas (Indians): 75, 87ff.

Pampas River: see Vilcas River

Pancorvo, Juan de: lxi, 228 & n.; 265n., 266

Panzaleo: 54

Paramonga fortress: 326–27 & n., 328

Parcos: 119, 120

Paria: 244 & n., 286

Pariacaca: l, 329–30 & n.

Parinacochas, Lake: 203n.

Pass of Huayna Capac: 299

Paucar-colla: 219

Paullu Inca (Paullu Tupac Yupanqui): 189–90n.; 197 & n.

Peranzúres: see Pedro Anzures

Pérez de Guevara, Juan: 100

Peru: general description, 17–19; early history of, 25ff.

Philip II of Spain: lxix, 146; marriage of, lxxii–iii; effect of accession on publishing, lxxiv

Picoy: 119, 121n.

Pillucho peak: 125 & n., 128, 231n.

Pincos: 133

Piquillacta, ruins of: described, liv–v; aqueduct and gate at, 262n.

Pisca (Indian): aids Cieza in history, lxii

Pisco: see Cangallo

Piscobamba, province of: 106–107; fortress at, 107

Piura, calley of: 297n., 302

Pizarro, Francisco: xxxii, xlvi, 95, 135, 255, 300n., 302, 324, 336, 338, 351; signs contract with Queen Juana the Mad, 51n.; and founding of Huánuco, 108n.; war with Manco Inca II, 122; founds Huamanga, 123; refounds Cuzco, 148; in Spanish civil wars, 162n.; founds Lima, 331

Pizarro Gonzalo: xliv, xlvii, 120n., 125; rebellion of, xlvi, 133; battle with Manco Inca II, 122; in Spanish civil wars, 162; in battle of Huarina, 285 & n.

Pizarro, Hernando: xxix, xxxiii, 109n., 255, 336f.; at Pachacamac, 335n.

Plate River: 112n.; discovery of, 288; see also La Plata River

Poechos: 302 & n.

Polygamy: 58, 69n., among the Yungas, 307

Pomallacta (Puma-llacta), lodgings of: 67n.

Pomatambo: Inca conquest of, 203–204, 231 & n.; natives of, 255

Popayán: xlv, 322

Porras Barrenchea, Raúl: on publication of Third Part of Chronicle, lxxix n.

Portents and auguries: 199, 315–16

Posts, system of highway: 139-40

Potatoes: 44, 317; dried (chuño), 271 & n.

Potosí: 249; discovery of silver at, lvi, 286–27n.; coca traffic in, 260; see also La Plata

Prescott, William H.: on Cieza, xxv; on Herrera and Cieza, lxxvii; on Second Chronicle, lxxviii n.

Priests, native: 147, 182, 183–84, 191–92; use of coca, 260n.; customs of, 313ff.; duties of, 335–36

Prisoners, Indian treatment of: xli

Pucará: 120, 238 & n.; description of, 277–78 & n.

Puelles, Pedro de: 108n.

Puerto Viejo: sodomy in, 179

393

THE CIVILIZATION OF THE AMERICAN INDIAN SERIES

of which *The Incas of Pedro de Cieza de León* is the fifty-third volume, was inaugurated in 1932 by the University of Oklahoma Press,
and has as its purpose the reconstruction of American Indian civilization by presenting aboriginal, historical, and contemporary Indian   395
life. The following list is complete as of the date of publication of
this volume:

1. *Forgotten Frontiers:* A Study of the Spanish Indian Policy of Don
   Juan Bautista de Anza, Governor of New Mexico, 1777–1787.
   Translated and edited by Alfred Barnaby Thomas. Out of print.
2. Grant Foreman. *Indian Removal:* The Emigration of the Five
   Civilized Tribes of Indians.
3. John Joseph Mathews. *Wah'Kon-tah:* The Osage and the White
   Man's Road.
4. Grant Foreman. *Advancing the Frontier, 1830–1860.*
5. John Homer Seger. *Early Days Among the Cheyenne and Arap-
   ahoe Indians.* Edited by Stanley Vestal.
6. Angie Debo. *The Rise and Fall of the Choctaw Republic.*
7. Stanley Vestal (ed.). *New Sources of Indian History, 1850–1891.*
   Out of print.
8. Grant Foreman. *The Five Civilized Tribes.* Out of print.
9. *After Coronado:* Spanish Exploration Northeast of New Mexico,
   1696–1727. Translated and edited by Alfred Barnaby Thomas.
10. Frank B. Speck. *Naskapi:* The Savage Hunters of the Labrador
    Peninsula. Out of print.
11. Elaine Goodale Eastman. *Pratt: The Red Man's Moses.* Out of
    print.
12. Althea Bass. *Cherokee Messenger:* A Life of Samuel Austin Wor-
    cester.
13. Thomas Wildcat Alford. *Civilization.* As told to Florence Drake.
    Out of print.
14. Grant Foreman. *Indians and Pioneers:* The Story of the Ameri-
    can Southwest Before 1830.
15. George E. Hyde. *Red Cloud's Folk:* A History of the Oglala
    Sioux Indians.
16. Grant Foreman. *Sequoyah.*

17. Morris L. Wardell. *A Political History of the Cherokee Nation, 1838-1907*. Out of print.
18. John Walton Caughey. *McGillivray of the Creeks*.
19. Edward Everett Dale and Gaston Litton. *Cherokee Cavaliers:* Forty Years of Cherokee History as Told in the Correspondence of the Ridge-Watie-Boudinot Family. Out of print.
20. Ralph Henry Gabriel. *Elias Boudinot, Cherokee, and His America.* '
21. Karl N. Llewellyn and E. Adamson Hoebel. *The Cheyenne Way:* Conflict and Case Law in Primitive Jurisprudence.
22. Angie Debo. *The Road to Disappearance*.
23. Oliver La Farge and others. *The Changing Indian*. Out of print.
24. Carolyn Thomas Foreman. *Indians Abroad*. Out of print.
25. John Adair. *The Navajo and Pueblo Silversmiths*.
26. Alice Marriott. *The Ten Grandmothers*.
27. Alice Marriott. *María:* The Potter of San Ildefonso.
28. Edward Everett Dale. *The Indians of the Southwest:* A Century of Development Under the United States. Out of print.
29. Adrián Recinos. *Popol Vuh:* The Sacred Book of the Ancient Quiché Maya. English version by Delia Goetz and Sylvanus G. Morley from the translation of Adrián Recinos.
30. Walter Collins O'Kane. *Sun in the Sky*.
31. Stanley A. Stubbs. *Bird's-Eye View of the Pueblos*.
32. Katharine C. Turner. *Red Men Calling on the Great White Father*.
33. Muriel H. Wright. *A Guide to the Indian Tribes of Oklahoma*.
34. Ernest Wallace and E. Adamson Hoebel. *The Comanches:* Lords of the South Plains.
35. Walter Collins O'Kane. *The Hopis:* Portrait of a Desert People.
36. *The Sacred Pipe:* Black Elk's Account of the Seven Rites of the Oglala Sioux. Edited by Joseph Epes Brown.
37. Adrián Recinos and Delia Goetz. *The Annals of the Cakchiquels.* Translated from the Cakchiquel Maya, with *Title of the Lords of Totonicapán,* translated from the Quiché text into Spanish by Dionisio José Chonay, English version by Delia Goetz.
38. R. S. Cotterill. *The Southern Indians:* The Story of the Civilized Tribes Before Removal.

39. J. Eric S. Thompson. *The Rise and Fall of Maya Civilization.*
40. Robert Emmitt. *The Last War Trail:* The Utes and the Settlement of Colorado. Out of print.
41. Frank Gilbert Roe. *The Indian and the Horse.*
42. Francis Haines. *The Nez Percés:* Tribesmen of the Columbia Plateau. Out of print.
43. Ruth M. Underhill. *The Navajos.*
44. George Bird Grinnell. *The Fighting Cheyennes.*
45. George E. Hyde. *A Sioux Chronicle.*
46. Stanley Vestal. *Sitting Bull: Champion of the Sioux, A Biography.*
47. Edwin C. McReynolds. *The Seminoles.*
48. William T. Hagan. *The Sac and Fox Indians.*
49. John C. Ewers. *The Blackfeet:* Raiders on the Northwestern Plains.
50. Alfonso Caso. *The Aztecs:* People of the Sun. Translated by Lowell Dunham.
51. C. L. Sonnichsen. *The Mescalero Apaches.*
52. Keith A. Murray. *The Modocs and Their War.*
53. *The Incas of Pedro de Cieza de León.* Edited by Victor Wolfgang von Hagen and translated by Harriet de Onis.
54. George E. Hyde. *Indians of the High Plains.*
55. George Catlin. *Episodes from* Life Among the Indians *and* Last Rambles. Edited by Marvin C. Ross.
56. J. Eric S. Thompson. *Maya Hieroglyphic Writing:* An Introduction.
57. George E. Hyde. *Spotted Tail's Folk:* A History of the Brulé Sioux.
58. James Larpenteur Long. *The Assiniboines:* From the Accounts of the Old Ones Told to First Boy (James Larpenteur Long). Edited and with an introduction by Michael Stephen Kennedy.
59. Edwin Thompson Denig. *Five Indian Tribes of the Upper Missouri:* Sioux, Arickaras, Assiniboines, Crees, Crows. Edited and with an introduction by John C. Ewers.
60. John Joseph Mathews. *The Osages:* Children of the Middle Waters.
61. Mary Elizabeth Young. *Redskins, Ruffleshirts, and Rednecks:* Indian Allotments in Alabama and Mississippi, 1830–1860.

399

The type in which this book is set is Granjon, designed by George W. Jones in 1924. It is based on the Garamond of the Egenolff specimen sheet but is considerably modified. Granjon is an adaptation that retains the Garamond character while being admirably suited to modern use. It has been said of Granjon that it is "a book face worthy to rank with Caslon for usefulness, with Centaur for beauty; sharp enough for publicity, clear enough for a dictionary."

University of Oklahoma Press : Norman